EDITION

5

STUDYING POLITICS
AN INTRODUCTION TO POLITICAL SCIENCE

Edited by
CHRISTOPHER G. ANDERSON
Wilfrid Laurier University

and

RAND DYCK

NELSON
EDUCATION

NELSON
EDUCATION

Studying Politics: An Introduction to Political Science, Fifth Edition

by Christopher G. Anderson and Rand Dyck

VP, Product and Partnership Solutions
Anne Williams

Acquisitions Editor:
Mark Grzeskowiak

Marketing Manager:
Terry Fedorkiw

Content Development Manager:
Jessica Freedman

Photo Researcher:
Marnie Lamb

Permissions Coordinator:
Marnie Lamb

Production Project Manager:
Christine Gilbert

Production Service:
Cenveo Publishing Services

Copy Editor:
Jessie Coffey

Proofreader:
Pushpa V. Giri

Indexer:
BIM Publishing Services

Design Director:
Ken Phipps

Managing Designer:
Franca Amore

Interior Design:
Sharon Lucas

Cover Design:
Sharon Lucas

Cover Image:
© REUTERS/Mohammad Ismail

Compositor:
Cenveo Publisher Services

Library and Archives Canada Cataloguing in Publication Data

Studying politics: an introduction to political science / edited by Christopher G. Anderson, Rand Dyck (Carleton University). — Edition 5.

Includes bibliographical references and index.
ISBN 978-0-17-653149-2 (paperback)

1. Political science—Textbooks.
I. Dyck, Rand, 1943-, editor
II. Anderson, Christopher G. (Christopher Gordon), 1969-, editor

JA66.S84 2015 320 C2015-902617-2

ISBN-13: 978-0-17-653149-2
ISBN-10: 0-17-653149-1

Politics is not just the domain of political scientists and politicians but of us all—it affects every one of us and every one of us can have an effect on it. This book is, therefore, dedicated to all those students and teachers who take up the challenges of studying politics—of learning how to appreciate and respond to the vital yet complex issues, however local or global, that give shape to the quality of our lives.

BRIEF CONTENTS

CONTENTS

PREFACE

The influence that Rand Dyck has had on the study (and thus the practice) of politics in Canada is, and I use the word advisedly, immeasurable. Between his editorship of the first four editions of *Studying Politics* and his authorship of seven editions of *Canadian Politics* (most recently with Chris Cochrane of the University of Toronto), never mind his decades of teaching and mentoring, Rand has possibly shaped the political thinking of more students in this country than anyone else. In part, he has done so by ensuring that each edition of this text has presented a fresh update on how we study politics, situating Canada within a global context and in a language that is readily accessible to each new generation of students—practices that we have worked to continue in this fifth edition.

I first became a part of this process when, on the friendly recommendation of my then-Chair Brian Tanguay at Wilfrid Laurier University, Rand offered me the opportunity to write a new chapter on "States and Governments" for the third edition. In doing so, he took a bit of a risk as I was an all but unpublished and freshly minted PhD student who had just entered the increasingly tight Canadian labour market for university professors in Political Science. As he shepherded me from first draft to final proofs, Rand was welcoming and supportive, and the experience was an extremely rewarding one that shaped my thinking and approach not just to the discipline and the study of politics but to teaching my large introduction to politics courses at Laurier. I became a better researcher and teacher, I think, by going back to basics to consider what it is we do in Political Science and how we explain this to students. At some point around the lead-up to the fifth edition, Rand generously raised the possibility of my taking over as editor. In accepting, I hope to extend and continue to develop the significant contributions that Rand has made through the first four editions in creating one of the most valued and valuable introductory politics texts in Canada.

Continuing and Developing the Traditions

There are two particular traditions that Rand has established during the first four editions that I want to continue and to develop. The first is to ensure that *Studying Politics* is crafted in a language that students find accessible and relevant—that speaks to the complexity of the political world in which they live (whether they realize it or not), and provides them with touchstones and tools to see patterns where others see confusion and to offer solutions where others offer resignation. While there is great merit in the idea that "forewarned is forearmed," it is also true that forearmed is forewarned, and to both of these ends this textbook introduces students to many of the traditions and tools of, and much of the knowledge that has been generated through, studying politics.

This book is not, however, written just for those who plan to pursue a career in political science or in politics. As everyone who has taught an introduction to politics course knows, the majority of students in the classroom have a more limited interest in or awareness of politics. While some are looking to gain a greater appreciation and understanding of, and to become more comfortable and conversant in, the world of politics, others do not really know why they are there except that they know that it somehow matters. In order to address these varied audiences, we have worked to adopt a tone and approach that is directed toward the more inclusive study of *politics* even as it encourages the study of *political science*. When I teach my introductory class, I aim to inspire and equip those for whom politics will be a deep and fulfilling lifelong commitment but I more generally want to convince the entire class that politics shapes their lives every single day and that they possess and can develop the skills and knowledge to influence it in turn. Our students are members of multiple (and often overlapping) communities with meaningful aspirations and concerns that can be aided and abetted through a more informed engagement with politics, and this textbook is written to start them, or to help them to continue, along that path.

A second tradition upheld in this fifth edition is to maintain a judicious mix of established and newer scholars. If you look at the table of contents and compare it with the previous edition you will see that there are nine new chapters. As is the case for myself as editor, all of these new authors have very big shoes to fill as those who came before them set very high standards to follow. However, even as previous generations of scholars have experience and wisdom to offer in spades, and often remind us that what may seem new is but a variant on an old theme, more recent scholars often see both the established canon and make connections with other fields of study in new and interesting ways. As a result, they can offer different ways of encouraging and mobilizing students to think about how politics intersects with their lives.

You will find, therefore, much that is familiar but also much that is new in this fifth edition. *Studying Politics* is still a textbook aimed at the students we teach, seeking to encourage them to see politics as an important and productive part of their lives, as a sphere of human behaviour that they can—and ought to—engage. Apart from the many new chapters that provide fresh perspectives on core features of the discipline, our returning authors have updated and revised their contributions to reflect recent developments in the discipline and to link them to important events in the world that the students of 2015 and beyond live in. There are also some important organizational changes that have been made. Our students are perhaps the most globally oriented and connected generation that we have ever seen, and they view the world in ways that readily transcend traditional borders and categories. Thus, each author has been encouraged to weave in comparative and global dimensions in their chapters, especially along lines that extend our understanding of politics beyond more traditional Western examples, even as they retain a core focus on Canada and Canadians. As well, the role of ideas—of concepts and theories—in shaping how we study politics has been privileged in this edition, especially in the first and second chapters.

Furthermore, two new types of pedagogical tools have been integrated into this new edition. Two **Think and Discuss** boxes appear in each chapter, with the aim of encouraging students to engage critically with the surrounding chapter content. These can also be used in the classroom (as can the discussion questions at the end of each chapter) to structure in-class breakout groups that help to move past the standard lecture format and promote active learning in the classroom. Each chapter also contains a **Photo Essay** box, which features an image that highlights a topical or controversial issue, along with an essay that explicates the significance of the image. In this way, students are further encouraged to take their learning from the classroom and the textbook and to apply it to the debates and issues that affect and interest them. Finally, the textbook has, as you can see, been significantly redesigned visually in an effort to meet the needs of today's instructors and students, who are ever more in need of ways to apply the tools and knowledge that can be found in the discipline of Political Science to the world around them. There is also, of course, a suite of pedagogical resources that instructors can use to extend and promote student learning both in and beyond the classroom.

Instructor Resources

 The **Nelson Education Teaching Advantage** (NETA) program delivers research-based instructor resources that promote student engagement and higher-order thinking to enable the success of Canadian students and educators. Visit Nelson Education's **Inspired Instruction** website at http://www.nelson.com/inspired/ to find out more about NETA.

The following instructor resources have been created for *Studying Politics,* Fifth Edition. Access these ultimate tools for customizing lectures and presentations at www.nelson.com/instructor.

NETA Test Bank

This resource was written by Nanita Mohan, University of Guelph. It includes approximately 230 multiple-choice questions written according to NETA guidelines for effective construction and development of higher-order questions. Also included are approximately 250 True or False questions.

The NETA Test Bank is available in a new, cloud-based platform. **Nelson Testing Powered by Nelson Cognero®** is a secure online testing system that allows instructors to author, edit, and manage test bank content from anywhere Internet access is available. No special installations or downloads are needed, and the desktop-inspired interface, with its drop-down menus and familiar, intuitive tools, allows instructors to create and manage tests with ease. Multiple test versions can be created in an instant, and content can be imported or exported into other systems. Tests can be delivered from a learning management system, the classroom, or wherever an instructor chooses. Nelson Testing Powered by Cognero for *Studying Politics,* Fifth Edition can be accessed through www.nelson.com/instructor.

NETA PowerPoint

Microsoft® PowerPoint® lecture slides for every chapter have also been created by Nanita Mohan, University of Guelph. There is an average of 12 slides per chapter, many featuring key figures, tables, and photographs from *Studying Politics,* Fifth Edition. NETA principles of clear design and engaging content have been incorporated throughout, making it simple for instructors to customize the deck for their courses.

Image Library

This resource consists of digital copies of figures, short tables, and photographs used in the book. Instructors may use these jpegs to customize the NETA PowerPoint or create their own PowerPoint presentations.

DayOne Slides

DayOne—Prof InClass is a PowerPoint presentation that instructors can customize to orient students to the class and their text at the beginning of the course.

MindTap

Offering personalized paths of dynamic assignments and applications, **MindTap** is a digital learning solution that turns cookie-cutter into cutting-edge, apathy into engagement, and memorizers into higher-level thinkers. MindTap enables students to analyze and apply chapter concepts within relevant assignments, and allows instructors to measure skills and promote better outcomes with ease. A fully online learning solution, MindTap combines all student learning tools—readings, multimedia, activities, and assessments—into a single Learning Path that guides the student through the curriculum. Instructors personalize the experience by customizing the presentation of these learning tools to their students, even seamlessly introducing their own content into the Learning Path.

Student Resources

The **Student Companion Website** for *Studying Politics,* Fifth Edition provides you with access to interactive study tools, including flashcards, games, and more. Visit NELSONbrain.com and access it today.

MindTap

Stay organized and efficient with *MindTap*—a single destination with all the course material and study aids you need to succeed. Built-in apps leverage social media and the latest learning technology. For example:

- ReadSpeaker will read the text to you.
- Flashcards are pre-populated to provide you with a jump start for review—or you can create your own.
- You can highlight text and make notes in your MindTap Reader. Your notes will flow into Evernote, the electronic notebook app that you can access anywhere when it's time to study for the exam.
- Refection and Discussion Board activities allow you to apply a theme or idea you've just studied.
- Questia.com is an online research and paper-writing tool, which helps you find and cite high-quality, scholarly research with emphasis on subjects related to the humanities and social sciences.

Visit http://www.nelson.com/student to start using **MindTap**. Enter the Online Access Code from the card included with your text. If a code card is *not* provided, you can purchase instant access at NELSONbrain.com.

ACKNOWLEDGMENTS

First and foremost, I want to thank Rand for providing me with this opportunity. As someone who has now taught at the introductory level for nine years, it has been a privilege first to write a chapter for this book and then assume its editorship. Next, I want to thank those authors who contributed to the last edition and who stepped aside to make room for new scholars to set their mark on how we define and explain core ideas and findings in the discipline—their role in making this textbook what it has become cannot be overstated: Andrew Heard, Brenda O'Neill, David Stewart, Miriam Smith, James Busumtwi-Sam, Peter Ferguson, and William D. Coleman. Third, I want to thank all the continuing authors from previous editions who have been so very supportive during this transition—they were receptive to any suggestions that I had and it has been a pleasure to get to know them through, and work with them on, this project. Fourth, I want to welcome on board and acknowledge the hard work of all the new authors for this edition—some of whom I already knew but many of whom I met for the first time through this process. To write for (primarily) first-year students is both a privilege and a challenge, and singularly and collectively they rose to the occasion. While we are professionally trained to write for our peers, it is another thing altogether to write for introductory students—it is necessary to think through and develop a new language for our material and this often requires extensive and numerous revisions. As with our returning authors, our new authors were very receptive to suggestions and I learned a lot from the many exchanges that we had in working from the first to final drafts.

A text that speaks on behalf of the political science community cannot do so without considerable assistance from that community, and many political science professors have helped us to develop a better textbook through their advice and comments as we have moved through to the fifth edition. Indeed, many important revisions and changes are a direct result of their suggestions. Among these reviewers are Todd Alway, McMaster University; Amanda Bittner, Memorial University of Newfoundland; Chris Erickson, University of British Columbia; Jay Haaland, Kwantlen Polytechnic University; Paul Hamilton, Brock University; Wayne A. Hunt, Mount Allison University; Brenda Lyshaug, Simon Fraser University; David G. MacDonald, University of the Fraser Valley; Bryan Peeler, St. John's College, University of Manitoba.

Finally, as a new author for an edited textbook, I want to express my deep appreciation for the cooperation, support, hard work, and patience of everyone at Nelson Education Ltd. In particular, I want to thank Anne-Marie Taylor (Publisher) and Jessica Freedman (Developmental Editor), with whom I worked most closely for the past two years, and as well with Mark Grzeskowiak (Acquisitions Editor), who took over from Anne-Marie in the later stages of the process, and Marnie Lamb, who was the Freelance Permissions Researcher. My thanks also extend to those with whom I am just beginning, even as I write this Preface, to work to take the chapters written and develop them to create the final result: Christine Gilbert (Production Project Manager), Rajachitra (Project Manager), and Jessie Coffey (Copy Editor).

As in any collective effort at a press, there are more people involved than I will ever know, and on behalf of both myself and the various authors assembled here, I want to thank all of them for their commitment and dedication in bringing you, the reader, the volume that you now hold in your hands (or are reading on your screen)!

Christopher G. Anderson
Wilfrid Laurier University

ABOUT THE CONTRIBUTORS

Yasmeen Abu-Laban is Professor of Political Science at the University of Alberta. She has published widely on issues relating to the Canadian and comparative dimensions of gender and racialization processes, border and migration policies, and citizenship theory. She is the co-editor of *Surveillance and Control in Israel/Palestine: Population, Territory, and Power* (2011); co-editor of *Politics in North America: Redefining Continental Relations* (2008); and editor of *Gendering the Nation-State: Canadian and Comparative Perspectives* (2008). She is also the co-author (with Christina Gabriel) of *Selling Diversity: Immigration, Multiculturalism, Employment Equity and Globalization* (2002).

Christopher G. Anderson is an Associate Professor in the Department of Political Science at Wilfrid Laurier University. He received his PhD from McGill University and his BA from the University of Toronto. His research encompasses both historical and contemporary studies of Canadian citizenship, multiculturalism, immigration, and refugee policy. His book, *Canadian Liberalism and the Politics of Border Control, 1867–1967* was published in 2013.

Amanda Bittner is an Associate Professor in the Department of Political Science at Memorial University. She studies elections and voting, and her broad research interests include the effects of knowledge and information on voter decision-making, as well as the institutional and structural incentives affecting voting behaviour in both Canadian and comparative contexts. She is the author of *Platform or Personality? The Role of Party Leaders in Elections* (2011), and the co-author (with Royce Koop) of *Parties, Elections, and the Future of Canadian Politics* (2013).

Michelle D. Bonner is an Associate Professor in the Department of Political Science at the University of Victoria. She specializes in comparative and Latin America politics with an interest in human rights, democratization, policing, social movements, and media. She is the author of two books, *Policing Protest in Argentina and Chile* (2014) and *Sustaining Human Rights: Women and Argentine Human Rights*

Organizations (2007), as well as many articles in academic journals such as the *Journal of Latin American Studies*, *International Journal of Press/Politics*, and the *International Journal of Transitional Justice*. She regularly teaches undergraduate courses in the politics of development.

Arjun Chowdhury is an Assistant Professor in the Department of Political Science at the University of British Columbia. He received his PhD from the University of Minnesota and his BA from Vassar College. His primary research interest is in international security. He is currently working on a book manuscript that explains why most states in the world are weak states.

David Docherty is President of Mount Royal University. He holds a PhD in political science and is evangelical about our Westminster Parliamentary system and the men and women who serve in it.

John Kurt Edwards is a graduate of the Policy Studies program of Mount Royal University. His research interests include democratic institutions, economic theory, and the mechanisms of social change throughout history.

Anna Esselment is an Assistant Professor in the Department of Political Science at the University of Waterloo. She earned her PhD at the University of Western Ontario, where she examined the role of partisanship in intergovernmental relations. Her areas of teaching and research interests include Canadian politics and institutions, campaigns and elections, political marketing, political advisors, and intergovernmental relations.

Rodney Haddow is an Associate Professor in the Department of Political Science at the University of Toronto, where he teaches Canadian and comparative politics. Among other publications, he has written *Comparing Ontario and Quebec: Political Economy and Public Policy at the Turn of the Millennium* (2015), *Poverty Reform in Canada* (1993), and co-authored *Partisanship, Globalization, and Canadian Labour Market Policy: Four Provinces in Comparative Perspective* (2006).

His research interests are in the fields of Canadian and comparative political economy and welfare state scholarship. He has published articles in the *Canadian Journal of Political Science*, *Canadian Public Policy*, *Canadian Public Administration*, the *Journal of Canadian Studies*, and the *International Journal of Canadian Studies*, and has contributed numerous book chapters.

Matthew Hennigar is an Associate Professor in the Department of Political Science at Brock University. His teaching and research focus on Canadian and comparative law and politics, constitutional law, judicial appointment, and government litigation in rights cases. He is the co-author (with Lori Hausegger and Troy Riddell) of *Canadian Courts*, and his work has appeared in such venues as the *Canadian Journal of Political Science*, *Law and Society Review*, *I-Con: International Journal of Constitutional Law*, *Osgoode Hall Law Journal*, *University of Toronto Law Journal*, *Canadian Public Administration* and *Comparative Politics*.

Sandy Irvine teaches political science at Wilfrid Laurier and McMaster Universities. He received his PhD from the University of Toronto and MA degrees from McMaster and St. Andrews Universities. He conducts research in the areas of international migration, global governance, global security, and Canadian refugee policy.

Rachel Laforest is an Associate Professor and head of the Public Policy and Third Sector Initiative in the School of Policy Studies, Queen's University in Canada. Her areas of expertise are the study of governance and welfare state restructuring. Her current research interests focus on poverty reduction strategies and welfare state restructuring. She is also interested in intergovernmental relations and Canadian politics. She is the author of *Voluntary Sector Organizations and the State* (2011). She is also the editor of *The New Federal Policy Agenda and the Voluntary Sector: On the Cutting Edge* (2009)

and of *Government-Nonprofit Relations in Times of Recession* (2013).

Stephen Phillips teaches political science at Langara College in Vancouver. Trained in law and political science, he teaches Canadian government and comparative politics. His research interests include comparative parliamentary systems, political parties, and the Crown in Canada. He has recently contributed chapters on BC politics to the *Canadian Annual Review of Politics and Public Affairs*.

Claire Turenne Sjolander is Vice-Dean (Graduate Studies) at the Faculty of Social Sciences, as well as Professor of Political Science, at the University of Ottawa. A student of International Relations Theory and Canadian Foreign Policy, she has many publications in these areas. Her recent publications include *Canada in the World: Internationalism in Canadian Foreign Policy* (2013), co-edited with Heather Smith; and "Through the Looking Glass: Canadian Identity and the War of 1812," *International Journal*, 69:2 (2014) (this article was awarded the 2014 Marcel Cadieux Distinguished Writing Award). Her teaching has gained her the University of Ottawa's Excellence in Education Award (2008–2009), and the Faculty of Social Sciences' Professor of the Year Award (2004). Her scholarship has earned her the 2012 Distinguished Scholar Award of the International Studies Association (ISA-Canada).

Richard Sigurdson is Dean of Arts at the University of Calgary, where he is also Professor of Political Science. His areas of academic interest include contemporary political theory, Canadian politics and government, and the history of political thought. He has published a book on Jacob Burckhardt's social and political thought and numerous articles and book chapters on topics including nationalism, immigration, the Canadian Charter of Rights, multiculturalism, and provincial party politics in Canada.

PART

1

INTRODUCTION

© TongRo Images/Alamy

CHAPTER 1

STUDYING POLITICS: AN INTRODUCTION

Christopher G. Anderson

© ANDREI PUNGOVSCHII/AFP/Getty Images

Protesters in Bucharest, Romania, protest against a 2013 government plan to allow a Canadian mining company to level four mountains, creating the largest open-pit mine in Europe, to extract gold and silver. This example reminds us of the complexity of politics, pitting—for example—environmental exploitation versus environmental protection, public policies versus public protests, and Canadian corporations versus non-Canadian communities.

CHAPTER OBJECTIVES

After you have completed this chapter, you should be able to:

- appreciate the scope and complexity of the political world in which we live
- identify tools and knowledge that you already possess, and those that you can gain and improve, in the study and practice of politics
- understand that defining politics is itself a political act, and that how we approach politics (for example, as a cynic or a skeptic) can influence both our engagement with politics and potential political outcomes
- identify the basic characteristics of an essentially contested concept and its relevance to key political concepts such as "power"
- view politics as an arena of lifelong study and practice

INTRODUCTION

Politics is the privileged domain of neither political scientists nor politicians. Rather, it is a vital area of study for us all as we are forever part of and affected by the world of politics. Thus, while this textbook is certainly directed toward those who want to become part of the discipline of **Political Science**—involving the study of the institutions and processes through which, and the ideas on the basis of which, individuals and groups make decisions that have consequences for the recognition, production, and allocation of public and private goods and goals—as well as those who plan to become active in politics (for some of the career paths that can stem from a degree in Political Science, see Box 1.1), it is also written for students who want to increase their ability to navigate the often complex and confusing debates and issues that surround them that can be found under the fairly broad umbrella of "politics." In an effort to meet these different but overlapping interests, this textbook is designed to help you to:

> **Political science:** The study of the institutions and processes through which, and the ideas on the basis of which, individuals and groups make decisions that have consequences for the recognition, production, and allocation of public and private goods and goals.

- become clearer about and in your own political beliefs;
- develop your capacity to be critical about politics along constructive paths (that is, not just to *criticize* but to understand and compare different ideas about politics and to raise, if not yet answer, relevant questions about them);
- explore and appreciate the diversity of approaches available in the study and practice of politics;
- identify and examine core concepts, debates, issues, and themes in Political Science; and,
- undertake all the above in reference to political events in the past as well as those unfolding around us.

After you finish this course, you will know more about the political world in which you live and will have developed more rigorous and productive habits when thinking about it. As well, you will come to see—or at least set yourself up to appreciate—how politics intersects not just with your daily life as a member of a community or a citizen of a country but with the study and practice of whatever career you choose to pursue while at school and beyond.

Over 2,000 years ago, in ancient Greece, the philosopher Aristotle called politics the "master science of the good" because he saw in it a form of inquiry that allowed for the determination of how the best ends of society—in which happiness was achieved while governed by reason—could be attained.[1] Certainly, politics is distinctive in that it has direct bearing on the decisions that we make together as individuals and groups to further our various objectives and goals. And while many areas of study can make strong claims on influencing our quality of life (after all, everyone is subject to biology, economics, and history,

BOX 1.1

COMMON CAREER PATHS FOR POLITICAL SCIENCE GRADUATES

Campaign/Elections Officer	Public Relations
Market Researcher/Analyst	Human Rights Officer
Diplomat/Embassy Officer	Urban Planner
Legislative/Parliamentary Assistant	Lobbyist
Journalist/Reporter	Political Activist
Public Policy Analyst	Intelligence/Security Agent
Public Opinion Pollster/Analyst	Consumer Advocate
Professor/Teacher	Media Analyst/Researcher
Political Strategist	Labour Organizer/Negotiator
Public Administration (all levels of government)	Law Enforcement
Lawyer/Paralegal	Program Evaluator
Community Worker	Immigration Officer

for example), one special feature of politics is that we all have the capacity to study and practice, and possess considerable experience in, politics. Indeed, every person reading this textbook has already acquired some basic political tools, although they may not recognize them as such. Moreover, your capacity and experience in this respect are constantly being engaged and refined. Of course, some individuals have developed these tools more explicitly and extensively than others through personal interest and inclination, opportunity and chance, as well as formal education, families and friends, among other influences. Nonetheless, each of you possesses some of the basic skills needed to reflect on and participate in politics in a meaningful way (look at the list provided in Box 1.2—when you think about your education and experience to date, you have probably used all of these skills in some form or another).

This is a really important point to keep in mind because a wide range of consequential political decisions are constantly being made on your behalf, with or without your involvement, by diverse actors both inside and beyond government. Whether or not you are interested in politics, rest assured that politics is interested in you! And while none of us can be aware of and engaged in all the politics that affects our lives (after all, as you will see it encompasses an extensive and complex terrain), by identifying and developing our political skills we can become better prepared to recognize when it is important to use them, and how to do so to better effect.

So, while every person can perform politics, we can all learn how to perform better: practice may not make perfect but it can certainly make for improvement. For example, despite the complexity of politics, all of us can express political opinions on most any subject that is brought to our attention. Take a look at the photograph that opens this chapter. If you and your friends or classmates sat down to talk about the sorts of issues that it raises—such as environmental exploitation versus environmental protection, public policies versus public protests, and Canadian corporations versus non-Canadian communities—all of you could form some political opinions. You could offer comments in reaction to the situation, put forward ideas as to how you feel about the issues that it generates, and even offer possible solutions. If you then went around the group or room, you would quickly

BOX 1.2

TRANSFERABLE SKILLS DEVELOPED IN THE STUDY OF POLITICS

Although politics is rooted in some degree of passion and commitment, it also requires an ability to step back from events in order to understand them. Drawing on and refining the skills that we possess, we can develop new ways of interpreting past and present circumstances, and identifying future possibilities.

An Analytical Capacity
- An ability to sort things, categorize them, or impose some scheme on what is otherwise an overwhelming set of materials
- An ability to draw relevant or significant distinctions between different classes of information
- An ability to comprehend and apply new and/or unfamiliar information to different situations and settings

A Synthetic Capacity
- An ability to identify and access a wide range of relevant information and resources
- An ability to see connections, including making surprising or unexpected connections by grouping like with unlike according to conceptual or classificatory schemes

The Skill of Critical Perspective
- An ability to engage with political events and gain a greater understanding of the processes involved in different political systems around the world
- An ability to separate oneself and one's emotions from events, and to escape the pressures of immediacy, to see the background to events, and to identify the broader chain of cause and effect
- An ability to appreciate the logical and empirical gaps not simply in the positions of others but in your own as well

others, at a more serious—and a more profound—level. Unless you were convinced by those with whom you had initially differed, you would have to try to explain in greater detail why you hold the positions that you do, and you would likely begin to move from making assertions about the issues at hand to developing arguments: putting forward more precise claims and backing them up with justifications and evidence in the face of counterarguments. Your friends and classmates would have to do the same. In the process, each of you would learn much more about what you think and believe. Indeed, you would probably shift a little (or even a lot) as you heard new ideas and had to respond to more precise questions about your own. You would be engaged in a lifelong practice of identifying, testing, and explaining your political ideas, sharpening the critical analytical and discursive skills that will stand you in good stead in the world of politics and beyond.

This textbook is designed to help you in this process of becoming more informed about the political world in which you live and, as a result, better able to think more systematically about it. An understanding of politics is not something that we are born with but rather is something that we must work at developing as we live our lives. That this undertaking will be lifelong should not be a cause for dismay any more than the fact that breathing is a lifelong practice! It simply is a reflection of the reality that we are surrounded by politics and that politics is implicated in the quality of our lives and our ability to achieve goals and objectives for ourselves, our families and friends, and our communities. Moreover, politics is a bit like a language: the more you study and practice it, the more comfortable you become using it, and the more you benefit as you reach new levels of communication and experience with others (take a look at Box 1.3, which gives you an idea of some of the dimensions of the language and knowledge of politics that you will gain). Thus, using the capabilities that you already possess—including your intelligence and creativity—you can, along with everyone else in your class, gain a good understanding of politics. This is, in fact, a significant feature of the study and practice of politics—it is never too late to become involved (and neither is it ever too early!) and the start-up costs are not very high at all.

In the pages that follow, we will explore two types of questions to help you in developing your

find that some agree with you and others disagree, while still others agree with some but not all of what you have to say. And this is where the more interesting work would begin: you would have to think through your initial comments, as well as those made by the

BOX 1.3

SPECIFIC KNOWLEDGE SKILLS ACQUIRED IN THE STUDY OF POLITICS

Although the exact list may differ, this is the sort of knowledge that you will acquire through the study of politics at college or university, all of which will be useful in your lives whether you want to become a Political Scientist, active in politics, or just more comfortable understanding the political world around you.

- Familiarity with central ideas and ideologies that animate political discussions and actions, and an appreciation of both their inherent complexity and tendency to evolve over time
- Recognition of ways in which societal and economic factors and forces influence politics, and vice versa
- Identification of factors that produce regime stability in more and less democratic political systems, both within and between different levels of government, and perpetual difficulties in appropriately apportioning power among different actors in all political systems
- Knowledge of the respective roles and powers of executive and legislative branches of government in different political systems, and of constitutions and the judiciary in defining both the scope of political authority held by executive and legislative actors, and in shaping society-state relations
- Understanding of formal and informal processes through which people seek to influence decision-makers, including elections, political parties, and civil society organizations
- Appreciation of global dimensions of contemporary politics as concerns questions of development, war and peace, and human security, for example, and of the role of theory in helping us to understand these connections

understanding of politics. The first type of question encompasses more traditional academic inquiries, the answers to which provide a common language and a shared history that facilitate our discussions about politics. What is politics? What does it mean to be political or to act in a political manner? How can politics be studied and why should it be studied? What are some of the core concepts and theories that we have developed to assist in describing and explaining the political world? What kinds of knowledge have we generated about politics? How relevant is that knowledge to the world in which we live? What are some of the areas where we need to develop a better understanding of how politics operates? The second type of question involves more personal lines of inquiry, the answers to which remind us that we all share a world of politics regardless of our level of commitment or interest. What are your own political beliefs? What political issues are important to you? In what ways do you or people you know engage in politics? What sorts of constraints and opportunities exist that affect your ability to pursue political goals and objectives? Should you become more involved in politics and how would you do so? What are some of the consequences of choosing instead to ignore politics? While no one textbook or course can provide complete answers to any of these questions (remember, politics is a lifelong practice), they will help you to develop a better grasp of what good answers to some of them might look like.

DEFINING POLITICS

Before going any further, there are three steps that we should take. First, it is important to get a sense of what politics entails, which will give us an appreciation of its scope. Second, we can then survey different definitions of politics, each of which tells us something different about its study and practice. Finally, and in taking these two steps, we can see how defining "politics" is itself a political act and identify implications of this insight.

Four dimensions of politics: We begin by considering certain dimensions of politics that give us an indication of what it entails. First, there is a formal (and most familiar) dimension. When people hear the word "politics," many immediately think of states and governments, presidents and prime ministers, parliaments and congresses, constitutions and courts, elections and political parties. These are some of the many specific institutions and processes that give shape to much of the political world around us. For example, when there is an election campaign

THINK AND DISCUSS

As you learn more about politics in this class, it will be useful for you to establish a personal bench-mark for your learning. Take a piece of paper and write down your own definition of "politics" in a few sentences. Next, write down three political issues that you think are the most important in the world today. Compare your responses with those of your classmates and consider the ways in which they are similar and different. Hold on to this piece of paper. At the end of the course, once again write down your own definition of politics and see whether and how much your ideas have changed.

underway—whether a contest for the presidency of a student union on campus or the presidency of a country—we know that we are in the middle of a political process. When a prime minister makes a speech on television, we know that she is making a political statement. When laws are passed by a legislature or interpreted by the courts, we know that political decisions are being made. And when people take to the streets to protest—or even overthrow—a government, we know that we are witnessing a political event. There are, then, certain places where we expect politics to unfold and certain actors that we expect to be involved in politics, and these constitute significant areas of study in the discipline of Political Science.

Second, in tandem with these formal institutions and processes there exists an informal dimension to politics. There is a common saying from the 1960s that partially reflects this idea: the personal is political.[2] Although first popularized within the feminist movement to call attention to how aspects of politics particularly germane to understanding the status of women in society were often hidden from view because they were deemed to be personal and therefore not political, it can be applied more generally to the question of the scope of politics. In this sense, there is an intersection between the formal world of politics and our personal lives that expands the space for the boundaries of politics to be defined, practiced, contested, and, as a result, redefined. In short, there is no inevitable and immutable division between the political and non-political but rather this changes over time as people make decisions about what matters to them and how to respond to perceived constraints on and opportunities for their scope of action. Politics can, therefore, be seen wherever people undertake actions that they (or we, as observers) consider to be

political, which can open up avenues of politics in both anticipated and unanticipated ways.

The idea of the intersection between the formal and informal in politics is reflected in the photograph of the Nishiyuu Walkers arriving on Parliament Hill in Ottawa on March 25, 2013 (see http://nishiyuujourney.ca/). On January 16, 2013, six Cree youth accompanied by an experienced trekker/spiritual guide began the 1,600 kilometre walk from Whapmagoostui (the northernmost Cree community in Quebec, consisting of some 900 people) on the Hudson Bay coast. The walk was originally conceived by 17-year-old David Kawapit as a way of supporting Attawapiskat First Nation Chief Theresa Spence of Victoria Island (near Ottawa), who was engaged in a hunger strike to protest the federal government's treatment of Aboriginal peoples, including various legislative proposals that would affect Aboriginal treaty rights and sovereignty. As well, the path chosen was seen as a way of building solidarity among Aboriginal groups along traditional trade routes. On the way, the youth were joined by many others and numbered some 270 by the time they reached Ottawa. At Parliament Hill, the walkers were greeted by hundreds more, who held a rally in support of Aboriginal peoples in general and the walkers' accomplishment in particular. When interviewed, David Kawapit spoke of the need for youth to become more engaged in politics: "This is to show the youth have a voice. It's time for them to be shown the way to lead. Let them lead the way," he said.[3] The photo, then, captures the informality of politics: how individuals who feel excluded and/or that they have something important to say can—using a wide range of skills stemming from their creativity and intelligence, their life experiences and commitment—develop new ways of raising issues in politics and mobilizing support from society. It also, quite literally through the Peace Tower on Parliament Hill in the background, underscores the formality of politics—the centrality (in this case) of the Canadian state in defining and shaping the status of Aboriginal peoples in Canada through such institutions as the Department of Aboriginal Affairs and Northern Development and the Indian Act, and through various policies and laws that affect Aboriginal ways of life.

In the study and practice of politics, then, it is important to look out for both formal and informal dimensions as well as the interplay between them. All the more so because the formal dimensions—despite the fact that they are more readily identifiable—often unfold in quite surprising ways, while the informal dimensions—despite their seeming fluidity—can congeal into predictable forms of behaviour. In order to appreciate and understand these tendencies better, however, we need to take note of two additional aspects of politics.

A third important dimension revolves around history. Politics never unfolds in a vacuum and important determining factors often stem from what has come before. Even in the most revolutionary periods the past is never simply overthrown but transformed and adapted to reflect new political demands and forces. It is no trite statement to observe, therefore, that in order to comprehend the present, and to anticipate where we might go in the future, we must

Nishiyuu Walkers arriving on Parliament Hill. While the Canadian flag flies atop the Peace Tower, the Nishiyuu Walkers hold aloft a flag of their own, with a warrior on horseback superimposed on the maple leaf, suggesting an alternate vision of Canada.

© The Canadian Press/Fred Chartrand

investigate the past. Or perhaps, better yet, the *pasts*, as there are many different ways of thinking about what has brought us to now at any given time, and we constantly revise and expand upon these understandings. So while it may not quite be true that, as the essayist George Santanya famously wrote, "[t]hose who cannot remember the past are condemned to repeat it,"[4] it is generally more difficult to navigate the present and future if we fail to either examine or seek to comprehend their roots.

Let's look again at the example of the Nishiyuu Walkers. It is impossible to understand what compelled these young people to undertake this action, or Chief Spence to go on her hunger strike, without examining the history of colonialism in Canada and its continuation into the present. When Prime Minister Stephen Harper declared, while extolling the virtues of Canada at an important international meeting in 2009, that Canadians "have no history of colonialism," he was probably thinking about the sort of extra-territorial colonialism practiced by many European countries over the centuries in Africa, Asia, the Caribbean, and Latin America (surveyed in Chapter 13).[5] His comment, however, serves as a reminder that Canadians often forget, or at least do not appreciate more fully, the historical legacy and continuing effects of colonialism on the economic, political, and social well-being of Aboriginal peoples in Canada.[6]

Finally, a fourth but by no means less consequential dimension of politics concerns ideas. Just as the word "politics" calls to mind a range of institutions, processes, behaviours, and issues—from the past and present—it also prompts words such as democracy and freedom, equality and liberty, justice and fairness, as well as their opposites. Ideas can operate as incredibly powerful, even transformative, tools in politics, but they have to be thought of and articulated before they can really serve to mobilize people. We constantly draw on ideas to help us navigate through the complex world of politics. (We will address this more extensively when we turn to look at the role of concepts in the study and practice of politics, further below.)

If we return one last time to the Nishiyuu Walkers, we can see that a range of important ideas give shape and definition to the ways in which politics concerning relations between Aboriginal peoples and the Canadian state unfold. For example, the vision statement of the

Department of Aboriginal Affairs begins by observing that "Our vision is a future in which First Nations, Inuit, Métis and northern communities are healthy, safe, self-sufficient and prosperous—a Canada where people make their own decisions, manage their own affairs and make strong contributions to the country as a whole."[7] In contrast, the Declaration of First Nations, found on the Assembly of First Nations' website, asserts that "The Creator has given us the right to govern ourselves and the right to self-determination" and that "The rights and responsibilities given to us by the creator cannot be altered or taken away by any other Nation."[8] There is a world of difference between self-sufficiency within a broader Canadian nation and self-determination within the context of equal nation-to-nation relations. In short, the ideas that motivate and propel Aboriginal politics on the part of the Canadian state are often strikingly different from—and at times incompatible with—those that motivate and propel many First Nations communities. It is possible, as Canadian author John Ralston Saul has argued, that we could learn a lot about how to govern Canada better if we worked harder to build bridges between Canadian and Aboriginal histories, knowledge, and philosophies.[9]

So what do these four dimensions tell us about the nature of politics at this stage? First, we can see that it is *complex*: the dynamics of politics are multidimensional, touching on institutions, processes, issues, actions, traditions, and histories as well as beliefs and ideas, to name but a few aspects. Second, it is *contested*: politics involves numerous and varied disagreements, disputes, and conflicts between and within states, governments, and communities, as well as individuals; contests over, for example, positions, resources, and ideas. Third, and at the same time, however, politics is *cooperative*: there needs to be a certain level of agreement as to who governs and the powers that they require, for example, so that we can identify what we want to do together and how we are going to do it. Last but not least, it is *crucial*: much is at stake on issues both great and small for us all in politics, since it touches upon most every aspect of our individual and collective well-being.

Different definitions of politics. Now that we have identified some key dimensions of politics, we can turn

to examine different definitions, each of which sheds additional light on what it means to study and practice politics. We can turn first, as we often do when we want to understand the meaning of a word, to dictionaries and encyclopedias. For example, according to *Merriam-Webster's Collegiate® Dictionary, 11th Edition*, politics is "… the art or science concerned with guiding or influencing governmental policy…"* This definition alerts us to the notion that politics involves both science and art, each of which can reflect regularity and spontaneity as well as orderliness and creativity. Politics is neither wholly predictable nor wholly random, otherwise there would be limited use in studying it (or at least there would be much less of it that would merit close study). Thus, when we examine politics we are looking for patterns that exist in the realm of probability rather than certainty. In the face of such bounded uncertainty, the study and practice of politics is a perpetually unfinished project but one about which we can forever discover something new.

For an alternate definition, we could turn to Wikipedia (although professors usually suggest that you avoid Wikipedia as an academic source for research, due to the lack of a peer review process that ensures sufficient reliability, it can be a useful tool to get your feet wet on a given subject or when you want a quick reminder of what you have previously studied), where politics is defined as a "process by which decisions are made within groups. Although the term is applied generally to behaviour within governments, politics is observed in all human (and many non-human) group interactions."[10] With this definition, the essential influence of the human being is introduced into the mix. Although research on chimpanzees suggests that they, too, engage in local politics,[11] and recent studies reveal the existence of interspecies warfare among bees,[12] politics is a vital human activity. As far back in time as we can go through written and archaeological records, wherever we find human beings living together, we find evidence of politics. Aristotle's famous (and gendered) assertion that "man is a political animal"[13] underlines this point. Given the sheer variation experienced in the lives of human beings, we can once again appreciate the intrinsic sources of the complexity of politics.

---

*By permission. From *Merriam-Webster's Collegiate® Dictionary, 11th Edition* ©2015 by Merriam-Webster, Inc. (www.Merriam-Webster.com).

We could continue to quote and unpack such definitions but we might do well to turn to political scientists themselves to see how they have dealt with the term. In 1939, Harold Lasswell published a book that today is probably better known for its title than its contents: *Politics: Who Gets What, When, How.* The book opens with an assertion that "the study of politics is the study of influence and the influential."[14] Politics often revolves around the ability of individuals and groups to affect and effect particular outcomes, in turn producing winners and losers. An important feature of the study of politics, therefore, involves identifying *who* is involved in contests over *what* kinds of ends or goods, and under what conditions—*when* and *how*—they are able to achieve their goals. We could usefully add *why* to this list, as there is usually an explanatory drive to our investigations: we are rarely satisfied with only uncovering what happens and also want to explain why it happens (and why something else does not happen). And if politics is neither predetermined nor random, then we ought to be able, with enough effort and appropriate tools, to identify some patterns. The hope that motivates much of Political Science as a science, then, is that if we can grasp, albeit imperfectly, the nature of these patterns then we can increase our ability not just to understand the world better but to change it for the better as well. As you will see throughout this textbook, although they may champion and employ different tools with which to study politics, political scientists are generally united in their attempts to identify important patterns in politics.[15]

Another influential work, *Bringing the State Back In*, raises the question of where we should focus our attention when we study politics. When Peter Evans, Dietrich Reuschmeyer, and Theda Skocpol published this collection in the mid-1980s they were reacting to what they perceived to be a predominant trend of studying politics through a narrow lens of "society-centred theories" of political behaviour (as exemplified in the work of Lasswell, for example) that overlooked or ignored the central role of state institutions, especially in terms of the capacity and autonomy of states to "formulate and pursue goals that are not simply reflective of the demands or interests of social groups, classes, or society."[16] In their work, Evans and his colleagues sought to rectify this situation by bringing state institutions toward the centre of political analysis.

People do not act in an open political environment; rather their behaviour is both informed by and channeled around and/or through political institutions. It is difficult, for example, to offer a convincing explanation of voter behaviour without taking into account the institutions that define how elections operate. And if you change those institutions, people will generally alter their behaviour in response to the new rules put into place. Although we can focus more on one or the other, behaviour or institutions, often we are most interested in the interplay between the two. If we focus too much on institutions, then we risk overlooking ways in which people act outside those boundaries, while if we stress the role of individuals unduly, then we may exaggerate the scope for autonomous action that people actually possess.

Apart from those who study politics, we can look to those who practice it—the politicians—and once again find an array of insights and ideas. For example, Mao Zedong, a leader in the revolution that resulted in the establishment of the People's Republic of China in 1949, wrote that "politics is war without bloodshed while war is politics with bloodshed."[17] Certainly, politics frequently seems to be related to conflict, to some winning and some losing. In a war, the parties engaged generally want to defeat one another in order to protect or gain some important good—resources such as land or oil, or perhaps independence. The same is often true in politics, as different actors seek to accomplish their goals at the expense of the goals of others. For example, the African-American Civil Rights Movement pitted those who sought to realize equality and liberty for African Americans against those who would continue to see them treated as second-class citizens on the basis of race. In this contest, neither side could envision giving up their goals in order to avoid conflict. While the struggle over civil rights stemmed from and often unfolded through violence (involving beatings, incarcerations, lynching, murders, and assassinations, for example, as well as fights, riots, and arson),[18] it also brought to the fore alternate means of politics, in particular the civil disobedience advocated by Martin Luther King and others, a tradition that had recently risen to prominence in the life and thought of Mahatma Ghandi in India and the work of the Russian novelist Leo Tolstoy, but which also had American roots through such individuals as Henry David Thoreau.[19]

Of course, politics is not just about zero-sum games, where the victory of one side is predicated on the defeat of the other. While conflict may seem inherent to politics, it certainly is not all there is, as captured by the well-worn phrase: "Politics is the art of compromise." Although the origins of this expression are not known, it contains a wisdom that is often overlooked in the hullabaloo of partisanship, where compromise is frequently portrayed (along with cooperation) as weakness rather than strength. Compromise, however, is an essential feature of democratic politics, as a wide range of ideas and interests can and need to find space in the political landscape if the type of stability that allows us to live fulfilled lives is to exist. In less democratic political systems, the room for compromise is much more constrained at every level—from limitations on the organization of political parties, for example, to those placed on the range of ideas that can be expressed in public without fear of punishment. Indeed, if we look back in history, we often find that great political instability has arisen when people feel that their interests and needs are not being met within the political system—when the system does not allow for sufficient compromise—and this can result in revolution, civil war, and other forms of extreme political action, including terrorism. This is true for democratic as well as non-democratic regimes.

Finally, we can turn to comedians and satirists for insight into the meaning of politics, as we often do through television shows such as Rick Mercer's *The Mercer Report* and John Oliver's *Last Week Tonight*. For example, we can look at the work of author Ambrose Bierce, who developed *The Devil's Dictionary* (originally published in 1906 as *The Cynic's Word Book*), in which he purported to provide the real definitions for words in common usage. Bierce defined politics, accordingly, as "a strife of interests masquerading as a contest of principles. The conduct of public affairs for private advantage."[20] This idea is similarly captured in a saying commonly attributed to author and critic Gore Vidal: "Politics is made up of two words: 'poli,' which is Greek for 'many,' and 'tics,' which are blood-sucking insects." These quotes, first of all, are funny, but they also speak to a profound issue in politics: To what extent can politics move beyond self-interest, and how do we, in small groups or large societies, accomplish this? What do we mean by, and how do we realize, the public good? If living together within a polity is in part a reflection of the desire to accomplish important goals together, then this is a vital—and vitally important—concern.

Defining politics as a political act. There are, then, many different ways of defining politics, and this leaves us with some good questions to address. First, why is there such variation? Why can we not just settle on one definition and be done with it? The answer lies in the fact that the world of politics includes the act of determining the definition of politics itself. Our definitions reflect our beliefs and values. If we believe that the personal is political, for example, then we will have a much more extensive understanding of politics than if we do not. The definition that we support is, in short, a reflection of who we are and therefore such variation is not such a surprise at all. Second, does this matter? Yes. It matters because "any definition, conception or understanding of politics is likely to carry with it quite far-reaching implications for how we study it."[21] Until quite recently, for example, what took place within the confines of a home with respect to relations between a man and a woman was deemed to be largely a private matter—and as a result, our conception of both violence against women and the responsibility of society (through the state) to intervene when such violence occurs was muted or absent. Thus, different definitions legitimate different types of political study and practice.

Finally, if the definition of politics is political and if this has important consequences for how we study and practice it, then what can or should we do about this? Well, one approach is to throw up our hands and declare that "anything goes"! Another approach, advocated here, is to accept the reality of this complexity and uncertainty, and to become engaged participants rather than more remote observers of the politics that surrounds us. While the challenges involved will seem daunting at times, there is comfort in the idea that— as Nobel Prize winning chemist Dudley Herschback is said to have observed—"You have to be confused before you can reach a new level of understanding anything." The world of politics *should*, given all that we have said to this point, appear a little overwhelming. After all, politics can be read in a wide range of ideas and events, it encompasses both formal and informal institutions and processes, it operates at a very individual level and yet includes communities that transcend national borders, and its pursuit can involve both conflict and cooperation. This produces a fair amount of debate within the discipline of Political Science over the meaning of politics, and thus the task of the political scientist. And if those trained to study these issues are beset by such uncertainties, then we can expect that reasonable people will disagree about a great number of things when it comes to politics. The more pressing issue is whether this situation convinces us to become engaged or disengaged as a result.

WHAT IS WRONG WITH POLITICS TODAY?

Most people today seem to have pretty negative views about politics. Ask yourself, or your family, friends, or classmates: Do you feel optimistic about politics, or do you feel more cynical? Do you feel that the political system is working well or do you feel that it does not deliver the sorts of leadership that we need? When you think about politics, do you want to get involved with a political issue or a political party, or do you feel that it is all a bit out of your control? When another political scandal appears in the media, are you surprised? If you or those you know have predominantly negative feelings toward politics, then you are certainly not alone. In Canada and more generally in liberal-democratic political systems—places where the voice of the people is supposed to be more influential—there is a discernible sense of unease over the state of politics (it is more understandable that such discontent exists in less democratic systems, since "the people" have a less autonomous role to play in collective decision-making). Sometimes this is referred to as a **democratic deficit**—a gap between our expectations of the political system and what we actually think happens within it.

> **Democratic deficit:** The perceived gap between the theoretical principles of democracy and the actual practice of ostensibly democratic institutions, including national governments and international organizations.

We can see this along many dimensions. Take, for example, the results captured in Table 1.1: politicians rank among the lowest of professions in terms of levels of societal respect. These responses are consistent with many studies over the past few decades. Books with titles such as *Disaffected Democracy* and *Imperfect Democracies* capture this sentiment and these findings in the literature.[22] Even in political systems ostensibly designed to represent a wide range of interests, then, there is a sense that too many people are excluded and too few are in control. Moreover, those in control are not generally deemed worthy of much respect. As you will see elsewhere in this textbook, we can find similar evidence of disconnect from the political system in the low numbers of people who vote in elections or join political parties. We can also see it in the Occupy movement (which opposes the concentration of wealth and its disproportionate influence on politics) and other forms of popular protest in both established democracies and, as with the Arab Spring movement in the Middle East and North Africa, the less democratic world. What needs to be recognized is that a negative perception of politicians, political systems, and politics more generally can be inspired by a hope for change but it can also reflect a rejection of the possibilities for politics to produce positive outcomes for society.

A cynic is "a person who has negative opinions about other people and about the things people do…"* Such an individual expects the worst from politics and finds this belief consistently confirmed whenever they hear about the latest problem or scandal. It is not that such cynicism has no real-world foundations, of course, but this outlook operates on a limited or partial understanding of that world. Take an example that has been prevalent in the media in recent years—the scandals surrounding the Canadian Senate. The Senate was created to perform certain functions in the Canadian political system. Most notably, it was to provide a chamber of sober second thought (that is, a place where the rough and tumble of partisan politics so prevalent in the House of Commons is partially held in check since Senators are appointed rather than elected and thus can operate with some freedom, seeing as neither citizens nor political parties can punish them for speaking their mind) and to ensure greater regional representation.

---

* By permission. From *Merriam-Webster's Collegiate® Dictionary, 11th Edition* ©2015 by Merriam-Webster, Inc. (www.Merriam-Webster.com).

TABLE 1.1 LEVELS OF RESPECT FOR VARIOUS PROFESSIONS	Canada	United States	United Kingdom
Nurses	96	92	93
Doctors	96	86	90
Farmers	95	93	84
Scientists	92	87	88
Teachers	88	88	80
Military Officers	86	85	82
Police Officers	85	81	78
Judges	76	70	64
Priests/Ministers	66	76	54
Journalists	63	53	20
Building Contractors	61	69	43
Lawyers	56	45	53
Business Executives	55	48	28
Bankers	55	53	15
Car Salespeople	28	30	14
Politicians	27	20	15

The following question was put to Canadian, American, and British respondents: "Generally speaking, do you tend to have a great deal of respect, a fair amount of respect, not much respect, or very little respect for each of the following professions?"

Percentage of respondents who answered "great deal" and "fair amount" shown.

Source: Angus Reid Public Opinion, "Nurses, Doctors Are Most Respected Jobs in Canada, U.S. and Britain," October 2, 2012, online at http://www.angusreidglobal.com/wp-content/uploads/2012/09/2012.10.02_Professions.pdf (accessed June 23, 2015).

There have been criticisms of the Senate for just about as long as there has been a Senate, including calls for its abolition. Some people, for example, argue that although the Senate has the power to defeat any bill passed by the House, it almost never uses this power. Instead, critics maintain, legislation is quickly and routinely "rubber-stamped" with little serious discussion or debate. When senators are more active on the legislative front, however, they are often criticized for delaying legislation sent to them by the democratically elected members of the House. The Senate is also held to be a type of "country club" for friends of the prime minister, who has the power to appoint them with no effective oversight. Senators are widely understood to receive numerous perks and a high salary for doing very little in return. There is, of course, some truth to these concerns. Senators are wary of playing too prominent a role in the review of legislation, and frequently confine themselves to improving the technical rather than challenging the political aspects of

the government's agenda. As for how seriously they take their jobs, numerous studies have shown that too many senators show up too infrequently for too little work (although there is also evidence of improvement over time), a criticism exemplified in the famous case of former Senator Andy Thompson, who spent much of the 1990s residing in Mexico while drawing his senatorial paycheck.[23] From late 2012 onwards, it has been the personal misconduct of senators that has been the primary focus of concern after Senators Patrick Brazeau, Mike Duffy, Mac Harb, and Pamela Wallin were found to have made inappropriate travel and/or housing expense claims. All four were ordered to repay funds, and Brazeau, Duffy, and Wallin were suspended without pay from the Senate (Harb retired in 2013).

As the issue hit the front pages of both the tabloid and broadsheet press, splashed across television screens, prompted a seemingly endless stream of blogs and tweets, and kept political cartoonists busy, it was reported that an impressively high 96.7 percent of Canadians had heard about the scandal.[24] But what, exactly, had they learned from the flood of details presented to them? Did Canadians have an informed context within which to assess the information and allegations that emerged, or did it just confirm the negative views that they already held about Canadian politics in general and the Senate in particular? These are significant questions, since by the middle of 2013, 41 percent of Canadians were said to be in favour of abolishing the Senate (another 49 percent supported its reform).[25] But what do Canadians really know about either the role of the Senate or the consequences of such a bold move as getting rid of it?

If what we know of the extent of Canadians' political and historical knowledge about their country is anything to go by,[26] chances are good that they do not know all that much about either. Even one of the foremost Canadian parliamentary scholars, C.E.S. Franks, expressed his surprise when he turned to look at the work of the Senate up close. According to the general portrayal in the academic literature, he ought to have found a Senate that played a relatively minor and unproductive role in the legislative process.

Images such as this reflect a common portrayal of the work of Canadian senators, and can feed into the cynicism of Canadians when it comes to the Senate or, more generally, politics.

© Tim Dolighan

Instead, he recounts, "I found myself time and again surprised and even taken aback by the thoroughness, level-headedness, insight and thoughtfulness of the Senate's review of legislation and investigations into a wide range of social, economic and other issues."[27] Its work, he concluded, was "vital to the effective functioning of Parliament" and at times exceeded the quality of that undertaken in the House. Thus, while abolishing the Senate might seem an expedient way of removing a particular problem (the personal indiscretions of some senators), a more effective response might be to develop a better way of appointing them in the first place. Moreover, if the Senate were to be abolished there is no guarantee that the House would do a better job at producing good government—we might find ourselves in an even worse situation (which would feed right into the cynic's expectations, however). It is not clear, therefore, that the negative views of Canadians—however well-entrenched—are either well-informed or well-purposed to improve the quality of our politics.

So why do so many people hold such negative views of politicians, political systems, and politics? Well, we can likely identify a range of reasons, many of which you might have thought yourself. For some people, politicians waste public resources (our tax money!), say anything to gain and remain in power, can be influenced or bought to work for private interests while in power, are disconnected from citizens and "the real world," mask self-interest as public interest, and approach complex political problems in simplistic zero-sum (win-or-lose) terms. Many consider that politics is rooted in conflicts over interests, values, and identities that reflect particular rather than general interests, suppresses our true potential as a society, and is too complex and confusing, leading people to feel that they cannot make a difference against the powers that be. As well, and less charitably toward ourselves, it may be that we have unrealistic expectations of politics—we want simple answers to complex questions, do not take the time to become informed about important issues and events (never mind the political system itself), and even share many of the same characteristics that we ascribed to politicians, such as being self-interested and seeing the world in zero-sum terms. It is not that we are bad people but we may not try hard enough at politics, and may, as a result, look for reasons to excuse our bad habits.

Indeed, it is possible that this habit of looking for the worst in our politicians and political systems and readily finding it confirmed (especially with a media that itself seems to prefer negative over positive stories when it comes to politics) has become a part of our **political culture**—the collection of the understandings, values, attitudes, and principles of a community or society that relate to its political organization, processes, disputes, and public policies. Like culture at a broader level, political culture—although difficult to define with precision—structures our behaviour and expectations, in this case about politics.[28] It is part of a shared outlook that helps to define who we are and what we do. Thus, we do not operate as purely autonomous individuals but are parts and reflections of society and its constituent communities. Although political culture is malleable (after all, in the early 20th century it was accepted in Canada that women, Aboriginal peoples, "Asians," and others should be denied the right to vote, a position that is no longer tolerated) and flexible (we can certainly challenge it and perhaps even operate outside parts of it), we are acculturated within it during our lives as a result of **political socialization**, a process through which attitudes toward knowledge about political matters are passed on within a society.

> **Political culture:** The collection of understandings, values, attitudes, and principles of a community or society that relate to its political organization, processes, disputes, and public policies. Out of a society's political culture come important beliefs and values that structure the citizens' attitudes and expectations toward such political concepts as legitimacy, power, authority, and obedience.

> **Political socialization:** The processes through which attitudes toward and knowledge about political matters are passed on within a society.

We are all socialized in a variety of ways throughout our lives by what are called **agents of political socialization**, those people or institutions that convey political attitudes and values to others in society. Think about how you have learned about how politics works in Canada or beyond its borders. Chances are that you would list such agents as your family, the schools that you have attended, the media (including social media),

your peers, the places you have worked and the organizations that you have belonged to or participated in (faith-based organizations, community groups, and so on), as well as the institutions and processes of the state itself. Sometimes our knowledge and habits have been passed on to us directly (perhaps your parents took you to a polling station during an election when you were young) while at other times it may have been indirect (perhaps you simply heard about a friend who volunteered for an environmental group). Such socialization can be both positive and negative, however, and if we are surrounded by people and institutions that encourage us to see the worst in politics—to be cynical about politics—then we may well come to view this as normal and appropriate, and subsequently take the negative examples that arise around us as confirmation of the validity of this approach.

> **Agents of political socialization:** Those groups of people or institutions that convey political attitudes and values to others in society.

Why is such cynicism dangerous? We have already touched on some of the ways in which it seems to discourage participation and awareness on the part of the citizenry. If politics is about, at some fundamental level, the people, then it is no small problem when we become disengaged from the political system in large numbers, and it is an even greater problem when we accept or even celebrate that disengagement. Moreover, such cynicism might convince politicians and those who aspire to political office that politics really is about self-interest rather than the public good, and thus we may encourage the sorts of behaviour that we so dislike. Indeed, given the low levels of respect with which we generally hold politicians, we may discourage those who really wish to serve the public from becoming involved, as it is unlikely that they will receive positive recognition for their efforts. All of this suggests that rather than looking in from the outside, criticizing those working on the inside, we may need to take a hard look at ourselves to see what we each can do to improve the situation. In short, we may need, like Walt Kelly's famous political cartoon character Pogo (see overleaf) observed long ago, to recognize that we must take some responsibility for being part of the problem.

In part, an introduction to politics course and its supporting textbook offer the opportunity to take

This is a play on a famous message sent by American Commodore Oliver Hazard Perry after his victory at the Battle of Lake Erie during the War of 1812: "We have met the enemy and they are ours." Walt Kelly, who pen and inked the classic political comic, *Pogo*, adapted this phrase for the first Earth Day poster in 1970 to remind us that we need to look closer to home to explain some of the great problems that we face as a society.

© *Okefenokee Glee & Perloo, Inc. Used by permission.*

such a step by shifting our gaze away from seeing politics as somewhere else and politicians as someone else. By increasing our knowledge about how political systems operate we can situate ourselves better within the political world of which we are, whether we know it or not and whether we like it or not, a part. So what would it take for us to become less cynical about politics (and thereby to perhaps make politics less worthy of cynicism)? A small step could be to develop in its place a sense of skepticism. A skeptic is defined as "a person who questions or doubts something (such as a claim or statement)…"* Unlike a cynic, a skeptic

does not presuppose the worst in the process of questioning politics. As a result, they do not preclude complex solutions to difficult puzzles. The skeptic seeks to understand rather than simply blame, and recognizes that we may not yet know enough to explain some things about politics. If done with a certain degree of modesty and humility, moreover, one can even become a healthy skeptic!

By adopting such an outlook, the reasons why we should want to study and practice politics become much clearer and a little more encouraging, opening up spaces within which the future can be determined. If we approach politics as a cynic, then we foreclose possibilities for action because we forestall understanding. If we approach it as a healthy skeptic, then we at least have the chance to contribute to the creation of a political world that is more closely aligned with our goals. We will, over the course of our lives, succeed to greater or lesser degrees on different issues, but at least in the effort we may become more part of a solution than part of the problem.

CONCEPTUALIZING POLITICS

Throughout this course and textbook, you will be exposed to a number of tools that can be used in the study and practice of politics, and that will assist you in both appreciating and handling its complexity. One of the most important tools that we will employ, one that we use every day in our lives, is concepts. It has been said that "[c]oncepts are to the student of Politics what maps and compasses are to navigators."[29] We use concepts to impose an order on the world so that we are not overwhelmed by the breadth and depth of its complexity, and so that we can navigate our way through politics in ways that help us to explain why some things happen and others do not. Our concepts, then, help us to develop the theories that we use to try to understand the past and present, and to plan for the future.

Whether we recognize it or not, we are constantly guided in our lives by concepts. The word "concept" is derived from the Latin *concipere*,

---

* By permission. From *Merriam-Webster's Collegiate® Dictionary, 11th Edition* ©2015 by Merriam-Webster, Inc. (www.Merriam-Webster.com).

which means to conceive. A concept is defined as "… something conceived in the mind: thought, notion … an abstract or generic idea generalized from particular instances."* Human beings depend on concepts. Indeed, not long after birth we seem to develop such concepts as magnitude, space, and time in processing information about the world.[30] As our cognitive abilities expand, we acquire and employ an extensive range of concepts about ourselves and the world in which we live in order to sort through the vast amounts of information and experiences that define our lives. This is just as true in the study and practice of politics. Concepts help us to describe, understand, and explain political phenomena, and in doing so allow us to not simply interpret the world but seek to change it as well. It is important to note, however, that as much as they can help us, concepts can also hinder us by leading us to describe, understand, and explain political phenomena poorly, and thus to interpret and seek to change the world in unfortunate ways.

With the stakes so high, then, we need to consider carefully the concepts that we use, exploring both their meaning and implications, seeking to identify and overcome their biases and imperfections. The better the concepts that we have at our disposal, the more general their application to the potential universe of cases to which they refer. Apart from helping us identify patterns in politics, concepts also provide us with a common language through which to interpret and debate the world. That being said, we should not—as we shall see—expect too much from concepts: having good concepts does not remove the

politics from Political Science, even if it provides a structure for it, and just because concepts give us a common language, this does not mean that we all use them the same way or communicate them clearly to one another.

So how do we employ concepts? We sort objects or experiences into concept categories by identifying their basic characteristics or critical attributes; that is, by assessing whether the attributes match the particular sequence, relationship, or patterns that are required by the concept's definition or rule. For some concepts, this is a relatively simple exercise. Take, for example, the following concept: "a woody plant having a single elongated main stem generally with few or no branches on its lower part."[31] Chances are that you would agree that this describes a tree. And if we went around your class, you and your classmates would all likely agree that this describes a tree—in fact, it is probable that each of you would picture a tree in your mind. With the help of this concept, we could readily and systematically divide the world into two categories: those objects to which the concept "tree" applies and those to which it does: not-trees and not-trees! Moreover, if everyone in your class was asked to use a digital camera to take a picture of a tree, then when we reviewed all the pictures taken, we would probably be able to recognize each submission as a tree. If someone tried to convince us that a lamp post was, in fact, a tree, we would say that it was an inappropriate example for the concept category.[32] With the help of the concept of a tree, then, we can speak in a more meaningful way about the world in which we live, distinguishing trees from, for example,

THINK AND DISCUSS

"Justice" can be defined as "… *(1)*: the principle or ideal of just dealing or right action *(2)*: conformity to this principle or ideal: righteousness…"** Discuss (and adjust if necessary) this definition with your classmates or friends until you all agree that it accurately captures the concept. Then, using a digital camera, go onto your campus or into your community and take a picture of something that you think constitutes justice. Meet again to share and discuss your photos. Do you all agree that all of the photos represent justice? If not, try to figure out why you disagree. What is it about the concept that you interpret or apply differently?

---

* By permission. From *Merriam-Webster's Collegiate® Dictionary, 11th Edition* ©2015 by Merriam-Webster, Inc. (www.Merriam-Webster.com).

** By permission. From *Merriam-Webster's Collegiate® Dictionary, 11th Edition* ©2015 by Merriam-Webster, Inc. (www.Merriam-Webster.com).

shrubs, and even distinguishing between different categories of trees according to their distinctive properties (e.g., coniferous and deciduous).

Not all concepts, however, represent subjects that take on a set physical shape (such as a tree), and as a result we often find much less agreement on their interpretation and application. For example, what if your class was instead instructed to take a picture of justice? You can imagine that we would receive a very wide array of images and that we might not always agree that what had been captured was justice.

Essentially Contested Concepts: In response to the challenges of grasping such non-tangible concepts, philosopher Walter Bryce Gallie introduced the idea of the essentially contested concept in a talk published in 1956.[33] In this work, Gallie sought to find a path away from an expectation that we could and should be able to resolve disputes over the meaning of certain important concepts, such as art and democracy. He cautioned against efforts to determine one authoritative definition as they would stifle productive discussions, as seen in three approaches: dogmatism, relativism, and eclecticism.[34] For example, when debating a concept such as social justice, some might slip into a dogmatic "I am right and you are wrong" outlook, while others might adopt a relativist "we are both right for our own reasons" view; others still might look to accommodate difference by stitching together eclectic parts of various arguments with the idea that "we are each right about different facets." Although these approaches often stem from good intentions, Gallie maintained, they frequently interfere with our ability to understand the world better because they deny rather than recognize the essential complexity of certain concepts, and thus they do not accurately capture the phenomena in question.

An essentially contested concept arises when there is basic agreement on the definition of a concept but legitimate disagreement as to how best to identify or realize it in practice. Such "perfectly genuine" disputes, Gallie claimed, "although not resolvable by argument of any kind, are nevertheless sustained by perfectly respectable arguments and evidence."[35] They are "concepts the proper use of which inevitably involves endless disputes about their proper uses on the part

of their users." These disagreements, therefore, do not emerge and are not perpetuated because some are right and others were wrong (although this may be the case to some degree), and they cannot be resolved by reframing the debate, constructing better arguments, or finding more evidence—their contested nature is essential to the operation of the concept itself. Gallie put forward several defining characteristics of such concepts, three of which we will note here. First, such concepts are internally complex; that is, they have numerous facets that can be emphasized in different ways and combinations. Second, their usage changes over time as circumstances and our ability to apprehend them evolve. Finally, we do not approach these concepts from a position of neutrality but instead from within our own value-based perspectives; we explore them on subjective rather than objective grounds. For these reasons, there is something inherently contestable about such concepts: the situation cannot be avoided.

In order to appreciate how this operates, consider art. Art is defined as "… the conscious use of skill and creative imagination especially in the production of aesthetic objects; *also*: works so produced…"* If we gather together a group of people it is quite likely that they could all agree that this definition captures the concept of art (if there were uncertainties, we could discuss and adjust the definition until we were all satisfied). If we then began to search online for art, however, we would soon find that there were significant differences in terms of how each person interpreted and applied the concept. If we looked, first, at Leonardo Da Vinci's *Mona Lisa*, everyone would doubtless accept that this is a work of art, and a similar level of agreement would probably arise if we viewed Emily Carr's *Big Raven*. If we then took a look at Jackson Pollack's *Convergence* or Kazimir Malevich's *Black Square*, however, we would hear people say things like "but anyone can do that" or "there is no real skill needed to come up with that!" All of a sudden, despite the fact that they agreed on the definition of the concept of art, they would disagree quite strongly in terms of how to assign such a designation to a particular example. And while we might, through discussion, find that some people would come to agree with

---

* By permission. From *Merriam-Webster's Collegiate® Dictionary, 11th Edition* ©2015 by Merriam-Webster, Inc. (www.Merriam-Webster.com).

one side or the other, we would ultimately be unable to achieve consensus, even if we revised the definition or studied the examples more closely. Intelligent people can and will reasonably disagree about art, and we lose something in our understanding of art (and thus ourselves) when this is denied.

We could repeat this process with other forms of art (go online and compare, for example, Myron's *Discus Thrower* with Jana Sterbak's *Meat Dress*, or Beethoven's *9th Symphony* with John Cage's *4'33*), but let's instead see how this can operate with a core concept in the study of politics—**power**.

> **Power:** The ability of one actor to impose its will on another, to get its own way, to do or get what it wants.

Power as an Essentially Contested Concept: Power is a core concept in the study of politics but it is by no means a simple one. Although we can often easily identify powerful individuals (a prime minister, for example) and powerful countries (such as the United States or Russia), we still have trouble when we try to map and understand how and when power is exercised, and by whom. For example, despite its evident military power, the United States failed to accomplish key military goals during the Vietnam and Iraq wars. And at times, an individual can have more power than might otherwise have been anticipated or imagined, such as Rosa Parks in Montgomery, Alabama, who refused to give up her seat on a bus in December 1955 for a white passenger, which resulted in the Montgomery Bus Boycott and, in December 1956, a Supreme Court decision that upheld a lower court ruling that had declared Alabama's bus segregation laws to be unconstitutional, an historic moment in the African-American Civil Rights Movement.

In the 1950s, a vigorous debate opened up in the United States among sociologists and political scientists about how to think about power in theory and how to study it in practice, one that would see two schools of thought—called Elitist and Pluralist—counter one another before they were joined by another—Class Analysis. While they all could agree on a core definition of power, each school interpreted it in different ways, and therefore looked for it in different places, with different implications for the study and practice of politics. Thus, as we explore the concept of power, we can see its complexity, its malleability, and its openness to subjectivity. In short, we can see how reasonable people can disagree as to how and where to look for power in politics.

At the start, sociologists Floyd Hunter, in *Community Power Structure* (1953), and C. Wright Mills, in *The Power Elite* (1956), argued that America was not a land of political equals but one in which a few individuals "occupy the strategic command posts of the social structure"[36] and use these posts to dominate public affairs. While Hunter explored the nature of the "power structure" in a regional city (Atlanta), Mills surveyed the nature of "the power elite" across a wide array of institutional positions, but especially within economic, political, and military circles. From these different vantage points, they each proposed that political power in the United States was concentrated in the hands of the few, and that this severely curtailed democratic politics by marginalizing or even excluding the interests and participation of the majority. This situation was held to be problematic on several levels, not least of which because it fostered a passive citizenry, wherein "obedience of the people to the decisions of the power command becomes habitual."[37] In short, rather than the common portrayal (at least in America) of the United States as a land of equality and freedom, Hunter and Mills maintained that the country's political landscape was dominated by elites.

This Elitist analysis sparked a reaction from a Pluralist school of thought amongst political scientists, as embodied most particularly in the work of Robert A. Dahl, and especially in his book *Who Governs* (1961). Elitists had, Pluralists proposed, misunderstood the nature of power in American society: power was more fluid and less stable (that is, the access points to the decision-making process were plural rather than singular; hence, the name of this school of thought) than Elitists suggested. Moreover, it was not enough to assume that reputed or positional power was the same as actual power: just because a person was high up in the military chain of command, you could not assume that they could command effective political power. In order to assess the Elitist position properly, Dahl argued, a more rigorous approach was needed to test whether (a) elites were in fact an identifiable group, (b) you could identify cases where elites and non-elites were at odds in terms of their political preferences, and (c) elite interests regularly prevailed in such circumstances.

This was precisely the behavioural-empirical approach that Dahl undertook in his study of decision-making in New Haven, Connecticut, published as *Who Governs?* In it, he explored what he called the first face of power: "A has power over B to the extent that he can get B to do something that B would not otherwise do."[38] Under such circumstances it could be said that A has power over B, as might be accomplished through such means as influence, coercion, or political authority. This is a common understanding of power, one that we can see, to pick a simple example, when the Allied forces defeated the Axis powers to end the Second World War. For Dahl, then, power was an observable relationship of control—an observable behaviour— and he concluded that it was sufficiently dispersed in New Haven: there was no entrenched political elite but instead power was relatively open as a range of people could mobilize and influence the political process and its outcomes.

This work prompted a fair number of critical responses, on both methodological and substantive grounds, which need not concern us here, as we want to focus more on the conceptualization of power itself. For this we can turn to the work of Peter Bachrach and Morton S. Baratz, published as "The Two Faces of Power" (1962). They agreed with Dahl's conceptualization but argued that it was incomplete as he had missed the second face of power: "power is also exercised when A devotes his energies to creating or reinforcing social and political values and institutional practices that limit the scope of the political process to public consideration of only those issues which are comparatively innocuous to A."[39] Thus, power is not just employed through decisions taken (à la Dahl) but through non-decisions as well, when issues and interests are removed from or never make it onto the political agenda. This still entails observable behaviour because these issues and interests have been articulated and perhaps even mobilized but are kept off the political agenda. Although more difficult to trace, this still reflects a form of power. For example, in the post-September 11, 2001 era, the idea that you are either "with us or you are with the terrorists" has been employed to frame public debate over state responses to terrorism (it was used, notably, by U.S. President George W. Bush in his September 20, 2001 address to Congress). Such polarizing rhetoric serves to delegitimize political positions that are neither for terrorism nor the government's response to terrorism (for example, those who sought forms of engagement beyond military intervention in Afghanistan and Iraq, or who opposed the use of torture by liberal-democratic states in the name of counter-terrorism), making it more difficult for people to propose never mind pursue alternate political agendas.

Following on Bachrach and Baratz, British philosopher Steven Lukes entered the debate, offering his ideas on a third face of power, which he explored in *Power: A Radical View* (1975). Lukes accepts the validity of the two previous faces of power but criticizes those who stop there on the grounds that they remain solely within the realm of observable behaviour. What if, he asks, people do not know what their real interests are? What if A is able to reinforce conventions and norms, for example, such that B does not or is not able to identify and consider

Prisoners held by American military forces at Guantanamo Bay Detention Camp (and elsewhere) raised important questions of whether liberal democracies should use torture in response to terrorism; however, the constrained political discourse within the United States at the time made it difficult for opponents to have their concerns taken seriously. A lengthy 2014 Senate intelligence committee report and subsequent comments by President Barack Obama subsequently legitimized their concerns, if well after the fact.

© REUTERS/U.S. Department of Defense/Petty Officer 1st class Shane T. McCoy/Handout/Files alternatives that are more closely aligned with their true interests? "Those subject to [such power]," Lukes later explained, "are led to acquire beliefs and form desires that result in their consenting or adapting to being dominated, in coercive and non-coercive settings."[40] In order to get at such exercises of power, he maintains, a much more difficult—and radical—analysis needs to be undertaken. In the third face of power, then, interests that people would, under different circumstances, objectively prefer are never identified, articulated, or mobilized, and thus are never even considered or discussed as part of anyone's political agenda. Within this conceptualization, power may be very hard to trace as the conflict with alternative interests is latent and thus unobservable in terms of observable behaviour. This does not simply occur because we are not smart enough to understand our own interests but because it is too difficult to figure out what they are on most political issues. As political critic Noam Chomsky phrased it in the 1988 documentary *Manufacturing Consent*:

> Very few people are going to have the time or the energy or the commitment to carry out the constant battle that's required to get outside the [mainstream media]. The easy thing to do … you come from home work, you're tired; you've just had a busy day and you're not going to spend the evening carrying out a research project. So you turn on the tube and say "it's probably right," or you look at the headlines in the paper… Sure, the other stuff is out there, but you are going to have to work to find it.

Without considering this third face of power, Lukes proposes, we are left with only a surface-level, if observable, understanding of power and thus of politics.

Now, the debate over the notion of power did not end with Lukes. British feminist Carole Pateman has explored the gendered nature of how power has been conceptualized,[41] while French philosopher Michel Foucault focused on how power is reflected and contained in the systems within which we operate.[42] Moreover, while the three faces of power capture various ways in which some have power *over* others, politics is also concerned with the power *to* accomplish

our goals. Think of the Rosa Parks example raised earlier, in which an individual had the ability to contribute to a process of profound political change. The fact that she did not do so alone recalls a definition of power proposed by political philosopher Hannah Arendt, who conceived it as "the human ability not just to act but to act in concert."[43] Indeed, the idea of empowerment is today very much in line with modern democratic thought, given its emphasis on the ability of "the people" to affect and effect meaningful political change. However, for the moment, we can stop here with the three faces of power because they allow us to draw certain conclusions about the nature of power, concepts, and thus the study and practice of politics.

First, power can be seen as an essentially contested concept, which forewarns us to handle our conceptual (and thus our theoretical) tools quite carefully in politics. Power is certainly complex: while some forms of power may become institutionalized in politics, other forms are much more mercurial, operating through and beyond formal institutions and processes. As well, both the concept and the examples of power that we identify in the world clearly change over time: think, for example, of the power that can come through the use of social media—power that was unimaginable even 10 years ago. Finally, the ways in which we approach power in politics reflect our value-based positions. While Dahl requires power to be expressed through observable behaviour, for example, Lukes is open to a much more expansive conceptualization. Thus, we are reminded, as Rand Dyck noted in an earlier version of this textbook, that "One of the charms of the discipline of political science is that almost every concept is open to debate."[44]

Second, how we interpret and study power—and thus politics—matters, a conclusion that builds on the earlier finding that defining politics is itself a political act. As we noted, the definitions that we use, and the ways in which we interpret them, influence how we study (and practice) politics. For example, for much of the Cold War the power of the Soviet Union was studied and analyzed in fairly narrow terms, often relating to its position vis-à-vis the United States in the arms race. As a result, the fall of the Berlin Wall and the subsequent dismantling of the Soviet Union took the Political Science community almost completely by surprise.[45]

The discipline has learned much about the nature of power as a result, but the example offers a healthy reminder that we often need to try to think outside our own conceptual and theoretical boxes if we are to understand the politics that unfolds around us. If power had been conceptualized differently, then perhaps we would have picked up on indications of what was to come earlier.

Finally, this examination of power as an essentially contested concept reminds us of the importance of developing a better understanding of politics if we are to study and practice it. Politics rarely presents us with simple issues or choices and, following on with the language metaphor introduced earlier, the more we engage with it—the more we learn about it and use what we learn—the more we can gain and contribute in our relations with others. Another good metaphor is that of riding a bicycle: although learning to ride is difficult at first, with practice it can become a life-long habit that presents all sorts of opportunities to get from one place to another, quickly or slowly, with others or by ourselves. The same is true of politics. The chapters that follow in this textbook will provide you with a solid foundation on which to develop such a better understanding, and offer numerous reasons why you should choose to do so.

THE STRUCTURE OF THIS TEXTBOOK

The study of politics involves many fields or areas of specialization, traditionally including Political Theory, Canadian Politics, Comparative Politics, the Politics of Development, International Relations, and Public Policy/Administration. This textbook introduces many key aspects and ideas relating to each, and your college or university will typically offer higher-level courses that allow you to dig deeper into these and other areas of specialization.

In Chapter 2, we turn first to investigate predominant ideas and ideologies that animate our political discussions and actions. You will find that these continually emerge as important features in both the study and practice of politics. Their influence in shaping the world of politics can hardly be exaggerated. Consider, for example, "democracy," which was

created, practiced, and debated by the ancient Greeks at various points, and to varying degrees, from the 6th to 4th centuries BCE, after which it practically disappeared from the historical record before returning to prominence during the political revolutions in the United States and France in the late 18th century. Since then, the idea and practice of democracy has spread the world over, and are now used as touchstones and benchmarks for almost every political regime, as well as many revolutionary movements that seek to create their own. Thus, ideas provide the foundation for conversations that we can have with one another and with the past, often stretching back centuries, as we try to figure out how best to live our lives in the present and future. Given what we now know about essentially contested concepts, we can anticipate that many of these ideas will prompt well-reasoned yet irresolvable disputes as to their meaning and realization. We can gain great insight into these disagreements by studying the nature and role of ideologies in our political discussions and actions. Based as they are on assumptions (often divergent) about human nature, ideologies operate as a sort of codebook that can help us to understand why people differ over crucial political ideas such as equality and liberty, and over how best to realize them.

We turn in Part II to explore core foundations in the study of politics: governments, societies, and markets, and how the state intersects with (defines and is defined by) each. Throughout history we find governments (long before we find states). As you will learn in Chapter 3, people have always, in smaller or larger groups, created mechanisms whereby **political authority** has been granted to some to act on behalf of others. The terms on which this has been done, however, and the ideas that have justified these terms, have evolved over the millennia and continue to do so. In keeping with the global spread of democracy, the notion that governments ought to be—as U.S. President Abraham Lincoln famously phrased it in his Gettysburg Address—"of the people, by the people, for the people" has clearly taken hold as a powerful idea, providing a justification for political authority that rests less on divine intervention, hierarchy, and tradition, and more on some kind of direct mandate from the society that is governed. The means by which we can best arrange this are far from self-evident, however, and governments find themselves increasingly challenged from below, as people lose faith that they are being governed well, and from above, as transnational economic, political, and social forces reshape and redefine the scope for government action.

> **Political authority:** The imposition of one's will on another by reason of legitimacy—because the subject regards the decision-maker as having a right to make such a binding decision.

Such global forces have done much to rearrange the terrain of politics, a reality that arises in every area covered in this textbook. For example, in recent years, older ideas of the nation-state, in which a relatively unified people was presumed to align with a given territorial state, have given way to a recognition that all countries are ever more plural in nature and along many politically salient dimensions, a process examined in Chapter 4. This reflects, in part, the recognition that most states have long suppressed their internal diversity, such as ethnic and racial diversity, in the name of a more limited self-understanding of the nation that privileges particular identities (reflecting dominant interests) over others. It also is a consequence of international migration, as a growing proportion of the world's population lives outside their country of birth. As previously marginalized groups raise their political voice and as new groups arrive to become equal members (at least formally) within the body politic, a much more complex notion of "the people" emerges. Indeed, the increasing reality and recognition of diversity prompts compelling questions concerning the meaning of such core ideas as equality and liberty. For example, Cecil Foster, a Black Canadian who has written on it means to be Canadian as a *Black* Canadian, asks whether "the immigrant who is a Canadian citizen of one day's standing would have the same rights and privileges as any other citizen. This would include the right to negotiate a change in the existing social relations."[46] We could extend this question through issues of ethnicity, race, religion, language, gender, sexual orientation, and any other significant category within society, including economic class.

In comparison with most other regions of the world, discussions about class have long been comparatively muted in North America. And while the 2011 Occupy movement, with its "we are the 99%" slogan, brought attention to the concentration of wealth in American society within the top one percent of earners, it has not prompted any fundamental economic reforms. In a period of heightened economic uncertainty, the toolkit employed by state and societal managers of the economy remains largely unchanged. This may be, in no small part, due to the ascendance of political ideologies that promote an ideal of "the market" with limited state intervention. Now, we have known for some time that the rise of the market economy was interwoven with the rise of the modern nation-state, a point demonstrated by political economist Karl Polanyi in his classic *The Great Transformation*.[47] This underscores the value in maintaining a political lens when examining what seem to be strictly economic phenomena, and vice versa. This is the approach taken in Chapter 5, where different conceptual and theoretical tools of political economy are introduced that can be used to compare and contrast how countries address the issue of the state's role in fostering citizen well-being. In using a comparative perspective, we can gain great insight not simply into how and why other people do things the way they do but how and why we do things the way we do, and whether we could benefit from changing our approach.

After having surveyed these core foundations for how we are governed—government, society, and the market as mediated through the state—we turn in Part III to explore core institutions and processes that define the state itself, each of which presents challenging political puzzles, for even as they serve core functions that provide for the possibility of good governance, they inevitably exhibit certain dysfunctions, impeding our ability to accomplish important political aims. We turn first in Chapter 6 to constitutions, which establish the fundamental rules for a given political system by enabling and limiting the scope of the state, both with respect to itself (demarcating, for example, the relative political authority of the executive, legislative, and judicial branches, as well as different levels of government) and to citizens as well as non-citizens. Constitutions can, moreover, anchor national attachment, sentiment, and ambition. For example, the constitution of East Timor (recognized as an independent state by the United Nations in 2002 after centuries of Portuguese colonization followed by some 25 years of Indonesian occupation, in which tens of thousands of Timorese died in what some call a genocide), affirms the country's

> determination to fight all forms of tyranny, oppression, social, cultural or religious domination and segregation, to defend national independence, to respect and guarantee human rights and the fundamental rights of the citizen, to ensure the principle of the separation of powers in the organisation of the State, and to establish the essential rules of multi-party democracy, with a view to building a just and prosperous nation and developing a society of solidarity and fraternity.[48]

Thus, even as they lay out a blueprint for governance, constitutions can also express the aspirations of a people for self-determination. As important as they are, however, constitutions are ultimately only words on paper (and sometimes, with constitutional conventions, not even that!) and therefore there is bound to be significant disagreement as to how to interpret and realize them appropriately and consistently.

For example, one of the functions of a constitution is to assign and contain the power of the executive, the topic of Chapter 7. The executive is the oldest of our three traditional branches of government. Before the emergence of democracy, the executive was usually centralized around particular individuals (such as an emperor/empress or king/queen—absolute rulers) and their close officials, who possessed the authority not only to enforce the laws but to create and adjudicate them as well, often on the basis of a claimed mandate from the gods. With the emergence of a tradition of constitutions and, as you will see, constitutionalism (a commitment to upholding the constitution), the political authority of the executive was balanced and contained by other political actors, such as legislatures and courts. However, because executives are so active—think of all the ways in which you interact with officials when it comes to your student loan, healthcare, passport, driver's licence, and so on—in our lives, they retain enormous power. Whether in parliamentary (with a prime minister), presidential (with a president), or hybrid forms, all political systems struggle with the question of how to ensure that the executive has the power to act on our behalf while remaining accountable for the exercise of that power.

This difficulty has been a major topic of debate in Canada, where concerns have been raised about the concentration of prime ministerial power from the time of Pierre Trudeau through to Stephen Harper.[49]

One of the ways in which the executive can be held to account for the use of its power is through legislatures, which are not only involved in the process of creating the laws under which we are governed but also have the function of representing us (our interests, values, goals, etc.) within the political system. Given ongoing concerns about the power of the executive in many political systems, we already have reason to suspect that legislatures face constraints on all these functions but the problem goes much deeper than that. For example, while it is possible to provide a fairly succinct definition of **political representation** in which citizen interests are re-presented within the political system it is actually quite a complex concept. In 1967, political scientist Hannah Pitkin published *The Concept of Representation*, a path-breaking investigation that remains widely influential. In it, she explored how and explained why it was so difficult to be definite about the nature of political representation, identifying four ways in which it can be undertaken, each comprising a different process and standard of assessment. Overall, she concluded, representation is like "a rather complicated, convoluted, three-dimensional structure in the middle of a dark enclosure," and that these four aspects are but "flash-bulb photographs of the structure taken from different angles."[50] This is another way of saying that representation constitutes an essentially contested concept, which may explain why we have such difficulty figuring out how to create political systems that represent the "will of the people" to our satisfaction.

> **Political representation:** In which the interests, values, goals, etc. of citizens (and in some cases non-citizens) are represented within the political system, especially the executive and legislature.

Alongside legislatures, another institutional actor—the judiciary—serves to contain executive power and hold it to account. As with government, we can go back quite far in history and find the existence of laws in human society. The oldest and most complete written example is the Code of Ur-Nammu, which dates from around 2100–2050

The legislature is often considered to be central to democratic governance because it is where, through elections, the people can choose their representatives, who can hold the executive to account, pass laws, and—more generally—represent citizen interests in collective decision-making. All legislatures, however, struggle to fulfil these functions well.

© Vlad G / Shutterstock.com

BCE in Sumeria (modern-day Iraq). As an absolute ruler, King Ur-Nammu not only had the authority to create and execute the law but to render authoritative decisions when disputes arose in its interpretation and application as well (although records suggest that he did so by fostering the consent of many of those over whom he ruled).[51] As you will see in Chapter 9, it is only with the concept of "the rule of law," in which both rulers and the ruled are subject to the law, that we see the emergence of courts that have the independent authority (grounded in the constitution) to provide a check on executive power. Despite their centrality and, as you can see in Table 1.1, the relatively high levels of respect (76 percent in Canada) that judges are given by society in comparison with politicians (26 percent), the existence of independent courts and powerful judges presents difficult questions for democratic government. As is the case with nominally "free markets," the law and those who interpret it are inherently political. By rendering authoritative and at times unpopular decisions, courts give definition to our values and beliefs through their interpretations of the laws of the land, but they are (with some few exceptions) appointed rather than elected. Thus, while democracy promotes accountability to "the people" and government as a reflection of the "will of the people," we often face situations in which parts of the political system (certainly the courts) need for

very good reason to be isolated from popular opinion so that we can be governed well.

In Part IV, we turn to look more closely at some of the spaces where "the people" can bring their interests, ideas, goals, values, and beliefs, as well as their concerns and criticisms, to bear on how they are governed. When democracy first took root in ancient Greece it was direct democracy: all citizens could participate directly in the deliberations that produced collective decisions. We now practise indirect democracy: most notably, we vote for people in elections who stand for us in the decision-making process, who represent us (with all the difficulties involved that we noted earlier). Elections are an incredibly efficient way of translating the voices of millions into a few hundred. However, despite their centrality within the modern democratic process, it seems that fewer and fewer people are willing to take the time to vote. Whether this reflects conscious non-participation,[52] disinterest, or something else altogether, it serves at least as an indication that a great many people do not think that elections are worth the time and effort. There are, however, alternate ways of conducting elections, which are reviewed in Chapter 10. Each method translates the "will of the people" in a different way, which can produce different types of politics. If some of the dissatisfaction that Canadians feel for politicians and the political system stems from a sense that they are not represented well, then perhaps a more extensive discussion of electoral reform and its consequences is in order.

Of course, changing how we conduct elections will not solve all the perceived problems within a given political system! Since politics is complex and often creates winners and losers, people will frequently be disappointed by the outcomes of politics. The important question is whether they turn away as a result. As Chapter 11 on political parties makes clear, just because important features of our political system are imperfect, this does not mean that they are not essential. Thus, even though fewer people seem willing to join political parties, and political parties themselves are more tightly controlled from the centre, they remain a central means of assigning legitimacy to those who govern us. We simply have not come up with a better way of doing democracy on a large scale (although the immediacy of digital technology and social media raise some interesting new options).[53]

Whether we are involved in them or not, political parties will continue to provide a primary means by which political power is attained in modern democracy.

For many people, dissatisfaction with elections and political parties has led them to look for more meaningful political engagement through civil society organizations. While political parties generally seek to aggregate a wide range of interests in order to attract broad support, civil society organizations are comparatively narrowly focused. For many people, then, such entities allow for a much more immediate form of representation and sense of participation, producing a greater feeling of political satisfaction. As you will see in Chapter 12, in providing such representation, civil society organizations—interest groups, social movements, voluntary associations—are very much in line with our notions of democracy as they provide alternate mechanisms whereby the voices of "the people" can be heard. However, whether they are equally heard or equally loud is important. As early as the 1960s, political scientist E.E. Schattschneider challenged the pluralist view promoted by Robert Dahl and others, which maintained that the political system was sufficiently open to different voices in modern democracy. If open, Schattschneider concluded, it was far

from equal: "the flaw in the pluralist heaven is that the heavenly chorus sings with a strong upper-class accent."[54] Moreover, while political parties can be held accountable through periodic elections, the same is not true of civil society groups. Thus, while some organizations can be extremely influential within the political system, they are accountable more to their membership than to society as a whole. This is rendered even more complicated by the fact that such groups and movements are not, unlike political parties, contained by national boundaries, and thus "the people" that they represent within the political system may not even be citizens of the country in which they hold influence.

This is in part a reflection of the fact that we live in a much more interconnected world than ever before—look, for example, at Figure 1.1, which shows that while Internet connectivity remains uneven around the globe, the gaps have been narrowing over time. In Part V, we thus move beyond the borders of Canada, North America, and even Europe to look directly at certain global dimensions of politics. Although the prominence of the term globalization is relatively recent, all sorts of global connections have existed for centuries. After all, as is recounted in

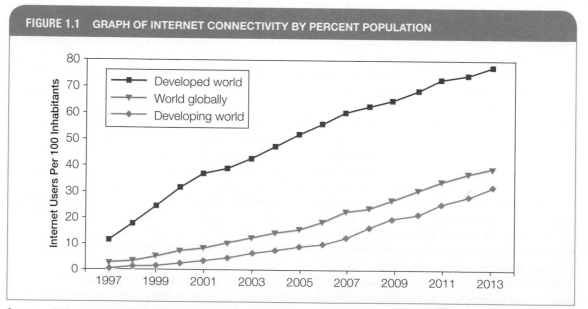

FIGURE 1.1   **GRAPH OF INTERNET CONNECTIVITY BY PERCENT POPULATION**

Chapter 13, there is a long history of colonial relations between what are now often called the countries of the Global North and those of the Global South (generally located in Africa, Asia, the Caribbean, and Latin America). Although Canada was never a colonial power in the way that Britain, France, and Spain, among other European powers, have been, seeking to control overseas territories physically to benefit themselves economically (although, as we were reminded earlier, colonial relations are still maintained with Aboriginal peoples within Canada), this does not mean that the country is not implicated in neocolonial relations today, in which countries (particularly in the Global South) are formally independent but remain constrained in their choices by foreign interests that may use their economic and/or military power to foster political and economic outcomes consistent with the interests of the neocolonial powers. For example, Canada has participated in numerous military interventions in recent years (e.g., the former Yugoslavia, Afghanistan, Libya, Syria, and Iraq), and is involved in an international economic order that is often seen as being disadvantageous to the countries of the Global South. At the same time, it has greatly reduced its commitments to longstanding Canadian activities, such as peacekeeping and overseas development assistance.[55] An important question is whether these new forms of intervention are fostering a more stable world, or whether Canadians should investigate other ways of determining their role in an increasingly interconnected and interdependent world.

Although we can certainly make a difference in other countries for better or for worse, any such intervention can be a very tricky business, as has been seen in the continued instability in parts of the world where the most direct military intervention on the part of the Global North has taken place in recent years, such as Afghanistan, Iraq, and Libya. Although the world has become more democratic over the course of the 20th and 21st centuries (there are more democracies, and a greater proportion of the world's population live in democracies), many new democracies remain politically unstable. It seems that it is easier to create than sustain democracy. Since Aristotle's time, political scientists have been interested in how to create stable political regimes, for stability is thought to increase

the opportunities for working together to determine and pursue our goals as a society (whether national or global). Although we can develop checklists of what is needed to establish a democratic form of government,[56] determining how to ensure that this form survives over the long haul is fraught with difficulties. In Chapter 14, this problem is tackled from the opposite end by exploring instead how and why non-democratic regimes such as North Korea are able to hold onto power, despite the fact that they do not represent—indeed, often brutally oppress—their citizens. If we can uncover the logic that sustains such regimes, then we may anticipate better and respond more appropriately to regime change—either toward or away from more democratic forms—when it occurs.

As observed at the outset of this chapter, whether we focus on what happens within states or between them, we are often looking for patterns that help us to understand the past and present in order to navigate the future. While concepts are vital tools in this process, Chapter 15 underlines the importance of theory as well, in this case in the realm of International Relations, which seeks to explain such vital questions as those relating to war and peace, to international stability and instability. We can define theory as "an idea or set of ideas that is intended to explain facts or events…"* There are two components worth underlining here, each of which can prompt considerable disagreement. First, we need to be able to identify the relevant facts or events. For example, "If we are to envision a less violent world, we must first understand how violent the world is."[57] Second, we need to offer an explanation of these facts and events; that is, to link them together in ways that help us to grasp what has happened and thus the conditions under which it could happen again. It should come as no surprise, given our earlier explorations of the definition of politics and essentially contested concepts, that we will often disagree on the relevant facts/events as well as how to explain them. These processes are necessarily open to our subjective and normative positions. The world is an incredibly complicated place and to make sense of it we must impose some kind of order on it, or else we will be overwhelmed with information. Our theories, like our concepts, help in this process but they do so with all the inevitable weaknesses and limitations of the human being, including

---

our biases and (in a non-pejorative sense) ignorance in the face of so much potential knowledge. However, in politics as in most everything else, we have to work with the tools that we possess while trying to improve upon them, and it is through the contest of different interpretations of the world around us—different theories—that we can hope to learn to understand and explain it better.

The urgency that lies behind doing so is underscored in Chapter 16, which examines the concept of security and its opposite, insecurity. Under conditions of greater interdependence we are not only more interconnected with events and people around the world but we also have much greater knowledge about them, which allows us more choices (and more informed choices) about how to respond. For example, during the Vietnam War, the United States was involved in extensive bombing of Cambodia that was neither widely known by the public nor reported much in the media. It was not until 2000, when President Bill Clinton released (incomplete) data so that Cambodia could look for unexploded ordinance throughout the country (which continued to kill and maim civilians decades later) that the extent of the bombing was made known: it began four years earlier

than previously understood and involved "2,756,941 tons' worth, dropped in 230,516 sorties on 113,716 sites. Just over 10 percent of this bombing was indiscriminate, with 3,580 of the sites listed as having 'unknown' targets and another 8,238 sites having no target listed at all."[58] While an estimated 50,000–150,000 civilians were killed and tens of thousands more were injured as a result of this bombing, it never became a significant political issue in the United States because of the lack of public knowledge and debate. In contrast, through the application of satellite and digital technology, it is possible for the public to become graphically aware of and to assess 21st century bombing campaigns such as those in Darfur (in Sudan) and Syria, which has in turn sparked vigorous political mobilization and extensive political debate about the responsibilities of the international community in the face of such suffering.[59] Awareness and knowledge about events half way around the world can therefore generate new and different forms of politics, and challenge us to develop more effective ways of thinking through the meaning and realization of what it means to be secure in a world in which the causes and consequences of security and insecurity are more tightly interwoven for us all.

CONCLUSION

The challenges that we face in the study and practice of politics, whether we come at them as political scientists, political activists, or community members and citizens, are many and varied, and none of us can possibly engage with more than a few at any given time. However, the message that I hope this chapter has put across is that each of us should think about what it is we want from politics and how we might make our mark in politics. No matter how disconnected or removed we may feel, the reality is that politics affects us every single day of our lives, sometimes to our benefit but other times to our detriment. Although the sheer scope of politics may cause us to hesitate, through a conscious application of the skills that we possess, and the knowledge that we gain by our involvement in politics, we can learn how

to respond in more positive and productive terms. Now, we may not see the effects of our actions immediately, or even in the short-to-medium term, since politics (with all the sorts of compromises that it requires) is often about the long-game. The renowned Canadian scientist and pacifist Ursula Franklin draws on the earthworm to underscore this point: "from earthworms we learn that before anything grows there has to be a prepared soil… [Our immediate effort] may not change minds, but it will provide the arguments for a time when minds are changed."[60] Hopefully, this textbook and the course that it supports will provide you with some ideas as to how you might make your own contributions to the preparation of this soil, and help you to select some of the tools that you will need to do so.

DISCUSSION QUESTIONS

1. When you think about politics, who do you think has the most power? What are the sources of their political power? Do they possess the right amount or too much?

2. Which groups in society, either in Canada or elsewhere in the world, do not have enough political power? What would need to change for them to acquire a more appropriate amount of power, and what kinds of power would this entail?

3. Are you optimistic about politics in Canada today? What would you like to see changed, if you could, to foster a more positive political environment?

4. Are you optimistic about politics in the world today? What would you liked to see changed, if you could, to foster a more positive political environment?

5. Do you believe, along with the Elitists, that the political system is controlled by a few in their own interests, or do you think, along with the Pluralists, that the system is sufficiently open to respond to a diversity of interests?

WEBSITES

Canadian Political Science Association
cpsa-acsp.ca

American Political Science Association
http://www.apsanet.org

International Political Science Association
ipsa.org
These three websites provide many windows onto the type of work that political scientists undertake around the world. They each contain links to many other sites that can broaden your appreciation of the study and practice of politics.

Centre for International Governance Innovation
https://www.cigionline.org/
This is the website of one of the many institutions, often called Think Tanks, that conduct and publish research on politics. For its part, CIGI seeks to understand and develop new ways of governing ourselves in a more complex and interconnected world.

iPolitics
http://www.ipolitics.ca/
There are many news websites out there, and from a wide range of ideological perspectives, that you can access to keep informed about political issues unfolding locally and globally. An important part of being engaged in politics simply involves remaining aware of events and issues around you in the news.

FURTHER READING

Janet M. Box-Steffensmeier, Henry Brady, and David Collier, eds., *The Oxford Handbook of Political Methodology*. Oxford: Oxford University Press, 2010.

Rand Dyck and Chris Cochrane, *Canadian Politics: Critical Approaches*, 7th ed. Toronto: Nelson Education, 2013.

Ursula Franklin with Sarah Jane Freeman, *Ursula Franklin Speaks: Thoughts and Afterthoughts, 1986–2012*. Montreal and Kingston: McGill-Queen's University Press, 2014.

Adrian Leftwich, ed., *What is Politics: The Activity and its Study*. Cambridge: Polity Press, 2004.

Alan Ryan, *On Politics: A History of Political Thought from Herodotus to the Present*. Toronto: Penguin Group, 2013.

ENDNOTES

1. This phrase is from a sub-heading provided in Aristotle, *Nicomachean Ethics*, trans. Martin Ostwald (Indianapolis: Bobbs-Merrill, 1962).

2. This phrase first gained widespread attention as the title of a 1970 article by feminist Carol Hanisch; the text is reproduced, alongside her observations on its meaning and significance some 25 years later, at http://www.carolhanisch.org/.

3. Quoted in "'Nishiyuu Walkers' complete 1,600 km trek to Ottawa," CTVNews.ca, March 25, 2013, online at http://www.ctvnews.ca/canada/

nishiyuu-walkers-complete-1-600-km-trek-to-ottawa-1.1209929.

4. George Santanya, *The Life of Reason: Reason in Common Sense* (New York: Scribner's, 1905), p. 284.

5. Quoted in David Ljunggren, "Every G20 nation wants to be Canada, insists PM," Reuters.com, September 25, 2009, online at http://www.reuters.com/article/2009/09/26/columns-us-g20-canada-advantages-idUS-TRE58P05Z20090926.

6. For a recent United Nations report that surveys some of these effects, see Human Rights Council, *Report of the Special Rapporteur on the rights of indigenous peoples, James Anaya, on the Situation of Indigenous Peoples in Canada*, July 4, 2014 [A/HRC/27/52/Add.2].

7. See http://www.aadnc-aandc.gc.ca/eng/1100100010023/1100100010027.

8. See http://www.afn.ca/index.php/en/about-afn/a-declaration-of-first-nations.

9. John Ralston Saul, *A Fair Country: Telling Truths about Canada* (Toronto: Penguin Canada, 2008); see also, Thomas King, *The Inconvenient Indian: A Curious Account of Native People in North America* (Toronto: Doubleday Canada, 2012).

10. As an indication of how fluid and transient Wikipedia can be, this definition has already been removed from the webpage! For the most recent version, see http://en.wikipedia.org/wiki/Politics.

11. Frans de Waal, *Chimpanzee Politics: Power and Sex among Apes* (Baltimore: Johns Hopkins University Press, 2007 [1982]).

12. John Paul Cunningham, James P. Hereward, Tim A. Heard, Paul J. De Barro, and Stuart A. West, "Bees at War: Interspecific Battles and Nest Usurpation in Stingless Bees," *The American Naturalist* 184 (6) (December 2014), pp. 777–86.

13. Aristotle, *The Politics*, trans. T.A. Sinclair, revised and re-presented by Trevor J. Saunders (London: Penguin Books, 1981 [1962]), p. 60.

14. Harold Lasswell, *Politics: Who Gets What, When, How* (New York: Peter Smith, 1950 [1936]), p. 1.

15. For a survey of methodological approaches and issues in Political Science, see Janet M. Box-Steffensmeier, Henry Brady, and David Collier, eds., *The Oxford Handbook of Political Methodology* (Oxford: Oxford University Press, 2010). There are numerous useful textbooks available that cover Political Science methodology. Ask your professor which one they think would be most useful for your class and program.

16. Theda Skocpol, "Bringing the State Back In: Strategies of Analysis in Current Research," in P.B, Evans, D. Rueschemeyer, and T. Skocpol, eds., *Bringing the State Back In* (Cambridge: Cambridge University Press, 1985), p. 9.

17. Mao Zedong, "On Protracted War," in *Selected Works, Volume 2*, May 1938, online at https://www.marxists.org/reference/archive/mao/selected-works/.

18. For an excellent repository of resources on the African-American Civil Rights Movement, see the digital collection available through the U.S. Library of Congress, http://www.loc.gov/rr/program/bib/civilrights/home.html.

19. On the history of civil disobedience and pacifism, see the work of Canadian historian Peter Brock, who wrote extensively on the subject for some 50 years, and for a good reader on pacifism, see Peter Mayer, ed., *The Pacifist Conscience* (Harmondsworth, Middlesex: Penguin Books, 1967). There are many online repositories of the works of Ghandi, Tolstoy, and Thoreau.

20. You can find this work online at http://www.thedevilsdictionary.com/.

21. Adrian Leftwich, "Thinking Politically: On the politics of Politics," in A. Leftwich, ed., *What is Politics: The Activity and its Study* (Cambridge: Polity Press, 2004), p. 5; the previous point is also drawn from this source.

22. Susan J. Pharr and Robert D. Putnam, eds., *Disaffected Democracies: What's Troubling the Trilateral Countries?* (Princeton: Princeton University Press, 2000), and Patti Tamara Lenard and Richard Simeon, eds., *Imperfect Democracies: The Democratic Deficit in Canada and the United States* (Vancouver: University of British Columbia Press, 2012).

23. For a critique of the Senate that recounts this story, see Claire Hoy, *Nice Work: The Continuing Scandal of Canada's Senate* (Toronto: McClelland and Stewart Inc., 1999).

24. Nanos Research, "Canadians views on Senate expenses," June 18, 2013, online at http://www.nanosresearch.com/library/opinion_2013.html.

25. Nanos Research, "Reform Outpaces Abolishment of Senate," June 20, 2013, online at ibid.

26. On the relatively low levels of political knowledge on the part of Canadians, see Elisabeth Gidengil, André Blais, Neil Nevitte, and Richard Nadeau, *Citizens* (Vancouver: University of British Columbia Press, 2004).

27. This and the following quote are from C.E.S. Franks, "The Canadian Senate in Modern Times," in S. Joyal, ed., *Protecting Canadian Democracy: The Senate You Never Knew* (Montreal and Kingston: McGill-Queen's University Press, 2003), p. 183.

28. An early attempt to explore the link between political culture and our negative view of politics can be found in Neil Nevitte, *The Decline of Deference* (Toronto: University of Toronto Press, 1996).

29. Georgina Blakeley and Valerie Bryson. *Contemporary Political Concepts: A Critical Introduction* (London: Pluto Press, 2002), p. 1.

30. Emory University, "Babies grasp number, space and time concepts," ScienceDaily.com, June 15, 2010, online at http://www.sciencedaily.com/releases/2010/06/100615141751.htm.

31. I first came across this example on the Internet many years ago but the site from which I obtained it has long since disappeared.

32. Similarly, we would object if someone tried to deny that a tree was a tree when it met the concept's definitional requirements. In the world of art, Réné Magritte famously presented a painting in 1929 called *Les trahison des images* (The Treachery of Images), in which the text below an image of a pipe states "ceci n'est pas une pipe" ("this is not a pipe"). When we look at the painting, however, our first thought is to say "yes, it is a pipe!"

33. This section is based on a course on "power" that I took as an undergraduate student in the late 1980s at the University of Toronto, which was taught by Professor Susan Soloman.

34. See Eugene Garver, "Rhetoric and Essentially Contested Arguments," *Philosophy and Rhetoric* 11 (3) (1978), pp. 156–72.

35. This and the following quote are from W.B. Gallie, "Essentially Contested Concepts," *Proceedings of the Aristotelian Society* 56 [New Series] (1955–56), p. 169. For recent explorations of Gallie's relevance to the study of politics, see David Collier, Fernando Daniel Hidalgo, and Andra Olivia Maciuceanu, "Essentially contested concepts: Debates and applications," *Journal of Political Ideologies* 11 (3) (2006), pp. 211–46, and David-Hillel Ruben, "W.B. Gallie and Essentially Contested Concepts," *Philosophical Papers* 39 (2) (2010), pp. 257–70.

36. C. Wright Mills, *The Power Elite* (New York: Oxford University Press, 1956), p. 4.

37. Floyd Hunter, *Community Power Structure: A Study of Decision Makers* (Chapel Hill: University of North Carolina Press, 1953), p. 247.

38. Robert A. Dahl, *Who Governs? Democracy and Power in an American City* (New Haven: Yale University Press, 1961), pp. 202–03.

39. Peter Bachrach and Morton S. Baratz, "The Two Faces of Power," *American Political Science Review* 56 (4) (1962), p. 948.

40. Steven Lukes, *Power: A Radical View*, 2nd ed. (Houndsmills, Basingstoke: Palgrave Macmillan, 2005 [1974]), p. 13.

41. Carol Pateman, *The Sexual Contract* (Bloomington, Indiana: Stanford University Press, 1988).

42. For an introduction to his ideas, see Michel Foucault, *Politics, Philosophy, Culture: Interviews and Other Writings 1977–1984*, edited and introduced by Lawrence D. Kritzman; trans. by Alan Sheridan and Others (New York and London: Routledge, 1988).

43. Quoted in Rein Peeters, "Against violence, but not at any price: Hannah Arendt's concept of power," *Ethical Perspectives* 15 (2008), p. 172.

44. Rand Dyck, ed., *Studying Politics: An Introduction to Political Science*, 1st ed. (Toronto: Nelson College, 2002), p. 19.

45. There was, as a result, considerable soul-searching during the immediate post-Cold War period, particularly among International Relations scholars, for whom the Cold War had been a central topic of study for decades; see, for example, *International Organization* 48 (2) (1994), which includes various papers prepared for a "The end of the cold war and theories of international relations" symposium.

46. Cecil Foster, *Where Race Does Not Matter: The New Spirit of Modernity* (Toronto: Penguin Canada, 2005), p. 171.

47. Karl Polanyi, *The Great Transformation*, foreword by Robert M. MacIver (Boston: Beacon Press, 1957).

48. See http://www.refworld.org/docid/3dd8dd484.html.

49. See, for example, Donald J. Savoie, *Governing from the Centre: The Concentration of Power in Canadian Politics* (Toronto: University of Toronto Press, 1999), Jeffrey Simpson, *The Friendly Dictatorship* (Toronto: McClelland and Stewart Inc., 2001), and Michael Harris, *Party of One: Stephen Harper and Canada's Radical Makeover* (Toronto: Viking Press, 2014).

50. Hannah Pitkin, *The Concept of Representation* (Oakland: University of California Press, 1967), p. 10.

51. Samuel Noah Kramer, *History Begins at Sumer* (London: Thames and Hudson, 1958 [1956]).

52. It certainly is a far cry from the plot of Nobel Prize recipient José Saramago's 2004 novel *Seeing,* in which a state of emergency is declared after 70 percent of voters purposefully leave their ballots blank, which the government interprets as an act of subversion rather than an expression of the will of the people.

53. This is a burgeoning area of study. On the role of technology in the recent Arab Spring movement, see Philip N. Howard and Muzammil M. Hussain, *Democracy's Fourth Wave? Digital Media and the Arab Spring* (Oxford: Oxford University Press, 2013); for a more skeptical view, see Matthew Hindman, *The Myth of Digital Democracy* (Princeton: Princeton University Press, 2008).

54. E.E. Schattschneider, *The Semisovereign People: A Realist's View of Democracy in America* (New York: Holt, Rinehart and Winston, 1960), p. 35.

55. For a critical perspective on these developments, see Yves Engler, *The Ugly Canadian: Stephen Harper's Foreign Policy* (Black Point, New Brunswick and Vancouver: Fernwood Publishing and RED Publishing, 2012).

56. See, for example, the materials produced though the Inter-Parliamentary Union's "Promoting Democracy Worldwide" project; online at http://www.ipu.org/dem-e/overview.htm.

57. P.H. Hynes, quoted in Christin Ormhaug with Patrick Meier and Helga Hernes, *Armed Conflict Deaths Disaggregated by Gender*, PRIO Paper 23, November 2009, online at http://file.prio.no/Publication_files/Prio/Armed%20Conflict%20Deaths%20Disaggregated%20by%20Gender.pdf.

58. Taylor Owen, "Bombs Over Cambodia," *Walrus Magazine*, October 2006, online at http://thewalrus.ca/2006-10-history. The political effects of this bombing in Cambodia are a subject of some debate. Owen argues that "Civilian casualties in Cambodia drove an enraged populace into the arms of an insurgency that had enjoyed relatively little support until the bombing began, setting in motion the expansion of the Vietnam War deeper into Cambodia, a coup d'état in 1970, the rapid rise of the Khmer Rouge, and ultimately the Cambodian genocide."

59. See, for example, the photos analyzed at https://www.google.ca/earth/outreach/stories/darfur.html and http://www.aaas.org/aleppo.

60. Ursula Franklin with Sarah Jane Freeman, *Ursula Franklin Speaks: Thoughts and Afterthoughts, 1986–2012* (Montreal and Kingston: McGill-Queen's University Press, 2014), p. 27.

2

THINKING ABOUT POLITICS: IDEAS AND IDEOLOGIES IN POLITICS

Richard Sigurdson

A papyrus fragment of Plato's *Republic* from the 3rd century CE, discovered among thousands of written fragments in buried rubbish dumps outside Oxyrhynchus, a city in ancient Egypt. Finds such as this allow us to carry on conversations across the centuries about the ideas that define the political worlds of our past, present, and future.

CHAPTER OBJECTIVES

After you have completed this chapter, you should be able to:

- discuss the ways in which one's view of human nature helps determine one's attitude toward government and politics

- define the term ideology and outline its functions in the contemporary world

- outline the different views on equality put forward by conservatives, liberals, and socialists

- distinguish between negative and positive concepts of freedom, and discuss the relevant policy implications in emphasizing one view of freedom over the other

- differentiate between the political left and right and define the following: progressive, liberal, conservative, reactionary, and far-right

INTRODUCTION

Political *theory* is the subfield of the discipline of political science that involves, rather simply, thinking about politics. Political theorists study the "big ideas" about things political, such as: the nature and function of the state; the role, legitimacy, and proper ends of government; the relationship between the individual and society; the meaning of liberty, obligation, and rights; and the connections between law, justice, authority, and power. Practically speaking, political theory involves the study of a number of key texts, mainly written by long-dead writers, most of whom were philosophers of other things as well, not just politics. (For instance, the Greek philosopher Aristotle [384–322 BCE], who famously classified types of government and is often considered the founder of political science, is equally renowned for his contributions to logic, physics, biology, and medicine.) Political theory is sometimes referred to as "political philosophy." But it is not really philosophy, strictly understood. (Or at least, it is not philosophy as it is understood by most professional philosophers of the analytical tradition.) For instance, political theorists are usually less likely to rely upon highly abstract ethical or epistemological theories (or meta-theories) and are more likely to be grounded in historical or empirical sources of evidence than are their counterparts in philosophy. Still, there is an obvious connection between the two, just as there is an affinity between political theorists and historians of ideas as well as with political sociologists. In the end, political theory might best be seen as the study of concepts and principles that people use to explain and understand political events, actions, and institutions, such as the state. Political theory is thus crucial to the study of politics, as it provides the tools for meaningful participation in crucial discussions in all sub-fields, from international relations to domestic politics.

Systematic political thinking is evident in various eras and cultures. In the Western world, it dates at least as far back as the ancient Greeks, whose philosophers debated the merits of most of the forms of government still known to us today: monarchy, aristocracy, democracy, tyranny, and oligarchy (see Box 2.1). As noted above (and as explored more in Chapter 3), Aristotle famously classified types of government according to the number of rulers (the one, the few, or the many), as well as the ends pursued by the rulers (illegitimate rule is for the benefit of the rulers alone and legitimate for the benefit of all).[1] Political philosophers in the East struggled with similar issues related to politics and statecraft. In ancient China, Confucius (551–471 BCE), Mencius (372–289 BCE), Han Fei (280–233 BCE), and others produced politically-informed philosophies during an era of political chaos and constant warfare. This tradition was sustained throughout the Middle Ages when Christian thinkers, such as Augustine (354–430) and Thomas Aquinas (1225–74), and Islamic philosophers, such as al-Farabi (872–951) and Ibn Khaldun (1332–1406), studied the Hellenic writers, reviving their ideas while also proposing new philosophies and visions of the ideal state. From the early modern period to today, political thinkers around the world

---

BOX 2.1

WHO RULES?

Rule by one: autocracy

Rule by the few: oligarchy

Rule by the hereditary king or queen: monarchy

Rule by the usurper of legal authority: tyranny

Rule by the best or the elite: aristocracy

Rule by the people: democracy

Rule by the most honourable: timocracy

Rule by the wealthy: plutocracy

Rule by thieves: kleptocracy

Rule by the masses: ochlocracy

Rule by no ruler or government: anarchy

Rule by the clerics: theocracy

Rule by men: patriarchy

Rule by women: matriarchy

Rule by technical experts: technocracy

Rule by administrators: bureaucracy

Indeed, the list of classic texts required for a good understanding of the tradition is not very long and will vary only slightly from one expert to another, primarily depending on how long you allow the list to be. The core, however, is seldom in dispute. (See Box 2.2 for a list of important primary texts.)

Some knowledge of the canon of Western political theory is generally regarded as fundamental to the discipline of political science in the Anglo-American academy. First-year survey courses often include some general overview of the key ideas of the Western tradition of political thought, and entry-level political theory courses are popular. Often, these are organized chronologically, helping to walk the student through a series of thinkers and their works—usually leading from the Greeks, who invented the ideal of political liberty, to the modern democracies of the post-Second World War period, in which political freedom has been institutionalized (to varying degrees of perfection). This way of covering the material is often dubbed "Plato to NATO" and indeed this was the title of a 1984 BBC Radio series, which was then published as a popular book of 14 essays spanning thinkers such as Plato (428/427 or 424/423–348/347 BCE), Niccolò Machiavelli (1459–1527), Thomas Hobbes (1588–1679), John Locke (1632–1704), Jean-Jacques Rousseau (1712–1778), and Karl Marx (1818–1883), before ending with the views of

---

BOX 2.2

THE MAJOR TEXTS OF WESTERN POLITICAL THEORY

1. Plato, *The Republic* (360 BCE)
2. Aristotle, *The Politics* (350 BCE)
3. Augustine, *The City of God* (413–26)
4. Thomas Aquinas, *Summa Theologiae* (1265–74)
5. Niccolò Machiavelli, *The Prince* (1513)
6. Thomas Hobbes, *Leviathan* (1651)
7. John Locke, *Second Treatise on Government* (1690)
8. Jean-Jacques Rousseau, *The Social Contract* (1762)
9. Karl Marx and Friedrich Engels, *The Communist Manifesto* (1848)
10. John Stuart Mill, *On Liberty* (1859)

---

and in many cultures have theorized about the foundations of power, issues of social welfare and equality, and the relative merits of different forms of political authority.

Typically, the study of political theory starts with a close reading of a given number of classic works by a few well-known thinkers. In the Western tradition, the foundational texts go back to the ancient Greek period and then can be found scattered across the following centuries. Some political theorists do not even regard anything written after the beginning of the 20th century to be worthy of inclusion in this "canon." It is for this reason that a colleague of the renowned professor of political theory, Alan Ryan, once said to him that political theorists are people "obsessed with two dozen books." Ryan's retort was that "two dozen might be a little on the high side."[2]

20th century philosophers such as Herbert Marcuse (1898–1979) and Hannah Arendt (1906–1975).[3] There is a general presumption that the main ideas of Western political thought expressed within this grand tradition have served, one way or another, to form the philosophical and ideological foundations for modern governments around the world.

Such an approach is not uncontroversial. It can be criticized for presenting a misleading narrative of a unilinear trajectory of political development in the West.[4] Moreover, the almost complete absence of women from the list of notable political writers is telling and indicates the extent to which a masculinist bias excludes women's experience from the history of political theory. Likewise, the "Plato to NATO" approach is relentlessly Occidental. This is problematic for a number of reasons. For one thing, it gives the impression that political theory is only a Western phenomenon, or at least that non-Western thought is not important. This is not the case. Non-Western thought has its own long and rich tradition—or more accurately "traditions," since Chinese, Islamic (and pre-Islamic Middle-Eastern), Indic-Hindi, and African traditions each offer a different philosophical framework, each with its own foundational texts. An understanding of one or more of these traditions of thought can particularly benefit the study of political science sub-fields such as comparative politics and International Relations. Another problem is that the grand tradition's Eurocentrism calls into question its claims to universality and objectivity, since the key authors' perceptions about what it means to be human or to belong to a political community come from a particular perspective. Finally, we might question, along with the seminal thinker Edward Said (1935–2003), the accuracy of the depictions of non-Western cultures and peoples that are found in the Western canon.[5]

Nevertheless, there is great value in studying the history of Western political thought, since the competing notions about political community, social justice, and human nature found in it continue to frame and inform our own conversations about such things as the proper design of government, the appropriate use of power, and the best distribution of resources. Moreover, this tradition informs politics not only in Western countries, but for a variety of reasons (colonialism, globalization, and so on) it has had an influence on virtually every political system worldwide. Students need to explore the ideas that shape their own subjective worldviews and that have helped form the institutions and frameworks that regulate their political lives. And it is clear that the ideas of many now-dead political philosophers profoundly influence the strategies and practices of actual political leaders, whose actions directly affect our daily lives.

Political thinking led to the ideologies that underlie all modern political systems: liberalism, conservatism, socialism, feminism, anarchism, political Islam, and so on. Here are just a few examples. The Chinese thinker Sun Tzu (544–496 BCE) is the attributed author of *The Art of War*, which has greatly influenced military strategists—first in East Asia and later in Europe after its translation into French in 1772. Particularly important is its theory about the economics of warfare and the ways in which one can wage warfare without the risks (and costs) of full battle. A similarly influential text—and one, like *The Art of War*, which has been applied beyond its original context—is Machiavelli's *The Prince*, a book that has become a key resource for any leader seeking knowledge of political strategy. The ideas of Locke and Baron de Montesquieu (1689–1755) more directly provided the intellectual underpinnings for the liberal democratic nation-state, informing such founding documents as the Constitution of the United States. The writings of Adam Smith (1723–1790) helped create the modern discipline of political economy and provide the rationale for capitalism, free trade, and libertarianism. Rousseau's contemplations on freedom and equality inspired the French Revolution of 1789, which had as its slogan the Rousseauian phrase: "*liberté, égalité, fraternité.*" A direct line can be drawn between the advocacy of women's equality of opportunity by Mary Astell (1666–1731) and Mary Wollstonecraft (1759–1797) and the feminist movement of the contemporary era. The radical ideas of Marx and Friedrich Engels (1820–1895) or Friedrich Nietzsche (1844–1900) aroused, often unwittingly, political movements—communist and fascist, respectively—that had a tremendous impact on the 20th century. Mao Zedong's (1893–1976) adaptation of Marxist notions to the Chinese context provided the blueprint for the creation of the People's Republic of China in 1949, while Frantz Fanon (1925–1961) used his knowledge of psychotherapy to help provide the inspiration for anticolonial liberation movements throughout the Third World.

For many reasons, then, political theorists can be seen to have had a profound impact on the world in which we live. Yet there is more to studying political theory than linking the meaning of what philosophers said with the role their ideas have played in later social or political struggles, or with identifying the historical consequences for which this or that political philosopher's ideas are commonly held responsible. The study of political ideas can also afford us the opportunity to think through, in our own mind and with our own experiences as points of reference, the big political questions that face humankind in all ages and territories. Our engagement with the writings of major political philosophers of the past is simply one way to help clarify for ourselves the precise meaning and utility of notions such as equality, freedom, power, and justice. This is more than merely an abstract thought experiment. It equips us with the tools to understand and attempt to resolve the conflicts that are at the root of contemporary political life everywhere on the planet. And ultimately, this involves an engagement with the overarching question of political theory: How can human beings best govern themselves?

Over the centuries, as we will see throughout this chapter, there have been several competing ways to answer this question. What is more, the recent past has seen a highly conflictual and often violent dispute among competing ideologies—liberalism, conservatism, socialism, communism, fascism—each of which contains its own answers to this question. Therefore, the goal of the following pages is to introduce some of the key ideas about politics and explore their meanings and consequences, both historically and in terms of our contemporary situation. In the latter part of the chapter, in particular, we will turn to the contemporary landscape by exploring how political ideas form the foundation for major world ideologies. But first we will examine some perennial issues and topics in political thought, organizing the material thematically by looking at the role of human nature in politics as well as the key concepts of equality and liberty—the two most influential ideas in Western liberal-democracies. While the specific theories of individual philosophers cannot be given the space they deserve in a single chapter, I hope that you will take up the challenge of reading

in their own words some of the great political thinkers from the past. At the same time, perhaps this interaction with the thoughts and philosophies of the long-dead will also spur you to read some of the most prominent political philosophers of the more recent era, such as Canada's C.B. Macpherson (see Box 2.3). I hope to show that political theory is by no means just a field of historical study. Ideas are alive today, and debates over political concepts and ideas are as important and lively now as they have ever been. In fact, there has been a powerful revival of political theory in the past 50 years or so, and this is evident across the world, not only in the West. Indeed, many of the key ideas of the Occidental tradition—particularly equality and liberty, which we will focus upon in this chapter—have been incorporated, perhaps in a modified version, in every part of the world. Hence, an understanding of the history of political theory—its key themes and ideas—is crucial for the study of politics in our era of globalization, with its unique mix of complementary and competing cultural and political values.

While it is the last part of the chapter that is intended to focus specifically on the concept of ideology and its role in political science, it will be impossible to avoid touching upon the key ideologies—conservatism, liberalism, socialism—in the earlier part as well. So some preliminary explanation of the leading ideologies of the modern West is in order, along with an indication of how they developed chronologically. First, it should be noted that terms like conservative, liberal, and socialist are appropriately reserved for thinkers and politicians of the modern period. What does that mean? Well, there is a lot of debate about this issue, but it is generally understood that the modern age is post-medieval and post-traditional, in the sense that with modernity the world came to be seen as open to purposeful change by the force of human intention. In terms of political theory, Machiavelli is often regarded as the first modern political thinker, due to his realistic analysis of how things are and how a cunning prince could tame the effects of fate and fortune. While his advice in *The Prince* was offered to a monarch, his *Discourses* reveal republican sentiments and a paramount interest in liberty. Likewise, we can find the germs of liberalism as an ideology in the 16th century opposition to traditional and hereditary powers

---

BOX 2.3

C.B. MACPHERSON: CANADIAN POLITICAL THEORIST

Crawford Brough (C.B.) Macpherson (1911–1987) was a prominent professor of political science at the University of Toronto and remains Canada's pre-eminent political theorist. He is known worldwide for his ground-breaking interpretation of **liberalism**, which has influenced generations of scholars in North America and abroad. His thought is commonly seen as a unique blend of T.H. Green's ethical liberalism and Karl Marx's political economy.[6]

> **Liberalism:** The ideology based on the paramount value of individual liberty. Liberalism assumes that all humans are free and equal by nature, and that society is a vehicle for the protection and enhancement of our natural rights. In its earlier form, often called classical liberalism, this ideology assumed a limited role for the state. In later years, liberals tended to advocate a larger role for the state to guarantee equality and to help foster the full development of the individual. In one form or another, liberalism is the most widely held political position across the West and has become increasing hegemonic worldwide, especially since the fall of the Berlin Wall in 1989.

Macpherson's best-known book, *The Political Theory of Possessive Individualism: Hobbes to Locke* (1962), is a critique of the specific sort of liberalism premised on what he dubbed "possessive individualism"—the idea that each of us is the sole owner of ourselves and the fruits of our labour, with the right to do with this possession what we wish. As Macpherson explains: "Its possessive quality is found in its conception of the individual as essentially the proprietor of his own person or capacities, owing nothing to society for them. The individual was seen neither as a moral whole, nor as part of larger social whole, but as an owner of himself." Under such a conception,

the essence of humanity is "freedom from dependence on the wills of others." Society, in this view, is little more than a system of economic relations, a place for "exchange between proprietors" (p. 3). And political society becomes a mere contrivance for the protection of individual property and for its free exchange within the market. This culture of possessive individualism supports only a very "thin" conception of the human person, Macpherson argues, one that keeps us from realizing our fuller human selves.

In subsequent publications, including the book of his 1964 Massey Lectures, *The Real World of Democracy* (Toronto: House of Anansi, 1965), Macpherson continued to explore the developments of liberal-democratic theory and its impact on national and international politics.

Often overlooked by political theorists is Macpherson's first book, *Democracy in Alberta: The Theory and Practice of a Quasi-Party System* (Toronto: University of Toronto Press, 1953). Here he explains the curious one-party dominant system in provincial politics in Alberta with reference to the Marxian theory of class division, especially the role of the petit-bourgeoisie, and the idea of the economic repression of the Western provinces by central Canada. More than 60 years after its publication, this thesis continues to pack explanatory punch, as pundits turn to Macpherson's ideas to help explain the remarkable phenomenon of one-party dominance in Alberta, re-affirmed most recently in December 2014 when the leader of the Opposition Wildrose Party, Danielle Smith, crossed the floor of the legislature along with eight of her MLAs to sit with the Government, further solidifying its hold on almost all seats in the province.[7]

The Canadian Political Science Association presents an annual C. B. Macpherson Prize for the best book on political theory written by a Canadian.

---

in England and Europe, especially in the challenge to monarchy justified by the divine right of kings. Still, it is not until the 17th century that we normally start to distinguish in thinkers such as Hobbes and Locke ideas that are unequivocally liberal, and which

supported a growing bourgeois social and economic class. Socialism comes later, only after the French Revolution and industrialization, and exists as a challenge to the hegemony of bourgeois liberalism and free market capitalism.

PERENNIAL ISSUES IN POLITICAL THOUGHT

Human Nature and Politics

In recent times, we have grown increasingly suspicious of the notion that there is a single conception of what it means to be a human. We are attuned to see diversity in humankind and a multiplicity of cultures, each with its own socially constructed view about the human essence. Thus, we might tend to agree with the distinguished ethnologist Clifford Geertz that "there is no human nature apart from culture."[8] I will come back to this approach later, but will start here with the fact that theories about human nature have historically played a key role in how various thinkers envision the best ordering of society. Simply in terms of method, political theory has operated on the assumption that a keen understanding of the innate characteristics of the human condition—derived from the study of human behaviour, including in history—provides the evidence for determining the best model for governance. For the Greeks, this exercise was linked explicitly to the study of what was "natural," since justice consisted of doing that which was in accord with nature. Likewise, modern thinkers adopted the scientific method to analyze human beings objectively in order to identify natural tendencies, attributes, and dispositions. These findings, in turn, provided a rational basis for the determination of what was best, or most practicable, for what political thinkers of the time called "the governance of men."

For instance, Thomas Hobbes was convinced that human activity could be explained much the same way as the workings of any other biological mechanism, in terms of what pushes them this way and pulls them that. In his view, humans are driven primarily by our natural "desires" and "aversions." Two basic postulates about human nature provide the basis for all his political theorizing: first, that human beings are inescapably engaged in a perpetual struggle for power over others that ends only in death; and second, that our strongest aversion is to violent death, which we will seek to avoid at all costs. Hobbes comes to these conclusions about human nature by imagining what people would be like if they lived in a "state of nature"—that is, in a condition free of any government or rule-making authority. Hobbes concludes

that a natural condition without authority or rules would be one of constant war "of every man against every man." Life in the state of nature, as Hobbes succinctly declares, would be "solitary, poor, nasty, brutish, and short."[9] Thus, the only rational thing for humans to do in order to avoid perpetual violence, or the constant fear of it, is to quit the state of nature, agreeing mutually to abdicate to a sovereign power all of one's natural rights to govern oneself. Civil society, the result of this covenant between rational human beings, is to Hobbes but an expedient. He says that while it is not natural for humans to live in society, their self-interest will compel them to bind together for the purposes of mutual security and benefit.

Aristotle presents an opposite point of view. For him, it is living in society that is natural—humans are *by nature* social and political animals. Only a beast or a god (the subhuman or the superhuman) could live without being a member of a political community. For us humans, it is in our nature to commune with our fellow citizens. More than that, political life is to Aristotle the highest form of self-actuality. We are most alive, most true to our nature, when we are participating in political activity, especially when we are governing in a good state. Because *polis* life is natural, the best states are ones in which the interests of one person are the same as the interests of all. Hence, a person who acts for his or her own good must also act for the good of all fellow citizens. Such a view was consistent with Plato's notion that reason can show us the truth about how we should live our lives. In contrast to modern liberal thinkers, the Greeks believed that the dictates of reason push us to what is good for the whole rather than what maximizes our self-interests as individuals. Plato does, however, identify sources of conflict within the body politic, analogous to what he sees as separate and competing elements within human nature. That is, along with the part of us that is motivated by reason (our brain), there is a part motivated by spirit or aggression (our heart), as well as a part driven, as Hobbes would have it, by appetites (our stomach and loins). Fortunately, people can control their appetites through reason, providing good health overall. In the same way, a well-ordered society is one governed by those few who can grasp the eternal and perfect reality—what he calls the "forms." It is for this reason that he famously argued that in the best polis a true "philosopher-king" would rule over the appetitive and spirited ranks of humanity, though he would do so for the good of the whole.

Again, this classical Greek view was in contrast to that put forward by Hobbes, who saw humans as avaricious and selfish by nature. Driven by self-interest, he said, humans will constantly seek their own satisfaction at the expense of others, rendering peaceful coexistence impossible in the absence of a single sovereign who will impose upon humanity an artificial order that must be followed, for fear of the harshest punishment for transgression. The rule of the sovereign envisioned by Hobbes does not seek to eliminate competition entirely, though. Rather, it seeks to control it within a set of known laws and rules. Likewise, Locke envisioned a society rife with competition but similarly controlled by rules. In his case, however, he believed that humans would only agree to follow rules that they had agreed to, explicitly or tacitly. In the Victorian era, armed with the discoveries of Charles Darwin, social thinkers such as Herbert Spencer (1820–1903) argued that competition is an essential part of human nature and championed it as a key value in society. Spencer coined the term "survival of the fittest" to describe the process whereby individuals and groups would fail or prosper, according to a societal version of natural selection. What came to be called "Social Darwinism" justified the policies of free market capitalism on the basis that government interference (e.g., welfare state programs) interfered with the natural competition between and among individuals in society. Unfairly perhaps, in the 1980s British Prime Minister Margaret Thatcher and U.S. President Ronald Reagan were labelled as followers of this largely discredited theory, since they both promoted deregulation and privatization of the economy.

An alternative, more optimistic perspective is found in the thought of Jean-Jacques Rousseau. He believed that humans are essentially decent beings but that they have been gradually led away from their natural, congenial condition toward one that is corrupt, unjust, and divisive. This misfortune occurred, Rousseau theorizes, because humans introduced into their lives private property, which led to inequality, selfishness, distrust, and the concentration of power in the hands of a few. Rousseau's thesis, put very simply, is that humans are basically good but have been corrupted by their sociopolitical environment: bad institutions have distorted the natural goodness of humankind. Rousseau offers us hope that human goodness can be rediscovered if social conditions are put right, specifically if an enlightened leader governs in a manner that reflects the will of all. This reasoning, which goes back at least as far as the Confucian philosophy of Mencius in the 4th century BCE, has struck a positive chord with a variety of thinkers and political actors over the years. For instance, most modern liberals believe that by reforming social and political institutions we can help develop the moral character of the individual members of society. T.H. Green (1836–1882) believed that humans are not only naturally inclined to advance their own welfare but those of others as well. Utopian socialists also stress the inherent human capacity for consensus and cooperation and imagine strategies for creating a world of peace and harmony. Marx's doctrine of historical materialism rests on a faith in inexorable historical progress toward the highest phase of communist society, in which there will be no social classes and therefore no destructive political conflict.

More will be said in a subsequent section about the concepts of the political left and right, but it can be noted at this stage that Western thinkers on the so-called left (liberals, socialists, communists) are more likely than those on the right (conservatives, Christian democrats, fascists) to hold the belief that human nature is good, or inherently perfectible, and that political ills stem from societal influences rather than essential human flaws. Thus, the goal of leftist or liberal political action is to create the sorts of institutions that would be most likely to provide the necessary positive

THINK AND DISCUSS

Based on your own observations, do you believe that those who rise to the top in society are generally those who are most talented, work the hardest, and so on? Or are there other factors that play a larger role in determining success in society?

influences to benefit humanity. Thinkers on the political right tend to share a belief in the imperfection of human beings, seeing in the individual varying degrees of weakness, irrationality, perfidy, and immorality. Indeed, conservatives think that humankind is not only morally imperfect but intellectually imperfect as well. Thus, they hold that humans simply cannot know enough to be sure that social experimentation and tinkering with the institutions of government will actually lead to positive change rather than to more problems.[10]

In the Western world, the conviction that humankind is morally imperfect is rooted in the Christian doctrine of original sin. According to this teaching, human beings are fallen creatures, alienated from the goodness of their Creator and divided against each other by selfishness. Most instructive on this topic is the work of St. Augustine, who regarded humans as invariably corrupt and helpless, driven by their most base passions to commit grievous wrongs and to suffer dearly for doing so. In contrast to Plato, Augustine regarded as naïve the idea that people will do what is right and good if they only know the truth. According to Augustine, human beings are from conception wicked and dangerous creatures driven by lust, including the lust for power. No amount of proper education or wisdom will reverse their fallen state. Not surprisingly, he believed that people need to be coerced and restrained by harsh laws, a strict code of behaviour, and brutal punishment for transgressions. Augustine accepted that temporal institutions, as creations of a sinful humanity, would always be inherently flawed and could never bring true happiness. Yet he concluded that secular political institutions, no matter how oppressive, must be respected, since they constitute the only earthly bulwark against disorder. A similar, though entirely secular, version of this notion of human nature can be found in the psychoanalytical theory of Sigmund Freud (1856–1939), who saw the human animal as a complex beast of primitive urges, desires, and passionate inclinations that are barely kept under control by peer pressure and the necessary repression of societal institutions, such as the church and the state.[11]

Another point of view on the issue of human nature is found in Islam, which does not presuppose any inherent wickedness in human nature. Instead, the Qur'an teaches that human beings are born in a state of *fitrah*, which denotes the inherent disposition toward goodness and virtue in humankind that is manifest in peaceful submission to the will of Allah. Thus, there is no concept of original sin in Islam.

People are not perfect, to be sure, and it is a struggle to remain on the right path. But any deviation from one's original virtuous state is due to external factors, suggests the Qur'an. True repentance of sin can return a person to the original, sinless state. According to Muslim theology, humankind's chief failings are pride and rebellion. In their pride, humans attempt to become equals of Allah, and this runs counter to the primary theological concept of Islam, the belief that there is only one God. Thus, pride is a cardinal sin. The chief virtue, again, is submission to divine will. In Islam, *sharia* is the expression of divine will and it forms a system of obligations and duties that are incumbent upon all Muslims. Politically, this is at the root of the Islamic adherence to a strict legal framework within which both public and private aspects of life are regulated for those living under **sharia law**. It is often pointed out that in political Islam there is no inherent separation between matters for the state and those for the church as there is in **liberal democracy**.

Sharia law: Sharia is the Islamic system of law, both civil and criminal, that is based on the Qur'an (the holy book of Islam); the life example and hadiths (sayings) of the Prophet Muhammad; and on subsequent scholarly interpretations and writings. This system of law prescribes the correct behavior for Muslims across different areas of life and the punishments for transgressions. Importantly, Sharia law is not uniform throughout the Muslim world as it is influenced by different schools of jurisprudence, among other factors.

Liberal democracy: A form of government common to Western political systems in which there is a combination of the "liberal" right to individual freedom and the "democratic" right to representative government. Decision-making power is subject to the rule of law as established by a constitutional system that recognizes fundamental rights and freedoms (e.g., free speech, freedom of the press and religion, and freedom of association) along with certain legal rights to property, privacy, equality under the law, etc. Liberal democracies are distinguished by free and fair elections within multi-party systems, civilian rule, separation of powers between the executive and legislative branches, an independent judiciary, and a political culture of tolerance and pluralism—including protection for minorities against potentially tyrannical majorities.

But should we take it for granted that human nature has such explanatory power that it can validate or invalidate normative theory? That is, should we accept the argument that a theory can be dismissed if it imposes standards or requirements that we think go against human nature? This is a popular move in political theory. For instance, a common criticism of Marxism, even by those who might grant that a classless society would be most just, is that it simply could not work, since its requirement that people forego private property is something that runs against our acquisitive nature and can only be imposed by brutal force. The most popular retort from the left is that these critics wrongly base their assumptions about human nature on observations of class-divided societies, and then impute as "natural" such characteristics as covetousness or individualism. That is, observing people in capitalist societies, where competition is rewarded, might lead one to read into the natural condition traits that are, in fact, culturally specific.[12] But here as well the argument often goes back to human nature, and to which version of it is most correct. Many who support a classless society argue, along with T.H. Green, that cooperation and not competition is what is natural to humanity, pointing to primitive societies where collaboration and sharing are the norm. Others dismiss all attempts to theorize politically from a concept of human nature, preferring a sort of *tabula rasa* approach whereby human beings offer a blank slate upon which is inscribed a set of values and preferences specific to a given culture or environment.[13] Change the environment, and you will get different normative practices. This brings us back to Geertz and his denial of a common human nature: "One of the most significant facts about us may finally be that we all begin with the natural equipment to live a thousand kinds of life but end in the end having lived only one."[14]

Equality

Political thinkers since Hobbes and Locke have presumed that human beings are equal in essence, though they have differed on what this means in practice. Indeed, **egalitarianism** has become not only a main pillar of liberal-democracy but a staple of almost all systems of government and political thinking. Aside from a small minority of extreme racists or anti-feminists, we are all egalitarians of some

sort now. To use the phrase popularized by Canadian political philosopher Will Kymlicka, we operate on an "egalitarian plateau".[15] That is, we grant everyone standing as moral equals, and extend to all members of the political community the rights of equal concern and respect. Yet we disagree quite drastically when it comes to determining what it means to treat people equally—with equal rights, equal recognition, and equal opportunity.

> **Egalitarianism:** The doctrine that advocates that people should be treated as equals regardless of differences of wealth, income, class, sex, religion, ethnicity, physical ability, and so on. At minimum, egalitarianism promotes the equality of social and political rights for all citizens; at maximum, egalitarianism calls for a much greater equality of wealth and income for all persons across all divisions in society. In this regard, liberals emphasize equality of opportunity, while socialists emphasize equality of condition.

For most of human history, however, there was no such agreement that humans were to be regarded as fundamentally equal. Quite the opposite was the case. Even the ancient Greeks, who created a political system in which full citizens shared equally the rights of power and participation, presupposed a rank order of humankind. Citizens in the Greek polis were always a very small proportion of the overall residents. Greek philosophers justified inequality on the grounds of people's unequal capacity for reason. On this basis, Aristotle excluded from citizenship whole categories of humanity—artisans, workers, women, slaves—on the grounds that they lacked the ability to reason for themselves. Plato was more willing to regard women as equal to men, but he was by no means an egalitarian. He designed an elaborate theory of government to justify the rule of a naturally superior individual, the philosopher-king.

Even in modernity, and in spite of the growing agreement among political philosophers that humans are by nature equal, there were very few prominent philosophers who proposed that this equality should translate into anything like equality of income or condition in society. Many theorists—most notoriously, Friedrich Nietzsche—argued that egalitarianism was itself a sign of the decline of civilization. Nietzsche was frustrated by the fact that philosophers and politicians in the modern age were increasingly promoting what he called the "slave" doctrine of equality and the values of the inferior "herd" over what he dubbed "master morality" and the noble doctrine of aristocracy. In his more fanciful moments, Nietzsche looked forward to the rise to power of a new breed of "supermen" who would reflect the highest potential for human creativity and vitality.

While few have been as bold as Nietzsche in announcing their anti-egalitarianism, many thinkers in the tradition of Anglo-American or European conservatism have assumed that humanity is naturally and hierarchically ordered. Conservatives often take their cue in this regard from Edmund Burke, who valued above all order and stability and feared that the egalitarian ethos arising from the French Revolution would undermine the current social structure. Burke held that the best government is an **aristocracy** in which the privileged orders—the high-born and well-bred—would rule wisely and for the good of the whole. This mindset is connected to the generally pessimistic view of human nature shared by traditional conservatives, who regard human beings as imperfect and easily corrupted. Of course, there is always a natural elite made up of individuals more able to control their passions and exercise sound judgment. In a well-ordered society, these superior talents will be rewarded with disproportionate material benefits. But with these advantages comes a greater obligation to act nobly and to serve the greater good. This is the concept known as "noblesse oblige."

> **Aristocracy:** Government by an elite or privileged class or by a minority regarded as those best fit to rule. For the Ancients, the term was reserved for the rule by the few "best" (*aristos* in Greek)—the most educated, wise, brave, and selfless people, who would rule in the interests of the whole society rather than their own. During the Middle Ages in Europe, the term became associated with hereditary rule by a particular social class, otherwise known as the "nobility." The term aristocracy has generally lost its original positive connotation and it now commonly carries a pejorative meaning in liberal democratic societies.

In contrast to Burke's aristocratic conservatism, the liberal position holds that humans are by nature free and equal creatures, equally in possession of their own natural rights (primarily, the right to preserve oneself, but also the right to individual freedom and the enjoyment of private property). Hobbes noted that in the state of nature (which was in essence a state of war, each person versus every other) individuals were more or less equal, since they were equally capable of killing each other. Locke put emphasis on individuals as equal possessors of rights and freedoms according to natural law, but similarly saw the lack of government as a potential source of chaos and thus as a serious impediment to the enjoyment of one's natural freedom. Rousseau, too, regarded the original condition as one of perfect equality, though his state of nature was a state of peace. He argued that it was the introduction of money that led to inequality in civil society, and that this inequality between people was the source of all conflict and violence. Even in these different conceptions, we find that the main emphasis of the liberal point of view was that humans naturally enjoyed equal rights. Ultimately, these ideas laid the intellectual foundations for the liberal-democratic states epitomized by the great republics arising out of the 18th-century revolutions in France and America. In the former, this ideal is captured in the national motto: *Liberté, Egalité, Fraternité.* Moreover, the Declaration of the Rights of Man and of the Citizen, passed by France's National Constituent Assembly in August 1789, states that the law "must be the same for all, whether it protects or punishes. All citizens, being equal in its eyes, shall be equally eligible to all high offices, public positions and employments, according to their ability, and without other distinction than that of their virtues and talents." In the case of the United States, the spirit behind the new order was nicely summed up by Thomas Jefferson (1743–1826) in the Declaration of Independence: "We hold these truths to be self-evident: that all men are created equal; that they are endowed by their Creator with certain inalienable Rights: that among these are Life, Liberty and the pursuit of Happiness."

As a statement of political ideals, the Declaration stakes out an inspiring egalitarian position that is rightfully revered by patriots as symbolic of America's democratic roots. Indeed, many a noble reformer—in America and elsewhere—has found motivation and strength in these powerful words. Yet, as many have pointed out, there is a huge gap between the ideals expressed in this great document and the social reality of the polity it created. Most glaring is the fact that when the Declaration was penned in 1776, and for almost a century thereafter, slavery was legal in America. Many of its signatories, including Jefferson himself, and many representatives to the Constitutional Convention, including George Washington (who once denounced slavery as "repugnant"), owned slaves. It was not until the Emancipation Proclamation and the passage of the 13th, 14th, and 15th Amendments in the wake of the Civil War that American constitutional law entrenched racial equality—and even then the courts were largely unwilling to enforce any of its provisions on state governments wishing to continue various forms of racial segregation and discrimination.

Nor should it escape our attention that the Declaration and the rights it champions were limited to "all men" and not to the female half of the population. American women did not receive equal political rights until the 19th Amendment was passed in 1920. Neither were the rights that were claimed by the male American colonists extended to Indigenous peoples, who were largely regarded as savages unfit for citizenship and equal treatment under the law. Finally, full political rights were not even enjoyed by all white men in the Thirteen Colonies, since those who did not own sufficient property were excluded. In spite of the Founders' lofty rhetoric, therefore, the notion that all human beings should be regarded as equal and treated so by law was not a practical reality in the U.S. at its inception.

In truth, neither France nor America nor any other nominally democratic state created in the 18th or 19th century has had a very good track record when it comes to equality. To be sure, in most quarters there was a steady expansion of the franchise, and one can trace a greater inclusion of previously excluded groups into the realm of the equal-rights-bearing citizenry in North America and Europe. But the trajectory was not always upwards. The most horrific case in point, of course, is the almost incomprehensible denial of full human status to Jews by the National Socialists in Germany. Adolph Hitler and other proponents of Nazi ideology rejected outright any notion of universal human equality. For members of their own nationality, defined racially as those sharing Aryan blood, there were equal legal and political rights, even extending to ethnic Germans outside the territory of the German state. But all non-Aryans were regarded as inferior and unworthy of equal rights, with Jews specifically targeted in policies such as the Nuremburg Laws. Jews were first stripped of their

rights, then their citizenship, and then their lives. Based on a racist ideology, the Nazi regime embarked upon an unprecedented program of extermination of members of the Jewish race throughout Germany and in other lands the Reich occupied. In the end, over six million Jews were murdered in the Holocaust.

Political theorists are implicated, though often only tangentially, in the rise of fascism and Nazism. Theorists of German nationalism, such as Johann Gottlieb Fichte (1762–1814), who promoted German exceptionalism and stressed the need for the German nation to be purified, are often cited as an inspiration for Nazism. French aristocrat Arthur de Gobineau (1816–1882) is widely regarded as the father of race theory, and his idea of an Aryan master race was enormously influential among the Nazis (although they had to account for the fact that he was not an anti-Semite, and in fact admired Jews for their contributions to civilization). Nietzsche's ideas about a new master race were also used (or misused) by apologists for Nazism who sought to justify Hitler's racist and nationalist doctrines (again, in spite of the fact that Nietzsche himself denounced racism and nationalism as perverted ideologies).[16] Oswald Spengler (1880–1936), a philosopher of the decline of Western civilization, is also often linked to the Nazis, though he never became one himself. On the other hand, some academics, such as the philosopher Giovanni Gentile (1875–1944), explicitly endorsed Italian fascism in their philosophical writing and became active members in fascist politics.

A more curious and controversial case is presented by the renowned philosopher Martin Heidegger (1889–1976), the author of *Being and Time*, one of the monumental works in 20th century philosophy. Heidegger was appointed Rector of the University of Freiburg in 1933 and promptly joined the Nazi Party. How far his affinity with the regime went, and to what extent his philosophy is related to Nazism, remain highly divisive matters among commentators.[17] Though the evidence is clear that Heidegger was not only a Party member but shared many views in common with the Nazis, he has had many supporters within the philosophic community who justify his party status as a move intended to protect the university and who see no connection between this party affiliation and his intellectual enterprise. Most notable in this regard is Hannah Arendt, the theorist of totalitarianism and herself a Jew who had to escape from Nazi Germany.

She was also Heidegger's student and former lover, and she ultimately defended him during his denazification hearings.[18] Recently, even more damning evidence against Heidegger has appeared with the release in German of his "Black Notebooks."[19]

In the period following the end of the Second World War and the full disclosure of the Nazi horrors, there was a significant rise in the philosophical and political analysis of human rights. On the political side, there was widespread acceptance of the values of the 1948 United Nations Declaration of Human Rights, with its affirmation of the "inherent dignity and of the equal and inalienable rights of all members of the human family." Indeed, most liberal-democratic states have formally eradicated any official obstacles to equality before and under the law. It is no longer legal to deny services to people based solely on their gender or race. But now that virtually all of the formal and legal obstacles to equal participation have been dismantled in places such as the United States and Canada, critics have turned their attention to ways in which women, visible minorities, Indigenous peoples, immigrants, the poor, and others continue to experience conditions of less than full equality even in the most advanced Western societies.

How can we justify inequalities in societies that are avowedly egalitarian? How much inequality is permissible, and of what sort? What, if anything, should society or the state do to address the problem of persistent social inequality? Here one finds diverging views among political theorists, even among those who regard themselves as liberal and egalitarian. For some, like Milton Freidman (1912–2006), the answer is typically that we should guarantee formal or legal equality and then rely on the free market to produce an equilibrium of societal benefits. Freidman, who is a leading inspiration for contemporary neo-liberals, held that we should make sure that there is no legal or official discrimination, and then accept that a fair system of market competition will eventually produce the best results. Beyond ensuring impartiality and nondiscrimination, the liberal state should not be used to provide specific advantages for any individuals or groups. Yet, as French economist Thomas Piketty has recently shown, post-welfare state capitalism has been marked by a sharp increase in inequality in Europe and North America, as the uncontrolled free market results in rapid accumulation of inherited wealth.[20] He argues that this concentration of wealth in the hands of a very few undermines liberty and democracy, and says that it can only be reversed by some form of state intervention. Piketty recommends an annual global wealth tax, along with a significantly progressive income tax, to reverse the trend. Proponents of redistribution, such as Piketty, tend to argue that for freedom and equality to be meaningful everyone must have an equal chance to compete fairly, on a level playing field with all others, for a share of the social and economic benefits that society has to offer. Judged by the results, these theorists say, the playing field is not at all level; it is still tilted very much in favour of members of certain groups (such as the upper-class or members of the majority racial or ethnic group). So in the name of equality, the power of the state must be used to ensure fair chances for all citizens (e.g., through **affirmative action** or employment equity policies). In this fashion, no one will be excluded from, nor unduly disadvantaged when engaging in, societal competition. Yet liberals of this sort would normally expect that once equality of opportunity is assured—once there is an even playing field—the most talented or industrious individual should still be able to reap the rewards of his or her own competitive efforts. As long as the competition between individuals is free and fair, the liberal will not deny that some can have more and others less. Social or "conventional inequality" will exist in a liberal society, since some individuals will gain more because they will work harder or have more ability than others. However, this conventional inequality is justifiable, from the liberal point of view, so long as no one is denied a meaningful opportunity to compete and to be successful, especially on the basis of attributes or identifiers over which they have no control, such as race or gender.

Affirmative action: An American policy and term designed to increase the representation of targeted groups in such areas as employment and education. Critics may view it as "preferential treatment" or "reverse discrimination" but proponents say it redresses the effects of past discrimination. Affirmative action began in the U.S. in the 1960s, focusing mainly on increasing opportunities for African-Americans. In the 1970s, it started to be used to increase the number of women in professional and managerial positions. In Canada, a policy of "employment equity" has been used to encourage the representation of women, visible minorities, Aboriginal people, and persons with disabilities in government or companies doing business with the government.

It is at this point that **socialism**, the doctrine advocating economic equality of the classes and the use of government to serve the collective good of the whole society, breaks with liberalism and insists that true egalitarianism demands more than equal opportunity or equal social and political rights. Socialists are most concerned with material inequality and equal access to the resources of the community. It is often said, then, that while liberals are content with an equality of opportunity, socialist justice requires an actual equality of condition. For those on the moderate left (e.g., social democrats), equality of condition is more of an ideal than a practical goal. That is, the objective is to narrow the gap as much as possible between rich and poor, gradually levelling out society's social and economic inequalities by raising the floor for those at the bottom and lowering the ceiling for those at the top. Socialists argue that the free market system, left unchecked, allows for the accumulation of enormous wealth by the very few at the expense of the majority. In the name of equality, social democrats want the state to intervene in the economy, adjusting the effects of the disparities between winners and losers that inevitably arise from market competition. Likewise, they support the rights of organized labour as a bulwark against unfettered capitalist exploitation of workers. The stronger the unions, the less power employers have to drive down wages in order to increase profits. In effect, social democrats want to see a redistribution of wealth and income, and so they promote such measures as steeply graduated income taxes, whereby the rich are taxed at a higher rate than the less affluent; extensive social welfare programs, which use public funds to provide services and benefits to those who cannot otherwise pay for them; and full employment or job guarantee policies, whereby all those willing and able to work can do so.

For radical socialists and communists, however, these social democratic strategies are insufficient, since they can never provide for an absolute equality of condition. For justice to be achieved, it is argued, the fundamental inequality of classes—most importantly, the gap between the bourgeoisie and the workers—must be addressed at its root. Redistributive economic policies and trade unionism will not, in themselves, bring about full equality. Indeed, they might even forestall it by improving conditions that would otherwise lead to the overthrow of capitalism. Vladimir Ilyich Lenin (1870–1924), Marxist theoretician and the leader of the Bolshevik Revolution in Russia, insisted that social democratic parties and their trade union partners could not be vehicles for truly revolutionary change. What was needed was not a redistribution of wealth and income through higher wage settlements for workers but the complete abolition of **capitalism** and its replacement with full public ownership of all of the means of production. In order for there to be real equality, he and other communists would say, the capitalist system must be replaced with a planned economy, one in which central authority decides what is to be produced and to whom it will be distributed. Communists envision a society organized around the principle: "From each according to their ability, to each according to their need."

Socialism: The doctrine advocating economic equality of the classes and the use of government to serve the collective good of the whole society. Socialists value the collective good over the private interests of individuals, and thus emphasize cooperation over competition. Socialists advocate public ownership of key industries, regulation of the market, redistribution of resources, and protection of fundamental social rights and freedoms. There is a wide variety of socialist practice. Social democrats insist on working within the parliamentary system and achieving socialism through democratic and evolutionary change, while communists and other radical socialists believe in the need for total, revolutionary change, often through the violent overthrow of the existing regime. Since 1989, however, officially communist regimes have either collapsed or reframed their ideological positions to provide for a greater role for the market in the economy.

Capitalism: An economic system in which the means of production (land, factories, technology, etc.) are privately owned and operated according to the profit motive. Decisions about production, investment, and distribution of resources are determined according to market forces (i.e., whether a profit can be made producing and marketing a product), rather than collective or community priorities. In capitalism, workers exchange their labour for wages or salary. Although it is often called the "free enterprise system," capitalism can exist even where there is little freedom, politically or socially, and where the state controls the system (i.e., in "state capitalism").

Of course, disparities in wealth and income are not the only forms of inequality that are of critical political consequence. In the North American context, the most contentious and historically significant debates regarding equality and social justice have involved race, gender, and sexuality. More than anything, slavery and the legacy of racial discrimination against African-Americans dominate the thinking about the politics of equality in the United States. Can there ever be racial equality in a country built on the enslavement of tens of millions of people? For many observers, the election in 2008 of Barack Obama—the first African-American president—marked a symbolic victory for racial equality. Yet, as Cornell West puts it, race still matters in America.[21] This has become especially evident recently in terms of relations between police officers and minority youth. The outbreak of riots in Ferguson, Missouri in 2014 after the police killing of black teenager Michael Brown echoed the Treyvon Martin shooting of two years earlier, which is part of a sad history that also includes the Rodney King incident and the riots in Los Angeles in 1992. As President Obama himself acknowledged in response to the Ferguson riots, "we've made extraordinary progress but we have not made enough progress."[22]

Surprisingly, race and racial discrimination have not been major themes for most political theorists in the Western tradition. As we saw above, Count Gobineau developed a racial theory in his book *An Essay on the Inequality of the Human Races*, which identifies three major races—white, black, and yellow—as "natural" categories. He argued that whites were superior, and also warned that "race-mixing" was the greatest threat to Western civilization. In response to Gobineau, Haitian writer Anténor Firmin (1850–1911) wrote *The Equality of the Races*, demonstrating the errors in race theory and presaging contemporary thinking by arguing that differences between races were not natural or even biological. A similar position was developed by W.E.B Du Bois (1868–1963), perhaps the most influential (and certainly the most prolific) writer on race. He argued that race theory was methodologically unsound, and demonstrated that there was no justification for using race as if it was a legitimate means of scientific classification. As contemporary theorists would put it (and as you will explore further in Chapter 4), race is a "socially constructed" phenomenon.

More so than race, ethnicity and culture have been the focus of much work in political theory in the last few decades. In particular, there have been heated debates about the rise of "identity politics"—a rather value-laden term that signifies various kinds of political movements that focus on demands for recognition and rights based on membership in, and identification with, a particular group within society. The Canadian political theorist, Charles Taylor (1932–), one of the world's leading scholars of multiculturalism, has argued that the modern concept of identity hinges upon a personal connection with an identity-conferring group such that one's authenticity depends on the recognition of this shared membership in a group.[23] Hence, the demand for equality based on group identity is different from the traditional, individual request to be treated the same as all others. Identity politics rejects the idea that everyone should be treated the same, regardless of their "difference," since this undermines the project of recognition for one's unique socio-cultural attributes. Rather than wishing to be treated as the same as everyone else, the identity-based recognition-seeker wants to be recognized for her difference. In terms of multicultural rights, then, equality-seeking groups want to have their specific practices, traditions, or values respected within society, which often means being allowed to operate separately from others within the public realm. This notion that treating everyone exactly the same might, in practice, be discriminatory is increasingly accepted in liberal democracies. For instance, the U.S. Supreme Court ruling in *Holt v. Hobbs* (2015) says that treating a Muslim prisoner equally means allowing him to grow a half-inch beard, for religious reasons, even though the state government does not otherwise allow prisoners to wear beards.

Feminist political movements have been similarly regarded as identity-based because they seek recognition for women's rights based on their identity as women—not just as individual, rights-bearing human beings. Feminist political theory arose out of these movements, and is characterized by the commitment to expand the frontiers of the "political" to include an interrogation of relations of power in areas previously regarded as "personal," such as family or work. Thus, feminism directly challenges Aristotle's definition of politics as strictly limited to matters of the polis. He explicitly excluded the "household" from the realm of the political, and this was one of his reasons for denying women equal political rights. Of course, he (and generations of other male political theorists) also relied on a biological determinism which viewed women as not only different from men, by nature, but as fundamentally unequal to them. As he said, "the relation of male to female is naturally that of the superior to the inferior—of the ruling to the ruled."[24] In various renderings, Aristotle's position held sway among political thinkers for centuries.[25] Mary Astell and Mary Wollstonecraft were among the first female authors who challenged this view, arguing that women and men are equally capable by nature. They regarded the exclusion of women from proper education as the main source of perceived inequity between the sexes. Another notable early proponent of women's rights was John Stuart Mill (1806–1873), who advocated for the full political equality of women and denied that there were any politically relevant differences between men and women. It is not due to nature, he said, but to social convention hardened by centuries of oppression that women are kept inferior to men. *The Subjection of Women*, published in 1869, was thought to be extremely radical in Mill's time but is now seen as a classic statement of democratic and liberal feminism.

Today, feminist political theory consists of a variety of schools of thought—liberal feminism, radical feminism, difference feminism, critical legal feminism, postcolonial feminism, anarcha feminism, and so on. This diversity helps keep feminist theory relevant and engaged in the current debates of political theory. But there is still a core. In all cases, for instance, feminist political theorists challenge the philosophies, practices, and institutions that subordinate women and perpetuate inequality through differential gender roles. In this regard, feminist theorists have successfully argued that gender, like race, is socially-constructed. This was an important move, as well, for the emergence of an identity politics related to homosexuals. Among those theorists promoting LGBT rights, there are important differences, in particular between the "anti-essentialists" who see sexuality as historicized, contingent, and dependent on the elaboration of particular "genealogies," and those who see sexual orientation as natural or essential and use this argument to advance the cause of equal rights for gay men and lesbians. The theorist best known for

articulating the non-essentialist or genealogical notion of homosexuality is Michel Foucault (1926–1984).[26] In this view, there are no fixed identities but only disciplinary discourses and societal power relationships. Fighting for gay and lesbian rights is a self-transformative action meant to destabilize and undermine the status quo, along with the liberal values it promotes.[27] Support for anti-essentialism can also be found in recent studies that debunk the notion that men and women, or straight people and LGBT people, are by nature different because they have different brains.[28] Still, there are those in the gay and lesbian movement who promote a more biologically determinist conception of sexuality. According to this view, gay people are "born that way" and have no more "choice" about their sexuality than do, say, Blacks about their skin colour. Because it is not a choice to be gay—since it is normal and natural—there is no rational or moral reason for discrimination based on sexuality. This argument in favour of equal rights has been quite persuasive in the public realm, if not always among queer theorists. In any event, LGBT rights have been increasingly accepted in recent years. Many of the final barriers to equal treatment, such as laws prohibiting same-sex marriage, have been falling (see Photo Essay Box); and it is no longer unusual to find members of the LGBT community elected to office in Western democratic countries. Of course, matters are different in other parts of the world, including Russia, where President Vladimir Putin in 2014 supported a law banning pro-gay "propaganda" or the public promotion of non-traditional sexual relations.

Liberty

Political theorists over the centuries tended to conclude that authority from above was necessary. Order had to be imposed by philosopher-kings, as Plato suggested; by divinely inspired kings, as the medieval philosophers presumed; by religious experts who know the will of God; by a spirited and ruthless prince, in the manner described by Machiavelli; or by the well-bred and naturally superior elite, as conservatives would have it. Liberalism emerged as a reaction against this will to impose power from above. It theorized a broader, more bottom-up notion of authority according to which government is empowered by the people to protect their freedom and rights.

PHOTO ESSAY

Same-sex marriage rights on the rise.

THE EXPANSION OF MARRIAGE EQUALITY

Liberal-democratic governments are founded on the principle that individuals are equal before and under the law. Yet, until very recently, this was not interpreted to include the equal right of same-sex couples to marry. Politicians were slow to act, fearing a backlash from traditional voters, and courts were more willing to extend equal spousal benefits and other forms of recognition to gay citizens than they were to mandate marriage equality.

All of this is changing, however, and doing so very rapidly. Marriage equality is expanding across many parts of the globe—along with growing support in public opinion. In 2001, the Netherlands was the first country to recognize same-sex marriage, though "civil unions" or "registered partnerships" were available in several jurisdictions prior to that. As of January 1, 2015, 16 other countries have joined the Dutch in formally recognizing same-sex marriage, and several sub-national units (e.g., states within the U.S.) have done the same.

In Canada, formal marriage equality dates to 2005 with the passage by the federal government of the Civil Marriage Act. This legislation was the culmination of a long process, driven primarily by the courts. In fact, by 2005 marriage equality was already recognized in Ontario, British Columbia, and Quebec due to superior court rulings holding that existing restrictions against it were discriminatory and contrary to Section 15, the equality clause, of the Canadian Charter of Rights and Freedoms.

In contrast to Canada, marital status under the American federal system is a state responsibility, and so the spread of marriage equality has been on a state-by-state basis. As of the beginning of 2015, same-sex marriages were recognized by the federal government and 35 states. Barack Obama, who was initially opposed to same-sex marriage, in 2012 became the first sitting president to endorse marriage equality. While his support did not change any law, it was a powerful symbol as well as a reflection of how far public opinion had shifted on this issue.

Indeed, liberals have always harboured a degree of uneasiness with the power of the state or with large social institutions because they can provide an opportunity for tyranny—a base for power-hungry individuals to usurp the rights of others. This is the reason for their belief in a limited government and in checks and balances. It was a liberal thinker, Lord Acton (1834–1902), who famously said that "Power tends to corrupt, and absolute power corrupts absolutely." But he and other liberals do not conclude from this that there should be no state authority—that each individual should be entirely free to do as he or she pleases. On the contrary, the liberal message is that one needs a properly working constitutional democracy. Arbitrary power and tyranny are the likely consequences of regimes without sufficient constitutional checks and balances. According to this logic, the power of one individual or group needs to be held in check by the countervailing powers of other individuals and groups. In addition, individuals need to be protected, as much as possible, from arbitrary authority and from pressures to conform to the majority viewpoint.

Liberals tend to conceive of freedom essentially as the absence of coercive authority. One is free to the extent that one can live as one chooses, seeking one's own happiness, pursuing one's own self-interest, striving to fulfil one's own goals and aspirations. In economics, this translates into the principle of **laissez-faire**, the idea that the economic system works best when there is the least interference from government. The virtues of this doctrine were first elaborated by Scottish political economist Adam Smith, who argued that if government abandoned its regulatory function, leaving individuals to enter or leave economic relations as they see fit, the "invisible hand" of the market would maximize individual well-being and ensure public welfare. This concept of laissez-faire became the distinguishing feature of modern capitalism and remains its most sacred principle.

> **Laissez-faire:** A French phrase meaning literally "let do"; this economic theory provides the intellectual foundation for the system of free-market capitalism. Following the principles of Adam Smith, proponents of laissez-faire believe that the economy works best when there is no government intervention. Thus, the theory rejects state ownership or control, advocates a free market, values individualism, and promotes free trade.

Again, even free-market liberals recognize some need for government authority. There is always a threat that unscrupulous individuals will pursue their selfish interests in ways that impinge upon the freedom of others. Consequently, the very freedoms that liberals hold most dear (i.e., the right to "life, liberty, and property") can survive only when people are defended against the violent, coercive, or fraudulent behaviour of others. Protecting people's lives and possessions by maintaining law and order is therefore a fundamental job of government. But is this all that government should do? For some, the answer is yes. The only legitimate role for the state is to be a guarantor of security and a protector of private property. Anything beyond this limited role for government becomes a threat to liberty. Such a minimalist government is often referred to as the "night-watchman state." It tends to be promoted by libertarians and neoliberals. But others doubt that such a state can serve the interests of all people. For them, freedom requires more than simply being left alone to do as you please because a certain amount of social and economic power is needed to exercise freedom.

To help us clarify this issue, it is worthwhile to turn to Sir Isaiah Berlin (1909–1997), who distinguished between negative and positive concepts of freedom.[29] The former is stressed by classical liberals and was discussed above—namely, freedom consists in the lack of external (usually governmental) restraints imposed on the individual. The greatest threat to personal freedom, from this point of view, comes from unwanted interference from other people, including governments acting on behalf of the people. Representative writers in this tradition include Locke and Mill, as well as the more recent theorist Robert Nozick (1938–2002), who took as his first principle that people have natural rights, and that any interference in one's activities on the part of the state is, prima facie, a violation of those rights. As for the concept of positive liberty, it consists in there being sufficient conditions for each individual to develop to his or her full potential. From this perspective, the greatest threat to personal freedom comes not from other people per se but from an insufficiency of resources, wealth, or the opportunity to act freely. Representative writers in this tradition include Rousseau and Marx, as well as the more recent theorist John Rawls (1921–2002), who took as his first principle that "justice is fairness," which means that the goods necessary to freedom—resources, wealth, and the opportunity to fulfil one's life plans—should be distributed equally unless an unequal distribution is to the advantage of the least favoured in society.

A common way to express Berlin's distinction is to say that negative liberty is freedom *from*, while positive liberty is freedom *to*. Examples of negative liberty are the "fundamental freedoms" protected in liberal democracies through such measures as the Canadian Charter of Rights and Freedoms. Among others, negative freedoms include freedom of religion, speech, association, and assembly, as well as such legal rights as freedom from cruel and unusual punishment or freedom from unlawful search and seizure. In these cases, we are free from unwanted interventions by external authorities. For instance, we are free from government restrictions on what we can write in a newspaper article; we are free from rules that instruct us on when and where we must worship; and we are free from unwarranted harassment by police officers as we walk or drive down a public street. On the other hand, positive liberty involves the power to develop to the fullest of one's potential, the capacity to take charge of one's own life and direct one's actions, and the freedom to enjoy all opportunities for self-realization and self-fulfilment that might be available. Positive freedom implies not just the existence of certain opportunities (e.g., freedom to pursue higher education) but also the means necessary to take advantage of them (e.g., the motivation to seek such an education and the funds for tuition). Since the achievement of positive liberty involves the removal of concrete obstacles to individual participation and human development, there is an implication that some persons (or more likely, some social institutions) must take responsibility for providing the conditions necessary for its realization. If one takes seriously the right to positive liberty, then one has to accept that it imposes on the collective the obligation to provide meaningful opportunities for self-determination in concert with others. Perhaps the best articulation of this concept of freedom is Rousseau's vision of a society in which all individuals find their freedom through participation in the process of self-government according to the general will.

Not surprisingly, use of the state in the name of positive freedom is often viewed as a potentially dangerous interference in private affairs. Even Berlin himself was wary of the possibilities for authoritarianism that might flow from attempts to implement a strategy of positive liberty. It may be fine, critics say, to encourage everyone to realize his or her own goals and to achieve self-actualization, but not if this comes at an unreasonable cost to others who might have to give up their freedom or some of their resources in order to provide the means necessary for the realization of someone else's life plans. The obvious concern here is that the pursuit of the equal right to self-realization will come at the expense of traditional individual liberties. In effect, there is a tension between positive and negative liberty, as the pursuit of one might require limitations on the other. Many contemporary debates about such things as taxation policy or affirmative action programs are, in effect, about getting the balance right in liberal societies between promoting positive and negative forms of liberty. Those whom we today call neo-liberals (or fiscal conservatives), argue that the balance has tipped away from the protection of individual rights against an intrusive state. They point to the deleterious consequences of high taxes, for instance, and argue that efforts at dramatic income or wealth redistribution are an offence to individual liberty. Indeed, many will argue that the pursuit of public solutions to what are essentially private problems (lack of self-respect, failure to succeed economically, and so on) is simply wrongheaded. Individuals, the argument goes, must take responsibility for their own choices and the satisfactory pursuit of their own life plans, and should not rely upon social institutions to solve their problems for them. For the most part, this is the view from the contemporary political right, and it stems from the presumption that the individual's liberty to do what he or she desires should almost always prevail over the state's authority to force individuals to do what they do not want to do—even if this activity will benefit the greater good of a majority of the people.

When it comes to social or moral issues, the political right and left also tend to disagree on the amount of freedom that should be allowed, say, in matters such as euthanasia, drug use, flag-burning, pornography, civil disobedience, and so on. Contemporary liberals often take their cue on matters such as these from John Stuart Mill. In his famous essay "On Liberty," Mill defended the thesis that only self-protection can justify either the state's tampering with the liberty of the individual or any personal interference with another's freedom—particularly with respect to freedom of thought and discussion. According to Mill's famous "harm principle," only conduct that might do harm to others (and not action that might do harm only to oneself) is susceptible to the authority of the state or society. "In the part which merely concerns himself," Mill emphatically stated, "his independence is, of right, absolute. Over himself, over his own body and mind, the individual is sovereign."[30] Mill used as an example the case of liquor prohibition, which he saw as an unwarranted infringement on liberty. In our day, we might use Mill's arguments to advocate for the decriminalization of marijuana possession, which has now occurred in various jurisdictions, including the U.S. state of Colorado. As mentioned above, Mill famously and vigorously defended freedom of speech. For him, any idea or doctrine should be allowed to see the light of day, no matter how immoral or offensive to others. Today we can see how complicated the protection of free speech can be. While supporting it in principle, both politicians and theorists have been increasingly sensitive, for instance, to the potential harm that can be done to vulnerable groups and have sought to protect them from "hate speech." Getting the balance right between freedom for those with controversial views and the protection of those who might be hurt or offended by such speech is difficult to achieve. And as the Danish cartoon controversy in 2005 (or the murder of staff at the office of the French satirical magazine, *Charlie Hebdo*, in Paris in 2015 by Islamic terrorists angered by depictions of the prophet Mohammad) has demonstrated, these are not simply abstract or theoretical matters.

Similarly, the appropriate balance between protecting individual liberty and securing personal security has become an increasingly problematic issue, in theory and in practice, since the terrorist attacks of 9/11 and the beginning of the seemingly endless "war on terror" that arose in response. In spite of their reputation as great lovers of liberty, Americans have been increasingly willing in recent years to accept the need for restrictions on long-cherished individual freedoms in the name of preserving democracy or maintaining national security. Given that the enemy is often racialized and depicted as dangerous to the very values of the state, governments in the U.S. and elsewhere have engaged in practices such as racial profiling at

John Stuart Mill (1806–1873), one of the most important philosophers of liberalism.
Library of Congress/LC-USZ62-2939

airports or, worse, the detention of suspected terrorists without trial. Even more troubling for many civil libertarians, an extensive Senate Intelligence Committee report, declassified in December 2014, documented the widespread use of torture by the United States ("enhanced interrogation techniques") under the administration of President George W. Bush. Prior to the release of this report, President Obama had already declared that the U.S. would no longer use such tactics, but these recent revelations of the sorts of abuses suffered by prisoners or suspected terrorists have also led many to question the value of such interrogation techniques and to seek a return to a more principled foreign policy.

The extent to which individuals in modern, liberal societies have a right to be "different" and to be free from majority pressure to assimilate to social and cultural norms is at the heart of numerous important political debates today. For instance, the anti-immigration backlash in many Western countries, and the general suspicion with which minority peoples, especially Muslims, are often held, exposes a number of tensions within liberal theory and democratic practice. Do majorities have a right to protect their way of life—their liberal-democratic culture—from the perceived threats that come from culturally different minorities? The troubling rise in Eastern Germany of a new mass movement opposed to immigration of Muslims, PEGIDA (in English, "Patriotic Europeans against the Islamization of the West"), is an indication of how hotly contested these debates can be, especially when they spill over into the streets. Meanwhile, in France, where the politics of headscarves worn by Muslim women and girls has been in hot debate for over a decade, the issue is presented as one that pits the preservation of the society's secular and liberal values against a minority's religious and illiberal opposition to societal norms.[31] Hence, a bill banning veils, including burqas and niqabs, in all public places was justified by the French government on the grounds that the liberal state must sometimes curtail individual practices or behaviours that are regarded as outside the mainstream culture and possibly injurious to the solidarity of the whole. The French government also turns to feminist theory—including the notion that private matters, such as clothing choices, are politically relevant—to help bolster its case that Muslim practice perpetuates inequality and limits the freedom of the women who are subject to male domination.

POLITICAL IDEOLOGIES
The Nature and Function of Ideology

You have already been introduced to the major political ideologies—conservatism, liberalism, and socialism. But what exactly is **ideology** as a social scientific concept? What does an ideology do? Put broadly, an ideology is a reasonably consistent system of political beliefs that aspires to explain the world, to justify certain power relationships, and to maintain or transform existing institutions. An ideology is a system of thought according to which we can orient ourselves politically and act accordingly. Political ideologies provide a link between the world of ideas and the concrete realm of political action—for example, political parties, interest groups, mass movements, and constitutional systems.

> **Ideology:** A fairly coherent set of beliefs that not only explains what may be wrong with society, but also provides a vision of what society should look like.

In its philosophical aspects, the function of an ideology is to explain the key problems facing a society and to interpret key events. In this way, an ideology provides meaning for human life and history. In its policy-oriented aspects, ideology shapes the objectives and priorities of political action—it encourages the identification of specific social problems and it influences the selection of the most desirable and feasible solutions. An ideology thus operates as a perceptual screen that accepts some alternatives but filters out others. Theorists have also pointed out the instrumental value of ideologies for those in power. That is, ideology helps those persons holding social and political power to gain acceptance for their deeds. Of course, ideology is also used by activists and opposition politicians who do not exercise governmental power. Ideology can challenge established authority, criticize existing policies, and offer proposals for change. Indeed, a primary function of an ideology is to mobilize human efforts behind a cause, such as ecological preservation (environmentalism) or freedom from government regulation of individual activity (libertarianism).

Brant Parker and Johnny Hart, *The King Is a Fink.*
"By permission John L. Hart FLP and Creators Syndicate, Inc."

Ideologies are espoused by intellectuals concerned with politics—writers, teachers, politicians, journalists, lawyers, and so on. But they are necessarily mass belief systems. An ideology must be accepted by a large number of people in order to be effective. Ideological messages are formulated in a manner that can be readily understood by potential followers who do not have the ability, interest, or inclination to become political experts. Ideological discourse therefore seeks to simplify the inherent complexity of the world, imposing on apparent disorder a more or less systematic body of concepts and moral beliefs that can be called upon to help people make sense of the political world. In this way, ideology helps people determine how to act appropriately, and how to distinguish right from wrong in political circumstances. To a certain extent, ideology is a necessary ingredient of modern political life; it helps individuals make their way in a complex world. In this regard, many experts follow Sigmund Freud in emphasizing the psychological function of ideology as a means of equipping individuals with an appropriate set of reactions to social and political demands, allowing them to cope with personal strain or anxiety. This sort of analysis would suggest that ideology is an ever-present element in political life, essential as it is to humankind's social and mental requirements.

Ideology can also be understood as a style of thought. Persons who think in terms of ideology tend to perceive and interpret events in the light of broad and abstract ideas, such as gender equality (feminism) or faith in the common people (populism). When we say that a particular viewpoint or line of argument is "ideological," we mean to suggest that it is based upon a general or abstract set of political principles or doctrines, rather than unique, specific, or concrete conditions. Used in this fashion, ideology refers to a specific manner or style of thinking. Sometimes this will apply to patterns of thought characteristic of a whole class or group of individuals. We might say, for example, that pride in one's consumer possessions is an attribute of "bourgeois ideology," since it is characteristic of the predominant ideas, values, and attitudes of the middle class in capitalist societies. Conversely, the principled refusal to live a life geared toward the accumulation of material wealth, on the basis that the production of unnecessary consumer goods does ecological harm, is an element of environmentalism as an ideological style.

In the history of political theory, Karl Marx developed one of the most influential conceptions of ideology. To Marx, ideologies, ideas, and values (religious, political, etc.) are part of what he calls the "superstructure," which is determined by the "base" or the concrete material relations within society, especially class relations. When we study aspects of the superstructure, including ideology, we are focusing on the distorted and usually misleading reflections of real class interests. In the capitalist mode of production, ideologies such as liberalism, conservatism, and social democracy serve merely to justify the system, including its unequal distribution of resources. Marx also added to the debate the notion of "false consciousness," which occurs when a group or class accepts an ideology that in reality is contrary to its "true" or objective interests. Marxists, such as Antonio Gramsci (1891–1937), use this concept to explain the curious fact that so many working-class individuals reject **communism** and instead share the ideological views of the capitalists. This is due to what Gramsci called "cultural hegemony"—the domination of a diverse and class-divided society through the manipulation of its culture by the ruling class.

> **Communism:** A political ideology based on eliminating exploitation through nearly complete public ownership, full state control, and central planning of the economy.

Karl Marx (1818–1883), the most famous philosopher of socialism.

© Henry Guttmann/Getty Images

The Political Spectrum: Right, Left, and Centre

In order to understand the significance and current standing of ideologies in Western politics, we should keep in mind two important dates: 1789 and 1989. The first, of course, marks the defeat of the Ancien Régime in France and the rise to power of the Revolutionists. The second marks the fall of the Berlin Wall and the subsequent crumbling of the communist regimes in the so-called Soviet Bloc.

The French Revolution unleashed an awesome upheaval in world affairs, and it solidified the position of the various ideologies of modernity along the classic spectrum of right and left. As we have seen, Conservatives like Edmund Burke were generally opposed to the ethos of the revolution, while liberals and socialists (or, more accurately, proto-socialists) generally approved of the spirit of the revolutionary movement. In fact, the terms right and left, in reference to political positions, come to us from the seating arrangements in the French National Assembly of 1789, where members of the nobility, who supported the retention of substantial powers for the monarchy, were seated on the right side of the presiding officer. Seated on the left were those who wished to reduce dramatically or eliminate entirely the powers of the monarch, favouring instead a pure republic in which the elected representatives of the people would be sovereign. Today we still say that the more conservative individuals, or those who desire the least radical change to the status quo, are on the right, in contrast to the progressives or radicals on the left, who seek far-reaching and often revolutionary change.

These political ideologies continued to interact and develop throughout the period of industrialization and into the 20th century, when they were further crystalized during the Cold War era. In essence, the Cold War amounted to a colossal and high-stakes confrontation between liberalism and communism. Within the liberal-democratic world, mind you, there were ideological differences that were reflected in competing party platforms offered by a wide array of office-seekers—liberal, conservative, social democrat, Christian democrat, nationalist, separatist, unionist, communist, Marxist-Leninist, Maoist, etc. But seen from a higher level, the Western world offered a particular model of society characterized by a liberal-democratic political system, a capitalist (or some sort of mixed) market economy, and individualism in rights and culture. This was opposed in theory and practice by the leaders and ideologues of the so-called communist world, anchored by the Soviet Union and the People's Republic of China. The idea here was of a one-party state, a planned economy, and a collectivist culture.

Since 1989, however, we have been living in an entirely different world, and the global division between two opposing ideological powers is no longer a factor. But how much has the end of the Cold War changed the ideological landscape within liberal-democratic societies? Many commentators claim that everything has changed, and that it no longer makes sense even to refer to left versus right as political signifiers. Some, such as Francis Fukuyama in his best-selling book *The End of History*, declared that the Western, liberal-democratic and capitalist ideal has proved victorious and that ideological conflict as we have known it for the past two centuries—even within liberal states—is henceforth over.[32] I will return to the "end of history" thesis a bit later, but it is important to add here that Fukuyama's specific take on post-communist era politics shares some ideas expressed by Western political theorists long before the Wall fell. For instance, Daniel Bell famously announced "the end of ideology" as early as 1965, arguing that the era of "total ideologies" with their all-inclusive systems and powerful hold on people's passions had come to an end.[33] Specifically, he was lamenting the end of Marxist socialism and predicting a period of general agreement on the bigger picture, with politics reduced to an increasingly technocratic matter of tinkering with the system here or there. Again, there is a similarity here with Fukuyama, who also highlights mainly the collapse of left-wing ideologies as viable alternatives in a post-1989 world.

An alternative interpretation of the current situation is offered by Italian political scientist Norberto Bobbio, who argues that the fundamental left/right political distinction is still very much relevant today.[34] Bobbio acknowledges that the distinction itself is historically relative but still finds that it holds up under scrutiny. Specifically, that which divides those on the left from those on the right is their view of equality. That is, the political left is still distinguished by its commitment to equality, even if this egalitarianism now includes a recognition of and appreciation for difference of various kinds. In the end, Bobbio says, the left is less willing than the right to tolerate the existence of inequality, especially extensive differences in income and social status. He further distinguishes between moderates and extremists. Put simply, moderates favour tolerant and democratic methods, whereas extremists prefer militaristic, authoritarian means. Moderates and extremists can be found on both the political left and right.

There are probably few who would object, in theory, to Bobbio's contention that those on the left, especially those who are avowedly socialist, are more egalitarian politically than those on the right. But this does not do much harm to the contention of commentators like Fukuyama, who says that the left/right distinction is losing effective explanatory power because of the decline of the left and the increasing similarities between the remaining parties. Politicians and their constituents, regardless of their nominal party position or even their location in the world, he says, are converging on key liberal-democratic values. But this too is relative. If one looks, for instance, at party politics in the United States today, one finds a highly polarized system and a deeply divided electorate.[35] While socialism per se has never been a prominent (or even valid) political position in the U.S., the Democrats are the representatives of liberal and left-liberal views, and they have continued to stake out a claim to a political territory far to the left of the Republicans, who might be seen under the influence of the "Tea Party" activists to have strayed even further right of their former position. Surely, left and right continue to make sense in this context, allowing us to conduct meaningful discourse about politics in Western societies and elsewhere.

Indeed, plotting the differences between those on the political left and right in terms of important issues or policies helps us to gain clarity about the divisions within our societies. Table 2.1 illustrates some of the key themes that differentiate leftists (e.g., Democrats in the U.S., Liberals and Social Democrats in Europe) from rightists (e.g., Republicans in the U.S., Christian Democrats in Europe). Admittedly, some of the issues I have chosen are more relevant to North American politics than European politics. Different societies will map somewhat differently, depending on historical and other variables. It should also be remembered that

these are generalizations and simplifications; they are not meant to capture all of the views of left- or right-wing people, politicians, or parties. Nevertheless, this sort of map highlights the ways in which ideology divides people along relatively consistent lines.

Another virtue of the left/right terminology is that it helps us to visualize the relationships between and among ideological perspectives. The notion of a spectrum or a continuum also helps us realize that there are overlapping values and ideals, and that being on the left or the right is very much a matter of degree. While there is more than one set of measures that can be used to place thinkers or parties along the spectrum, a popular measure of placement is attitude toward societal change, including both the degree of change deemed necessary and the direction of the change preferred. On the left, progressives (anarchists, communists, socialists) tend to be discontented with the status quo and demand rapid and extensive change. The term "progressive" indicates that the political change desired tends to be forward-looking and inclusive, intended to improve the general lot of all people in society, especially the poor and disadvantaged. Sometimes, these individuals are called "radicals." The word radical comes from a word for root, and so in political circumstances what the radicals want to do is to get to the roots of societal injustice and, if need be, to uproot the entire economic and political system in order to remake society along more egalitarian lines. For example, radicals in capitalist societies see the private ownership of the means of production as the root source of injustice. Hence, they wish to eradicate capitalism itself and replace it with some version of communal property ownership. Radicals often believe that only through violent revolutionary upheaval will society be changed in total. But not all progressives are committed to the use of revolutionary tactics and most do not condone violence as a strategic option for realizing their political goals. There is a range of progressive beliefs depending on the extent of change desired and the means deemed appropriate to achieve it. Hence, anarchists and communists are considered to be farther to the left than socialists, and social democrats and reform liberals closer to the centre. Since the late 1990s, "progressive" has become a more popular term to refer to left or left-liberal positions in American politics. Progressive has replaced "liberal" in campaign literature and political discourse because

TABLE 2.1 LEFT/RIGHT POLITICAL DIFFERENCES		
	Left (Liberal/Social Democrat)	Right (Conservative)
Role of Government	Positive role in providing for needs of majority through activist policies	Negative role, limited to protecting citizens and enforcing laws
Business	Mix of public and private enterprise, with strict regulations	Free enterprise with few or no public corporations; minimal regulation
Labour	Pro-union, more worker protection	Pro-employer, fewer worker entitlements
Taxes	Maintain or increase, as needed	Decrease or eliminate, as possible
Trade	Fair trade	Free trade
Minimum wage	Government-mandated, as high as practicable	Non-binding, as low as practicable
Family values	Progressive	Traditional
Affirmative action	Promote	Oppose
Abortion	Pro-choice	Pro-life
Same-sex marriage	Support legalization	Oppose legalization
Law and order	Focus on social causes of crime; protect rights of accused	Tough punishment for criminals; protect rights of victims
Death penalty	Oppose	Support
Gun control	Support	Oppose
Religion	Separation of Church and State; no faith-based government initiatives	Allow religion in schools and support other faith-based government initiatives
Freedom	Freedom from inequality	Freedom from intrusive government
Equality	Level playing field for all groups, free of systemic discrimination	Individual opportunity to achieve or fail, depending on skills and effort
International relations	Diplomacy, pacifism, internationalism	Might, militancy, patriotism
Immigration	Open and inclusive; multiculturalism; support amnesty for illegal aliens,	Closed and exclusive; assimilationist; oppose amnesty for illegal aliens,
Highest value	Justice	Order

politicians and activists on the left of the American political spectrum feel that "liberal" has become a negative term.

It is customary to label as "liberal" the moderate range that fits somewhat between the socialist/communist left on the one hand and the conservative/reactionary right on the other. Here again, one must be sensitive to the extent of the subtle range of different viewpoints captured within this middle category. On the left of this range one finds reform-oriented or left-liberals who, like social democrats, favour progressive social change that can be seen as quite radical. They share the view that government

should be used to improve social and political life through various types of social planning and policy experimentation. Left-liberals champion freedom from inequality in all its forms, and are willing to use the state to achieve the goal of improving the lives of the less advantaged. Historically, reform liberalism was associated in the United States with proponents of President Franklin Roosevelt's New Deal legislation in the 1930s and with the civil rights movement and the "war on poverty" in the 1960s. In Canada, reform liberalism brings to mind the use of a mixed economy (private ownership along with some public corporations), a Keynesian approach to fiscal policy (the use of public funds to "prime the pump" of economic development), and a far-reaching **welfare state** system (characterized by old age pensions, universal medical coverage, unemployment insurance, social assistance programs, and the like). Indeed, one will still find the term welfare liberal used to designate these left-of-centre liberals and to distinguish them from more business-oriented liberals. More often, however, they are simply called left-liberals, since they support extensive reforms or changes to existing institutions or practices in a manner similar to social democrats and other leftists.

> **Welfare state:** A concept that stresses the role of government as a provider and protector of individual security and well-being through the implementation of interventionist economic policies and social programs. This positive role for government stands in contrast to the minimalist government (or "night-watchman state") that has as its only function the protection of personal property and individual security. The welfare state is regarded as having a positive role in promoting human welfare and in shielding the individual against the economic and social consequences of unemployment, poverty, sickness, old age, disability, and so on.

On the right within the liberal range are those who might be dubbed classical liberals or business liberals (and now more often "neoliberals"). These people are concerned, first and foremost, with the right to private property and with the protection of individual liberty against intrusive government action. As is often noted, there is not much of a difference on economic matters between the classical liberal position and the views of those we would today call conservatives, including members of Conservative parties in the United Kingdom or Canada or the Republican Party in the United States. This overlap between classical liberalism and contemporary conservatism can cause confusion, especially in those places where a liberal is clearly someone on the left of the political spectrum and not one who, like a classical liberal, promotes a limited state and a laissez-faire style of capitalism.

Conservatism, which defends the status quo against major social, economic, and political change, is usually understood to be on the right of the political spectrum. But again, there are many sorts of conservatives.

Typically, conservatives place order and authority above liberty and equality in their hierarchy of values, stressing the duties of citizenship and not just the rights or entitlements of citizens. Conservatives tend to be traditionalists who venerate the beliefs and moral values that have been passed down from generation to generation within a culture. Conservatives instinctively defend existing institutions against challenges from reformers on the basis that it took a long time and a lot of common-sense wisdom to create what we now have. Change should be measured, incremental, and respectful of the values of the past. Indeed, conservatives are largely skeptical about the human ability to improve life through social engineering on a grand scale. In an odd twist, this viewpoint can at times put them at odds with the status quo and even make them look like the "radicals" in society. For instance, after Western liberal democracies established extensive and often experimental welfare state systems in the 1960s and 1970s, conservatives became the ones who challenged the status quo and called for a rolling back of the expansionist state put in place by liberal reformers. Likewise, conservatism today is evident among those who decry the many progressive social changes that are associated with such 1970s and 1980s movements as feminism, gay and lesbian rights, multiculturalism, and so on. We often refer to these people as social conservatives, since they are most concerned with preserving traditional cultural or social values and virtues. In contrast, fiscal conservatives (or neo-liberals) are worried mainly about progressive changes to the economy. They fear growth of government, over-regulation of the economy, and rising taxation rates—especially on corporations and the wealthy.

> **Conservatism:** An ideology defending the status quo against major social, economic, and political change. Conservatism became a clearly articulated philosophy in reaction to the upheavals caused by the French Revolution. The classic statement of this attitude can be found in the speeches and writing of the English statesman Edmund Burke (1729–1797). He argued that political order and stability will be maintained only if change is gradual and evolutionary rather than rapid and revolutionary. Today, conservatism is often used to label those who wish to protect established economic interests and social norms.

Neoliberalism and Neoconservatism

The terms neoliberalism and neoconservatism are regularly used today to refer to individuals or groups on the political right. **Neoliberalism** is an economic philosophy that holds that a system of free markets, free trade, and the free flow of capital is the best way to ensure the greatest social, political, and economic good. It argues for reduced taxation, reduced government regulation, and minimal state involvement in the economy. Neoliberals support the privatization of health and welfare benefits, the weakening or dismantling of trade unions, and the general opening up of the economy to foreign competition. Neoliberalism can be found in most advanced capitalist societies around the world. Indeed, some argue that there has been an astonishing consensus among political and economic leaders across a large variety of states on the need for some sort of neoliberal solution to economic challenges. Nevertheless, opposition to neoliberalism is on the rise, as people negatively affected by austerity measures ask at what cost comes the global tightening of public spending. The term neoliberalism itself is not normally used by proponents of such policies; rather, it is widely employed by academics and other commentators.

> **Neoliberalism:** An economic philosophy that holds that a system of free markets, free trade, and the free flow of capital is the best way to ensure the greatest social, political, and economic good. It argues for reduced taxation, reduced government regulation, and minimal state involvement in the economy.

Neoconservatism, an older term, is applied to politicians on the political right who combine neoliberal economic policies (low taxes, smaller government, limited social spending) with conservative social policies (opposition to abortion, gay rights, feminism) and a "hawkish" foreign policy (increased military spending, pro-nuclear weapons, vigilant "war on terror"). The term is used primarily in the U.S., and had its greatest currency during the Reagan years. It was also often used to describe British Prime Minister Margaret Thatcher and her policies. An important element of the neoconservative viewpoint was an almost Manichean vision that saw the West as the embodiment of goodness and freedom and the East (Soviet Russia and China, at any rate) as the home to empires of evil. The events of 1989 were widely regarded as a victory of good over evil, and President Reagan was given a great deal of credit for having kept up the pressure on the Soviet Union until it finally crumbled. Neoconservatism has lost some of its focus and purpose in the post-Cold War environment, though some of its hawkish tendencies are evident among those who rely upon a stark "us/them" attitude in foreign policy—whether in terms of relations with the so-called "Muslim World" or with Russia under President Putin.

> **Neoconservatism:** A term applied to those on the political right who combine neoliberal economic policies (low taxes, smaller government, limited social spending) with conservative social policies (opposition to abortion, gay rights, feminism) and a "hawkish" foreign policy (increased military spending, pro-nuclear weapons, vigilant "war on terror"). The term is used primarily in the U.S., and had its greatest currency during the Reagan years in the 1980s.

U.S. President Ronald Reagan: "Defender of the Free World."
© Paul Shambroom/Science Source via Getty Images

Contemporary Conservatives

Again, contemporary conservatives in countries such as Canada have not been averse to radical change in cases where they believe that liberal reforms have gone too far and are in need of drastic overhaul. In the 1980s, conservative leaders such as Ronald Reagan and Margaret Thatcher, along with Prime Minister Brian Mulroney in Canada, launched extensive programs of deregulation and privatization that radically altered the status quo. More recently in Canada, Prime Minister Stephen Harper has similarly embarked upon an extensive project of state retrenchment. Yet he, like his mainstream conservative colleagues elsewhere, has brought about change—even dramatic change—by moderate, democratic, and constitutional means. To the extreme right along the ideological continuum, however, one finds various sorts of radical political ideas that are often referred to as "far-right" or "reactionary." The level of discontent and frustration is very high among reactionaries, and they are usually willing to go to extreme lengths to change things. In this regard, they resemble radicals on the extreme of the political left. But unlike leftists, they disavow the ideals of egalitarianism and inclusiveness characteristic of the contemporary era. There is an intense antidemocratic core to reactionary politics. Indeed, reactionaries will often say that many contemporary problems stem from an excess of democracy, an overabundance of choices and options that lead people away from the proper values of society. Hence, reactionaries tend to favour stern government that is unafraid to enforce strict rules. For many reactionaries, not surprisingly, the best government is found in authoritarian military rule.

The ideology of the far-right is intimately linked to the history of European **fascism** and totalitarianism. The Nazi and fascist movements of the 1920s and 1930s in Germany and Italy are the exemplars of far-right politics. In Europe today, far-right movements, some of which openly take their inspiration from fascism, have been on the rise. Far-right and ultranationalist political parties give voice to a growing discomfort among majority populations with the large numbers of ethnically-different residents in Western European countries. The largest and most successful European party of the far-right is the National Front in France, which promotes economic protectionism, law and order, and ethnic nationalism. Many other Western European countries have similar, though less popular, right-wing, anti-immigration parties, such as the Party for Freedom of the Netherlands, which wants to ban all mosques, and the Swiss People's Party, which wanted to ban construction of minarets, the spires of mosques. The United Kingdom Independence Party (UKIP), associated mostly with the desire to withdraw the UK from the European Union, also wants to impose a five-year ban on immigration. German political leaders have been surprised by the rise of PEDIGA, which in 2015 began organizing large rallies, originally in Dresden but spreading throughout Germany and elsewhere (Sweden, Austria, Switzerland). In Eastern Europe, too, there has been a rise of far-right parties, such as Jobbik in Hungary, which seeks to capitalize on popular resentment of the country's Roma population. Some would also identify the governing party in Hungary, the Fidesz Party led by Prime Minister Viktor Orban, as right-wing and antidemocratic.

> **Fascism:** A political system of the extreme right, based on the principles of the strong leader (dictator), a one-party state, nationalism, total control of social and economic activity, and arbitrary power, rather than constitutionalism. In 1922 in Italy, Benito Mussolini created the first fascist regime, soon emulated by Adolf Hitler in Germany. Fascist regimes also held power in Spain and Argentina. Today there are numerous neofascist movements advocating ultranationalist, racist, and anti-immigrant political positions.

In North America, the electoral system is not very conducive to the creation of small, fringe parties (see Chapter 10). The anti-immigrant and ultranationalist minority is more marginalized and struggles to find room within the larger parties of the political right, the Republicans in the U.S. or the Conservatives in Canada. On social issues, however, the right in North America has had a certain amount of power and influence. In both the U.S. and Canada, the right is generally skeptical about the role of the courts and objects to judicial activism—the process whereby courts strike down laws that violate constitutional rights, as has happened repeatedly, for instance, regarding laws denying rights to LGBT citizens. In the end, however, attitudes toward economic issues are still the best way to differentiate the right from the left. The Tea Party, for all of its social conservatism, is still most strongly distinguished by its opposition to big government and high taxation.

A popular way to conceive of the left/right split is to use a scale charting attitudes toward the use of the state as an instrument for effecting social and political policy (see Figure 2.2). On the whole, those on the political right are less comfortable with the use of state power to promote collective political purposes than are people on the left. Free-market capitalists would therefore be regarded as right-wingers, while socialists and communists would be leftists. Still, as we have already seen, there are differences of degree on each end of the spectrum. On the right, more ideologically driven fiscal conservatives will oppose almost all government regulation and intervention, while more traditional conservatives will allow for a considerable degree of state control or direction in order to ensure order and stability for the community as a whole. On the political left, social democrats, with their faith in a mixed economy, will be closer to the moderate centre than those adhering to various brands of hard-line communism, which calls for total public ownership and full state control of the economy.

Moreover, if we use attitude toward the role of the state as the only means of determining the left/right split, we have to deal with certain anomalies. First, fascists and communists are both in principle willing to use a strong state to impose their philosophical views throughout the entire society. If we used a "freedom/authority" scale, they would both be on the side of strong authority. Yet these ideologies are clearly on opposite ends of the spectrum in terms of the goals they wish to achieve. Historically, fascists and communists have been mortal enemies. In fact, fascism first arose as an extreme reaction against socialism and communism. Much of the initial fascist violence was directed at trade unions and other progressive organizations in society. Likewise, economic libertarianism and anarchism could appear to fit on the same side of the scale, since they both stand for the maximization of individual freedom and the absence of a coercive state. Yet, if one turns to the motivation for opposing state power, these ideologies clearly belong on the opposite ends of the left-right spectrum (more in line with Figure 2.1). Libertarianism defends the unfettered individual right to acquire and enjoy personal property without interference.

THINK AND DISCUSS

What is your ideology? Are you liberal, conservative, socialist? Or do you see yourself aligned more with a non-traditional ideology? To what extent, and how, is your behaviour influenced by this ideological position?

FIGURE 2.1   THE TRADITIONAL IDEOLOGICAL CONTINUUM

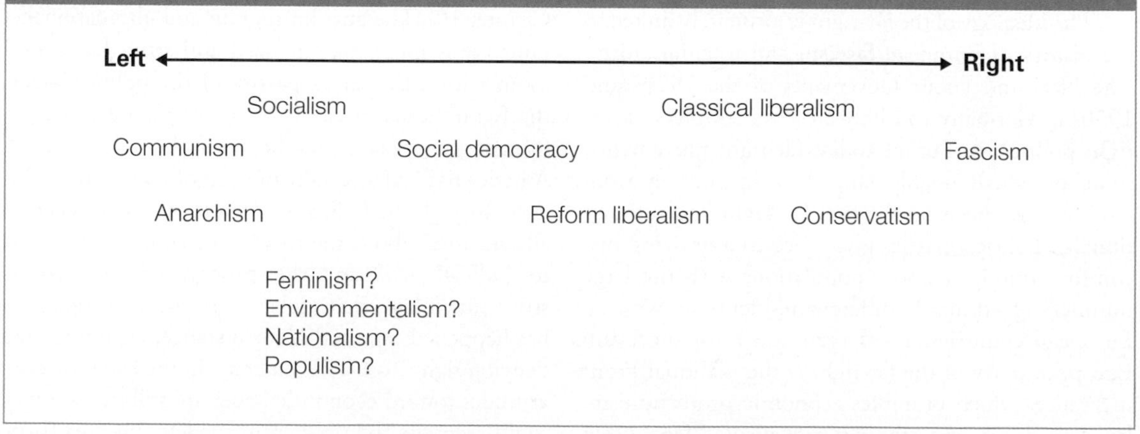

Left ←————————————————————————→ Right

Socialism   Classical liberalism

Communism   Social democracy   Fascism

Anarchism   Reform liberalism   Conservatism

Feminism?
Environmentalism?
Nationalism?
Populism?

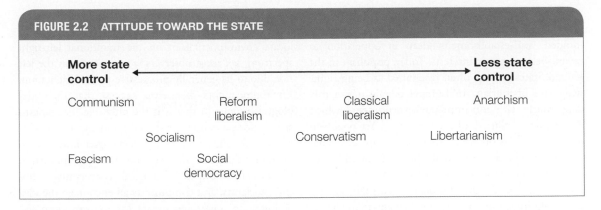

FIGURE 2.2   ATTITUDE TOWARD THE STATE

More state control ← → **Less state control**

Communism	Reform liberalism	Classical liberalism	Anarchism
Socialism		Conservatism	Libertarianism
Fascism	Social democracy		

In this regard, it is quite similar to classical liberalism or fiscal conservatism, ideologies of the political right. Anarchism, on the other hand, shares many of the general values of radical socialism and communism. Many leading anarchists, such as Mikhail Bakunin (1814–1876) and Emma Goldman (1849–1940), began their political lives as communists and later broke with their comrades over the latter's insistence on the heavy use of state power.

Finally, we should note that there are several "isms" that do not fit comfortably on the left-right spectrum, including nationalism, populism, environmentalism, and feminism. While these ideologies can be either leftist or rightist in orientation, it is probably most accurate to suggest that the former two—nationalism and populism—are today more associated with conservative or right-wing politics, such as the anti-immigration movements discussed above, while the latter—environmentalism and feminism—are more often seen as progressive, left-wing movements.

Take nationalism, which is explored in greater detail in Chapter 4 of this book. As we have seen, the Nazis and their precursors were proponents of a vehement nationalism. That is, they promoted the interests and values of their own ethnocultural nation (or race) above all others, and regarded the autonomy of their national unit as a primary political good. The far-right political parties spreading throughout Europe today take a similar stance. When Jobbik members chant "Hungary belongs to the Hungarians," they are expressing a patriotism that is often motivated by animosity towards the non-ethnic Hungarian population, specifically Jews and Roma. This is clearly a right-wing ultranationalism in action. Yet nationalist convictions can be exhibited by various groups, many of whom see national independence or autonomy as a means by which to construct a progressive society organized around the principle of equality for all members of the political community, regardless of ethnicity, race, or religion. The national liberation movements that arose in the mid-20th century to fight against Western colonialism and create independent states in Africa and Asia were often led by communists. The nation-states that emerged once colonial rule was thrown off were comprised of multicultural citizens who seldom shared a common language, but did share a colonial heritage of racial and imperial exploitation. The states constructed out of the national liberation struggle were almost invariably leftist in economics and finance. Still, a survey of nationalist movements today would more likely result in a list dominated by right-of-centre leaders and parties, intent not on creating a socialist state in their homelands but ethnically pure ones.

Populism—the faith in the wisdom of the common people—is regarded as being neither inherently right-wing nor left-wing. Populists tend to struggle against the elites and the big interests in the name of the people. This can take either a left- or right-wing slant. In Canada, left-wing populism was a major influence in the first major social democratic party in Canada—the Co-operative Commonwealth Federation (CCF), forerunner to today's New Democratic Party. Populism of the political right expressed itself in the Alberta Social Credit Party in the 1930s, and more recently it inspired the founders of the federal Reform Party in the 1990s. Populism has been an essential feature of American political culture, playing an explicit role in party politics in the late 19th and early 20th centuries in parties such as the People's Party (popularly known as the

"Populists") and Theodore Roosevelt's "Bull Moose" or Progressive Party, each of which espoused reform-minded, anti-establishment ideals in opposition to established economic interests. Today, populism in the United States is most often recognized as being right-wing and libertarian. In Europe, populism can mix dangerously with anti-immigration sentiments, which are usually a hallmark of the far-right.[36] Yet populism often cuts across otherwise solid party positions. That is, workers who might normally have supported labour or social democratic parties have been attracted to the populist disdain for the "Eurocrats" and their techno-cratic solutions, and fear of losing their jobs to foreigners makes them open to populist calls for an end to immigration. Finally, scholars of Latin America have used the term "neo-populism" to describe the emergence of a political strategy in which a charismatic leader seeks popular support directly from "the people," creating a justification for action that bypasses traditional parties and institutional mechanisms of power. A curious element of neo-populism is that it can be used by a strong leader to impose neo-liberal economic solutions, which are otherwise not regarded as advantageous to the people as a whole.[37]

One of the fastest-growing and most truly global political movements in the 21st century is environmentalism. As with feminist theory, environmentalism has involved a broadening of the boundaries of the political; its supporters argue "that the natural world—normally 'invisible' to political theory—affects, and is affected by, political decisions in a way which makes it necessary to consider it a site of political activity."[38] While concerns about the connection between the environment and politics go back a long way in human history, the distinctive stance that our human embeddedness in the natural world requires a thoroughly integrated theory of ecology and politics is relatively recent.[39] Environmental political theory has focused on the concept of nature itself, and its relationship to the human essence, as well as on the limitations of traditional liberalism and the need for new ways to theorize liberty and democracy beyond an individualistic paradigm.

This brings up the phenomenon of environmentalism as an ideology and as a political movement—sometimes referred to as "green" politics or "ecologism." First, we should note that proponents of environmentalism often refuse to see it as an ideology like the others, and proudly claim to be "neither left nor right, but green." Indeed, it can be somewhat difficult to locate environmentalism on the traditional left-right spectrum; yet most observers would put it on the left side due to its generally progressive policy orientation. Environmentalists themselves suggest that their ideology is unique in that it is the only one that repudiates the idea that humans should dominate and subdue nature. Although they may disagree over how best to distribute the goods derived from human exploitation of the environment, ideological conservatives, liberals, socialists, and communists all encourage the idea of humanity mastering nature for its own purposes. Environmentalists alone challenge this "human-centred" approach and promote an alternative "Earth-centred" philosophy. As Peter Hay points out, and as we have seen with other ideologies, there is a range of opinion, or of political positioning, among adherents to environmentalism, spanning from liberal environmentalists through to more radical ones.[40]

The ideology of feminism is also somewhat independent of traditional ideologies, although it is by definition a progressive ideology calling for a change to the status quo of male domination. As we have seen, feminism affirms the equality of the sexes and decries the subjugation of women in all of its forms. Again, there is a continuum of sorts along which one can imagine placing different feminist theorists. Liberal feminists regard the key ideals of liberalism—freedom, equality, justice for all—to be the central aims of feminism. The liberal feminist program calls for various concrete measures aimed at producing an equality of opportunity for women—for instance, by advocating affirmative action plans or pay equity legislation.[41] In its more radical variants, feminism regards the systematic oppression of women by men through violent patriarchy as the most fundamental moral problem. From this point of view, all of the traditional ideologies are implicated, since they are inherently male-centred.[42] Many leading feminist theorists have been middle-class and white, but specific brands of feminist political thought have arisen to speak more directly to African-Americans or to the post-colonial experience.[43] At the same time, feminism and queer theory—often influenced by Michel Foucault's genealogical approach—have combined to encourage a redefinition of the relations between sex, gender, sexuality, and power.[44]

CONCLUSION

As this survey of key political theories and ideologies should have demonstrated, ideas continue to play a large role in politics. Our understanding of political events and our orientation toward the political world are informed by a long tradition of political thinking, stretching back in the West at least as far as the ancient Greeks. The types of laws we live under, and the sorts of governments we support, were developed under the influence of leading political thinkers. By examining the works of the great thinkers of the past, we can better comprehend our own societies as well as equip ourselves to participate as active citizens in our own communities. And ideology plays a continued role in our lives as students and citizens. Even if we do not see ourselves as ideologues, most of us have strongly held political beliefs about who should rule and what should be done by those in positions of political power. Moreover, contemporary political elites—government officials, politicians, media representatives, interest group leaders, and others active in the political process—represent ideological points of view, in spite of their frequent reluctance to be seen to do so. Conflicting ideologies offer us a means of understanding our society, situating ourselves in the political world, and participating in actions intended to advance our interests and those of our communities.

DISCUSSION QUESTIONS

1. Given the nature of human beings, is it possible for all people to be united in a conflict-free society?

2. In what cases are you willing to see the state interfere in society, in particular by limiting the right of individuals to live as they choose? Consider issues such as euthanasia, abortion, and pornography.

3. Are the terms *right* and *left* still relevant today, given the global changes that have occurred since the fall of the Berlin Wall in 1989?

4. How is the far-right different from traditional conservatism?

5. Where do ideologies like environmentalism or feminism fit on the traditional ideological spectrum?

WEBSITES

The Stanford Encyclopedia of Philosophy
http://plato.stanford.edu/index.html
Includes articles by scholars from around the world on topics in philosophy and related disciplines to create and maintain an up-to-date reference work.

Online Library of Liberty
http://oll.libertyfund.org/
An online collection of works about individual liberty and free markets.

Marxists Internet Archive
http://www.marxists.org/
A collection of texts, biographies, and historical archives related to Marx and Marxist thought.

Political Philosophy: A Small Companion to Cyberspace
http://lgxserver.uniba.it/lei/filpol/filpole/indicere.htm
A site that groups resources into historical periods and areas of enquiry.

Women's Human Rights Resources
http://www.law-lib.utoronto.ca/diana/
A repository of research, teaching, and cooperative materials available through the Bora Laskin Law Library, University of Toronto.

FURTHER READING

In its Very Short Introductions Series, Oxford University Press publishes small books on a variety of topics, including the following on issues related to this chapter:

MARX: A Very Short Introduction, by Peter Singer (2000)

MACHIAVELLI: A Very Short Introduction, by Quentin Skinner (2000)

DEMOCRACY: A Very Short Introduction, by Bernard Crick (2002)

HOBBES: A Very Short Introduction, by Richard Tuck (2002)

IDEOLOGY: A Very Short Introduction, by Michael Freeden (2003)

POLITICAL PHILOSOPHY: A Very Short Introduction, by David Miller (2003)

ANARCHISM: A Very Short Introduction, by Colin Ward (2004)

SOCIALISM: A Very Short Introduction, by Michael Newman (2005)

FREE SPEECH: A Very Short Introduction, by Nigel Warburton (2009)

Other general books of interest on political ideas and ideologies include:

Terrence Ball and Richard Dagger, *Political Ideologies and the Democratic Idea*, 6th ed. New York: Longman, 2005.

Leaon P. Baradat, *Political Ideologies*, 11th ed. New York: Longman, 2011.

Colin Bird, *An Introduction to Political Philosophy*. Cambridge: Cambridge University Press, 2006.

Terry Eagleton, *Ideology*. New York: Verso Press, 2007.

David Harvey, *A Brief History of Neoliberalism*. New York: Oxford University Press, 2006.

Will Kymlicka, *Contemporary Political Philosophy: An Introduction*, 2nd ed. Toronto: Oxford University Press, 2003.

Iain Mackenzie, *Politics: Key Concepts in Philosophy*. London: Continuum International Publishing, 2009.

Allan Ryan, *On Politics: A History of Political Thought from Herodotus to the Present*. New York: Liveright Publishing Corporation, 2012.

ENDNOTES

1. See Aristotle, *The Politics*, trans. Ernest Barker (London: Oxford University Press, 1958), bk. III, chs. 6–7.

2. Alan Ryan, *On Politics: A History of Political Thought from Herodotus to the Present* (New York: Liveright Publishing Corporation, 2012), p. xx.

3. Brain Redhead, ed., *From Plato to NATO* (London: Houghton Mifflin Harcourt, 1988).

4. See, for instance, David Gress, *From Plato to NATO: The Idea of the West and Its Opponents* (New York: Simon and Shuster, 1998).

5. In his famous book, *Orientalism* (New York: Vintage, 1978), Said locates Western prejudices and stereotypes about Asian, Middle Eastern, and North African peoples in early justifications for colonialism and disputes the very basis of the distinction between "West" and "East."

6. Peter Lindsay, *Creative Individualism* (Albany, New York: State University of New York Press, 1996).

7. Paul Fairie, "Democracy in Alberta is about management, not ideology," *The Globe and Mail*, December 18, 2014. However, the electoral victory of the New Democratic Party in the 2015 Alberta provincial election reminds us that politics, alongside our understanding of politics, is constantly evolving!

8. Clifford Geertz, *The Interpretation of Cultures* (New York: Basic Books, 1973), p. 35.

9. Thomas Hobbes, *Leviathan*, C.B. Macpherson, ed. (Harmondsworth, Middlesex: Penguin English Library, 1981), ch. 13, pp. 185–86.

10. See Anthony Quinton, *The Politics of Imperfection: The Religious and Secular Traditions of Conservative Thought in England from Hooker to Oakshott* (London: Faber and Faber, 1978).

11. See especially, Sigmund Freud, *Civilization and Its Discontents* (New York: W.W. Norton and Company, 1989).

12. This is the case made by C.B. Macpherson, *The Political Theory of Possessive Individualism: Hobbes to Locke* (Oxford: Oxford University Press, 1962).

13. The popular psychologist Steven Pinker argues persuasively that contemporary social scientists are afraid of arguments based on human nature,

a position he thinks is misguided. He criticizes those who take the tabula rasa approach, as well as those who follow Rousseau with a "noble savage" view (people are born good but are corrupted by society) or who adopt what he calls the "ghost in the machine" idea (each of us has a soul that makes choices free from biology). See *The Blank Slate: The Modern Denial of Human Nature* (London: Penguin Books, 2002).

14. Geertz, *The Interpretation of Cultures* p. 45.

15. Will Kymlicka, *Contemporary Political Philosophy* (Oxford: Clarendon Press, 1990), p. 5.

16. See Jacob Golomb and Robert S. Wistrich, eds., *Nietzsche, Godfather of Fascism? On the Uses and Abuses of Philosophy* (Princeton: Princeton University Press, 2002).

17. See Victor Farias, *Heidegger and Nazism* (Philadelphia: Temple University Press, 1989); Hugo Ott, *Martin Heidegger: A Political Life*, trans. by A. Blunden (New York: Basic Books, 1993).

18. Elzbieta Ettinger, *Hannah Arendt/Martin Heidegger* (New Haven: Yale University Press, 1997).

19. Written between 1931 and the early 1970s, the writings in these notebooks put to rest any doubts that Heidegger was strongly anti-Semitic and that many of his key philosophical concepts are intertwined with Nazi beliefs. See Peter E. Gordon, "Heidegger in Black," *New York Review of Books*, October 9, 2014, online at http://www.nybooks.com/articles/archives/2014/oct/09/heidegger-in-black/.

20. Thomas Piketty, *Capital in the Twenty-First Century* (Cambridge, Mass.: Harvard University Press, 2014).

21. Cornell West, *Race Matters* (New York: Vintage Books, 1994).

22. The White House, Statement by the President, August 18, 2014, online at http://www.whitehouse.gov/the-press-office/2014/08/18/statement-president.

23. Charles Taylor, "The Politics of Recognition," in Amy Gutmann, ed., *Multiculturalism:* *Examining the Politics of Recognition* (Princeton: Princeton University Press, 1992), pp. 25–73.

24. Aristotle, *The Politics*, bk. I, ch. 5, para. 6.

25. See Susan Moller Okin, *Women in Western Political Thought* (Princeton: Princeton University Press, 1979).

26. Michel Foucault, *A History of Sexuality, Volume 1: An Introduction*, trans. Robert Hurley (New York: Vintage Books, 1978).

27. See Ladelle McWhorter, *Bodies and Pleasures: Foucault and the Politics of Sexual Normalization* (Bloomington: Indiana University Press, 1999).

28. See Rebecca Jordan-Young, *Brain Storm: The Flaws in the Science of Sex Differences* (Cambridge, Mass.: Harvard University Press, 2010).

29. Isaiah Berlin, "Two Concepts of Liberty," in *Four Essays on Liberty* (New York: Oxford University Press, 1969).

30. John Stuart Mill, *On Liberty* (New York: Bobbs-Merrill, 1956), p. 13.

31. See John R. Bowen, *Why the French Don't Like Headscarves: Islam, the State, and Public Space* (Princeton: Princeton University Press, 2006).

32. Francis Fukuyama, *The End of History and the Last Man* (New York: Penguin, 1992).

33. Daniel Bell, *The End of Ideology: On the Exhaustion of Political Ideas in the Fifties* (Cambridge, Mass.: Harvard University Press, 1962).

34. Norbert Bobbio, *Left and Right: The Significance of a Political Distinction*, trans. and introduced by Allan Cameron (Chicago: University of Chicago Press, 1996).

35. A Pew Research Center report, "Political Polarization in the American Public," June 12, 2014, demonstrates that Republicans and Democrats are now more divided along ideological lines than at any time within the last two decades; online at http://www.people-press.org/2014/06/12/political-polarization-in-the-american-public/.

36. Hans-Georg Betz, *Radical Right-Wing Populism in Western Europe* (London: Palgrave Macmillan, 1994).

37. Kurt Weyland, "Neopopulism and Neoliberalism in Latin America: Unexpected Affinities," *Studies in Comparative International Development* 31 (3) (1996), pp. 3–31.

38. Andrew Dobson, "Afterword," in A. Dobson and P. Lucardie, eds., *The Politics of Nature: Explorations in Green Political Theory* (London: Routledge, 1993), pp. 229–34 at 230.

39. Key texts include William Ophuls, *Ecology and the Politics of Scarcity* (San Francisco: W.H. Freeman, 1977), Murray Bookchin, *The Ecology of Freedom: The Emergence and Dissolution of Hierarchy* (Pal Alto: Cheshire Books, 1982), John S. Dryzek, *Rational Ecology: Environment and Political Economy* (New York: Basil Blackwell, 1987), and Andrew Dobson, *Green Political Thought* (London: Routledge, 1995).

40. See Peter Hay, *A Companion to Environmental Thought* (Edinburgh: University of Edinburgh Press, 2002), especially chs. 7–10.

41. A leading example would be Martha Nussbaum, *Sex and Social Justice* (Oxford: Oxford University Press, 1999).

42. Examples would include Mary Daly, *Gyn/Ecology: The Metaethics of Radical Feminism* (Boston: Beacon Press, 1978), Andrea Dworkin, *Intercourse* (New York: Free Press, 1987), and Catharine MacKinnon, *Toward a Feminist Theory of the State* (Cambridge, Mass.: Harvard University Press, 1989).

43. See Stanlie M. James and Abena P. A. Busia, eds., *Theorizing Black Feminisms: The Visionary Pragmatism of Black Women* (New York: Routledge, 1993), and Chandra Talpade Mohanty, *Feminism without Borders: Decolonizing Theory, Practicing Solidarity* (Durham, North Carolina: Duke University Press, 2003), respectively.

44. See Judith Butler, *Gender Trouble: Feminism and the Subversion of Identity* (New York: Routledge, 1999).

PART

2

FOUNDATIONS OF POLITICS

3

STATES AND GOVERNMENTS: PERPETUAL WORKS IN PROGRESS

Christopher G. Anderson

© Sean Pavone / Shutterstock.com

The General Assembly of the United Nations, where the 193 member states of the world meet and discuss issues of local, regional, and global importance. Although these states, and the governments that direct them, can vary greatly one from another in terms of size and power, here they meet on formal terms of equality.

After you have completed this chapter, you should be able to:

- understand governments and states as crucial yet imperfect and ultimately transient institutions
- differentiate basic functions and forms of government
- discuss principal features of democratic and non-democratic governments
- identify possible conditions and consequences of statehood and state fragility
- consider the role of government and state in a globalized world

INTRODUCTION

Imagine a political system in which there is no government and no state, a society where each person has an equal say over decisions that affect individuals, groups, or the full political community, in which people hammer out the details of these decisions in person and on a regular basis. Although there have been repeated attempts throughout history to create such political systems based on the principles of **anarchy**, where authority is not entrenched in established institutions and practices but can be made to justify itself over and again, they have proved to be difficult to set up (never mind maintain) and have remained more an approach to politics than a sustained reality.[1] Instead, governments and states—as structures and processes of governance—have long been prevalent in the lives of human beings, locally, nationally, and internationally. Indeed, as noted in Chapter 1, it is difficult to contemplate modern life without taking into account the role of governments and states. No matter where we live, governments and states figure extensively and intensively in our very existence, in both positive and negative ways, and for this reason they are essential focal points when studying politics.

Anarchy: A system of social, political, and economic relations without formal institutions of governance to define enforceable rules or exact obedience from the governed. Realist scholars use this term to characterize the international system, where there is no authority above the state that can solve inter-state conflict. Anarchy does not mean chaos.

In part we study governments and states because we want to understand why some things happen and others do not. In short, we seek to create and accumulate knowledge about how politics unfolds around us. Such knowledge can help us to become better informed as citizens, locally and globally, empowered not only to interpret the world but to change it as well. In the process, we soon learn that no political system will ever be perfect but that each can be improved. Governments and states can be powerful vehicles for positive and negative change both in individual and collective terms, and in order to appreciate better the roles that they play in our lives we need continually to ask what they do, why they do it, and how they might do it better.

While pondering these questions, we will repeatedly encounter the fact that governments and states are often subject to considerable criticism. For example, in many of the long-established democracies of the world, including Canada, there is evidence of a **democratic deficit**, whereby citizens feel that the actions of government and state do not meet their expectations, either in terms of the accountability of the political system to "the people" or its responsiveness to their interests.[2] In political systems where there are far fewer mechanisms through which public preferences can be brought to bear on those who rule, we often find widespread human rights violations. In some countries there is talk of fragile or even failing states, where violent conflicts rage between and among state and non-state forces, and governments are unable to provide basic services in such areas as education and health. Sometimes such struggles are rooted in the demands of people looking to create their own state as part of a process of liberating themselves from oppression. At the global level, in turn, there are increasing discussions about the necessity—or even inevitability—of a system of **global governance** to bind both state and non-state actors more closely to a commonly derived set of laws and norms of behaviour in order to provide for a more fulfilling and sustainable life for all.

> **Democratic deficit:** The perceived gap between the theoretical principles of democracy and the actual practice of ostensibly democratic institutions, including national governments and international organizations.

> **Global governance:** Collective policy-making aimed at addressing global problems in the absence of a formal governing structure for the whole world.

In this chapter, we will explore these and many other features of governments and states at the outset of the 21st century, and this will require that they be placed within both historical and comparative contexts. Governing institutions do not appear before us wholly formed, and neither do they remain the same for very long—rather, they are constantly evolving within a variety of economic, social, and political circumstances. An historical perspective reminds us that the institutions and practices through which we are governed are not—and never have been—set in stone. In a global age, when barriers between states are thought to be ever more permeable, the task of tracing such patterns of continuity and change is both more difficult and perhaps more important. In an increasingly interconnected world, we can gain perspective by thinking about the foundations of governing institutions and practices that differ from our own, rooted in alternate political traditions. As the Canadian political scientist Alan C. Cairns suggests, societies, governments, and states are embedded in one another, both nationally and internationally, and an important part of studying politics lies in determining the nature of this embeddedness and its effects on how we live our lives.[3] While we cannot cover the great variety and complexity of forms that

this might take fully, we can nonetheless establish some basic terms and ideas to help us study governments and states in a more systematic manner.

STUDYING GOVERNMENTS

Humans and **government**—the set of institutions and practices that make and enforce collective public decisions for a society—have long been related in close, complicated, and enduring ways. Indeed, everyone in the world today falls under the purview of some governing authority. Even those who have been rendered stateless, or who live in one of the estimated 100 "uncontacted" tribes left in the world (http://www.uncontactedtribes.org), are within the ambit of one government or another, even if they are unaware of it! Because governments can affect most every aspect of our lives, the ways in which they are set up and in which we interact with them are multiple and complex. An important first step, therefore, is to identify what governments do: their functions within a political system.

> **Government:** The set of institutions and practices that make and enforce collective public decisions for a society.

We can start by turning to the work of the political scientist Gabriel Almond, who provides a useful list of functions performed by all governments regardless of their particular form: rule-making, rule-application, and rule-adjudication.[4] While citizens in democracies can readily connect these functions with the three main branches of government—the legislature, the executive, and the judiciary—they may not be so clearly assigned to separate institutions in other political systems. For example, in the last remaining **absolute monarchy** in Africa—the Kingdom of Swaziland—the king has extensive powers to make and interpret rules, and to see them implemented through a process of rule by decree. Even among democracies, significant variations exist in how these functions are institutionalized, as seen in Chapters 6, 7, and 8, which explore the structure and operations of government.

> **Absolute monarchy:** A system of government ruled, at least in name, by one individual whose authority is unchecked, final, and permanent.

The prevalence of the word "rules" among the functions listed above suggests that governments and states exist to a significant extent to determine and impose order on a given population. As we will see later in this chapter, the ways in which this is done can be more or less open to popular participation—more or less democratic, if you will. We should never lose sight of the fact, however, that all governments and states stand apart to some degree from "the people" and that this inevitably creates tensions between "the will of the people" and presumed "reasons of state." For some thinkers, such as Thomas Hobbes and John Locke, governments and states represented a path away from the disorder inherent in the "state of nature"— a bargain or social contract whereby authority was granted to political institutions in exchange for societal security and prosperity. For others, governments and states represent more a significant restraint on human freedom. As political economist Pierre-Joseph Proudhon phrased it in his 1851 publication, *General Idea of the Revolution in the Nineteenth Century:*

To be GOVERNED is to be watched, inspected, spied upon, directed, law-driven, numbered, regulated, enrolled, indoctrinated, preached at, controlled, checked, estimated, valued, censured, commanded, by creatures who have neither the right nor the wisdom nor the virtue to do so. To be GOVERNED is to be at every operation, at every transaction noted, registered, counted, taxed, stamped, measured, numbered, assessed, licensed, authorized, admonished, prevented, forbidden, reformed, corrected, punished. It is, under pretext of public utility, and in the name of the general interest, to be place under contribution, drilled, fleeced, exploited, monopolized, extorted from, squeezed, hoaxed, robbed; then, at the slightest resistance, the first word of complaint, to be repressed, fined, vilified, harassed, hunted down, abused, clubbed, disarmed, bound, choked, imprisoned, judged, condemned, shot, deported, sacrificed, sold, betrayed; and to crown all, mocked, ridiculed, derided, outraged, dishonored. That is government; that is its justice; that is its morality.[5]*

Critics of both the ideological left and right continue in this day to question the role of government and state in our lives, and their effects on our freedoms as human beings. Regardless of one's ideological perspective, the central point to keep in mind is that it is important to bring a critical eye to the actions of governments and states and to be cognizant of their capabilities as well as their limitations when studying politics.

The diversity that we find with respect to how the functions of government are institutionalized and practiced, and thus how they are interpreted and understood, can be explained by the fact that each system has evolved within its own historical conditions and political traditions, some of which stretch far back in time. Indeed, in some parts of the world— such as China, India, and the Middle East—we can trace histories of government for several millennia. Thus, the forms that governments have taken, and the justifications advanced to support them, have varied greatly over time and continue to do so.

A BRIEF HISTORY OF GOVERNMENT

Our knowledge of how people have been governed only really stretches as far back as the written word. We can certainly speculate about what happened before that time—based, for example, on archaeological evidence or more contemporary forms of tribal societies—but this leaves us with enormous gaps in our understanding of the economic, social, and political lives of such communities, and of the institutions and practices through which they were governed. Even where written records and archaeological findings coexist—as they do for the first time with the Sumerian and Egyptian civilizations (now parts of the Middle East) as early as c. 3500–3000 BCE—our knowledge remains impressionistic.[6] In both cases, we know that absolute monarchs with a mandate said to come from the gods ruled over large peasant populations and at times quite extensive territories with the support of increasingly professional militaries and a relatively small number of court officials and temple priests, alongside a select and well-trained staff

---

* Pierre-Joseph Proudhon, *General Idea of the Revolution in the Nineteenth Century,* trans. by John Beverley Robinson (London: Pluto Press, 1989 [1923, 1851]), p. 294.

of accountants and scribes. While certain features of these early governments would seem familiar to us today—there were, for example, repeated reform efforts to improve government administration and concerns over corruption—there were significant differences. Perhaps most importantly, these governments were not constituted *of the people* but instead ruled *over the people* to ensure their obedience to the gods. Thus, the people were subjects, not citizens, as they had little or no say in how they were governed. Although the precise configurations changed over time, and while new governments emerged, evolved, and disappeared in the Middle East (e.g., in Assyria, Babylonia, and Persia) and beyond (e.g., in present-day India and China), each presents us with a variation on this original form—absolute monarchy. It was not until the formation of the **republics** of ancient Greece that a significantly different type of relationship between the rulers and the ruled took root in the historical record.

> **Republic:** A system of government ruled by a head of state who is not a monarch (generally, in modern times, a president), in which citizens are entitled to participate in decision-making.

The Seat of Athenian Democracy: At the general assembly in ancient Athens, the *Pnyx*, citizens debated and decided important issues of the day in sight of the Temple of Athena, the Goddess of Wisdom, on the nearby Acropolis.
sirylok © 123RF.com

The Legacy of Government in Ancient Greece

Within the broad scope of the history of government, from the ancient Sumerian city-states to the recognition of South Sudan as the latest (and 193rd)

member state of the United Nations in 2011, the rise and fall of democracy in ancient Greece from about 600 BCE to 300 BCE constitutes a relatively brief moment in time—but it has nonetheless had a profound influence on how we think about and practice government.[7] Most of the approximately 1,500 city-states that existed within ancient Greece were already notable for having instituted and developed republican governments, in which subjects (at least some of them) were transformed into citizens. Thus, government in the Greek city-states had generally shifted from the palace of the monarch to the *polis*, which consisted of both the city (along with lands surrounding it) and its citizens. This was in and of itself a radical break with the past. The Greeks, however, also originated the word (formed by joining *demos* [people] and *krátos* [power or rule]) as well as the practice of democracy, both of which have come to permeate modern politics, albeit with important modifications. Although earlier political systems (in Mesopotamia and India, for example) displayed certain democratic features,[8] it is with the ancient Greeks that we first see democracy named, described, analyzed, debated, and even celebrated (see Box 3.1).

In broad strokes, the institutional arrangement of the *polis* consisted of a select council, a general assembly, and the courts, and as democracy took hold decision-making shifted toward the assembly. For example, in Athens, which was considered the centre of democratic life in ancient Greece, all citizens could participate in the assembly, where they would discuss and decide important issues of the day, including those relating to war and peace. Moreover, some citizens would be chosen by lot to participate in the Council of 500 and the courts. Although similar to modern democracy in privileging the voice of "the people" in the political process, this was nonetheless a very different democracy than we find in the world today.

First, it occurred on a much smaller scale: at the height of democratic Athens there were perhaps 30,000 citizens, and only a few thousand participated in the meetings of the assembly or were selected to serve as potential jury members, and just a few hundred were assigned to various public posts. In contrast, most modern democracies consist of millions of citizens. Second, citizen involvement was much more immediate—this was direct democracy

---

BOX 3.1

PERICLES' FUNERAL ORATION

In *The History of the Peloponnesian War*, Thucydides (460–395 BCE) recounts a speech given by Pericles (495–429 BCE), who ruled in Athens for more than 30 years, in memory of those who had died during the first year of what would become a 27-year-war between Sparta and Athens.

> Our constitution does not copy the laws of neighbouring states; we are rather a pattern to others than imitators ourselves. Its administration favours the many instead of the few; this is why it is called a democracy. If we look to the laws, they afford equal justice to all in their private differences; if to social standing, advancement in public life falls to reputation for capacity, class considerations not being allowed to interfere with merit; nor again does poverty bar the way, if a man is able to serve the state, he is not hindered by the obscurity of his condition. The freedom which we enjoy in our government extends also to our ordinary life. There, far from exercising a jealous surveillance over each other, we do not feel called upon to be angry with our neighbour for doing what he likes ... But all this ease in our private relations does not make us lawless as citizens. Against this fear is our chief safeguard, teaching us to obey the magistrates and the laws ... whether they are actually on the statue book, or belong to that code which, although unwritten, yet cannot be broken without acknowledged disgrace.

Source: Robert B. Stassler, *The Landmark Thucydides: A Comprehensive Guide to the Peloponnesian War* (New York: Free Press, 1996), 112.

---

in which citizens participated as rulers as well as the ruled. That is, there were opportunities for all citizens to be involved personally and routinely in collective debate and decision-making, and a greater expectation that they would do so. Today, apart from voting in elections and perhaps in referenda and plebiscites, there are relatively few institutionalized mechanisms for or expectations of regular citizen participation. Third, citizenship was generally limited to adult males whose ancestors were citizens, thereby excluding some 220,000 foreigners, women, slaves, and children. Modern citizenship is much more inclusive, and some countries even allow non-citizens to vote in local electoral contests. Finally, just because the *polis* was democratic did not mean that there was broad consensus that it was the best system of government (it was even overthrown for a period in Athens). While the historian Thucydides provides an indication of the pride that democracy could engender, it was not uncommon to hear it denounced as an unstable, and therefore dangerous, form of government. At the outset of the 21st century, there is by no means universal consensus as to the superiority of democracy, but it is perhaps the one political ideal for which support can be found around the globe.[9] As British Prime Minister Winston Churchill is alleged to have observed: "It has been said that democracy is the worst form of government except all the others that have been tried."

Although numerous figures from ancient Greece discussed and wrote on the nature of government (along with Thucydides we could add the playwright Sophocles and the philosopher Plato, for example), Aristotle provides one of the more systematic analyses of the different forms of government known to the Greeks during this period. In *The Politics*, he famously states that "man is a political animal in a sense in which a bee is not, or any other gregarious animal," because men possess a "power of speech" that allows them "not only to feel pleasure and pain but to communicate these feelings to each other."[10] As a result, they have a unique ability to consider what is right and what is wrong, what is just and unjust, and do so to greatest effect in association with one another. While this leads Aristotle to claim that government is, therefore, a natural phenomenon—that it is the means by which citizens can not only live but also pursue the "good life"—there remains the vital question of which form of government is best.

TABLE 3.1 ARISTOTLE'S TYPOLOGY OF GOVERNMENT FORMS		
RULE IN THE INTERESTS OF:		
Number of Rulers	All Citizens (common interests)	The Rulers (particular interests)
One	Monarchy	Tyranny
A few	Aristocracy	Oligarchy
The many	Polity	Democracy

Source: Adapted from Nicolas Baxter-Moore, Terrance Carroll, and Roderick Church, *Studying Politics: An Introduction to Argument and Analysis* (Toronto: Copp Clark Longman Ltd., 1994), 4. Reprinted with permission of Nicolas Baxter-Moore.

To address this issue, Aristotle undertook a political analysis to determine which form of government was most likely to produce the stability required for the contemplation and achievement of the good life. He did so by collecting and comparing the political constitutions of 158 city-states. Aristotle divided these cases according to whether they were defined by the rule of one, a few, or the many, and then he distinguished systems where those in power ruled in the common interest from those where they ruled in their own particular interest. This produced a six-fold classification (see Table 3.1) from which—after having considered the nature of the constitutions in each—he drew a number of conclusions. While democracy was not considered by Aristotle to be the worst form of government (this was tyranny, which replicated a master–slave relationship between ruler and ruled), neither was it the best because it was prone to instability when demagogues courted popular support against the wealthy few, eventually leading to an **oligarchy** as the rich seized power and governed to protect their own interests. Aristotle wrote, nonetheless, of the need to incorporate democratic elements into any stable system of government. As for monarchy and aristocracy, they were ideal forms only when controlled by people truly able to define and reflect the common interest. However, when this was not the case, they were likely to slide into tyranny and oligarchy, respectively. Instead, Aristotle pointed to the benefits of a **polity**, with the rule of the many (but not all), on the grounds that their deliberations were more likely to reflect the common interest consistently over time: "As a larger amount of water is less easily polluted, so the multitude is less easily corrupted than the few."[11] Thus, he saw in a polity the potential to balance the interests of poor and wealthy citizens, thereby increasing the likelihood of political stability.

Oligarchy: A system of government ruled by a few and, according to Aristotle, in their own interests.

Polity: A system of government ruled by the many but not—as in a democracy—by all; according to Aristotle, this was the most stable system of government when it was able to balance the interests of the wealthy with those of the poor.

Because he approached the study of government systematically—as a comparative examination of political institutions and behaviour—Aristotle's work is often seen as an early example of political science in action. Moreover, as was the case with other Greek thinkers of the day such as Plato, the vocabulary he employed and the ideas he explored have influenced political thinkers through to the present. As just one example, take the term *oligarchy*. Robert Michels, a German sociologist, was confronted with an important puzzle when he noticed that all the political parties he studied—even those that were democratically structured—wound up being dominated by party leaders. In an effort to explain this puzzle, he proposed the existence of an "iron law of oligarchy," in which all organizational forms eventually become oligarchic, not simply because leaders seek to consolidate power but because those who are led permit them to do so. "Who says organization," he famously concluded, "says oligarchy."[12] This idea, while offering an explanation of a particular aspect of organizational behaviour, speaks directly to the study of governments and states, especially those that are democratic, because it challenges the idea that modern democracies are simply based in the will of the people and suggests instead that collective decision-making can often reflect the narrower interests of those in power.

Other Ancient Government Traditions

What is most surprising about ancient Greek democracy is not that it ended, as the various city-states were eventually subsumed within the expanding power of Rome around 150 BCE, but that it so completely disappeared as a form of political organization for centuries before rising to such prominence in the recent past. While Rome itself emerged with a republican form of government, it never became a democracy but resembled more an oligarchy, in which an entrenched elite dominated public affairs, before it took on more tyrannical forms with the arrival of emperors claiming to descend from the gods. Nonetheless, Rome also left its mark on the subsequent development of government, initially at least in Europe. Aside from providing the staging ground for the eventual expansion of Christianity as a major religious and political force in the world, the Romans developed complex systems of both public and private law—the former giving definition to the scope of legitimate government action, and the latter setting out rights and responsibilities between persons—that were both secular and rationally developed. This began the process of transforming government from something personal (e.g., embodied in the person of the monarch, as captured in the famous declaration attributed to King Louis XIV of France: "L'État, c'est moi") to something more abstract (i.e., embodied in the law itself, as captured in the concept of the **rule of law**, covered in greater detail in Chapter 9). Thus, the essence of political authority increasingly came to be seen to be vested in the institutions of government (and later the state) rather than the individuals who controlled them. When European nation-states began to emerge in the 16th century, they drew deeply on this tradition.

> **Rule of law:** The principle that government must act through laws that are made known to the public before they are enforced and that are applied equally to all, and where disputes under law are heard by fair and impartial judges. In short, no one is above the law, even leaders.

However, with the decline and eventual fall of the Roman Empire from about the 5th to 7th centuries, political life in Europe became much more fragmented and local. Meanwhile, alternate large-scale forms of political organization elsewhere in the world thrived, some of which continue to shape the nature of governments and states, and thus politics, at the outset of the 21st century. For example, the roots of Chinese political life can be traced back thousands of years to around 2000 BCE, after which it became one of the most developed and durable forms of political organization until the late 18th century. By the time of the Han dynasty (206 BCE–220 CE), the basic contours of a form of government that combined an absolute monarchy with a Confucian system of belief were in place, from which have evolved a number of democratic and non-democratic political systems in Asia today, including those found in North and South Korea, Singapore, Taiwan, Vietnam, and China itself.

Confucianism is not a religion or a systematic code of law but instead is rooted in a set of ethical assertions originating with the Chinese sage/philosopher Confucius (551–479 BCE) concerning the correct ordering of society. According to his teachings, the best way to achieve social harmony, and therefore the best form of government, is through rituals that reflect and reinforce ordered and hierarchical relationships—between government and the people, between parents and children, and between friends, for instance. Those in positions of authority are duty-bound to lead by example and to care for those under their charge, while those subject to such authority should revere and obey those in command. As opposed to the ancient Greeks, then, there is no sense of political power residing within a citizenry of equals; at the same time, however, the existence of boundaries around the power of rulers is more clearly defined than was the case in many other monarchical systems. In part, this stemmed from another distinctive feature of government in China: the elevation of scholars into the highest ranks of social and political life on the basis of merit. This left them in a relatively privileged position from which to influence public decision-making. In comparison, the idea of a merit-based bureaucracy would not really take hold in the West until the 19th century, some 2,000 years later. Of course, the history of Chinese government reveals periods of stability and instability (stemming from both internal and external causes), and many Confucian ideas were explicitly rejected with the rise to power of the Communist Party in 1949.

Some of these ideas have experienced resurgence in recent years, however, as an emphasis on harmony and order, as well as hierarchy and responsibility, have been seen to offer the possibility of greater stability as the massive social upheaval that has accompanied China's rise to prominence as one of the foremost economic and military powers in the world unfolds.

Elsewhere, with the emergence and consolidation of Muhammad as a prophet and political leader at the outset of the 7th century, the roots of a new religion and a new form of political organization took hold. From its origins in what is now Saudi Arabia, Islam rapidly spread within 100 years to encompass the Middle East, Northern Africa, and parts of South and Central Asia, Portugal, and Spain, and in doing so provided the foundations for one of the most extensive empires in human history. Although the Empire of the Caliphate lasted for just about 250 years (c. 630–870 CE), it has had a lasting influence on politics and government in these regions and beyond. Indeed, today there are nearly 50 countries in which Muslims represent a majority of the population, mostly in the Middle East, Northern Africa, Central and South Asia, and Southeast Asia, constituting about a third of the world's population. A number of these countries—such as Indonesia and Senegal—are relatively stable democracies, while the Arab Spring protests that began in 2010 are seen by some to have forged close and perhaps inseparable links between modern political Islam and democracy.[13]

One distinctive feature of Islam's influence on government has been the role of **sharia law**, which—as the command of God—regulates aspects of both public and private life, including features of worship and interpersonal relations. Since its inception, the existence of sharia law, and the role of religious scholars in interpreting its meaning, has raised a question of great significance, namely, that of the appropriate balance between political and religious authorities in governing. In practice, from the Empire of the Caliphate to modern-day Islamic republics such as Iran and Pakistan, this has not been easy to settle: Should a more secular political authority exist, and, if so, should its authority be higher than or merely different from that of religious authorities? Even states that are founded upon an explicit separation of church and state, such as France and the United States, struggle in this regard.[14] As with political systems based on Confucianism, the Islamic world experienced periods of stability and instability over time, but we can certainly contrast the often high degree of sophistication of its government forms up until the 17th century with those prevalent in Europe during much of this time.

> **Sharia law:** Sharia is the Islamic system of law, both civil and criminal, that is based on the Qur'an (the holy book of Islam); the life example and hadiths (sayings) of the Prophet Muhammad; and on subsequent scholarly interpretations and writings. This system of law prescribes the correct behavior for Muslims across different areas of life and the punishments for transgressions. Importantly, Sharia law is not uniform throughout the Muslim world as it is influenced by different schools of jurisprudence, among other factors.

EUROPEAN NATION-STATES

Indeed, the contrast with Europe (excepting the Byzantium Empire, which from its base in Constantinople would last almost 1,000 years as an absolute monarchy after the fall of the Roman Empire) was stark. It was not really until the late Middle Ages that government began to coalesce around a series of feudal kingdoms on the continent, and these, despite

THINK AND DISCUSS

It is often argued that Western political systems are defined by a separation of church and state, and in some countries this has been used to justify bans on Muslim women wearing either a full head and face (*burqa*) or head (*hijab*) covering in public spaces. How clear do you think the separation between politics and religion is in Western states such as Canada, and do you think that this can be used to limit the religious rights of certain segments of the citizenry?

their diversity, shared several common characteristics. Although the pinnacle of political authority resided with kings, they often depended on the support of powerful and armed landholders who could choose with whom they wished to align. In such a relatively decentralized system of power, towns came to take on great importance, often acting as essentially self-governing republics. In general, however, the vast majority of the population remained subjects of their respective feudal lords. Alongside this more secular system of political organization, Christianity became an integral thread in the weave of European political life during this period, as the Catholic Church worked to carve out and develop a political space for itself that was superior to that of kingly governments, representing—in the person of the Pope—a higher (indeed, heavenly) authority. Thus, the Middle Ages were defined by a complex, evolving patchwork of relations of authority, responsibility, and rights, and it was often far from democratic. Indeed, it was only in a few small areas, such as a handful of Swiss cantons, that democracy flourished.

Nonetheless, within a few centuries, key features of modern democratic government had emerged and challenged the political authority of established monarchies as well as the papacy, and a new form of political organization—the **nation-state**—had appeared. This occurred at a time when European governments were beginning once again to become active on the world stage, and when European society was experiencing an incredibly dynamic period of economic, social, and political development. It is difficult to do justice here to the breadth and speed of the changes that took place in Europe from the 14th to 18th centuries. With the rise of Protestantism, the religious and political authority of the Catholic Church came under attack. When combined with a new age of secular thought that blossomed throughout the Reformation and Renaissance, radical transformations took place in terms of how authority was conceptualized. This process was facilitated by the invention of the printing press, which resulted in widespread debate about competing economic, political, religious, and social ideas. The emergence of capitalism, industrialization, urbanization, and a period of rapid technological development in such areas as transportation and weaponry can be added to this mix, which facilitated both commerce and conquest. Indeed, during this period European governments began not only to centralize and institutionalize their authority as nation-states but to expand their economic and political ambitions vis-à-vis the rest of the world. By the 19th century much of Africa, the Americas, and South and Southeast Asia had been forcefully brought under European control under the aegis of colonialism. Altogether, this constituted perhaps the most rapid and extensive spread of political ideas and influence since the Empire of the Caliphate.

> **Nation-state:** A term sometimes used synonymously with state but which implies that citizens share a common ethnic or cultural background. In the modern world, few such homogeneous states remain, most either being multicultural, multiethnic, or multination states.

A good example of the cumulative effects of these rapid changes can be found in 17th-century England, during which time a number of ingredients came together to challenge the monarchy's domination of English politics. First, the enclosure movement produced profound changes in society, as landlords were allowed to "enclose" or fence off public use lands in order to increase their agricultural production and wealth. As people were, consequentially, forcibly displaced from the country to the cities, a ready-made working class for the Industrial Revolution was created. Second, a new entrepreneurial or bourgeois class began to oppose the power of the monarchy to control lands and impose taxes. As their demands for greater private property protection increased, so did tensions with the landed aristocracy, which had long benefited from its allegiance to the crown. In their mobilization against one another, and vis-à-vis the crown, the origins of the party system that defines modern democratic government can be found. Third, religious toleration became socially and politically more acceptable. The political liberation that came with the uncoupling of England from the power of the Catholic Church in Rome unfolded in conjunction with a scientific freedom that assisted in shifting attention away from the divine right of kings and toward the terrestrial and rational interests (individual and collective) of society.

These ingredients came together to produce new political demands that traditional political institutions associated with the monarchy could not address. Although the power of the crown had been circumscribed—and many of the rights of the people asserted—through the Magna Carta as early as 1215, it was not until the 17th century that the institutions and practices of government began to reflect this more accurately. The calls and struggles for political reform that emerged from both workers (soon to be labelled the proletariat) and the bourgeoisie, which were encouraged by the development of powerful ideas concerning liberty and authority, put into motion a series of important transformations. The concepts of representative democracy, free speech, the right to rebel against bad government, freedom for the accumulation of profit, human rights—all of which are now hallmarks of many modern systems of government—developed in a political renaissance that found inspiration in ancient thinkers and innovation in an emergent intellectual class that promoted ideas that would underpin a new age of democracy. A prime example is found with John Locke, a philosopher and activist whose thinking would be reflected in both the American Revolution and its Declaration of Independence. In his *Two Treatises on Government*, Locke contested the notion of the divine right of kings, arguing instead that against the uncertainty inherent in a "state of nature" a people will submit to government as long as it is directed toward "the mutual preservation of their lives, liberties and estates, which I call by the general name, property."[15] When such property rights were not respected, however, Locke argued that the people had the right to rebel against the government—that is, the right of revolution.

Two of the most significant political revolutions of the period took place during the late 18th century in the American colonies and France, respectively. In each, a fiery rhetoric arose in which the rights of citizens within and over the government were placed at the foundation of a new political system (see Box 3.2). Moreover, as can be seen in the American case in particular, this was to be a democratically elected government, a notion that resonated with the democracy of the ancient Greeks but altered it in significant ways. The commitment to what Abraham Lincoln would call in his famous Gettysburg Address "government of the people, by the people, for the people" certainly harked back to ideas of the ancient Greeks, as did the notion that only a select group of citizens (in this case, property and/or taxpaying white males) could participate. It was radically different, however, in two related ways: first, it was to be a large-scale political system, and second, it would be based not on direct but indirect or **representative democracy**. Thus, the vast majority of citizens would be ruled but not—at least in any routine way—rulers as well, instead electing those who would rule on their behalf. Although it would take some time, democratic forms of government emerged in many parts of Europe after the American and French revolutions within a new organizational form—the nation-state.

> **Representative democracy:** A system of government in which voters elect candidates to represent them in government and make collective decisions on their behalf.

BOX 3.2

RIGHTS, GOVERNMENT, AND REVOLUTION

The American Declaration of Independence of 1776 is quite a radical document, both for its time and in the present day. Building on the ideas of philosophers such as John Locke, its authors provided a justification for the removal of any government that did not adequately reflect the people's will:

> We hold these truths to be self-evident, that all men are created equal, that they are endowed by their Creator with certain unalienable Rights, that among these are Life, Liberty and the pursuit of Happiness. That to secure these rights, Governments are instituted among Men, deriving their just powers from the consent of the governed. That whenever any Form of Government becomes destructive of these ends, it is the Right of the People to alter or to abolish it, and to institute new Government….

A similar commitment to the sanctity of political rights can be seen in the French Declaration of the Rights of Man and of the Citizen of 1789:

> Law is the expression of the general will. Every citizen has a right to participate personally, or through his representative, in its foundation. It must be the same for all, whether it protects or punishes.

STUDYING STATES

Just as it is difficult to imagine modern life without governments, it is hard to overlook the presence of states in our world, especially when we discuss international politics. However, the historical survey presented above reveals that the world has not always been organized into a system of states. Indeed, for centuries—millennia, even—vast areas of the globe were left relatively unstructured in political terms, even during the rule of some of the most highly developed governments of the ancient world. This began to change with the emergence and expansion of European nation-states from the 17th century onwards, although, as will be seen below, degrees of uncertainty remain. What, then, are the basic features of a state?

First and foremost, a **state** needs a constitutive population; there must be a people over which rulers can rule. In the contemporary period, we can point to the need for a group of people whose status as citizens links them to a particular state, creating unique ties of responsibilities and rights between them. Often, the people are seen to be the equivalent of a **nation**, but in reality very few states have ever existed within such a singular ethnocultural environment (and current international migration trends make this even less likely). For example, at Confederation in 1867 it was understood that four national groups made up the Canadian people: English, French, Irish, and Scottish. It is now accepted that numerous Aboriginal peoples also existed as nations at that time, even if they were not recognized as such, while the process of immigration has since produced extensive cultural diversity—or multiculturalism—that now gives definition to what it means to be Canadian.

State: A modern form of organizing political life that is characterized by a population, territory, governing institutions, and a government that claims a monopoly of legitimate force; recognition by the international community of states (most often by the United Nations) may also be key.

Nation: A community of people, normally defined by a combination of ethnicity, language, and culture, with a subjective sense of belonging together.

Elsewhere, colonialism and subsequent processes of decolonization often resulted in borders being drawn in ways that created numerous multiethnic if not multination states, sometimes with tragic consequences. For example, while a range of economic, social, and political factors help to explain the 1994 genocide in Rwanda, during which an estimated 800,000 Tutsis were killed by Hutus within a period of about 100 days, as hundreds of thousands more fled to neighbouring countries as refugees, the uneasy coexistence of these two groups during and after the colonial period that preceded the country's independence in 1961 remains a central factor. The politics of national identity, then, has affected and continues to affect both the behaviour and forms of all states, as you will see in greater detail in Chapter 4.

Second, a state requires an established territory over which to govern. Although conflicts about land stretch back millennia in human history, it is only relatively recently that set boundaries have become such a defining feature of political organization. For example, while the ancient Chinese dynasties claimed and controlled vast territories, precise borders remained undefined (the Great Wall of China notwithstanding). The relationship between political organization and land was changing when the 1648 Treaty of Westphalia brought an end to the Thirty Years' War in Europe, which was fought against the backdrop of the competing religious claims of Catholicism and Protestantism. One of the significant outcomes of the treaty was the principle that rulers could determine the religion for the territory over which they ruled. It followed that the ruler would no longer need to submit to an external religious or political authority. Thus, the sovereignty of the state became a legal condition, with political authority being embedded in domestic institutions and practices. Of course, this has not eliminated disputes over where borders lie between various sovereign states of the world. For example, Canada still has a number of maritime boundary disagreements with the United States (in the Beaufort Sea, at the Dixon Entrance between Alaska and British Columbia, and in the Strait of Juan de Fuca between Washington State and British Columbia, as well as around Machias Seal Island and North Rock, both of which lie between Maine and New Brunswick). More recently, the issue of Arctic sovereignty has come to the fore as Canada, the United States, Denmark, Norway, and Russia all lay claim to parts of the Arctic (see Box 3.3). While many border disputes are maintained or resolved peacefully, others can explode into violence, as occurred in 1982 when Argentina took the Falkland Islands (known more for sheep farming than strategic importance, although offshore oil exploitation may change that) in the South Atlantic Ocean by force, which had been under British control since their own forcible occupation in 1833. By the time the British subsequently retook the islands, 900 combatants from both sides were dead.

In recent years, a number of states have increased their military presence and capability in the Arctic, as the ice shields continue to melt and new questions of territoriality—and control over valuable natural resources—arise.

© The Canadian Press/Sean Kilpatrick

Third, a state requires sufficient political institutions to govern the population within its territory. As noted earlier, these are often associated with the rule-making, rule-enforcing, and rule-adjudicating functions of government. For these to be undertaken in a well-ordered fashion, a capable **bureaucracy** (or civil service) is required, that is, some form of public administration that can advise decision-makers on policy and both interpret and implement their decisions. While politics within a given country will provide more precise definition to the purposes to which such activities are turned, there is a general expectation that a sovereign state will use these institutions on behalf of its citizens. This idea has been made more concrete with the concept of the responsibility to protect (R2P), which holds that states have responsibilities toward their own citizens, and that under certain circumstances the international community can violate state sovereignty to protect a people when a state cannot or will not (see Chapter 16).

> **Bureaucracy:** The expert, permanent, non-partisan, professional officials employed by the state to advise the political executive and to implement government policies.

BOX 3.3

ARCTIC SOVEREIGNTY

As long as it remained frozen, it seemed possible to contain Canada's longstanding disagreement with the United States over who had sovereignty over the Arctic, especially the Northwest Passage. As with other border disputes between the two countries, they had more or less agreed to disagree for the time being, as seen in the 1988 Arctic Co-operation Agreement. Recently, however, other states have begun to weigh in more heavily with claims of their own. Although Canada's diplomatic dispute with Denmark over who controls tiny Hans Island (which lies between Ellesmere Island and Greenland) often generates amusement, if not bewilderment, Russia's 2007 decision to lay a flag on the seabed floor beneath the North Pole is seen as a more assertive attempt to bolster its claims in the Arctic. The economic payoff in this sovereignty game will likely be quite significant. With ice sheets melting, control over the previously hidden bounty of up to one-fourth of the untapped petroleum resources in the world, along with a wealth in valuable minerals, is at stake. Thus, even as the countries involved pursue scientific and diplomatic routes to secure their control over the North, they have been increasing their military capabilities in the region as well.

Source: Adapted from CBC.ca, "Arctic sees military buildup"; available at http://www.cbc.ca/canada/north/story/2010/03/25/arctic-military025.html; accessed September 29, 2010.

Fourth, a state must have, as sociologist Max Weber famously phrased it, a "monopoly of the legitimate use of physical force within a given territory."[16] Such force can be used not only to defend the country's interests but also to enforce collective decisions. It usually involves the military and police, although a small number of states only have the latter. For example, Costa Rica abolished its standing army in 1948 after a civil war that left some 2,000 dead. The country still maintains police and public security forces, however, and has contributed soldiers to peacekeeping missions. The relationship between the development of the modern state and the military has been, some argue, quite close. For example, American sociologist Charles Tilly proposes that the emergence and development of European nation-states occurred as they extended their military control and control over their militaries.[17] As states increasingly came to rely on standing armies to preserve and expand their political authority, large bureaucracies were created to extract the funds necessary to maintain national armies and administer conquered territories. Moreover, with the state drawing ever more heavily on the resources of the populations under its control, Tilly suggests, the people came to feel that they had the right, in turn, to make demands upon the state—especially with respect to some form of participation in collective decision-making. At a global total of more than $1.7 trillion (U.S.) in 2013, some 40 percent higher than in 2003 (although 1.9 percent less than in 2012), it is worth considering whether military expenditures continue to shape the nature of the state.[18] While it pales in comparison to the $188 billion spent by China or the $640 billion spent by the United States, Canada nonetheless ranked within the top 20 in the world at $18.7 billion in military spending in 2013, an increase of 11.3 percent over 2003.

Finally, a state must be able to function within a community of states. Certainly, without international recognition an entity that possesses all the other characteristics of a state noted above will not be able to engage as an equal on the world stage, whether at the **United Nations** or with respect to other international institutions. As can be seen in the case of South Sudan (see photo essay), statehood creates opportunities for people to determine their own futures and produces tangible benefits such as gaining control over local resources and the possibility of receiving international assistance on a bilateral (i.e., country-to-country) or multilateral basis, although usually not without significant challenges. In a sense, international recognition provides a state with the **legitimacy** to act as a sovereign state, giving a *de facto* state a *de jure* or legal status under international law.

United Nations: An international organization formed in 1945 as a successor to the League of Nations; it has become the largest and most ambitious international governmental organization in world history, consisting of a vast array of organs and agencies. Its membership now includes almost every country in the world. Less than a world government, it attempts to promote peaceful relations among states and economic and human rights for all people.

Legitimacy: A measure of the degree to which citizens accept and tolerate the actions and decisions of social and political actors such as governments, states, international organizations, and civil society groups themselves, usually based on the notion that the decision-makers have a right to such power.

THINK AND DISCUSS

During 2004–2013, Canada allocated almost $200 billion to military expenditures (the total figure for military-related spending is likely higher). If Charles Tilly is right, and there is a close connection between states and their militaries, then what kind of state might Canada have created if it had directed some or all of these expenditures elsewhere? What sorts of effects, in other words, does military expenditure have on defining a Canadian way of life?

PHOTO ESSAY

The Republic of South Sudan was formed in July 2011 following a referendum on independence, but it was beset by civil war in 2013, which led to at least 10,000 deaths and hundreds of thousands of displaced persons.

FRAGILE STATEHOOD FOR SOUTH SUDAN

In January 2011, the people of southern Sudan turned out en masse to vote in a referendum on national independence from the Republic of the Sudan—more than 97 percent of the population cast a ballot, of which more than 98 percent supported separation. Sudan was a construction of colonialism, enduring long years of Egyptian and British rule before gaining independence in 1956. However, the new country experienced considerable internal conflict, often along cultural, ethnic, and religious lines, including two major civil wars that pitted the north (which houses the national capital of Khartoum) against the south. These conflicts left millions dead and millions more displaced over the years, lasting from 1955–1972 and 1983–2005. At the end of the second civil war, a peace agreement was reached, which paved the way for the 2011 referendum. Apart from questions of self-determination for the people of southern Sudan, one of the significant issues at stake in the conflict between the north and south was control over substantial natural resources that lie between them, especially oil. Although not without controversies,

the referendum process was relatively peaceful and closely monitored by the international community, and the Sudanese government in Khartoum quickly recognized the new Republic of South Sudan. Within an independent state, the people of South Sudan now have much greater potential to determine their own future, but this has not come without challenges, including continued disputes over oil revenues and territorial disagreements with Sudan, and the outbreak of a civil war which has unfolded along communal lines and left some 10,000 dead. For its part, Sudan is still beset by internal conflicts, most notably in the region of Darfur, which has received considerable attention in the West due to a mobilization campaign spearheaded by activist groups (e.g., see http://savedarfur.org/), many on university campuses, and high-profile celebrity support from George Clooney, Mia Farrow, and Don Cheadle, among many others. The example of Sudan/South Sudan serves as a reminder that formal recognition by the international community only tells us so much about the nature of states and the governments that attempt to control them.

For more, see the resources contained at the BBC's "South Sudan profile," online at http://www.bbc.com/news/world-africa-14069082.

Although every state generally displays these basic features, few possess them to the fullest possible extent. Moreover, even though some states clearly do not meet these standards (especially those, explored later in the chapter, identified as "fragile states"), they are still considered to be states. This underscores the point that states are not all the same. At a broad level, we can separate states into **regimes** that are democratic and those that are non-democratic, or authoritarian. Although each type raises definitional difficulties—especially concerning the point at which regimes cross over from one to the other—they nonetheless exhibit distinguishing characteristics that are important to the study of politics.

> **Regime:** The constitutional principles and arrangements according to which government decisions are made; the political system.

MODERN DEMOCRATIC REGIMES

In its 2002 *Human Development Report*, the United Nations Development Program observed that an incredible burst of democratization had occurred since the 1980s: "Some 81 countries took significant steps toward democracy, and today 140 of the world's nearly 200 countries hold multiparty elections—more than ever before."[19] Notwithstanding this shift, the report recommended caution in considering whether this marked an irreversible turn toward democracy. As you will see in more detail in Chapter 14, not only has the expansion of democracy been much more modest of late, but the strength of democracy has been weak in a number of transitioning countries, and thus the possibility of a return to authoritarianism remains. Indeed, despite expressions of popular aspirations for more democratic rule in many countries where it does not prevail, there is evidence in both long-established and newer democracies that publics have been growing disillusioned with the seeming inability of democratic institutions to meet their expectations. While this often arises in established democracies through a decline in voter turnout and trust in public institutions, in some cases it has resulted in calls for a return to more authoritarian forms of government.[20]

The need to probe in greater detail how to make democracies work is not simply a question of addressing a democratic deficit in long-standing democracies, or of testing the democratic claims of other states, although these are valuable undertakings; it is also an issue of considerable international importance. In recent years, **democratization** has become a component part of the foreign policies of a number of countries, including Canada, and recent efforts to institutionalize democracy in Afghanistan and Iraq, and to support democratization movements more generally in the Middle East, reveal how difficult this process can be. Moreover, the language of democracy has come to permeate, if not dominate, political discourse, even in countries where it is practised least. What do we mean, then, when we talk about democracy?[21]

> **Democratization:** A group of transitions from non-democratic to democratic regimes, involving the relaxation of authoritarian political control by political leaders, the expansion of political and civil liberties, and the creation of institutional mechanisms that open up the political system to greater public representation and participation.

First, a government must be established, and it must be possible to replace it, through free and fair elections. It is in this way that power can be said to reside with the citizenry. Moreover, it is through their elected representatives that the people can (indirectly) govern. The rulers, therefore, receive their power on loan from the people and must return it when asked to do so. For elections to be free and fair several conditions need to be met, including the possibility of competition between different political parties, accessible information on both party and candidate positions as well as the issues, and the regulation of elections themselves by a nonpartisan agency whose job it is to ensure that everyone adheres to the law. Furthermore, votes should be cast through a secret ballot and people should not be intimidated or harassed at the polls. Thus, an election is not democratic if it is not free and fair. Even established democracies can have difficulties in administering elections fairly, as the United States found in 2000 when the contest between George W. Bush and Al Gore ultimately had to be settled (and not without controversy) by the Supreme Court.

Second, the people need to constitute an active citizenry. On the one hand, they ought to be engaged politically, by participating in elections, keeping abreast of important political issues, supporting a political party, or running for office. On the other hand, they should be engaged civically, getting together with fellow citizens to volunteer or participate in a range of social organizations as members of civil society. Through such means—often voluntary, ideally peaceful—citizens can mobilize around issues of importance to them, scrutinize government actions, and attempt to influence state behaviour. Moreover, through the multitude of forms of participation open to citizens in a democratic system, bonds of social trust and commitment to the political system itself may be strengthened.[22]

Finally, a democracy must be based on the rule of law, through which both citizens and the state are subject to fair judicial proceedings. In a democratic system, the people are protected by the law, which limits state power and provides avenues of redress against illegal state activities. For their part, the courts should serve as impartial arbiters and interpreters of the law, and must have independence from other branches of government and society (for more on these essential principles, see Chapter 9). Thus, all individuals, regardless of their economic, political, or social position, are equal before the law. The rule of law must also incorporate provisions for human rights protections. Everyone must be protected from such practices as arbitrary arrest or imprisonment, inhumane treatment or torture, or summary execution. People should have the right to know any charges brought against them and to defend themselves in a public trial. Thus, within a democracy every citizen possesses basic rights as a human being that cannot be taken away. Often these are enshrined in a constitution, and may also be supported under international law. Of course, no state, even the most democratic, respects all **human rights** all the time. This can be seen with a quick look through Amnesty International's annual report, the 2013 edition of which lists human rights violations in 159 countries, many of which—such as Canada—are longstanding democracies.[23] Particularly noteworthy is the recent increase in counter-terror and security-related rights restrictions in established democracies, which can affect both citizens and non-citizens (such as immigrants and asylum seekers) alike.

> **Human rights:** Rights enjoyed by individuals simply because they are human beings, primarily including the prevention of discrimination or coercion on grounds of ethnicity, religion, gender, or opinion.

MODERN NON-DEMOCRATIC REGIMES

Clearly, while democracy exhibits several basic institutional features, which require a certain level of commitment on the part of the people to sustain them over time, it is no simple matter to create one. This complexity is increased by the fact that most states in the world make some kind of claim to be democratic. For example, the constitution of the People's Republic of China states that "the Chinese people of all nationalities will continue to adhere to the people's democratic dictatorship and the socialist road, steadily improve socialist institutions, develop socialist democracy, improve the socialist legal system, and work hard and self-reliantly … to turn China into a socialist country with a high level of culture and democracy." While China nonetheless lacks many core features commonly associated with a modern democracy, the language used in its constitution underlines the point that many governments that we label authoritarian have some element or elements that can be called democratic. In the Islamic Republic of Iran, for example, the president is elected through a competitive process, but the supreme leader (who controls the military and shapes the direction of policy, among other significant powers) is elected by an Assembly of Experts (Islamic scholars), which itself is created through an electoral contest in which only government-approved candidates can compete. Such states are often called dictatorships, are commonly divided between **authoritarian** and **totalitarian** regimes,[24] and lack several key democratic characteristics.

> **Authoritarian government:** A non-democratic form of government that is not based on free and fair elections, severely curtails public participation in political life, and holds the actions of the state to be above the law; such regimes often commit gross human rights violations in order to maintain their power.

> **Totalitarian government:** A non-democratic form of government that seeks to control and transform the people though an all-encompassing ideology that speaks to their cultural, economic, political, and social roots and destiny. Totalitarian regimes were responsible for two of the worst genocides of the 20th century, in Europe during the Second World War and in Cambodia in the 1970s.

While elections may be held they are neither free nor fair when, for example, parties cannot compete freely or ballots are not counted accurately. For its part, the citizenry is often discouraged or prevented from debating and promoting issues outside official channels, and may be subject to harassment or even face execution for doing so. Meanwhile, the state seeks to control all forms of mass media closely, especially new social media technologies that challenge the state's ability to contain political mobilization. As for the rule of law, it is generally undermined by a lack of judicial independence, while the government itself often acts with impunity. As a result, such regimes feature prominently in the work of organizations like Amnesty International and Human Rights Watch, which call attention to those who sustain their rule through human rights violations. Moreover, corruption is frequently systemic in such political systems. As a result of such practices, citizens are treated like the subjects under an absolute monarchy, as the people are ruled over with few opportunities to influence how they are governed. In order to remain in power, the regime's leadership is often closely associated with military, police, and other security forces—indeed, the leadership might have emerged from the ranks of such organizations—and these may receive considerable public funding to maintain the government in power against public opposition. Because so much power is centred on the leader, their role is often glorified as the interests of the country are equated with those of its leadership. Thus, while the vast majority of people are likely to live in poverty, the rulers and their supporters are rarely found wanting. Because of such personification of power, when governments do change it can be a very violent process as different factions compete for control.

There are, however, important differences between authoritarian and totalitarian regimes. For example, authoritarian regimes tend to have a much less clearly defined ideological orientation and reflect, instead, a more pragmatic approach to power. Thus, they may adopt and promote discourses and policies aimed at economic development, national independence, public order, or social justice, among others. To these ends, authoritarian regimes seek to mobilize particular segments of the population—to allow forms of political mobilization that bolster the regime. In contrast, totalitarian regimes seek to control and transform the people wholly through an all-encompassing ideology that speaks to their presumed cultural, economic, political, and social roots and destiny. Rather than distancing itself from society, a totalitarian regime seeks to absorb it. In the 20th century, prominent totalitarian regimes include Nazism in Hitler's Germany, **fascism** in Mussolini's Italy, Soviet communism, especially under Stalin, and the agrarian communism in Pol Pot's Cambodia, which resulted in the death of an estimated two million civilians within half a decade. Although the number of authoritarian and totalitarian governments has been in decline over the past 25 years, the material introduced in Chapter 14 reveals that they still have a marked presence in world politics and will likely continue to do so for many years to come.

> **Fascism:** A political system of the extreme right, based on the principles of the strong leader (dictator), a one-party state, nationalism, total control of social and economic activity, and arbitrary power, rather than constitutionalism. In 1922 in Italy, Benito Mussolini created the first fascist regime, soon emulated by Adolf Hitler in Germany. Fascist regimes also held power in Spain and Argentina. Today there are numerous neofascist movements advocating ultranationalist, racist, and anti-immigrant political positions.

Indeed, some of the new democracies that have emerged during the past few decades have retained attributes of their former authoritarian selves, which may help to explain the tenuousness of their processes of democratization. Early hopes that the end of the Cold War would lead to a stable democracy in Russia, for example, have been disappointed by evidence of its transformation into an authoritarian capitalist regime.[25] Moreover, the growth of legislation and policies to counter terrorist threats in recent years—which frequently involve the suspension of liberties that otherwise remain central to democratic political life—has opened up an increasing debate over a "creeping authoritarianism" in established democracies.

NON-STATE GOVERNMENTS

If you take a map of the world and overlay it with the 193 member states of the United Nations, some more democratic and some more authoritarian, you would not have an accurate representation of the full range of either governments or state-like entities in the world. Not only would you miss areas where it is not quite clear who is sovereign but you would also overlook places where other types of government or state-like entities operate. To understand more fully the nature of governments and states, we should consider a few of these situations.

Traditional Governments

Human history is replete with instances of some groups dominating others, perhaps absorbing them into their own populations through conquest or maintaining them as dependencies in order to extract valued resources, for example. European colonialism from the late 15th century onwards provides countless such examples, as Western explorers, militaries, and rulers searched the globe for new trade routes, areas for settlement, and riches. As they moved through Africa, Asia, Latin America and the Caribbean, and beyond, they often encountered—and conquered or displaced—Indigenous peoples. Some, such as the Aztecs (of present-day Mexico), had long-standing and complex political systems, based in highly developed city-states ruled through kings and tributary relations that impressed Europeans. Thus, although he sacked it in 1521, the Spaniard Hernán Cortés praised the sophistication and splendour of Tenochitlán (which was perhaps larger than any other European city aside from Paris at the time) in letters to his king. In North America, democratic forms of government could be seen among some Aboriginal groups, such as those that made up the Iroquois Confederacy, which promoted consensus decision-making between five (later six) participating tribes and was inclusive of both men and women. Although nomadic peoples, such as the Maasai (now of Kenya and Tanzania) and the Bushmen (in southern Africa), had less observable political structures they nonetheless possessed complex understandings of societal norms and political relations, some of which had likely developed over centuries. It is in such small-scale and relatively isolated communities that political anthropologists have found real world examples of anarchist principles practiced.[26]

While Europeans often depended upon the knowledge of such groups for survival in climates and terrains unfamiliar, they generally held Indigenous peoples to be less "civilized" (or even "uncivilized") in comparison. In some instances an assertion of cultural

and racial superiority served to justify—in their own eyes—their domination over such groups, while in others, subtle arguments were developed to show that these "new lands" could be considered *terra nullius* (empty lands), as Indigenous peoples did not use systems of law or property that conformed to European models of governance. In either case, it was often argued that these groups existed in a pre-political "state of nature" that justified European control. After centuries of marginalization and even outright oppression, there is now a world movement of Indigenous peoples that promotes the recognition of spheres of independent Indigenous political authority in many states. To this end, the Declaration on the Rights of Indigenous Peoples, adopted by the United Nations General Assembly in 2007, states that "Indigenous peoples have the right to maintain and strengthen their distinct political, legal, economic, social and cultural institutions, while retaining the right to participate fully, if they so choose, in the political, economic, social and cultural life of the State" (Article 5).

It is impossible to do justice here to the great variation of such arrangements that have been or might be made, as there are some 370 million Indigenous people in the world, constituting some 5,000 different groups in more than 90 countries (see http://www.culturalsurvival. org/). The struggles that they face are diverse and are no longer simply a product of colonial times (although colonialism remains a necessary framework through which to study them). For example, the Yanomani lived in near seclusion within the Amazon rainforest until the 1970s, when the discovery of gold led to (sometimes deadly) conflicts with miners. Although land was set aside for the Yanomani in 1992, miners continue to work illegally within the territory, resulting in environmental and health threats that undermine the Yanomani way of life. In Canada, progress has been made in recognizing the diverse cultural, economic, environmental, and social challenges faced by Aboriginal peoples. This has largely been due to the political organization and involvement of Aboriginal peoples themselves since the 1960s, which has produced increased calls for **Aboriginal self-government.** Given that there are more than 600 different Aboriginal groups in Canada (consisting of more than 1.4 million people, according to the 2011 National Household Survey conducted by Statistics Canada), with varying degrees of political organization, territorial cohesion, and self-government ambition, the models that might be developed vary greatly.

A recent example was instituted with the Nisga'a Treaty of 2000, which recognized the authority of a Nisga'a government in British Columbia within the context of the Canadian constitutional structure. The emergence of the Idle No More movement in 2012 in opposition to numerous federal legislative and policy actions that were seen to infringe upon Aboriginal treaty rights and ways of life (http://www.idlenomore.ca/), as well as protests over the muted federal government response to the issue of missing and murdered Aboriginal women and girls,[27] serve as reminders that Indigenous peoples continue to struggle against the legacy and perpetuation of colonialism.

> **Aboriginal Self-Government:** Diverse arrangements whereby the authority of Aboriginal or Indigenous groups to govern themselves is recognized; such authority (over various aspects of community life) would have to be consistent with the laws operating within existing states.

Other Non-State Governments

Aside from such traditional governments without states, there is also one area of the globe with neither government nor state, Antarctica, which has no permanent population but is the fifth-largest continent in the world. Although seven countries claim parts of the Antarctic, these claims have been laid aside for the time being under the 1959 Antarctic Treaty, created to ensure that Antarctica remains demilitarized and accessible for peaceful scientific research. There are also various entities around the world that have state-like attributes but do not possess state sovereignty. For example, numerous colonies, dependencies, and external territories are linked and in some way subordinate to an established state. Often, such relationships have grown out of particular colonial histories, while at other times they reflect geographic proximity. At present, there are more than 50 dependencies and areas of special sovereignty in the world (according to the U.S. State Department), including such well-known examples as Bermuda, the Cayman Islands, and Puerto Rico. Although they tend to be associated with western states such as Australia, the Netherlands, Norway, the United Kingdom, and the United States, two are linked to China (Hong Kong and Macau). For its part, Canada does not possess any such territories but can point to the case of the islands that make up the Territorial Collectivity of Saint Pierre and Miquelon, which lie just off the coast of Newfoundland and have been under the control of France since the 1763 Treaty of Paris.

We can also find examples of what might be called *de facto* states that have not received *de jure* recognition from the United Nations. For example, Palestine is recognized at the United Nations as a non-member entity. It maintains—like the Holy See of the Catholic Church in Vatican City State—a permanent mission at UN headquarters in New York and is allowed to participate as an observer in the General Assembly. Other cases are less clear-cut: Taiwan is claimed by China, and the Sahrawi Arab Democratic Republic effectively controls a significant amount of territory otherwise claimed by Morocco in the Western Sahara. Only a minority of states have been willing to establish diplomatic relations with either entity. Elsewhere, while the United States and many European countries support statehood for Kosovo, this is opposed both by Serbia and Russia, among others. There are also several possible *de facto* states that are not really recognized by anyone else. These include the areas of Northern Cyprus (which is recognized only by the Turkish government), Abkhazia and South Ossetia (in Georgia), Nagorno-Karabakh (in Armenia-Azerbaijan), Somaliland (in Somalia), and Transnistria (in Moldova). By challenging the authority of ruling governments from within, such state-like entities might one day become sovereign in their own right; however, they might also produce state failure.

Failed and Fragile States

The issue of state failure became particularly acute in the post-Cold War era and even more so in the wake of September 11, 2001. Although the international system of states had seen major shakeups before, what has happened since the Cold War has been especially dramatic. With the demise of the Soviet Union, 16 new states were recognized by the United Nations, while the breakup of the former Yugoslavia has resulted in six new member states and Kosovo could soon constitute a seventh. In some instances, such as the 1989 Velvet Revolution in Czechoslovakia, this process was fairly peaceful. In others, it was extremely turbulent, as in the former Yugoslavia, which was beset by violent interethnic conflict between 1991 and 2001, resulting in the death of perhaps 120,000 people and the displacement of more than two million others. The issue of state failure took on heightened resonance following September 11, when a more explicit link was proposed between such states and **terrorism**. In short, it was argued that failed or failing states could provide a safe haven for terrorists when no central authority was willing or able to confront them. A good example of this can be seen in the rise of the Islamic State of Iraq and the Levant (ISIL), which calls for an Islamic State in parts of Iraq and more extensively in the Middle East. In the absence of an effective political or military response from the Iraqi government, a wide range of local and international states and actors (including Canada) have initiated, with the cooperation of the Iraqi government, a military response against ISIL. This follows on the heels of similar actions in Iraq, Afghanistan, and Libya, as well as calls for more extensive intervention to support opposition forces in the Syrian civil war, which has seen a death toll of perhaps 200,000 as well as the creation of some 4 million refugees since its onset in 2011. For these and other reasons, the international community has been paying (along with those who study politics) increased attention to identifying the conditions of state failure and trying to determine how best to respond.

> **Terrorism:** The threat or use of violence, usually directed at civilian populations, in order to create some form of political change.

The conditions of state failure might at first seem fairly obvious: a state is no longer a state when it loses one or more of the five characteristics of statehood. Thus, a failed state would be one, for example, that no longer had "a monopoly of the legitimate use of physical force within [its] given territory."[28] This answer, however, does not take us very far because, as we saw above, very few states match the full ideal of statehood, and even states that clearly do not meet certain criteria are still considered to be states by the international community. For example, although no national government was able to control the country's territory from 1991 until 2012, when a Federal Government of Somalia was instituted, the international community still recognized the existence of a state of Somalia. As opposed to stateless governments, those in power in a recognized state at least nominally have a territory over which they possess jurisdiction under international law.

The factors at play in state failure are diverse and can combine in various ways. This has led the researchers behind the Failed States Index, a joint project of *Foreign Policy Magazine* and the Fund for Peace since 2005, to rebrand their work as the Fragile States Index, to capture and reflect better the complexity of the serious challenges that confront states (and as a result their citizens). In constructing the index, numerous economic, political, and social indicators are gauged (see Box 3.4), and in 2014, the five states for which a "Very High Alert" was issued were South Sudan, Somalia, Central African Republic, the Democratic Republic of the Congo, and Sudan, followed by Chad and Afghanistan (http://ffp.statesindex.org). Each indicator represents a range of complex issues that defy easy understanding or solution, and to address any of them requires political will from both the state in question and the international community. Moreover, as can be seen in Box 3.5, a new twist has been added to the issue of state fragility with global warming.

While state fragility is generally discussed in terms of countries in the Global South, the concept is applicable to any political system, many of which can experience "pockets of fragility" (the 2014 Fragile States Index includes 178 countries, with Finland listed as the least fragile and Canada ranking 168). For example, when Hurricane Katrina hit New Orleans in 2005, the United States was unable to mount an effective reaction for several days; that same year, France declared a state of emergency after weeks of

Syrian civilians searching through the debris of destroyed buildings in the aftermath of a strike by Syrian government forces, in the neighbourhood of Jabal Bedro, Aleppo, Syria.
© AP Photo/Aleppo Media Center AMC, File

BOX 3.4

INDICATORS OF STATE FRAGILITY

Social Indicators

1. Mounting demographic pressures
2. Massive movement of refugees or internally displaced persons creating complex humanitarian emergencies
3. Legacy of vengeance-seeking group grievance or group paranoia
4. Chronic and sustained human flight

Economic Indicators

1. Uneven economic development along group lines
2. Sharp and/or severe economic decline

Political Indicators

1. Criminalization and/or delegitimization of the state
2. Progressive deterioration of public services
3. Suspension or arbitrary application of the rule of law and widespread violation of human rights
4. Security apparatus operates as a "state within a state"
5. Rise of factionalized elites
6. Intervention of other states or external political actors

Source: *CAST: Conflict Assessment Framework Manual* (Washington, DC: Fund for Peace, 2014), 4.

BOX 3.5

CLIMATE CHANGE AND STATE FAILURE

As public recognition of the threat of global warming grows, new possibilities of state failure have been identified. Take, for example, the case of the tiny island state of Tuvalu (consisting of four reef islands and five atolls), which is the least populated and fourth-smallest member state of the United Nations. This Polynesian country, located between Australia and Hawaii, gained independence from Britain in 1978 and has survived mainly on foreign aid ever since. Although it is a fully functioning constitutional monarchy, with a democratically elected parliament, the state faces the prospect of failure due to rising sea levels as the country is—on average—just six feet above sea level. Tuvalu is one of a number of island states where not only the physical existence of the territory but the existence of the way of life of a people is under threat.

Source: "Tuvalu NAPA—Essential Adaptation: Planning for Climate Change," a documentary by the United Nations Development Program, online at https://www.youtube.com/user/AdaptationLearning, accessed December 12, 2014.

---

rioting in Paris and beyond. In 2014, concerns arose that the spread of the Ebola virus might turn into a pandemic, which could overwhelm states if hospital systems became overloaded. By expanding the concept of state fragility, of course, the point is not to equate the political situation in Canada, for example, with that of South Sudan, for clearly differences in the degree, nature, and consequences of fragility are significant. It does, however, remind us that every state is confronted by both external and internal challenges, and that these could eventually produce a situation of state failure.

Postnational States?

While questions of state failure still seem remote for the more established states of the world, there has been considerable talk of their transformation since the late 20th century, often in the context of a process of **globalization**. According to one scenario, in an era of increased international migration, the old notion of the nation-state, while never an accurate depiction, has become an especially inappropriate term for increasingly diversified societies around the world today. This might, in fact, change the meaning of citizenship that lies at the heart of the definition of a state. In another scenario, states are being challenged both from within and from without, as the power generally associated with the national state is transferred upwards to international governing structures or devolved downwards to regional or municipal levels. With respect to powers transferred upwards, analysts often focus on institutions such as the **World Trade Organization**, which is supposed to ensure that national economic activities conform to certain shared standards of behaviour, or the **European Union (EU)**, through which a range of administrative, executive, judicial, and legislative functions have been passed from member states to a higher political authority. With respect to powers devolved downwards, the focus often shifts to the rise of "global cities" such as New York, London, and Tokyo, which—while existing within sovereign states—operate through global economic and social networks that create powerful and distinctive subnational political interests and forces. In either case, pressing and challenging questions are raised as to the nature and functions of governments and states, and it suggests that their evolution is far from over.

> **Globalization:** The movement of goods, capital, ideas, and people across geopolitical boundaries today and in the past. Contemporary patterns of globalization involve a deepening constellation of economic, technological, and cultural changes that are worldwide in scope and that challenge the sovereignty of the state. These processes are leading to ever closer economic relations among the countries of the world, based on increased trade, foreign direct investment, activity by multinational corporations, and financial flows.

> **World Trade Organization (WTO):** An organization created during the Uruguay Round of GATT negotiations whose goal is to provide liberal trading practices and to reduce protectionism through the development and enforcement of global laws and regulations.

> **European Union (EU):** A unique supranational organization made up of 28 member states, characterized by increasing economic and political integration.

CONCLUSION

As will become evident as you work your way through this textbook, governments and states do not define the entire scope of the study of politics, but they are often important factors and are rarely very far removed from modern political life. Clearly, whether we live under a democratic or an authoritarian regime quite literally shapes our prospects for living—as Aristotle observed—the good life. It also affects the types of politics that surround us and in which we become engaged. It is important, therefore, that we study the governments under and the states within which we live to understand how they operate, determine whether they work well, and decide how they need to be altered. Indeed, history informs us that no political regime is perfect—that each, indeed, has important limitations—but that each might be improved. In an age of increasing globalization, moreover, it is ever more difficult to isolate ourselves from what is going on in the rest of the world, making it essential to study the nature of other governments and states, how they are similar to or different from our own and why, and what kinds of ties—whether of self-interest or shared responsibility—might bind us together.

DISCUSSION QUESTIONS

1. Can you imagine a world without governments or states? What would it look like, and what would be its advantages and disadvantages?

2. In what ways are modern democracies less democratic than they might be, and how might they become more democratic?

3. Should we be concerned about fragile states halfway around the world? If so, what should we do in response?

4. Is Aboriginal self-government compatible with state sovereignty? Why or why not?

5. In what ways might global governance support, and in what ways might it challenge, democratic political life in a country like Canada?

WEBSITES

The United Nations
http://www.un.org/en/
A vast archive of studies and data related to governments, states, and peoples around the world, addressing an extraordinary range of economic, social, and political issues.

International Institute for Democracy and Electoral Assistance (International IDEA)
http://www.idea.int/about/
A useful library of analysis related to democracy and democratization, including an innovative program for citizen-led assessments of democracy.

Human Rights Watch
http://www.hrw.org/
A repository of information on human rights conditions around the globe (see as well the webpage for Amnesty International cited in the text).

International Workgroup for Indigenous Affairs
http://www.iwgia.org/
An important resource on the challenges and opportunities that face Indigenous peoples around the world, and actions that could help reduce the former and seize the latter.

FURTHER READING

Mark T. Berger, ed., *From Nation-Building to State-Building*. New York: Routledge, 2007.

Ian Buruma, *Taming the Gods: Religion and Democracy on Three Continents*. Princeton: Princeton University Press, 2012.

Larry Diamond, *The Spirit of Democracy: The Struggle to Build Free Societies Throughout the World*. New York: St. Martin's Griffin, 2009.

Lotte Hughes, *The No-Nonsense Guide to Indigenous Peoples*. Toronto: Between the Lines Press, 2003.

James C. Scott, *Seeing like a State: How Certain Schemes to Improve the Human Condition Have Failed*. New Haven: Yale University Press, 1999.

ENDNOTES

1. A comprehensive account can be found in Peter Marshall, *Demanding the Impossible: A History of Anarchism* (Oakland: PM Press, 2010).

2. Patti Tamara Lenard and Richard Simeon, eds., *Imperfect Democracies: The Democratic Deficit in Canada and the United States* (Vancouver: University of British Columbia Press, 2012).

3. Alan C. Cairns, "The Embedded State: State-Society Relations in Canada," in D.E. Williams, ed., *Reconfigurations: Canadian Citizenship & Constitutional Change, Selected Essays by Alan C. Cairns* (Toronto: McClelland and Stewart Inc., 1995), pp. 31–61, 358–61.

4. Gabriel A. Almond, "A Functional Approach to Comparative Politics," in G.A. Almond and J.S. Coleman, eds., *The Politics of the Developing Areas* (Princeton: Princeton University Press, 1960), pp. 3–64.

5. Pierre-Joseph Proudhon, *General Idea of the Revolution in the Nineteenth Century*, trans. by John Beverley Robinson (London: Pluto Press, 1989 [1923, 1851]), p. 294.

6. "In a world-historical perspective, then, the Middle East is the cradle of organized government, and it was to retain its cultural, political, and military supremacy … for over 2,000 years." S.E. Finer, *The History of Government from the Earliest Times, Volume I* (Oxford: Oxford University Press, 1997), p. 99.

7. See John Dunn, *Democracy: A History* (Toronto: Penguin Canada, 2005).

8. For some pre-Athenian examples, see Eric W. Robinson, *The First Democracies: Early Popular Government Outside Athens* (Stuttgart: Steiner, 1997).

9. As Amartya Sen, winner of the Nobel Prize in Economics, frames it: "I would argue that universal consent is not required for something to be a universal value. Rather, the claim of a universal value is that people anywhere may have reason to see it as valuable." See his "Democracy as a Universal Value," *Journal of Democracy* 10 (3) (1999), pp. 12.

10. Aristotle, *The Politics*, trans. T.A. Sinclair, revised and re-presented by Trevor J. Saunders (London: Penguin Books, 1981 [1962]), p. 60. Aristotle viewed men to be by nature superior to women, and on this ground justified the rule of the former over the latter, and the exclusion of women from politics.

11. Ibid., p. 222.

12. Robert Michels, *Political Parties: A Sociological Study of the Oligarchical Tendencies of Modern Democracy* (New York: Collier Books, 1962 [1911]), p. 365.

13. Robin Wright, ed., *The Islamists are Coming: Who They Really Are* (Washington, DC: United States Institute of Peace, 2012).

14. There is a burgeoning comparative literature on these issues; see, as but one example, Alfred Stepan and Charles Taylor, ed., *Boundaries of Toleration* (New York: Columbia University Press, 2014).

15. John Locke, *Second Treatise of Government*, ch. 9, sec. 123, originally published in 1689 and accessible online through *Project Gutenberg* at http://www.gutenberg.org/etext/7370.

16. Max Weber, "Politics as a Vocation," originally delivered as a speech in 1918 and online at http://anthropos-lab.net/wp/wp-content/uploads/2011/12/Weber-Politics-as-a-Vocation.pdf. He famously defined a state as "a human community that (successfully) claims the monopoly of the legitimate use of physical force within a given territory."

17. See Charles Tilly, *Coercion, Capital and European States, AD 900–1990* (Cambridge, Mass.: Basil Blackburn, 1990).

18. See the website of the Stockholm International Peace Research Institute, online at http://www.sipri.org/. The information on military spending in this chapter comes from this website; for comparability, all figures are in constant U.S. (2011) dollars.

19. United Nations Development Program, *2002 Human Development Report* (New York: Oxford University Press, 2002), p. 1.

20. See Kathryn Stoner and Michael McFaul, eds., *Transitions to Democracy: A Comparative Perspective* (Baltimore: The Johns Hopkins University Press, 2013).

21. See Larry Diamond, "What Is Democracy?," lecture at Hillah University for Humanitarian, Scientific and Religious Studies, January 21, 2004, online at http://web.stanford.edu/~ldiamond/iraq.html. Diamond advised the Coalition Provisional Authority in Baghdad in its efforts to establish a democratic political system in Iraq, and delivered this speech on the basic characteristics of a democracy to some 1,500 Iraqi leaders in 2004.

22. This is the basic thrust of Robert Putnam's *Bowling Alone: The Collapse and Revival of American Community* (New York: Simon and Schuster, 2000).

23. Amnesty International, *Amnesty International Report 2013*, online at http://www.amnesty.org/en/annual-report/2013.

24. See James Malloy, "Contemporary Authoritarian Regimes," in M. Hawkesworth and M. Korgan, eds., *Encyclopedia of Government and Politics, Volume I* (London: Routledge, 1992), pp. 229–46.

25. See Azar Gut, "The Return of Authoritarian Great Powers," *Foreign Policy* 86 (4) (July/August 2007), pp. 59–69.

26. Harold Barclay, *People Without Government: An Anthropology of Anarchy* (London: Kahn and Averill, 1996).

27. Royal Canadian Mounted Police, *Missing and Murdered Aboriginal Women: A National Operational Overview*, 2014, online at http://www.rcmp-grc.gc.ca/pubs/mmaw-faapd-eng.pdf.

28. Weber, "Politics as a Vocation."

4

STATES AND NATIONS: CULTURAL PLURALISM, NATIONALISM, AND IDENTITY

Yasmeen Abu-Laban

© REUTERS/Charles Platiau

In an age of international migration and resettlement, cultural pluralism constitutes a significant challenge to traditional forms of nationalism centred on the idea of ethnocultural homogeneity. In many Western countries (as in France, pictured here), this debate has focused specifically on the compatibility of liberal values with those that stem from Islam, especially with respect to women who wear a headscarf or veil for religious reasons.

INTRODUCTION

According to demographic statistics, only about 10 percent of countries can be said to be ethnically homogeneous.[1] The fact that cultural pluralism is a reality in most countries has important implications for politics. As noted in Chapter 3, modern government has come to rest largely with the state. Given that 90 percent of the countries of the world are characterized by having a heterogeneous population (see Table 4.1), it is easy to see why political scientists are interested in cultural and ethnic diversity. The sense of identity that people have, the relations between different cultural and ethnic groups, and the possibility of different and even conflicting demands made by groups can all affect the terrain of state governance. A better understanding of these issues has considerable practical significance, affecting people's quality of life and helping decision-makers who wish to enact effective public policies.

In this way, the attempt to describe ethnic, cultural, and other forms of diversity is not merely an abstract theoretical exercise. The research findings of political and other social scientists on issues pertaining to diversity are extremely relevant. This fact has been recognized at the highest levels internationally, as exemplified by the mandate of the Management of Social Transformations (MOST) program, launched in January 1994 by the United Nations Educational, Scientific and Cultural Organization (UNESCO). MOST is an ongoing project designed to promote international comparative social science research, with the aim of transferring policy-relevant findings to governmental and nongovernmental decision-makers. A central goal of MOST in its first phase of operation (1994–2003) was to understand multicultural and multiethnic societies better, precisely because of the potential implications for a host of policy areas. Accordingly, it was argued,

> The major challenge facing policy-makers in the fields of education, health, social welfare, and justice is to formulate policies in such a way as to promote and sustain peaceful multi-ethnic and multi-cultural co-operation and to rebuild such co-operation in societies undergoing post-war political, social and economic reconstruction.[2]

This quest continued in the second phase of operation (2004–2013) with an explicit focus on "International Migration and Multicultural Policies," and in its latest phase, since 2014, there is a stress on "intercultural dialogue," as well as harnessing the findings of social science research conducted through MOST to assist policymakers with social development.[3]

This chapter examines the internal diversity of nation-states in light of a belief system that profoundly shaped politics and events in the 20th century: nationalism. For political scientists today, a major research question concerns the salience of nationalism in the 21st century, given contemporary patterns of globalization. The economic, cultural, and

TABLE 4.1   DIVERSITY IN SELECTED COUNTRIES

Drawing on national census data and other statistical information, *The World Factbook* of the U.S. Central Intelligence Agency lists ethnic groups present in all countries of the world.

Country	Ethnic groups
Afghanistan	Pashtun 42%, Tajik 27%, Hazara 9%, Uzbek 9%, Aimak 4%, Turkmen 3%, Baloch 2%, other 4%
Australia	White 92%, Asian 7%, Aboriginal and other 1%
Belgium	Fleming 58%, Walloon 31%, mixed or other 11%
Brazil	White 47.7%, mulatto (mixed white and black) 43.1%, black 7.6%, Asian 1.1%, Indigenous 0.4%
China	Han Chinese 91.6%, Zhuang 1.3%, other (includes Hui, Manchu, Uighur, Miao, Yi Tujia, Tibetan, Mongol, Dong, Boyei, Yao, Bai, Korean, Hani, Li, Kazakh, Dai, other nationalities) 7.1%
Finland	Finn 93.4%, Swede 5.6%, Russian 0.5%, Estonian 0.3%, Roma (Gypsy) 0.1%, Sami 0.1%
Gaza Strip	Palestinian Arab
Germany	German 91.5%, Turkish 2.4%, other (made up largely of Greek, Italian, Polish, Russian, Serbo-Croatian, Spanish) 6.1%
India*	Indo-Aryan 72%, Dravidian 25%, Mongoloid and other 3%
Iraq	Arab 75%–80%, Kurdish 15%–20%, Turkoman, Assyrian, and other 5%
Iran	Persian 61%, Azeri 16%, Kurd 10%, Lur 6%, Baloch 2%, Arab 2%, Turkmen and Turkic tribes 2%, other 1%
Israel	Jewish 75.1% (of which Israel-born 73.6%, Europe/America/Oceania-born 17.9%, Africa-born 5.2%, Asia-born 3.2%), non-Jewish (mostly Arab) 24.9%
Mexico	Mestizo (Amerindian-Spanish) 60%, Amerindian or predominantly Amerindian 30%, white 9%, other 1%
South Africa	Black African 79.2%, white 8.9%, coloured 8.9%, Indian/Asian 2.5%, other 0.5%
Sudan	Sudanese Arab (approximately 70%), Fur, Beja, Nuba, Fallata
Switzerland	German 65%, French 18%, Italian 10%, Romansch 1%, other 6%
Syria	Arab 90.3%, Kurds, Armenians and other 9.7%
United Kingdom	White 87.2%, black/African/Caribbean/black British 3%, Asian/Asian British: Indian 2.3%, Asian/Asian British: Pakistani: 1.9%, mixed 2%, other 3.7%
United States	White 79.96%, black 12.85%, Asian 4.43%, Amerindian and Alaska native 0.97%, native Hawaiian and other Pacific Islander 0.18%, two or more races 1.61%*
West Bank	Palestinian Arab and other 83%, Jewish 17%

Note: a separate listing for Hispanic is not included because the U.S. Census Bureau considers Hispanic to mean persons of Spanish/Hispanic/Latino origin including those of Mexican, Cuban, Puerto Rican, Dominican Republic, Spanish, and Central or South American origin living in the U.S. who may be of any race or ethnic group (white, black, Asian, etc.); about 15.1percent of the total U.S. population is Hispanic.

Source: *The World Factbook 2013-14* (Washington, DC: Central Intelligence Agency, 2013); available at https://www.cia.gov/library/publications/the-world-factbook/index.html, accessed December 6, 2014.

technological processes associated with globalization now seem to challenge both national identity as the only or main form of identity experienced by people, as well as the **nation-state** as a form of political organization. In this chapter, it is argued that while national identity is not disappearing, its primacy is being challenged by contemporary globalization.

Nation-state: A term sometimes used synonymously with state but which implies that the citizens share a common ethnic or cultural background. In the modern world, few such homogeneous states remain, most either being multicultural, multiethnic, or multination states.

In the first section of this chapter, key concepts pertaining to nationalism are explained. The second section contains an overview of theories of nationalism with reference to historic nationalist liberation struggles in the developing world. In the third section, the tension between nationalism and other forms of identity (especially gender) is examined in light of Apartheid and post-Apartheid South Africa. Finally, the tension between nationalism and globalization is addressed, and contemporary expressions of nationalism and identity claims that are not based on a single national identity are explored in relation to Canada.

KEY CONCEPTS IN THE STUDY OF NATIONALISM

Connotation of Nationalism

What comes to mind when you think of the word *nationalism*? Are your reactions positive or negative? No matter how you answer these questions, you will enter into a debate that has raged among analysts and historians for over two centuries. This momentous force has been viewed as the root cause of such diverse events as the emergence of the European state system, the First World War, the rise of fascism in Europe, Third World anticolonial struggles, reassertions of national identity by minorities in industrialized countries (e.g., in Scotland and Quebec), post-Cold War conflict in both the former Soviet bloc countries (e.g., the Balkans and Central Asia) and in the developing world (e.g., South Sudan and Afghanistan).

Some consider nationalism as a positive force. It has been suggested, for example, that the existence of nations is associated with the existence of ties of love or kinship.[4] Frequently, we may speak of nations as "motherlands" and "fatherlands." Citizens form a national "family." Immigrants are said to "adopt" countries that are not their native homes. In the United States, the president and the president's spouse are referred to as the "First Family." In Canada, the first two lines of the national anthem (at least in English, as the Canadian anthem's meaning is different in French!) are "O Canada! Our home and native land! True patriot love in all thy sons command." When the late Nelson Mandela became the first president of post-apartheid South Africa, his wife at the time, Winnie Mandela, was honoured as South

Africa's "Mother of the Nation," and this moniker has continued in spite of any personal or political controversies she has stirred.[5]

Probably more often, however, nationalism has been associated with hatred. Some have viewed nationalism as the most destructive force of the 20th century—the cause of violence, atrocity, and incalculable human misery.[6] The Nazi regime in Germany and the evils of the Holocaust stood as the mid-century's horrifying example of this scourge. Responding to the tragedy of the Holocaust, Polish jurist Raphael Lemkin coined the term **genocide** (from the Greek word *genos*, meaning race, and the Latin word *caedere*, meaning to kill).[7] An international prohibition against genocide was established in 1948 when the United Nations adopted the Convention on the Prevention and Punishment of the Crime of Genocide. In the 1990s, the violence, bloodshed, and killing that occurred among rival ethnic and religious groups in the former Yugoslavia (Serbs, Croats, and Muslims) and also in Rwanda (Hutus and Tutsis) emerged as new horrors that led many to reaffirm that nationalism was one of the most destructive forces imaginable and to refocus international attention on genocide.

> **Genocide:** The deliberate and systematic extermination of a national, ethnic, or religious group. The term was developed in response to the horrors of the Holocaust.

The 1992–1995 war in Bosnia-Herzegovina was the key segment in the dissolution of Yugoslavia, which began when the republics of Croatia and Slovenia seceded in 1991, leaving open the possibility of an independent Bosnia. There was no clear ethnic majority in Bosnia; the three constituent peoples (as defined by earlier Yugoslav constitutions) were the Muslims (most numerous at 42 percent of the population), followed by the Serbs and the Croats.[8] In this climate of uncertainty in Bosnia, President Slobodan Milosevic of Serbia used the crisis to consolidate his power by sending in his paramilitary troops bent on ethnic cleansing.[9] While the United Nations attributes violence in Bosnia-Herzegovina to all sides, the term **ethnic cleansing** was used specifically to refer to a slate of violent measures and policies designed to eliminate or dramatically reduce the Muslim and Croat populations in Serb-held territory.[10] Ethnic cleansing included the systematic rape by Serbian soldiers of

Muslim and Croat women, whose captivity, torture, and forced pregnancies were designed to reproduce "Serbians."[11] The term "ethnic cleansing" is controversial because it is seen as somewhat euphemistic (in contrast to *genocide*) and serves to mask the impact of this nationalist violence.

> **Ethnic cleansing:** The removal of one or more ethnic groups from a society by means of expulsion, imprisonment, or killing. The term entered the political lexicon in reference to the former Yugoslavia; it was first used to describe the violent measures and policies designed to eliminate or dramatically reduce the Muslim and Croat populations in Serb-held territory.

The Rwandan genocide began on April 6, 1994, when a small group of Hutu political and military leaders targeted and began the slaughter of more than a half a million Tutsis—a group that constituted about 10 percent of the population—along with thousands of Hutus who opposed the elite in power. This genocide differed from others in its rapidity (lasting about a hundred days) and in the number of ordinary people who were mobilized by a small elite to kill.[12]

The travesties in Rwanda and the former Yugoslavia, which clearly included both the direct and indirect involvement of governments, led to renewed calls within the international community for more effective means to prosecute such crimes. To this end, the United Nations created the International Criminal Court, whose jurisdiction includes the ability to prosecute the crime of genocide, as defined in the 1948 Convention on the Prevention and Punishment of the Crime of Genocide. These tragic events of the 1990s also had an impact on the study of nationalism. Michael Ignatieff (who would later assume the leadership of the Liberal Party in Canada between 2008 and 2011) wrote an international bestseller in 1993, tellingly entitled *Blood and Belonging*. In this book he argues that the end of the Cold War has been replaced by a new age of violence based on nationalism and ethnic particularism.[13]

Some see the continuation of this age of violence in the 21st century through the prism of the "war on terrorism." Here, many longstanding national conflicts have come to be viewed as somehow reflecting a "clash of civilizations"—a term popularized by the late political scientist Samuel Huntington (see also the photo essay). Following the end of the Cold War, as marked by the collapse of the Berlin Wall in 1990, Huntington predicted that the main characteristic of international politics would be that of a civilizational clash involving Western societies on the one hand and non-Western societies on the other.[14] Huntington's thesis enjoyed a period of renewed currency following the September 11, 2001 attacks in New York and Washington because it seemed to explain a divide between the East (specifically, Islam) and the West (specifically, Christianity). However, the "clash of civilizations" thesis has also been subject to criticism for treating the West and the non-West as homogeneous and, as a result, not accounting for the complexity of either, never mind the ways in which "cultures" (as well as people) intermix.[15] Notably, Huntington's 2004 book dealing with the United States and immigration, particularly from Mexico, entitled *Who are We? The Challenges to America's National Identity*,[16] drew very similar criticisms since it suggested that Catholic and/or Spanish influences were seemingly incompatible with the British and/or Protestant settler foundation and national identity of the U.S.[17] Such debates, whether about domestic or international politics, suggest the need for a careful definition of nationalism.

Denotation of Nationalism

While there are radically different readings of the impact of nationalism as a force, political scientists are on less contentious ground in delineating what nationalism is. At root, **nationalism** may be defined as an ideology or belief system that contains three major assumptions.[18] The first assumption is that certain identified populations contain characteristics that make them nations. The second is that the world is divided into nations. The third is that a nation should be able to establish its own institutions, laws, and government and to determine its future—this is really what lies behind the idea of self-determination. The doctrine of self-determination holds that a group of people who call themselves a nation have a right to have control over territory or domains that immediately concern them, normally through statehood. The idea of self-determination may be traced back to the emergence of the European state system in the middle of the 17th century. In the 20th century, it became enshrined in the principles of international institutions such as the United Nations, and self-determination is now considered a human right under international law.[19]

> **Nationalism:** An ideology used by state leaders to promote the interest of the nation, including defence of the state in times of war. Alternatively, it can be used by secession movements against the state. In the extreme, nationalism can be used to motivate ethnic cleansing and genocide. Nationalism has been a leading cause of conflict.

Other Associated Concepts: State, Nation, Multination State, Diaspora

Unpacking the ideology of nationalism requires a closer examination of several associated concepts. The first concept is that of the state. Political scientists have theorized much about the state, but there is no clear consensus about whose interests it promotes. For example, as noted in Chapters 2 and 5, the 19th-century thinker Karl Marx (1818–1883) argued that in a capitalist society the state was a class instrument that served the interests of the owners of the means of production (the bourgeoisie) over the interests of the workers (the proletariat). For Marx, the state was central in the functioning of the capitalist system and the perpetuation of class inequality. This is why Marx called on workers to unite, overthrow the state, and usher in a more egalitarian (in this case, communist) society. More recently, radical feminists have argued that the state is central in perpetuating patriarchy (the rule of males) by privileging men in law and public policy.[20] Other (mainly liberal) theorists assert that the state operates in the interests of different individuals or groups at different times.

Although there is considerable debate about whose interests are represented by the state, most political scientists do agree on what the **state** is and use the definition first provided by Max Weber (1864–1920), who proposed that the "state is a human community that (successfully) claims the monopoly of legitimate use of physical force within a given territory."[21] For Weber, the state is characterized by territory (existing in a given geographical boundary), by sovereignty (the state is the highest authority and can back up its claims with force),

and by institutions (including the bureaucracy, the military and the police, and the legislature). Many political scientists would also subscribe to the idea that a state must have recognition by the international community, an idea explored in Chapter 3.

> **State:** A modern form of organizing political life that is characterized by a population, territory, governing institutions, and a government that claims a monopoly of legitimate force; recognition by the international community of states (most often by the United Nations) may also be key.

It should be noted that the way political scientists use the term "state" to refer to territory, sovereignty, and institutions is very comprehensive and precise; the term "state" is not synonymous with country or government. The term "country" describes geographical units of the globe. When you look at the divisions of the world in an atlas, you are looking at countries. As discussed in Chapter 3, the term "government" refers to the set of institutions and/or individuals that makes and enforces collective public decisions.

The ideology of nationalism holds that territory, sovereignty, and institutions ought to be allocated to people of a single nation. While belonging to a state may be a simple matter of citizenship, belonging to a **nation** rests on a subjective sense of identity and belonging, marked by distinct cultural or linguistic traditions, which is usually in turn marked by membership in a distinct ethnic group. A leading theorist of nationalism, Benedict Anderson, refers to nations as "imagined communities" precisely because the idea of a nation rests on a subjective sense of belonging to a community that is neither voluntary nor organizationally defined. Joining an organization such as an undergraduate students' association (which likely holds elections for those willing to run for president, vice-president, and the like) is not like being part of a nation. In contrast, belonging to a nation is somewhat similar to belonging to a family—it is seemingly "natural" and involuntary.[22] For this reason, according to Anderson, dying for one's nation "assumes a moral grandeur which dying for the Labour Party, the American Medical Association, or perhaps even Amnesty International cannot rival, for these are all bodies one can join or leave at easy will."[23]

Undoubtedly, we could put campus student associations in this same "voluntary" category as political parties or interest groups.

> **Nation:** A community of people, normally defined by a combination of ethnicity, language, and culture, with a subjective sense of belonging together.

Although the ideology of nationalism implies that there ought to be a correspondence between territory, a single nation, and governance, this is not the case with most countries. Some states contain more than one nation; such a state is called a **multination state**. For example, Canada has been variously described as containing two nations (the French and the British), three nations (the French, the British, and Aboriginal peoples), and even numerous nations (particularly when the multiple traditions and languages among Aboriginal peoples in Canada are considered). This is where the problems of the doctrine of self-determination become apparent. Often in real-world politics the same territory is claimed by more than one group. This is especially apparent in a country such as Canada—a settler colony with an Indigenous population and a minority francophone population located primarily in Quebec. The fact that Aboriginal peoples have land claims all over the country, including Quebec, became very apparent during the 1995 Quebec referendum on sovereignty. Although separation from the rest of Canada was rejected by a very narrow margin of Quebecers (50.6 percent to 49.4 percent), some Aboriginal groups, including the Cree and the Montagnais, held their own referendums on the issue of sovereignty, in which the proposal was also rejected by a much wider margin. Another international example of competing national claims to the same land is seen in the conflict zone of Israel–Palestine (see the photo essay).

> **Multination state:** A state that contains more than one nation.

PHOTO ESSAY

© JAAFAR ASHTIYEH/AFP/Getty Images

A member of the Israeli security forces stands guard while Palestinian farmers plough their land as Israeli settlers protest and try to prevent them from cultivating their fields in the northern West Bank village of Jalod on December 31, 2014.

TWO NARRATIVES: "PALESTINE" AND "ISRAEL"

Both Palestinian Arabs (Muslims and Christians) and Israeli Jews lay claim to the territory of Palestine/Israel as their national home on the basis of history, religion, and long residence. The area known as Palestine was, until the First World War, part of the Turkish Ottoman Empire. Following the war, the League of Nations (the forerunner to the United Nations) granted Britain a mandate over Palestine. Flowing from the 1917 Balfour Declaration, the British government viewed "with favour the establishment in Palestine of a national home for the Jewish people," and promised to use immigration to support this objective.

While Palestinian Arabs remained a majority in the area until the late 1940s, the goal of creating a Jewish state in Palestine was further developed in the United Nations Partition Plan in 1947. The Partition Plan sought to divide Palestine into an Arab state and a Jewish state, with the city of Jerusalem designated as an international zone. The Partition Plan was viewed as unacceptable and unfair by Palestinian Arabs, who believed that it threatened the geographical integrity of Palestine and disagreed with the manner in which Palestine was to be divided. Hostility between Arabs and Jews mounted in Palestine, and civil war broke out. On May 14, 1948, the British mandate came to an end and an independent state of Israel was declared. As a result, open warfare between the surrounding Arab states and Israel erupted. By the end of the war, there was more land taken by Israel than had been allotted under the Partition Plan. In the meantime, Israel rapidly gained the recognition of both the world's superpowers—the United States and the Soviet Union. Israeli leaders immediately indicated that the new state belonged to all the Jewish people around the world and invited immigration from the Jewish diaspora. This is codified as the Israeli state's "law of return."

The events of 1948 are subject to very different national narratives on the parts of Palestinians and Israelis. For many Israelis, the years 1947 and 1948 are seen as a period in which the birth of a national state was made possible after the Holocaust and after what Israelis call the War of Independence of 1948. In contrast, for most Palestinians, the year 1948 represents a disaster (in Arabic the *Nakba*) characterized by half of the Arab population losing homes and property and becoming stateless refugees outside of mandatory Palestine. Today Palestinians make up one of the world's largest and oldest refugee groups. Indeed, from 1949, the Palestinian national identity crystallized around the loss of homeland, the longing to return, and the desire for self-determination. This is symbolized in the quest for a "right of return."

A series of wars in the region (in 1956, 1967, 1973, and 1982) served to reconfigure control of the land in favour of the state of Israel. For example, after the 1967 war, the territories of the West Bank and Gaza (known as "the occupied territories") came under Israeli control. The Oslo agreement signed in 1993 by Israel and the Palestine Liberation Organization (PLO) allows for parts of these two territories to be handed over to Palestinian rule. Nonetheless, disputes over land persist as Israeli settlers continue to build settlements (residential outposts) in the West Bank, East Jerusalem, and the Golan Heights. Peace has therefore remained elusive between Israelis and Palestinians as well as in the larger region.

This case provokes a number of questions of interest for studies of pluralism, nationalism, identity, and contemporary politics, including:

1. Can competing claims to the same territory be adequately resolved by the doctrine of self-determination?
2. Outside the region, American President Barack Obama has called for renewed peace talks between Israeli and Palestinian leaders aimed at fostering a "two state solution," wherein it is envisioned that an Israeli state and a Palestinian state will co-exist in peace and security. However, some Palestinian and Israeli leaders and intellectuals have instead advanced the idea of a "one state solution" based on equal rights and citizenship for all regardless of ethnicity, national origin, or religion. How feasible are either the one state or two-state options?
3. Since September 11, 2001 there has been renewed interest in the "clash of civilizations" thesis forwarded by Samuel Huntington. In what ways does the thesis apply or not apply to the case of Israel/Palestine?

A further complication to the doctrine of nationalism is the fact that nations may spill out across state boundaries—a feature encapsulated in the concept of **diaspora**. The term was originally applied to Jewish people, but today it is used to describe any ethnic group that has experienced or currently experiences dislocation across multiple states, and yet typically nurtures narratives and political projects about a "homeland" as a place of eventual return at some opportune time.[24] In contemporary usage it has been applied to such diverse groups as Palestinians, Armenians, and Cubans.[25]

> **Diaspora:** An ethnic group that has experienced or currently experiences dislocation across multiple states, yet typically nurtures narratives and political projects about a specific "homeland" as a place of eventual return.

Racial Discrimination and the Politics of Multiculturalism

Finally, as part of understanding nationalism it should also be noted that ethnic groups can have many different political demands and points of mobilization that do not take the form of nationalism and self-determination but instead stress gaining acceptance and equality.[26] In particular, some groups may struggle against discrimination based on race (racism) as well as processes of **racialization** (the historically and contextually specific ways in which certain groups come to be seen as separate and inferior on the basis of biology and/or culture).

> **Racialization:** The historically and culturally specific processes associated with representations or assertions of superiority by one group over another on the basis of purported biological and/or cultural characteristics.

In the past, the term **race** has been used in many different ways. During the 19th century, biologists used it to refer to different "subspecies" of humans. The inspiration behind eugenics movements—which advocated the use of "scientific" breeding techniques to improve the genetic potential of humans—was the supposed existence of biological differences between distinct and hierarchically ordered "racial" groups. In the early 20th century, the term "race" was often used as a synonym for nation and ethnic group. This can be seen in the metaphor of the United States as a "melting pot," popularized in the 1908 play *The Melting Pot* by Israel Zangwill. Zangwill spoke of different "races" (by which he meant Germans, Russians, the English, the French, and the Irish) jumping into a common melting pot and emerging as Americans.[27] By the middle of the 20th century, as a result of the atrocities of the Holocaust, the use of "race" to refer to biological differences between people was completely discredited; instead, many began to talk about "the human race" to indicate that eugenics was wrong, as all people are of the same species.

> **Race:** Historically, the term "race" was used to speak about differences between people that were supposedly biologically based. Today social scientists completely reject the idea that there are any significant biological differences between people that warrant the use of the term. While some suggest that in light of this the term should not be used at all, many contemporary social scientists put the term in quotation marks to refer to differences that are socially constructed and historically specific, but have important consequences in the form of racism. Contemporary discussions of racism assume that it involves a biological and/or cultural assertion of superiority by one group over another.

Today, social scientists use the term "race" to refer to socially constructed rather than biologically inherited differences. In other words, race is viewed as significant only because of socially created beliefs about differences between people, not because biology itself determines culture or personality. In particular, social scientists are interested in examining how the experiences and impact of racism (and processes of racialization) are manifested in practices and institutions to the detriment of particular groups in particular times and places. Some have advocated rejecting the term "race" altogether, or at least putting it in quotation marks to signify that there are no inherent differences between people.[28]

The idea that "race" and processes of racialization are socially constructed and temporally specific can be readily documented. For example, historically, the Irish were held to be a separate and inferior "race" to the British; they experienced discrimination in a host of spheres in Britain, Canada, and the United States. Today, groups struggling with racial discrimination include African-Americans in the United States. African-Americans overcame slavery in the 1800s, and through the civil rights movement in the 1950s and 1960s successfully challenged segregation in public schools and private establishments, yet discrimination against them remains a fact of life and a source of conflict. One example of this conflict was seen in the protests and riots of 2014 in Ferguson, Missouri following a grand jury decision to not indict a white police officer (Darren Wilson) in the shooting and killing of Michael Brown, a black 18-year-old.

The continued inequality in employment and earnings between African-Americans and other groups in the U.S. has led to public policy measures such as affirmative action. **Affirmative action** is designed to equalize the chances of members of minority groups or groups traditionally discriminated against, such as African-Americans, women, and people with disabilities, in accessing education and jobs by setting goals for ensuring the statistical representation of these groups. Affirmative action has become increasingly controversial in the United States, as has, to a lesser extent, the Canadian version known as employment equity. Critics charge that affirmative action is essentially "reverse discrimination," while proponents argue that it helps put into practice the principle that all people are of equal worth. In the United States, affirmative action has tended to be supported by African-Americans more than by other groups.[29] Given the historical and contemporary social context of that country, categories such as "black" and "white" (and increasingly, "mixed race") are important politically. Indeed, the legacy of slavery has been so profound that the 2008 election of President Barack Obama, the country's first African-American President, was widely interpreted as an historic moment.

Contemporary theoretical discussions of racism are further complicated by the fact that analysts have increasingly sought to identify the relationship between culture (not just biology) and processes by which groups can experience differentiation, discrimination, and disadvantage. For example, British political theorist Tariq Modood distinguishes "colour racism" (as seen in hierarchically distinguishing "black" and "white") and "cultural racism." For Modood, the primary example of cultural racism today can be seen in how Muslims in Britain face discrimination and their religion is vilified (also captured in the more popularized concept of Islamophobia).[30] Modood states, as well, that this tendency predates the events of September 11, 2001.

Whether looking at African-Americans in the United States or British Muslims, the projects of such groups tend to be different from groups seeking national self-determination. Political theorist Will Kymlicka suggests that in Canada and elsewhere many minority and immigrant groups have mobilized to demand **multiculturalism**. He points out that this pursuit of multiculturalism is geared primarily to achieve inclusion in the dominant culture, rather than to attempt to live separately from it. For Kymlicka, multicultural responses to minority and immigrant group claims might involve such diverse policies as affirmative action, guaranteed seats in legislatures, curriculum changes in schools, work schedule changes to accommodate diverse religions, flexible dress codes, literacy programs in the first language of immigrants, and bilingual education programs for the children of immigrants.[31] In this way, multiculturalism may be seen as a very different kind of demand than national self-determination.

Affirmative action: An American policy and term designed to increase the representation of targeted groups in such areas as employment and education. Critics may view it as "preferential treatment" or "reverse discrimination" but proponents say it redresses the effects of past discrimination. Affirmative action began in the U.S. in the 1960s, focusing mainly on increasing opportunities for African-Americans. In the 1970s, it started to be used to increase the number of women in professional and managerial positions. In Canada, a policy of "employment equity" has been used to encourage the representation of women, visible minorities, Aboriginal people, and persons with disabilities in government or companies doing business with the government.

Multiculturalism: A policy sometimes adopted in a state characterized by cultural pluralism that supports ethnic and cultural groups in maintaining their customs and traditions, often with public financial assistance.

EXPLAINING NATIONALISM: NATIONAL LIBERATION MOVEMENTS AND DECOLONIZATION

So far in our discussion, two main themes have emerged. First, nationalism has been associated with many different—even opposite—phenomena in the

20th century: war, violence, hate, oppression, liberation, family, and love. Second, political scientists have defined the ideology of nationalism and related concepts in a precise way that seems to capture the essence of most, if not all, expressions of nationalism. The areas of agreement and disagreement help account for two very distinct approaches to studying nationalism that political scientists have used in explaining its emergence in very different times and locales.

Because the ideology of nationalism is fairly consistent across its various expressions, political scientists have tried to determine whether there is one primary factor that can explain the emergence of nationalism in so many different places. Those searching for this all-purpose general explanation have engaged in *universalizing comparisons*; that is, they have attempted to show how all instances of nationalism follow the same patterns. In contrast, other political scientists have postulated that, partly because of the sheer variety of phenomena associated with nationalism (from oppression to liberation), there may be many different explanations for why nationalism emerges in different locales— that is, that there is no universal explanation. Those searching to discover such differences have engaged in *individualizing comparisons*, which attempt to show the unique characteristics of a given instance of nationalism.

To evaluate these two different approaches, it is helpful to consider how each might account for the same manifestation of nationalism, namely that of 20th-century Third World anticolonial movements. During the 19th century, **imperialism**—in the form of colonization of other countries and the establishment of empires—led to the expansion of Western power over the rest of the world (for more on this, see Chapter 13). However, during the 20th century, the formal control of Western states in different parts of the world largely came to an unexpected end in a relatively short period of time. Consider that in 1945, when the United Nations emerged as the primary international organization to promote peace and human rights, 51 states obtained membership. As can be seen in Table 4.2, out of these 51 states, only three were located in Africa (Ethiopia, Liberia, and South Africa), three in Asia (of which only China was independent of colonial rule), and seven in the Middle East. Initially, then, the great majority of member states in the United Nations were the countries of North America, the Commonwealth, and Europe, including the former Soviet Union. Notably, most observers in the 1950s did not expect

TABLE 4.2 THE ORIGINAL 51 MEMBER STATES OF THE UNITED NATIONS, 1945

Argentina	Cuba	Haiti	Nicaragua	Turkey
Australia	Czechoslovakia	Honduras	Norway	Ukraine
Belgium	Denmark	India	Panama	United Kingdom of Great Britain and Northern Ireland
Bolivia	Dominican Republic	Iran	Paraguay	United States of America
Brazil	Ecuador	Iraq	Peru	Uruguay
Belarus	Egypt	Lebanon	Philippines	Venezuela
Canada	El Salvador	Liberia	Poland	Yugoslavia
Chile	Ethiopia	Luxembourg	Russian Federation	
China	France	Mexico	Saudi Arabia	
Colombia	Greece	Netherlands	South Africa	
Costa Rica	Guatemala	New Zealand	Syrian Arab Republic	

European power to end in their lifetime.[32] However, by the end of 1965, 66 new states had joined the United Nations, bringing the number up to 117; in 2011 South Sudan became the 193rd member.

> **Imperialism:** A broader term than colonialism that literally means "empire building," imperialism occurs when one country dominates another with the aim of controlling and/or exploiting the latter. This domination can be economic, political, social, and/or cultural.

The addition of 66 new states by 1965 symbolized a dramatic political change: the formal transfer of power from Europeans to non-Europeans and the liberation of some one billion people from colonial rule in Asia and Africa. The emergence and successes of Third World nationalist anticolonial movements might be explained in different ways depending on the approach one uses.

Universalizing Comparisons

Traditionally, many political scientists used universalizing comparisons to try to establish that all forms of nationalism follow the same patterns or rules. This approach was widely accepted during the 1950s, 1960s, and 1970s, and there are still people who use it today. Its popularity may be related to how political science, as a discipline, has been influenced by developments in the United States. In that country, during the first two to three decades after the Second World War, political analysts were very much concerned with developing generalizations that could be applied to all societies at all times. This was part and parcel of developing a "science" of social and political life.[33]

The accounts that address nationalism from the vantage point of universalizing comparisons generally suggest that nationalism was rooted in the European experience, dating from the French Revolution and gaining speed with the unification of Germany and Italy in 1870. In this view, nationalism was somehow related to the processes of industrialization. What exactly is highlighted as important about industrialization varies in different accounts that make use of universalizing comparisons. Some have argued that technological developments in mass communication and the introduction of mass education made it possible for people to communicate easily with each other across vast distances.[34] As a result, people started to identify with one another in a new way—as part of national communities. Others have proposed that capitalism accompanied industrialization, and with capitalism came uneven development, such that, when there were pockets of poverty in distinct regions, expressions of nationalism emerged.[35] Both of these scenarios that use industrialization to explain nationalism have a universalizing quality to them—a sense that the ideology of nationalism developed in Europe and was simply exported to Africa and Asia on the back of European colonialism.[36]

More recently, such universalizing explanations have been criticized for being Eurocentric—that is, focused only on the experience of Europe. Critics also argue that they are ahistorical—that is, they tend to ignore the unique historical contexts of different countries outside Europe in accounting for nationalism. There is value to these criticisms, since political scientists have never been able to produce one general theory that accounts for the emergence of nationalism everywhere and for all time.

Individualizing Comparisons

Individualizing comparisons, then, take into account both historical and geographical specificity. They seek to uncover that which is unique about a given form or instance of nationalism. Broadly speaking, the suggestion that comes out of such accounts is that many expressions of Third World nationalism may be viewed as a political reaction against colonialism.[37] This political reaction occurs in societies where traditional modes of social and political organization have collapsed as a result of the changes introduced by colonialism.

One way to understand how Third World expressions of nationalism were a reaction against the oppressive effects of colonial rule is to consider how colonized people were treated and depicted by colonial powers. The famous lines by British poet Rudyard Kipling on "The White Man's Burden" provide a literary example of this broader phenomenon. Kipling's poem, written in 1899, describes the need for British men—and more broadly white men—to go out to the colonial world and rule the peoples there, whom Kipling describes as "half devil and half child."[38]

Unequal power relations that rested upon the dehumanized depiction of the colonized by the colonizer are key to understanding the motivation behind Third World nationalist movements for liberation. Imperialism and colonialism worked to erode the dignity of peoples of the Third World, but nationalism formed a part in the recovery of that dignity.[39] Consequently, one of the things that tends to surface in such expressions of Third World nationalism aimed at liberation is an attempt to invert and put value on the identity of the colonized. For example, Léopold Sédar Senghor, a poet who became the first president of Senegal after it achieved independence from France in 1960, is associated with a literary and political movement known as négritude. The négritude movement, which began in the 1930s and reached its zenith in the 1960s, launched a critique of Western society for suppressing blacks and for cutting African blacks off from their roots. Négritude aimed to rediscover ancient African values so that Africans could feel pride and dignity in their heritage and culture.

Likewise, Frantz Fanon, a West Indian-born psychoanalyst and philosopher who spent time in Algeria when it was under French colonial rule, went on to write about the necessity of creating or recreating a national cultural consciousness as a means of achieving true independence. In contrast to the négritude movement Fanon saw an important, almost redemptive, role to be played by violence. He describes this idea in his famous 1963 book *The Wretched of the Earth*, which deals with the situation in Algeria. Between 1954 and 1961, there was a bitter and violent war between France and Algeria, as a result of which Algeria gained its independence in 1962. For Fanon, the lessons of the Algerian war of independence suggest the value of violent struggle as a means to empower colonized people. Violence, he argues, is a cleansing force that "frees the native from his inferiority complex and from his despair and inaction."[40] Yet, ultimately, the development of a genuine national consciousness leading to real liberation is difficult to achieve, Fanon points out, because the forces of domination are internalized by indigenous elites.[41] Even after decolonization, the unequal social and economic structures inherited from colonialism might well continue. Fanon sensed very early on that the national liberation movements in countries that experienced colonization might be successful in overthrowing foreign rulers, but that this might not necessarily in and of itself lead to an egalitarian future.

The basic idea behind individualizing comparisons is that while nationalism might be a single ideology, it contains several subvarieties.[42] From the vantage point of individualizing comparisons, manifestations of nationalism in the Third World in the context of national struggles for liberation may be seen as unique because the factors that motivated nationalism were unique. Universalizing explanations, in contrast, fail to take into account the specificity of the situation in the Third World. In an attempt to fit all manifestations of nationalism into one pattern, they neglect to consider the historical effects of imperialism and colonialism in the countries of the developing world, and to consider ways in which explanations may apply to some countries, but not necessarily all countries—this might also be called a middle-range explanation. A focus on more middle-range (as opposed to universal explanations), along with attention to context, which are a hallmark feature of individualizing comparisons, provide a useful way into understanding nationalism in the contemporary period.

THE NATION VERSUS OTHER FORMS OF IDENTITY: CONSIDERING SOUTH AFRICA

The advantages of individualizing comparisons do not completely negate the need to theorize about the nation in relation to internal forces. The warnings of Frantz Fanon about the future of liberated (postcolonial) states highlight the complexities present in any nation. Any population that calls itself a nation is inevitably internally diverse and divided along some combination of class, gender, age, and rural–urban lines. As one prominent example of the relevance of this kind of internal diversity within nations, it is useful to consider the more recent work of feminist scholars who have insisted on the importance of gender diversity in the study of national identity and relations of power. We have noted how nationalist discourses often make use of metaphors relating to kinship—motherlands, fatherlands, and the like. Such "familial" depictions of the nation have been the starting point for the work of these feminist scholars who stress that nationalist movements can act to subordinate women. For example, whether women have children, how women socialize children, and even how women dress are often extremely important to most nationalist movements.[43] In recent years, political debates in Canada and other Western countries about the appropriateness of some Muslim women wearing the *hijab* (a head cover) or the *niqab* (a head and face cover) underscore the fact that how women dress is not simply a question of individual choice but can tap into wider issues of identity, community, and nation.

Because women frequently play a central role in transmitting and reflecting cultural traditions across generations, the argument has also been made that it is women who play the primary role as "bearers of the nation," rather than schools or forms of mass communication (as has been suggested by some accounts focusing on explaining the rise of nationalism in relation to industrialization).[44] In this way, women can become specific targets as both the "property of men" and the "embodiment of the nation," as attested to by the systematic use of rape in the name of ethnic cleansing.[45] While, typically, nationalist movements themselves are tied to gendered relations, this does not always mean that they specifically improve the position of women. Indeed, according to feminist scholars, those who assume that nationalist movements generally improve the lot of the disadvantaged often neglect to attend to specific social and political structures and belief systems that can keep women in subordinate positions.[46]

In the context of nationalist movements aimed at liberation, South Africa provides a noteworthy example of a country where gender equality came to be considered explicitly. The history of the African National Congress (ANC) illustrates this point. The ANC was created in 1912 as the principal organization reflecting indigenous black South African interests. Although it was outlawed in 1960, the ANC was later instrumental in ending the racist policies of apartheid (or apartness) that had supported white (European) colonial political and economic dominance.[47] Nelson Mandela, once branded a "terrorist" by the South African government, emerged from a long prison term to lead a successful anti-apartheid movement and then become the first president of post-apartheid South Africa in 1994.

The history of politics in South Africa and the reaction of black women there to the long years of resistance and hope for liberating the country from white control demonstrate that black women's relation to nationalism has undergone changes.[48] Initially, when the ANC was created, women were denied formal representation in the organization, yet, gradually, as a result of women's own insistence, they were granted full participation. Nevertheless, calls for women's emancipation were generally seen as secondary to national revolution, sometimes even by women themselves. Over the late 1970s and 1980s, however, the issue of women's empowerment began to be raised as a project distinct from national, democratic, and social revolution. By the early 1990s, female ANC nationalists carried placards with the slogan "A nation will never be free until women are free."[49]

Such women's demonstrations were successful in leading to formal recognition of women's rights within the ANC, which in 1990 issued a Statement on the Emancipation of Women. The statement argued that the experience of other societies with successful national liberation struggles showed that the emancipation of women does not necessarily follow from national liberation. The statement asserted that, given this historical record, women's emancipation had to be addressed within the ANC, the mass democratic national movement, and society as a whole. It went as far as to say that all "laws, customs, traditions and practices which discriminate against women shall be held unconstitutional."[50] Indeed, under Nelson Mandela a new constitution was passed that emphasized not only formal but also substantive equality for women.[51] Formal equality refers to the idea that everyone has the same rights; substantive equality refers to the idea that everyone is actually able to access the same opportunities by holding and exercising those rights.

While it has been observed that no other country has a constitution with such progressive ideas to eliminate sexism,[52] constitutions do not in and of themselves necessarily guarantee all the rights they proclaim. For this reason, in the context of "national liberation" and the transition to democracy in South Africa, gender equality and issues relating to women's inequality remain on the agenda for analysts as well as women's organizations.[53] Additionally, profound economic inequalities in post-Apartheid South Africa today (commonly referred to as "economic apartheid") have also drawn analytical attention to forms

Nelson Mandela's death in December 2013 rekindled discussions inside and outside South Africa about his example and legacy.

© AP Photo/Tsvangirayi Mukwazhi

of inequality on the basis of class and race, as well as gender.[54] Overall then, the case of South Africa and the ANC demonstrates how nationalism still matters, how nations are internally diverse, and how national movements and even successful liberation projects may be affected by diversity.

NATIONALISM VERSUS GLOBALIZATION

Given the internal diversity of nations and the fact that what motivates nationalism might vary depending on the time period and geography, it seems clear that the idea of a universal theory of nationalism is problematic. The limitations of universalizing explanations should be kept in mind as we turn to the grand question concerning the future of national identity and nationalism in light of contemporary globalization.

In an important way, as attested to by the examples of imperialism and colonialism, **globalization** is not a completely new phenomenon. For centuries, people, money, ideas, goods, and corporations have crossed geopolitical boundaries. But the processes associated with contemporary globalization (since 1945) have some distinct features. Globalization before the end of the Second World War was based on imperialism, colonialism, and coercion practised by institutions of empires (such as the British or French Empires). Contemporary globalization processes rest on a multitude of multilateral institutions (such as the World

Trade Organization) and, since the collapse of the Soviet Union, the political and economic dominance of the United States.[55] As well, the contemporary economic, technological, and cultural flows associated with globalization today are more intense than in earlier periods.[56] The unprecedented speed with which capital (in the form of cash, stocks, and shares, for example) can move around the world as a result of new information technologies illustrates how economic flows have changed in the past several decades. The speed with which information can flow across the planet as a result of the Internet, social networking (like Facebook and Twitter), and other developments in communications (such as the advent of CNN, which is based in Atlanta in the United States but has overseas operations and services, or Al Jazeera, based in Doha, Qatar, which carries Arabic and English language operations and services, including Al Jazeera America) means that information flows are not simply national but global. As well, while people may always have moved from place to place, now migration is more widespread and multidirectional. Currently all regions and countries both send and receive people.[57]

> **Globalization:** The movement of goods, capital, ideas, and people across geopolitical boundaries today and in the past. Contemporary patterns of globalization involve a deepening constellation of economic, technological, and cultural changes that are worldwide in scope and that challenge the sovereignty of the state. These processes are leading to ever closer economic relations among the countries of the world, based on increased trade, foreign direct investment, activity by multinational corporations, and financial flows.

The combination of all of these developments has led some political scientists to question the future viability of the state as a form of organization, because one of its key aspects is sovereignty, the assumption that it is the highest authority. But sovereignty may be transforming in the face of the contemporary worldwide reorganization of economic, technological, and cultural flows. For example, states now have much more difficulty controlling the flow of information across and within their borders (such as the information leaked through WikiLeaks, an organization dedicated to releasing secret (state) information).

Globalization and National Identity

Globalization also raises questions concerning national identity. The late Stuart Hall was a British analyst of culture. He argued that the developments associated with contemporary globalization that appear to challenge the state and its sovereignty also raise issues about the future of nationalism. Hall suggested that the seemingly "natural" priority given to national culture (and identity) was in fact an historical phenomenon tied to the emergence of the nation-state. He argued that contemporary globalization appears to have the effect of "contesting and dislocating the centred and 'closed' identities of a national culture."[58] Globalization raises many uncertainties about the future of national identity, not only because people who move across national boundaries may bring with them different cultural influences, but also because there are forms of culture (from Mickey Mouse to world music) that are not simply national but global. Furthermore, there are elements of identity (gender, for example) that may assume as much importance for some people as national identity, if not more.

According to Stuart Hall, the 21st century ushered in three possibilities for national identity.[59] One possibility is that national identity might actually be strengthened in response to globalization. Another possibility is that national identity might be weakened. The third possibility is the emergence of new, shifting, and even hybrid forms of identity that challenge a singular national identity.

Drawing from our discussion on the advantages of individualizing comparisons, it is probably more useful to attend to specific cases when considering these propositions rather than to attempt to make universal claims. We will therefore turn our attention to the cases of the **European Union (EU)** (see Box 4.1) and Canada to gain insight into the possibilities that contemporary globalization raises for the future primacy of national identity.

> **European Union (EU):** A unique supranational organization made up of 28 member states characterized by increasing economic and political integration.

The Canadian Case

In Canada, the daily news reminds us that people of many different backgrounds reside here—that is, that Canada is a country that reflects a reality of cultural pluralism. Among a host of possible demographic statistics that might be used to illustrate this reality are those on ethnic diversity (Table 4.3) and religious diversity (Table 4.4). A dominant issue that structured Canada's history as a settler-colony concerned the rights of Catholics versus those of Protestants. For example, the 1774 Québec Act granted the freedom to practise the Catholic faith in Canada, and retained the French civil law and seigneurial landholding systems. While the Québec Act did not say anything about the use of the French language, the appointed council (overseen by a colonial governor) allowed for Roman Catholics to hold office. Today, this particular division between Catholics and Protestants has less obvious resonance. Instead, Canadian electoral and other political debates have often revolved around the place of the province of Quebec, and the future of the sovereignty movement still supported by many francophones there.

Beyond the potential secession of Quebec, other issues related to cultural identity frequently cause heated debates. For example, what about the right of francophones outside Quebec to speak French in public institutions? What about Aboriginal peoples and their quest for self-government and cultural preservation? What of non-French/non-British immigrants and their offspring—to what extent should the maintenance of languages other than French and English be encouraged and to what extent should Canadian institutions change to reflect and accommodate peoples of all backgrounds? And what about those who want to define themselves as simply "Canadian"—should the Canadian state foster only this kind of allegiance?

All of these questions lie at the heart of the politics of multiculturalism, national recognition, and nationalism in Canada, and there is an ebb and flow about which ones assume prominence in public debate. Since the events of September 11, 2001, and the fallout from the U.S.-led "war on terrorism," there has been a strong shift to thinking of accommodation and multiculturalism through the lens of religious difference, and to the question of accommodating religious minorities (i.e., non-Christian faith groups, in contrast to the historic focus on Catholics versus Protestants), especially Muslims. The focus on religious minorities was in evidence in Ontario during the 2005 debate over religious-based

A NEW "EUROPEAN" IDENTITY?

The modern nation-state system arose in Europe, so it is particularly relevant to consider developments in that region when examining the question of whether national identity is weakening. The European Union (EU) is an international organization dating back to the 1950s, created with the specific goal of weakening national rivalries (especially between France and Germany) through greater economic cooperation. Initially consisting of only Western European countries, in May 2004 the EU gained 10 new members, including for the first time former Soviet-bloc countries of Central Europe. As of 2013, membership stood at 28: Austria, Belgium, Denmark, Finland, France, Germany, Greece, Ireland, Italy, Luxembourg, Spain, Sweden, the Netherlands, Portugal and the United Kingdom were joined by Cyprus, the Czech Republic, Estonia, Hungary, Latvia, Lithuania, Malta, Poland, Slovakia, and Slovenia in 2004, Bulgaria and Romania in 2007, and Croatia in 2013.

Over the 1980s and 1990s, economic cooperation in Europe deepened significantly, which also affected the political sphere. A European flag, anthem, and parliament were created, and in 1993 the Maastricht Treaty introduced a citizenship of the European Union. The rights associated with EU citizenship include the right of free movement; for example, a Dutch citizen has the right to move to and work in Belgium or any other member country. EU citizens also have the right to vote and stand for elections at the local level and at the European level in any member state. Finally, EU citizenship entitles one to consular protection when abroad from any embassy of a member country.

Every citizen of an EU member state is considered to be an EU citizen. However, the rights of EU citizenship, and especially the right of free movement, were not fully implemented across all EU countries (for a period of anywhere from two to seven years) for citizens of the countries that joined in 2004, 2007, and 2013.

The EU, its citizenship, and its projected continued enlargement with six recognized candidate countries (Albania, Iceland, Macedonia, Montenegro, Serbia, and Turkey) raise many interesting questions. Does EU citizenship contribute to a new form of belonging or identity—that of being "European"? If so, how does that differ from national identity? Does EU citizenship really weaken national citizenship? Should EU citizenship have been automatically and fully granted to the citizens of the 13 countries that joined between 2004 and 2013, or was it reasonable to do this over time? Should full EU citizenship be granted to any person who permanently lives in Europe regardless of citizenship (including some 18.5 million legally residing migrant workers and their families who have come mainly from countries of the developing world)? Does the EU provide a model for other world regions, like North America?

arbitration (especially as it concerned **sharia law**) as well as the 2007 electoral discussion over faith-based schools. In Quebec in 2007, Premier Jean Charest formed a commission, headed by two prominent academics—historian Gérard Bouchard and political theorist Charles Taylor—to address the question of "reasonable accommodation" as it concerns religious minorities and practices in relation to public institutions. The Bouchard-Taylor Commission traced the growing fixation on the idea of "reasonable accommodation" found in print media coverage, and broadly set its discussion in relation to the theme of secularism, even calling for more explicit attention to be paid by the Quebec National Assembly to outlining Quebec's secular model.[60] Although the recommendations of the Bouchard-Taylor Commission were largely not implemented, issues of religion and governance have remained salient in the province, and have been deeply entwined with the still unresolved "national question" regarding sovereignty. This was seen when the former Parti Québécois (PQ) government of Pauline Marois attempted to pass a Quebec "Charter of Values," which would have prohibited the wearing of "ostentacious" religious symbols by public sector employees (this would have included, for example, orthodox Sikh men wearing a turban, or those Muslim women who choose to wear a hijab). The proposed Charter was controversial, and widely

TABLE 4.3   ETHNIC GROUPS SURPASSING 1 MILLION IN CANADA, STATISTICS CANADA 2011 NATIONAL HOUSEHOLD SURVEY ESTIMATES

The following are the totals for responses to the ethnic origin question (respondents were allowed to name more than one origin).

	Total Response	Single Responses	Multiple Responses
Total population	32,852,320	19,036,295	13,816,025
Canadian	10,563,805	5,834,535	4,729,265
English	6,509,500	1,312,570	5,196,930
French	5,077,215	1,170,620	3,906,595
Scottish	4,714,970	544,440	4,170,530
Irish	4,544,870	506,445	4,038,425
German	3,203,330	608,520	2,594,805
Italian	1,488,425	700,845	787,580
Chinese	1,487,580	1,210,945	276,335
North American Indian	1,369,115	517,550	851,565
Ukrainian	1,251,170	276,055	975,110
Dutch	1,067,245	297,885	769,355
East Indian	1,165,145	919,155	245,985
Polish	1,010,705	255,135	755,565

Source: Statistics Canada. 2011 National Household Survey, Statistics Canada Catalogue no. 99-010-X2011028. Available at http://www12.statcan.gc.ca/nhs-enm/2011/dp-pd/dt-td/Rp-eng.cfm?LANG=E&APATH=3&DETAIL=0&DIM=0&FL=A&FREE=0&GC=0&GID=0&GK=0&GRP=1&PID=105396&PRID=0&PTYPE=105277&S=0&SHOWALL=0&SUB=0&Temporal=2013&THEME=95&VID=0&VNAMEE=&VNAMEF= (accessed 10 December, 2014).

TABLE 4.4   MAJOR RELIGIOUS DENOMINATIONS IN CANADA (AS PERCENT OF POPULATION), STATISTICS CANADA 2011 NATIONAL HOUSEHOLD SURVEY ESTIMATES

Christian Faith Communities	
Roman Catholic	38.7
United Church	6.1
Anglican	5.0
Christian	1.9
Christian Orthodox	1.7
Non-Christian Faith Communities	
Muslim	3.2
Hindu	1.5
Sikh	1.4
Buddhist	1.1
Jewish	1.0
No Religious Affiliation	
No Religion	23.9

Source: Adapted from Statistics Canada, National Household Survey 2011, "Immigration and Ethnocultural Diversity in Canada" (prepared by Tina Chui). Catalogue No. 99-010-X2011001. Minister of Industry, 2013. http://www12.statcan.gc.ca/nhs-enm/2011/as-sa/99-010-x/99-010-x2011001-eng.cfm#a6 (accessed December 10, 2014).

seen to differentially impact religious minorities. With the 2014 electoral defeat of the PQ government, the Liberal government of Premier Philippe Couillard promised a new era of "religious accommodation."[61] Whether framed in relation to "accommodation" or not, it can be anticipated that religion will remain a key feature of Canadian discussions in the second decade of the 2000s. Still, it is only one facet of diversity that has entailed questions of governance.

> **Sharia law:** Sharia is the Islamic system of law, both civil and criminal, that is based on the Qur'an (the holy book of Islam); the life example and hadiths (sayings) of the Prophet Muhammad; and on subsequent scholarly interpretations and writings. This system of law prescribes the correct behavior for Muslims across different areas of life and the punishments for transgressions. Importantly, Sharia law is not uniform throughout the Muslim world as it is influenced by different schools of jurisprudence, among other factors.

Indeed, diversity and governance were relevant prior to European colonization in the early 17th century, as Aboriginal societies were characterized by a rich range of cultural, linguistic, social, and political practices.[62] The Iroquois Confederacy, formed long before first contact with Europeans, united five, and later six, separate nations with principles relating to consensus and respect for diversity. When the French and the British established their settlements and expropriated land from Aboriginal peoples, they brought with them their own cultures and languages. Since then, there have been many waves of immigration from other European countries, and increasingly, since the late 1960s, from countries outside Europe. For much of Canada's history, government policies

reflected an emphasis on the model of **dominant conformity** and, specifically, Anglo conformity. The idea behind dominant conformity is that all groups should assimilate to the language, culture, and values of the dominant group, and in the case of Anglo conformity in Canada, that all groups should conform to the British group.

> **Dominant conformity:** A model of ethnic group integration holding that all groups in a society should conform to the language and values of the dominant group. In the case of Canada, this is the idea behind historical policies emphasizing Anglo conformity, which aims to have all groups assimilate by speaking English and holding the values of the dominant British-origin group.

In the last few decades, as a result of pressures from different minority groups, the Canadian state has adopted a series of public policy measures designed to deal with diversity in a different way. In 1969 a national policy of official bilingualism (French and English) was introduced. In 1971 a national policy of official multiculturalism within a bilingual framework was established, giving recognition to the multiplicity of ethnic groups present in the country. In recent years, both the federal and provincial governments have been involved in discussions pertaining to settling Aboriginal land claims and fostering forms of Aboriginal self-government. For their part, Canadian human rights commissions and courts have highlighted the need for employers, landlords, and public officials to make "reasonable accommodation" for a range of groups (including persons with disabilities and religious minorities) in such areas as job duties and expectations, building design, or even school

THINK AND DISCUSS

In 2013, the Parti Québécois government of Pauline Marois introduced Bill 60, the "Charter Affirming the values of State secularism and religious neutrality and of equality between women and men, and providing a framework for accommodation requests" (informally known as the Quebec Values Charter). Amongst other things the bill sought to ban the wearing of "conspicuous" religious symbols by public sector employees, a feature that set off a huge debate in and outside Quebec. The bill died as of the 2014 election win of the Quebec Liberal Party which campaigned against Bill 60. In light of the ideas of secularism and cultural pluralism, how might Bill 60 be justified and how might it be critiqued?

rules. For instance, in March 2006 the Supreme Court of Canada ruled that a Quebec schoolboy, who is an orthodox Sikh, could wear the *kirpan* (ceremonial dagger) to school, and that refusing to allow this on the basis of a general prohibition against students carrying "weapons" was a violation of the religious freedom guaranteed by the Canadian Charter of Rights and Freedoms.[63]

Does the shift since the 1960s suggest that national identity is weakening? If that identity is defined in terms of Anglo conformity, then the answer is yes. These kinds of initiatives reflect Canada's commitment to a variant of the model of **cultural pluralism**. Beyond the existence of diverse ethnic and cultural groups within a country, the cultural pluralism model specifically aims at promoting peaceful cooperation and recognition among these groups. The model suggests that groups can maintain distinct features without being marginalized economically or socially. Moreover, it contends that the cultivation of differences does not necessarily produce conflict; rather, it can produce peaceful coexistence through overarching values and institutions.

> **Cultural pluralism:** The coexistence of many ethnic and cultural groups within a country. Such diversity is the starting point in arguing that all groups in a society can maintain their linguistic, cultural, and religious distinctiveness without being relegated to the economic or cultural margins, and is achieved through the creation of a common set of values and institutions.

The models of dominant conformity and cultural pluralism represent opposite methods of dealing with ethnic and cultural diversity within a country. While many federal policies in Canada today reflect the model of cultural pluralism, it should also be noted that these policies have been controversial and subject to challenge. For example, members of the Reform Party and Canadian Alliance (the precursors to the Conservative Party of Canada) and some intellectuals have argued that multiculturalism is leading to the fragmentation of Canada and should therefore not be publicly recognized or funded. In a related way, it has been suggested that a policy emphasis on "being Canadian" would contribute to the unity of the country and the loyalty of citizens toward the Canadian state.[64] It is interesting that the federal

Conservatives of Prime Minister Stephen Harper, while accepting multiculturalism, have placed a new emphasis on patriotism and Canadian identity. This has involved the promotion of Canada's ties with Britain and the monarchy, as well as military history emphasizing Canadian battle triumphs; these features are graphically seen in *Discover Canada*, a 2009 government guide given to new immigrants to study for the citizenship test.[65] These developments illustrate that there are those who would like to see the strengthening of a singular national identity in Canada.

Finally, there is evidence that Canadians identify in many ways that are not captured adequately by the idea of belonging to any one group, whether defined by gender, ethnicity, or other factors. Indeed, by the 1990s the Canadian women's movement (and feminist scholars) began increasingly to take the position that there is a complex heterogeneity among Canadian women along racial, ethnic, class, and other lines. Likewise, we see that Canadians self-identify in complex ways. For example, in the 2011 census over 42 percent of Canadians gave multiple responses to the ethnic origin question.[66] It is clear that many Canadians describe themselves as having multiple heritages, such as writer Lawrence Hill, who has referred to himself as a "zebra" to describe the hybrid experience of having a white mother and a black father.[67] It could be anticipated that such kinds of multiple and mixed identities might increase as a result of contemporary globalization, since people

Members of Team Canada celebrate after winning the gold medal game against Sweden in the men's hockey final at the 2014 Winter Olympic Games in Sochi: for many Canadians, the ultimate expression of their nationalism.

© *The Canadian Press/Paul Chiasson*

may migrate several times in a lifetime, and since a growing number of people appear to be at ease with multiple national attachments and fluid and shifting identities.[68]

The case of Canada therefore suggests that an argument can be made that the salience of a single national identity (particularly in the form of Anglo conformity) has lessened with time. Although there are still debates about the desirability of having one dominant national identity, there is evidence that many Canadians see themselves as having multiple origins and identities. This suggests that while national identity is not about to disappear, it may be increasingly less dominant in the 21st century. In light of this tension, this may be why the politics associated with diversity—as seen in the recent turn to looking at "reasonable accommodation" in Canada—has been and continues to be so vexed.

CONCLUSION

This chapter examined key terms and concepts pertaining to the politics of cultural pluralism. It surveyed different theoretical approaches to the study of nationalism, arguing that helpful insights are gleaned by attending to specific cases and using contemporary approaches that consider issues such as gender and different forms of identity. The central question raised in this chapter concerns the future of the nation-state and the salience of national identity in the contemporary era of globalization. It was suggested that there are three possibilities: national identity may be strengthened; national identity may be eroded; or new, shifting, and even hybrid forms of identity may emerge. The chapter tested these three possibilities by examining the case of Canada. The findings suggest that while national identity is not disappearing, its primacy is indeed being challenged by contemporary globalization.

Given the internal diversity of most countries around the world today, and given the fact that contemporary globalization itself may create the conditions for new and evolving forms of identity, it seems that political scientists will have much to examine in the years ahead. As well, because the already heterogeneous national populations of the world are increasingly (and perhaps differently) affected by the larger international context, policymakers will have to think creatively to enact effective public policies.

DISCUSSION QUESTIONS

1. Is nationalism primarily a negative or a positive force? Why?

2. It has been suggested that the gendered aspects of nationalism are particularly apparent when it comes to war, the transmission of culture, and dress. Can you provide examples supporting this idea? Can you think of other ways in which men and women are called upon differently or similarly in the name of "the nation"?

3. Are people attached primarily to a singular national identity, or is there another form (or are there other forms) of identity to which people are meaningfully attached?

4. Does contemporary globalization weaken or strengthen nationalism? What examples would you use to support your position?

5. Are the demands made by minority ethnic groups for policies such as affirmative action or flexible work or dress codes easier or more difficult to resolve than claims for self-determination?

WEBSITES

The Nationalism Project
http://www.nationalismproject.org
The Nationalism Project is a nationalism studies Internet resource that provides scholarly information and resources.

The World Factbook
https://www.cia.gov/library/publications/-world-factbook/
The World Factbook of the U.S. Central Intelligence Agency provides statistical information on countries and territories around the world.

The Ethnicity and Democratic Governance Project
http://www.queensu.ca/edg/index.html
The Ethnicity and Democratic Governance project was a five-year international scholarly project, based in Canada, designed to examine the comparative governance of diversity and best practices.

EUROPA
http://europa.eu
EUROPA is the official website of the European Union, and provides useful information about issues pertaining to the EU and its 28 member states.

MOST Program
http://www.unesco.org/new/en/social-and-human-sciences/themes/most-programme/about-most/
The Management Of Social Transformations (MOST) program of UNESCO supports social science research to generate policy-relevant information to further UNESCOs' goals.

FURTHER READING

Yasmeen Abu-Laban, ed., *Gendering the Nation-State: Canadian and Comparative Perspectives.* Vancouver: University of British Columbia Press, 2008.

Isabel Altamirano-Jimenz, *Indigenous Encounters with Neoliberalism: Place, Women and the Environment in Canada and Mexico.* Vancouver: University of British Columbia Press, 2013.

Keith Banting, Thomas J. Courchene, and F. Leslie Seidle, eds., *Diversity, Recognition and Shared Citizenship in Canada.* Montreal: Institute for Research on Public Policy, 2007.

Paul Bramadat and Lorne Dawson, eds., *Religious Radicalization and Securitization in Canada and Beyond.* Toronto: University of Toronto Press, 2014.

Canadian Journal of Political Science 43(2) (2010). (This special issue of the journal is devoted to "diversity and democratic politics").

Alain-G Gagnon, *The Case for Multinational Federalism: Beyond the All-Encompassing Nation.* London and New York: Routledge, 2010.

David Theo Goldberg, *The Threat of Race: Reflections on Racial Neoliberalization.* Malden, Mass.: Blackwell, 2009.

Jack Jedwab, ed., *The Multiculturalism Question: Debating Identity in 21st Century Canada.* Montreal and Kingston: School of Policy Studies, Queen's University and McGill-Queen's University Press, 2014.

Will Kymlicka, *Multicultural Odysseys: Navigating the New International Politics of Diversity.* Oxford and New York: Oxford University Press, 2007.

Tariq Modood, *Still not easy being British.* Stoke-on-Trent: Trentham Books, 2010.

Jill Vickers and Annette Isaac, *The Politics of Race: Canada, Australia and the United States*, 2nd ed. Toronto: University of Toronto Press, 2012.

Elia Zureik, David Lyon, and Yasmeen Abu-Laban, eds., *Surveillance and Control in Israel/Palestine: Population, Territory and Power.* London and New York: Routledge, 2011.

ENDNOTES

1. *MOST Newsletter* 3 (June 1995), p. 1, online at http://www.unesco.org/most/newlet3e.htm.

2. *MOST Newsletter* 1 (December 1994), p. 5, online at http://www.unesco.org/most/ newlet1e.htm.

3. UNESCO, "The Future of UNESCO's Management of Social Transformations (MOST) Programme," (June 16, 2014), online at http://www.unesco.org/new/en/social-and-human-sciences/themes/most-programle:/sv10/news/the_future_of_unescos_management_of_social_transformations_most_programme/#.VJSxrZ0AM.

4. See Benedict Anderson, *Imagined Communities: Reflections on the Origin and Spread of Nationalism*, rev. ed. (London: Verso, 1991).

5. Geoffrey York, "South Africa's 'Mother of the Nation' a Tarnished Icon," *The Globe and Mail*, November 7, 2013, online at http://www.theglobeandmail.com/news/world/south-africas-mother-of-the-nation-a-tarnished-icon/article15331345/.

6. See Elie Kedourie, *Nationalism* (London: Hutchinson, 1985).

7. Danilo Türk, "Genocide," in Joel Krieger, ed., *The Oxford Companion to Politics of the World* (Oxford: Oxford University Press, 2001), p. 316.

8. Srda Trifkovic, "Bosnian War," in Krieger, *The Oxford Companion to Politics of the World*, p. 79.

9. Ibid.

10. Elizabeth Philipose, "Ethnic Cleansing," in Lorraine Code, ed., *Encyclopedia of Feminist Theories* (London: Routledge, 2001), pp. 192–93.

11. Ibid., p. 193.

12. Allison Des Forges, "Rwandan Genocide," in Krieger, *The Oxford Companion to Politics of the World*, p. 749.

13. Michael Ignatieff, *Blood and Belonging: Journeys into the New Nationalism* (Toronto: Penguin Books, 1993).

14. Samuel Huntington, "The Clash of Civilizations," *Foreign Affairs* 72 (3) (Summer, 1993), pp. 22–49.

15. Yasmeen Abu-Laban, "Humanizing the Oriental: Edward Said and Western Scholarly Discourse," in Naseer Aruri and Muhammad A. Shuraydi, eds., *Revising Culture, Reinventing Peace: The Influence of Edward W. Said* (New York and Northampton: Interlink, 2001), pp. 85–103.

16. Samuel Huntington, *Who Are We? The Challenges to America's National Identity* (New York: Simon and Shuster, 2004).

17. Louis Menand, "Patriot Games: The New Nativism of Samuel P. Huntington," *The New Yorker*, May 17, 2004, online at http://www.newyorker.com/archive/2004/05/17/040517crbo_books?currentPage=all.

18. E. Ellis Cashmore, *Dictionary of Race and Ethnic Relations* (London: Routledge and Kegan Paul, 1984), p. 182.

19. Pereket Hablte Selassie, "Self-Determination," in Krieger, *The Oxford Companion to Politics of the World*, pp. 760–61.

20. Janine Brodie, "State Theory," in Code, *Encyclopedia of Feminist Theories*, p. 462.

21. Quoted in Ronald H. Chilcote, *Theories of Comparative Politics: The Search for a Paradigm Reconsidered* (Boulder: Westview Press, 1994), p. 98.

22. Sometimes the term "civic nationalism" is used to refer to an inclusive form of national belonging based on participation in a shared public sphere, as contrasted with "ethnic nationalism," which privileges shared ethnicity or blood ties. However, the utility of this dichotomy has been called into question on a number of grounds, including the claim that civic nationalism can serve to mask the power of the dominant ethnic group(s) in organizing public life in the first place. See Claude Couture, *Paddling with the Current: Pierre Elliott Trudeau, Étienne Parent, Liberalism and Nationalism in Canada* (Edmonton: University of Alberta Press, 1998), p. 112.

23. Anderson, *Imagined Communities*, p. 144.

24. James Clifford, "Diasporas," in Montserrat Guibernau and John Rex, eds., *The Ethnicity Reader: Nationalism, Multiculturalism and Migration* (Cambridge: Polity Press, 1997), pp. 283–90.

25. Ibid., p. 284.

26. Tomas Hylland Eriksen, "Ethnicity, Race and Nation," in Guibernau and Rex, *The Ethnicity Reader*, pp. 33–41.

27. Yasmeen Abu-Laban and Victoria Lamont, "Crossing Borders: Interdisciplinary, Immigration and the Melting Pot in the American Cultural Imaginary," *Canadian Review of American Studies* 27 (2) (1997), p. 33.

28. Robert Miles and Rudy Torres, "Does 'Race' Matter? Transatlantic Perspectives on Racism after 'Race Relations,'" in Vered Amit-Talai and Caroline Knowles, eds., *Re-situating Identities: The Politics of Race, Ethnicity and Culture* (Peterborough: Broadview Press, 1996), pp. 25–46.

29. Lucius J. Barker and Mack H. Jones, *African Americans and the American Political System* (Englewood Cliffs: Prentice Hall, 1994), pp. 30–49.

30. Tariq Modood, *Multicultural Politics: Racism, Ethnicity and Muslims in Britain* (Minneapolis: University of Minnesota Press, 2005).

31. Will Kymlicka, *Finding Our Way: Rethinking Ethnocultural Relations in Canada* (Don Mills: Oxford University Press, 1998), p. 42.

32. John Isbester, *Promises Not Kept: The Betrayal of Social Change in the Third World* (West Hartford: Kumarian Press, 1995), p. 109.

33. For an example, see Karl W. Deutsch, *Nationalism and Social Communication: An Inquiry into the Foundations of Nationality* (New York: John Wiley, 1953).

34. See Ernest Gellner, *Nations and Nationalism* (Oxford: Basil Blackwell, 1983) on these points, and see Anderson, *Imagined Communities*, regarding the significance of the printing press.

35. See Tom Nairn, *The Break-up of Britain* (London: New Left Books, 1979).

36. See especially Kedourie, *Nationalism*, p. 145.

37. Isbester, *Promises Not Kept*, p. 106.

38. Ibid., p. 102.

39. Ibid., pp. 105–48.

40. Frantz Fanon, "The Wretched of the Earth," in Omar Dahbour and Micheline R. Ishay, eds., *The Nationalism Reader* (New Jersey: Humanities Press, 1995), p. 283.

41. *Ibid.*, pp. 274–83.

42. Anthony D. Smith, *Theories of Nationalism*, 2nd ed. (London: Gerald Duckworth, 1983), p. 193.

43. Nira Yuval-Davis and Floya Anthias, *Woman-Nation-State* (Basingstoke: Macmillan, 1989).

44. Nira Yuval-Davis, "Gender and Nation," in Rick Wilford and Robert L. Miller, eds., *Women, Ethnicity and Nationalism* (London: Routledge, 1998), pp. 23–35.

45. Elizabeth Philipose, "Ethnic Cleansing," in Code, *Encyclopedia of Feminist Theories*, p. 183.

46. For a discussion of these issues, see Deniz Kandiyoti, "Identity and Its Discontents:

Women and the Nation," in Patrick Williams and Laura Chrisman, eds., *Colonial Discourse and Post-Colonial Theory: A Reader* (New York: Columbia University Press, 1994), pp. 376–91.

47. For an overview of apartheid, see the chapter by David Theo Goldberg on "Racial South Africanization," in David Theo Goldberg, *The Threat of Race: Reflections on Racial Neoliberalization* (Malden, Mass.: Blackwell, 2009), pp. 245–326.

48. See Sheila Meintjes, "Gender, Nationalism and Transformation: Difference and Commonality in South Africa's Past and Present," in Wilford and Miller, *Women, Ethnicity and Nationalism*, pp. 62–86.

49. This account of women's organizing and the placard example are adapted from Anne McClintock, *Imperial Leather: Race, Gender and Sexuality in the Colonial Context* (New York: Routledge, 1995), pp. 379–86.

50. McClintock, *Imperial Leather*, p. 384.

51. Meintjes, "Gender, Nationalism and Transformation," pp. 82–83.

52. Ibid., p. 83.

53. Ibid., p. 84.

54. See David Theo Goldberg, *The Threat of Race*, pp. 245–326.

55. David Held et al., *Global Transformations: Politics, Economics and Culture* (Stanford: Stanford University Press, 1999), pp. 425–26.

56. Ibid.

57. Ibid., p. 297.

58. Stuart Hall, "The Question of Cultural Identity," in Stuart Hall et al., eds., *Modernity: An Introduction to Modern Societies* (Cambridge: Polity Press, 1995), p. 628.

59. Ibid., pp. 596–634.

60. Québec, Commission de consultation sur les pratiques d'accommodement reliées aux diffé-rences culturelles, *Building the Future: A Time for Reconciliation Report*, 2008.

61. "Philippe Couillard Pledges Transparency, Integrity," CBCNews.ca, April 8, 2014, online at http://www.cbc.ca/news/canada/montreal/quebec-votes-2014/philippe-couillard-pledges-transparency-integrity-1.2602822.

62. Olive Patricia Dickason, *Canada's First Nations: A History of Founding Peoples from Earliest Times* (Toronto: McClelland and Stewart, 1992), pp. 63–83.

63. Yasmeen Abu-Laban and Baha Abu-Laban, "Reasonable Accommodation in a Global Village," *Policy Options* 28 (8) (September 2007), pp. 28–33.

64. For this position, see Rhoda Howard-Hassmann, "Canadian as an Ethnic Category: Implications for Multiculturalism and National Unity," *Canadian Public Policy* 25 (4) (1999), pp. 523–37. For a critique of this position, see Yasmeen Abu-Laban and Daiva Stasiulis, "Constructing 'Ethnic Canadians': The Implications for Public Policy and Inclusive Citizenship," *Canadian Public Policy* 26 (4) (December 2000), pp. 477–87.

65. Yasmeen Abu-Laban, "Reform by Stealth: The Harper Conservatives and Canadian Multiculturalism," in Jack Jedwab, ed., *The Multiculturalism Question: Debating Identity in 21st Century Canada* (Montreal and Kingston: School of Policy Studies, Queen's University and McGill-Queen's University Press, 2014), pp. 149–72.

66. Statistics Canada, National Household Survey 2011, "Immigration and Ethnocultural Diversity in Canada," (prepared by Tina Chui) [No. 99-010-X2011001], May 2013, p. 13, online at http://www12.statcan.gc.ca/nhs-enm/2011/as-sa/99-010-x/99-010-x2011001-eng.cfm#a6.

67. Lawrence Hill, "Zebra: Growing Up Black and White in Canada," in Carl E. James and Adrienne Shadd, eds., *Talking About Difference: Encounters in Culture, Language and Identity* (Toronto: Between the Lines, 1994), pp. 41–47.

68. See, for example, Parminder Bhachu, "The Multiple Landscapes of Transnational Asian Women in the Diaspora," in Vered Amit-Talai and Caroline Knowles, eds., *Re-situating Identities: The Politics of Race, Ethnicity and Culture* (Peterborough: Broadview Press, 1996), 283–303, and Ayse S. Caglar, "Hyphenated Identities and the Limits of 'Culture'," in Tariq Modood and Pnina Werbner, eds., *The Politics of Multiculturalism in the New Europe* (London: Zed Books, 1997), pp. 169–85.

5

STATES AND ECONOMIES: STUDYING POLITICAL ECONOMY IN POLITICAL SCIENCE

Rodney Haddow

donvictorio / Shutterstock.com

In 2013, almost $20 trillion (2005 U.S. dollars) was traded in goods and services around the world. With increased global economic integration, all countries are experiencing new opportunities as well as constraints on the political choices that they make, both domestically and abroad.

CHAPTER OBJECTIVES

After you have completed this chapter, you should be able to:

- explain what political economy is, and what it can contribute to the study of politics

- indicate how and why countries produce and redistribute wealth differently

- illustrate what it means for students of politics to explain something in terms of "big structures, large processes, [and] huge comparisons"

- show how the development of Canada's political economy compares with what has happened in other affluent countries

- appreciate the importance of globalization for understanding how the well-being of citizens may change in the future

INTRODUCTION

Canada and most other affluent societies are now commonly referred to as liberal democracies because each of their citizens has an equal chance to cast a vote to determine who governs them. Yet most observers would agree that these citizens do not, in the final analysis, have an equal say in how they are governed. One reason for this is the enormous disparity in wealth and income among residents of these countries. Individuals and groups that have more economic resources at their disposal can expect to influence government much more extensively than their less well-endowed fellow citizens.[1] Moreover, some interests are systematically favoured by government actions because of the position they occupy in our private sector-dominated economy. Politics is therefore intimately connected with economic realities. This relationship between politics and economics is the focus of scholarship on political economy. This chapter argues that this field of research has a great deal to offer to our understanding of political life.

More formally, **political economy** is defined here as the study of the relationship between the **state**, as the leading authoritative actor in affluent societies, and the economy, the site in these societies where wealth is produced, exchanged, and distributed. Political economy scholars usually stress how much this state–economy relationship varies among countries. The countries examined in this chapter all have capitalist or private-market economies, that is, economies in which most production takes place in the private sector, not under state ownership, and where the exchange of goods takes place in primarily private markets. Most people work for firms that are not owned by the government, or work for themselves.[2] They buy goods from retail stores that are run by non-governmental interests that hope to make a profit. Despite having this in common, these countries differ fundamentally in how they organize economic life. In some cases, the state is very active in guiding the private sector in a certain direction; it might, for instance, provide strong incentives to private firms to invest in one industry rather than another. In other cases the state shies away from this role, seeking to create a "level playing field" for all investment choices, which firms will choose among for themselves. Moreover, private economic interests coordinate with each other substantially in some cases, but not much elsewhere. And in some countries the state does a great deal to reduce the inequalities of income and wealth that result from market activities in the private sector, using the welfare state to redistribute extensively from the rich to the poor and providing extensive health and social services to all citizens. In other countries, activities of this kind are much more modest and citizens are expected, and expect, to rely on the market to provide for their well-being. Political economists study these variations, and seek to identify their causes and to ascertain what impact they have on the lives of citizens.

Political economy: The study of the relationship between the state, as the leading authoritative actor in affluent societies, and the economy, the site in these societies where wealth is produced and exchanged.

State: A modern form of organizing political life that is characterized by a population, territory, governing institutions, and a government that claims a monopoly of legitimate force; recognition by the international community of states (most often by the United Nations) may also be key.

Political economy is also distinguished by its tendency to study "big structures, large processes, [and] huge comparisons."[3] Like other scholars who study politics, political economists examine specific topics—such as the development of new bank regulations or child care programs. But the concepts they use to explain these developments usually refer to the broadest or *macro* level of a society, rather than features of only the particular field or sector (banking, child care) where they take place (an "intermediate" or *meso* approach) or of the specific individuals and organizations directly involved in events (the *micro* level). This point is explained more fully below. For reasons of length, our attention will be directed mainly to political economy as it is used in the study of particular countries—including Canada—and in comparisons between countries. The political economy of the international system, or of relations between countries, is a much-studied topic in its own right, but it is not treated here.[4] For the same reason, we concentrate on the political economy of now-rich (or developed) countries.

Political economy is not always defined in the manner indicated above. A reader must examine closely how the term is used by an author to determine which meaning is intended. This issue is addressed in the first section below, which discusses definitions of political economy that are the main alternatives to this one, indicating their strengths but also how relying on one of these would narrow our focus too much. These alternative definitions have much to say to students of politics and they overlap in important ways with the one used here. They therefore deserve our attention but must be distinguished carefully from each other

and from the definition used here if we are to fully appreciate their import. The following section then expands on the definition provided above and explains the field's origins, development, and current main features. The third and fourth sections discuss in greater detail the approaches to understanding variable relations between the state and the economy that have been proposed by comparative political economists. The chapter then looks at the political economy of Canada and asks what impact globalization is having on the political economies of developed countries.

POLITICAL ECONOMY AS A METHOD

Political economy, as defined above, is a *focus* within the study of politics—one that attends to the relationship between state and economy. The main alternative definitions instead treat it as a *method* or a *theory* that can be applied to a wide range of topics, sometimes well beyond this particular focus. One such method is called *rational choice*; a prominent alternative is *Marxian political economy*. Both of these methods are widely used in the study of politics but scholars who do so will not usually indicate explicitly that they are employing them. This must often be inferred from their general approach and the concepts they use. Once a scholar's approach is identified, it is much easier to appreciate what she or he has to offer.

To understand why these different meanings emerged, it helps to refer to some history. During the 17th and 18th centuries, many European societies witnessed the extensive development of private markets in which goods were bought and sold by profit-seeking merchants who were relatively free from control by the state or by the traditional aristocracy. For instance, a flourishing trade emerged in southern England that was based on merchants there finding a profitable market for wool on the European continent. These merchants were seeking an advantage for themselves rather than being directed by government, or being bound to do so because of a traditional obligation to a feudal lord. Such private and self-regarding activities had existed for a long time but had now gradually become the dominant form of economic activity. Ever-larger segments of society in this emerging **capitalism** consisted of people who depended on such market activities for their livelihood. Especially in England, where an industrial revolution began in the late 18th century, working people increasingly depended on earning money wages for their survival, rather than producing enough food themselves to subsist or depending on the kinds of feudal ties of long-term mutual obligation that were once common.

> **Capitalism:** An economic system in which the means of production (land, factories, technology, etc.) are privately owned and operated according to a profit motive. Decisions about production, investment, and distribution of resources are determined according to market forces (i.e., whether a profit can be made producing and marketing a product), rather than collective or community priorities. In capitalism, workers exchange their labour for wages or salary. Although it is often called the "free enterprise system," capitalism can exist even where there is little freedom, politically or socially, and where the state controls the system (i.e., in "state capitalism").

In this setting a new discipline of political economy emerged; it focused on how these market activities worked and how they might be organized so as to maximize well-being. Adam Smith's *The Wealth of Nations*, published in 1776, was the most prominent contribution to this new study. Smith's book is often treated as the first comprehensive effort to understand the newly emergent capitalism and to advocate on its behalf. While focusing on wealth, these early political economists nevertheless paid close attention to how wealth-creation related to the activities of the state, and how it affected and depended upon different groups and classes in society. They also examined these questions historically, as they held that what happens today can only be understood in terms of what came before. This early political economy therefore included much of what we would now call the social sciences: it touched upon what is currently included in economics, political science, sociology, and history.[5] During the late 19th and 20th centuries, however, the study of wealth-creation became narrower and more technical. The modern discipline of economics emerged, which sought to understand markets in more abstract terms, with extensive resort to higher mathematics and to

formal models, and without nearly as much attention to history and to the market's political, social, and historical contexts. The separate and equally-specialized disciplines of sociology and political science also emerged at this time. In Canada, this process of specialization unfolded more slowly, but it happened here too.[6] For example, at the University of Toronto, the study of economics, politics, and society remained united within a Political Economy Department until well after the Second World War. When that department was finally abolished in 1982, its remaining Economics and Political Science components were reconstituted as separate units.

Today's **rational choice** approach to political economy essentially takes the method of modern economics, rather than its broader 18th and 19th century antecedents, and applies it to both economic and non-economic phenomena, including politics. Modern mainstream economists stress the extent to which individuals are motivated by a desire to maximize their *utility*, calculated mostly in terms of wealth and income, when they engage in market activities. A market works well, they argue, if it is structured in such a way as to offer individuals ample opportunities to pursue this goal while producing something of value to (equally utility-maximizing) consumers. Rational choice scholars extend the economist's idea of utility to include power, status, and so forth, as well as wealth. The institutions they examine may lie well outside of what we normally call politics; for instance, rational choice has been used to explain why people marry and form families. But we will concentrate here on its application to **government**. A pioneering study of this kind explained why the major political parties in countries often differ only modestly in their proposals. It argued that politicians' utility is maximized by winning elections. This leads all parties to move their proposals closer to those of their main opponents in order to capture the same *marginal voter*, the hypothetical single voter in the middle of the political spectrum whose support can make the difference between winning and losing an election.[7] The alleged tendency of government bureaucracies to grow over time has been explained by referring to bureaucrats' desire to maximize their utility in the form of income and organizational power.[8] The success of an interest group has been accounted for in terms of its ability to ensure that individuals who might benefit (derive utility) from the group's activities help finance it as a condition for receiving these benefits.[9]

> **Rational choice:** An approach to political economy, and the study of politics more generally, that derives from economics, and in which social processes, including politics, are said to reflect the outcome of interaction among individuals and organizations that each seek to maximize their own self-interest or utility, which may include power and status as well as wealth and income.

> **Government:** The set of institutions and practices that make and enforce collective public decisions for a society.

Karl Marx's 19th century contributions to political economy, most prominently in the first volume of his *Capital* (1867), offer the main method-based alternative to rational choice. Here the focus is on social **classes** and their interests and resources. According to **Marxian political economy**, society is made up of different classes, which consist of persons who share a common relationship to the economic property system or *means of production.* In a capitalist economy, the dominant social class is the capitalist one, which consists of those who own and control substantial amounts of productive property (in manufacturing, transportation, banking, and so forth). The working class consists of those who do not have access to property of this kind, and who must sell their labour to capitalists to earn a living. The interests of these classes are opposed. In the long term, the main non-economic institutions of society can be expected to favour the interests of capitalists, and to preclude the emergence of a

non-capitalist alternative that would be in the interest of workers. But these institutions nevertheless can also embody some concessions to workers' interests, so as to legitimate the capitalist system as a whole. Thus, Marxian political economy was used in the 1970s to account for the large welfare states that had emerged by then: these were depicted as a necessary concession to the working class in view of its significant (though still subordinate) power at that time.[10]

> **Class:** A concept that describes hierarchical groupings within societies based on social and economic factors such as income, occupation, education, and status.

> **Marxian political economy:** An approach to political economy that stresses the importance of social classes and class conflict, and that identifies the interests of the dominant class, the capitalist one under capitalism, as the main influence on social institutions, including the state.

How popular is each of these currents today? Rational choice is among the most prominent approaches to the study of political science, especially in the United States, where it is often treated as synonymous with political economy.[11] It has great appeal to scholars and students who are attracted to the idea that the self-regarding behaviour of individuals, however much these might be aggregated by organizations and institutions, is the foundation of political life. The standing of rational choice is somewhat lower elsewhere, particularly in Canada, where its adherents contribute a smaller body of scholarship. The Marxian

THINK AND DISCUSS

Some critics believe that rational choice scholars are wrong to explain behaviour in terms of self-interest. They argue that cultural norms guide behaviour by telling people what actions are appropriate in particular situations. For instance, people may avoid taking actions that are in their self-interest (make them wealthier, or increase their individual happiness in some other way) because they live in a society that defines those actions as inappropriate or morally wrong. It is on this basis that many people refuse to steal from others or to cheat on an exam, even if there is no chance of being caught. Do you agree that evidence of this kind of behaviour calls into question the value of rational choice theories?

approach, on the other hand, was important during the 1970s but has since declined to a quite marginal presence in American political science. It remains more significant in Europe.[12] It is often employed by scholars who adopt a critical view of contemporary capitalism, and who are deeply skeptical of its ability to meet fundamental human needs, now or in the future. While Marxian scholarship is also less prominent in both Canada and the study of Canadian politics than it was a couple of decades ago, it nevertheless remains a more significant current here than in the United States.

POLITICAL ECONOMY AS A FIELD OF STUDY

If we adopt one of the above definitions of political economy, then we exclude valuable research contributed by practitioners of the other. We also ignore what might be termed the "broad middle" of contemporary political economy. Most self-described political economists rely primarily on neither rational choice nor Marxism, though they may make use of them. They instead adhere to the definition given at the beginning of this chapter: they study the relationship between state and economy. The questions they address are among the most important treated in political science: What patterns of state–economy relationship, and of connection among organizations and actors within the economy, have been conducive to economic prosperity? Why is there persistent variety of such patterns? German, American, and Japanese affluence, for example, have quite different origins and remain distinct. What are the implications, moreover, of these different state–economic contexts of growth for the level of inequality and poverty in a country? It seems clear, in fact, that some patterns consistently are associated with higher inequality and poverty than others. These are much higher in the U.S., for instance, than in Sweden. What are the implications of these differences for the economic and social situation of women? Does inequality- and poverty-reduction go further in countries with particular kinds of welfare states than in others? What are the causes of these variations?

As these questions indicate, much contemporary political economy seeks to return to the broader approaches that typified early political economy; it brings together political, economic, and social questions that the various social sciences now treat separately, and it often examines them historically. While many political economists work in political science departments, therefore, others are sociologists, and some are management or industrial relations scholars or institutional economists. As the above queries also suggest, contemporary political economy typically is *comparative*: it identifies multiple cases (usually countries) with similar or different state–economy patterns, and enquires about the origins and consequences of these similarities and differences. Again, one cannot emphasize too much the focus of comparative political economists on variety. For instance, the pattern of economic growth in the United Kingdom or the United States has typically not relied on extensive planning and intervention by the state. But we know that such a **laissez-faire** approach is not a prerequisite for prosperity because other now-affluent economies, such as Japan and France, have at times relied heavily on such intervention. Political economists will then ask: What characteristics do the Anglo-Saxon (English-speaking) cases have in common, replaced by alternative features in Japan and France, that might explain why the former succeeded with a laissez-faire approach? Conversely, what features of the Japanese and French state–economy settings allowed them to benefit from intervention? The approach to explanation is not primarily the application of a particular methodological insight but the use of comparisons between appropriately-selected and carefully-observed cases.

> **Laissez-faire:** A French phrase meaning literally "let do"; this economic theory provides the intellectual foundation for the system of free-market capitalism. Following the principles of Adam Smith, proponents of laissez-faire believe that the economy works best when there is no government intervention. Thus, the theory rejects state ownership or control, advocates a free market, values individualism, and promotes free trade.

As noted earlier, these comparisons usually are made at the *macro* level of the countries studied, rather than the more narrowly-defined *meso* level of the sector or the *micro* level flow of day-to-day events. For example, the forces that shape labour market training policies could be studied in different ways. At the least aggregated or *micro* level, one might examine the short-term factors that led to a specific program change, such as a new measure to help unemployed workers acquire the skills they need to find a new job. The beliefs and actions of individuals who can make these changes would be the focus of attention: What did the minister of education and training think? What were the opinions of her senior bureaucrats? Did these decision-makers have career or social ties with outside experts or interested "stakeholders" in the training system who favoured the changes? Did they simply find some of these non-governmental representatives more congenial personally? Scholarly studies often refer to factors of this kind, but primary reliance on these individual-level factors is more common in writing by journalists.[13]

A *meso* or intermediate level account looks for more enduring features of the context in which this new training initiative was discussed. But these features would be sought within the particular sector of policy-making that deals with training.[14] In a Canadian province, such a study might ask: Does the ministry of education and training habitually have the autonomy from other ministries, the budget, and the expertise to pursue innovations? To what extent do non-governmental organizations with a stake in the training sector, such as the community colleges and their unionized employees, have an important policy role and the resources to defend their interests? In this case, do these interests (such as maximizing college budgets and protecting teachers' careers and salaries) favour or oppose reform? Is the federal government an important actor in this field, and does it typically encourage independent provincial initiatives? Are there non-governmental think-tanks with expertise and prestige in the training sector? Are the proposed reforms consistent with established views in these organizations?

Political economy scholarship may include these kinds of micro- and meso-level data. But its distinctive focus is at the *macro* level, on long-term and slowly-changing features of the countries being studied as a whole, features that are relevant to understanding changes across many policy sectors as well as the interconnection between these different domains. For instance, one recent comparative study found that where union movements are strong (because many workers belong to them) and are linked to strong left-wing parties, retraining programs are pursued aggressively.[15] Retraining is seen by these organizations to be in workers' interests, providing them with access to an alternative livelihood if they lose their jobs. By contrast, where unions are weaker and Catholic institutions are strong (they have a major presence in many European countries), the focus of policy has been in entirely different sectors: using regulations to protect now-employed workers from lay-offs and maintaining expensive unemployment insurance programs that are not closely linked to training. Where neither strong union movements nor strong Catholic traditions exist, policy instead reflects the views of business and free market-oriented political parties. In this case, there is a preference for program cuts. In each of these scenarios, outcomes reflect broad features of a country's setting: the overall strength of unions, business, religious institutions, and different kinds of political parties are factors whose importance goes well beyond any one policy sector. Moreover, developments in different sectors are linked: strong labour movements prefer retraining workers, so they do not foster policy developments in other sectors, such as job protection or even some kinds of unemployment insurance. As this example illustrates, political economy can provide more integrated and comprehensive explanations of political phenomena than is possible with less encompassing alternatives. Its focus on "big structures, large processes, [and] huge comparisons" can pay off.

STRONG AND WEAK STATES; CORPORATISM VS. PLURALISM

This section and the next discuss the main currents in contemporary political economy internationally. In this section, I discuss the main building-block ideas developed during the 1970s and 1980s for understanding different political economies. The next section deals with refinements that have been introduced in recent years. After that, the chapter turns to a discussion of Canada.

Between the end of the Second World War and the 1970s, social scientists mostly assumed that economic development occurred similarly in different countries. Moreover, underdeveloped countries in Africa, Asia, and Latin America could achieve affluence, these social scientists argued, if they modernized in the same way as now-rich European and North American countries did during the 19th and early 20th centuries. For example, in his highly influential book, W.W. Rostow detailed the common *stages of economic growth* that he claimed countries had gone through, or would experience, en route to prosperity.[16] Mainstream theory in economics, similarly, contended that countries would converge on common "equilibrium" institutions, as they moved toward the most efficient way of organizing their economies.[17]

As has been stressed already in this chapter, comparative political economy scholarship generally rejects this view. Political economists do not agree on how much capitalist countries differ, or on whether these differences will persist in the future. But they concur in saying that variation remains very important. Starting in the 1970s, two bodies of scholarship emerged to challenge the post-war consensus. One focused on the fact that the state was more active in promoting industrialization in some now-affluent countries than it had been in others, and argued that current arrangements still reflect these differences. A comparison of England and France can illustrate this point. Badie and Birnbaum argue that the transition to a market economy occurred relatively smoothly and without government guidance in England during the 16th and 17th centuries, with the result that the country retained a **weak state**: it did not require, or develop, a capacity to guide the economy.[18] In France, by contrast, the transition to market capitalism lagged behind England and encountered obstacles from within French society that only state intervention could overcome; as a result, France acquired a *strong state* able and willing to intervene in the economy. Bertrand Badie and Pierre Birnbaum argue that the economic roles of the British and French states continue to diverge between these weak and strong models. More recent research often agrees that this is the case, but stresses that strong states in Europe are not as interventionist as they used to be. During the two decades after the Second World War, for instance, France's state provided very firm guidance to the private sector, pushing it to invest in specific industries, to develop certain technologies, and so forth. Nowadays, however, the state is likely to use a much lighter approach, negotiating with companies about their future plans, and listening carefully to feedback that it receives from them.[19] In East Asia, strong state guidance remains firmer, though there too it is more relaxed than it was a few decades ago.

> **Weak state:** The form of state that exists in countries where it did not play an important role in fostering the transition to a market and industrial economy, and in which it continues to play a modest role in guiding overall economic development. This does not mean that the institutions of government work badly or have "failed" in such states; but they do not intervene extensively and systematically.

The second stream of research that crystallized in the 1970s distinguished two kinds of relationships *among* the major interests in the economy, rather than *between* the economy and the state. In many Northern European countries the economy depends on close cooperation among organizations that speak for big business and other producer interests (such as farmers), on the one hand, and unionized workers, on the other.[20] In these corporatist countries, business, labour union, and other economic interests are highly organized: they have well-staffed national organizations and they have a certain amount of power over lower-level business and labour groups within particular firms, regions, or economic sectors. Labour unions are much stronger in most of these countries, representing a quite high percentage of all workers. Much government policy concerning the economy and social programs is formulated after extensive discussions among the leaders of these organizations, who acquire a habit of compromising with each other. By contrast, other countries, in the English-speaking world but also in Southern Europe, are termed *pluralist*. In these nations, business and labour are not nearly as well organized above the level of individual companies. Labour unions typically are weaker than in corporatist countries, which is one reason why business does not bother to develop strong national organizations to respond to them. In pluralist countries, business is more likely to get what it wants without having to organize extensively. The different interests, and even individual firms, tend to see each other as rivals in a competitive struggle for higher profits and wages. Government policy is made without the formal involvement, let alone cooperation, of the major economic interests.

The two approaches described above can be combined to provide an overall account of how countries that share a market economy nevertheless organize

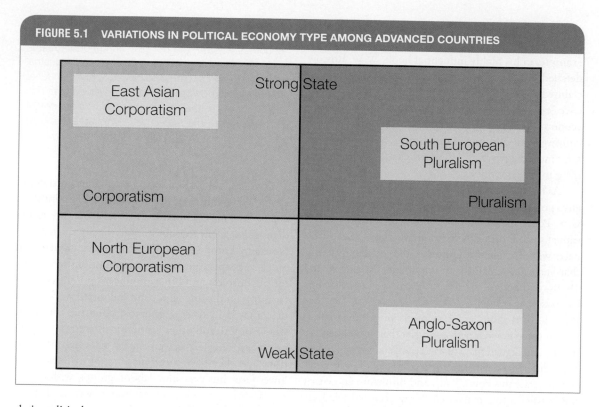

FIGURE 5.1   VARIATIONS IN POLITICAL ECONOMY TYPE AMONG ADVANCED COUNTRIES

their political economies very differently. Figure 5.1 illustrates how this can be done. On the north–south (up-and-down) axis it distinguishes strong from weak states. At the bottom are those countries where the state mostly follows a laissez-faire path, allowing the private sector to pursue its own preferences. At the top are countries where the state seeks to guide firms to an important extent, even if not as much as it would have a few decades ago. The east–west axis divides countries between corporatist (on the left side of the figure) and pluralist (on the right side). In the former, business and labour are well-organized, unions are generally stronger, and there is significant policy coordination among these actors. These features are much less present in pluralist cases. The richer countries of the world can be distinguished into four broad clusters, based on these distinctions. We should keep in mind, however, that these distinctions are quite general, and simplify what is, in fact, a very complex pattern of variation among the political economies of rich countries. Anglo-Saxon countries are in the lower right-hand corner of the figure, signifying that they combine a laissez-faire (weak state) approach to the economy with pluralism. Southern European nations also have weak business and labour organizations, and are therefore pluralist, but combine this with a state that is stronger than in Anglo-Saxon countries (though not as strong as it once was). On the left side of the diagram, Northern European countries combine very highly developed **corporatism** with states that are below-average in their degree of intervention (strength). Near the upper-left corner, finally, are richer East Asian countries, such as Japan, South Korea, and Taiwan, where the state remains quite strong, and where there is also a considerable amount of corporatism, but in a setting where business is much stronger, relative to organized labour, than in Northern Europe. Table 5.1 identifies the 10 most prominent examples of corporatist and pluralist countries today, based on political scientist Alan Siaroff's classification; it also sub-divides these countries into two categories with different degrees of state strength.

Corporatism: A political economy in which formal bargaining and compromises among leading societal interests, above all business and labour, are very important for social and economic outcomes.

TABLE 5.1 CORPORATIST AND PLURALIST POLITICAL ECONOMIES

Corporatist Countries	Pluralist Countries
Northern European Variant: (with weaker state)	Anglo-Saxon Variant: (with weak state)
Austria	United States
Norway	Canada
Sweden	United Kingdom
Netherlands	Australia
Denmark	Ireland
Germany	Southern European Variant: (with stronger state)
Switzerland	France
Finland	Greece
Belgium	Italy
East Asian Variant: (with strong state)	Spain
Japan	Portugal

Source: Adapted from Alan Siaroff, "Corporatism in 24 Industrial Democracies: Meaning and Measurement," *European Journal of Political Research*, vol. 36, no. 2 (1999), p. 198. Reprinted by permission of John Wiley and Sons.[21]

Table 5.2 shows how much the strength of labour unions varies between corporatist and pluralist countries today, indicating that these two types of market economy remain very different from each other, just as the original writers found them to be in the 1970s and 1980s. On average a much larger proportion of workers belong to a labour union in Northern European corporatist countries (43.3 percent) than in pluralist ones (22.6 percent in Anglo-Saxon countries and 20.8 percent in Southern Europe). The one East Asian case in the table (Japan) has a quite low unionization level, consistent with its distinctive variant of corporatism.

THE NEW GENERATION OF COMPARATIVE POLITICAL ECONOMY

Contemporary comparative political economy has incorporated the concepts discussed above into new frameworks to deal with recent trends, including the globalization discussed later in this chapter. The leading two of these are treated here.

One is called **Varieties of Capitalism (VoC)**. It again starts with a distinction between two models,

Coordinated Market Economies (CMEs) and *Liberal Market Economies* (LMEs). These will be called *Coordinated* and *Liberal* for short. They differ in terms of how much individual firms collaborate with other economic actors. In Coordinated countries, the success of firms depends on having long-term relations with other firms to develop new products and technologies, with financial institutions to obtain financing for new projects, and with their workers regarding skills. Firms in Liberal countries instead pursue a firm-centred strategy where competition and responding to short-term price signals are the norm instead of cooperation.[22]

> **Varieties of Capitalism (VoC):** The foremost contemporary political economy approach to developed countries. These are divided between Coordinated Market Economies (CMEs), where firms rely on coordination with other actors, and Liberal Market Economies (LMEs), where they do not.

VoC divides rich countries into categories that strongly overlap with those treated above. We can therefore use the categories set forth in Figure 5.1 to distinguish the political economy types discussed by this new research. Thus, the Coordinated category

TABLE 5.2	UNIONIZATION LEVELS IN ADVANCED POLITICAL ECONOMIES			
Corporatist Countries	%	Pluralist Countries	%
Northern European: (weaker state)		**Anglo-Saxon: (weak state)**	
Austria	28	United States	11
Norway	55	Canada	27
Sweden	68	United Kingdom	26
Netherlands	18	Australia	18
Denmark	68	Ireland	31
Germany	18	**Southern European: (stronger state)**	
Switzerland	16	France	8
Finland	69	Greece	25
Belgium	50	Italy	36
East Asian: (strong state)		Spain	16
Japan	18	Portugal	19
Average for Northern European Variant	43.3	*Average for Anglo-Saxon Variant*	22.6
		Average for Southern European Variant	20.8

Source: Based on data from OECD, Trade Union density in OECD.StatExtracts http://stats.oecd.org/, accessed on July 28, 2014.

includes Northern European countries that formed the main body of *corporatist* cases in the earlier research. The East Asian countries are a different variant of this category, in which the state plays an important role in facilitating coordination. Anglo-Saxon *pluralist* countries fit into the Liberal category. The Southern European pluralist countries form a mixed cluster, characterized by limited private sector coordination but an active state.

VoC has been used to explain persistent differences between countries of the Coordinated and Liberal types during the 21st century. Three of these are discussed here. First, most Coordinated economies, including Germany and Japan, are particularly successful in manufacturing sophisticated products, including high-end automobiles and heavy machinery. Liberal economies like the U.S. and the U.K. are much better at advanced services, including finance and information technology. Why? VoC scholars point out that these specializations are suited to what each type does well:[23] manufacturing benefits from ongoing and

step-by-step improvements in products. The reliance of Coordinated economy firms on constant collaboration facilitates such incremental progressions. In contrast, high-end services tend to improve intermittently, by means of sudden and radical innovations. Introducing these is easier in Liberal settings, where firms are not encumbered by commitments to each other and to their workers, and where sudden changes therefore face fewer obstacles. Governments play an important role in perpetuating these very different specializations. In Coordinated countries, the state encourages firms to cooperate on research and discourages foreign takeovers of domestic firms that would disrupt existing collaboration. In Liberal countries, in contrast, governments promote competition among firms to maximize efficiencies, and use anti-trust laws to impede them from colluding with each other.

Second, education and training systems also differ substantially. Coordinated economies in Central and Northern Europe have extensive vocational apprenticeship schemes, which offer a route to well-paying employment for many young people. Liberal economies offer far fewer such options but instead provide access to a liberal arts post-secondary education to a larger share of their populations. What explains this variation? Coordinated economies require a large supply of technically-skilled workers for their manufacturing sectors.[24] These sectors' high productivity also means that employers can afford to pay high wages and offer considerable job security to workers in exchange for their willingness to commit considerable time and effort to acquiring needed skills. The flexibility that is prized in Liberal economies, in contrast, means that workers must be able to adjust to very different requirements from one task or job to the next. A liberal arts education is more likely to cultivate this kind of adaptability. Here too, the state plays a key role in perpetuating differences, by overseeing and partly financing apprenticeships in Coordinative countries and by generously funding university education in Liberal ones.

Third, Liberal countries often respond to a recession, in which the economy shrinks and unemployment rises, with stimulus policies. As advocated by John Maynard Keynes, this requires the government to run a deficit (allow spending to exceed revenues); the central bank (the Bank of Canada, for instance) also must keep interest rates low. These policies encourage consumers to borrow, and firms to invest and produce more goods. This creates jobs and growth, and may pull the economy out of the recession. Once this is done, Keynesians stipulate that the deficits must be replaced by surpluses, and interest rates rise, in order to prevent excessive inflation. In Coordinated economies, on the other hand, governments are reluctant to use this Keynesian strategy. They often prefer to keep deficits low, and interest rates higher, even in a recession. Since the financial crisis of 2008, this approach has been closely identified with Germany, the dominant European economy. Why? Many media commentators argue implausibly that it is because Germans are still afraid of inflation due to the extreme levels they experienced during the 1920s, a time that no living German can possibly remember. VoC scholars instead point out that Keynesian policies have the potential to upset the equilibrium between business and organized labour in a country that needs them to collaborate.[25]

This need means that unions can effectively "hold the economy to ransom" by refusing to cooperate. They may respond to Keynesian policies by raising their wage demands substantially, worried that future inflation will eat away their value. If unions are able to impose this goal on employers, the price of German goods will rise, even before the recession has ended, making these goods less competitive abroad. In contrast, unions are much weaker in Liberal countries, and their cooperation is not as likely to be solicited or required. Governments in Liberal countries can stimulate the economy without worrying as much that it will lead to rising wages and excessive inflation even before the recession has ended.

The second leading current approach to comparative political economy is Gøsta Esping-Andersen's framework for studying social policy.[26] He argues that advanced capitalist countries continue to have very different social security systems (or **welfare state regimes**). The main factor explaining these persistent variations is the strength of organizations that represent workers, and how effective they were in forming alliances with other interests when the welfare state was first developed in the late 19th and 20th centuries. In particular, social democratic (left-of-centre) political parties typically support larger **welfare states** that spend more money, redistribute more from the rich to the poor, and reduce poverty substantially. Their main opponents are pro-business parties that usually oppose these goals, or Christian democratic parties, which are strong in many European countries. While favouring larger welfare states than pro-business parties, Christian democrats accept more inequality than do social democrats. Consistent with the Catholic social teachings that heavily influence them, Christian democratic parties see an important role for government to pursue collective goals on behalf of society but also accept social hierarchy as inevitable and perhaps desirable.

Welfare state regimes: The welfare states of affluent, capitalist countries are said to come in three variants—social democratic, Christian democratic, and liberal (Anglo-Saxon)—which originated through different political party and social coalitions. These regimes are associated with different levels of poverty and inequality.

Welfare state: A concept that stresses the role of government as a provider and protector of individual security and well-being through the implementation of interventionist economic policies and social programs. This positive role for government stands in contrast to the minimalist government (or "nightwatchman state") that has as its only function the protection of personal property and individual security. The welfare state is regarded as having a positive role in promoting human welfare and in shielding the individual against the economic and social consequences of unemployment, poverty, sickness, old age, disability, and so on.

As Table 5.3 indicates, the strength of social democratic parties differs substantially across countries. In particular, they have been in power at the national level much more in the Northern European corporatist group of countries than in either variant of pluralist countries, on average, though there is much variation within each category, especially the Anglo-Saxon group. In the Northern European corporatist countries, social democrats governed, on average, for 30 of the 66 years between 1946 and 2011; in Anglo-Saxon and Southern European countries, in contrast, they averaged 12 and 17.6 years in power, respectively.

Esping-Andersen did not find that welfare states were always larger, and poverty lower, in countries where social democrats were often in power. Equally importantly, social democrats may have formed strategic alliances with other parties, for instance those representing small farmers or white collar workers, when the welfare state was developing. If they did this, as was typically the case in the Nordic countries (Sweden, Norway, Finland, Denmark, and Iceland), then they exercised an influence that was even greater

TABLE 5.3   THE VARIABLE STRENGTH OF SOCIAL DEMOCRATIC AND SOCIALIST PARTIES IN ADVANCED POLITICAL ECONOMIES

Corporatist Countries	Years	Pluralist Countries	Years
Northern European: (weaker state)		**Anglo-Saxon: (weak state)**	
Austria	36	United States	0
Norway	47	Canada	0
Sweden	51	United Kingdom	30
Netherlands	16	Australia	24
Denmark	33	Ireland	6
Germany	21	**Southern European: (stronger state)**	
Switzerland	16	France	18
Finland	27	Greece	20
Belgium	23	Italy	11
East Asian: (strong state)		Spain	21
Japan	2	Portugal	18
Average for Northern European Variant	*30.0*	*Average for Anglo-Saxon Variant*	*12.0*
		Average for Southern European Variant	*17.6*

Cumulative years of "left" party government, 1946–2011.

Source: David Brady, Evelyne Huber, and John D. Stephens, Comparative Welfare States Data Set, University of North Carolina and WZB, Berlin Social Science Center, 2014.

than their own electoral support would have justified. This resulted in very well-funded welfare states that also reduced inequality and poverty substantially. In English-speaking countries, on the other hand, social democratic parties have either been very weak at the national level (the United States and Canada) or failed to form strong alliances with parties representing other groups in society. The latter was true, for instance, of the British and Australian Labour Parties. Both have governed their countries for over 20 of the 66 post-war years but never obtained the support of a large share of middle class voters. They were therefore unable to push through more expensive and poverty-reducing programs. A third kind of welfare state developed in many Continental European welfare states where Christian democratic parties governed most of the time after the Second World War. Here, social spending usually is not much lower than in the Nordic countries. But because Christian democrats are less interested than social democrats in promoting equality, these welfare states do not reduce poverty as much as the Scandinavian ones. Nevertheless, even the Christian democratic cases are not all the same: social democrats have tended to be stronger in Northern than in Southern Europe, so that welfare states are more egalitarian in the former than in the latter.

These patterns are illustrated in Tables 5.4 and 5.5. First, Table 5.4 indicates that when it comes to spending money on social programs, the main dividing line is between the Anglo-Saxon countries on the one hand, and all European countries on the other. The Anglo-Saxon countries, whose welfare states disproportionately reflect the influence of business-oriented parties that oppose welfare state expansion, spend on average 20.8 percent of their Gross Domestic Product (GDP) on social security. In the Northern and Southern European countries, spending is much higher, respectively 26.9 percent

TABLE 5.4   VARIATIONS IN THE SIZE OF WELFARE STATES, 2013

Corporatist Countries	%	Pluralist Countries	%
Northern European: (weaker state)		**Anglo-Saxon: (weak state)**	
Austria	28	United States	20
Norway	23	Canada	18
Sweden	29	United Kingdom	24
Netherlands	24	Australia	20
Denmark	31	Ireland	22
Germany	26	**Southern European: (stronger state)**	
Switzerland	19	France	33
Finland	31	Greece	22
Belgium	31	Italy	28
East Asian: (strong state)		Spain	27
Japan	22	Portugal	26
Average for Northern European Variant	*26.9*	*Average for Anglo-Saxon Variant*	*20.8*
		Average for Southern European Variant	*27.2*

Total social security expenditures as a % of Gross Domestic Product (GDP).

Source: Based on data from OECD, Social Expenditure - Aggregated data in OECD.StatExtracts http://stats.oecd.org/, accessed on July 28, 2014.

TABLE 5.5 POVERTY IN ADVANCED POLITICAL ECONOMIES			
Corporatist Countries	**%**	**Pluralist Countries**	**%**
Northern European: (weaker state)		**Anglo-Saxon: (weak state)**	
Austria (CD)	7	United States	18
Norway (SD)	7	Canada	13
Sweden (SD)	6	United Kingdom	15
Netherlands (CD)	5	Australia	12
Denmark (SD)	6	Ireland	9
Germany (CD)	10	**Southern European: (stronger state)**	
Switzerland (CD)	8	France	8
Finland (SD)	7	Greece	14
Belgium (CD)	8	Italy	12
East Asian: (strong state)		Spain	15
Japan	11	Portugal	N.A.
Average for Northern European Variant	*7.1*	*Average for Anglo-Saxon Variant*	*13.4*
		Average for Southern European Variant	*12.3*

Source: LIS Inequality and Poverty Key Figures, http://www.lisdatacenter.org (July 29, 2014). Luxembourg: LIS.

and 27.2 percent of GDP. The countries in these categories formed welfares states either under social democratic (Nordic countries) or Christian democratic (all the others) dominance. Either way, these welfare states are relatively expensive.

To distinguish between the Northern and Southern European cases, we need only turn to Table 5.5. As expected, poverty levels are highest in the Anglo-Saxon countries, with their small welfare states; poverty averages 13.4 percent for this group of countries. Despite their high spending, however, the Christian democratic welfare states of Southern Europe, formed under weak social democratic influence, also have a relatively high average rate of poverty, at 12.3 percent (though France's level is quite a bit lower). The Northern European countries, either social democratic or formed by Christian democrats in countries where centre-left parties and labour unions nevertheless were generally much stronger than in Southern Europe, have a much lower average level of poverty, 7.1 percent. The social democratic

cases in Table 5.5 (marked with an SD) average 6.5 percent, while the Northern European Christian democratic countries (marked with a CD) have an average poverty level of 7.6 percent. If we look at statistics on overall inequality (not reproduced here), rather than poverty, we see more of a distinction between the social democratic cases and the Northern European Christian democratic ones, with inequality being significantly lower in the Nordic countries. Predictably, inequality is higher in Southern Europe than in either the Nordic or Northern European Christian democratic countries, and highest of all in the Anglo-Saxon countries.[27]

Welfare regimes also differ in the extent to which they offer equal opportunities to women, the focus of a growing body of research.[28] Social democratic welfare states include an extensive social service administration that offers many employment opportunities to women. As Table 5.6 indicates, a very high percentage of women are employed in these countries—on average, 71.3 percent of women between 15 and 64 in 2013.

TABLE 5.6 EMPLOYMENT RATE FOR WOMEN IN ADVANCED POLITICAL ECONOMIES, 2013			
Corporatist Countries	**%**	**Pluralist Countries**	**%**
Northern European: (weaker state)		**Anglo-Saxon:** (weak state)	
Austria (CD)	68 (+6)	United States	62 (-6)
Norway (SD)	74 (—)	Canada	70 (+5)
Sweden (SD)	73 (+1)	United Kingdom	66 (+1)
Netherlands (CD)	70 (+6)	Australia	66 (+6)
Denmark (SD)	70 (-1)	Ireland	56 (+2)
Germany (CD)	69 (+9)	**Southern European: (stronger state)**	
Switzerland (CD)	74 (+4)	France	60 (+2)
Finland (SD)	68 (+5)	Greece	40 (-1)
Belgium (CD)	57 (+7)	Italy	47 (+9)
East Asian: (strong state)		Spain	50 (+11)
Japan	63 (+6)	Portugal	58 (-1)
Average for Northern European Variant	*69.2 (+3.9)*	*Average for Anglo-Saxon Variant*	*64 (+1.6)*
		Average for Southern European Variant	*51 (+4)*

Source: Based on data from OECD, LFS by sex and age - indicators in OECD.StatExtracts http://stats.oecd.org/, accessed on July 28, 2014.

Female employment is lower in Liberal welfare states—64.0 percent in that year. Until the 1990s it nevertheless was much higher in these countries than in most Christian democratic ones because of the large supply of private sector service jobs in Liberal countries, and because their free-market policies made it comparatively easy for women to seek employment. Most Christian democratic welfare states lagged far behind until the 1990s. They often actively encouraged women to remain at home to raise children and to rely for support on a male bread-winner. Female employment was also stymied by the prevalence of male-dominated manufacturing jobs. But most Northern European Christian democratic countries subsequently tried to remove barriers to female employment; it now averages 67.6 percent in these welfare states, having increased by an average of 6.8 percent since around 1999. In contrast, barriers to female employment remain substantial in many Mediterranean Christian democratic countries, where it averaged 51 percent in 2013, although here too it is rising.

To what extent do the more expensive welfare states in non-English speaking countries hamper economic growth? Would their economies grow faster if, as media commenters often suggest, they cut social spending and allowed poverty to rise? In fact, it is not true that larger welfare states necessarily result in lower economic growth.[29] Growth since the 1980s has been about as strong, on average, in the costly social democratic Nordic countries as in the much cheaper and less generous liberal regimes of the Anglo-Saxon world. Growth is generally lower, however, in the Southern European countries which have expensive welfares states that nevertheless do not redistribute very extensively. In recent years, financial crises in Portugal, Greece, Spain, France, and Italy have precipitated significant reforms and heated debates in these countries. But the Nordic cases show that, contrary to much press coverage, it is not the cost and overall generosity of a welfare state that creates a major problem for economic growth.[30] An expensive welfare state will not undermine economic prosperity if it is properly structured. Well-designed comprehensive social programs may even enhance the economy.[31]

WHAT ABOUT CANADA?

How does Canada fit into these comparative typologies? Most scholars consider that Canada belongs to the Anglo-Saxon (LME or Liberal) category of the VoC typology and that the country has a typically Anglo-Saxon, relatively-small welfare state. The data in the tables discussed above generally support this view. Yet observers also qualify this characterization, noting that some features of the Canadian case depart in important ways from what one would expect in an Anglo-Saxon setting. These unusual features of Canada's political economy have drawn the attention of a distinctive scholarly tradition. Its formative figure was Harold Innis, who argued during the 1940s and 1950s that Canada's colonial dependency upon France and then the United Kingdom caused its economy to develop along quite different lines than did the United States.[32] The **staples thesis** argues that rather than moving from raw material production to manufacturing and then to services, Canada remained locked in a *staples trap*, as a result of which its exports continued to be dominated by raw materials. These were what the European "mother countries" wanted from Canada, while manufacturing was discouraged. Canada has long since become a politically sovereign country but, for Innisians, remains locked into this pattern of exporting raw materials and importing higher value added goods and services from a dominant external economy. By the mid-20th century, the latter role had passed from the U.K. to the United States. Data on Canada's pattern of exports does, in fact, show that the country is still by a wide margin a net exporter of raw materials, such as energy, minerals, and lumber, and that it also remains a net importer of manufactured goods.

Staples thesis: An interpretation of Canadian economic development that holds that, unlike most other now-affluent countries, the production of raw materials for export markets has remained central for the Canadian economy. It has not been replaced by a focus on manufactured goods and then services.

A number of important departures from the Anglo-Saxon norm of a laissez-faire, non-interventionist state are associated with this staples pattern in Canada's history. The cost of infrastructure (such as railways and electricity) needed to facilitate resource extraction, in a country with a huge land mass but a small population, was immense. Canadian governments therefore were much more active in promoting the economy's development than is typical in weak state settings. For instance, the trans-Canadian railway network built during the later 19th century, starting with the Canadian Pacific Railway, was heavily subsidized by government funds; private entrepreneurs were not attracted to the idea of building it without government assistance. During the 20th century, similarly, the federal government was responsible for the beginnings of radio and television broadcasting in Canada, as well as for commercial air travel. Since the 1980s, the federal government has become much less involved in the economy; for example, it has sold Air Canada and the Canadian National Railways to the private sector, and reduced its regulatory role in the economy. For some observers, this shift has marked an end to its earlier pattern of interventionism, making Canada much more typical of a weak state, laissez-faire economic model than ever before. Other observers disagree, arguing that Canada's state nevertheless remains more involved in the country's economy than is typical in the Anglo-Saxon cluster of countries.

Other features of Canadian political life were also heavily marked by the country's pattern of economic development. For instance, raw materials are distributed unevenly across the Canadian landmass and were exploitable at different points in the country's history. When an internally-focused manufacturing sector did develop after Confederation (designed to produce manufactured goods for sale within the country but not, for the most part, for export to other countries), moreover, it was concentrated in a corridor between Windsor, Ontario, and Montreal. Resource-based provinces outside this region came to perceive their own circumstances as representing a dependency on the central provinces that was analogous to that of Canada as a whole on its American partner.[33] For political economists, this acute economic heterogeneity accounts for the often-noticed tensions among the Canadian regions as much as, or more than, the more commonly-discussed cultural and linguistic differences. Regional sensitivity, in its turn, fostered a decentralized federalism, where citizens' loyalties are divided between the country and their own province. In this setting, after 1945 provincial states embarked on *province-building*, motivated to intervene in the economic and social life of their residents and to prevent the federal government from exercising undue influence in areas of provincial jurisdiction.[34]

Regarding its welfare state, Canada again departs in important ways from the Anglo-Saxon norm of limited spending and little poverty-reduction. Unlike the United States, for instance, Canada's welfare state developed an employment insurance scheme that was quite generous, especially in poorer regions. It also includes important universally-available income security measures and universal public health insurance. According to the best available statistics, inequality is now much lower in Canada than in either the United States or the United Kingdom, and lower than in several European countries.[35] Working class political pressures, especially through the New Democratic Party (NDP), encouraged these developments. But until 2011 the NDP was a minor party at the federal level in Canada. Working class power likely cannot, therefore, account for these features alone. Political economists instead have turned to an account of Canada's party system first developed by Frank Underhill. In his view, Canada's diverse political economy and the resulting inter-regional frictions required the main political parties (the Liberals and Conservatives) to perform a *brokerage* role, resulting in a **brokerage party system**.[36] Rather than advancing an **ideology** of either the left or the right, these parties seek to assemble (or broker) large enough coalitions of heterogeneous voters from different regions to win elections. The main parties therefore have differed little overall in their attitude to redistribution, and both have had strong links to the business community. Yet both Conservatives and Liberals also have needed the support of non-business, including working class, voters to win. It was in response to this imperative, expressed in terms of regional demands as much as class ones, that Canada developed a more ample welfare state than did the United States.[37] The fact that regional and federal–provincial sensitivities remain acute in Canada may also explain why welfare state cutbacks have been more muted here since the 1980s than in either the U.S. or the U.K.

Brokerage party system: A description of Canada's national party system, which holds that ideological polarization is less pronounced in Canadian politics than in many other countries; instead, the main political parties are said to attempt to aggregate enough diverse interests to win elections.

Ideology: A fairly coherent set of beliefs that not only explains what may be wrong with society, but also provides a vision of what society should look like.

TABLE 5.7 UNIONIZATION RATES IN THE CANADIAN PROVINCES, 2012	
Province	**%**
Newfoundland	39
PEI	34
Nova Scotia	31
New Brunswick	30
Quebec	40
Ontario	28
Manitoba	36
Saskatchewan	35
Alberta	24
British Columbia	31

Source: Statistics Canada. *Table 282-0078 - Labour force survey estimates (LFS), employees by union coverage, North American Industry Classification System (NAICS), sex and age group, annual (persons)*, CANSIM (database). (accessed: 2015-06-19)

Canada's fragmented political economy begat a decentralized federation in which sub-national (provincial) governments have more autonomous power than elsewhere. This suggests another potentially distinctive avenue for Canadian research. The political economy literatures reviewed in the previous sections identify sovereign countries as the level at which to study macro-level factors that shape wealth-creation and redistribution. The ample resources available to Canadian provinces, and their diversity, imply that we might want to adapt such cross-national typologies for use in inter-provincial comparisons. In this vein, Rodney Haddow and Thomas Klassen argue that the political economies and party systems of Canada's largest provinces differ significantly, and diverge from the national pattern for Canada.[38] Tables 5.7 and 5.8 indicate the extent of differences among the provinces in the strength of their labour movements and in the importance of their social democratic parties—two important potential causes of policy variations. For instance, the unionization rate is much higher in Quebec (at 40 percent) than in Alberta (24 percent). Alberta's figure is certainly typical of a pluralist, Anglo-Saxon country, but Quebec's level is much more comparable to those in Northern European corporatist countries. Similarly, Table 5.8 indicates that social democratic parties (NDP or Parti Québécois) have been in power in some provinces far more than in others since 1970. Based on Esping-Andersen's account, we would expect better developed welfare states in the provinces with more frequent social democratic government and stronger union movements.

Haddow and Klassen conclude that, indeed, policy-making in Quebec differs significantly from the pattern in Canada's three most populous Anglo-Saxon provinces, including some features that resemble the more corporatist settings found in Europe. This was not the case in Ontario, British Columbia, or Alberta. Reflecting its weak labour movement and the absence of an effective social democratic force, Alberta's policies were particularly consistent with the laissez-faire, low-spending norm in Anglo-Saxon countries.[39] More recent research by Haddow indicates that Quebec's social programs also reduce inequality and poverty more than such programs do in other Canadian provinces, while Alberta's programs do less than is the case in almost all other provinces.[40] In light of these findings, Canadian political economy might benefit from more comparative provincial research.

As with the ideas reviewed earlier, one might ask how relevant this Canadian scholarship remains in the current era of globalization-induced change. The next section turns to this question.

GLOBALIZATION AND CHANGE

National political economies are changing dramatically in the 21st century. Globalization is a major reason. From a political economy perspective,

TABLE 5.8 VARIABLE STRENGTH OF SOCIAL DEMOCRATIC PARTIES IN CANADIAN PROVINCES

Province	Years
Newfoundland	0
PEI	0
Nova Scotia	4
New Brunswick	0
Quebec	21
Ontario	5
Manitoba	30
Saskatchewan	27
Alberta	0
British Columbia	13

Total number of years that social democratic parties were in power, 1971–2014.

Source: Compilation by the author using http://www.electionalmanac.com/ea/ (accessed July 30, 2014). Figures report number of years of New Democratic Party (English Canada) or Parti Québécois (Quebec) government.

globalization has a particular meaning:[41] since the 1970s, the economies of different countries have become much more integrated. Specifically, the proportion of each country's production that is exported to other countries, or imported from them, has increased substantially. Moreover, although foreign investment has always been very important in Canada, it has become much more salient around the world; there is now much more Foreign Direct Investment (FDI) than there was 30 years ago. Firms are also now more likely to be multinational or **transnational corporations**, that is, to locate different parts of their production in different countries. Finally, there has been an explosion in the global flow of capital, subject to little or no restraint by national governments. The impact of these changes is reinforced by increasingly-powerful inter-governmental organizations (IGOs), such as the World Trade Organization (WTO), the **International Monetary Fund (IMF)**, and the **G8** and G20, which encourage, or push, countries to open up their economies evermore to international forces.

Globalization: The movement of goods, capital, ideas, and people across geopolitical boundaries today and in the past. Contemporary patterns of globalization involve a deepening constellation of economic, technological, and cultural changes that are worldwide in scope and that challenge the sovereignty of the state. These processes are leading to ever closer economic relations among the countries of the world, based on increased trade, foreign direct investment, activity by multinational corporations, and financial flows.

Transnational corporation: Business firms that are headquartered in one country but have plants or places of operation around the world, permitting them to integrate their business activities on a global scale.

International Monetary Fund (IMF): A sister of the World Bank and a branch of the United Nations that regulates the international monetary system in order to stabilize national currencies, and that, subject to certain conditions, makes loans to developing countries.

Group of 8 (G8): Canada, France, Germany, Italy, Japan, Russia (prior to 2014), the United Kingdom, and the United States, whose leaders meet once a year to discuss how they might coordinate their economic activities to ensure that the global economy functions well.

Of all of the above, the trade and FDI changes are the most frequently-cited aspects of globalization. Tables 5.9 and 5.10 indicate how much more "exposed" countries are to these global economic currents today than they were in 1980. The most common measure of how much a country trades is its trade "openness," calculated by adding together the value of its exports and imports, and dividing this sum by its GDP. As Table 5.9 indicates, for the top 10 countries reported in the earlier tables in this chapter, trade openness has increased substantially since 1980—on average from about one-half of the value of a country's GDP to about three-quarters of GDP. This means that a larger share of what is produced in each country is subject to competition from goods and (less often) services produced elsewhere. Table 5.10 indicates that the share of FDI in these countries has increased even more dramatically. In 1980, on average, the value of direct investments by foreigners equalled 6.3 percent of the GDP in these countries; by 2012, this figure had risen six-fold to 38.5 percent. In both cases this increase has been more modest for Canada, which has always been very exposed to external economic interests.

How will these changes affect national political economies? One frequent answer is that it will cause a *race to the bottom*; that is, states that intervene more in their economies, or that take greater steps to redistribute income or to provide social services, will feel compelled to reduce these market-curtailing activities drastically. Such a development would eventually eliminate, or at least dramatically reduce, the variations among political economies that have been the focus of comparative political economy scholarship since the 1970s. Because firms and countries increasingly have to compete with each other to export, and also have to compete to attract foreign investors, who might otherwise take their capital (and the resulting jobs) somewhere else, they are now determined to cut costs. Non-Anglo-Saxon political economies, which have relied on cooperation among economic actors, and which have maintained more expensive welfare states, will abandon these and move toward the less

TABLE 5.9	HOW MUCH HAS TRADE INCREASED FOR ADVANCED POLITICAL ECONOMIES?	
Corporatist Countries	**1980**	**2013**
Austria	69%	110%
Sweden	61%	86%
Netherlands	105%	167%
Germany	45%	95%
Japan	28%	31%
Pluralist Countries		
United States	21%	30%
Canada	54%	62%
United Kingdom	52%	64%
France	44%	56%
Italy	45%	58%
10-country average	*52.4%*	*75.9%*

Trade openness = exports + imports as a % of GDP.

Source: Based on data from OECD, Gross domestic product (GDP) in OECD.StatExtracts http://stats.oecd.org/, accessed on July 28, 2014. German figures for 1980 are for West Germany. Latest Japan and United States data is for 2012. Trade openness = International Trade Exports + International Trade Imports / GDP (expenditure approach).

TABLE 5.10	HOW MUCH HAS FOREIGN OWNERSHIP INCREASED IN ADVANCED POLITICAL ECONOMIES?	
Corporatist Countries	**1980**	**2012**
Austria	4%	40%
Sweden	2%	72%
Netherlands	11%	74%
Germany	4%	21%
Japan	> 1%	3%
Pluralist Countries		
United States	3%	25%
Canada	20%	36%
United Kingdom	12%	54%
France	5%	42%
Italy	2%	18%
10-country average	*6.3%*	*38.5%*

Stocks of inward Foreign Direct Investment (FDI) as % of GDP.

Source: *UNCTADSTAT,* online at http://unctadstat.unctad.org/wds/TableViewer/tableView.aspx?ReportID=89 (accessed July 30, 2014). German figures for 1980 are for West Germany.

costly and interventionist arrangements that typify, for instance, the United States. Abetted by IGOs, which often preach the virtues of laissez-faire and of low taxation and spending, this view concludes that these globalization pressures will undermine the **sovereignty** of independent states, making them less able to constrain the rising power of big business or impede rising inequality and poverty.

Sovereignty: A legal authority over a population and territory commonly claimed by the government of a state but ultimately sanctioned by the international system of states. In other contexts, sovereignty can be said to reside in the people or in parliament.

Many political economists disagree. For them, globalization is having a more complex impact.[42] Depending on the circumstances, it might reinforce the ability and determination of countries to defend what is distinctive about their political economies. Even if it does curtail national sovereignty in some areas, it might strengthen it in others—for instance, by enhancing the influence of states on international decision-making.

Nevertheless, political economists agree that globalization is likely to affect existing political economies *somehow*. Approaches to political economy that appear to rule out fundamental change are therefore highly questionable. Some recent contributions try to modify (without abandoning) the approaches reviewed earlier in this chapter to accommodate the idea that political economies might be forced to change in an era of globalization. Wolfgang Streeck and Kathleen Thelen hypothesize that political economies are constantly the site of conflict among organized groups and economic interests, even after they develop to a quite advanced level.[43] They argue that political economies experience constant gradual change, as different interests adjust their goals and gain or lose power in new circumstances, such as those presented by globalization. Moreover, these stimulants to constant change mean that a country may no longer conform to a "pure" type of the kind proposed by the theories discussed earlier in this chapter. Countries may acquire "hybrid" features that mix elements of one type with aspects of another. Even if a country's political

economy looks like a pure Coordinated one today, it may look quite different five years from now. Political economy scholarship may in the future have to tolerate more "messiness," with less room for dividing the world into a few clearly-distinguishable categories.

What this more change-sensitive and "messy" comparative political economy can look like is illustrated here with an example. By 2000, there was much criticism inside Germany—supported by business—that its political economy, which the VoC typology characterizes as Coordinated (or CME), was in trouble. It was experiencing chronically high unemployment alongside rising social security taxes and expenditures. According to the critics, this was happening because Germany could not create enough high skill/high wage jobs to prevent unemployment levels from becoming unacceptably high. Employers were reluctant to create more work because regulations made it hard to fire unproductive employees. The solution, for the critics, was to make it easier for employers to fire people, and to change regulations and the tax system so that low-wage jobs could be created for people who lacked high skills. Labour unions opposed these changes but unsuccessfully, a sign that business had gained in power at labour's expense. In fact, the changes, commonly called the *Hartz IV reforms*, were passed by a social democratic party-led government. In the reforms' wake, unemployment declined in Germany, even after a global recession began. However, many of the new jobs created pay low wages by German standards, and are in low skill occupations; few of these new workers are unionized. This new sector strongly resembles what one would find in an Anglo-Saxon or Liberal (LME) political economy. But Germany's Coordinated model otherwise remains in place, and the economy has rebounded. At the time of writing it is fairly robust. This is based on a resurgence of exports from its very competitive

THINK AND DISCUSS

There have always been powerful tensions among the regions and provinces of Canada. Scholars often claim that this friction is explained by differences of language (in the case of Quebec) and culture, and by the geographic distance between provinces. But the provinces also vary importantly in terms of the political economy and welfare state models discussed in this chapter. Quebec stands out as especially distinctive; it intervenes much more in its economy, and has a more extensive welfare state. Do you think that these differences in political economy might explain as much, or even more, of the regional tensions in Canada than the linguistic, cultural, and geographic factors that usually receive attention?

PHOTO ESSAY

French Union Solidaires protesting in the Place du Martroi in Orléans.

THE FUTURE OF THE LABOUR MOVEMENT

Unions still represent many workers, though their strength varies across countries and provinces (see Tables 5.2 and 5.7). The unionization rate nevertheless has fallen considerably since the 1970s in most industrial societies, though there is again much inter-country variation on this score.[44] Individual unions are now far less likely to launch industrial strikes, which are designed to improve wages and benefits for their members.[45] For many observers, this signifies that unions are inexorably becoming less relevant in contemporary political economies.

Some political economists nevertheless have noticed a surprising counter-trend since the 1990s. While industrial strikes are in decline, political strikes have become more common in many Continental European countries, though not in Anglo-Saxon ones.[46] Political strikes differ from industrial ones. They are launched by more than one union; indeed they are often "general strikes," instigated by the main national labour federations. Moreover, their objective is to force a government to change its social or economic policies, rather than to address the specific needs of union members. The strike depicted above, for instance, was launched by multiple French unions in 2010 to prevent the government from cutting public pension benefits.

What does this trend tell us about the labour movement's future? It could mean that unions have found a new role. As they become less able to advance their members' immediate economic interests, they may compensate by becoming more active champions of broader societal needs that only governments can meet. On the other hand, the very fact that unions now take on such a political role could instead be further evidence of their weakness. As they lose their ability to influence governments quietly, labour movements may have had to become more confrontational in attempting to protect the diminishing government benefits available to working people.

manufacturing sector, where high skills and wages, and strong unions, persist. Consequently, there is little reason to believe that the main elements of Germany's core Coordinated model are currently in danger, even as a significant Liberal-type labour market emerges alongside it. The resurgence might even restore some of the unions' lost power (even as their role continues to evolve, as seen in the Photo Essay above). Indeed, they may be able to increase their membership again, a prospect that is more likely when unemployment rates are lower.

The narrative in the above paragraph includes several of the elements recommended for a messier but more change-sensitive comparative political economy: attentiveness to the importance of changing objectives among key societal groups (usually business and labour), and shifts in the balance of power between them; and an appreciation that change may lead to mixed results, with the outcome not corresponding clearly to one or another model but blending elements of each.

How might such an approach be applied to Canada? We saw that earlier generations of political economists were reluctant to situate Canada fully in the laissez-faire category alongside other Anglo-Saxon countries. Have recent developments justified seeing Canada as more purely laissez-faire and low-spending than before? On the one hand, one is struck by how much Innis's staples thesis remains relevant. Canada continues to rely on raw materials for a large part of its exports. On the other hand, it is no longer clear that Canada's national state plays a larger role in the country's economic development than is the case in other Anglo-Saxon countries. Since the 1980s, most tariffs have been abandoned, state enterprises privatized, and many economic sectors deregulated. Trade agreements signed since that time, culminating with the WTO in 1994, now preclude many forms of state intervention.

Changes in Canada's welfare state have also been important, though perhaps less dramatic. Inequality has risen in Canada but by less than in most Anglo-Saxon countries. Market income inequality (inequality before we measure the impact on it of taxes and government transfers) has increased significantly since the 1980s. But taxes and social transfer payments redistribute about as much today as they did three decades ago. We can therefore conclude that the ability of federal and provincial governments to curtail inequality and poverty has not weakened during this period, but neither has it strengthened. Consequently, final income inequality (inequality as measured after taxes and government transfers have affected market income) has risen by about as much as has market income inequality.[47] The elements that supported redistribution during the post-war era arguably remain in place, including a brokerage national party system and a union movement that is now much stronger than its American counterpart; but they have not become stronger. Our welfare state may therefore have reached the limit of its ability to stymie rising market inequality, which has accompanied globalization in almost all affluent capitalist countries.

CONCLUSION

Political economy has been examined in this chapter as a focus of scholarship, though alternative definitions that treat it as a method have also been discussed, as these remain very important within the study of politics. This focus draws our attention to the highly-variable nature of the relationship between authority-wielding states and market-based economies in affluent countries, and to equally diverse relations among economic actors in them. Political economy treats much that is exciting and important for students of politics. By tackling political questions from a macro perspective, one that draws our attention to broad and fundamental features of social life, political economy addresses institutions and forces that can remain hidden to meso- and micro-level scholarship. It also permits us to deal with influences that extend beyond any one sector, and to trace to their origins influences on political change that affect various areas of public policy and political life simultaneously.

Examining the relationship of state and economy also has an important practical value for us as citizens. The main traditions of political economy have for a long time stressed the variety of ways in which people produce and redistribute wealth. The modern world is not an "iron cage," to borrow a term from the classical sociologist Max Weber, in which we are compelled to accept as inevitable certain ways of organizing our lives, and to acquiesce to particular levels of inequality in power and wealth. Political economy reminds us that there has always been much variation in how states intersect with economies. Since this variety is at least in part the result of distinctive *choices* made by different peoples throughout their histories, they are revealed to be not inevitable. And since macro-level scholarship is particularly suited to drawing our attention to the uneven distribution of political power and economic wealth, it encourages us to think critically about our societies. For as Thomas Picketty's recent best-selling study of wealth-concentration has documented emphatically, our political economies fall well short of achieving the equality of opportunity much cherished by modern democracies,[48] though to degrees that vary considerably among nations and over time.

DISCUSSION QUESTIONS

1. Why is there so much disagreement about the right definition of political economy, and is a focus on political economy more or less useful than other approaches to the study of politics that you have looked at?

2. Coordinative political economies celebrate collaboration and compromise; Liberal ones champion competition and individual initiative. Which of these distinctive values do you prefer as a basis for political and economic life?

3. By international standards, Canada's federation is quite decentralized. Economic opportunities are also distributed very unevenly across the country. In light of this, would greater centralization (more power for Ottawa over the provinces) be a good or a bad thing?

4. Is Canada disadvantaged because natural resources still make up a very large part of its exports? Should governments pursue interventionist policies to change this by increasing the international competitiveness of Canadian manufactured goods and services?

5. The chapter shows that countries organize their political economies quite differently. In light of this variety, what kinds of changes should Canadians consider making, if any, in terms of their political economy, based on the experience of other countries?

WEBLINKS

Canadian Council of Chief Executives
http://www.ceocouncil.ca/
The leading association for big business in Canada.

Canadian Labour Congress
http://www.canadianlabour.ca/home
The national labour union federation.

Canadian Social Research Links
http://www.canadiansocialresearch.net/
A good source of links to information on Canadian social policy.

Luxembourg Income Study
http://www.lisdatacenter.org/
The main source for internationally-comparable inequality and poverty data.

Organization for Economic Cooperation and Development (OECD)
http://www.oecd.org/
A leading provider of data on affluent capitalist countries.

FURTHER READING

Keith Banting and John Myles, eds., *Inequality and the Fading of Redistributive Politics*. Vancouver: University of British Columbia Press, 2013.

Stephen Clarkson, *Uncle Sam and Us: Globalization, Neoconservatism and the Canadian State*. Toronto: University of Toronto Press, 2002.

Gøsta Esping-Andersen, *The Three Worlds of Welfare Capitalism*. Princeton: Princeton University Press, 1990.

Jacob Hacker and Paul Pierson, *Winner-Take-All Politics*. New York: Simon and Schuster, 2010.

Torben Iversen and Frances Rosenbluth, *Women, Work, and Politics*. New Haven: Yale University Press, 2010.

Thomas Picketty, *Capital in the Twenty-First Century*. Cambridge, Mass.: Harvard University Press, 2014.

Jonas Pontusson, *Inequality and Prosperity: Social Europe vs. Liberal America*. Ithaca: Cornell University Press, 2005.

ENDNOTES

1. See, for instance, Jacob Hacker and Paul Pierson, *Winner-Take-All Politics* (New York: Simon and Schuster, 2010).

2. Of course, many people nevertheless work in the public sector in all of the affluent capitalist democracies that we consider in this chapter.

3. Charles Tilly, *Big Structures, Large Processes, Huge Comparisons* (New York: Russell Sage Foundation, 1984).

4. A good textbook on this literature is John Ravenhill, ed., *Global Political Economy*, 3rd ed. (Oxford: Oxford University Press, 2011).

5. C.B. Macpherson, "Politics: Post-liberal democracy?," in Robin Blackburn, ed., *Ideology in Social Science* (London: Fontana, 1972).

6. Daniel Drache, "Rediscovering Canadian Political Economy," in Wallace Clement and Daniel Drache, eds., *A Practical Guide to Canadian Political Economy* (Toronto: Lorimer, 1978).

7. Anthony Downs, *An Economic Theory of Democracy* (New York: Harper, 1965).

8. William Niskanen, *Bureaucracy and Representative Government* (Chicago: Aldine, Atherton, 1971).

9. Mancur Olson, *The Logic of Collective Action* (Cambridge: Harvard University Press, 1965).

10. Ian Gough, *The Political Economy of the Welfare State* (London: MacMillan, 1979).

11. See, for instance, the definition of political economy in Barry Weingast and Donald Wittman, "The Reach of Political Economy," in Weingast and Wittman, eds., *The Oxford Handbook of Political Economy* (New York: Oxford University Press, 2006), p. 3.

12. See, especially, Bob Jessop, *The Future of the Capitalist State* (Cambridge: Polity, 2002).

13. For an excellent example, see Edward Greenspon and Anthony Wilson-Smith, *Double Vision: The Inside Story of the Liberals in Power* (Toronto: Doubleday, 1996).

14. See, for instance, William Coleman and Grace Skogstad, eds., *Policy Communities and Public Policy in Canada: A Structural Approach* (Mississauga: Copp Clark Pitman, 1989).

15. Jingjing Huo, *Third Way Reforms: Social Democracy after the Golden Age* (Cambridge: Cambridge University Press, 2009).

16. W.W. Rostow, *The Stages of Economic Growth*, 2nd ed. (Cambridge: Cambridge University Press, 1971).

17. John Myles and Paul Pierson, "The Comparative Political Economy of Pension Reform," in Paul Pierson, ed., *The New Politics of the Welfare State* (Oxford: Oxford University Press, 2001), p. 312.

18. Bertrand Badie and Pierre Birnbaum, *The Sociology of the State* (Chicago: University of Chicago Press, 1983), pp. 73–76.

19. Vivien Schmidt, *The Futures of European Capitalism* (Oxford: Oxford University Press, 2002).

20. Philippe Schmitter, "Still the Century of Corporatism," *Review of Politics* 36 (1974), pp. 85–131; Peter Katzenstein, *Small States in World Markets* (Ithaca: Cornell University Press, 1985).

21. Rankings in the original source were based on a scale of 1 (pure pluralism) to 5 (pure corporatism). In this table, countries are listed as "corporatist" if their score, rounded to the nearest whole number, was 4 or 5. They are identified as "pluralist" if this number was 3 or less.

22. Peter Hall and David Soskice, "An Introduction to Varieties of Capitalism," in Hall and Soskice, eds., *Varieties of Capitalism* (Oxford: Oxford University Press, 2001), pp. 1–68.

23. Ibid, pp. 36–44.

24. Margarita Estevez-Abe, et al., "Social Protection and the Formation of Skills," in Hall and Soskice, eds., *Varieties of Capitalism*, pp. 145–83.

25. Robert Franzese and Peter Hall, "Institutional Dimensions of Coordinating Wage Bargaining and Monetary Policy," in Torben Iversen, et al., eds., *Unions, Employers and Central Banks*

(Cambridge: Cambridge University Press, 2000), pp. 173–204.

26. Gøsta Esping-Andersen, *The Three Worlds of Welfare Capitalism* (Princeton: Princeton University Press, 1990).

27. Inequality is usually measured with the Gini index. The higher the Gini index, the greater is the social inequality. The most recent Gini averages for the four groups of countries discussed here are as follows: Nordic, .247; Northern European Christian democratic, .272; Southern European Christian democratic, .319; and Anglo-Saxon, .331. Luxembourg Income Study, *LIS Key Figures*, online at http://www.lisdatacenter.org/data-access/key-figures/download-key-figures/.

28. See Torben Iversen and Frances Rosenbluth, *Women, Work, and Politics* (New Haven: Yale University Press, 2010).

29. Jonas Pontusson, *Inequality and Prosperity: Social Europe vs. Liberal America* (Ithaca: Cornell University Press, 2005), especially ch. 7.

30. The problem in the Southern European countries, more likely, is that they deliver unsustainably high benefits to certain privileged categories of citizens, impede people from entering and moving around the job market, especially young people and women, and use inefficient forms of taxation.

31. For more on this theme, see Lane Kenworthy, *Jobs with Equality.* (Oxford: Oxford University Press, 2008).

32. Harold Innis, *Essays in Canadian Economic History*, edited by Mary Innis (Toronto: University of Toronto Press, 1956).

33. Vernon Fowke, *The National Policy and the Wheat Economy* (Toronto: University of Toronto Press, 1957).

34. Edwin R. Black and Allan Cairns, "A Different Perspective on Canadian Federalism," *Canadian Public Administration* 9 (1966), pp. 27–44.

35. The Gini index for inequality (see fn. 23) was .317 for Canada in 2010. In the same year it was .357 in the U.K. and .373 in the U.S. It was also somewhat higher in Italy (.327) and Spain (.334) than in Canada. Luxembourg Income Study, *LIS Key Figures*, online at http://www.lisdatacenter.org/data-access/key-figures/download-key-figures/.

36. Frank Underhill, *Canadian Political Parties* (Ottawa: Canadian Historical Association, 1957).

37. Jane Jenson, "Representation in Crisis: the Roots of Canada's Permeable Fordism," *Canadian Journal of Political Science* 23 (4) (1990), pp. 655–83.

38. Rodney Haddow and Thomas Klassen, *Partisanship, Globalization, and Canadian Labour Market Policy* (Toronto: University of Toronto Press, 2006). Haddow has developed this premise further in *Comparing Quebec and Ontario: Political Economy and Public Policy at the Turn of the Millennium* (Toronto: University of Toronto Press, forthcoming).

39. Haddow and Klassen, *Partisanship, Globalization, and Canadian Labour Market Policy.*

40. Rodney Haddow, "Labour Market Income Transfers and Redistribution: National Themes and Provincial Variations," in Keith Banting and John Myles, eds., *Inequality and the Fading of Redistributive Politics* (Vancouver: University of British Columbia Press, 2013), pp. 389–98.

41. See Harman Schwartz, "Round Up the Usual Suspects: Globalization, Domestic Politics and Welfare State Change," in Paul Pierson, ed., *The New Politics of the Welfare State* (Oxford: Oxford University Press, 2001), pp. 17–44.

42. Linda Weiss, *The Myth of the Powerless State* (Cambridge: Polity Press, 1998).

43. Wolfgang Streeck and Kathleen Thelen, "Introduction," in Streeck and Thelen, eds., *Beyond Continuity: Institutional Change in Advanced Political Economies* (Oxford: Oxford University Press, 2005), pp. 1–39.

44. Andrew Glyn, *Capitalism Unleashed: Finance, Globalization and Welfare* (Oxford: Oxford University Press, 2006), pp. 121–23.

45. During the 1990s, strike days per worker fell to half their 1950s level and one quarter of their 1970s level in 15 affluent political economies; James Piazza, "Globalizing Quiescence: Globalization, Union Density and Strikes in 15 Industrialized Countries," *Economic and Industrial Democracy* 26 (2) (2005), p. 290.

46. Kerstin Hamann, Alison Johnston, and John Kelly, "Unions against Governments: Explaining General Strikes in Western Europe, 1980-2006," *Comparative Political Studies* 46 (9) (2013), pp. 1030–57.

47. Keith Banting and John Myles, "Introduction: Inequality and the Fading of Redistribution," in Banting and Myles, eds., *Inequality and the Fading of Redistributive Politics*, pp. 27–32.

48. Thomas Picketty, *Capital in the Twenty-First Century* (Cambridge, Mass.: Harvard University Press, 2014).

PART

3

INSTITUTIONS AND STRUCTURES OF GOVERNMENTS

© Len Staples/Getty Images

6

DESIGNING AND LIMITING GOVERNMENTS BY CONSTITUTIONS

Stephen Phillips

ELIZABETH THE SECOND

By the Grace of God of the United Kingdom, Canada and her other Realms and Territories Queen, head of the Commonwealth, defender of the faith.

To all to whom these presents shall come or whom the same may in anyway concern

GREETING:

A PROCLAMATION

Attorney

WHEREAS
in the past certain amendments to the Constitution of Can... ...made by the
Parliament of the United Kingdom at the request...
AND WHEREAS it is in accord with th... ...independent state...
Canadians be able to amend their... ...in all respects;
AND WHEREAS it is desirable to... ...of Canada by...
ion of certain fundamental rights... ...make other amendments...
Constitution;
AND WHEREAS the Parliament of t... ...the... ...request...
the consent of Canada, enacted th... ...for the pat...
amendment of the Constitution...
AND WHEREAS section 58 of the Co... ...1982 set out in schedule...
Act, provides that the Constitution...
force on a day to be fixed by proclam...
NOW KNOW you that We, by and with the...
this Our Proclamation, declare that the Constitution Act, 1982 sh...
59 thereof, come into force on the Seventeenth day of April, in the Year...
Thousand Nine Hundred and Eighty-two.
OF ALL WHICH Our Loving Subjects and all others whom these Presents may con...
required to take notice and to govern themselves accordingly.

IN TESTIMONY WHEREOF We have caused these Our Letters to be made Patent and the Great Seal of Canada to be hereunto affixed.
At Our City of Ottawa, this Seventeenth day of April in the Year of Our Lord One Thousand Nine Hundred and Eighty-two and in the Thirty-first Year of Our Reign.

ELIZABETH D

par la grâce de dieu reine d...
canada et de ses autres rou...
chef du commonwealth, dé...

à tous ceux que les présen...
manière concerner,

SALUT:

PROCLAMATIO...

...Canada

...ec le consentement du Cana...
...sieurs reprises la Consti...
...à un État souverain, les...
...titution au Canada_;
...la Constitution du C...
...s fondamentaux et c...
...la demande et avec...
...Canada, qui prévoit...
...candienne...
...xe B de la Loi sur le C...
...nelle de 1982 entrera e...
...eau du Canada_,
...sur l'avis de Notre Conseil privé...
...nelle de 1982 entrera en vigueur, sous réserv...
...mois d'avril en l'an de grâce mil neuf cent quatre-...
...DEMANDONS À Nos loyaux sujets et à toute autr...
...de la présente proclamation_.

...N FOI DE QUOI, Nous avons rendu les présentes lettres pate...
grand sceau du Canada_.
Fait en Notre ville d'Ottawa, ce dix-septième jour du moi...
neuf cent quatre-vingt-deux, le trente et unième de...

The Proclamation of the Constitution Act of 1982, signed by then prime minister Pierre Trudeau and Queen Elizabeth II, stained with red ink a year later by a protester who objected to American cruise missile testing in Canada. The document brought about the repatriation of the Canadian constitution, which provides the foundation for the Canadian political system, and gives formal recognition to the sovereignty of Canada.

INTRODUCTION

Until recently constitutions were a neglected topic of research by political scientists. This is not altogether surprising given the fact that in most states the constitution itself is rarely at the centre of political debates. After all, while constitutions allocate political power to core institutions of government, such as executives, legislatures, and judiciaries, they do not state with precision the political ends to which such power is to be applied. Thus, while a constitution may assign wide powers of taxation to the national government, it does not specify how the proceeds of such taxation must be spent. Should the government provide free university tuition for qualified students or allocate more funds to municipalities for public transport? Should it spend more money on its armed forces or increase old age pensions? In most states, it is questions such as these, rather than those of constitutional authority, that chiefly engage the attention of governments, political parties, pressure groups, politically attentive citizens, and the media.

Moreover, for many years constitutions were thought to have no obvious effect on the policy choices of governments. Rather, such choices were presumed to hinge primarily on socioeconomic factors such as class, political culture and ideology, and the influence of organized interest groups.[1] Consequently, these subjects became the principal focus of political studies, especially in the United States, while the study of constitutions was left to legal scholars.

Today there is renewed interest in constitutions among political scientists, generated by two major developments. The first is a growing recognition that the design of state institutions can have an important bearing on political outcomes and on political behaviour itself. In other words, what governments do, or fail to do, may be shaped to a considerable extent by their constitutional structure. This insight is part of an approach to studying politics known as neo-institutionalism. In recent years, there has been a growing interest among scholars in the design of political institutions and the special challenges of governing multination states.[2]

The second development sparking interest in the study of constitutions has to do with the drafting of new constitutions in many states in the past two decades, such as post-apartheid South Africa and the post-communist states of Eastern Europe. Established democracies, such as France, the United Kingdom, and Australia, have also undergone or debated important constitutional reforms since the late 1990s. Indeed, the U.K. recently embarked on a national debate about potentially far-reaching reforms to the country's basic political institutions following an historic referendum on independence held in Scotland in September 2014. In short, there are sound reasons for students of politics to take a closer look at the once-neglected subject of constitutions.

WHAT IS A CONSTITUTION?

The term **constitution** has two generally accepted meanings. In its broader sense, the constitution of a state is that body of fundamental laws, rules, and practices that defines the basic structures of government, allocates power among governmental institutions, and regulates the political relationship between citizens and the state.[3] In this sense, all states have an identifiable constitution, whether they be established liberal democracies (such as Canada and the United Kingdom), communist states (such as North Korea and the People's Republic of China), or authoritarian states of various kinds (such as Nigeria, Myanmar, and Iran). In its second, narrower sense, the term constitution refers to a specific document or collection of documents that embody the legal rules of the constitution. Examples of such constitutional documents include the Constitution of the United States, the Basic Law of Germany, and Canada's Constitution Acts, 1867 and 1982.

> **Constitution:** The body of fundamental laws, rules, and practices that defines the basic structures of government, allocates power among governmental institutions, and regulates the relationship between citizens and the state.

In either case, constitutional rules are binding on political actors, taking precedence over non-constitutional rules. This is made clear in Section 52 of Canada's Constitution Act, 1982, which declares the Constitution to be "the supreme law of Canada" such that any law that is inconsistent with its provisions "is, to the extent of the inconsistency, of no force or effect." Constitutions also embody norms and understandings about the appropriate exercise of political power. For example, if Canada's governor general were to refuse to sign a bill duly passed by Parliament, he or she assuredly would be accused of acting unconstitutionally, despite having the legal authority to withhold giving assent to bills.

EMERGENCE OF MODERN CONSTITUTIONS

The idea that constitutions should limit the exercise of governmental power is closely associated with the rise of liberalism in the 17th and 18th centuries. Nevertheless, its origins can be traced to an older doctrine, that of the rule of law, which holds that political authority should be based on law and not the arbitrary choices of rulers: in short, a government of laws, not of men. This idea was boldly asserted at Runnymede in 1215 when English barons forced King John to set his royal seal to a document affirming that the sovereign is bound to exercise his or her powers in accordance with the established laws of the land. That document came to be known as Magna Carta (the Great Charter). In one of its most celebrated provisions (clause 39), it declares:

> No free man shall be taken or imprisoned or dispossessed or outlawed or exiled or in any way ruined, nor will we [the King] go or send against him, except by the lawful judgements of his peers or by the law of the land.[4]

King John renounced the Charter almost immediately, claiming that he had signed it under duress. However, the spirit of Magna Carta lived on, gaining renewed importance in the 17th century when Parliament began openly to challenge the autocratic rule of the Stuart kings. The struggle for supremacy between Crown and Parliament plunged England into civil war in 1642. Following the defeat of the Royalists by the Parliamentary forces in 1649, Charles I was put on trial, convicted of treason, and executed. Parliament finally achieved supremacy over the Crown in 1688 through a series of events known as the Glorious Revolution.[5] The Revolution brought about the transfer of lawmaking authority from the king alone to the "King-in-Parliament," meaning that henceforth laws were to be enacted by the king with the advice and consent of the two houses of parliament, the House of Commons and the House of Lords. Meanwhile the power to execute laws was left to the king and ministers of the crown, while the power to resolve disputes about the law was to be exercised by an independent judiciary.

The liberal theorist John Locke provided a justification for the Glorious Revolution and the system of constitutional monarchy to which it gave rise. Building on the earlier idea of the rule of law, Locke held not only that rulers are bound by the law but also that government itself is limited by fundamental laws—the law of the constitution—that constrain what it may and may not legitimately do.[6]

This idea, known as **constitutionalism**, was elaborated by later liberal theorists. It holds that constitutions limit governments in several ways. First, by allocating power to various institutions of government, the constitution avoids an undue concentration of power in the hands of a single person or group of officeholders. England's constitution was lauded by the French political philosopher Montesquieu, who saw in its partial separation of executive, legislative, and judicial powers an effective safeguard against tyranny. His most important work, *The Spirit of the Laws* (1748), elaborated a theory of the separation of powers that profoundly influenced the framers of the U.S. Constitution of 1787.

> **Constitutionalism:** The idea that the constitution should limit the state by separating powers among different branches and levels of government and by protecting the rights of individuals and minorities, such as through a bill of rights.

Second, constitutions limit government by requiring certain procedures to be followed in the making and implementing of decisions. For example, police in Canada may not ordinarily enter a private residence without a judge's warrant. Constitutions may also limit government by imposing restrictions on the content of prospective laws or executive actions through a constitutional bill of rights. Such substantive limits include the 1st Amendment of the U.S. Constitution, which prohibits Congress from passing laws to establish a state religion or to abridge freedom of speech. Such guarantees are designed to protect the **civil rights and liberties** of citizens.

> **Civil rights and liberties:** Those legal and constitutional guarantees, such as freedom of speech, the right of *habeas corpus*, and non-discrimination rights, that govern the conduct of the state, and some private sector actors, in their relations with individuals and certain minority groups.

It must be acknowledged that while all states today have a recognizable constitution, not all of them adhere to the principle of constitutionalism. Here it is useful to distinguish between nominal and façade constitutions. A nominal constitution, rather than limiting the power of the state, simply describes and legitimizes "a system of limitless, unchecked power."[7] Such a constitution does not embody constitutionalism because even the most capricious and oppressive measures of the state would always be in accordance with the constitution. From this point of view, a constitution that vested all executive, legislative, and judicial powers in an elected assembly would violate the principle of constitutionalism no less than one that vested all political power in an absolute monarch. A façade constitution, in contrast, is one whose provisions are routinely ignored. The arbitrary arrest, torture, and extrajudicial execution of civilians carried out by certain regimes professing to respect the rule of law attests to the sham nature of their constitutions. The real purpose of such constitutions is to serve as window dressing for the international community. Nevertheless, even if the constitution of a state does not accurately describe how political power is used in all circumstances, it may perform other functions that reveal something about the political character of the state.

FUNCTIONS OF CONSTITUTIONS

Constitutions perform a variety of functions, the most common of which are as follows:

1. *To define the structure of major institutions of government.* Constitutions typically identify the principal offices and institutions of the state, specify who is eligible to hold office, and indicate how officeholders are to be selected—for example, by election or appointment—and for what term.
2. *To divide powers and responsibilities among the various institutions of government.* The constitutions of most states divide powers and responsibilities horizontally among the executive, legislative, and judicial branches of government. The constitutions of federal and confederal states (discussed later) also specify how powers and responsibilities are to be allocated vertically between different levels of government.
3. *To regulate the exercise of power by the state in relation to individual citizens or members of minority groups.* These rules are usually characterized as rights and codified in a constitutional charter or bill of rights. Such rights fall into two broad categories: negative rights and positive rights.

Negative rights are designed to protect the interests of individuals and minorities by restricting the scope of allowable government action. For example, constitutions guaranteeing freedom of religion do so by limiting the power of the state to ban or unduly restrict religious worship. Positive rights, in contrast, impose a duty on the state to provide certain benefits to citizens. Canada's constitution, for example, requires the federal government to deliver services to the public in English or French. Many constitutions adopted since 1945 enshrine social and economic rights, such as the right to education, social security, and housing. The inclusion of this category of rights in post-war constitutions reflected the rise of the welfare state and the influence of social democracy.[8]

4. *To serve as a political symbol.* A constitution is meant to vest legitimacy in the state and may even serve as a focus for the allegiance of its citizens. To these ends many constitutions expressly invoke values and touchstones embedded in the history of a nation or people; others seek to produce a break with the past and to proclaim the advent of a new political era. The preamble of the constitution of the Republic of Ireland, adopted in 1937, pays tribute to past generations for "their heroic and unremitting struggle to regain the rightful independence of our nation."[9] The preamble of the 1954 constitution of the People's Republic of China declares that the Communist Revolution of 1949 marked the end of "imperialism, feudalism, and bureaucratic capitalism" and the beginning of a process of social transformation leading "to the attainment of a socialist society."[10] Other constitutions emphasize order and continuity; for example, the Canadian constitution, in its most memorable phrase, authorizes Parliament "to make laws for the Peace, Order, and Good Government of Canada."

5. *To specify a method for amending the constitution.* The procedure for amending most constitutions is usually more onerous than that for amending ordinary laws. The relative difficulty of amending constitutions maintains the stability of the political order and prevents transitory democratic majorities from abolishing too easily the constitutional rights of minorities.

ORIGINS OF CONSTITUTIONS

The introduction of a new constitution or the significant amendment of an existing one often follows tumultuous and sometimes bloody events. Among the circumstances that give rise to new constitutions, we may count the following:

1. Revolution. **Revolutions** bring about extensive political, social, and/or economic change. The American Revolution of 1774, the French Revolution of 1789, and the Bolshevik Revolution of 1917 overthrew the existing political order and ultimately produced new constitutions. More recent events include the revolutions in Eastern and Central Europe in 1989 that brought an end to communist rule.

2. Decolonization. Most of the states in existence today came into being after 1945 as colonies in Asia, Africa, the Caribbean, and elsewhere gained their independence from European powers. In many cases, as in French Algeria and Portuguese Angola, independence was achieved after bloody wars of national liberation.

3. Aftermath of war. The defeat of a state in war may so discredit the political regime that the old constitution is scrapped and a new one adopted. In some cases, such action is driven by a new balance of domestic political forces. For example, Germany's defeat in the First World War brought an end to the authoritarian Prussian-dominated Second Reich and led to the founding of the Weimar Republic in 1919, based on a liberal-democratic constitution. In other cases, such as in Japan and in Germany following the Second World War, a new constitution was adopted by the defeated state at the behest of foreign military occupiers.

4. Secession. New constitutions also result from the breakup of a state following the secession of one or more of its constituent regions. In 1971, an uprising in East Pakistan against rule by West

> **Revolution:** A sudden, drastic, and usually violent change in the government of a state; the overthrow and replacement of existing political institutions and principles, not merely the forcible removal of the current ruler or government.

Pakistan led ultimately to East Pakistan's secession and the founding of the new state of Bangladesh. A more peaceable breakup occurred in Czechoslovakia in 1993, resulting in the establishment of the Czech Republic and Slovakia. Attempted secessions may also give rise to constitutional change. A case in point is the defeat in the U.S. Civil War of the Confederate States of America, which had attempted to secede from the United States. The postwar (or Reconstruction) period saw passage of the so-called Civil War amendments to the U.S. Constitution, which outlawed slavery and extended the provisions of the U.S. Bill of Rights to state governments.

Not surprisingly, the circumstances under which new constitutions are adopted have a major influence on their content. The U.S. Constitution, for example, affirms the ideals of liberal constitutionalism that were beginning to gain ground in Europe in the late 18th century. However, so thorough was their repudiation of monarchy that the drafters went much further in restricting and diffusing governmental power than most other liberal democracies have since thought necessary. As Harold Laski observed, "The American system, in its ultimate foundations, is built on a belief in weak government."[11]

Many national constitutions reflect an intention to remedy the perceived defects of past constitutions. Examples of such reactive constitutions include the West German constitution of 1949 and the French constitution of 1958. West Germany's constitution, known as the Basic Law, was drafted with a view to addressing the shortcomings of the Weimar Constitution of 1919 and preventing a recurrence of the political extremism that preceded the rise to power of the Nazis. It was thought, for example, that one source of political instability in Weimar Germany was the ease with which parliament could defeat a government on a vote of non-confidence. Under the Basic Law, therefore, the Bundestag (German Parliament) may remove the chancellor only on a constructive vote of non-confidence. This provision requires parliamentarians simultaneously to install a successor, a more difficult undertaking than merely bringing down the government. The Basic Law also authorizes the Federal Constitutional Court to ban political parties that seek to undermine democratic institutions.

France's constitution of 1958 reflects the accumulated experience of the many constitutions adopted and discarded since the French Revolution. The constitution of the Fifth Republic established a mixed presidential-parliamentary system in which executive power is divided between a president who is elected directly and a prime minister and the cabinet who are responsible to parliament. It is designed to avoid an excessive concentration of executive power in one person (a tendency known in France as "Bonapartism") and an excessive diffusion of power among political parties and factions in the National Assembly.

TYPES OF CONSTITUTIONS
Written Versus Unwritten Constitutions

A traditional basis of classifying constitutions is to distinguish between **written** and **unwritten constitutions**. A written constitution is one whose fundamental rules have been reduced to a single document or limited set of documents. An unwritten constitution is one whose subject matter is dispersed across a variety of statutes, court rulings, and unwritten political practices known as **constitutional conventions**. Though widely used, this terminology is unsatisfactory for at least two reasons. First, since only a handful of states today have an unwritten constitution—notably the United Kingdom, New Zealand, and Israel—it follows that the overwhelming majority of constitutions cannot usefully be classified under this scheme. Second, the term unwritten constitution wrongly implies that most if not all of the state's constitutional rules exist in the form of conventions. Yet much of the "unwritten" British constitution is written down, chiefly in leading common law cases and various acts of parliament, such as the Bill of Rights (1689), the Act of Settlement (1701), and the Parliament Acts of 1911 and 1949. At the same time, many of the constitutional rules of states having a written constitution exist in unwritten form.[12] It is perhaps more appropriate to distinguish between codified and uncodified constitutions. In each case, the constitution consists of both written and unwritten rules.

> **Written constitution:** A constitution whose fundamental provisions have been reduced to a single document or set of documents.

> **Unwritten constitution:** A constitution whose subject matter is dispersed across a variety of statutes, court rulings, and unwritten political practices known as constitutional conventions.

> **Constitutional convention:** An unwritten rule of constitutional behaviour that fills in gaps in the written constitution and conditions the exercise of legal powers under the constitution. While considered obligatory, such rules are not legally enforceable.

Constitutional Conventions As noted above, conventions are an important element of all constitutions. A constitutional convention, according to K.C. Wheare, is "a binding rule, a rule of behaviour accepted as obligatory by those concerned with the working of the Constitution."[13] Because conventions are not entrenched in a constitutional document or enacted in statutory form, they lack legal status and are not enforceable by the courts. Nevertheless, they are indispensable to the operation of modern constitutions, providing "the flesh which clothes the dry bones of the law."[14] Conventions not only provide guidance where the written constitution is silent, but specify how the legal powers set out in the written constitution are to be exercised.

Many of the principles of parliamentary government in Canada are defined by convention rather than by the Constitution Act, 1867. For example, the role of the prime minister and the cabinet is nowhere spelled out in the written constitution. Similarly, the Act is silent on one of the central features of parliamentary government: the obligation of the government to resign or seek a dissolution of Parliament if defeated in the House of Commons on a vote of confidence. These institutions and practices were well-established conventions of British parliamentary government by the late 1700s and well known to the Canadian politicians who drafted the British North America Act (later renamed the Constitution Act, 1867) between 1864 and 1866. Accordingly, it was felt sufficient to declare in the preamble of the BNA Act Canada's desire to adopt

a constitution "similar in principle to that of the United Kingdom."

In addition to filling gaps in the written constitution, conventions indicate how its legal powers are to be exercised. For example, Section 50 of the Constitution Act, 1867 refers to the power of the governor general to dissolve the House of Commons for a general election. By convention, however, it is understood that this power is only exercised on the advice of the prime minister. In Westminster systems, control over the timing of general elections (within the maximum term of a Parliament) is one of the most formidable powers that prime ministers have at their disposal.[15] In Canada, this conventional power of the PM was ostensibly curtailed in 2007 when Parliament passed a law providing for fixed election dates. Under the terms of the new law, general elections are to be held every four years; accordingly, the PM may only request an early dissolution if the government loses a vote of confidence. Ignoring the intent, if not the strict letter, of his government's fixed election date law, Prime Minister Stephen Harper requested, and was granted, a dissolution in September 2008, two years ahead of schedule.[16]

It should be noted that not all established political practices constitute conventions. Practices that are not generally thought to embody important constitutional principles are known as usages. Although neither conventions nor usages are legally enforceable, "there is a stronger moral obligation to follow a convention than a usage," such that the breach of a convention is liable to attract greater criticism.[17] For example, in naming a chief justice of the U.S. Supreme Court, it is customary for presidents to appoint someone who has previous judicial experience. When President Eisenhower departed from this practice in 1953 by nominating Earl Warren, former governor of California, the nomination was mildly criticized but ultimately ratified by the Senate.[18] Breach of a convention is viewed more gravely, as proved to be the case when Franklin D. Roosevelt broke a U.S. convention limiting presidents to two terms of office by seeking (and winning) an unprecedented third term in 1940, followed by a fourth term in 1944. Controversy about Roosevelt's breach of the term-limit convention led to its being entrenched in the U.S. Constitution in 1951 as the 22nd Amendment.

THINK AND DISCUSS

What are the advantages and disadvantages of using constitutional conventions to define and regulate key institutions and processes of government, rather than codifying these rules in a formal constitutional document?

Vertical and Horizontal Divisions Of Power

Another way of classifying constitutions turns on the allocation of governmental authority within the state. Constitutions allocate such authority both vertically and horizontally among the leading institutions of the state. When referring to the vertical division of power, we are concerned with the allocation of sovereign or supreme lawmaking authority between national and subnational governments. Depending on how sovereignty is divided between different levels of government, we may identify three major types of constitution: confederal, federal, and unitary, as illustrated in Figure 6.1. Constitutions may also be classified on the basis of the horizontal division of governmental authority between the executive and legislative branches; such a schema, discussed in Chapter 8, allows us to identify three additional forms of government: parliamentary, presidential, and semi-presidential systems.

Confederal States In a confederal state (or **confederation**) sovereignty is retained by numerous existing states that agree to cooperate in order to achieve certain common purposes.[19] Under a confederal constitution, the central government exercises only such powers as are delegated to it by the constituent states. That is to say, any powers transferred to the central government may be modified or revoked by the subnational governments. Typically, the powers of the central government are limited in number and scope. For example, the central government usually lacks the power to levy taxes and relies instead on periodic financial contributions from the constituent states. Moreover, the states may exercise a power of veto over certain decisions taken by the central government or reserve the right to opt out of decisions with which they are unwilling to comply. Finally, states belonging to a confederation retain the right of secession.[20]

Confederation An association of sovereign states that have agreed by treaty to delegate certain powers to a central governing authority. In principle a looser political union than a federation, a confederation's member-states retain the right of secession.

Today there are few examples of functioning confederations. In North America, the oldest confederal form of government is the Iroquois Confederacy, an association of six Iroquoian First Nations.[21] Some confederations evolve into federations, as in the case of the 13 American states that established a confederal association under the Articles of Confederation in 1781. The chronic inability of the central government to take action in the common interests of the states led to the drafting of a federal constitution in 1787.

The **European Union**, an association of 28 sovereign states, embodies many of the characteristics of a confederation, as does the Commonwealth of Independent States, an association of former Soviet republics established in 1991 to promote cooperation in areas of mutual interest.[22] The confederal nature of the EU is reflected in the fact that any member state may opt out of key decisions agreed to by the others. For example, Britain, Sweden, and Denmark chose to retain their national currencies and to refrain from participating in the launching of the common EU currency, the Euro, in 2002. Also consistent with the confederal principle is the fact that the EU does not directly tax the citizens of its member states but relies instead on revenue transferred to it by national governments.[23]

European Union (EU): A unique supranational organization made up of 28 member states, characterized by increasing economic and political integration.

The structure of the EU and its governing bodies is defined by a series of treaties that have been signed by each member state. The earliest treaty, the Treaty of Rome,

FIGURE 6.1 CONFEDERAL, FEDERAL, AND UNITARY CONSTITUTIONS

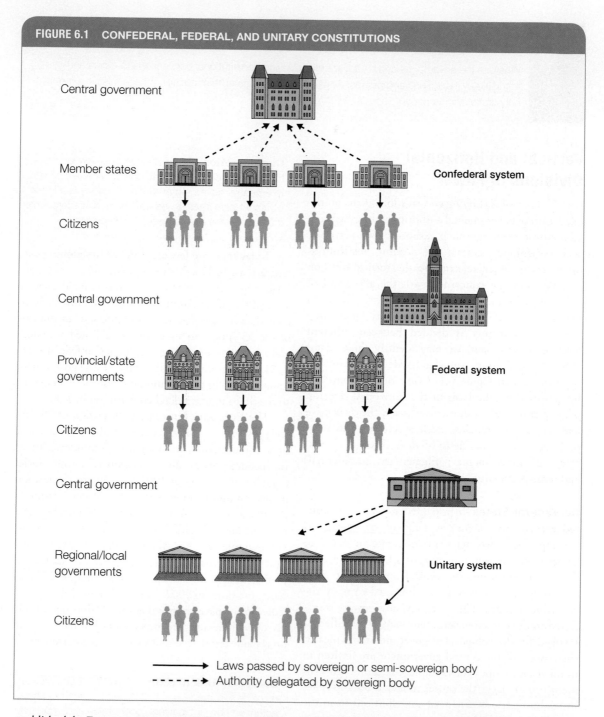

Central government

Member states — Confederal system

Citizens

Central government

Provincial/state governments — Federal system

Citizens

Central government

Regional/local governments — Unitary system

Citizens

⟶ Laws passed by sovereign or semi-sovereign body
⟶ Authority delegated by sovereign body

established the European Economic Community (EEC) in 1957. Drafted by the EEC's six founding members, it has been supplemented and amended many times over the years, most notably by the Treaty on European Union of 1992 (better known as the Maastricht Treaty) and, most recently, the Treaty of Lisbon of 2007. Each new treaty must be ratified by every member state before it can take effect. In 2005 this unanimity requirement doomed efforts to adopt a constitution designed to consolidate the EU's various treaties into a single document and to simplify its increasingly cumbersome decision-making rules. In May of that year voters in France and the Netherlands rejected the proposed constitution in separate referendums.[24]

Federal States Under a federal constitution, sovereignty is formally divided between two levels of government: a national (or central) government and a number of subnational governments. Both levels of government exercise legislative authority over the territorial units that make up the federation, such that neither level is subordinate to the other. These territories are known variously as provinces, states, cantons (in Switzerland), or Länder (in Germany).[25]

While unitary constitutions outnumber federal constitutions by a ratio of nine to one, federalism is a significant form of government nonetheless. Approximately one-half of the world's population lives in federal states, and **federalism** tends to be the constitutional system of choice for geographically large countries such as Canada, Australia, Brazil, India, Russia, and the United States, as can be seen in Table 6.1.

> **Federalism:** A form of government in which the sovereign powers of the state are formally divided under a constitution between two levels of government, neither of which is subordinate to the other.

Federal unions are formed for a variety of purposes. For small states, membership in a federation may offer the advantage of a common military defence against external threats. It may also offer economic advantages in the form of a larger internal market for trade and the building of national economic infrastructure by a central government that has superior financial resources. Both of these factors had a bearing on the decision of several of Britain's North American colonies to establish a federal union (the Dominion of Canada) in 1867 and on that of the Australian colonies to do likewise in 1901. At the same time, federalism allows the territorial units to retain their separate identities and to continue to exercise decision-making authority over a range of local matters. Canada's adoption of a federal constitution in 1867 was, in large part, a concession made to French-Canadian political leaders anxious to retain authority at the provincial level over matters vital to the preservation of their culture, religion, and language.

Division of Intergovernmental Powers Under a federal form of government, the written constitution allocates authority to each level of government to pass laws in relation to particular subjects. This division of powers may be effected by enumerating separate heads of authority for the national and subnational governments. For example, the Canadian constitution assigns to the federal parliament the authority to pass laws in relation to such matters as national defence and marriage and divorce. It assigns to the provincial legislatures, in their list of **enumerated powers**, authority over such matters as hospitals and municipal government. Other constitutions, such as those of the United States and Australia, allocate lawmaking power over certain subjects to the national government and declare all non-enumerated subjects to be the responsibility of the subnational governments. In either case, the constitution grants the power to deal with matters not clearly assigned to either level of government to one or the other. This **residual power** belongs to the federal government in Canada and India and to state governments in Germany and Switzerland.

TABLE 6.1	FEDERATIONS OF THE WORLD	
Argentina	Germany	South Africa
Australia	India	Switzerland
Austria	Malaysia	Tanzania
Belgium	Mexico	United Arab Emirates
Brazil	Nigeria	United States of America
Canada	Pakistan	Venezuela
Comoros	Russia	

Source: Barry Turner, *Statesmans Yearbook 2008*, published 2007 [Palgrave Macmillan]; reproduced with permission of Palgrave Macmillan.

> **Enumerated powers:** Those areas of legislative authority in a federal state that are specifically listed in the constitution and assigned to one level of government or the other, or to both.

> **Residual power:** The power in a federal state to pass laws in relation to any matters that the constitution does not expressly assign to either level of government. This power is assigned either to the federal or provincial governments.

Most fields of legislative authority listed in federal constitutions are to be occupied exclusively by one level of government or the other. In other words, if banking is assigned to the federal government, a provincial government may not pass laws in relation to banks. However, federal constitutions may also grant **concurrent powers**—that is, designate certain areas in which both levels of government can pass laws. Where there is a conflict between a federal and a provincial law in a jointly occupied field, the constitution specifies which law shall prevail.

> **Concurrent powers:** Those fields of shared jurisdiction under a federal constitution in which both the national and subnational governments can act and pass laws.

Responsibility for administering, enforcing, and interpreting laws does not necessarily reflect the intergovernmental division of legislative powers. For example, most civil servants in Germany are employed by the *Länd* governments and are responsible for implementing both Länd and federal laws. In Canada, the power to enact criminal law is a federal responsibility; the provinces, however, are responsible for the administration of justice within their respective territories, which includes the provision of police services, the handling of most criminal prosecutions, and the administration of a unitary system of courts that adjudicates disputes falling under provincial and federal jurisdiction. In the United States, in contrast, the federal principle is reflected in a dual system of state and federal courts, each of which is restricted to adjudicating cases of state law and federal law, respectively.

Judicial Review As a practical matter, no constitution divides legislative powers between the two levels

of government with absolute precision. Inevitably, there is functional overlap between the broad categories of federal and provincial jurisdiction. For example, in Canada, the Constitution Act, 1867, assigns responsibility for unemployment insurance to the federal parliament (Section 91[2A]) and responsibility for education to the provincial legislatures (Section 93). Who, then, has jurisdiction to establish job training programs, involving classroom instruction, for recipients of federal Employment Insurance benefits? Similarly, does a province's jurisdiction over health and welfare allow it to apply occupational health and safety standards to industries such as national airlines and broadcasting, which are otherwise subject to federal regulation? In federal systems, disputes of this kind typically are resolved by courts armed with the power of judicial review (explored further in Chapter 9). If the courts find a particular law to be in violation of the constitutional division of powers, or in conflict with some other aspect of the written constitution, such as a bill of rights, they have the authority to declare it invalid.

> **Judicial review:** When judges determine whether state actions are legally permissible, for example, in light of rights protections or the federal division of powers.

Evolution of Federal Systems As noted above, a literal reading of a state's written constitution paints an incomplete and often inaccurate portrait. This is especially true of federations, in which power may be considerably more centralized or decentralized than the written constitution would lead one to suppose. How, then, do federal constitutions evolve over time, if not by formal amendment? Three agents of change may be identified.

First, through judicial review, the courts may interpret particular fields of jurisdiction narrowly or expansively. For example, the Judicial Committee of the British Privy Council, which served as Canada's final court of appeal between 1867 and 1949, tended to give a restrictive reading to powers assigned to the federal parliament and a comparatively wide reading to powers assigned to the provinces. In contrast, the U.S. Supreme Court enlarged many areas of federal jurisdiction, especially in cases decided after 1937.

These divergent judicial legacies explain in part why American federalism is decidedly more centralized today than its Canadian counterpart, contrary to the intentions of each country's founders.

A second factor shaping the nature of federalism is the political legitimacy attached to the exercise of certain federal and provincial powers. In other words, is the vigorous use of certain legal powers held by one level of government or the other widely accepted as being appropriate? In Canada, strong regional and provincial loyalties, overlaid by a robust defence of provincial autonomy by successive Quebec governments, has inhibited federal governments from exercising the full range of their legal powers. For example, the federal cabinet has the unrestricted legal authority to disallow any provincial law within a year of its passage.[26] However, owing to strenuous objections by the provincial premiers to the use of the disallowance power, it has long since fallen into disuse. In Australia and the United States, in contrast, there is a broader acceptance of political initiatives by the federal government.

A third agent of change in federations has to do with social and economic developments and their impact on financial relations between national and subnational governments. Federations established in the 19th century tended to assign constitutional responsibility for health and social welfare to subnational governments. These subjects were not considered to be matters of national importance in an era in which hospitals and welfare services were largely provided by religious and private charitable institutions. By the 20th century, however, with the rise of the welfare state, governments began to assume responsibility for the provision of a wide array of public services and benefits. In federations, these burgeoning responsibilities often exceeded the revenue-raising capacity of the provincial or state governments, creating a problem of **fiscal imbalance**.

> **Fiscal imbalance:** In federal states the constitutional responsibility of subnational governments to deliver a wide range of public services often exceeds their financial capacity, thus requiring cash and other transfers from the national government.

In most federations, the central government's financial resources are superior to those of the subnational governments; after all, it has a broader tax base than that of any single province or state and typically has access to a wider range of tax instruments (such as customs duties, excise taxes, and corporation taxes). As a result, the problem of fiscal imbalance in federations is usually addressed through the transfer of federal funds to the subnational governments (see Table 6.2). Such transfers give the central government the potential to influence the content and administration of laws falling outside its jurisdiction. This is most obviously the case where the central government attaches conditions to transferred funds. The use of such conditional grants has had the effect of centralizing power in many federations by giving the federal government leverage over the policies and programs of the subnational governments. Such grants are used extensively in the United States to ensure the compliance of state and local governments with a variety of federal laws, from civil rights legislation to environmental regulations.[27]

Strictly speaking, conditional grants do not impair the constitutional authority of subnational governments because the latter are free to decline them. Politically, however, it is difficult to refuse such federal largesse; after all, local citizens have contributed to these funds through federal taxes. Less intrusive federal fiscal transfers include unconditional grants and federal tax abatement agreements, whereby the federal government partially vacates a field of taxation jointly occupied by both levels of government in order to create additional "tax room" for the provincial or state governments. The degree of reliance on fiscal transfers from the federal government is a useful benchmark for measuring the effective degree of centralization of a federation.

Intrastate Federalism So far we have been discussing the intergovernmental division of powers. This aspect of federalism is known as interstate federalism. Another feature of federal systems has to do with the representation of the subnational units within the institutions of the central government. This aspect of federalism, known as intrastate federalism, is typically reflected in the formal representation of states or provinces in the upper house of the national legislature. For example, in the U.S. Senate, each of the 50 states has two senators, who are elected to six-year terms. In Germany, the governments of each of the 16 Länder appoint between three and six members to the

TABLE 6.2	CONDITIONAL GRANTS AS A PERCENTAGE OF FEDERAL TRANSFERS TO SUBNATIONAL GOVERNMENTS IN SELECTED FEDERATIONS, 2004
Federation	**Percentage**
United States	100.0
Austria	78.9
Switzerland	73.1
Spain	66.1
Canada	64.9*
Germany	64.5
Mexico	55.5
Australia	40.9
India	40.7
Malaysia	39.3
Brazil	25.0
South Africa	11.5
Russia	9.0
Belgium	5.7

The CHT/CST transfer is included here as conditional; if treated as unconditional given the very general nature of the conditions, the figure for Canada would be 26.8 percent.

Source: Ronald L. Watts, *Comparing Federal Systems*, 3rd Ed. (Montreal and Kingston: McGill-Queen's University Press, 2008), 107.

Bundesrat (or Federal Council), who act as delegates of the *Länd* governments. The Länder are also represented in Germany's central bank, the Bundesbank.

Other forms of intrastate federalism may form part of the unwritten constitution or of established political practice. For example, in Canada, it is customary for a prime minister to ensure that their cabinet contains members of parliament representing each of the regions, if not every province. Similarly, when appointing judges to the Supreme Court of Canada, prime ministers strive to maintain territorial balance.

The Case for and against Federalism Leading arguments in favour of federalism include the liberal idea that federalism provides an institutional safeguard for individual liberty and minority rights by ensuring that political power is not concentrated exclusively in the hands of the central government. Indeed, by dividing political authority between two levels of government, federalism arguably acts as a second check on the potential abuse of power, along with the constitutional separation of powers within each level of government. James Madison expressed this idea in *The Federalist Papers* as follows:

In the compound republic of America, the power surrendered by the people is first divided between two distinct governments, and then the portion allotted to each subdivided among distinct and separate departments. Hence a double security arises to the rights of the people. The different governments will control each other, at the same time that each will be controlled by itself.[28]

The interests of a national minority group are best served under a federal constitution where its members are concentrated in a particular region of the country. In that way, they may hope to have effective political influence and may even constitute a majority in the legislature and government of that region. This is the case in Canada with regard to francophones, 85 percent of whom live in the province of Quebec.

Likewise, the Sikh and Muslim populations of India constitute majorities in the states of Punjab and Kashmir respectively, but are heavily outnumbered at the national level by the majority Hindu population.

A related strength of federalism is that it permits subnational governments to adopt policies that reflect the preferences of local populations, whereas the central government may tend to reflect the interests of a dominant section of the national electorate. For example, governments of regions of the country in which conservative social values are prevalent might choose to maintain stricter liquor licensing and Sunday trading laws than those of regions where more liberal values hold sway. Similarly, federalism would allow states or provinces whose populations attach a high priority to the environment to implement more stringent measures to combat pollution and global warming. In the United States, for example, California has long taken the lead in enacting strict controls on automobile emissions.

By allowing for a diversity of policies across the country in areas assigned to the subnational government, federalism may foster policy innovation. As the provinces take different approaches to addressing problems common to them all, they serve as laboratories of policy experimentation. Policies that prove to be successful and popular in one jurisdiction may then be emulated by others. For example, Saskatchewan's CCF–NDP government pioneered Canada's first comprehensive public health insurance program in 1962 in the face of fierce opposition from the province's doctors and the Saskatchewan Liberal Party. Yet the program, once implemented, proved to be such a success that it was soon embraced by the federal government and adopted by every other province.

There are, of course, potential drawbacks to federalism. Federalism does not necessarily serve the interests of minorities that are geographically dispersed. In fact, it may be inimical to their interests by making them vulnerable to hostile local majorities. Despite the abolition of slavery in the United States in 1865, African-Americans remained subject to many forms of discrimination for decades to come. In numerous southern states, this discrimination was institutionalized in the form of racial segregation of schools and other public services, and systematic efforts by state officials to thwart the registration of black voters. In these circumstances, African-Americans applied to the national government, including the federal courts, to

challenge oppressive measures in their home states.

This aspect of federalism remains contentious today in the United States, where states have jurisdiction over the conduct of national elections. Both the 2000 and 2004 U.S. presidential elections were marred by charges of political partisanship and racism in several states, most notably Florida and Ohio. More recently, Republican-controlled legislatures in numerous states have adopted stringent rules on voter identification. Though ostensibly designed to combat voter fraud, critics say that their real purpose is to suppress turnout at the polls by racial minorities and the poor. The most egregious restrictions on voting rights are state laws that disenfranchise citizens having a past criminal conviction. Such laws deny 5.3 million U.S. citizens the right to vote, four million of whom have completed their sentences. African-Americans are disproportionately affected by these laws.[29]

Federalism can also give rise to intergovernmental conflicts over jurisdiction and may obstruct or delay decisions requiring joint action by both levels of government. In this regard, federalism has been a factor impeding the development of social security programs.[30] By the same token, federalism may make it equally difficult to curtail programs over which both levels of government have some say. For example, in Canada, contributory public pensions are an area of concurrent jurisdiction. As a result, the federal government cannot make changes to the Canada Pension Plan without the consent of two-thirds of the provinces representing at least two-thirds of the population.

Finally, as an institutional response to the challenges of governing a large, culturally heterogeneous state, federalism may be a double-edged sword. Rather than merely accommodating existing territorial differences in the country, it may reinforce and even magnify them as subnational governments compete with the central government for power and prestige. In Canada, the effect of such "province-building" strategies may be to strengthen the parochial identities of citizens at the expense of their attachment to the national political community.[31] In extreme cases, this tendency may give rise to secessionist movements.

Unitary States

Under a unitary form of government, sovereignty is vested in the central government alone. Other levels of government, such as regional, county, or municipal governments, exercise only those powers that have been delegated to them by the national government. Consequently, such powers may be modified or withdrawn as the national government sees fit. Britain, France, Japan, and New Zealand are all examples of unitary states.

By centralizing constitutional authority, a unitary state enables the national government to make decisions on a full range of matters of importance to the nation as a whole, unimpeded by the jurisdictional conflicts to which federations so often are susceptible. This capacity for decision-making at the centre offers the potential for uniformity and consistency in the design of social and economic policies. Over time, the leading role taken by the national government in public affairs may promote national unity by fostering among citizens a stronger sense of allegiance to the national political community. This was a principal aim of the Jacobin leaders of the French Revolution, and their heirs, who set about establishing in Paris a strong central government that would enact laws for all of France. So centralized became the French state that in the 1930s Education Minister Anatole Monzie claimed to know at any time what was being taught in every classroom in the country![32]

However, excessive centralization of authority can also have undesirable consequences. The national government may be insensitive to regional differences arising from diverse local conditions. The imposition of uniform national policies may provoke resentment and undermine the legitimacy of the national government and, ultimately, that of the constitution itself. In practice, all unitary states delegate at least some authority to subnational governments. This delegation of authority, known as **devolution**, can be broad or narrow in scope. Under administrative devolution, local authorities are responsible for delivering services and implementing policies made by the central government. Legislative devolution, sometimes known as home rule, involves a partial transfer of lawmaking authority to regional governments.[33]

> **Devolution:** The delegation of administrative or legislative powers by a central government to regional or local governments.

Unless the terms of devolution are entrenched in the written constitution, the central government can alter them by ordinary legislation. As a result, the vertical distribution of power in a unitary state may shift back and forth between periods of relative centralization and decentralization, depending on changing political conditions both locally and nationally. This point can be illustrated by reference to the politics of devolution in the United Kingdom during the past 30 years. In the 1980s, the British Conservative government of Margaret Thatcher imposed severe restrictions on local government authorities in furtherance of its program of reducing government expenditure and privatizing public services. For example, local governments were required to offer for sale government-owned council houses to their renter-occupiers and were prohibited from using the proceeds to build new public housing units. Legal restrictions were also placed on local rate (or property tax) increases in order to prevent local councils from avoiding cuts to public services made necessary by reductions in central government grants. When the Greater London Council (GLC) openly campaigned against these policies, the government responded by passing legislation abolishing the GLC itself![34]

At the same time, the Conservative government was steadfastly opposed to devolving power to regional assemblies for Scotland and Wales, a long-standing demand of Scottish and Welsh nationalists and of sections of the British Labour Party. The Conservatives feared that regional devolution would produce a "dis-United Kingdom."

In 1997, the Labour Party, led by Tony Blair, was elected to office on a platform that included support for regional devolution and enhanced authority for local governments. After the new government's devolution proposals were approved by voters in separate referendums held in Scotland and Wales in 1997 and in Northern Ireland in 1998, it established regional assemblies, each structured differently to reflect the unique conditions of each region. As originally designed, the Scottish Parliament exemplified home rule because it was granted lawmaking powers in designated fields, including a limited power of taxation. The Welsh Assembly was an example of administrative devolution since it lacked the authority to pass primary legislation.[35]

The Northern Ireland Assembly was established as part of a larger agreement addressing many aspects of the 30-year political conflict in Ulster. A unique feature of that agreement is the requirement for power sharing within the Northern Ireland executive between the Protestant Unionist and Roman Catholic Nationalist parties. Despite several false starts, during which direct rule from London was temporarily reinstated, a stable power-sharing executive has been in place since the Assembly elections of March 2007.

The experience of devolution evidently whetted the appetite of the people of Wales and Scotland for wider powers of self-government. In 2006, the Welsh Assembly acquired additional administrative powers from Westminster; then, in a referendum held in March 2011, 65 percent of voters approved the devolution of full legislative powers to Wales. A commission was then established to make recommendations on the enactment of a third devolution law for Wales.[36] Meanwhile, the Scottish National Party, having formed a majority government in the Scottish Parliament after the elections of May 2011, announced plans to hold a referendum on outright independence in September 2014 (see Photo Essay Box below).

PHOTO ESSAY

© Simon Dawson/Bloomberg via Getty Images

Scotland's First Minister Alex Salmond addresses supporters at a rally in Perth on the eve of the 2014 referendum on Scottish independence.

SCOTLAND'S REFERENDUM ON INDEPENDENCE

The Scottish National Party (SNP), a party committed to the goal of political independence for Scotland, formed a majority government following the Scottish elections of May 2011. It proceeded to hold an historic referendum on Scottish independence on September 18, 2014. An affirmative vote would have begun the process of ending the political union of Scotland and the United Kingdom formed in 1707. Advocates of Scottish independence, led by SNP leader Alex Salmond (pictured above), argued that an independent Scotland would have the lion's share of North Sea oil revenues; they also contended that Scotland's social democratic political culture put it at odds with the more neo-liberal political culture prevailing in England, whose preponderant population—54 million compared to Scotland's 5.3

million—ensures its domination of national politics. Opponents of independence warned that an independent Scotland stood to lose political clout on the world stage—including membership in the European Union—as well as valuable social and economic benefits, such as the National Health Service and use of the pound sterling as Scotland's currency.

Toward the end of the referendum campaign, when opinion polls showed the two sides to be neck and neck, the three pro-unionist party leaders at Westminster (Conservative Prime Minister David Cameron, Labour Party leader Ed Miliband, and Liberal Democrat Deputy PM Nick Clegg) issued a joint statement promising to devolve wider powers of self-government to Scotland in the event of a No vote.[37] On polling day, the people of Scotland chose to remain part of the U.K. by a margin of 55 percent to 45 percent.[38]

These developments have opened a far-reaching debate about the constitutional future of the U.K. While the immediate task facing Westminster politicians is to work out the details of a new devolution law for Scotland, other reforms are also under discussion, including adopting a federal constitution for the U.K. or granting a form of devolution to England. Another proposal would deny Scottish MPs at Westminster the right to vote on matters affecting England which have been devolved to the Scottish Parliament. Meanwhile, SNP leaders have sent mixed signals since the referendum about the circumstances that might trigger the holding of another referendum on Scottish independence.[39]

CONSTITUTIONAL CHANGE

How does a constitution change over time, short of being replaced by a new constitution? Under conditions of relative political stability, there are three principal mechanisms of constitutional change: evolving usages and conventions, judicial review, and formal amendment.

Usages and Conventions

Since all constitutions consist of both written and unwritten components, changes in the latter may transform a constitution in significant ways. For example, the role and powers of the president under France's Fifth Republic were powerfully shaped by the two longest-serving occupants of the office, Charles de Gaulle (from 1958 to 1969) and François Mitterrand (from 1981 to 1995). As president, de Gaulle established the pre-eminence of the presidency, even in areas that the written constitution appeared to assign to the prime minister and government. De Gaulle was able to enlarge the scope of presidential power as long as his political allies in parliament commanded majority support and he was free to appoint prime ministers who would defer to him. In 1986, a Socialist president, François Mitterrand, was forced to appoint a Conservative prime minister and government when the Left lost its majority in the National Assembly. It was unclear whether the constitution could accommodate such a bifurcation of political authority; some even speculated that Mitterrand would resign and force early presidential elections. Instead, a *modus vivendi* was reached between the president and prime minister, under which the former retained paramount responsibility for foreign affairs while the latter took responsibility for most aspects of domestic policy. This pattern, once established, guided subsequent "cohabitations" in the 1990s.[40]

Judicial Review

Through judicial review the words of the written constitution may be reinterpreted by the courts to reflect changing times and circumstances (see also Chapter 9). This approach to constitutional interpretation was memorably captured in 1930 by Britain's Lord Chancellor, Viscount Sankey, who described Canada's constitution as "a living tree, capable of growth and expansion within its natural limits."[41] The particular case before the court had to do with whether women were "qualified persons" within the meaning of the British North America Act and thereby eligible for appointment to the Canadian Senate. The Supreme Court of Canada had ruled that women were not qualified persons for this purpose since the act, drafted in

"Do you ever have one of those days when every-thing seems unconstitutional?"

Joseph Mirachi The New Yorker Collection/The Cartoon Bank

1867—decades before women acquired the right to vote—refers to members of parliament in masculine terms only. In overruling that judgment, the Judicial Committee of the British Privy Council said that constitutions should be interpreted in the light of contemporary circumstances rather than being frozen in time. This view is not universally accepted. For example, in the United States some conservative jurists contend that the courts should interpret the constitution strictly in accordance with the "original intent" of its 18th-century drafters. A more widely held concern, addressed with humour in the cartoon above is that unchecked powers of judicial review may invite judges to substitute their own views for those of elected legislators.

Constitutional Limits in an Age of Counter-Terrorism In recent years, governments throughout the world have invoked the war against terrorism as a justification for the enactment of stringent new security measures, many of which infringe civil liberties and other constitutionally protected interests. For example, special counter-terrorism laws were passed in the United States, Britain, and Canada following the September 11, 2001 attacks on the U.S. and the terrorist bombings of July 7, 2005 in London. Some of these measures restricted or suspended altogether rights of due process for terrorism suspects, including the right of *habeas corpus* and the right to counsel. The surveillance powers of police and security services were also widened at the expense of privacy rights.

This enlargement of the state's executive powers is said to be necessitated by the demands of national security and public safety. In that respect many leaders today echo the words of the Roman statesman Marcus Tullius Cicero, who said: "The safety of the people is the supreme law."[42] The difficulty confronting democratic societies is how best to preserve public safety without unduly encroaching on civil liberties and, in doing so, threatening the survival of constitutional government itself.

This dilemma is not new. In times of national crisis, such as war or epidemic, we expect governments to take extraordinary measures, albeit within the confines of the law. During the First and Second World Wars, and, more controversially, during the FLQ Crisis of October 1970, Canada's Parliament granted sweeping powers to the federal government under the terms of the War Measures Act. The War Measures Act authorized the cabinet to issue regulations providing for arrest without trial, the banning or censorship of publications, the internment or deportation of entire classes of persons, and the confiscation of property. In 1942, yielding to long-standing anti-Asian prejudice in British Columbia, the federal government ordered the forcible removal of 22,000 Canadians of Japanese descent—men, women, and children, many of whom were Canadian citizens by birth or naturalization—from communities within 160 kilometres of the west coast. The government also ordered the seizure and sale of fishing boats, farms, and sundry items of personal property belonging to the evacuees. The racist nature of the policy is suggested both by the fact that military officials and the RCMP considered the mass round-up of Japanese Canadians to be unwarranted by the requirements of national security and by the fact that comparable measures were not taken against Canadians of German and Italian descent.[43] Nevertheless the lawfulness of the government's draconian treatment of Japanese Canadians was later confirmed by the courts.[44]

After the Second World War there was a heightened consciousness of the fragility of human rights in many parts of the world. This sentiment helped lay the foundation of a new international legal order, beginning with the Nuremberg Trials and the adoption in 1948 of the UN Universal Declaration of Human Rights.[45] In Canada, these developments gave impetus to the campaign for a constitutional bill of rights. However, as events of recent years have disclosed, security concerns can quickly take their toll on civil liberties—and not always in ways that comply with legal and constitutional rights.

Following the attacks of September 11, 2001 by agents of Al-Qaeda, U.S. President George W. Bush authorized the extraordinary rendition of persons suspected of supporting the work of terrorist organizations. This policy provided for the kidnapping of suspects and their delivery to countries or territories beyond the reach of American law. By this means suspects could be interrogated using extreme measures (including torture), detained indefinitely, and otherwise denied due process of law.[46] Maher Arar, a Canadian citizen of Syrian descent, became entangled in this extra-legal twilight zone in 2002. On a stopover in New York on his way home to Canada, Arar was detained by U.S. authorities. After receiving intelligence supplied by the RCMP—intelligence later found to be inaccurate and misleading—U.S. officials deported Arar to Jordan and thence to Syria, where he was imprisoned for a year and tortured. Following his release and return to Canada, a judicial inquiry found no evidence Arar had committed any offence or had ever posed a security threat. He later received a formal apology from the Canadian government and an award of $10 million in compensation.[47]

Courts have sometimes upheld the constitutionality of such counter-terrorism laws, thereby sanctioning restrictions on civil liberties; in other cases judges have declared such measures to be unlawful, in whole or in part. An example of the latter was a ruling by the Supreme Court of Canada in February 2007 declaring security certificates to be a violation of certain provisions of the Charter of Rights and Freedoms.[48] Originally enacted in 1978, security certificates empowered the state to conduct secret trials of noncitizens living in Canada and deemed to pose a threat to national security. Significantly, the accused were not allowed to see the evidence against them or to retain legal counsel. The Supreme Court found this aspect of the law to be a denial of the principles of fundamental justice as guaranteed by Section 7 of the Charter. In response, Parliament passed several amendments to the law governing security certificates. Based on a comparable U.K. law, the revised Canadian statute provides for the appointment of special advocates to represent the accused; vetted for security, they would have access to secret evidence. The constitutionality of the revised security certificates was upheld by the Supreme Court of Canada in May 2014.[49]

Another issue of importance concerns the allowable scope of surveillance activities by security intelligence agencies. Such agencies, operating covertly for the most part, do vital work to safeguard national security. But who is to guard the guardians? As a general rule, intelligence agencies such as the American CIA, the Canadian Security Intelligence Service (CSIS), and Britain's MI5 are empowered to conduct surveillance operations against foreign nationals, not their own country's citizens. Investigations of domestic threats to public order are instead the responsibility of police forces operating within the stricter framework of criminal law. The reason for prohibiting spy agencies from monitoring domestic populations is to prevent the creation of a secret police force, like the Gestapo of Nazi Germany or the Soviet KGB.[50] Nevertheless, in the absence of effective oversight by legislatures, or by agencies answerable to them, intelligence services in many liberal democracies have engaged in political spying. In the 1970s, a U.S. Senate Committee headed by Frank Church found evidence of extensive illegal surveillance by the CIA against American citizens engaged in legitimate political activities. The Church Committee's report led to the adoption of new restrictions on CIA activities and the formation of congressional oversight committees.[51] Likewise, evidence that came to light in the U.K. in the 1980s about unlawful activities of MI5 led to the creation of an oversight committee of parliamentarians, the Intelligence and Security Committee (ISC).[52]

The effectiveness of these oversight bodies has come into question in the wake of the extraordinary disclosures of Edward Snowden. In June 2013, Snowden, a former intelligence contractor for the U.S. National Security Agency (NSA), released confidential documents which revealed the existence of a massive data mining operation by the NSA, using data obtained from IT companies such as Microsoft, Google, and Facebook. The sheer scale of this program, code-named PRISM, is prompting demands in the United States and other countries for new laws to prohibit the indiscriminate collection of personal information by security services and technology companies, and to better protect the privacy rights of online users. Among the advocates of such measures are the major technology companies themselves, eight of which directed an open letter to U.S. lawmakers in December 2013 calling for a ban on bulk data collection in order to maintain the public's "trust in the Internet."[53]

Constitutional Amendment

If the constitution is a framework of fundamental laws of the state, it follows that it should not be easy to amend. After all, it would be disruptive if the rules of a hockey game could be changed by the home team in the middle of the third period, or if the bylaws of a students' council were altered every few weeks. Nevertheless, there are occasions when a constitutional amendment is thought to be necessary. In most states, the constitution prescribes a procedure for its own amendment that requires a higher threshold of support than that required for ordinary laws. Even so, not all **amending formulas** are equally onerous; some are relatively flexible while others are more rigid.

> **Amending formula:** The procedure by which a constitution can be amended; it is usually more onerous than procedures in place to amend ordinary legislation.

Not surprisingly, the most flexible amending procedures are found in those states that have unwritten constitutions; in such cases the constitution may be amended through ordinary legislation. Unitary states having a written constitution usually specify the need for an extraordinary parliamentary majority for constitutional amendments. For example, Finland's constitution provides for the approval of proposed amendments by at least two-thirds of the membership of the country's unicameral parliament. In 2008, France's parliament ratified a package of constitutional reforms sponsored by President Nicolas Sarkozy by the required three-fifths majority of both houses. One of the amendments restricts the President of the Republic to serving a maximum of two terms.

Amending formulas employed in federal systems are among the most rigid because of the requirement to secure agreement at more than one level of government. For example, the U.S. Constitution requires that constitutional amendments be approved by two-thirds majorities of both houses of Congress and ratified by three-quarters of the states. Since the ratification of the first 10 amendments to the U.S. Constitution in 1791 (known collectively as the Bill of Rights), only 17 amendments have been ratified.

Until 1982, the principal component of Canada's written constitution was the British North America Act. Since it was a British statute, most parts of it could be amended only by the U.K. parliament; in practice, however, the British willingly enacted amendments requested by the Canadian government. Within Canada, a constitutional convention developed to the effect that the consent of a substantial number of provinces was required before the federal government could legitimately request amendments affecting the fundamental interests of the provinces. In 1982, with the patriation of its constitution, Canada acquired a revised constitution, which included a domestic amending formula that codified the requirement for provincial ratification of key amendments (see Box 6.1).

A feature of the formula used in some states is the requirement that amendments be ratified by citizens in a national referendum. For example, one of the two methods of amendment set out in France's constitution of 1958 states that a proposed amendment, after being approved by a simple majority of both houses of parliament, must be ratified by referendum. This procedure was employed most recently in September 2000 to reduce the term of the president from seven years to five. A similar procedure exists in the Republic of Ireland. In 2013, voters narrowly defeated a proposed amendment to abolish the Seanad, the upper house of the Irish parliament.

Australia's constitution requires amendments that have been approved by parliament to be ratified by a national majority of voters; that national majority, in turn, must consist of majority votes in at least four of the six Australian states. For example, a November 1999 proposal was submitted to Australian voters to establish a

Political banners outside a polling booth in Canberra for the 1999 Australian referendum on whether to become a republic.

Loui Seselja, National Library of Australia, nla.pic-an22931296

BOX 6.1

AMENDING CANADA'S CONSTITUTION

Canada's amending formula is found in Part V of the Constitution Act, 1982. Strictly speaking, it consists of five different formulas. The formula that applies in a given case depends on the subject matter of the proposed amendment.

General Amending Formula

The general amending formula (Section 38) applies to most types of constitutional amendments, including the federal-provincial division of powers. It requires that an amendment be approved by Parliament and by the legislatures of at least two-thirds (or seven out of 10) of the provinces whose combined population is equal to at least 50 percent of the population of all the provinces. This means, in effect, that either Ontario or Quebec must give its consent to the amendment; otherwise the remaining provinces would fail to meet the stipulated population requirement.

Interestingly, Section 38 contains an opt-out clause designed to protect the interests of dissenting provinces. Under subsection (3), if a majority of provinces agree to an amendment transferring a certain field of provincial authority to Parliament, up to three provinces may opt out of the transfer.

Unanimity Formula

Certain matters require the unanimous consent of Parliament and all 10 provinces. These matters, listed in Section 41, include amendments affecting the monarchy and changes to the amending formula itself.

Amendments to Provincial Constitutions

Section 45 gives each provincial legislature the power to amend the constitution of the province. Pursuant to this authority, a province may increase (or decrease) the number of seats in the provincial legislature. It might even use this power to create a bicameral legislature—a legislature consisting of two chambers. Canada's provincial legislatures are unicameral (single-chamber) assemblies, unlike their counterparts in the United States and Australia.

Amendments to Central Government Institutions

Section 44 gives Parliament a parallel power to amend central government institutions that form part of "the Constitution of Canada" (narrowly defined). The Conservative Government of Stephen Harper proposed to use this section to establish a limited term for newly appointed senators and to provide for the holding of Senate primary elections in the provinces. However, the Supreme Court of Canada ruled in 2014 that such reforms to the Senate would require the formal approval of two-thirds of the provinces under the General Amending Formula. The Court went on to find that an amendment to abolish the Senate would require the approval of Parliament and that of all 10 provinces.[54]

Province-Specific Amending Formula

Pursuant to Section 43, amendments that would only affect one or two provinces may be made with the consent of Parliament and the province (or provinces) affected. Among the amendments made in the 1990s pursuant to this section were changes to the school systems of Newfoundland and Quebec.

republic by replacing the Queen with an Australian head of state. The amendment was rejected by 55 percent of voters on a national basis and defeated in all six states.[55] Many Australians who favoured a republic nevertheless voted to retain the status quo because they disapproved of the particular republican model on offer. That model proposed the election of a president by members of the Australian parliament, whereas most supporters of a republic favoured a popularly elected president.

Republic: A system of government ruled by a head of state who is not a monarch (generally, in modern times, a president), in which citizens are entitled to participate in decision-making.

Referendums are sometimes used to establish the legitimacy of controversial constitutional proposals, even where there is no constitutional requirement for one. As discussed earlier, the devolution measures implemented in the United Kingdom in 1998 were enacted by parliament only after they had been approved by voters in separate referendums held in Scotland, Wales, and Northern Ireland. Though not legally binding, the national referendum held in Canada in October 1992 on a package of constitutional amendments known as the Charlottetown Accord effectively sealed its fate when the Accord was decisively rejected by voters.

THE POLITICS OF CONSTITUTIONAL AMENDMENT

Formal constitutional amendment in most states is not as significant an agent of constitutional change as judicial review or evolving constitutional conventions. In many states this has to do, at least in part, with the rigidity of the amending formula. A mere fraction of the thousands of proposed amendments to the U.S. Constitution has made it past the first hurdle—that of approval by Congress—while less than 20 percent of the amendments approved by the Australian parliament since 1906 have been ratified in national referendums.[56] However, the difficulty of amending a constitution in democratic states also has to do with the fiercely contested nature of constitutional politics. After all, the stakes involved in constitutional change are often higher than those involved in the passage of ordinary legislation. Whereas a controversial law may be repealed, or an unpopular government defeated at the polls, a constitutional amendment, once adopted, is considerably more difficult to undo.

Constitutional politics also tend to arouse passions when a proposed amendment seeks to enshrine values in the constitution that are not firmly embedded in a country's national political culture. This was evident in Canada in the 1980s and early 1990s, when Quebec's

desire for constitutional recognition as a "distinct society" was fiercely resisted by many English-speaking Canadians. Antipathy to the "distinct society" clause in the Charlottetown Accord was one of the factors contributing to the accord's defeat in the 1992 constitutional referendum (see Box 6.2). Conflicting constitutional visions also doomed the European Union Constitution in the French and Dutch referendums of 2005.

Governments sometimes seek to entrench particular social or economic policies in the constitution so as to put such policies beyond the reach of future governments. For example, following the Portuguese Revolution of 1974, the left-wing provisional government proceeded to nationalize key industries and large land holdings. A new constitution, adopted in 1976, declared Portugal to be in "transition to socialism" and referred to the property nationalized since the revolution as "irreversible conquests of the working classes."[57] In the 1980s, a centre-right majority government was elected on a program that included the privatization of some state-owned industries. However, lacking the two-thirds majority in parliament necessary to amend the constitution, the government was unable to implement these promises. It was finally able to act in 1989, when the opposition Socialist Party agreed to the necessary constitutional amendments.

Conservative parties also seek the constitutional entrenchment of elements of their social and economic programs. In the United States, conservatives have responded to court decisions mandating same-sex marriage by proposing a constitutional amendment that would enshrine the traditional (heterosexual) definition of marriage. In Canada, in 1980–1981, Progressive Conservative MPs advocated the entrenchment of a property rights provision in the proposed Canadian Charter of Rights and Freedoms to protect the economic interests of property owners better. The Liberal government ultimately rejected this idea in response to opposition from New Democrat

THINK AND DISCUSS

Liberal constitutions largely enshrine negative rights—rights which afford protection against wrongful interference by the state. Should constitutions also include positive rights—rights which impose positive obligations on the state—such as the right of all citizens to housing, education, and health services?

BOX 6.2

THE POLITICS OF THE CANADIAN CONSTITUTION

An essential starting point from which to understand the nature of the constitutional debate in Canada today is the tortuous process that led to the patriation of the Constitution in 1982. Prime Minister Pierre Trudeau considered patriation to be the crowning achievement of his premiership. Others suggest that the country paid too high a price for it. Whatever history's ultimate verdict, there is no question that Canada is still living with the legacy of patriation.

The Road to Patriation (1968–1982)

When Canada acquired its independence from Britain in 1931 with the passage of the Statute of Westminster, it was presumed that the federal and provincial governments would shortly agree on a new constitution to replace the British North America Act (BNA), an act of the British parliament. Such a constitution would require a domestic amending formula. However, various attempts to reach agreement on these matters between Ottawa and the provinces ended in failure.

By the 1960s, the emergence of a powerful nationalist movement in Quebec raised the constitutional stakes for Canada. Unless relations between English and French Canada could be put on a more stable foundation, it was widely feared that Quebec's separation from Canada would just be a matter of time. The federal government took a major step toward accommodating the French fact by designating English and French the official languages of Canada in 1969.

The Liberal government of Pierre Trudeau then set out to achieve the constitutional entrenchment of bilingualism, including guarantees of access to minority-language education in the provinces. Despite numerous attempts, however, intergovernmental agreement proved elusive.

The first Parti Québécois (PQ) government was elected to office in 1976. Committed to the founding of a sovereign Quebec state, the PQ called a referendum on independence for May 1980. Toward the end of the referendum campaign, Prime Minister Trudeau pledged that if Quebeckers voted "No" his government would seek to renew Canadian federalism. When the ballots were counted, Quebeckers had rejected independence by a vote of 60 percent to 40 percent.

After the referendum the federal government made fresh overtures to the provinces. When talks with the provinces reached yet another impasse, Trudeau stunned everyone by declaring his government's intention to go to London unilaterally—without the consent of the provinces—to request the constitutional changes it deemed necessary. The federal government's position was staunchly opposed by eight of the 10 provincial premiers.

The standoff ultimately reached the Supreme Court of Canada, which was asked to rule on the constitutionality of the federal government's unilateral action. In a split decision, the judges ruled that while the federal government's action was legal, it violated a constitutional convention requiring the consent of a "substantial number" of provinces to major constitutional amendments.[58] The decision enabled both Ottawa and the provinces to claim at least a partial victory; it also allowed both sides to reach a compromise without losing face—always an important consideration in politics.

At a conference held in Ottawa in November 1981, agreement was reached between Trudeau and nine of the premiers. The provinces would accept the proposed Charter of Rights and Freedoms, provided it contained a "notwithstanding clause" that would allow legislatures to override certain sections of it. For its part, the federal government agreed to substitute the provinces' draft amending formula for its own.

Quebec Premier René Lévesque not only refused to sign the agreement but also angrily denounced his fellow premiers for having struck a deal behind his back. He pointed out that the new constitution eroded Quebec's jurisdiction over language and education while failing to recognize Quebec's right to veto constitutional amendments to which it objected. Lévesque accused English Canada of betrayal, a view that was shared by many Quebeckers.

Aftermath of Patriation

With the proclamation of the Canada Act (U.K.) on April 17, 1982, the Canadian constitution ceased to be a British statute; at the same time it acquired a domestic amending formula and a Charter of Rights.

However, patriation had been achieved at a high price: Quebec's further estrangement from the rest of the country. In the mid-1980s, the Progressive Conservative Government of Brian Mulroney attempted to achieve a rapprochement with Quebec in two further rounds of constitutional negotiations. Both the Meech Lake Accord of 1987 and the Charlottetown Accord of 1992 proposed, among other things, to give formal constitutional recognition to Quebec as a "distinct society." However, these proposals aroused considerable opposition across the country, and neither agreement was implemented.

The Meech Lake Accord expired in June 1990 when it failed to secure the unanimous provincial consent required for ratification. Many Quebeckers took the failure of Meech Lake to signify the futility of efforts to achieve a constitutional agreement between Quebec and the rest of Canada. This sentiment fuelled a resurgence of support in Quebec for political independence and led to the founding of the separatist Bloc Québécois, a party that went on to win a majority of federal seats in Quebec in the six general elections held between 1993 and 2008.

In August 1992 at Charlottetown, Prime Minister Mulroney reached agreement with the premiers on a new package of constitutional proposals. The Charlottetown Accord largely replicated the Meech Lake proposals, but also embraced a wide range of new issues, from Senate reform to Aboriginal self-government. Nevertheless, the Accord was soundly defeated in a national referendum held in October 1992. Interestingly, while many Canadians rejected the Accord because they believed that it gave too much power to Quebec, most Quebeckers were of the view that it gave Quebec too little!

The constitutional roller-coaster ride was not yet over. In 1994, the PQ returned to power in Quebec, promising to call another referendum on independence within a year of taking office. The results of the referendum of October 1995 were much closer than before; indeed, only a thin majority of Quebeckers voted against separation—50.6 percent to 49.4 percent.

Following the defeat of the Charlottetown Accord and the uncomfortably close results of the second Quebec referendum, federal politicians were unwilling to reopen the Pandora's Box of constitutional reform. Since then the preferred approach has been to pursue common objectives through political rather than constitutional means.

MPs, who feared that a property rights clause would be used by corporations to challenge legitimate forms of economic regulation.[59]

Trade Agreements as Supraconstitutions

Nowadays, private property rights increasingly are codified in international trade and investment agreements, such as the **North American Free Trade Agreement (NAFTA)**, and in the rulings of international bodies such as the **World Trade Organization (WTO)**. Through such agreements, states undertake to refrain from enacting laws that may be construed as interfering with international trade and investment. Some scholars consider the constraints imposed on governments by these agreements to be analogous to constitutional limitations, even though states retain the right to opt out of such agreements on giving the required notice. On this view trade and investment agreements may properly be regarded as **supraconstitutions**.[60] However, while national constitutions confer rights on citizens, both as individuals and as members of minority groups, trade agreements confer rights on transnational corporations. For example, NAFTA—an agreement between Canada, the United States, and Mexico—prohibits national governments from requiring foreign investors to meet performance requirements, such as local hiring or domestic investment in research and development, as a condition for doing business in the country.[61] More controversially, Chapter 11 of NAFTA enables corporations to seek financial compensation from governments whose policies are alleged to diminish the value of their investments. In an early NAFTA case, Ethyl Corporation, a U.S. chemical manufacturer, challenged a ban by the Canadian government on imports of MMT, a toxic fuel additive. In response, Canada lifted the ban and paid the company $13 million in compensation.[62]

North American Free Trade Agreement (NAFTA): An agreement ratified by the United States, Canada, and Mexico that contains rules to promote the freer movement of goods, capital, and services between these countries.

World Trade Organization (WTO): An organization created during the Uruguay Round of GATT negotiations whose goal is to provide liberal trading practices and to reduce protectionism though the development and enforcement of global laws and regulations.

Supraconstitution: In imposing on national governments a set of rules, norms, and principles from which domestic laws may not derogate, international trade and investment agreements are said by some scholars to be a form of transnational constitution.

The inclusion of comparable investor-state dispute settlement provisions in the proposed Transatlantic Trade and Investment Partnership (TTIP) between the United States and the European Union has elicited opposition from many quarters. Farmers, consumers, and environmentalists have expressed concern that laws requiring the labelling of genetically modified foods (GMOs) may be characterized as trade barriers.[63] After all, an earlier EU moratorium on the importation of GMOs was found to be contrary to international trade rules in a ruling by the WTO in 2006.[64] Neo-liberal norms pervade modern trade agreements as well as the domestic policies of many states around the world. However, in an era of growing concern about global climate change and the plight of the Earth's environment, the preoccupation of trade agreements with private property rights strikes many as incongruous. On this view the parlous state of the environment requires bold new measures, including the entrenchment in national constitutions and international agreements of a new category of rights and duties—most notably, the right of citizens to a healthy environment and the duty of governments to protect the environment.[65] Perhaps the time has come for constitutions to ensure that the public interest in a healthy environment takes precedence over the property rights of business corporations.

CONCLUSION

This chapter discussed the origins of modern constitutions, outlined their major political functions, and examined the relationship between written and unwritten elements of constitutions. It then described and assessed the principal types of constitutions—confederal, federal, and unitary—which allocate power on a territorial basis. The chapter concluded with an examination of the major processes of constitutional change. It demonstrated that constitutions, as well as the government institutions they authorize, are an indispensable part of the larger subject of politics. In the next three chapters, we take a closer look at these core institutions.

DISCUSSION QUESTIONS

1. In what circumstances is federalism likely to preserve the unity of a territorially diverse state? In what circumstances is it likely to exacerbate territorial differences?

2. What is the best method for amending a constitution? Should the method used in a unitary state differ from that used in a federal state? Explain.

3. How much detail should a written constitution provide with regard to each of the following matters?

   a) the structure of government institutions
   b) the values and principles on which the state is based
   c) the rights of citizens vis-à-vis the state
   d) social and economic policies

4. Are the interests of minorities better protected under federalism (or a decentralized unitary system) or a centralized unitary state? Does the existence of a constitutionally entrenched bill of rights make a difference to your answer?

5. What new issues and interests do constitutions of the 21st century most urgently need to address? Does the historic concern of liberal constitution-alism—to impose limitations on the state—provide a sufficient basis for the design or re-design of constitutions today?

WEB LINKS

Constitute
https://www.constituteproject.org
A compendium of national constitutions from around the world, developed by the Comparative Constitutions Project.

Europa.eu
http://europa.eu
The official website of the European Union.

Institute of Intergovernmental Relations, Queen's University
http://www.queensu.ca/iigr
The Institute conducts research on federalism and inter-governmental relations in Canada and other federations.

The Constitution Unit, School of Public Policy, University College London
http://www.ucl.ac.uk/constitution-unit
The Constitution Unit publishes studies on consti-tutional reform in the United Kingdom and other countries.

FURTHER READING

David R. Boyd, *The Right to a Healthy Environment: Revitalizing Canada's Constitution.* Vancouver: University of British Columbia Press, 2012.

Sujit Choudhry, *Constitutional Design for Divided Societies: Integration or Accommodation?* New York: Oxford University Press, 2008.

Andrew Heard, *Canadian Constitutional Conventions: The Marriage of Law and Politics.* Toronto: Oxford University Press, 1991.

M.J.C. Vile, *Constitutionalism and the Separation of Powers.* Oxford: Clarendon Press, 1967.

Ronald L. Watts, *Comparing Federal Systems,* 3rd ed. Montreal and Kingston: McGill-Queen's University Press, 2008.

ENDNOTES

1. Vernon Bogdanor, "Introduction," in Vernon Bogdanor, ed., *Constitutions in Democratic Politics* (Aldershot: Gower, 1988).

2. See Peter B. Evans, Dietrich Rueschmeyer, and Theda Skocpol, eds., *Bringing the State Back In* (Cambridge: Cambridge University Press, 1985), R. Kent Weaver and Bert A. Rockman, *Do Institutions Matter? Government Capabilities in the United States and Abroad* (Washington, DC: Brookings Institution, 1993), and Sujit Choudhry, *Constitutional Design for Divided Societies: Integration or Accommodation?* (New York: Oxford University Press, 2008).

3. S.E. Finer, ed., *Five Constitutions* (Harmondsworth, Middlesex: Penguin, 1979), p. 15.

4. Ralph V. Turner. *Magna Carta Through the Ages* (Harlow: Pearson Education, 2003), pp. 71–72.

5. Edward Vallance. *The Glorious Revolution: Britain's Fight for Liberty* (London: Little, Brown, 2006).

6. John Locke, *Two Treatises of Government,* edited by Peter Laslett. (New York: Mentor, 1965), reprint of Cambridge University Press edition of 1963. Original work published 1689–90. See Lee Ward, "Locke on Executive Power and Liberal Constitutionalism," *Canadian Journal of Political Science* 38 (3) (September 2005), pp. 719–44.

7. Giovanni Sartori, "Constitutionalism: A Preliminary Discussion," *American Political Science Review* 56 (4) (December 1962), pp. 853–64.

8. See generally T.H. Marshall, *Class, Citizenship, and Social Development* (Garden City, New York: Doubleday, 1964).

9. Quoted in Ivo D. Duchacek, *Power Maps: Comparative Politics of Constitutions* (Santa Barbara: American Bibliographical Center, 1973), p. 18.

10. Ibid., p. 23.

11. Harold Laski, *The American Presidency: An Interpretation* (New York and London: Harper and Brothers, 1940).

12. K.C. Wheare, *Modern Constitutions*, 2nd ed. (London: Oxford University Press, 1966), p. 15.

13. Ibid., p. 122.

14. W. Ivor Jennings, *The Law and the Constitution*, 5th ed. (London: University of London Press, 1959), p. 81.

15. Although the governor general ordinarily grants the prime minister's request for dissolution, there are circumstances in which he or she would be justified in denying such a request. See Chapter 7.

16. The legality of the 2008 dissolution was challenged in court by Democracy Watch, a public interest advocacy group. In September 2009, the Federal Court of Canada rejected the claim on the grounds that the law did not restrict the governor general's legal prerogative to dissolve Parliament (*Conacher* v. *Canada (Prime Minister)* 2009 FC 920). This ruling was upheld in May 2010 by the Federal Court of Appeal.

17. Peter W. Hogg, *Constitutional Law of Canada*, student ed. (Scarborough: Thomson Carswell, 2006), p. 25.

18. Henry J. Abraham, *Justices and Presidents* (New York: Oxford University Press, 1992), pp. 257–58.

19. While Canada styles itself as a confederation, it is more accurately classified as a federation. The error stems from the fact that in the 19th century the terms confederation and federation were often used interchangeably.

20. Karl W. Deutsch, *Politics and Government: How People Decide Their Fate* (Boston: Houghton Mifflin, 1970), pp. 181–82.

21. Donald S. Lutz, "The Iroquois Confederation Constitution: An Analysis," *Publius* 28 (2) (Spring 1998), pp. 99–127.

22. Daniel J. Elazar, *Constitutionalizing Globalization: The Post-Modern Revival of Confederal Arrangements* (Lanham, Maryland: Rowman and Littlefield, 1998), pp. 126–30.

23. Ronald L. Watts, *The Spending Power in Federal Systems: A Comparative Study* (Kingston: Institute of Intergovernmental Relations, Queen's University, 1999), pp. 40–46.

24. Many opponents of the constitution feared it would pave the way to European federalism or enshrine neoliberal economic doctrines at the expense of Europe's social market model of capitalism. Sara Binzer Hobolt and Sylvain Brouard, "Contesting the European Union? Why the Dutch and French Rejected the European Constitution," *Political Research Quarterly* 64 (2) (June 2011), pp. 309–22.

25. Part of the land base of the federation may be under the exclusive authority of the central government. Examples include the Canadian federal government's authority over the country's three northern territories (Yukon, the Northwest Territories, and Nunavut) and the Australian Commonwealth government's authority over the Northern Territory, the Australian Capital Territory of Canberra, and the various island territories.

26. See Sections 56 and 90 of the Constitution Act, 1867.

27. Thomas O. Hueglin and Alan Fenna, *Comparative Federalism: A Systematic Inquiry* (Peterborough: Broadview Press, 2006), pp. 330–35.

28. Clinton Rossiter, ed., *The Federalist Papers* (New York: Mentor, 1961), p. 323.

29. Wendy R. Weiser and Lawrence Norden, *Voting Law Changes in 2012* (Brennan Center for Justice, New York University School of Law, 2011), p.34, online at http://www.brennancenter.org; Jeff Manza and Christopher Uggen. *Locked Out: Felon Disenfranchisement and American Democracy* (New York: Oxford University Press, 2006).

30. Keith G. Banting, *The Welfare State and Canadian Federalism*, 2nd ed. (Montreal and Kingston: McGill-Queen's University Press, 1987), p. 41.

31. The term province-building was coined by Edwin R. Black and Alan C. Cairns in "A Different Perspective on Canadian Federalism," *Canadian Public Administration* 9 (1) (March 1966), pp. 27–44.

32. David S. Bell, *French Politics Today* (Manchester: Manchester University Press, 2002), p. 158.

33. Andrew Heywood, *Politics*, 4th ed. (Houndsmills, Basingstoke: Palgrave Macmillan, 2013), p. 390.

34. Eric J. Evans, *Thatcher and Thatcherism*, 3rd ed. (London: Routledge, 2013), pp. 62–69.

35. Russell Deacon, *Devolution in Britain Today* (Manchester: Manchester University Press, 2006).

36. Charlie Jeffrey. "Devolution in the United Kingdom," in John Loughlin, John Kincaid, and Wilfried Swenden, eds., *Routledge Handbook of Regionalism and Federalism* (London: Routledge, 2013).

37. "The Vow," *The Daily Record*, September 16, 2014.

38. Ibid.

39. See generally Robert Hazell, ed., *Constitutional Futures Revisited: Britain's Constitution to 2020* (Houndsmills, Basingstoke: Palgrave Macmillan, 2008).

40. David S. Bell, *Presidential Power in Fifth Republic France* (Oxford: Berg, 2000).

41. *Edwards v. A.-G. Can.,* [1930] A.C. 114.

42. Cicero, *The Laws*, Bk. 3, cited in J.S. Maloy, *Democratic Statecraft Political Realism and Popular Power* (New York: Cambridge University Press, 2013), p.24.

43. J.L. Finlay and D.N. Sprague, *The Structure of Canadian History*, 6th ed. (Scarborough: Prentice-Hall, 2000), pp. 425–26; Thomas R. Berger, *Fragile Freedoms: Human Rights and Dissent in Canada*, revised ed. (Toronto: Irwin, 1982), pp. 105–26.

44. *The Co-operative Committee on Japanese Canadians* v. *The Attorney General of Canada.* [1947] A.C. 87.

45. Geoffrey Robertson. *Crimes Against Humanity: The Struggle for Global Justice* (New York: New Press, 2000).

46. Tom Bingham, *The Rule of Law* (London: Allen Lane, 2010), pp. 138–39.

47. Ibid., p.140; Jeff Sallot, "How Canada Failed citizen Maher Arar," *The Globe and Mail*, September 19, 2006.

48. Kirk Makin, "A Big Thumbs-Up for Civil Libertarians," *The Globe and Mail*, February 24, 2007, p. A4.

49. *Canada (Citizenship and Immigration)* v. *Harkat.* [2014] S.C.C. 37.

50. Kate Martin, "Domestic intelligence and civil liberties," in Christopher Andrew, Richard J. Aldrich, and Wesley K. Wark, eds., *Secret Intelligence: A Reader* (London: Routledge, 2009), pp. 358–70.

51. M.C. Ott, "Partisanship and the decline of intelligence oversight," in Andrew et al., *Secret Intelligence*, 318–36.

52. Mark Phythian, "The British experience with intelligence accountability," in Andrew et al., *Secret Intelligence*, 337–56.

53. "Twitter, Facebook and more demand sweeping changes to U.S. surveillance," *The Guardian*, December 9, 2013.

54. *Reference re Senate Reform* [2014] 1 S.C.R. 704.

55. John Warnhurst and Malcolm Mackerras, eds., *Constitutional Politics: The Republic Referendum and the Future* (St. Lucia: University of Queensland Press, 2002).

56. Gwyneth Singleton et al., *Australian Political Institutions*, 8th ed. (Frenchs Forest, New South Wales: Pearson Education Australia, 2006), p. 57.

57. Kenneth Maxwell, *The Making of Portuguese Democracy* (Cambridge: Cambridge University Press, 1995), p. 159.

58. *Re: Resolution to Amend the Constitution* [1981] 1 S.C.R. 753.

59. The proposed property rights clause was also opposed by a majority of the premiers, who feared that it would encroach on the legislative authority of the provinces. See Alexander Alvaro, "Why Property Rights Were Excluded from the Canadian Charter of Rights and Freedoms," *Canadian Journal of Political Science* 24 (2) (June 1991), pp. 309–29.

60. Stephen Clarkson and Stepan Wood, *A Perilous Imbalance: The Globalization of Canadian Law and Governance* (Vancouver: University of British Columbia Press, 2010).

61. Clarkson and Wood, *A Perilous Imbalance*, p. 75.

62. Alex Michalos. *Trade Barriers to the Public Good: Free Trade and Environmental Protection* (Montreal and Kingston: McGill-Queen's University Press, 2008), chs. 11–12.

63. Michael Lipsky. "Will European Requirements for Labeling GMO Foods Survive New Trade Negotiations?," *Huffington Post*, July 13, 2013.

64. Stephen Castle, "GM food must be allowed into Europe, WTO rules," *The Independent*, February 8, 2006.

65. David R. Boyd. *The Right to a Healthy Environment: Revitalizing Canada's Constitution* (Vancouver: University of British Columbia Press, 2012).

7

THE POLITICAL EXECUTIVE AND BUREAUCRACY: ON TOP AND ON TAP

Stephen Phillips

© REUTERS/Charles Dharapak/Pool

World leaders, including Prime Minister Stephen Harper and American President Barack Obama, gather at the 2010 G-20 meeting in Toronto. The power of the Canadian executive was on display during this meeting, including an estimated 25,000 police officers, 1,000 security officials, as well as members of the Canadian military, at the cost of around $1.8 billion.

CHAPTER OBJECTIVES

After you have completed this chapter, you should be able to:

- identify the main functions of the executive branch
- distinguish the role of head of state from head of government
- compare parliamentary, presidential, and semi-presidential executives
- describe the political role of the bureaucracy
- recognize the various means by which the executive is held accountable

INTRODUCTION

The main functions of modern states are carried out by the three main branches of government: the executive, the legislature, and the judiciary. Of the three, the executive is unquestionably the least specialized. In fact, the sheer number and variety of tasks to which the executive sets its hand is truly remarkable. Consider the many circumstances that routinely bring citizens into direct contact with the state. Every year, millions of Canadians send their income tax returns to the Canada Revenue Agency. If they are lucky enough to qualify for a refund, it will be delivered to them by an employee of Canada Post or deposited directly in their bank account. Workers who lose their jobs and wish to claim unemployment benefits must submit an application to Service Canada. Business owners must ensure their compliance with regulations having to do with such matters as land use, product safety, and employment standards. In each of these cases, citizens interact directly with the executive branch of government.

By way of contrast, citizens rarely, if ever, come into contact with the judiciary. Few citizens have occasion to attend the local courthouse to appear before a judge or to be called upon for jury duty. A larger number of citizens—albeit still a minority— may have direct dealings with their member of parliament or their member of the provincial legislature. Citizens may write to their member of parliament (MP) to seek assistance with a local problem or to convey their views on a political issue of concern to them. However, many citizens would be hard pressed even to name their MP.

The importance of the executive branch goes beyond its extensive reach into the daily lives of citizens. The executive is first and foremost the nerve centre of the state, having responsibility both for proposing and implementing a full spectrum of public policies, from national defence and foreign policy to budgetary decisions on taxation and public spending to the regulation of TV broadcasting and agricultural pesticides. In other words, the executive is both on top and on tap: it is on top by providing political leadership for the nation, and on tap by supplying political leaders with the wherewithal to accomplish their aims. For this reason, the study of executives is a central preoccupation of political scientists.

In this chapter, we shall discuss the main types of executive found in modern democratic states and raise a number of questions about the exercise of executive power. A key issue to be addressed is the appropriate balance to be struck between the goals of effective governance and democratic accountability.

THE EXECUTIVE DEFINED

The term **executive** is rather broad and imprecise. Strictly speaking, the executive branch is concerned with the implementation and enforcement of laws and other authoritative decisions of the state. However, the executive also plays a leading role in formulating

public policy and providing political leadership. It is customary, therefore, to distinguish between the political executive and the administrative (or bureaucratic) executive. The political executive consists of those public officeholders who have political responsibility for making public policy. Presidents, prime ministers, and cabinet ministers constitute the core of the political executive. In ordinary parlance, the political executive is synonymous with the government of the day.[1] In democratic states, the political executive may undergo a wholesale change of personnel following a general election.

> **Executive:** The branch of government concerned with the implementation and enforcement of laws and other authoritative decisions of the state. The executive also formulates public policy and provides political leadership.

> **Public policy:** A course of action or inaction selected by public officials, usually in response to a specific problem or set of problems.

The administrative executive comprises a vast array of bureaucratic institutions that support the work of the political executive and ensure the smooth operation of the machinery of government. The administrative arm

of the state assumes a variety of organizational forms. However, most public servants (or bureaucrats) have certain common characteristics. Unlike politicians, public servants are nonpartisan and enjoy security of tenure. That is to say, they are obliged to carry out their duties impartially and are not liable to lose their jobs if a general election produces a change of government. In other words, bureaucrats, like judges, form part of the permanent apparatus of the state.

It should be noted that the term *bureaucrat* ordinarily denotes a public official who works in a government department headed by a minister (a member of the political executive). Beyond this bureaucratic tier, a host of other public institutions operate with more autonomy from the government on a day-to-day basis. Such institutions include state-owned corporations and regulatory agencies. Collectively, these institutions are often referred to as the *public sector*. Other distinctive components of the executive branch include the military and the police. Operating at a further remove from the political direction of ministers is the wider *para-public sector*, which includes public hospitals, public schools and postsecondary institutions, and a range of social service agencies. While these institutions derive the bulk of their financing from the state, they typically have wide discretion to manage their own internal affairs (See Figure 7.1).

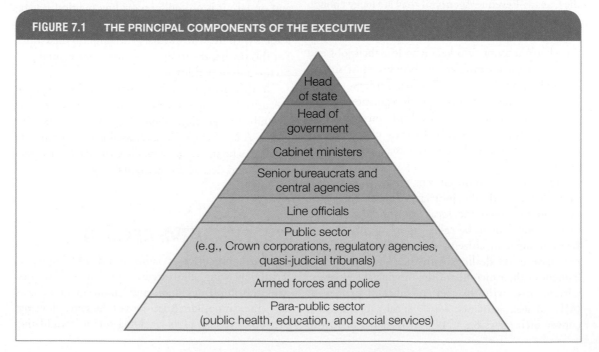

FIGURE 7.1   THE PRINCIPAL COMPONENTS OF THE EXECUTIVE

Head of state
Head of government
Cabinet ministers
Senior bureaucrats and central agencies
Line officials
Public sector (e.g., Crown corporations, regulatory agencies, quasi-judicial tribunals)
Armed forces and police
Para-public sector (public health, education, and social services)

THE EMERGENCE OF MODERN EXECUTIVES

The executive is the oldest branch of government. Before the rise of legislative assemblies and independent courts, all of the functions of government were discharged by, or in the name of, absolute monarchs. Before the rise of constitutional government, kings made law by issuing decrees, edicts, and other proclamations, which they enforced through a network of officials. As servants of the Crown, these officials held office at the pleasure of the sovereign and could be dismissed at will. Meanwhile, justice was dispensed through the King's Courts. Most routine cases were decided by local customary law or, in medieval England, by a uniform body of common law applicable throughout the realm.[2] The sovereign nevertheless retained wide prerogatives, including the power to grant pardons in criminal cases and to dismiss (and even to arrest) judges whose rulings displeased him!

The struggle for constitutional government was a struggle to limit the power of the Crown. As noted in Chapter 6, the prerogatives of English monarchs were narrowed considerably after the Glorious Revolution of 1688, in which parliament established its supremacy over the Crown. In the decades that followed, constitutional safeguards were put in place to protect the judiciary from improper interference by the executive branch. By the middle of the 19th century, the British monarchy had been transformed; it now belonged to the "dignified part of the constitution." According to Walter Bagehot, the "efficient secret" of the British Constitution was the fusion of executive and legislative power in the cabinet, which he described as a

> board of control chosen by the legislature, out of persons whom it trusts and knows, to rule the nation.... A Cabinet is a combining committee—a hyphen which joins, a buckle which fastens, the legislative part of the State to the executive part of the State.[3]

In an influential commentary on Bagehot's classic work, *The English Constitution*, Richard Crossman observed that with the rise of disciplined political parties in the late 19th century, the cabinet came to dominate parliament. Crossman and others went on to describe a significant centralization of power within the executive branch itself which has occurred since the end of the Second World War. In their view, prime ministers and senior bureaucrats exercise such wide-ranging powers nowadays that, in many respects, the cabinet has joined parliament and the Crown in forming part of the dignified (or decorative) part of the constitution.

FUNCTIONS OF THE EXECUTIVE

Today the main functions of the executive can be stated as follows:

- *To provide political leadership to the nation.* It is to the executive branch that citizens look to take the initiative to address political problems. Most of those problems are of a routine, ongoing nature, but citizens also expect the political executive to respond swiftly, decisively, and competently to national crises, both domestic and foreign. Note that while the approval of parliament (or the legislature) is often required in order to give formal, legal effect to the policies of the government, the initiative for most legislation lies with the executive.
- *To implement laws formally approved by the legislature.* The political executive dominates the early stages of the policy process, at which policy is formulated, as well as the latter stages, at which policy is implemented. In regard to the latter function, executive agencies of the state (chiefly, the bureaucracy) are responsible for ensuring that taxes are collected, that public services are delivered, and that a host of regulatory laws are enforced. In Canada, the prime minister and his or her government have ultimate political responsibility for the efficiency, effectiveness, and fairness with which such functions of the state are carried out.
- *To make rules and regulations.* In modern democratic states, the government needs legal authority from the legislature to carry out most of its operations. Legislative grants of authority to the executive tend to vest wide powers in the government to draw up detailed regulations that flesh out the often skeletal framework of legislation. In Canada, for example, statutes give authority to the Minister of Immigration to establish a procedure to process

claims for refugee status and to the Minister of Agriculture—or agencies that report to the ministry—to set production quotas for dairy and poultry farmers.

- *To administer government departments and other agencies.* As in any large organization, governments need to be organized into specialized units that are responsible for performing particular functions. A key task of the political executive is to organize the apparatus of the state, including its personnel, which may number in the hundreds of thousands. In carrying out this managerial role, the political executive relies heavily on the advice of high-ranking public officials within the bureaucracy.

Head of State versus Head of Government

The political executive sits at the apex of the executive branch. On closer examination, we may distinguish between two leading offices of state: the **head of state** and the **head of government**. In parliamentary and semi-presidential systems, these posts are filled by separate officeholders. This arrangement is known as a **dual executive**. In presidential systems, the two positions are combined and held by a single office-holder, an arrangement known as a **single executive**. For now, let us take a closer look at the respective roles of the head of state and the head of government under a parliamentary system of government.

> **Head of state:** Officeholder, such as a constitutional monarch, who symbolizes and represents the state but does not exercise effective political power.

> **Head of government:** Officeholder, such as the prime minister in a parliamentary system, who is in effective charge of the executive branch of government.

> **Dual executive:** A form of executive in which the posts of head of state and head of government are divided, each being held by a separate officeholder. In parliamentary systems, the head of state is a constitutional monarch or an elected president, and the head of government is the prime minister.

> **Single executive:** A form of executive in which the posts of head of state and head of government are combined and held by a single officeholder. This arrangement is characteristic of presidential systems, such as those of Argentina, Mexico, and the United States.

King Willem-Alexander of the Netherlands and Queen Maxima flank the former monarch, Queen Beatrix, who abdicated in April 2013 after reigning for 33 years.
© REUTERS/Paul Vreeker

In parliamentary systems, the office of head of state is held either by a constitutional monarch or an elected president. Spain, Japan, and the Netherlands are examples of parliamentary democracies having a monarchical head of state. Heredity is the principle governing succession to the throne, although the rules of succession vary somewhat among national monarchies. For example, in Norway the eldest child of the reigning monarch is deemed the heir apparent, whether male or female, whereas in Japan only males may accede to the throne. In Britain until recently, the line of succession privileged male heirs; under male-preference primogeniture, women could accede to the throne only in the absence of a male heir. The law also excluded Roman Catholics from the line of succession as well as heirs who married a Roman Catholic. Not surprisingly, there was much debate about repealing these laws as neither of them could easily be reconciled with contemporary views about equality. In 2013, the British Parliament amended the law to provide for the succession of the eldest heir to the throne, regardless of gender.

The new law also lifts the ban on heirs marrying a Roman Catholic, although it retains the requirement that the heir belong to the Church of England.

Queen Elizabeth II is head of state not only of the United Kingdom but also of some 15 other countries belonging to the Commonwealth, including Canada, New Zealand, and Jamaica.[4] However, with the exception of the United Kingdom, the Queen's duties in each of these countries are carried out by her representative, known as the governor general. In federal states, such as Australia and Canada, the Queen also has representatives at the state or provincial level of government. They are known as governors or lieutenant governors. These officials are appointed by the Queen or governor general, on the advice of the prime minister—or the state premier, as the case may be—and usually serve a five-year term.[5] Interestingly, there is a convention dating from 1931 according to which changes to the rules of succession must be assented to by each of the countries (or realms) in which the Queen is head of state. Such approval was obtained prior to the enactment of the recent amendments described above.[6]

A parliamentary **republic** is headed by an elected president, but despite the use of this latter title, we should not confuse it with a presidential system such as that of the United States. In a parliamentary republic, the president may be directly elected by the people, as in Portugal, Austria, and the Republic of Ireland. In other states, including Greece and Italy, the president is chosen by members of the national parliament. In Germany, the president is chosen by an electoral college (called the Federal Convention) comprising all members of the lower house of the federal parliament and an equal number of delegates elected by the state parliaments.

> **Republic:** A system of government ruled by a head of state who is not a monarch (generally, in modern times, a president), in which citizens are entitled to participate in decision-making.

The second part of the parliamentary dual executive is headed by a prime minister or premier (known in Austria and Germany as the chancellor). The prime minister is appointed by the head of state, usually following a general election, and is invited to form a government by naming a cabinet. In most cases, the prime minister is the leader of the party having the largest number of seats in parliament. As head of government, the prime minister advises the head of state on the exercise of the legal powers held by the latter, and, except in highly unusual circumstances, the head of state is obliged to comply with the prime minister's advice.

What then is the point of having a head of state separate from the head of government? There are three generally accepted roles for the head of state.

1. *To carry out ceremonial duties.* Part of the role of a head of state consists in dedicating new bridges and hospital wings, conferring awards and other honours, formally receiving and accrediting new ambassadors to the country, and hosting state banquets for visiting heads of state. By performing these duties, the head of state lightens the burden of the prime minister, allowing him or her to concentrate on government business.

2. *To serve as the nonpartisan representative of the state.* Unlike the prime minister, the head of state is expected to represent the nation as a whole, even if, as in many parliamentary republics, he or she was elected to office as the official candidate of a political party. Being above the partisan fray, the head of state has the potential to represent all shades of political opinion and to serve as a focus for national unity. To this end the head of state, in public pronouncements, tends to address broad, unifying themes and can even act as a kind of moral compass for the nation. As president of the Federal Republic of Germany from 1999 to 2004, Johannes Rau made a series of speeches reflecting on the nation's Nazi past and warning of a recurrence of political extremism in Germany.

3. *To act as guardian of the constitution.* If the prime minister seeks to undermine the constitution, the head of state may take corrective action by using the wide legal powers at his or her disposal. This is the so-called "fire extinguisher" function of the head of state.[7] For example, if the prime minister were to ignore a parliamentary vote of non-confidence, the head of state would be within his or her rights to dismiss the prime minister. In an even rarer and more extreme situation—a temporary vacuum of governmental authority—the head of state could assume effective control of the state pending the formation of a new government. Such an event occurred in the Caribbean island

nation of Grenada in 1983 when then-governor general Sir Paul Scoon assumed the reins of government following the murder of Prime Minister Maurice Bishop in an attempted *coup d'état*. The coup was thwarted, controversially, by a U.S. military invasion of the island.[8]

In the normal course of events, the head of state exercises his or her formal powers only on the advice of the prime minister or the cabinet as a whole. Nevertheless, there are certain situations in which the head of state has some discretion and is not bound to follow the advice of the ministry. In constitutional monarchies such as Canada and Australia, the head of state may exercise what are known as reserve or prerogative powers. These are residual powers of the Crown that have not been abolished by parliament or the written constitution. However, the head of state does not have an entirely free hand in exercising such powers; rather, he or she is expected to follow any applicable constitutional conventions.

Two of the main prerogative powers held by the head of state in a parliamentary system are the power to appoint or dismiss the prime minister and the power to dissolve parliament for a general election.

Appointment and Dismissal of the Prime Minister

In appointing a prime minister, the head of state is guided in most cases by well-known constitutional conventions. For example, if an incumbent government is re-elected in a general election, the current prime minister stays on, usually with a reshuffled cabinet. If the ruling party is decisively defeated, the outgoing prime minister tenders his or her resignation to the head of state, who then appoints as the new prime minister the leader of the party that won a majority of parliamentary seats. Sometimes, however, it may not be immediately apparent which party leader is in a position to form a government following a general election. In such cases, the head of state may have to hold discussions with parliamentary leaders and to exercise his or her own judgment in naming a prime minister, subject to any applicable conventions. Situations of this kind commonly arise in European democracies where multiple parties are represented in parliament and coalition governments are the norm.

Another well-established convention arises when a prime minister chooses to resign before the government is obliged to go to the polls. Given the reality of party government, prime ministers who wish to retire before the next election will usually announce that their resignation is to take effect as soon as the party has elected a successor—a process that may take days or months, depending on the procedure by which the governing party selects its leader. In Canada, governing parties elect their leaders by conducting a vote of the entire membership of the party. By this method it can take months to select the successor to a retiring prime minister; in the meantime, the incumbent typically remains in office until the party has made its choice.[9]

A more controversial power of the head of state is the power to dismiss the head of government. This power is to be used only in the most extraordinary circumstances, if at all. In parliamentary democracies the general rule is that a prime minister and a cabinet are responsible to parliament—more specifically, to the lower house—and ultimately accountable to the electorate.[10] In 1975, the governor general of Australia created a firestorm of controversy when he dismissed the prime minister, who headed a majority government at the time (see photo essay).

The Dissolution Power

The other main prerogative power is the power of dissolution—the power to dissolve parliament and call a general election. As a general rule, the head of state exercises this power on the advice of the prime minister in one of two circumstances: when the prime minister (still having the confidence of parliament) sees the need for an early election or when the government has been defeated in parliament on a confidence motion. However, the head of state is not bound to dissolve parliament in either of these cases: he or she retains some discretion.

In 1926, the refusal of Canada's governor general, Lord Byng, to grant a dissolution requested by the prime minister, William Lyon Mackenzie King, created a political uproar that came to be known as the King–Byng Affair. In that case, King had sought a dissolution in order to pre-empt an imminent vote in Parliament on a motion of censure against his minority government—a motion that, if passed,

PHOTO ESSAY

Gough Whitlam addresses a large crowd of supporters from the steps of Parliament House following his dismissal as prime minister, November 11, 1975.

THE DAY A GOVERNOR GENERAL FIRED A PRIME MINISTER

On November 11, 1975, Australians were shocked to learn that then-governor general Sir John Kerr had fired the prime minister, Mr. Gough Whitlam, despite the fact that Whitlam's Labor Government held a majority of seats in the House of Representatives, the lower house of the Australian parliament. The ostensible reason for this unprecedented use of the reserve powers of the Crown was the government's inability to secure passage in the Senate of its supply bills—bills giving the government legal authority to spend public money. For three weeks, the Liberal and National Country parties in the Senate had refused to approve supply unless Whitlam agreed to call early elections for the House of Representatives. This Whitlam refused to do on the grounds that the government is responsible to the "People's House" (the House of Representatives), not the Senate. He also contended that in blocking supply the Senate was violating a long-standing convention of British parliamentary government. Adding fuel to the fire was the fact that the opposition parties had recently gained control of the elected Senate by flouting another constitutional convention.*

Whitlam resolved to break the deadlock between the two houses by advising the governor general to call early elections for one-half of the Senate. When the prime minister arrived at Government House, the governor general's official residence, he was unaware that Sir John had already summoned the opposition leader, Mr. Malcolm Fraser. While Fraser waited in an adjacent room, out of view of the prime minister, Sir John abruptly informed Whitlam of his dismissal from office. He next invited Fraser to form a new government on condition that Fraser ensure the passage of supply and then advise a double dissolution of Parliament—the simultaneous election of both houses. Fraser agreed to these terms.

After the Senate had passed the supply bills, Fraser entered the House of Representatives to inform members that the governor general had just appointed him the new prime minister. In response, Labor members, who were still in the majority, passed a motion of non-confidence in Fraser and called on the governor general to reappoint Whitlam! The Speaker of the House attempted to deliver the resolution to Government House but was kept waiting while the governor general dispatched his secretary to read the proclamation dissolving Parliament and fixing the date of the general election. The proclamation ended with the words, "God Save the Queen." Taking his cue from those words, an indignant Gough Whitlam famously declared: "Well may we say God save the Queen because nothing will save the Governor General!"

Most Australians had disapproved of the Opposition's obstructionist tactics and were stunned by Kerr's response. Many accused him of staging a *coup d'état*. Indeed, as news of Whitlam's dismissal spread, thousands of workers walked off the job in protest. Nevertheless, once the election campaign was under way public attention began to focus on other issues—notably the parlous state of the economy—and on polling day Fraser's Liberals won sizeable majorities in both Houses.

Kerr considered the election results to be a vindication of his actions. However, most political analysts fault the governor general for having resorted to such a drastic measure as the dismissal of an elected government, especially as the government still had three weeks of supply. Moreover, in the face of mounting public disapproval of its tactics, the Liberal opposition was thought to be on the brink of giving way—a perception that was later confirmed by several Liberal senators. Others, however, applaud Kerr's conduct, including Sir Garfield Barwick, then-chief justice of the Australian High Court and a former (Liberal Party) attorney general, and Sir David Smith, Kerr's official secretary.[11]

The events of 1975 left a bitter legacy and remain a *cause célèbre* to this day, some 40 years later. Today "the Dismissal" serves as a reminder of the vast reserve powers of the Crown in many parliamentary democracies. It also underscores the importance of conventions that preclude the use of such powers in all but the most extraordinary circumstances. Finally, it sounds a cautionary note about the difficulty of combining a powerful elected Senate—one capable of blocking a budget—with a parliamentary system of responsible government.

* When two Labor-held seats in the Senate had become vacant several months earlier, convention dictated that the vacancies be filled by nominees of the Australian Labor Party (ALP); that way, party standings in the Senate, as of the 1974 election, would be maintained. Instead, the state governments of New South Wales and Queensland, both ruled by opposition parties, appointed opponents of the ALP. As a result of these breaches of constitutional convention, the Opposition gained effective control of the Senate.

would have constituted a vote of non-confidence. Following the denial of his request, King resigned as prime minister and Lord Byng invited the Leader of the Opposition, Arthur Meighen, to form a new government. Meighen's government took office but was defeated days later on a confidence vote. In the ensuing election campaign, King openly criticized the actions of the governor general. When the Liberals were returned to office—albeit with another minority government—many took the result to be a vindication of King's position.

But is the lesson of the King–Byng Affair that the governor general may never again refuse the request of a prime minister for a dissolution? That view is certainly wrong. Constitutional experts agree that there are still circumstances in which the governor general would be perfectly entitled to refuse a dissolution request.[12] What if a prime minister insisted on calling a series of elections merely because he was dissatisfied with the results?[13] As such a course of conduct would constitute an abuse of parliament, the governor general arguably would be duty-bound to put a stop to it.

Such arguments were advanced more recently in an analogous case when, on December 4, 2008, Conservative Prime Minister Stephen Harper stunned the nation by asking the governor general to prorogue the First Session of the 40th Parliament, a mere 16 days after the session had begun following the general election of October 14, 2008. Like dissolution, prorogation is one of the prerogative powers of the governor general. As in the King–Byng Affair, the government was anxious to avoid imminent defeat in Parliament on a non-confidence motion. Meanwhile, the Liberal and New Democratic parties had announced their intention, following the government's defeat, to form a coalition government with support in Parliament from the Bloc Québécois (which the BQ undertook to provide for a minimum of 18 months). Amid much controversy, Governor General Michaëlle Jean agreed to prorogue Parliament until January 26, 2009.

Prorogation is a routine procedure used by prime ministers to end a session of parliament when the government, having carried out the bulk of its legislative agenda, wishes to begin a fresh session with a new set of legislative priorities. However, Harper's use of prorogation in this case was far from routine. In the view of many observers, it was an improper, even unconstitutional, move by the prime minister to prevent Parliament from exercising its right to defeat the government. On this view, the governor general should have refused the prime minister's request.[14] Others contend that it would have been improper, if not unconstitutional, of the governor general to have refused the request of a prime minister who still, technically at least, had the confidence of Parliament. On this view, parliament's privileges would not have been infringed since the opposition parties would still have had an opportunity to defeat the government when the new session opened in January.[15] By that time, however, the Liberals had chosen a new leader, Michael Ignatieff, who was no longer intent on defeating the government.

> **Prorogation:** A prerogative power of the Crown in Westminster systems to end the current session of parliament for a certain period. Nowadays, it is generally exercised only on the advice of the prime minister.

Twelve months later, Prime Minister Harper abruptly prorogued the Second Session of the 40th Parliament and delayed its return for a period of six weeks beyond the scheduled Christmas break. This time the prime minister was apparently intent on shutting down a parliamentary committee that was inquiring into the government's policies and actions in Afghanistan regarding the transfer of detainees by Canadian forces to Afghan authorities. Again, the prime minister was accused by many of evading accountability to Parliament and of undermining responsible government.[16] Nevertheless, Governor General Jean granted the requested prorogation.

PARLIAMENTARY, PRESIDENTIAL, AND SEMI-PRESIDENTIAL SYSTEMS

As discussed in Chapter 6, the distinction between confederal, federal, and unitary states has to do with the vertical distribution of power between national and subnational governments. But what about the horizontal distribution of power within one level of government or the other? Here we may distinguish between parliamentary, presidential, and semi-presidential systems.

Parliamentary Systems

Parliamentary government, in its modern form, originated in Great Britain in the 18th century and has been widely imitated throughout the world. Countries having a parliamentary system include Canada, Australia, Germany, Japan, and Sweden. While there are important national variations in the form and function of parliamentary systems, certain essential features may be identified. First, parliamentary systems have a dual executive consisting of a separate head of state and head of government. A second feature has to do with the relationship between the executive and the legislative branches of government.

THINK AND DISCUSS

In view of the important constitutional role of the head of state in a parliamentary democracy, is this office better suited to a monarch or an elected president? What are the advantages and disadvantages of each?

In parliamentary systems based on the British (Westminster) model, there is an overlapping of powers and personnel between the two branches, which arises from the fact that the prime minister and members of the cabinet simultaneously hold office in both. As elected members of the legislature, the prime minister and the cabinet are intimately involved in parliamentary affairs, from introducing government bills to responding to questions from opposition MPs. Indeed, the prime minister and the cabinet dominate the parliamentary agenda, starting with the **Speech from the Throne**, an outline of what the government hopes to achieve in any given session of parliament. At the same time, the prime minister and the cabinet are responsible for discharging the executive functions of the state. As such, their duties include administering the daily operations of government departments and exercising a host of executive powers, from conducting foreign relations with other states to appointing hundreds of public officeholders, such as judges, ambassadors, senior civil servants, and the heads of various agencies, boards, and commissions. This intersection of the two branches of government in the prime minister and the cabinet is known as the **fusion of powers**.

> **Speech from the Throne:** The document prepared by the prime minister and cabinet and read by the head of state at the opening of each session of parliament; it outlines the government's legislative proposals for the session to follow.

> **Fusion of powers:** In parliamentary systems, the joint exercise of legislative and executive powers by the prime minister and members of the cabinet, who simultaneously hold office in the legislative and executive branches of government.

A third feature of parliamentary systems is the doctrine of **responsible government**, according to which the government may hold office only as long as it maintains majority support in the legislature. As noted earlier, in bicameral parliaments the lower house is the confidence chamber, not the upper house. If the government loses a confidence vote, it must resign or seek early elections. In Westminster systems, the prime minister also has the discretion to call an early general election, even if the government retains the confidence of parliament. This point is discussed further below.

> **Responsible government:** A defining principle of the Westminster model of parliamentary government, according to which the cabinet may only hold office as long as it has majority support in the legislature on votes of confidence. In a bicameral parliament the government is responsible to the lower house, not the upper house.

Parliamentary systems based on the Westminster model entail an enormous concentration of power in the hands of the prime minister and the cabinet. This is especially so in cases where the governing party has an absolute majority of seats in parliament: that is, a **majority government**. Moreover, political parties tend to be highly disciplined and cohesive in parliament; after all, the governing party cannot afford to lose a vote of confidence. As a result, it is customary for MPs belonging to the same party to vote as a bloc on bills and resolutions before parliament.

> **Majority government:** A government in which a single party holds a majority of seats in parliament and has exclusive control of the cabinet.

Advantages of Parliamentary Government

Parliamentary constitutions have many advantages. First, a government with a stable parliamentary majority is able to act decisively to implement its legislative program. This is equally true whether the government is formed by a single party or by a durable multiparty coalition. More specifically, parliamentary governments are well equipped to adopt measures designed to serve the national interest, even if such measures be opposed by powerful sectional groups in the country. Indeed, disciplined parties, while disparaged by many Canadians, provide individual MPs with some degree of protection against the efforts of powerful lobby groups to influence the votes they cast in parliament.[17] Second, by concentrating political power in the prime minister and the cabinet, parliamentary systems clarify political responsibility. The opposition parties in parliament hold the government to account both for its policies and its administrative competence. Equally, general elections in parliamentary systems tend to offer electors a choice between parties campaigning on national issues, rather than being a series of contests among individual candidates on local issues.

Third, the mechanism of the **non-confidence vote** allows for the removal of a government that has lost support in parliament. Such was the fate of the minority governments of Paul Martin in November 2005 and Stephen Harper in March 2011.

> **Confidence (or non-confidence) vote:** An explicitly worded motion indicating that the legislature either has or does not have confidence in the government; a vote on a matter that the government has previously declared to be a matter of confidence; or a vote on important measures central to the government's plans, such as the budget.

Disadvantages of Parliamentary Government

A leading criticism of parliamentary systems is that they vest excessive power in the hands of the government. According to Lord Hailsham, a former British politician, a majority government constitutes an "elective dictatorship," since it faces no effective check on its power in parliament. This is especially true of parliamentary systems such as those of Canada and Great Britain, in which the electoral system tends to give one party an absolute majority of seats and in which the upper house of parliament lacks effective power.

Another criticism of parliamentary systems is that by engendering disciplined national parties, they leave MPs less free to represent local interests, particularly where those interests conflict with the policy of the party to which an MP belongs. MPs affiliated with the governing party are especially constrained in this regard.[18]

Finally, parliamentary government can be unstable if no party is able to secure majority support in parliament. This has been the experience of Italy, where there have been over 50 changes of government since 1945. Governments in France under the Fourth Republic (1946–1958) were also notoriously short-lived. On the other hand, as many commentators have noted, postwar governments in Italy and Fourth-Republic France were less unstable than they appeared. Typically, the same coalition partners

remained in office following a change of government, key ministers were reappointed, and major government policies continued in force.

Presidential Systems

The presidential (or congressional) form of government originated in the United States in the 1780s. Although not as widely practised as its parliamentary counterpart, it has been adopted by most Central and South American states. The U.S. presidential system was designed with a view to avoiding an undue concentration of political power in any single branch of government. Consequently, there is a strict **separation of powers** among the executive, the legislature, and the judiciary.

> **Separation of powers:** A principle of constitutional government that is usually taken to mean that the legislative, executive, and judicial functions of the state should be carried out by separate branches of government. No one may hold office in more than one branch at the same time.

Under a presidential system, executive functions are consolidated in the president, who is both head of state and head of government (known as the *administration*). Legislative powers are assigned to the bicameral Congress, which comprises the Senate and the House of Representatives. On the relationship between the legislature and the executive, it is more accurate to say that there is a separation of personnel and a sharing, rather than a separation, of powers. For one, the president and all members of the cabinet are barred from sitting in Congress while holding executive office.[19] In addition, presidential elections are held independently from congressional elections. In the U.S., the president is elected every four years while members of the House of Representatives must face the electorate every two years; as a result, congressional elections are held in tandem with presidential elections, followed two years later by "mid-term" elections of the House held halfway through the president's four-year term of office. Senators, meanwhile, serve six-year terms, with one-third of the Senate being up for election every two years.

The exercise of executive and legislative powers is subject to a complex system of **checks and balances**.

Bills passed by both houses of Congress may be vetoed by the president. Congress, in turn, may override a presidential **veto** by a two-thirds majority vote of both houses. This sharing of legislative power by the two branches is also reflected in the joint exercise of certain executive powers. For example, key presidential appointments, from cabinet secretaries to federal judges to the heads of key executive agencies, must be formally confirmed by the Senate. Similarly, treaties negotiated by the president must be ratified by a minimum two-thirds majority vote of the Senate.

> **Checks and balances:** A constitutional system of power-sharing under which powers are assigned to the three branches of government (the executive, legislative, and judicial) so as to enable each branch to curb the unilateral exercise of power by the others.

> **Veto:** The authority to block a decision or piece of legislation, especially that of a president to reject a law passed by congress or that of a province to reject a proposed constitutional amendment.

Since both branches have fixed terms of office, the president may not dissolve Congress to hold early elections; by the same token, Congress may not remove a president in whom it no longer has confidence, except by the extraordinary procedure of impeachment. Under Article II (Section 4) of the U.S. Constitution, the president may be impeached for "Treason, Bribery, or other high Crimes and Misdemeanors." If articles of impeachment are approved by the House of Representatives, the matter proceeds to the Senate, where the president can be removed from office on a two-thirds majority vote. No U.S. president has been successfully impeached, although Richard Nixon resigned the presidency in 1974 after articles of impeachment were passed by the House Judiciary Committee.[20] The most recent attempt at impeachment, brought against Democratic President Bill Clinton by the Republican-controlled Congress in 1998, fell well short of the two-thirds majority required in the Senate. The political, as opposed to judicial, nature of impeachment was clearly revealed in that case as members of Congress voted strictly along party lines.[21]

The Advantages and Disadvantages of Presidential Government

Proponents of presidentialism cite various points in its favour. Among other things, it is argued that presidential executives are stable owing to their constitutionally fixed terms and to the provision made for the automatic installation of the vice-president in case the president is unable to complete his or her term. At minimum, these features of presidentialism help to avoid the frequent changes of government to which parliamentary systems may be susceptible. It has also been observed that presidents have a larger pool of talent from which to make cabinet appointments than do prime ministers in Westminster systems. Not being restricted to persons who have been elected to parliament, presidents may appoint cabinet secretaries from the ranks of business, academia, or other institutions.

Presidentialism also gives the legislature a more meaningful role as a lawmaking body by allowing members of Congress to defeat, or substantially amend, a bill sponsored by the president without automatically removing the president from office. Parliamentary executives, in contrast, too often hold the latter prospect like a hammer over the heads of MPs to cow them into supporting the government's measures. Congressional legislators therefore enjoy greater freedom from party discipline and have more scope to represent local interests. But the leading argument made in support of presidentialism is that the dispersal of political authority safeguards individual liberty against unreasonable encroachment by the state.[22]

Critics of presidentialism deplore its tendency to produce deadlock between the two branches of government. This feature of presidential systems arises from the diffusion of decision-making authority and the reciprocal vetoes held by the executive and legislative branches. Moreover, being separately elected, each branch can claim to have a mandate from the people and, for that reason, may be unwilling to reach a compromise with the other branch. And since the president lacks the power to dissolve Congress, there is no effective means to end the impasse. In the United States, the fragmentation of political authority arguably has helped well-funded lobby groups to block or significantly water down such measures as effective gun control and universal public health insurance.

A related shortcoming of presidentialism is the difficulty that voters face in assigning responsibility for political decisions (or political inaction) under a system of dispersed decision-making authority. This difficulty is compounded by the organizational looseness of national parties and by the tendency for congressional candidates to campaign for election on local rather than national issues.[23]

Proponents of presidential government reply to these points by noting the capacity of a strong president to unify the nation and to command considerable political authority. As the only officeholder to be elected by the nation as a whole, the president can claim to have a truly national mandate. In addition, presidents derive much authority from their dual status as head of state and head of government, not to mention their role as commander-in-chief of the armed forces. Indeed, the prestige of the presidency can bestow on even a mediocre occupant of the office considerable stature and gravitas in the eyes of ordinary citizens. In times of national crisis, this symbolic resource can be a significant asset for presidents as they seek to mobilize support from Congress and the nation. On the other hand, critics are quick to note the vulnerability of presidential systems when the chief executive brings the office into disrepute. When U.S. President Richard Nixon was implicated in criminal behaviour in the Watergate affair of 1972–1974, his status as head of state created a crisis of legitimacy in the institution of the presidency. Presidentialism can also exhibit antidemocratic features, as when presidents (and their supporters) equate legitimate political opposition to the head of state with disloyalty to the state itself. To critics of presidentialism, such as Juan Linz, it is no coincidence "that most of the countries with presidential constitutions have been unstable democracies or authoritarian regimes."[24]

Another point of contention between advocates of parliamentary and presidential government concerns the question of prior political experience. In parliamentary systems, prime ministers usually come into office after many years of service in parliament and in senior cabinet positions. As such, they bring to the office direct knowledge of national politics and the inner workings of a cabinet government. In presidential systems, the chief executive is more likely to take office with little or no prior experience in national government. In the U.S., three of the last five presidents—George W. Bush, Bill Clinton, and Ronald Reagan—were state governors prior to their election to the White House. While presidential candidates often seek to make a virtue of their status as Washington "outsiders," it is debatable whether inexperience in national government is a desirable quality for the leader of a major democracy, let alone a world superpower.

Semi-Presidential Systems

A halfway house between parliamentary and presidential systems is the so-called semi-presidential form of government. Semi-presidential systems combine elements of parliamentary and presidential government; broadly speaking, they combine a popularly elected president with a parliamentary prime minister.[25] Unlike the head of state of a parliamentary republic, the president has real power and the authority to use it. The quintessential example of a semi-presidential system is France under the Fifth Republic, especially since 1962, when the presidency became a popularly elected office. Other examples of semi-presidential systems include Finland, Russia, and several of the new democracies of Eastern Europe, including Poland, Romania, and Bulgaria (see Table 7.1).[26]

Sometimes the label semi-presidential is applied to any parliamentary system having a directly elected president. By this broad definition, countries such as Austria and the Republic of Ireland would be classified as semi-presidential systems. But as Arend Lijphart points out, the real test of a semi-presidential system is whether the president, rather than the prime minister, is the pre-eminent head of government.[27] In states such as Russia and France, the president is usually in charge. While leaving the day-to-day business of government in the hands of the prime minister, the president reserves the right to intervene in matters of policy and administration. The president may even sack a prime minister who still has the confidence of parliament.[28]

France is an interesting case because the president's wide powers, which are largely unwritten, are significantly curtailed when parties opposed to the president win control of the National Assembly. In cases like these, the president is obliged to appoint a prime minister acceptable to the new parliament. In such periods of cohabitation, France functions much

TABLE 7.1 SELECTED PARLIAMENTARY, PRESIDENTIAL, AND SEMI-PRESIDENTIAL STATES		
Parliamentary	**Presidential**	**Semi-presidential**
Australia	Argentina	Belarus
Belgium	Brazil	Bulgaria
Canada	Chile	Finland
India	Costa Rica	France
Italy	Indonesia	Lithuania
Jamaica	Mexico	Poland
Japan	Nigeria	Romania
Norway	Philippines	Russia
Spain	United States	South Korea
United Kingdom	Venezuela	Ukraine

Source: Based, inter alia, on Robert Elgie, "The Classification of Democratic Regime Types: Conceptual Ambiguity and Contestable Assumptions," *European Journal of Political Research*, vol. 33, no. 2 (1998), p. 228. Reprinted by permission of John Wiley and Sons.

like a parliamentary republic, with the notable exception that the president retains responsibility for foreign affairs and can dissolve the National Assembly on his own initiative before the expiration of its five-year term.

THE CHIEF EXECUTIVE: PRIME MINISTERS VERSUS PRESIDENTS

Prime ministers and presidents sit at the apex of power in parliamentary and presidential systems of government. As chief executives, they are widely seen to have ultimate responsibility for the executive branch as a whole, even though much of their decision-making authority is formally shared with other political actors. This point was famously made by U.S. President Harry S. Truman: a sign on Truman's desk proclaimed, "The buck stops here." In this section we consider the powers of prime ministers and presidents as well as various factors which condition the exercise of those powers. In doing so we must take into account the very different institutional settings in which prime ministers and presidents are obliged to operate.

The Prime Minister

In parliamentary systems, the political executive consists of the **prime minister** and the **cabinet**. In fact, parliamentary government is sometimes called a **cabinet government**, a phrase that denotes the fact

that government policy is formally set by the cabinet through a collective and collegial process of decision-making. According to the theory of a cabinet government, the prime minister is *primus inter pares* (first among equals) at the cabinet table.

Prime minister: The head of government in a parliamentary system, who provides political leadership and makes the major decisions, usually in concert with a cabinet.

Cabinet: The group of people chosen by the prime minister or president to provide political direction to government departments; in Canada, cabinet members act collectively to make the key government decisions.

Cabinet government: A system of government in which the major political decisions are made by the cabinet as a whole, as opposed to one in which the prime minister or president acts with considerable autonomy.

The office of prime minister originated in Great Britain in the 18th century. Sir Robert Walpole is generally considered Britain's first prime minister. During Walpole's long premiership (1721–1742) certain conventions of the cabinet government began to take form. Nevertheless, well into the 19th century, monarchs continued to exert personal influence over affairs of state because of their capacity to buy the allegiance of members of parliament elected from "pocket boroughs" (parliamentary districts containing small numbers of eligible voters). The Reform Act of 1832 abolished most of the pocket boroughs, thereby requiring MPs to reflect more faithfully the views of their constituents. Henceforth, the king would be obliged to appoint a prime minister who was Parliament's first choice, if not necessarily the king's.[29] As a result of these developments, the prime minister emerged as the effective head of government. According to Bagehot, the rights of the monarch in relation to the prime minister could now be summed up as follows: "the right to be consulted, the right to encourage, and the right to warn."[30] The monarch no longer had the right to refuse the advice of a prime minister having the confidence of the cabinet and of parliament.[31]

If the 19th century saw political power shift decisively from the Crown to parliament, the 20th century saw a comparable power shift from parliament to the political executive. Meanwhile, within the executive itself in recent years, more and more power has become concentrated in the hands of the prime minister at the expense of the cabinet as a whole. Before exploring this trend let us identify the principles of a cabinet government and discuss the formal role of the prime minister.

Principles of a Cabinet Government The following are three core principles of a cabinet government in Westminster systems such as Canada's:

- **Collective responsibility**. The principle of **collective responsibility** means that all members of the government ("the ministry") are collectively responsible to parliament for government policy and for the overall performance of the government. Thus, when a minister introduces a bill into parliament, that bill is taken to be a statement of government policy. The defeat in parliament of a bill introduced by a particular minister is therefore treated as a repudiation of the policy of the government as a whole. As noted earlier, if the vote on an important government bill is regarded as a confidence vote, the bill's defeat would have the effect of bringing down the government.

> **Collective responsibility:** In Westminster parliamentary systems, members of the political executive are collectively responsible to parliament for government policy and for the overall administrative performance of the government.

- **Cabinet solidarity**. The principle of **cabinet solidarity** refers to the constitutional obligation of all ministers publicly to support the policy of the government. Cabinet meetings are held behind closed doors and are subject to strict rules of cabinet secrecy. Ministers may speak candidly about proposed government policies and actions; however, once the cabinet has reached a decision, all ministers are obliged to explain and defend it in public. This practice enables parliament to identify the policy of the government and thus to hold the cabinet collectively responsible for it.

> **Cabinet solidarity:** The constitutional duty of ministers to publicly support the policy of the government. Ministers who openly dissent from government policy must resign from the government.

- Any minister who is unable to support the decisions of his or her colleagues must resign from the cabinet. In Britain, it is not uncommon for ministers to resign from the cabinet on matters of principle. For example, in 2003, Robin Cook and Clare Short, two members of Tony Blair's government, resigned from the ministry to protest the government's decision to participate in the U.S.-led invasion of Iraq. In 1990, Geoffrey Howe, a senior minister in Margaret Thatcher's government, resigned in protest against the prime minister's policy toward Europe and her autocratic style of leadership.
- In Canada, ministers rarely resign because of philosophical or policy differences with their colleagues. An exception to that rule occurred in November 2006, when Michael Chong resigned from the Cabinet of Stephen Harper to protest the Government's decision to designate the Québécois as a nation (see Chapter 6). However, it is more common for ministers to resign as a result of their being caught up in political scandals.

- **Ministerial responsibility**. The principle of **ministerial responsibility** refers to the responsibility of individual ministers to parliament. Under this doctrine, a minister is responsible not only for his or her own actions and decisions but also for those of officials in the department—whether or not the minister was aware of them. In other words, the minister is the public face of the department and must take *political* responsibility for it.

> **Ministerial responsibility:** The responsibility of individual ministers to answer to parliament for the administration of their departments, including the actions of public officials employed in such departments.

Holding Government to Account

In formal terms, there are various mechanisms for holding the executive accountable for its conduct in parliamentary systems. The oldest form of parliamentary control of the executive is the power of the purse—that is to say, the requirement that parliament authorize public spending and the imposition of new taxes by the executive. Parliament also has the opportunity to scrutinize public expenditures after the fact when ministries prepare detailed public accounts; in Canada, these records are examined by an independent officer, the Auditor General, whose annual report is then submitted to Parliament. Shortly before Jean Chrétien stepped down as prime minister in 2003, Auditor General Sheila Fraser delivered a scathing indictment of the ways in which federal advertising and sponsorship contracts had been tendered by the Department of Public Works in the years following the 1995 Quebec referendum on independence. The political outcry that ensued led Chrétien's successor, Paul Martin, to appoint a judicial enquiry into the so-called sponsorship scandal.

On a day-to-day basis, ministers are obliged to explain and defend government policy and executive actions through the oral Question Period as well as through routine debates in parliament. Ministers and senior civil servants are also expected to appear before parliamentary committees.

From time to time, opposition parties demand the resignation of a minister for maladministration. While such demands are rarely complied with, ministers are more likely to resign if they are deemed to be personally responsible for a questionable action than if the fault lies with subordinates in the minister's department. In either case, the minister is obliged to answer to parliament. This dilution of the doctrine of ministerial responsibility has led some to identify a new doctrine of ministerial answerability.[32] The general rule nowadays appears to be that the prime minister decides whether to request the minister's resignation, on the basis of an assessment of the minister's overall usefulness to the government.

Beyond the formal institutions of parliament, the news media can act as an important agent of government accountability. While the media are usually drawn to the more sensational and melodramatic aspects of political life, investigative journalists nevertheless can expose serious cases of executive misconduct or bring to light the consequences of ill-conceived government policies. Adverse news coverage, in turn, can act as a spur to corrective action.

Prime Ministerial Government

The prime minister occupies a position of preeminent power in Westminster systems. As noted above, many observers have detected a long-term trend toward the growing concentration of decision-making power in the hands of the prime minister at the expense of the cabinet. On this view, cabinet government has been superseded by **prime ministerial government**.[33] An early cartoon depicting this phenomenon is included in this chapter.

> **Prime ministerial government:** The notion that the prime minister is now so pre-eminent that the term "cabinet government" no longer accurately describes how decisions are made in the political executive, especially those based on the Westminster model. This idea is also known as the presidentialization of the parliamentary executive.

Others dispute this dire assessment; in their view, there remain significant checks on the powers of prime ministers. Nevertheless, it cannot be doubted that prime ministers have wide decision-making powers. Some of these powers are based on written or unwritten rules of the constitution while others have a legal basis in collective decisions of the cabinet to delegate authority directly to the prime minister.

'And now that we're reshuffled—onwards and upwards!'

This 1967 cartoon depicts the governing style of British Prime Minister Harold Wilson in his first term of government (1964–1970). Wilson adopted a more collegial style of governing in his second term (1974–1976).

Copyright Guardian News and Media Ltd 1967

Among the most important powers that are wielded by the prime minister we may count the following:

- *To make appointments to the cabinet.* The prime minister names the members of the cabinet, who are then sworn into office by the head of state. In Westminster systems, the only constitutional requirement to be met is the need for ministers to have a seat in parliament (normally the lower house of a bicameral legislature). The prime minister also has the power to remove ministers from the cabinet or to reassign them to other portfolios (called a cabinet shuffle).
- *To determine the organization of the cabinet and of government departments.* Every prime minister has the discretion to determine how large the cabinet shall be. In a small cabinet, some ministers will have responsibility for two or more departments of government. Alternatively, the prime minister may choose to merge separate departments into a smaller number of large departments. In such cases, cabinet ministers may be assisted by one or more junior ministers (ministers without cabinet rank), under-secretaries, or parliamentary secretaries.
- *To call a general election.* By convention, the prime minister has sole authority to advise the head of

state on the timing of a general election, within the normal lifespan of a parliament. As noted, this advice is almost invariably followed. Armed with this power, the prime minister may choose an election date that maximizes the governing party's chances of re-election. As the opposition parties are not privy to the prime minister's intentions, it is difficult for them to prepare their election campaigns with certainty.

Some have argued that the prime minister should not be able to take advantage of election timing in this way. They contend that elections should be held at fixed intervals, as in the United States. In Canada, several provinces have passed laws establishing fixed election dates. As noted in Chapter 6, a similar law governing federal elections was adopted by Parliament in 2007. In all of these cases, an early election may still be triggered by the defeat of the government on a confidence vote.

- *To make appointments to various posts within the government.* In addition to appointing cabinet ministers, the prime minister also chooses a host of other public officials, such as high-ranking civil servants, senior members of the judiciary, ambassadors, and the heads of state-owned enterprises. Some of these appointments are made on the basis of patronage; that is, the appointee's main qualification being his or her past political services to the governing party.
- *To convene and chair cabinet meetings.* The prime minister can call cabinet meetings at any time, and has various means of influencing its decisions. First, through control of the agenda, prime ministers can ensure that no item of business can come before the cabinet without their approval. Thus, if prime ministers are unsure that an important issue will go their way in the cabinet, they can keep it off the agenda until they have mobilized sufficient support for their preferred outcome. Second, the prime minister controls the establishment of cabinet committees and determines their membership. The recommendations of these committees go to the full cabinet, where they are usually ratified. Third, instead of calling a vote within the cabinet—in which case the prime minister would cast but one vote among many—the prime minister sums up discussion by articulating

the predominant mood of the cabinet—as the prime minister sees it. Even if the prime minister's definition of consensus does not reflect the majority view, the prime minister's summation becomes the official position of the government and is recorded as such in the minutes. At that point, the doctrine of cabinet solidarity obliges all ministers to defend the policy of the government or to resign from the cabinet.

• *To act as chief spokesperson for the government.* When journalists pose questions to ministers about the pressing issues of the day, a minister may go out on a limb and state a position that is inconsistent with that of the prime minister. In that case, the prime minister will usually make a statement purporting to explain what the errant minister really intended to say! The minister then invariably endorses the prime minister's view; as a result, all members of the government are once again in the happy position of singing from the same hymnbook. In the case of a fundamental disagreement between the prime minister and a senior minister, it is understood that the minister must give way. Shortly after the election of the Socialist–Green coalition government in Germany in 1998, a serious disagreement about economic policy broke out between Chancellor Gerhard Schroeder and his finance minister, Oskar Lafontaine. As a consequence of this breach, Lafontaine resigned his post in March 1999.

Limits on Prime Ministerial Power

Despite their undoubted power, prime ministers cannot act with impunity. To be a successful leader, the prime minister needs to be aware of important political constraints and to exercise power with discretion. The nature of such constraints varies from one state to another and can even vary over time within a single state.

In the matter of cabinet formation, the prime minister may wish to appoint all of his or her closest political allies, but there are other considerations that cannot be ignored. For example, in most European countries national elections are conducted using some form of proportional representation (PR). One of the characteristics of PR-based elections is that single-party majority governments are rarely formed (as detailed in Chapter 10); instead, one of the major parties is obliged to enter into a coalition with one or more of the other parties represented in parliament. In such cases, prime ministers must reach agreement with their coalition partners on the allocation of cabinet posts. Even if the government is formed by a single party, the prime minister must be mindful of certain political realities. If the governing party contains distinctive ideological camps, party unity may demand that major currents of opinion be adequately represented in the cabinet. (The role of expertise in cabinet formation is covered in Box 7.1)

In other countries, the importance of ideology may be overshadowed by the need to ensure that major social groups and regional populations are represented in the cabinet. In Canada, the prime minister is expected to ensure that MPs from all regions of the country, if not every province, have a seat at the cabinet table. Canadian prime ministers must also maintain an appropriate balance of anglophone and francophone ministers. It should be added that in all Western democracies today, prime ministers are expected to ensure that women have at least some representation in the cabinet.

BOX 7.1

WHAT ABOUT EXPERTISE?

Odd as it may seem, prime ministers are not unduly concerned, when forming a cabinet, that a minister possess expertise in the subject matter of his or her portfolio. Thus, it is not thought necessary to appoint a physician minister of health or a retired general minister of defense. The role of the minister is to act as political head of the department; accordingly, he or she is expected to defend its interests at the cabinet table, to explain and promote government policy in parliament and the country, and to ensure that the department is soundly administered. To fulfill these functions, the minister requires *political* skills, which are usually honed as a result of years of parliamentary experience.

To the extent that ministers need to acquire specialized knowledge to perform their tasks, they rely on the expertise of permanent officials in the department. Critics contend that this reliance on senior bureaucrats is a recipe for ministers to become captive to the interests of their departments.

Interestingly, the internal rules of the governing party may also curtail the power of the prime minister. For example, under the constitution of the Australian Labor Party (ALP), members of the cabinet are to be elected by members of the Labor caucus in parliament. A Labor prime minister may, however, assign cabinet members to specific portfolios. Party constitutions also determine the procedure by which a party leader may be removed. If the party is in power, removal of the leader entails a change of prime minister. In some parties, the leader can be removed by his or her parliamentary colleagues with remarkable dispatch. In this way, Margaret Thatcher was forced to step down as British Conservative Party leader and prime minister in 1990. Likewise, Australian Prime Minister Kevin Rudd was ousted by his Labor colleagues in 2010, shortly before a scheduled general election that the Party was expected to lose. Rudd's successor, Julia Gillard, led Labor to a narrow victory in the ensuing general election. Three years later, supporters of Kevin Rudd ousted Gillard and restored him as party leader and prime minister. Rudd's comeback proved to be short-lived, however. Several months after regaining the premiership he led his party to defeat in the general election of September 2013 and promptly resigned.

In other parties, the leader is elected by a vote of the party's rank-and-file or by a vote of elected delegates at a party convention. These extra-parliamentary methods of selecting and deselecting leaders are said to promote internal party democracy and to make party leaders more accountable to their members. Paradoxically, leaders who are elected outside parliament appear to have a more secure grip on power.[34]

While there has undoubtedly been a long-term trend toward the concentration of power in the hands of prime ministers, not all first ministers are able or willing to centralize power to the same degree. The balance of power between the prime minister and the cabinet is conditioned by such factors as the prime minister's personality and governing style. While some prime ministers choose to centralize power in their office, others prefer a more collegial style of governance in which the advice of the cabinet is both sought and heeded. The prime minister's ability to dominate the cabinet is also conditioned by the calibre of the ministers. If there are strong personalities around the table, prime ministers are less likely to be successful in bending the cabinet to their will. The prime minister's authority also hinges on the government's position in parliament. Other things being equal, a prime minister must be more conciliatory toward cabinet (and caucus) colleagues when the government is in a minority position in parliament; in such cases, the prime minister must also exercise more tact in dealing with the opposition parties. On the other hand, prime ministers who have just led their party to a resounding election victory are in a strong position to assert their authority in the cabinet, in caucus, and in parliament.

The President

In certain respects, presidents command wider authority than prime ministers. For example, Article II of the U.S. Constitution vests executive power in the president alone. Accordingly, "[t]he president is not first among equals; he is explicitly 'number one,' the person in charge."[35] The cabinet is not, therefore, a body for collective decision-making. While the president may consult individual members of the cabinet (called "cabinet secretaries" in the U.S.), he or she is under no obligation to do so. In other words, the policy of the administration on all matters is ultimately that of the president. The president also derives considerable political authority from the fact of being directly elected by the people, unlike a prime minister.[36]

On the other hand, as noted earlier, presidents are subject to a host of formal checks and balances. For example, the president must formally submit cabinet nominees to the Senate for confirmation. This requirement also applies to other senior executive

THINK AND DISCUSS

What factors have contributed to the emergence of prime ministerial government in Canada in recent years? What steps, if any, do you think could be taken to redress the imbalance of power between the prime minister, the cabinet, and Parliament?

appointments, including ambassadorships and the heads of major federal agencies such as the FBI, the CIA, the Federal Communications Commission, and the Supreme Court bench. Senate confirmation hearings are no mere formality; indeed, it is not unheard of for the Senate to reject presidential nominees. In 2005, President George W. Bush was forced to withdraw his nomination of Harriet Miers for the Supreme Court in the face of strong opposition from members of the Senate Judiciary Committee. The president's substitute nominee, Samuel Alito, met with the approval of most senators and was duly confirmed. Likewise, Larry Summers, President Obama's preferred choice to head the Federal Reserve, the U.S. central bank, withdrew his name from consideration in 2013 in the face of widespread opposition from Senate Democrats. Critics faulted him for having promoted bank deregulation during his tenure as Treasury Secretary in the 1990s.[37] In place of Summers, Obama nominated Janet Yellen, who was confirmed in January 2014 as the first woman to head the Federal Reserve.

One striking difference between presidential and parliamentary executives lies in the field of foreign affairs. In Westminster parliamentary systems, the political executive has exclusive authority over foreign relations, including the power to conclude treaties, to commit troops overseas, and even to declare war. The formal approval of parliament is not required in these cases; it must be said, however, that governments will often allow parliament to vote on such matters in order to lend greater legitimacy to the decisions taken by the prime minister and the cabinet. For example, the parliament of Canada formally approved a resolution declaring war on Germany in September 1939. In 2003, British Prime Minister Tony Blair yielded to pressure from backbench MPs on both sides of the House to hold a debate in Parliament on the impending deployment of British troops in Iraq.[38] On that occasion Parliament endorsed the government's plan. A decade later, Parliament rejected Prime Minister David Cameron's case for British military action in Syria against forces loyal to the regime of President Bashar al-Assad.[39] In presidential systems, the president must submit treaties to the legislature for ratification; in the United States, they must be approved by at least two-thirds of the Senate. Ratification is not guaranteed in all cases. In 1999, the Republican-controlled Senate delivered a setback to President Bill Clinton when it rejected the Comprehensive Nuclear Test Ban Treaty.[40] Article I (Section 8) of the U.S. Constitution gives Congress, not the president, the power to declare war. In practice, this formal limitation has not significantly hampered the ability of presidents to send troops into combat. During the Vietnam War, the Johnson and Nixon administrations committed tens of thousands of troops to Indochina without a formal declaration of war. Instead, following an attack on U.S. ships in the Gulf of Tonkin in 1964, Johnson sought, and obtained, broad congressional approval for combat operations in Southeast Asia. The Gulf of Tonkin resolution authorized the president "to take all necessary measures to repel any armed attack against the forces of the United States and to prevent further aggression."[41]

In 1973, Congress attempted to curtail the president's power to send U.S. troops into combat with the passage of the War Powers Resolution. It requires the president to consult with Congress prior to the start of hostilities and to remove U.S. troops from theatres of combat within 60 days if Congress has not declared war or passed a resolution authorizing the use of force. In practice, this limitation on the power of presidents to wage war has proven to be ineffective. As chief executive and commander-in-chief of the armed forces, the president is in a powerful position to define threats to the security interests of the state. Among other things, the president has access

Janet Yellen testifying before the Banking Committee of the U.S. Senate on November 14, 2013, prior to her confirmation as Chair of the Federal Reserve.

© AP Photo/Jacquelyn Martin

to intelligence information to which most members of Congress are not privy. Moreover, the president in most cases can appeal successfully to the patriotism (if not jingoism) of citizens when embarking on military operations abroad. This point is illustrated by the U.S. Senate's 77–23 vote in October 2002 authorizing the president to use military force against the regime of Saddam Hussein. At that time, the White House insisted that Iraq possessed "weapons of mass destruction" and thereby posed a clear and present danger to the stability of the Middle East, a claim later proven false.[42] Equally unfounded were administration claims that Iraq was behind the September 11 attacks on the World Trade Center and the Pentagon. Figure 7.2 is an organization chart of the whole U.S. government apparatus.

CENTRAL AGENCIES

Political executives face a formidable challenge in developing public policy and managing the multifaceted operations of the modern state. In an attempt to establish a more efficient and rational system of decision-making, governments have increasingly come to rely on **central agencies**. Unlike government departments, central agencies do not, in the main, have regulatory or program responsibilities. Rather, their mandate is to support the work of the political executive. Three key functions of central agencies are to prepare strategic plans for government, to develop and integrate economic and budgetary policies, and to allocate and manage the human and other resources of government.[43] Central agencies assumed a larger role in Canada and other Western democracies beginning in the 1970s as governments sought to fashion a more coordinated approach to policy-making and to exert more effective control over public spending.

> **Central agencies:** Those agencies of the state that assist the political executive to coordinate and control overall government operations. They provide both policy advice and administrative support.

In Canada, three key central agencies are the Privy Council Office, the **Prime Minister's Office**, and the **Department of Finance**.[44] The Privy Council Office (PCO) is staffed by civil servants seconded from various government departments. The PCO is headed by the clerk of the Privy Council and secretary to the Cabinet, who is the highest-ranking civil servant in Ottawa. Being a nonpartisan agency, the PCO serves the government of the day, regardless of its political stripe. The main roles of the PCO are to coordinate the flow of information to the prime minister and the cabinet and to provide analysis of major policy proposals. The PCO also advises the prime minister on the organization of government and on the appointment of senior civil servants in government departments and of officials who serve on various agencies, boards, and commissions.

> **Prime Minister's Office (PMO):** In Canada, the office that provides political advice to the prime minister. Staffed by partisan appointees, its chief concern is to protect and promote the PM's political interests.

> **Department of Finance:** Chief economic advisor of the government of Canada, this department is responsible for managing the national economy, raising revenue, preparing economic forecasts, and determining public expenditure levels. Its British counterpart is the Treasury.

The Prime Minister's Office (PMO) is staffed by political appointees of the prime minister. Its task is to provide partisan political advice to the prime minister—advice that civil servants are precluded from giving. Among other things, it assists the prime minister in developing overarching goals for the government as well as writing speeches and organizing the prime minister's busy schedule. Not surprisingly, members of the PMO can expect to be replaced when a new prime minister is sworn into office.

The Department of Finance provides economic expertise to the government. It is responsible for managing the national economy, raising revenue through taxation and other measures, fixing public expenditure levels, and making economic forecasts. In the 1990s, the Department of Finance had a large say in determining the fate of a wide range of public programs as governments sought to reduce the federal budget deficit through public spending cuts.

In the United States, the president relies on a myriad of central agencies. These include the

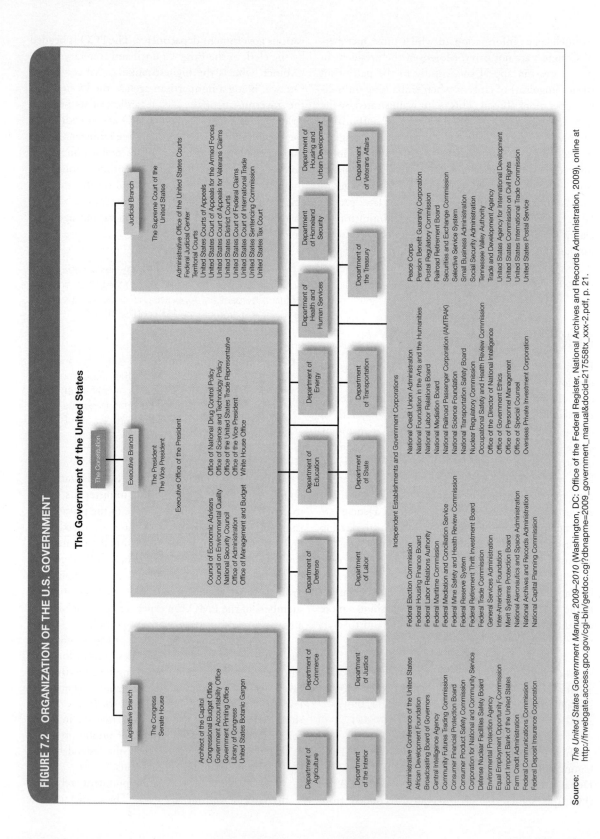

FIGURE 7.2 ORGANIZATION OF THE U.S. GOVERNMENT

The Government of the United States

The Constitution

Legislative Branch

The Congress
Senate House

Architect of the Capitol
Congressional Budget Office
Government Accountability Office
Government Printing Office
Library of Congress
United States Botanic Gargen

Executive Branch

The President
The Vice President

Executive Office of the President

Council of Economic Advisers
Council on Environmental Quality
National Security Council
Office of Administration
Office of Management and Budget

Office of National Drug Control Policy
Office of Science and Technology Policy
Office of the United States Trade Representative
White House Office

Judicial Branch

The Supreme Court of the
United States

Administrative Office of the United States Courts
Federal Judicial Center
Territorial Courts
United States Courts of Appeals
United States Court of Appeals for the Armed Forces
United States Court of Appeals for Veterans Claims
United States District Courts
United States Court of Federal Claims
United States Court of International Trade
United States Sentencing Commission
United States Tax Court

Department of Agriculture

Department of Commerce

Department of Defense

Department of Education

Department of Energy

Department of Health and Human Services

Department of Homeland Security

Department of Housing and Urban Development

Department of the Interior

Department of Justice

Department of Labor

Department of State

Department of Transportation

Department of the Treasury

Department of Veterans Affairs

Independent Establishments and Government Corporations

Administrative Conference of the United States
African Development Foundation
Broadcasting Board of Governors
Central Intelligence Agency
Community Futures Trading Commission
Consumer Financial Protection Board
Consumer Product Safety Commission
Corporation for National and Community Service
Defense Nuclear Facilities Safety Board
Environmental Protection Agency
Equal Employment Opportunity Commission
Export Import Bank of the United States
Farm Credit Administration
Federal Communications Commission
Federal Deposit Insurance Corporation

Federal Election Commission
Federal Housing Finance Board
Federal Labor Relations Authority
Federal Maritime Commission
Federal Mediation and Conciliation Service
Federal Mine Safety and Health Review Commission
Federal Reserve System
Federal Retirement Thrift Investment Board
Federal Trade Commission
General Services Administration
Inter-American Foundation
Merit Systems Protection Board
National Aeronautics and Space Administration
National Archives and Records Administration
National Capital Planning Commission

National Credit Union Administration
National Foundation in the Arts and the Humanities
National Labor Relations Board
National Mediation Board
National Railroad Passenger Corporation (AMTRAK)
National Science Foundation
National Transportation Safety Board
Nuclear Regulatory Commission
Occupational Safety and Health Review Commission
Office of the Director of National Intelligence
Office of Government Ethics
Office of Personnel Management
Office of Special Counsel
Overseas Private Investment Corporation

Peace Corps
Pension Benefit Guaranty Corporation
Postal Regulatory Commission
Railroad Retirement Board
Securities and Exchange Commission
Selective Service System
Small Business Administration
Social Security Administration
Tennessee Valley Authority
Trade and Development Agency
United States Agency for International Development
United States Commission on Civil Rights
United States International Trade Commission
United States Postal Service

Source: *The United States Government Manual, 2009–2010* (Washington, DC: Office of the Federal Register, National Archives and Records Administration, 2009), online at http://frwebgate.access.gpo.gov/cgi-bin/getdoc.cgi?dbnapme=2009_government_manual&docid=217558tx_xxx-2.pdf, p. 21.

Executive Office of the President (EOP), which employs over 2,000 officials and serves as the functional equivalent of the PMO. Other executive agencies that report directly to the president include the Office of Management and Budget, the National Security Council, and the Council of Economic Advisers. Given the unitary nature of the U.S. political executive, cabinet secretaries, advisors, and other officials constantly seek the ear of the president. The president's chief of staff therefore occupies a position of great importance since it is his or her role to act as gatekeeper to the president. Ideally, the chief of staff and other key officials in the White House Office keep the president's workload within manageable bounds while ensuring that he or she keeps abreast of crucial issues across the full range of government operations.

> **Executive Office of the President:** Offices and agencies attached directly to the President of the United States that provide advice on decisions and help develop and implement policies and programs.

THE BUREAUCRACY: THE ADMINISTRATIVE ARM OF GOVERNMENT

So far, we have looked at the upper echelons of the executive branch—the formal executive, the political executive, and the central agencies that support the work of the latter. In numerical terms, these institutions make up but a small fraction of the total membership of the executive branch of government. On a day-to-day basis, the functions of government are carried out by thousands of public servants, commonly called bureaucrats (or functionaries). In this section, we consider some of the functions carried out by bureaucrats and distinguish the role of senior officials from that of line officials. We also identify the organizing principles of the public service and the main structural forms through which bureaucratic authority is exercised. Finally, we address the question of political control of the bureaucracy.

To many people, the term **bureaucracy** carries a negative connotation. It is popularly associated with a rigid adherence to routine, a lack of imagination and

compassion in dealing with ordinary citizens, and an obsessive preoccupation with arcane rules and procedures ("red tape"). In North America in particular, disparaging references to the public service are regularly featured in the popular press, where examples of bureaucratic rigidity or incompetence are portrayed as the norm rather than the exception. The rise of neoconservative parties in Western democracies in the 1980s gave added momentum to this unflattering view of the public service.[45] As part of their larger critique of Big Government, neoconservatives routinely denounce the inefficiency of the public sector while extolling what they take to be the inherent superiority of private enterprise. Building on these assumptions, many critics of the public sector insist that government should be run like a business. To others, it is far from clear that the application of business principles to government is either appropriate or desirable.

> **Bureaucracy:** The expert, permanent, non-partisan, professional officials employed by the state to advise the political executive and to implement government policies.

The German sociologist Max Weber considered bureaucracy to be the most rational form of organization for modern states. He identified the following essential characteristics of a well-ordered bureaucracy:[46]

- hierarchical organization of public offices
- specialization of labour
- decisions based on the application of impersonal rules
- a clear demarcation of legal authority between public offices
- recruitment to the public service on the basis of technical qualifications
- promotion based on seniority or achievement (or both)

On the relationship between bureaucrats and political leaders, Weber did not doubt that the former should be subordinate to the latter. In that respect, he agreed with Woodrow Wilson, a professional political scientist prior to becoming president of the United States. Wilson contended that there should be a clear division between politics and administration—politics being the concern of elected politicians and administration the purview of bureaucrats.[47] In practice, the line between politics and administration is not so clear. Politicians rely heavily on the expertise and advice of senior bureaucrats in formulating public policy. At the same time, bureaucrats must exercise discretion in executing their duties.

Senior Bureaucrats versus Line Officials

It is useful to distinguish the role of senior bureaucrats from that of subordinate officials. In Canada, the highest-ranking officials in government departments are called **deputy ministers**. In Britain, such officials are called permanent secretaries. They, along with a cadre of senior administrators, have a dual role—they are responsible both for developing policy advice for ministers and for overseeing the administration of government departments. Such officials are sometimes called *mandarins*, a term originally used to denote the senior bureaucrats of Imperial China. Line officials, on the other hand, are concerned with the delivery of government programs and the enforcement of regulations.

> **Deputy minister:** A senior civil servant who acts as chief policy advisor to the minister and as general manager of the department. Known in Britain as the permanent secretaries, deputy ministers play a key role in the collective management of government operations.

Deputy Ministers In Westminster systems, deputy ministers are appointed directly by the prime minister. While they are usually career public servants with a wealth of experience in government service, they may, on occasion, be recruited from outside the public service, usually from academia, nongovernmental organizations, or the corporate world.

Some of the leading functions of senior officials include the following:[48*]

• *Policy initiation.* A key role of deputy ministers is to advise the political head of the department (the minister) on policy matters. Having expertise in the subject matter of their respective departments, deputy ministers identify issues that need to be addressed and then present their minister with various options for addressing them. In cases where the minister himself or herself takes an active interest in policy, it is the responsibility of the deputy minister to provide expert advice on the ways and means by which the minister's goals can be realized.

• *Channel for inputs.* Senior officials serve as a channel for transmitting information, advice, and political demands from pressure groups (and civil society in general) to the minister. Since most government policy originates in departments, it makes sense for organized groups wishing to influence public policy to seek access to senior departmental personnel. In fact, it is usually more fruitful for pressure groups to intervene at this pre-legislative stage of the policy process than to lobby for legislative changes at the parliamentary stage.

• *Rule-making.* After a law has been enacted by parliament, it falls to senior bureaucrats to draft detailed rules and regulations to flesh out the broad strokes of legislation. This post-legislative function is highly significant and is often conducted in close consultation with interested groups. While the minister has final authority to give legal effect to draft regulations, he or she relies heavily on the advice of departmental officials.

• *Management.* Deputy ministers manage government departments on a day-to-day basis. While the minister has political responsibility for the department, it is the deputy minister who manages departmental budgets and personnel and ensures the efficient delivery of public programs and services.

Line Officials Line officials are those bureaucrats who interact with the public in the course of delivering government services and enforcing rules and regulations. Two of their leading functions include:

• *Implementation and enforcement.* Most public servants are engaged, directly or indirectly, in the delivery of public programs and services and in

---

* Inwood, *Understanding Canadian Public Administration*, pp. 145–49, 191–97.

the implementation and enforcement of rules and regulations. This is true of tax collectors, customs officers, food safety inspectors, and a host of other functionaries.

- *Interpretation and adjudication.* In the process of implementing public policies and enforcing regulations, bureaucrats necessarily exercise some discretion. Does a claimed expense qualify for a tax deduction? Does a disability pension application meet the eligibility criteria? Has a prison inmate satisfied the conditions for parole? In all such cases, bureaucrats must exercise their judgment in applying rules of general application to specific fact situations.

Organizing Principles

As with other aspects of its parliamentary system of government, bureaucracy in Canada is closely modelled on the British civil service. Key defining principles of the Anglo-Canadian administrative state are set out below.

Merit The **merit principle** governs recruitment to, and promotion within, the bureaucracy. It stipulates that positions within the public service should be filled by the best-qualified persons on the basis of competitive entry requirements. This principle is to be distinguished from the earlier spoils system, under which most public offices were filled by **political patronage** appointments. Political patronage worked reasonably well as long as the role of government was fairly limited. However, by the early 20th century the nature and scope of governmental activity in many countries began to undergo a radical change, with the development of public health measures, the establishment of government-run research labs, the introduction of social security programs, and the growing need for government regulation of various kinds. These new responsibilities required the state to recruit public officials with specialized knowledge and expertise. Competence, not party affiliation, became the new imperative for recruitment.

> **Merit principle:** A system of hiring and promoting public servants on the basis of their merit (education, training, experience, and so on), rather than on the basis of party affiliation or other considerations.

> **Political patronage/patronage appointment:** When those in power favour political supporters or party members in making appointments to state offices.

In Canada, the merit principle was formally enshrined in legislation with the establishment of the Civil Service Commission (CSC) in 1918. In the decades that followed, well-defined procedures were laid down for recruitment to the civil service and for promotion within its ranks. Senior managers are responsible for hiring and promotion within the public service, subject to the procedures laid down by the Public Service Commission, or PSC (successor to the CSC). Any breach of the rules can be appealed to the PSC.

This is not to say that patronage has been, or arguably should be, banished entirely from government service. There remain a number of exempt positions within government departments that may be filled at the discretion of ministers.

Security of Tenure Public servants are protected from arbitrary dismissal by governments. The principle of security of tenure reinforces the idea that the public service is a professional corps of men and women pledged to execute faithfully the functions of the state. In this context, security of tenure does not mean that public servants can never be dismissed. On the contrary, public servants who are found to be negligent, incompetent, or corrupt are subject to a range of disciplinary sanctions, including dismissal. However, discipline is meted out not by the minister but by disciplinary bodies within the public service that operate at arm's length from government in order to ensure their impartiality.

It should also be noted that governments have wide powers to lay off public servants for budgetary reasons or as part of a reorganization of government departments. However, in reducing the number of public servants, the government is not allowed to single out a particular individual for dismissal in a deliberate and punitive way.

Political Neutrality The modern era demands strict political neutrality on the part of public servants. This principle goes hand in hand with the previous points about merit and security of tenure. Public servants are expected to serve the government of the day, whether or not they personally support the party in power or are in accord with its policies. It is the politicians, after all, who must answer for the wisdom and effectiveness, or lack thereof, of the government's policies.

Anonymity Public servants work in relative obscurity. Indeed, when political controversy envelops a government department, it is the minister who answers for the department, pursuant to the doctrine of ministerial responsibility. In such cases, the identity of particular public servants is generally not disclosed; as a result, they avoid being drawn into the political crossfire in parliament and the press. If instead beleaguered ministers were to point the finger of blame at their officials, then ministers, and the government as a whole, would cease to carry political responsibility. Such finger-pointing would also tend to prejudice any internal disciplinary proceedings against the officials in question. All the same, the veil of anonymity is lifted from time to time. This chiefly occurs when public officials are called to testify before parliamentary committees and public inquiries.

Representative Bureaucracy While merit remains the paramount guiding principle of the public service, it has been complemented in recent years by the goal of creating a more representative bureaucracy. The idea here is to foster the development of a public service that more accurately reflects the demographic composition of society. In Canada, the Official Languages Act (1969) was designed in part to promote the recruitment of francophones into the federal public service at a time when its higher levels were almost exclusively populated by anglophones. In more recent years, the federal government has striven to promote the recruitment of various groups that are underrepresented in the public service, particularly at managerial levels. Four groups have been targeted since the mid-1980s: women, Aboriginals, people with disabilities, and visible minorities.[49]

Bureaucratic Structures

Government bureaucracies are organized into a bewildering variety of institutions. Three of the organizational forms through which bureaucratic authority is exercised are government departments, regulatory agencies, and state-owned corporations. A key distinction among them has to do with the extent to which each is subject to ministerial control and direction. The extent of ministerial direction runs along a continuum; it is highest in the case of departments and lowest in the case of state-owned industries.

Government Departments Government departments are formally headed by a minister, who is responsible both for policy and administration. In reality, ministers rely heavily on their deputy minister in discharging both functions. As political head of the department, the minister takes the department's policy proposals to the cabinet while explaining and defending its existing policies in parliament and to the country. The deputy minister, as noted, assumes responsibility for the day-to-day administration of the department, a task for which most ministers have neither the time nor the skill.

In Westminster systems, departments are required to draw up detailed spending plans for the year (known as Estimates) which are tabled in parliament. The Estimates are then sent to parliamentary committees, where MPs have an opportunity to grill the minister, and sometimes the deputy minister, not only about the department's spending plans but also about the operations of programs and services delivered by the department. The Estimates must be formally approved by Parliament before the government can appropriate and spend public money. At the end of the financial year, departments must report to Parliament on how they spent their budgets.

Because the minister is the political head of the department, departmental affairs frequently become the target of opposition party attacks in parliament. For example, in the years when the post office was a government department, the Postmaster General would always be bombarded by opposition questions in Parliament during a national postal strike. In the early 1980s, the post office was converted into a Crown corporation. This change of organizational form gave the managers of Canada Post more freedom from ministerial control to manage the postal service. At the same time, by establishing an arm's-length relationship between the government and the post office, the government was better able to deflect at least some of the political flak resulting from unpopular decisions taken by Canada Post—such as increased postal rates, the closure of rural post offices, and recent plans, announced in late 2013, to replace door-to-door delivery in urban areas with community mailboxes.

Regulatory Agencies   The term "regulatory agency" or **administrative tribunal** embraces a wide range of agencies, boards, and commissions. A task common to all of them is the interpretation and application of regulations under various statutes (acts of parliament). To the extent that this role involves court-like functions, certain regulatory agencies are referred to as quasi-judicial bodies. For example, the Immigration and Refugee Board acts like a court in determining whether an applicant for landed immigrant status or refugee protection has met the relevant statutory and regulatory requirements and has been dealt with properly by the bureaucracy.

> **Administrative tribunals:** Boards or commissions established by the government to adjudicate certain disputes by applying laws to the facts; also called quasi-judicial tribunals or regulatory agencies. Not being proper courts, these tribunals are not headed by judges.

Members of regulatory agencies are appointed by the prime minister, the relevant minister, or the cabinet as a whole, depending on the enabling legislation. Given the quasi-judicial nature of many regulatory bodies, however, they must be free from ministerial interference to decide individual cases. It is improper, therefore, for a minister to direct, or even to lobby, a regulatory agency as to how it should decide a particular application that is before it. Alternately, it is permissible for the cabinet to issue policy directives to regulatory agencies. The purpose of such directives is to clarify the policy objectives underpinning a particular body of regulations. Legislation may provide a right to appeal the decision of an agency to the minister or the full cabinet. In any event, regulatory agencies are subject to less searching scrutiny by parliament than government departments.

State-Owned Corporations   State-owned corporations (known in Canada as **Crown corporations**) are established by government to fulfill a variety of public policy purposes, such as the promotion of regional economic development, the advancement of arts and culture, or the provision of transportation services. Such corporations are subject to the least ministerial control.

The cabinet appoints a board of directors, which in turn appoints a president and other senior executives to manage the corporation. Unlike a publicly traded company owned by shareholders, a Crown corporation is wholly owned by the government.

> **Crown corporation:** A corporation owned by the government that assumes a structure similar to that of a private company and that operates semi-independently of cabinet.

Compared to their counterparts in government departments, the managers of Crown corporations have a freer hand in personnel matters, such as hiring and promotion. While some Crown corporations are directed to act like a commercial corporation and to turn a profit, many of them require subsidies from the public treasury. For example, every year the CBC receives a subsidy, formally approved by Parliament, to carry out its mandate.

Political Control of the Bureaucracy

According to constitutional theory, the bureaucracy is subject to control by the government, which in turn is responsible to parliament. Many observers contend that this theory does not always correspond to reality. In particular, it underestimates the inherent power of the bureaucracy. Table 7.2 sets out the respective characteristics of senior bureaucrats and ministers.

The relationship between senior bureaucrats and their ministers can sometimes be highly unequal. Ministers often come to office knowing little or nothing about the workings of their department or the subject matter of their portfolio. Being novices, they must rely on the experience and expertise of their officials. Moreover, because of their relatively short tenure, most ministers are not in a position to pursue far-reaching policy changes. Innovation also carries political risks. While ministers can expect to be blamed for any teething problems that a new initiative experiences in its early stages, they may not receive credit for its success in the long run. It may take years for a new program or policy to bear fruit, by which time the minister will likely be in another portfolio or back on the opposition benches.

Winston Churchill once remarked that experts should be "on tap, not on top."[50] Yet many students

TABLE 7.2 COMPARISON OF CHARACTERISTICS OF BUREAUCRATS AND MINISTERS	
Bureaucrats	**Ministers**
Expert knowledge	General knowledge
Long tenure	Short tenure
Anonymity	Political responsibility

of bureaucracy—and some former politicians—contend that it is all too easy for ministers to be captured by their senior officials. Such was the premise of *Yes, Minister*, a popular British TV satire of the 1980s about the relationship between a fictional cabinet minister, James Hacker, and his Machiavellian permanent secretary, Sir Humphrey Appleby.

Countervailing Power

Recognizing the danger that ministers, and the government as a whole, may become unduly influenced by the interests and preferences of the bureaucracy, governments have attempted to enhance their political control of the bureaucracy. Steps toward this end include the following:

- *Turnover of senior officials by a new government.* A new prime minister—particularly one who has just led his or her party to victory at the polls after a long spell in opposition—can signal an intention to pursue a new agenda by replacing some of the top-ranking bureaucrats. While it is inadvisable for a new government to dispense with too many experienced hands at the top, a certain amount of turnover can reinvigorate the bureaucracy as a whole. This practice is more characteristic of changes in administrations in the United States than at the federal level in Canada.
- *Use of political staff.* Nowadays, all governments make use of political advisors to provide them with advice that is independent of that generated by the bureaucracy. Such advisors are called "exempt staff" because they are hired outside the normal rules that govern recruitment to the public service. This practice is highly developed in France, where ministers have their own "ministerial cabinet," a body of appointed advisors who serve the minister's political interests and monitor the activities of departmental officials.[51]

- *Enhanced role of central agencies.* One of the functions of central agencies is to counteract the influence of individual departments on the formulation of government policy. In Canada, the enlarged role of the PCO, the Department of Finance, and other central agencies reflects, in part, a strategy of using bureaucrats to check the power of other bureaucrats.
- *Election of a party with clear policy aims.* Other things being equal, a government will be better able to overcome bureaucratic inertia if it comes to office with a clear idea of what it intends to accomplish. This point is well illustrated by the records of reform-minded governments across Canada over the years. Examples include the Saskatchewan CCF government of T.C. Douglas (1944–1961), the Quebec Liberal government of Jean Lesage (1960–1966), and the federal Conservative government of Stephen Harper (2006–). Likewise, the British governments of Clement Attlee (1945–1951) and Margaret Thatcher (1979–1990) instituted sweeping, and sometimes controversial, changes in economic policy and the delivery of public services.

Citizens generally believe that in a democracy elected representatives have the final say over public policy; they also take it for granted that crucial policy decisions have a rational basis, supported by a preponderance of evidence. In other words, while we may applaud political leaders who act in accordance with their principles, we expect their decisions, at minimum, to be lawful and to have a reasonable possibility of achieving their stated goals. Thoughtful citizens are less likely to admire political leaders whose ideological convictions, or mere prejudices, lead them to ignore expert advice as to the lawfulness or feasibility of their proposed measures. Nevertheless an excessive politicization of the executive branch may produce such a result. A case in point is the neo-conservative government of Stephen Harper, which has been taken to task by a variety of critics, from environmental scientists to criminologists to legal scholars, for sacrificing sound public policy to the imperatives of ideology or short-term political gain.[52]

NEW PUBLIC MANAGEMENT: RUNNING GOVERNMENT AS A BUSINESS

The downsizing of government in many countries in the 1990s did much to mitigate concerns about all-powerful bureaucracies. This development formed part of a larger reconfiguration of the role of government that saw the dismantling of certain elements of the postwar **welfare state**, the **privatization** of many state-owned industries, and the diffusion of **neoliberal**, anti-statist norms embodied in global trade agreements. In English-speaking countries in particular, a renewed faith in the efficacy of the capitalist marketplace in recent decades had important effects on the organization and functioning of the executive branch of government. Increasingly, government services have been outsourced to private contractors, public–private partnerships, or other forms of alternative service delivery. The expectation is that public services can be delivered more efficiently by the private sector or by the application of business principles. The advent of this philosophy, known loosely as the **New Public Management**, has brought in a new emphasis on the use of quantifiable measures of performance, the expansion of public choice, and the achievement of efficiency gains, usually expressed in terms of financial cost savings.[53]

Welfare state: A concept that stresses the role of government as a provider and protector of individual security and well-being through the implementation of interventionist economic policies and social programs. This positive role for government stands in contrast to the minimalist government (or "night-watchman state") that has as its only function the protection of personal property and individual security. The welfare state is regarded as having a positive role in promoting human welfare and in shielding the individual against the economic and social consequences of unemployment, poverty, sickness, old age, disability, and so on.

Privatization: Transferring a government program, agency, or Crown corporation to the private sector, for example, by selling shares in the corporation to the public at large or to a private firm.

Neoliberalism: An economic philosophy that holds that a system of free markets, free trade, and the free flow of capital is the best way to ensure the greatest social, political, and economic good. It argues for reduced taxation, reduced government regulation, and minimal state involvement in the economy.

New Public Management: A bureaucratic transformation occurring in many states over the past 15 years involving downsizing government, technological change, providing public services in new (alternate) ways, and forming partnerships with private sector agencies.

The New Public Management (NPM) is more advanced in some countries, such as Britain and Australia, than in others, including Canada. Proponents of NPM point out that the goal of using public resources with maximum efficiency is shared by conservative and social democratic governments alike. They also reassert the view that politics should be separated from the technical business of administration.[54]

Critics reply that politics and administration cannot be neatly compartmentalized. Democratic governments must accommodate many different, and often conflicting, political demands. Such demands have to do not only with the ends of public policy but also with the means of realizing them. In choosing among alternative courses of action, efficiency is just one consideration among many.[55] As one observer aptly put it, "one person's red tape is another's due process."[56]

In any case, it may be difficult to measure quantitatively the performance of public bodies. For example, the benefit of health and safety regulations lies in the harm that is avoided, even if the financial costs of regulation can easily be measured. Conversely, the costs of deregulation may only become evident in the long run. This point was powerfully underscored by the global financial crisis that unfolded in late 2008, a consequence in large part of the deregulation of capital markets that began in the United States in the 1980s and was emulated by other countries. Today western governments are imposing new regulations on the financial industry and seeking to crack down on offshore tax havens used by transnational corporations to avoid the payment of income tax.[57]

CONCLUSION

The executive branch of government is powerful and pervasive. It provides political leadership for the nation while also having responsibility for the day-to-day administration of government operations. The executive assumes a wide variety of institutional forms, even among states having a shared commitment to democratic values. In this chapter, we considered three main types of executive: parliamentary, presidential, and semi-presidential. In evaluating these different forms of government, it is useful to consider the relative weight each assigns to the goal of firm and effective government and the need for the legislature to hold the executive to account. We should also be mindful of the capacity of the political executive to assert control over the administrative executive.

DISCUSSION QUESTIONS

1. Where does power lie in parliamentary systems?

2. Where does power lie in presidential systems?

3. Discuss the advantages and disadvantages of separating the head of state from the head of government.

4. Are the traditional governing principles of Anglo-Canadian bureaucracy still relevant today?

5. Should governments be run like a business?

WEBSITES

American Presidency
http.//www.whitehouse.gov
Official website of the U.S. President.

Policy@Manchester
http://www.policy.manchester.ac.uk/resources/civil-servant/
This section of the Policy@Manchester website provides information on the U.K. civil service, much of it applicable to other Westminster parliamentary systems.

Privy Council Office
http://www.pco.bcp.gc.ca
Website of the Privy Council Office, the central agency responsible for supporting and advising the prime minister and the cabinet in Canada.

Australian Constitutional Crisis of 1975
http://moadoph.gov.au/exhibitions/online/dismissed
This section of the website of the Australian Museum of Democracy at Old Parliament House recounts the events surrounding the Australian constitutional crisis of 1975.
http://whitlamdismissal.com
A useful archive on the crisis compiled by Malcolm Farnsworth.

FURTHER READING

Carl Dahlström, B. Guy Peters, Jon Pierre, eds., *Steering from the Centre: Strengthening Political Control in Western Democracies.* Toronto: University of Toronto Press, 2011.

Robert Elgie and Sophia Moestrup, eds., *Semi-presidentialism Outside Europe: A Comparative Study.* London: Routledge, 2007.

Paul Kelly, *November 1975: The Inside Story of Australia's Greatest Political Crisis.* St. Leonard's, New South Wales: Allen and Unwin, 1995.

Arend Lijphart, ed., *Parliamentary Versus Presidential Government.* Oxford: Oxford University Press, 1992.

Juan J. Linz, and Arturo Valenzuela, eds., *The Failure of Presidential Democracy: Comparative Perspectives,* Volume 2. Baltimore: Johns Hopkins University Press, 1994.

B. Guy Peters, *The Politics of Bureaucracy: An Introduction to Comparative Public Administration*, 6th ed. New York: Routledge, 2009.

ENDNOTES

1. Andrew Heywood, *Politics*, 4th ed. (Houndsmills, Basingstoke: Palgrave Macmillan, 2013), p. 285.

2. J.H. Baker, *An Introduction to English Legal History*, 4th ed. (London: Butterworths, 2002), chs. 1–2.

3. Walter Bagehot, *The English Constitution*, introduced by R.H.S. Crossman (Ithaca, New York: Cornell University Press, 1966), pp. 67–68. Originally published in 1867.

4. The Commonwealth is a voluntary association of 53 states that were once colonies of the United Kingdom. After achieving political independence, many chose to retain the Queen as their head of state, although the majority, including India and all of the African members, chose to become republics.

5. In Canada, lieutenant governors are appointed by the governor general on the advice of the prime minister. In Australia, governors are appointed by the Queen on the advice of the state premier. See David Butler and D.A. Low, eds., *Sovereigns and Surrogates: Constitutional Heads of State in the Commonwealth* (Houndsmills, Basingstoke: Macmillan, 1991), and Peter Boyce, *The Queen's Other Realms: The Crown and Its Legacy in Australia, Canada, and New Zealand* (Annandale, New South Wales: Federation Press, 2008).

6. In June 2013, two Laval University law professors filed a motion in Quebec Superior Court challenging the constitutionality of the Conservative government's statute giving Canada's assent to the U.K. bill altering the law of succession. The main basis of the claim is that the enactment amounts to a constitutional amendment "in relation to the office of the Queen" under Section 41 of the Constitution Act 1982; if so, it would require the formal approval of all 10 of the provinces. Rhéal Séguin, "Change to royal succession faces legal challenge in Quebec," *The Globe and Mail*, June 7, 2013.

7. Frank MacKinnon, *The Crown in Canada* (Calgary: McClelland and Stewart, 1976).

8. Peter Fraser, "A Revolutionary Governor General? The Grenada Crisis of 1983," in D.A. Low, ed., *Constitutional Heads and Political Crises: Commonwealth Episodes, 1945–1985* (New York: St. Martin's Press, 1988).

9. On the other hand, if the prime minister is in a hurry to step down, the government caucus can select an interim leader to hold the reins of office pending the holding of a leadership convention.

10. Peter W. Hogg, *Constitutional Law of Canada*, student ed. (Scarborough: Thomson Carswell, 2006), p. 278.

11. George Winteron, "1975: The Dismissal of the Whitlam Government," in H.P. Lee and George Winterton, eds., *Australian Constitutional Landmarks* (Cambridge: Cambridge University Press, 2003); Colin Howard and Cheryl Saunders, "The Blocking of the Budget and Dismissal of the Government," in Gareth Evans, ed., *Labor and the Constitution, 1972–1975: Essays and Commentaries on the Constitutional Controversies of the Whitlam Years in Australian Government* (Melbourne: Heinemann, 1977); Garfield Barwick, *Sir John Did His Duty* (Wahroonga, New South Wales: Serendip, 1983); David Smith, *Head of State: The Governor-General, The Monarchy, The Republic and The Dismissal* (Paddington, New South Wales: Macleay Press, 2005).

12. Hogg, *Constitutional Law of Canada*, pp. 290–91.

13. J.R. Mallory, "Crises That Didn't Happen: Canada 1945–1985," in Low, *Constitutional Heads and Political Crises*, pp. 229–31. The situation in Ontario after the 1985 provincial election is generally regarded as an instance in which the lieutenant governor would have been justified a refusing a dissolution had the premier, Frank Miller, requested one. Instead, following the defeat of his Conservative government in the

Legislature, Miller tendered his resignation and the lieutenant governor invited the Leader of the Opposition, David Peterson, to form a minority government. Peterson's Liberal government remained in office for two years with the support of the New Democratic Party.

14. Andrew Heard, "The Governor General's Suspension of Parliament: Duty Done or a Perilous Precedent?," in Peter H. Russell and Lorne Sossin, eds., *Parliamentary Democracy in Crisis* (Toronto: University of Toronto Press, 2009), pp. 47–62; Gary Levy, "Confidence Game," *Inroads* 25 (Summer/Fall 2009), pp. 48–59.

15. C.E.S. Franks, "To Prorogue or Not to Prorogue: Did the Governor General Make the Right Decision?," in Russell and Sossin, *Parliamentary Democracy*, pp. 31–46; Peter Neary, "Confidence: How Much is Enough?," *Constitutional Forum* 18 (2) (September 22, 2009), pp. 51–54.

16. "The Americas: Halted in mid-debate; Canada without Parliament," *The Economist,* January 9, 2010, p. 39.

17. C.E.S. Franks, *The Parliament of Canada* (Toronto: University of Toronto Press, 1987), p. 96.

18. See generally Christopher J. Kam, *Party Discipline and Parliamentary Politics.* (Cambridge: Cambridge University Press, 2009).

19. An exception to that rule in the U.S. concerns the vice-president, who presides over the Senate and casts the deciding vote in case of a tie.

20. In 1868, impeachment proceedings against President Andrew Johnson failed by a single vote to meet the two-thirds threshold in the Senate.

21. See generally William B. Perkins, "The Political Nature of Presidential Impeachment in the United States," in Jody C. Baumgartner and Naoko Kada, eds., *Checking Executive Power: Presidential Impeachment in Comparative Perspective* (Westport: Praeger, 2003).

22. See Matthew Soberg Shugart and John M. Carey, *Presidents and Assemblies: Constitutional Design and Electoral Dynamics* (Cambridge: Cambridge University Press, 1992); Antonia Maioni, *Parting at the Crossroads: The Emergence of Health Insurance in the United States and Canada* (Princeton: Princeton University Press, 1998).

23. See Juan J. Linz, "Presidential or Parliamentary Democracy: Does It Make a Difference?," in Juan J. Linz and Arturo Valenzuela, eds., *The Failure of Presidential Democracy: Comparative Perspectives*, Vol. 2 (Baltimore: Johns Hopkins University Press, 1994).

24. Linz, "Presidential or Parliamentary Democracy," p.4. See also John Gerring, Strom C. Thacker, and Carola Moreno, "Are Parliamentary Systems Better?," *Comparative Political Studies* 42 (3) (March 2009), pp. 327–59.

25. Maurice Duverger, "A New Political System Model: Semi-presidential Government," *European Journal of Political Research* 8 (2) (June 1980), pp. 165–87.

26. Karen Henderson and Neil Robinson, *Post-communist Politics: An Introduction* (Hemel Hempstead: Prentice Hall, 1997), p. 168.

27. Arend Lijphart, *Patterns of Democracy: Government Forms and Performance in Thirty-Six Countries* (New Haven: Yale University Press, 1999), p. 121.

28. Robert Elgie, ed., *Semi-presidentialism in Europe* (Oxford: Oxford University Press, 1999).

29. John P. Mackintosh, *The British Cabinet*, 2nd ed. (London: Methuen, 1968), ch. 3.

30. Bagehot, *The English Constitution*, p. 111.

31. Mackintosh, *The British Cabinet*, p. 118.

32. Paul G. Thomas, "The Changing Nature of Accountability," in B. Guy Peters and Donald J. Savoie, eds., *Taking Stock: Assessing Public Sector Reforms* (Montreal and Kingston: McGill-Queen's University Press, 1998). See also Donald J. Savoie, *Court Government and the Collapse of Accountability in Canada and the United Kingdom* (Toronto: University of Toronto Press, 2008).

33. For a good overview of this debate, see Patrick Weller, *First Among Equals: Prime Ministers in Westminster Systems* (London: Allen and Unwin, 1985). For a recent Canadian perspective, see Peter Aucoin, Mark D. Jarvis, and

Lori Turnbull. *Democratizing the Constitution: Reforming Responsible Government* (Toronto: Emond Montgomery, 2011).

34. Thomas M.J. Bateman, "Party Democracy Increases the Leader's Power," *Policy Options* (September 2001), pp. 20–23, and Christopher Moore, "Backbenchers Fight Back," *National Post*, February 13, 2001, p. A16.

35. Norman C. Thomas and Joseph A. Pika, *The Politics of the Presidency*, 4th ed. (Washington, DC: Congressional Quarterly Press, 1997), p. 259.

36. Strictly speaking, U.S. presidents are indirectly elected by the Electoral College, a body of men and women, elected in each state, who are pledged to cast their votes for the presidential candidate who wins the most votes in their state. Ordinarily, the candidate who wins the most votes nationwide also wins a majority of Electoral College votes. However, this was not the case in the presidential election of 2000, when Democratic candidate Al Gore won half a million more votes than Republican candidate George W. Bush. Bush nevertheless won a majority of votes in the Electoral College.

37. Zachary A. Goldfarb and Yian Q. Mui, "Larry Summers withdraws name from Fed consideration." *Washington Post*, September 15, 2013.

38. Andrew Grice and Ben Russell, "Parliament to be Recalled after Blair Bows to Pressure for Debate," *The Independent*, September 11, 2002.

39. The government had sought to justify military action as a humanitarian intervention in response to allegations that the Assad regime had used chemical weapons against its opponents. Nicholas Watt and Nick Hopkins, "Cameron forced to rule out British attack on Syria after MPs reject motion," *The Guardian*, August 29, 2013.

40. Helen Dewar, "Senate Rejects Test Ban Treaty," *Washington Post*, October 14, 1999.

41. Walter LaFeber, *America, Russia, and the Cold War, 1945–2006*, 10th ed. (New York: McGraw-Hill, 2008), pp. 250–52.

42. Neither UN nor subsequent U.S. weapons inspectors were able to find evidence of WMDs in Iraq.

43. Colin Campbell, *Governments Under Stress* (Toronto: University of Toronto Press, 1983).

44. Gregory J. Inwood, *Understanding Canadian Public Administration: An Introduction to Theory and Practice* (Toronto: Pearson Education, 2009), pp. 138–42.

45. Donald J. Savoie, *Thatcher, Reagan, Mulroney: In Search of a New Bureaucracy* (Toronto: University of Toronto Press, 1994), pp. 88–94.

46. Max Weber, *The Theory of Social and Economic Organization* (New York: Oxford University Press, 1947). Originally published in 1922.

47. Woodrow Wilson, "The Study of Administration," *Political Science Quarterly* 2 (2) (June 1887), pp. 197–222.

48. Inwood, *Understanding Canadian Public Administration*, pp.145–49, 191–97.

49. Patrick von Maravić, B. Guy Peters, Eckhard Schröter, eds., *Representative Bureaucracy in Action: Country Profiles from the Americas, Europe, Africa, and Asia* (Cheltenham: Edward Elgar, 2013).

50. Randolph S. Churchill, *Twenty-One Years* (Boston: Houghton Mifflin, 1965), p. 140.

51. Alistair Cole, *French Politics and Society* (London: Prentice-Hall, 1998), pp. 110–11.

52. These criticisms are documented in Michael Harris, *Party of One: Stephen Harper and Canada's Radical Political Makeover* (Toronto: Viking, 2014); Donald Gutstein, *Harperism: How Stephen Harper and His Think Tank Colleagues have Transformed Canada* (Toronto: James Lorimer, 2014); Lawrence Martin, *Harperland: The Politics of Control* (Toronto: Viking, 2010).

53. Allan Tupper, "New Public Management and Canadian Politics," in Janine Brodie and Linda Trimble, eds., *Reinventing Canada: Politics of the 21st Century* (Toronto: Pearson Education, 2003), pp. 231–42; Peter Aucoin, "New Public Management and New Public Governance: Finding the Balance," in David Siegel and Ken

Rasmussen, eds., *Professionalism and Public Service: Essays in Honour of Kenneth Kernaghan* (Toronto: University of Toronto Press, Institute of Public Administration of Canada, 2008), pp. 16–33.

54. David Osborne and Ted Gaebler, *Reinventing Government* (Reading, Mass.: Addison-Wesley, 1992).

55. Janice Gross Stein, *The Cult of Efficiency* (Toronto: Anansi, 2001).

56. Donald J. Savoie, "What Is Wrong with the New Public Management?," *Canadian Public Administration* 38 (1) (Spring 1995), p. 116.

57. Justin Baer, "Wall Street: From Recession to Regulation," *Financial Times*, September 24, 2010; "G8 leaders agree tax evasion measures," *BBC News*, June 18, 2013.

8

LEGISLATURES: CENTRE STAGE BUT NOT TOP BILLING

David Docherty and John Kurt Edwards

© The Canadian Press/Jeff McIntosh

Unlike those that exist at the federal and provincial levels in Canada, where government and opposition face each other across a central dividing aisle, the legislative assembly of Nunuvut—which was formally opened in 2002—is circular. This reflects the absence of political parties at the territorial level and the practice of consensus—rather than oppositional—government.

After you have completed this chapter, you should be able to:

- understand the different functions of a legislature

- differentiate between two main types of legislative systems (Westminster and Congressional)

- identify factors that can change how effectively a legislature operates

- appreciate the role of representatives in a legislature

- consider the challenges that modern legislatures and representatives face, and what, if any, reforms are needed to address them

INTRODUCTION

A **legislature** can be considered the "heart" of a democracy. At its most basic, the legislature serves as the *law-making* institution of a government. It is the legislature that largely decides what will be made into law, which can directly determine the policies that a government can pursue. At the national level, legislatures can make decisions that are critical to the future of a country: whether to go to war, whether to sign major trade agreements, whether to support large-scale social programs (such as universal healthcare), and so on. At the sub-national level (such as a province or a state), legislatures can address pressing local issues that might otherwise be overlooked by a larger national government. Locally or nationally, legislatures provide a forum for the needs and wants of average citizens to be brought forward, debated, and met through the passing of laws.

> **Legislature** The major lawmaking institution in a democracy. Legislatures can either be unicameral or bicameral.

Making law, however, is not the only function of a legislature. It is also the "democratic battlefield" on which **representatives** (or "members") duke it out over how the government should be run. Representatives in the legislature frequently have the power to debate (or introduce) **bills**, bargain with the government for laws more favourable to their interests, and hold the government to account by criticizing its actions in a public space. This battlefield can sometimes become a literal one, as in the Taiwanese **parliament** of 2007, where a brawl broke out over the issue of a delay in the passing of the budget bill.[1] While passionate debates are more common than outright melees in the United States and Canada, both cases show how much representatives care about legislative outcomes, and how much of their own lives they invest in its day-to-day operations. Despite this (or perhaps because of it), national publics often take a dim view of representatives and legislatures. For example, in the United States, a December 2013 Gallup poll found that only lobbyists (at six percent) scored lower in terms of honesty and ethics than did members of Congress (nine percent). Members of state legislatures (14 percent) can take little comfort in the fact that they were perceived as more honest than car salespeople (9 percent). They were fourth and third from the bottom of the list, respectively. Approval of Congress sat at the same level as it members.[2] The status of politicians in Canada is hardly better, with a mere 10 percent of Canadians trusting politicians.[3] Such findings point to serious problems with legislatures and representatives in our society, but what are the causes? And what sorts of solutions are available?

> **Representative:** A person who has been selected, usually through an election, to serve in a legislature. Representatives perform numerous tasks in a legislature, such as debating and proposing bills, attacking/defending the government, and meeting with constituents and lobbyists.

> **Bill:** A proposed law introduced into a legislature. Bills must go through a long review process, usually involving several votes and numerous amendments (additions to the bill), before being passed into law.

> **Parliament:** In a Westminster system, this is a common, informal name for the national lower house, though it formally encompasses both the upper and lower houses (such as in Canada, where it includes both the House of Commons and the Senate).

To help us begin the search for answers, this chapter examines the functions and roles of legislatures and legislators. First, we investigate the two main types of democratic systems—the **Westminster system** and the **Congressional system**—and see how legislatures differ between them. Then, we examine the actual role of a legislature, analyzing the key functions that it performs and the roadblocks that can prevent it from performing these functions. Finally, we survey the composition of legislatures: their size, their make-up, and the role of political parties within them. The chapter concludes by suggesting that legislatures should not necessarily be faulted for some of the negative outcomes that they produce, nor should most representatives be blamed for governing in the style that the rules encourage. Indeed, it may be that the real cause of citizen discontent is to be found more in the institutional design of our legislative systems than their outputs.

> **Westminster system:** A style of democracy, characterized by having a bicameral national legislature and the inclusion of the executive within the legislature. This system is found in countries like Canada and the United Kingdom.

> **Congressional system:** A style of democracy, characterized by having a bicameral national legislature and the separation of the executive from the legislature. This system is found, notably, in the United States.

This, really, is a key question for those who live in democratic countries. Why are the institutions that sit at the core of our politics, and the men and women who serve in them, held in such low regard? There are a lot of potential reasons. We sometimes elect the wrong people, who may perform poorly or act out of self-interest rather than the public interest. Some legislatures, meanwhile, are too rooted in outdated rules. Our legislatures in Canada are governed by rules that

were created to address 19th century problems. Are they the right rules to deal with problems that we face in the 21st century? Outdated rules can stifle innovation, which can cause legislatures to fail to address new issues or take advantage of the vast leaps in technology since that time.

While we cannot deny the credibility problem of our democratic bodies and the men and women who seek to serve in them, we also cannot deny that they are essential to our success as a society. Legislatures are the heart and soul of our democracies. With the exception of infrequent referenda (or, in some U.S. states, frequent and numerous referenda), legislatures are the vehicles that drive bills to become laws. It is on the floor of legislatures that citizen grievances are publicly addressed in an authoritative way. It is within the confines of the legislature that critical democratic oversight functions take place. Like it or not, legislatures not only matter but they are crucial. Until we determine a better method of representing citizen interests, and actually agree to adopt this new approach, we are left with—and must work through—legislatures.

The challenges that our legislatures face are significant, and the difficulties of reforming them should not be underestimated. This should not prevent us, however, from suggesting ways to improve the work and standing of these institutions and striving to gain a better appreciation of the men and women who serve in them. In order to measure the effectiveness of legislatures we must first understand what their functions are and if they are actually performing them, and, if not, what tools would allow them to do their jobs properly.

TYPES OF LEGISLATURES

Every legislature has its own unique identity, typically a product of how members are selected, the size of the assembly, whether it is **unicameral** or **bicameral**, the role of political parties, and the relationship between the assembly and the other branches of government. Broadly speaking, democratic countries today use one of two legislative systems: the Westminster system (sometimes called the "parliamentary system") or the Congressional system (sometimes called the "presidential system"). The Westminster system, having originated in Britain, is more commonly found in

Commonwealth countries (generally countries that were either a part of, or in alliance with, the British Empire). The Congressional system, meanwhile, is mainly found in the United States and in some nearby countries, such as Mexico. While other, more unique legislative systems exist in the world (such as in Switzerland), these two basic systems are in majority use worldwide and they shall thus be our focus in this chapter.

> **Unicameral/bicameral:** A unicameral legislature has only a single legislative house that handles all lawmaking in a state, province, or country. A bicameral legislature has two houses, such as the Canadian House of Commons (the "lower house") and Senate (the "upper house"), that handle the lawmaking in a state, province, or country.

While the two systems share similar features regardless of the country they're used in, each country has its own unique rules or **constitutional conventions** that make them operate differently than in other countries. Despite coming from relatively similar British roots, for example, the Canadian parliament and the United Kingdom (U.K.) parliament have numerous distinctions as a consequence of their separate histories. To simplify our analysis, the major comparisons in this chapter will be between Canada, which uses a Westminster system, and the United States (U.S.), which uses a Congressional system.

> **Constitutional convention:** An unwritten rule of constitutional behaviour that fills in gaps in the written constitution and conditions the exercise of legal powers under the constitution. While considered obligatory, such rules are not legally enforceable.

There are three important and closely linked differences between the U.S. Congressional system and Westminster-styled legislatures. The first, and perhaps most obvious, difference is that the United States is a republic while Canada is a constitutional monarchy. This distinction underpins the most significant foundations of each system. As a republic, the United States has an elected head of state, who is democratically accountable to the people he or she serves, and who has strict limits on how long they can serve in office.

A constitutional monarchy, meanwhile, has an unelected, hereditary monarch as the head of state, who (barring revolutions or death) can reign for as long as they wish. This remains the reality for many Westminster countries today: in Canada, for example, Section 9 of the original British North America Act specifies that all executive authority over Canada "is hereby declared to continue and be vested in the Queen [of Great Britain],"[4] a state of affairs which persists to this day. The patriation of the Constitution in 1982 and the addition of the Charter of Rights and Freedoms did nothing to change this foundation of political authority. It is important to note, however, that a constitutional monarchy makes an important distinction between the head of state (the Queen) and the head of government (the prime minister). This distinction has major political and procedural implications, especially today.

For example, when a foreign head of state visits Canada, they should be met by the Queen because she is the head of state. As the Queen is understandably absent from Canada most of the time, they are instead met by the Queen's representative. At the national level, this is the governor general, while at the subnational (provincial) level this is the lieutenant governor. Furthermore, even after it has been debated and passed by Parliament, a law in Canada is not official—is not proclaimed law—until it receives Royal Assent through the signature of the Queen or her representative. Many citizens of the U.S. might perceive this as being undemocratic but it lies at the heart of Canadian democracy. The **Crown** is above partisan politics and a law is therefore not enacted until the Queen's signature signifies that the legislation is in the best interests of the country. The signature, admittedly, constitutes a symbolic gesture today, rather than a political one. While the Crown was once intimately involved in the legislative process, changes in the relationship between the monarch and the legislature have meant that the Crown now has little practical power when it comes to passing laws. Although the Queen (or her representative) has the constitutional authority to withhold their signature, constitutional convention (or practice) has long been to sign off on all legislation passed by Parliament. Thus, even if a decision not to sign a bill would be legally valid, outrage would ensue if a provincial lieutenant governor, for example, were to balk at providing Royal Assent on legislation today.

Crown: An often-overlooked but critical part of Westminster parliaments. Officially the head of state, the Queen (or in her absence her representative) provides non-partisan continuity in governance, including such vital aspects as proroguing and dissolving parliament and, following an election, identifying who can command the confidence of the assembly to form the government.

Perhaps the most important roles of the governor general are the appointment of the prime minister and the **cabinet** and the calling and dissolution of parliament. Canadians often forget that we do not elect a government. Rather, we elect members to serve in parliament, and parliament then chooses a government. The role of the governor general is to ensure that parliament can work: namely, that the government has the support of the House of Commons.[5] Typically, the governor general selects the party with the most **seats** to form a government, with the cabinet being decided by the prime minister. The party with the second-most seats is called "Her Majesty's Loyal Opposition." While seemingly counter intuitive, the title is important. Westminster systems institutionalize opposition in a manner that makes clear that it is opposed to the government but not the state (recall the separation of the head of government and the head of state), and that it can provide an alternate government should it be required.

Cabinet: The group of people chosen by the prime minister or president to provide political direction to government departments; in Canada, cabinet members act collectively to make the key government decisions.

Seats: Refers to the territorially defined area that an elected representative serves. In most "first-past-the-post" electoral systems, there is only one elected official per seat or district, although at the provincial level, Prince Edward Island had 16 ridings that each elected two members until 1996. The distribution of seats among the different parties will determine whether any one party can form a majority government.

In comparison, the President of the United States is both head of state and head of government.

The president is ultimately responsible for all government action (save for that undertaken by the legislature), represents the country in all international matters, and meets with other heads of government and state. The president is the one who appoints the cabinet, and it is his or her signature that ultimately transforms a bill into law. The president has a lot more choice than the governor general does when it comes to which bills will see their signature, as they have the ability to veto (that is, refuse to sign) a bill, something which has been used frequently over the history of the United States up to the present day. Unlike the figurehead position of the governor general in Canada, which performs a largely ceremonial role in a modern constitutional monarchy, the President of the United States is highly involved in the running of the government and is the "public face" of the United States to the world.

The second significant difference is in the relationship between the political executive (as defined in Chapter 7) and the legislature. The Congressional system maintains the political executive and legislature as two separate branches of government. In Canada and other Westminster democracies, the political executive actually sits in the legislature. Moreover, in Canada, the cabinet members are generally drawn from those who have been elected in constituencies by voters—thus, the cabinet members are parliamentarians as well.[6] As a result, they enjoy far greater authority and influence than other members of the assembly, one of whose primary responsibilities is to hold the executive to account. By contrast, members of the political executive in a Congressional system are selected by the president (or, in the states, by governors) and ratified by the legislative branch. These members of the cabinet, alongside the president, do not sit in the legislature, unlike in the Westminster system. This **separation of powers** lies at the heart of the Congressional system.

Separation of powers: A principle of constitutional government that is usually taken to mean that the legislative, executive, and judicial functions of the state should be carried out by separate branches of government. No one may hold office in more than one branch at the same time.

Each method has its strengths and weaknesses. The presence of the executive in the legislature in the

Westminster system makes it easier for opposition parties to hold the executive to account, as they can directly and routinely question the government in full view of the public eye within the legislature during **Question Period**. This task is far harder in the Congressional system, primarily because neither the U.S. cabinet nor the president step foot in the legislature (save for during certain special events, such as the State of the Union address), meaning that legislators have no opportunity to question government actions directly—there is no Question Period for U.S. legislators. The power granted to the executive in the legislature in the Westminster system, however, is much greater than anything the President of the United States can muster, especially under a majority government. A key example of this in recent years is the power of **prorogation,** a special procedure that can be initiated only by the governor general of Canada on the advice (that is, by the request of) the prime minister.[7] Unlike an election, prorogation simply ends the current "session" of the legislature (the period of time when the legislature is sitting and thus performing its functions). The current MPs retain their seats and return to Ottawa when a new session of parliament starts up after a few weeks or months. Prorogation is significant because it brings about the termination of all bills and committees currently under way, which then have to be reintroduced or re-established, respectively, after the next session begins. Thus, prorogation temporarily removes one of the major public forums that opposition parties have for criticizing the government.

> **Question Period:** A period of time in a Westminster-style lower house when the opposition can ask questions of the government. This is the most common way that the opposition attempts to hold the government accountable, as Question Period is public and thus under the scrutiny of the media and ordinary citizens.

> **Prorogation:** A prerogative power of the Crown in Westminster systems to end the current session of parliament for a certain period. Nowadays, it is generally exercised only on the advice of the prime minister.

In practice, a parliament usually prorogues about half way into its mandate, or every two years.[8]

This gives both the government and opposition parties an opportunity to reprioritize which bills and issues they wish to focus on, and it provides the government the chance to introduce fresh ideas via a new Speech from the Throne at the opening of the next session. In theory, however, this also gives prime ministers a rather extraordinary power: to shut down the operation of parliament when they desire. During Prime Minister Stephen Harper's first seven years in office, Parliament has so far been prorogued a total of four times (in 2007, 2008, 2010, and 2013). The opposition parties have accused Harper of using prorogation to deflect criticism of the government (since Parliament, you will recall, allows opposition parties to hold the government to account), a charge that Harper has denied.[9]

The most contentious use of prorogation under Harper occurred in 2008, when he sought to shut down Parliament to avoid a **vote of non-confidence** that was sure to pass. In doing so he placed then-governor general, Michaëlle Jean, in a no-win situation. A refusal on her part would have marked the first time that such a request had been rejected by a governor general in Canada, but agreeing would have marked the first time that a governor general had allowed a prime minister to avoid a vote that could defeat the government and either trigger an election or lead the opposition parties to power in a coalition. In the end, the governor general granted the prorogation, and the prime minister used the time to undermine the chances of a combined opposition vote succeeding.[10] The government survived, but the office of the Queen's representative was placed in a constitutionally awkward situation by the prime minister. Not only was this not an incident for a highlight reel on good governance but the vote-avoiding prorogation was deeply unpopular with the public and triggered a serious national debate over how much power a prime minister is able to wield with little oversight beyond voter scrutiny. Such a situation is impossible within the Congressional system due to the separation of powers between the executive and the legislature. Deeply unpopular presidents can do little to oppose the will of a legislature united against them, and in certain exceptional circumstances can even be removed (impeached) from office by a vote from the legislature.

> **Confidence (or non-confidence) vote:** An explicitly worded motion indicating that the legislature either has or does not have confidence in the government; a vote on a matter that the government has previously declared to be a matter of confidence; or a vote on important measures central to the government's plans, such as the budget.

The third significant difference is in the level of voting that takes places in each of the two systems. Westminster systems generally concentrate the votes made during an election, such that a typical voter is only voting for a single individual or party to represent them. Certain Westminster countries, such as Australia, have an elected national upper house (the Senate), meaning that citizens also vote to select their upper house representatives. Canada, however, has an unelected Senate, meaning that citizens only get a single vote for a single representative during each federal election. Votes in the Congressional system, meanwhile, tend to be much less concentrated. In the United States, citizens vote for their local member every two years, their president every four years, and two senators every six years. Thus, in some elections, a voter has three votes to cast at the national level alone (Senate elections are staggered such that only one of a state's two seats in the Senate is in contest during a given election), and with each vote comes a different set of expectations. Broadly speaking, members of the House of Representatives are responsible for local issues, senators represent the interests of the state in the national capital, and the president is responsible for national and international matters. In Canada, the Senate is nominally meant to represent regional matters, while the House of Commons represents national and international matters. In practice, however, it is the House of Commons that tends to serve as the most prominent forum for subnational, national, and international concerns.

At the subnational level, there are usually differences between the national and provincial/state legislatures, even within the same legislative system. In Canada, for example, the national legislature is bicameral: it has a lower house (the House of Commons) and an upper house (the Senate). The provinces, however, are all unicameral, with only a single legislative house that handles all lawmaking for the province. In the U.S., the national legislature is bicameral (with the House of Representatives and the Senate), while the states are either bicameral or unicameral. Even within a single country, the legislative system used can vary greatly, as can be seen in the Canadian case with the legislature in Nunavut (pictured at the outset of this chapter), which operates on a consensus model.

It should be clear by now that the two main types of legislative systems are very distinct compared to one other, mainly in terms of how they divide power among different government branches and the concentration of votes. These differences are not solely because of the system used, but also because of historical events, political culture, and numerous other factors that are particular to each country. Each legislature, to put it simply, reflects the unique history of the country it belongs to. These distinctions greatly affect how a legislature performs its primary functions: making law, representing constituents, and upholding accountability.

THE FUNCTIONS OF LEGISLATURES

There are many ways of describing the functions of legislatures. For example, Canadian scholar C.E.S. Franks has argued eloquently and persuasively that legislatures have four primary and two secondary functions, though some of these are distinctive to parliamentary governments.[11] For comparative purposes, we will suggest that there are three primary functions of legislatures: they are *representative bodies* that *debate and pass/defeat/amend laws* while *holding the executive accountable* for how they use (or do not use) public resources and state power.

First, legislatures are representative institutions. Members are elected by citizens to both represent local interests and provide leadership on matters on which elected officials are (theoretically) better informed and/or better able to balance local concerns with national interests. In his now famous address to the voters of Bristol, England, British philosopher and would-be politician Edmund Burke made an impassioned, impressive, and ultimately unsuccessful plea to voters in 1774 to elect him for his wisdom and not simply to be a mouthpiece of local demands (see Box 8.1).

Burke's speech highlights the conundrum in which representatives often find themselves, as they can generally perform one of two roles: either as a *delegate*, directly bringing the interests and concerns of constituents to the government with no alteration or broader concerns applied, or as a *trustee*, who while not ignoring such interests and concerns promotes laws and policies that may—in the name of the "public good"—go against the expressed desires of their constituents. Both roles can work well in different circumstances. Delegates can bring issues that might otherwise be ignored to the forefront if they believe that it is their duty, no matter the consequences, to ensure that local voices are heard. For their part, trustees can pass laws that protect minorities, even in the face of the objections of the majority of their constituents. On the other hand, each type of representative can also have a negative impact on the legislature. Delegates can refuse to budge on issues that, while impacting their constituents negatively, benefit a larger number of people (such as with tax increases). Trustees, meanwhile, can mistakenly believe that they "know what's best" for their constituents, especially if they belong to a political party, where the influence of a group of your peers can easily convince you that you are voting for the "public good," even if it truly is not.

In more modern times, we have seen reactions against such a party-centred approach to representation. For example, Canada's Reform Party, successful in the 1990s, argued against **party discipline** and was proudly in favour of members voting in the legislature according to the perceived collective (or at least majority) views of their respective constituents. The fact that most Reform banner carriers shared an ideology of a smaller state and lower taxes made the pledge of free votes somewhat easier, though there were issues of divergence within the caucus.

> ### BOX 8.1
>
> #### EXCERPT FROM EDMUND BURKE'S "SPEECH TO THE ELECTORS OF BRISTOL," 1774[12]
>
> "Parliament is not a *congress* of ambassadors from different and hostile interests, which interests each must maintain, as an agent and advocate, against other agents and advocates; but Parliament is a *deliberative* assembly of *one* nation, with *one* interest, that of the whole—where not local purposes, not local prejudices, ought to guide, but the general good, resulting from the general reason of the whole. You choose a member, indeed; but when you have chosen him, he is not member of Bristol, but he is a member of *Parliament*. If the local constituent should have an interest or should form an hasty opinion evidently opposite to the real good of the rest of the community, the member for that place ought to be as far as any other from any endeavor to give it effect."

Party discipline: Refers to the reality of all members in a political party voting along the same lines inside a legislature. The level of party discipline varies between countries and parties. Some parties require their members to always vote along the same lines, while others only enforce party discipline for important votes (such as during a vote of non-confidence).

Even without these competing models, representing constituents can be tricky. Members are first selected by their party (with the exception of the few independent legislators who get elected to office), a group that is often more ideologically driven than the

THINK AND DISCUSS

Some people believe that representatives should only try to represent the direct interests of the citizens they serve, while others believe that representatives should focus on promoting the "public good," even if it conflicts with the interests of the people who voted for them. What interests should a representative ultimately promote in the legislature? In either case, how can citizens ensure that representatives remain accountable?

general public. They must then get elected by at least a **plurality** of citizens in their ridings—a somewhat broader group, but still likely to vote at least partially based on party platform and ideology. Yet, once elected, they must represent all their constituents, and not simply those who voted for them, even if they could identify them.

> **Plurality:** Where a party or candidate has more seats or votes than its rivals, though not a majority (50 percent or more). In a Westminster system, a government with a plurality of seats is known as a *minority government*, since it must rely on the support of opposition parties and MPs in order to pass legislation.

Moreover, it can be difficult to determine exactly what a majority of citizens wants on any given issue that members must vote upon. Not every citizen pays attention to each issue that is brought to a vote, even if that issue will have a significant effect on them. Representatives might only end up hearing from citizens with enough time and dedication to contact their representative directly, or from powerful interest groups and organizations with more resources than the average person. As well, members are often privy to more information than the general public, have the opportunity to discuss matters thoroughly with their caucus colleagues, and understand that what the public claims to want might not be in the public's best interest. All of this combined means that representatives are frequently caught between a rock and a hard place: whichever way they vote, someone will dislike them for it. Party discipline can be useful here, as it provides a convenient vehicle to allow members to vote in the broader public interest (because they have no choice but to vote along the party line) when it conflicts with the most vocal or organized demands of constituents.

As a result, we should not be surprised that members of the legislature might prefer to "represent" their constituents on personal grievances with the government, where ideology is less present and the pay back—both in terms of support and a sense of personal accomplishment—is greater. One can easily imagine that trying to influence the government on behalf of a constituent who wants a visitor visa for a relative, for example, could be more rewarding in both personal and political terms than trying to identify

and address local needs by bringing forth motions on more mundane and impersonal (though still important) legislation in an area such as energy policy.

Despite the conventional wisdom that elected representatives in the United States are not as beholden to their party leaders when it comes to casting ballots in the legislature as their Westminster counterparts, party affiliation still explains a great deal of voting behaviour in the national House of Representatives. While the number of times that each of the two major political parties (the Republicans and the Democrats) voted strictly along party lines against the opposing party are relatively modest by Canadian standards, they still, by the 1990s, made up at least half of all votes in the House. In other words, representatives voted along with what their party wanted half the time they were in Congress.[13] Thus, parties tend to dominate inside legislatures, even in an age when people do not identify with or necessarily respect political parties, regardless of whether it is a Westminster or Congressional system.

The second major function of a legislature revolves around the fact that elected officials are responsible for introducing, debating, and—with enough support— passing legislation. In the United States, members of Congress initiate and shepherd legislation though their respective chambers. By contrast, authority over the introduction of legislation is more restricted in Westminster systems. Notably, only members of the cabinet have the authority to introduce legislation that causes an expenditure of tax dollars (a "money bill").

A negative portrayal of a politician: while saying that he cares only about the public, he is really only concerned about himself. The reality is often more complex, with representatives having to balance their personal beliefs and interests with those of voters, lobbyists, and their own political party.

© John Larter. Reproduced with permission of Simon Fraser University Library.

This is a historic convention. The executive represents the Crown in parliament, and thus only the Crown can authorize the spending of Crown dollars. Non-cabinet members, or private members, have much more limited scope on the types of legislation they can introduce, especially as private members' bills cannot involve direct public expenditure or any kind of increase in public taxes.[14] As one might expect, this significantly narrows the potential for bills introduced by private members to have a real impact on

the direction of government policy. Major legislation is crafted in the cabinet, not parliament. Thus, parliament does not create legislation: it debates, amends, and then either passes or defeats legislation.

Despite these differences, the process for passing legislation in each system is not dissimilar. In Canada, the Crown (or the cabinet) introduces legislation that must pass three **readings** before going to the Senate, where it receives an additional three readings (Figure 8.1).[15] In the United States, individual

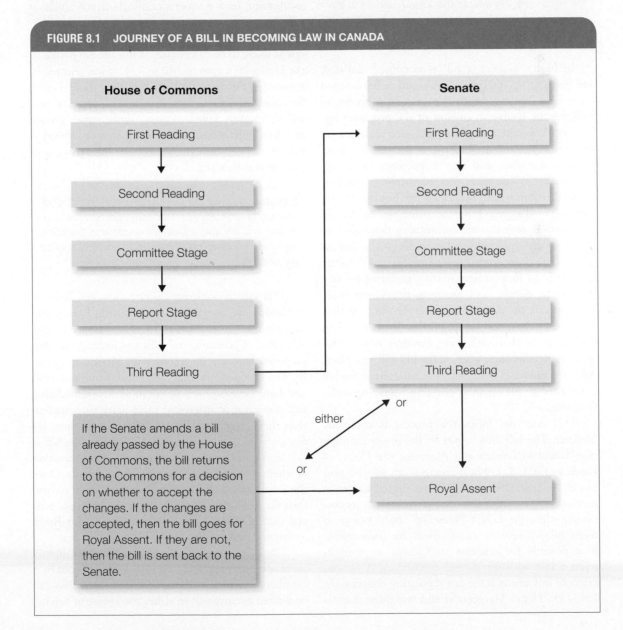

FIGURE 8.1   JOURNEY OF A BILL IN BECOMING LAW IN CANADA

members sponsor legislation, though legislation is often co-sponsored by a number of members in the hopes of garnering greater support across the floor. This may be more tradition than reality, however, as some studies point to co-sponsoring being no more effective than single sponsorship.[16]

> **Reading:** The general stages that a bill goes through in a legislature in the process of becoming a law. This includes the introduction of the bill to the legislature, as well as the formal debate in the legislature on the bill's components and any amendments to it.

In both countries, a bill is examined, debated, and voted on several times. In Canada, a bill is voted on at First Reading, which is more of a formality to facilitate the further discussion of the proposed legislation. A second vote takes place after a debate on the "principles" of the bill (what the bill is setting out to accomplish, and how it proposes to do so). This debate is known as Second Reading, and it is where divisions within the legislature first appear. By agreeing or disagreeing on the principles of the bill at this stage, members are committing themselves to their respective positions and providing a real indication of bill's chances of success. After Second Reading, most bills go to a parliamentary committee for further study, debate, and amendments. Committees meet outside the floor of the assembly and are thus followed by the media and public less frequently than debates in the House. They are, however, where some of the most important work on the bill will take place. After any proposed changes by the committee, the bill is returned to the assembly for Third Reading and a final vote.

This does not mean the process is complete, however. The bill then moves to the upper chamber (the Senate in Canada and Australia; the House of Lords in the U.K.), where changes can also be proposed. Australia's Senate, due to its elected nature, is more willing to reject bills that pass through its corridors, while the U.K.'s House of Lords' power to reject bills is severely constrained. By comparison, it is possible for **senators** in Canada to outright reject a bill, with few formal constraints. A famous example in Canada is the law regulating abortion. In 1983, Dr. Henry Morgentaler and two other doctors

were charged with unlawfully providing abortions for women at Morgentaler's Toronto clinic. His case went all the way to the Supreme Court, where the parts of the federal Criminal Code that made abortion (in most cases) illegal were ruled unconstitutional under the Canadian Charter of Rights and Freedoms and struck from the law. In 1989, the federal government introduced a new bill regulating abortion: Bill C-43. If passed by both the House of Commons and the Senate, the bill would have made performing an abortion on a woman a criminal offence, unless it was done by (or under the direction of) a physician who believed that the woman's life or health was otherwise likely to be threatened. While the bill passed in the House by a vote of 140 to 131, it was rejected in a stunning tie vote of 43 to 43 in the Senate. Under Senate rules, a tie vote is considered a negative, and Bill C-43 thus failed to pass. While other private members' bills aimed at restricting access to abortion have since been brought forth, none has managed to pass Second Reading.[17]

> **Senator:** A member of the Senate (the "upper house") of a country. In Canada, senators are unelected, and are appointed on the advice of the prime minister. In Australia and the United States, senators are elected.

This sort of occurrence is rare, however. Senators in Canada are wary of drawing too much attention to their non-elected status and instead spend valuable effort in "cleaning up" bills and making sure that proposed laws are in accord with previously passed legislation. Senators may also hear from witnesses and have been known to be more accommodating and respectful of interested third-party participation than their busy lower house colleagues. If there are any proposed amendments by the Senate, the bill is sent back to the House of Commons for consideration of whether to accept or reject the amendments. Once the Senate and the House of Commons are in accord, then the legislation is passed on to the governor general (acting as the Queen's representative) for Royal Assent and passage into law.

The U.S. Congressional system follows a slightly more complex path. Bills can only be introduced by a member of Congress (though the bills themselves can be drafted by anyone), in either the House or Senate.

A bill is sent to a committee or sub-committee immediately after being introduced, prior to a vote on the principles of the bill. U.S. House and Senate committees are far more powerful (and independent) than their Canadian counterparts, and many committee members are experts in their respective policy areas. Generally, the committee work of an American legislator is closely tied to their district's economic and social interests. A committee member who directly promotes bills or amendments that benefit their district does so in the hopes that they will garner greater public support going into the next election. Thus, there is a strong incentive to become a committee member, as it helps boost the representative's public image and may improve their chances of re-election.

Seniority dictates status on Congressional committees, with some members choosing to serve for several terms to become a sub-committee or committee chair. These positions are far more powerful than some cabinet posts in the executive, which is the complete opposite of the career structure in Canada. The combined incentive of power and electability makes committee service a desirable prospect in the United States. In Canada, by comparison, it is often seen as a distraction from more important work, such as debating in the legislature or performing constituency duties.

Once a bill has been reported on by the committee, it is voted on in the chamber that initiated it (either the House of Representatives or the Senate). If it passes the vote, then the proposed legislation is sent to the opposite house, where the bill can be debated and amendments added. Bills travelling from the House to the Senate in the U.S. (or vice versa) are far more likely to face substantial changes compared to Canadian bills going from the House of Commons to the Senate. This is primarily due to the lax requirements for amendment proposals. Amendments to bills in the second chamber in the Congressional system do not have to be relevant to the bill's purpose, meaning that senators can add items that have nothing to do with the bill itself. Amendments like these can be a sneaky way of getting laws or regulations in place that might not otherwise be so easily passed, as the president or the other chamber may face considerable political risk if they oppose particularly important bills, even if the proposed legislation has a number of totally irrelevant and problematic

amendments stapled to them.[18] If the opposite chamber approves the bill, then any major disagreements over new amendments are smoothed out by a conference committee until a final version, approved by both chambers, is created.[19]

Finally, the bill is sent to the president's office, where he or she can either sign the law or veto it and send it back to Congress. The veto is a potentially powerful tool for a president, allowing them to turn back legislation that they disagree with, unless both Congress and the Senate are able to muster a two-thirds majority vote to override the veto. A good example of this entire process is the Medicare Improvements for Patients and Providers Act of 2008 (legally known as H.R.6331), which was introduced in the House of Representatives on June 20, 2008. Containing a long list of recommended amendments and additions to federal Medicare and Medicaid programs, H.R.6331 was passed by the House with a vote of 355 to 59 in favour, and then by the Senate with unanimous consent. Upon being presented to then-president George W. Bush, however, H.R.6331 was vetoed by him and returned to the House of Representatives, along with a thousand-word message explaining his decision. His message failed to be persuasive, however, and H.R.6331 subsequently passed through both the House and the Senate with the required two-thirds majority vote in favour. This was sufficient to override the presidential veto.[20] In comparison, Canadian prime ministers operate under no such threat of an override, as the executive effectively controls the parliamentary agenda (unless, of course, it is a minority government).

Within the Westminster system, the prime minister (or premier) must hold the confidence (or support) of the legislature. Failure to hold this support could cost the government its power due to a vote of non-confidence, resulting in either the opposition being called upon to form the government or, more frequently, an election being called. (see Photo Essay box) This is not the case in Congressional systems, where the president might not be a member of the governing party and is often at complete odds with the majority in the Senate and/or the House of Representatives.

In Canada, the general practice in the legislature has been to treat virtually any piece of government legislation as a matter of confidence. By doing so, the government effectively requires its own caucus members to support every bill that the government introduces, even if the legislation would adversely impact their own ridings. Party discipline in Canada and Australia is much stronger than it is in the United Kingdom. In the U.K.'s House of Commons, members often vote against the party leadership, but only under certain conditions. The party leadership will normally indicate to caucus members on which votes they can choose how to vote and on which ones they are required to follow the party line (typically known as "three-whip" votes). The only matters that by constitutional convention would necessitate an election should they lose in the House are the Speech from the Throne that opens a legislative session, budget bills or other monetary matters, and specific motions of confidence. If a government introduces a budget or a Speech from the Throne and it is defeated, the head of government must visit the Queen or her representative, who determines if an election is necessary or if another group (typically one of the opposition parties or several parties in a coalition) can form a government.

In contrast, the United States government was effectively "shut down" in 2011 and 2013 when Congress and the president could not agree on a budget, yet no elections were called as a result and politicians did not really have to defend their inaction in the legislature. The U.S. president neither has a seat in Congress nor the ability to tempt members with promotion. Only during times of high popularity does the president enjoy the ability to persuade representatives, especially those of a different political party, to take the legislative path that he or she wants. By contrast, sitting in the same chamber as their members, the prime minister and opposition leaders can use their positions to encourage greater party discipline and stronger executive control. Their presence, however, also makes them more accountable to opposing parties, and puts them more firmly in the public eye with regards to their statements and actions. Congressional systems, meanwhile, encourage deadlock and unproductive posturing, but do not afford the executive the same level of control over the day-to-day operations of the legislature and the actions (how people vote, what they say, etc.) of the representatives therein. Both systems, as can be seen, have their benefits and drawbacks.

The third and final function of legislatures is to provide oversight and to attempt to hold the government accountable. They do this by making sure that the executive is keeping its election promises, delivering necessary public services, and not squandering the public purse. In the Westminster system, cabinet ministers are responsible for the departments they head and private members are responsible for holding ministers to account. All elected officials are ultimately responsible to the people who decide whether to re-elect them or to throw the rascals out. The fused executive and legislature provides members with unique oversight tools. Both opposition and government members can respond to the Speech from the Throne, speak freely about any topic they desire during members' statements, question the government during Question Period, challenge the government with motions of confidence, and make effective use of **opposition days**.[21] The beauty of the Westminster system is the requirement that the executive must stand across the aisle from the opposition parties and either answer for its actions or attempt to shift the focus away from itself in front of the nation.

> **Opposition days:** Also known as allotted days. In a Westminster system, opposition days are when a member of an opposition party is allowed to decide the topic for debate on that particular day. This gives the opposition a tool to "set the agenda" in the legislature, and to direct attention to specific areas of government policy for scrutiny.

The rose of executive accountability, however, is not without its thorns. Because of the often heated nature of debates in legislatures, rules on the general decorum (behaviour) of representatives are established to try to calm passions and keep representatives from personally attacking each other. In the Canadian House of Commons, for example, representatives in the legislature do not refer to each other by their names (instead using titles, positions, or their constituencies), and must always address their comments to the **Speaker**. They are not allowed to criticize either of the chambers or the Speaker while within the legislature, and must refrain from using "unparliamentary language" (offensive, provocative, or threatening language).[22]

PHOTO ESSAY

A vote of non-confidence in the House of Commons. The threat of a non-confidence vote encourages minority governments to seek compromises with opposition parties when it comes to passing bills.

VOTE OF NON-CONFIDENCE: HIGH RISK, HIGH REWARD

A vote of non-confidence in the Canadian legislature can be a risky gamble for opposition parties. When a vote coincides with a major scandal, opposition parties have the opportunity to seize the reins of power from the government. Without a scandal (or some other event that causes negative public opinion toward the government), such a vote can backfire, weakening the standing of the opposition parties overall. For example, the public may view the subsequent election as being unnecessary and wasteful, or may have more confidence in the current government than the opposition believes.

In 2005, the federal Liberal Party found itself embroiled in a "sponsorship scandal" over the apparent payment of hundreds of thousands of dollars to Liberal-aligned companies. While the money was ostensibly to be used to promote national unity and federalism in the wake of the narrowly defeated 1995 Quebec referendum (where Quebec voted on whether it was going to separate from Canada and become

its own country), it was instead put into "make-work" projects that had little benefit to Canadians. Sensing an opportunity, the opposition parties eventually passed a vote of non-confidence in the legislature, forcing the governor general to call a new election. The 2006 election ended the 12-year reign of the Liberal Party in federal politics, ushering in a minority federal Conservative Party government.[23]

By comparison, in 2011, the opposition parties misread the public mood toward the Conservative Party. The opposition parties called and passed a vote of non-confidence over the government's budget bill, flinging the country into a new election.[24] This proved to be a serious misstep. The Conservative Party pulled ahead in the 2011 election, gaining enough seats in the legislature to form a majority government. The other big winner was the New Democratic Party, which gained 66 seats, making it the new official opposition. For its part, the Liberal Party lost 43 seats, while the Bloc Québécois lost a staggering 45 seats, leaving them with a mere four.[25] The majority status of the Conservative government, however, now limited the influence that the opposition parties could have on the overall direction of policy.

Speaker: The Speaker is a member of a legislature (usually elected by their fellow representatives) who is responsible for the general day-to-day procedures of the legislature, such as debates and voting on bills. They are also usually responsible for maintaining the decorum of the legislature.

The existence of the rules, of course, does not always keep people from breaking them or toeing the line. In a famous incident, former prime minister Pierre Trudeau was accused by the opposition of mouthing an unparliamentary phrase in the House of Commons. Trudeau, in response, asserted that he had mouthed nothing worse than the words "fuddle-duddle."[26] Things have improved little since that time, although they still, thankfully, almost never devolve into fisticuffs.

Pity, then, the poor teacher who takes their students on a field trip to our national parliament to see the House of Commons in action during Question Period! Public school teachers demand a respectful, polite, and productive classroom, but what their class tends to see during Question Period looks more like a shouting match than a forum of thoughtful and inspired debate. What sort of lessons do the students take home with them? The students, and all other Canadians, will only respect our legislatures when members themselves respect each other and the democratic process, and the best place to start is inside the House itself.

The separation of powers in the United States means that oversight takes on a markedly different format. Oversight refers to checking or reviewing bureaucratic or executive actions "after the fact." Members of Congress, either individually or via committees or sub-committees, review government actions to ensure that the powers delegated to the bureaucracy by the executive have been properly exercised. Walter J. Oleszek suggests that there are seven requirements for effective oversight, including effective chairship of oversight committees, bi-partisanship (when legislators work across party lines for a greater purpose), willingness to dedicate adequate time and resources, and follow-up on any committee recommendations.[27] Committees are particularly important in the Congressional system, as members cannot question cabinet members or the president on the floor of the legislature. It is only through committee work that effective questioning of senior administration and bureaucrats can take place.

If these are the primary functions of legislatures—that they are *representative bodies* that *debate and pass/defeat/amend laws* while *holding the executive accountable* for how they use (or do not use) public resources—and if legislatures themselves are suffering from low levels of public support, then we are left with one fundamental question: Do our legislative assemblies have the tools to perform their functions adequately? Or to put it another way: Are legislatures, and those non-executive members in them, equipped to represent, legislate, and question the government effectively? If they are, then the problem may lie in the men and women (and political parties) that we elect to represent us. It may be that the motivations of these individuals (such as re-election and personal ambition) are taking priority over proper representation. This would require voters to re-think the role of their representatives and to vote for individuals both willing and able to perform a stricter interpretation of their roles.

Conversely, the problem might lie in the rules and tools that members have at their disposal. If legislatures are not set up to allow members to perform their proper roles, then the solution to the problem may lie in institutional reform. This is a much more difficult task, as changes to one set of rules or institutions can have serious ramifications for other forms of representation and can produce unintended consequences. Part of this reform may entail ensuring that legislatures have enough seats to do their jobs properly, and that they are sufficiently representative to ensure that the concerns of all constituents are properly heard.

THE SIZE AND COMPOSITION OF LEGISLATURES

Are legislatures large enough to do the work required of them? Or are they too large to work effectively? The size of assemblies is an important question as it impacts each of the three functions of assemblies explored above. We turn, then, to explore the relationship between legislative size and representation, legislation, and scrutiny.

A small legislature in a populous state may be more efficient but can also result in elected officials struggling to represent their constituents adequately. In turn, a large legislature in a less populous region might mean that members find themselves with too much time on their hands and can be less efficient. In single member districts, legislatures that are small are more likely to produce assemblies that have a less diverse party membership. Larger assemblies may be more likely to consist of a broader range of parties, but that could come at the cost of effective representation, with assemblies more prone to partisan gridlock. A quick comparison of five countries reveals some of the variation on the ratio of representatives to citizens that can occur in lower assemblies.

Canada has a smaller ratio of representatives to citizens than Australia (see Table 8.1). However, the Australian lower house is complemented with an elected upper house (the Senate), while Canada's upper house remains an appointed body. Great Britain and Italy have similar populations and lower house sizes, although Italy does have a regionally based upper chamber of over 300 members.

The largest outlier is the United States, with nearly three-quarters of a million residents per district. However, even this figure is misleading. Seats are distributed via states in a way that's roughly proportionate to their population but there is a relatively fixed number of total seats. This, combined with a growing population, produces wild variances in the representative-to-citizen ratio depending on the state. A state like Montana, with a resident population of 989,415 people, has only a single representative (a ratio of 1 representative per 989,415 people), whereas California, with a resident population of 37,253,956, has 53 representatives (a ratio of 1 representative per 702,905 people).[28] These differences mostly stem from an unwillingness to tackle the issue of a larger assembly. The House of Representatives

has not increased in size since before the First World War. The number 435 was put into law in 1929.[29] As a result, the United States simply "re-apportions" seats in its assembly and this decennial process sees some states gain seats at the cost of states with stable or shrinking populations. In the case of states like Montana, the attractiveness of the lower house as a political career path may be much lower than in a more populated state like California. After all, the representatives of these smaller states are charged with looking after the same number of voters as the two state senators but must be re-elected every two years, which is three times more than the six-term senators.

Within Canada, district population variations also exist. Like the United States, we do not have constituencies (or districts) that cross provincial/state borders. Unlike the United States, our elected officials are not averse to making the case for more politicians. In 1929, when Congress locked in the 435 number for the House of Representatives, the Canadian House of Commons had 245 seats, nearly a hundred fewer than Canada will have after the 2015 federal election. Canada has maintained some semblance of balance by increasing the size of the Commons to reflect a growing national population; however, there are two important points to note.

First, in typical Canadian fashion, we are loathe to produce losers or to impact smaller provinces adversely. Thus, not only do we increase the size of the assembly to accommodate provinces with increasing populations but we act as creatively as possible to ensure that no province loses any seats. For example, Prince Edward Island, with a population that should

TABLE 8.1	LOWER HOUSE ASSEMBLY SIZE AND POPULATION IN FIVE DEMOCRACIES		
Country	Assembly size	Population Estimate (2013)	Representative: Citizen Ratio
Australia	150	23,319,400	1:155,463
Canada	308	35,158,300	1:114,150
Italy	630	60,782,668	1:96,480
United Kingdom	650	64,100,000	1:98,615
United States	435	309,487,186	1:710,767

Population figures are based on 2013 estimates. Assembly size is based on actual number of seats available in 2013. The Canadian House of Commons will increase to 338 for the projected 2015 election.[30]

Source: "New House of Commons Seat Allocation," *Elections Canada*, December 19, 2011, online at http://www.elections.ca/content.aspx?section=med&document=dec1911&dir=pre&lang=e, accessed January 14, 2015.

only justify two elected federal members if it were kept on par with the ratios in more populous provinces, actually has four. Why is this? Well, Section 51 of the Constitution Act, 1867 states that provinces must have at least as many members of the Commons as they have senators, *regardless of population*.[31] Thus, Prince Edward Island, with four senators, gets to double the representatives that it would otherwise receive in the House. The other three Atlantic provinces also benefit from the "Senatorial Floor" clause. Other "grandfather clauses" in the Representation Act protect provinces from losing the seats that they already have.

As a result, only three provinces (British Columbia, Alberta, and Ontario) actually have the number of seats that their populations warrant. At the same time, these most populous provinces are still technically "under-represented" as the various clauses "over-represent" the other seven provinces and the three territories. For those up in arms thinking that this somehow provides a net advantage to smaller Prince Edward Island or New Brunswick, you can rest easy. Even with twice as many federal seats as it deserves, Prince Edward Island holds less than two percent of all House seats, while New Brunswick has less than three percent. A vote might be worth more in the smaller provinces, but their collective voice is still relatively quiet.

Second, the growing House is a positive move in accountability and representation. After all, smaller districts can provide a closer relationship between an elected official and the public that they serve. Meeting the needs of a population of 100,000 is easier than doing so for three-quarters of a million people. American legislators require much larger staffs and the local member has a more difficult time attending the myriad of local events he or she is invited to on a regular basis. Members can more easily get a sense of community needs and desires when there are fewer people to represent. This depends, of course, on whether the creation of new districts is able to outpace a growing population. There is a difference between making new districts for a relatively stable population (to provide better representation) and making new districts to keep up with a rapidly expanding population (to keep the same level of representation as before).

A larger house (with smaller districts) may also lead to greater member independence from party leaders.

One of the greatest carrots that a prime minister can hold over a caucus member is the possibility of a cabinet post. There is nothing like the hint of satisfied ambition to keep a member in line! But in the U.K., where the House of Commons is far larger, most members get elected knowing that they will never be in the cabinet. Once that carrot is removed, members have fewer constraints when it comes to pursuing parliamentary careers focusing on legislation and accountability rather than career advancement. If the ideal role of both opposition and government private members is to hold the government accountable for its actions, then a larger, more independent legislature can only be a good thing. This is particularly true when one examines the smaller provincial assemblies.

As Table 8.2 suggests, there is great variation in sub-national assemblies in Canada, from a low of 19 in two territories to a high of 125 in the Quebec National Assembly. Given the different population sizes involved, this is to be expected. More interesting, however, is the variation on the population of the riding per member. Setting aside the less populous territories, members represent as few as 5,400 citizens in Prince Edward Island to over 128,000 in Ontario.

The size of these ridings can provide some challenges to representation. For example, elected officials in Ontario and Quebec require larger staffs to assist them in constituency work. At the same time, we need to recognize that different jurisdictions have different needs. The territorial ridings have relatively few people but cover vast areas, with many remote communities only accessible by air. All elected members represent people and not rocks, trees, and lakes, but a greater number of rocks, trees, and lakes can make visiting communities difficult, particularly compared to densely populated urban ridings where members can travel from one end to the other in less than an hour. In other jurisdictions (such as New Brunswick), many ridings have areas that are unincorporated, meaning that there is no local government. In these cases, members act not just as provincial representatives but also as mayors, dealing with potholes and broken street lamps as often as they deal with education and health, matters that fall under provincial jurisdiction.[32]

One particular challenge in smaller assemblies is that of scrutiny. Official opposition parties are often the same size as the cabinet, and third parties are even smaller. Why does this matter? In order to hold

TABLE 8.2	ASSEMBLY SIZE AND POPULATION IN CANADIAN ASSEMBLIES[33]				
Jurisdiction	Assembly Size	Residents per Member	Cabinet Size	Size of Official Opposition	Legislative Sittings Days (2013)
Alberta	87	46,265	20	16	49
British Columbia	85	53,906	20	34	36
Manitoba	57	22,193	18	19	103
New Brunswick	55	13,746	13	21	52
Newfoundland and Labrador	48	10,972	16	13	50
Northwest Territories	19	2,291	7	12	40
Nova Scotia	51	18,447	16	7	45
Nunavut	22	1,618	9	13	34
Ontario	107	126,523	27	28	100
Prince Edward Island	27	5,379	11	3	40
Saskatchewan	58	19,109	18	9	65
Quebec	125	65,243	28	29	84
Yukon	19	1,931	8	11	60

Refers to total number of seats available in the legislature, rather than total number actually filled at this time.

The Northwest Territories and Nunavut do not have political parties. The cabinet is formed via collective voting in the legislature, and the "official opposition" is simply anyone who isn't a part of the cabinet.

the government to account, opposition parties give their members critic or "shadow cabinet roles." For example, the opposition will have a critic for the minister of health. This critic's role is to question the minister on actions or inactions of the government, act as a specialist when legislation related to health are introduced, and produce alternative health policies so that voters have a meaningful choice come election time. Ministers not only have their own staff to assist them but they also have the weight of their ministry when drafting legislation and policy. By contrast, critics have much smaller staffs, something which makes attending to their constituency duties at the same time a challenge. This is exacerbated when opposition members hold down two or three critic roles, which stretches both resources and time even further. Minor parties face even greater challenges.

The Northwest Territory and Nunavut offer a unique variation on Westminster government by not having political parties. All members meet after an election to select who will serve in the cabinet. Party discipline is not an issue as there are no parties and no leaders to keep members in line. A person's ambition of getting a cabinet position requires them to have the respect of all their peers, rather than merely having the respect of the leader of their own party.

Sub-national assembly size in the United States varies even more than in Canada, though assemblies tend to be larger south of the border. Table 8.3 illustrates some select state assemblies.

The case of New Hampshire speaks well to the nature of the Congressional system. At first blush, a large assembly for a small population indicates a close relationship between voters and legislators. With just over 3,000 constituents per district, members are indeed close to those that voted for or against them, and with 400 members in the lower house, New Hampshirites are nothing if not well represented. Despite this excellent ratio, the effectiveness of their legislature may be less than that of districts with a far higher ratio of representatives to constituents. State legislators in New Hampshire are, at best, part-time representatives.

	TABLE 8.3	SIZE AND SITTING DAYS IN SELECT U.S. ASSEMBLIES			
State	**Total Legislative Seats**	**Constituents per Senate District**	**Constituents per House District**	**Sitting Day Limits**	
Texas	181	811,147	167,637	140 days with biennial sessions	
New Hampshire	424	54,853	3,291	45 per year	
New York	212	307,589	129,187	No limit	
Nebraska	49	N/A	37,272	On odd years, 90 per year, on even years 60 per year	

Source: Adapted from "2010 Constituents per State Legislative District Table," *National Conference of State Legislatures*, available at http://www.ncsl.org/research/about-state-legislatures/2010-constituents-per-state-legislative-district.aspx, accessed June 19, 2015.

The assembly does not convene very often, committees rarely meet, and members rely on outside sources of income to supplement their legislative salary. Such assemblies have been described as a "dead-end," where members have to look outside the legislature to satisfy career goals, leaving the legislatures with a constant "brain drain" and new recruits more concerned with career advancement than citizen representation.[34] By contrast, the state of New York has a lower house of 150 members and a 63-member Senate. Here, members are full-time legislators: they enjoy a full staff complement to assist them with legislation, oversight, and assisting the approximately 129,000 constituents that they each represent (roughly the same population per member ratio as many Canadian assemblies), and they meet—as we will see—more frequently.

Given the separation of the executive and the legislature, oversight in the United States often takes place both on the floor of the legislature and through the committee system. In Canada, it occurs via debates, motions of confidence, Opposition Days, members' statements, and, most critically, Question Period. The common thread in all of these mechanisms is that they take place only when the legislature actually meets. When the assembly is not in session, sitting members can dedicate almost all their time to constituency matters, thus enabling greater opportunities for representation of a wider range of constituents' interests and concerns. Critics would be wrong to say that when an assembly is not meeting, members are not working. They are often working just as diligently, just not necessarily on legislation and accountability (though they may well be doing work that relates to these as

well). In order to engage on these latter two functions actively, legislatures must sit.

Measuring actual sitting days can be tricky, however. In Westminster parliaments, sessions can last two or more years, and the yearly calendar is not the reference for accounting for sitting days. Moreover, certain events, such as elections, can mean that the legislature sits for fewer days during the year than it would otherwise as the members are on the campaign trail. Nonetheless, with the exceptions of the Ontario and Manitoba assemblies, there is some uniformity in the frequency of legislative sessions, with the Atlantic provinces meeting between 40 and 50 days, the prairie provinces between 50 and 60, and the Central Canadian provinces more frequently.

Among other things, this means that there are more chances to hold the government accountable in provinces where the assembly gathers more frequently. This is especially true of Question Period. Despite the deserved reputation that it earns at every level as a forum for venom, dirty politics, and outlandish behaviour, Question Period serves a critical role in accountability, as it provides a regular time when opposition members can stand and ask unscripted questions of the government. The questions can be about the personal conduct of ministers, matters that have occurred in their ministries, misspending, underspending, overspending, and just about any other matter that the opposition can try to hang on the government.

Students would be wise to recognize that this accountability mechanism is not called Answer Period. The government is not compelled to provide specific answers (although they must respond) and

---

BOX 8.2

REPRESENTATIVES RECONSIDERED

It can be easy to think of representatives—especially ones in national legislatures—solely in terms of the common stereotypes of politicians: lazy, selfish, and arrogant, without any real connections to or understandings of the people they represent. This perception likely comes in large part from the fact that we rarely interact with our representatives, and only briefly see them in news reports or during election campaigns, if at all.

In truth, however, they are busy people. When not sitting in legislatures, representatives are still working hard at addressing their constituency's concerns, meeting with voters and interest groups, attending important local events, and so on. This is the work that can be the most rewarding for a representative, as it has a direct and meaningful impact on the lives of the people they represent. Instead of abstractly attempting to advocate for their constituents in a

legislature, they are performing hands-on, face-to-face work that provides real benefits to citizens, helping them to obtain neglected public services and work through government bureaucracy, for example, or even bringing the well-wishes of the government to an 85th birthday party.[35]

Unfortunately, this is also the work that is far less well-covered. The eyes of the media tend to be focused more on the theatrical stage of the legislature or on brewing private scandals, rather than on the humdrum day-to-day work of a representative meeting with constituents or attending charity events. This "invisible work," despite forming a core part of what a representative does, rarely influences the general public's view toward their reputation. This may well be why so many politicians get such a bad rap: a huge portion of the work that they do is work that we never see.

---

often looks to deflect questions in order to paint the opposition parties in a negative light. It is perhaps the abuse of the answer process that makes mild-mannered Canadians—and possibly professional wrestlers—cringe at the antics on television. Yet to dismiss Question Period as merely theatre of the absurd would be to give it short shrift. More than one political career has been terminated by a member's inability to defend their actions during Question Period. This regular time slot provides the Opposition with unparalleled opportunities to highlight government mismanagement, and opposition parties seldom let that chance slip by them. The conundrum of Question Period is that it works best when it looks worst. Members resort to poorer behaviour when the stakes are at their highest, and they are at their highest when the light of transparency shines on indefensible behaviour. As citizens, we may not like the tone of Question Period, but we should appreciate the role it plays in promoting a more honest and accountable government. (Negative stereotypes of elected representatives are reconsidered in Box 8.2.)

No such mechanism exists in the United States. When the government shutdown occurred in 2013,

for example, there were no public debates between the Republican leadership and the president. Any such meetings were held behind closed doors. During the awkward first days of President Obama's healthcare reforms, the battered president did not have to face tough and unpredictable questions on the floor of the legislature. Instead, he and his office could more effectively stage-manage their appearances and messages. A prime minister could only look on with envy.

Perhaps the most startling aspect of Table 8.3 is the number of states that constitutionally limit the number of sitting days. The legislature in Texas, the second-largest state in the United States, can only meet every other year by law. In New Hampshire, with more representatives than any other state, the house can only meet for a maximum of 45 days a year. By contrast, New York, which has one of the most professional assemblies, is one of only 10 of the 50 states that has no limits on the number of days that it can meet.

The reason for the difference between sitting days in Westminster assemblies and the U.S. Congressional system reflects inherent differences in political culture and institutional design. Congressional systems diffuse power across government branches and even within Congress itself. If you want to limit government (and government spending), then you limit the amount of time during which the legislature can meet.

Westminster systems, meanwhile, concentrate power within the cabinet, which constitutes approximately 10 percent of the assembly.[36] Legislatures do not spend money; the cabinet does. The 90 percent of legislators who are not in the cabinet are charged with keeping it honest. It is harder to do that from home. Members are their most effective at performing their legislative and accountability functions when they can face those that they are charged with scrutinizing. Even government caucus, where members have the opportunity to question their leaders in privacy and with (at least in theory) no fear of reprisal, meets far less often when the House is not in session. Meeting more often in Westminster assemblies is a small and worthwhile price to pay for good government.

Finally, it is worth reflecting on the difference in the legislative calendars of Westminster and Congressional governments. The regularity of the timing of U.S. federal elections has been established since 1845. The vote is always held on the Tuesday following the first Monday in November (in other words, if November begins on a Tuesday, the vote is held a week later). The regularity of these elections provides a level playing field for government and opposition alike. The morning after an election, everyone knows when the next general vote will take place.

Fixed election dates are a much more recent phenomena in many Westminster systems. In both the United Kingdom and Canada it is only in the past decade or so that legislation for fixed election dates has been passed. This should not be surprising, given the continual requirement that the government leader must always have the confidence of the assembly. The Canadian Constitution stipulates that elections must be held at least every five years but does not specify when, allowing for governments to fall at any time. Until recently, it was generally thought that any attempt to establish fixed dates would run counter to this rule.

In 2001, British Columbia became the first Canadian jurisdiction at either the provincial or federal level to introduce fixed election dates. In doing so, it was made clear that the fixed date was an outside limit and that a general election could be held whenever the lieutenant governor did not believe anyone could maintain the confidence of the chamber. This

simple change was remarkable. Among other things, it provided a more level playing field, on which premiers had less opportunity to stage-manage the timing of an election to their party's benefit as easily as before. Without such complete control over determining the timing of an election, the premier could no longer simply call elections at politically convenient times, or hold off on doing so when his or her party was low in the polls. The fixed date effectively took an arrow from the quiver of the premier (though the option of prorogation was still left open for them).[37] Since then, all other jurisdictions have adopted some form of fixed election date. This trend demonstrates the wonderful ability of the Westminster system to adapt to changing ideas about democracy.

Overall, it is clear that there is great variation in the size of legislatures and the frequency of their meetings. Hiding behind these two is a third major difference: the *composition* of a legislature. This refers to the types of people who serve as representatives (in terms of such characteristics as occupation, gender, ethnicity, religion, and sexual orientation), and how much they actually reflect the makeup of the country. This is an interesting and important question. After all, if our legislators are to represent us well, then it is not unreasonable to hope that the membership of the legislature would look a little like the demographic profile of the country. The problem, of course, is that even with a large cohort of representatives (such as the 338 members of the Canadian House of Commons as of the 2015 election) it is difficult to reflect the many different characteristics of a country. While having improved remarkably along some dimensions, Canada still has yet to create a truly representative legislature in this regard.

For example, let's look at occupational representation. In 1941, only around 0.2 percent of Canadians were in the legal profession, yet over one third of all MPs were lawyers.[38] Why such over-representation? For one thing, politics in 1941 was a part-time profession and MPs required outside sources of income to get by. The legal profession was far more conducive to this type of lifestyle than, say, a shop clerk or teacher. It was not necessarily a matter of competence. With all due respect to lawyers, it is not clear that laws created by lawyers are any better than those created by poets, teachers, bankers, and small businesspeople. The legislature now has a much broader range of occupational backgrounds than it did over 70 years ago; therefore a broader range of experiences and perspectives are brought to bear on the legislative process. The present House of Commons has lawyers, teachers, engineers, journalists, and farmers,[39] although with the growing range of new careers that our modern society creates, the House may always be playing catch-up.

While the diversity in professions has improved, gender and ethnic representation in the House of Commons remains rather lackluster. Using the same 1941 baseline, when only two of the 262 sitting members were women, by 2014 nearly one quarter of the House was female, the highest total in Canadian history. (Percentages of seats held by women in other national legislatures are shown in Figure 8.2.) Still, that is less than half of what it should be if MPs mirrored the broader Canadian public. Moreover, less than 10 percent of the present House of Commons

are members of visible minority groups, despite the concerted efforts of all political parties to attract more visible minorities (and women) to seek office.[40]

Increases in gender representation often come during large electoral swings in Canada. For example, 40 of the 105 New Democrats elected in 2011 were women. This should be gratifying for the NDP, as it has been more proactive than other parties in recruiting female candidates. Yet 27 of the 40 were elected in Quebec, a province in which the party had no real history of electoral success, and no expectation of winning 59 seats at the start of the election. This is consistent with a more general pattern, in which women are more frequently found running in ridings where the party is not expected to win a seat.[41] A similar outcome of unexpected growth in female representation occurred in the wake of the election of Brian Mulroney's large Conservative majority government in 1984.

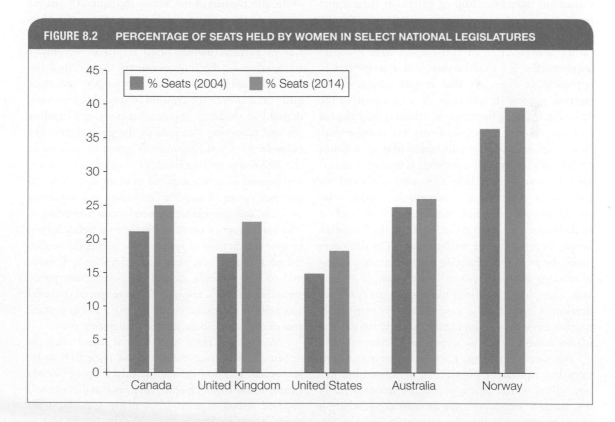

FIGURE 8.2   PERCENTAGE OF SEATS HELD BY WOMEN IN SELECT NATIONAL LEGISLATURES

This graph shows the number of seats held by women in national legislatures as a percentage of the total seats filled.

Source: Data from "Women in National Parliaments: 30 November 2004," *Inter-Parliamentary Union*, available at http://www.ipu.org/wmn-e/arc/ classif301104.htm, accessed Jan. 7, 2015; "Women in National Parliaments: 1 November 2014," *Inter-Parliamentary Union*, available at http://www.ipu.org/wmn-e/classif.htm, accessed Jan. 7, 2015.

Ironically, the unelected Canadian Senate has historically been far more diverse than the House of Commons (or, for that matter, most provincial assemblies). In 2000, for example, 20.9 percent of all MPs were women, compared to 33.3 percent of senators; while only 1.7 percent of MPs were of Aboriginal origin, compared to 5.0 percent of senators.[42] It may seem a bit of a stretch to argue this, but one beauty of the appointed Senate is that it provides prime ministers with opportunities to make up for gaps in our representative diversity as created by the collective will of the electorate. This potential benefit of the Senate's unelected nature, however, has not been enough to deflect the frequent calls for significant reform to—and even abolishment of—that chamber.

Reforming Legislatures

Canadians have been hoping to reform their upper house for almost as long as they have had a Senate. On the one hand, we can hardly blame those advocating change. It is an elitist body, with property requirements for membership and a near-lifetime appointment (age 75) that is not subject to an election process. It stands in direct contrast to the Australian Senate, for example, which is fully elected and has no special requirements for membership. Australian senators are constantly held to account by the public through elections. Canadian senators are held to account only by their own ethics and the scrutiny of their peers. A senator in Canada who contributes only the most minimal effort to hold on to their salary has nothing to fear from the Canadian people beyond a poor public image. On the other hand, the process of changing a legislature, regardless of whether it's the upper or lower house, is no easy task. Complex institutions like legislatures that have developed over decades can respond in completely unexpected ways to even minor changes, making legislative reform largely an issue of risk versus reward.

For some Canadians, a Senate appointment must seem the equivalent of winning a cash-for-life lottery.[43] Part of this perception is the consequence of the Senate's "secondary" role in lawmaking, where it serves mostly to polish the legislation brought forward in the House of Commons. The unelected and secondary nature of the Canadian Senate means that its work is rarely caught by the public eye, and usually only when senators hold up or reject a major House of Commons bill or are the focus of a major scandal. One such scandal in 2014 involved the revelation, during an audit of the Senate, of apparently faulty expense claims by Senator Mike Duffy and Senator Pamela Wallin. Duffy was subsequently charged by the RCMP of fraud, bribery, and breach of trust over housing and travel expenses, as well as an apparent monetary "gift" from Nigel Wright, the former chief of staff to Prime Minister Stephen Harper.[44] For her part, Wallin eventually repaid close to $140,000 for numerous disputed travel expense claims.[45] Needless to say, these sorts of events do nothing for the Senate's public image and help to keep the flames of Senate reform burning.

Such exposure often paints the Senate in a very negative light, while positive aspects of its work are rarely highlighted, yet there are numerous examples of the effectiveness of the Senate throughout Canada's history. In the process of debating and amending legislation, the Senate's attention to detail beyond the fray of partisan politics often results in significant technical and other improvements that escaped the notice of the House. The Senate's strengths have especially been seen in the creation of special committees, devoted to studying important aspects of Canadian life and proposing solutions to the government. For example, the Croll Committee's report on poverty in the 1970s was well-received, as senators went above and beyond what was required of them to understand the root causes of poverty (including visiting slums and jails) and provide recommendations for ending it. The Lamontagne Committee on science policy helped to spur the creation of government bodies devoted to the advancement of science and technology in Canada and to start a public debate on government policy regarding scientific research.[46] These special committees enjoyed clear success and highlight the important role of the Senate in guiding and analyzing policy.

Nonetheless, there have been repeated attempts at Senate reform over the years, but none have so far succeeded. The now defunct Reform Party of Canada (under whose banner Stephen Harper was first elected) received strong support from many Canadians for their "Triple-E" Senate proposal. The Senate was to be equal (each province would have the same number of senators), elected (via public votes), and effective (greater powers to protect provincial interests).

THINK AND DISCUSS

The unelected nature of the Canadian Senate means that, while it is not directly accountable to citizens through elections, it is also not directly accountable to political parties, since senators can sit for almost their entire lives. Should the Senate remain unelected? What are the advantages and disadvantages of such a system?

Alternatively, some parties and representatives, New Democrats among them, think that the best reform is to simply abolish the Senate and move to a unicameral system. However, it is unlikely that we will see any large-scale reform (or deconstruction) of our existing Senate for some time. Why?

For better or worse, any large-scale Senate reform would require amending our constitution, and that would open up a political Pandora's Box that would pre-maturely age all but the hardiest of prime ministers! Here is but one example. Suppose a proposal for an equal Senate—say, 10 senators per province—was put on the table. This would require a constitutional amendment and unanimous consent from the provinces and the federal government. Prince Edward Island would go from four to 10 senators and love it. Ontario would go from 24 to 10 senators and would want something in return for this sacrifice. It gets even more complicated. There is another provision in the Constitution which states that every province *must* have as many members of the House of Commons as it has senators. Prince Edward Island would go from four MPs to 10. Unless this constitutional provision was also changed, this would mean that Prince Edward Island would have one MP for every 14,700 people compared to one MP for every 108,554 persons in Ontario.[47] This is something Ontario would simply not tolerate.[48] The only way this could be accomplished would be constitutional amendment **logrolling** between the provinces and between the provinces and the federal government. This is the political death knell for prime ministers and premiers alike.

Logrolling: A method of strategic voting in which a representative agrees to vote in favour of another representative's bill or amendment in return for a vote in favour of their own bill or amendment.

As a result, the best way to change our Senate is probably to do so outside the constitution, and here we can look to Alberta for leadership. During each provincial election, voters in Alberta select "senators in waiting." When a vacancy occurs in Alberta the premier "recommends" the winner to the prime minister. If every province were to follow this method and if prime ministers were to follow Stephen Harper's example of appointing the winners, senators would soon be "elected" across the country. What seems like a small step could very well pave the way for further democratic reform.

Though there have been plans to reform the Senate to make it more democratic, none has yet been completed. In this cartoon, Stephen Harper is shown tip-toeing his way toward Senate Reform, a place that's still very far away.

© Bob Krieger. Reproduced with permission of Simon Fraser University Library.

This would, however, also remove a unique aspect of the Senate: its unelected nature. It would, essentially, serve as a "second" House of Commons, where the same political parties would do battle, though perhaps with different dominant parties elected in each one. Would such a change be for the better? The uncertainty surrounding the Senate is what makes reforming legislatures tricky. Whatever path is taken, incremental reforms may be the best way forwards, as major institutional changes can lead to unintended consequences. Taking things one step at a time and analyzing the problems and solutions as we go makes more sense than jumping in head-first with reforms and hoping for the best.

As for the House of Commons, calls for reform are commonplace but they rarely take on a solid form. The aforementioned lack of trust that Canadians display in their politicians points toward a need to change how the House works in some substantive way, but how to go about it remains a largely unanswered question. Still, there have been concrete suggestions for changes to the lower house. Generally, these follow along the lines of reining in the power of the prime minister and preventing the abuse of prorogation for political ends,[49] an increased role for committees in the legislative process (similar to what the U.S. has), and loosening party discipline to allow for more independent voting. These proposals remain largely theoretical, though, with no current plans for implementation, and no other big ideas on how the chamber might otherwise be reformed. Westminster and Congressional systems both seem stuck in similar situations: aware that trust in the legislature is plummeting, but with no plans for how to restore that lost faith.

CONCLUSION

This chapter has sought to make clear that legislatures, like any other human institutions, are not perfect. They are, however, undoubtedly important institutions in the context of a democracy. Legislatures provide the opportunity for the views and opinions of people without the ability to participate in the day-to-day work of government to be heard. They allow political parties and concerned citizens to challenge government actions in full view of the public. They feature numerous checks and balances designed to make the passing of laws and spending of tax dollars more than just a "rubber stamp" process. They provide, all-in-all, what is most important to any democracy: a way of keeping the government accountable to the people that it is supposed to serve.

But legislatures suffer from numerous problems. Their structures can make them standoffish and adversarial, as political parties seemingly spend more time fighting each other than governing. They can give the executive significant powers that can minimize the effectiveness of measures designed to hold them accountable. Representatives can fall prey to their own selfish desires, misusing their powers for personal gain, or implementing policies that they think are "for the public good" over the real objections and concerns of their constituents. Legislatures can be composed of people representing only a small fraction of the religions, ethnicities, genders, and sexual orientations of a country. At their best, legislatures promote accountable government that earnestly responds to the views of citizens and acts to balance both private and public interests. At their worst, legislatures are used to disguise oligarchy, in which a small number of individuals hold most of the power and the legislature is used to legitimize their rule under the name of "democracy."

What can be done about the challenging issues that our legislatures face? How can we restore the confidence of citizens in their effectiveness as a key part of a democracy? These are tough questions, and tough questions rarely have easy answers waiting around. First, we must try to understand *why* there is such a crisis of confidence with regards to legislatures in our own countries. Why do people view representatives the way that they do? How do these sorts of views develop, and are they well founded? Is it that citizens feel that their own views are not being represented or that they are being represented poorly? Do people simply feel as though they are unable to affect the course of legislation, even if done through the actions of a representative? If we feel like we cannot control something, after all, we tend to ignore it or find ways of simply learning to live with it. We cannot control the weather, so we shrug our shoulders and put on a coat when it starts snowing, and perhaps grumble about it to our friends and coworkers. Is the solution, then, to somehow give more power in the legislature to ordinary citizens (such as through the use of citizens' committees that are consulted on bills, or more frequent referendums), or would this simply create a new set of problems without solving the old ones? Should there be more legislatures and representatives, or fewer? Second, and perhaps most importantly, how would any changes be implemented? What are the challenges that would face such reform efforts? What sort of laws or people would stand in the way of such changes, whatever they might be?

Again, there are no simple solutions to any of these questions. Figuring out what changes an institution as complex as a legislature needs (or does not need) is a long process. It is important, however, that we start thinking about these issues, even in a very small way. Do you think that current legislatures are doing a good job? What are the big problems that you see in legislatures today? Even though they might seem very far removed from our own private worlds, the actions of legislatures have far-reaching consequences. They can decide how much support you receive if you are ever out of a job, or how much you have to pay out of your own pocket when you go see a doctor. They can decide how much maintenance the road outside your home receives, or whether your school gets its badly-needed repairs. They can decide what is and is not a crime, and how those crimes and the people involved in them are dealt with. They can decide how much of the wealth of society goes toward tanks and bombs, and how much to hospitals and homes. There is little that legislatures do not, at some level, have a hand in.

These are decisions that will not only affect you, but your friends, family, fellow students, and coworkers. What a legislature decides affects all of us in one way or another, even if it is not always obvious until well after a law has been passed. Having a legislature that remains responsible to its citizens, then, is of vital importance. Figuring out ways of keeping and improving its accountability, and advocating for the changes needed, is our shared responsibility.

DISCUSSION QUESTIONS

1. While democratic legislatures are the "normal" way of making laws in countries today, there have been numerous other methods of creating laws throughout history. Can you think of some historical examples? What were their strengths and weaknesses compared to a modern democratic legislature?

2. Are regular elections the best tool for ensuring that representatives perform their jobs well? What other methods could be used to ensure that representatives remain accountable to citizens?

3. Do you think that the Westminster method of having the executive sit in the legislature is better or worse than the Congressional method? Which method do you think best helps to hold executive power in check?

4. While legislatures have gradually become more representative of the overall population in descriptive terms, they still fall short. What, if anything, should be done to promote a more diverse, representative legislature?

5. More "direct democracy" (where citizens vote on new laws directly, rather than delegating this authority to their representatives) has been proposed to increase citizen input into the legislative process. What benefits would there be to having more direct democracy in your country? What problems might nonetheless arise?

WEBSITES

PARLINFO
http://www.parl.gc.ca/parlinfo/
Official database of information on Canada's legislatures.

NCSL – National Conference of State Legislatures.
http://www.ncsl.org/
Information on legislatures in the United States.

Elections Canada
http://www.elections.ca/home.aspx
Information on the process of voting for representatives and election results.

CanLII

https://www.canlii.org/en/

Online database of Canadian legislation and court cases.

Congress.gov

https://www.congress.gov/

Contains online database of U.S. legislation.

FURTHER READING

Robert A. Dahl, *Who Governs? Democracy and Power in an American City*, 2nd ed. New Haven: Yale University Press, 2005.

David Docherty, *Legislatures*. Vancouver: University of British Columbia Press, 2007.

Gerhard Lowenberg, Peverill Squire, and D. Roderick Kiewiet, eds., *Legislatures: Comparative Perspectives on Representative Assemblies*. Ann Arbor: University of Michigan Press, 2002.

Peverill Squire and Gary Moncrief, *State Legislatures Today: Politics Under the Domes*. New York: Pearson Education, 2010.

ENDNOTES

1. "Taiwanese MPs in parliament brawl," *BBC News*, May 8, 2007, online at http://news.bbc.co.uk/2/hi/asia-pacific/6636237.stm.

2. Art Swift, "Honesty and Ethics Rating of Clergy Slides to New Low," *Gallup,* December 16, 2013, online at http://www.gallup.com/poll/166298/honesty-ethics-rating-clergy-slides-new-low.aspx.

3. Deborah Coyne, "Canadians Don't Trust Politicians – Let's Strive to Change That," *Huffington Post*, September 19, 2013, online at http://www.huffingtonpost.ca/deborah-coyne/canadians-trust-in-politicians_b_3617666.html.

4. *Parliament of Canada, Constitution Act, 1867, 30 & 31 Victoria, c. 3. (U.K.). CanLII.* April 1, 1999.

5. Ronald I. Cheffins, "The Royal Prerogative and the Office of Lieutenant Governor," *Canadian Parliamentary Review* 23 (1) (Spring 2000), pp. 14–19.

6. Members of cabinet can also serve from the upper chamber (the appointed House of Lords in the U.K., or the appointed Senate in Canada—Australian senators are elected).

7. "Prorogation of Parliament," *Library of Parliament*, Parliament of Canada, March 2006.

8. David Docherty, *Legislatures* (Vancouver: University of British Columbia Press, 2007), pp. 141–42.

9. "Stephen Harper to seek prorogation of Parliament." *CBC News*, August 19, 2013, online at http://www.cbc.ca/news/politics/stephen-harper-to-seek-prorogation-of-parliament-1.1378924.

10. Steven Chase, "Jean feared 'dreadful crisis' when Harper sought prorogation: ex-adviser," *The Globe and Mail*, June 25, 2012, online at http://www.theglobeandmail.com/news/politics/ottawa-notebook/michaelle-jean-feared-dreadful-crisis-when-harper-sought-prorogation-ex-adviser/article4370133/.

11. C.E.S. Franks, *The Parliament of Canada* (Toronto: University of Toronto Press, 1987), p. 4.

12. Edmund Burke, *The Works of the Right Honorable Edmund Burke, Vol. II.,* Project Gutenberg, February 28, 2005, online at http://www.gutenberg.org/ebooks/15198.

13. James Q. Wilson, John J. Dilulio, Jr., and Meena Bose, *The Essentials: American Government: Institutions & Policies*, 12th ed. (Boston: Cengage Learning, 2011), pp. 333–35.

14. Docherty, *Legislatures*, p. 110.

15. While bills are far more commonly introduced in the House of Commons, it is possible to introduce a (non-money) bill in the Senate instead.

16. Anthony Clark, "DC's favorite time-wasting scam: Cosponsoring bills," *Salon*, August 2, 2013, online at http://www.salon.com/2013/08/02/congress_favorite_time_wasting_scam_co_sponsoring_bills/.

17. Mollie Dunsmuir, "Abortion: Constitutional and Legal Developments," *Library of Parliament,* Parliament of Canada, November 1989.

18. Wilson, Dilulio, Jr., and Bose, *The Essentials: American Government*, p. 348.

19. Ibid., p. 349.

20. United States Congressional Senate, 110th Congress, 2nd Session. H.R.6331, Medicare Improvement for Patients and Providers Act of 2008.

21. "Glossary of Terms: allotted day," *Library of Parliament*, Parliament of Canada, September 2011.

22. Parliament of Canada, "Rules Regarding the Content of Speeches," *House of Commons Procedure and Practice*, 2nd ed. (2009).

23. "Indepth: Sponsorship Scandal," *CBC News*, October 26, 2006, online at http://www.cbc.ca/news2/background/groupaction/.

24. "Government's defeat sets up election call," *CBC News*, March 25, 2011, online at http://www.cbc.ca/news/politics/government-s-defeat-sets-up-election-call-1.1068749.

25. "Electoral Results by Party," *Library of Parliament*, Parliament of Canada, October 7, 2011.

26. CBC, "CBC Archives: Fuddle Duddle 1971." *YouTube*, September 18, 2008, online at https://www.youtube.com/watch?v=YXKSGRyZtz8.

27. Walter J. Oleszek, "Congressional Oversight: An Overview," *Congressional Research Service*, February 22, 2010, online at http://fas.org/sgp/crs/misc/R41079.pdf.

28. Kristin D. Burnett, "Congressional Appointment (2010 Census Briefs C2010BR-08)," *U.S. Department of Commerce, Economics, and Statistics Administration*, November 1, 2011, online at http://www.census.gov/prod/cen2010/briefs/c2010br-08.pdf.

29. Bruce Bartlett, "Enlarging the House of Representatives," *The New York Times*, January 7, 2014, online at http://economix.blogs.nytimes.com/2014/01/07/enlarging-the-house-of-representatives/?_r=0.

30. "New House of Commons Seat Allocation," *Elections Canada*, December 19, 2011, online at http://www.elections.ca/content.aspx?section=med&document=dec1911&dir=pre&lang=e.

31. Dunsmuir, "Abortion."

32. David Docherty, "Representation in New Brunswick: Capital and Constituency Concerns," in Bill Cross, ed., *Democratic Reform in New Brunswick* (Toronto: Canadian Scholar's Press, 2007), pp. 152–53.

33. Residents Per Member: This number was derived by dividing the population estimates for 2013 by the Assembly Size in 2013. Data for this calculation was obtained from these sources: http://www.statcan.gc.ca/daily-quotidien/130926/t130926a002-eng.htm; "Canada's total population estimates, 2013," Statistics Canada, 26 September 2013. Web. 13 January 2015; Statistics Canada. Estimates of population, Canada, provinces and territories, quarterly (persons), Statistics Canada. Web, 25 January 2015. Table 051-0005. Cabinet Size: This number was calculated by visiting each of the provincial legislature websites on January 13, 2015 and calculating the total cabinet size at that time. Data for this calculation was obtained from these sources: http://www.parl.gc.ca/Parlinfo/compilations/ProvinceTerritory/PartyStandingsAndLeaders.aspx; "Cabinet Ministers," Government of Newfoundland and Labrador, Web. 13 January 2015; "Cabinet Ministers." The Legislative Assembly of Manitoba. 14 November 2014. Web. 13 January 2015; "Cabinet," Alberta Government. Web. 13 January 2015; "Cabinet." Government of Nunavut, Web. 13 January 2015; "Cabinet." Government of Prince Edward Island. 18 October 2011. Web. 13 January 2015; "Cabinet." Government of Saskatchewan. Web. 13 January 2015; "Cabinet." The Nova Scotia Legislature. Web. 13 January 2015; "Current MPPs." Legislative Assembly of Ontario, Web. 13 January 2015; "Members of the Executive Council," Government of New Brunswick, 9 Jan. 2015. Web. 13 January 2015; "Parliamentary and Ministerial Office Holders." Assemblée Nationale Quebec. 10 October 2012. Web. 13 January 2015; "Premier and Ministers," Legislative Assembly of the Northwest Territories, Web. 13 January 2015;

"Premier's Team." Yukon Government. Web. 13 January 2015; "The Executive Council of the Government of British Columbia." Government of British Columbia. Web. 13 January 2015. Size of Official Opposition: Data compiled from the following sources: https://web.archive.org/web/20150120213515/http://www.parl.gc.ca/ParlInfo/Compilations/ProvinceTerritory/PartyStandingsAndLeaders.aspx; Library of Parliament. "Party Leaders and Standings." Parliament of Canada. 20 January 2015. Web. 13 January 2015. Accessed via Internet Archive Wayback Machine. Legislative Sitting Days (2013): Library of Parliament. "Sitting Days of the Provincial and Territorial Legislatures by Calendar Year." Parliament of Canada. 12 January 2015. Web. 13 January 2015.

34. Peverill Squire, "Career Opportunities and Membership Stability in Legislatures," *Legislative Studies Quarterly* 13 (1) (February 1988), pp. 65–82.

35. Docherty, *Legislatures*, p. 73.

36. The 10 percent figure is approximate. As Table 8.2 suggests, the smaller assemblies have up to a third or more of the assembly in cabinet. Larger assemblies fall somewhere between 10 and 20 percent.

37. This wonderful line deserves to be credited to its author, Ken Carty from the University of British Columbia. I have no real citation for this line, but recall hearing it from Ken at a conference in Ottawa in 2002 or 2003. It is a wonderfully apt description.

38. Docherty, *Legislatures*, p. 39.

39. "Edging Towards Diversity: A Statistical Breakdown of Canada's 41st Parliament, with Comparisons to the 40th Parliament," *Public Policy Forum*, June 2011, p. 13.

40. Ibid., p. 8.

41. David Docherty, *Mr. Smith Goes to Ottawa: Life in the House of Commons* (Vancouver: University of British Columbia Press, 2011), p. 63.

42. Docherty, *Legislatures*, p. 42.

43. For the record, this is NOT the author's view. The vast majority of senators are hardworking, dedicated servants of the people. But in an appointed (and somewhat anachronistic) institution, a few rotten apples can spoil the appearance of the entire barrel.

44. Janyce McGregor, "Mike Duffy Senate expenses trial set for 41 days starting in April," *CBC News*, September 23, 2014, online at http://www.cbc.ca/news/politics/mike-duffy-senate-expenses-trial-set-for-41-days-starting-in-april-1.2774968.

45. "Pamela Wallin writes cheque to pay back Senate more than $100k in disputed travel claims," *National Post*, September 13, 2013, online at http://news.nationalpost.com/news/canada/canadian-politics/pamela-wallin-writes-cheque-to-pay-back-senate-more-than-100k-in-disputed-travel-claims.

46. Brian O'Neal, "Senate Committees: Role and Effectiveness," *Government of Canada Publications,* June 1994, online at http://www.parl.gc.ca/Content/LOP/researchpublications/bp361-e.htm.

47. Statistics Canada, *Estimates of population, Canada, provinces and territories, quarterly (persons)*, Table 051-0005, online at http://www5.statcan.gc.ca/cansim/a26?lang=eng&id=510005; "New House of Commons Seat Allocation," *Elections Canada,* December 19, 2011, online at http://www.elections.ca/content.aspx?section=med&document=dec1911&dir=pre&lang=e.

48. Figures are based on Statistics Canada population numbers for 2014 and the proposed 121 seats in Ontario for the 2015 election.

49. Mark D. Jarvis, "The House: Three-part reform," *Maclean's*, April 11, 2011, online at http://www.macleans.ca/politics/ottawa/the-house-three-part-reform/.

9

THE JUDICIARY: POLITICS, LAW, AND THE COURTS

Matthew Hennigar

© REUTERS/Stephane Mahe

The courts are often represented by a set of scales as the judiciary must balance both support and opposition for each case that appears before it. In doing so, the courts play an inherently political role as they interpret—sometimes with quite significant policy implications—the laws crafted by executive and legislative bodies.

INTRODUCTION

Contrary to what some people believe—and what many judges and lawyers assert—courts and the law are inherently political. Law is primarily the product of political actors in legislatures and executives, and reflects power relations within society, the state, and, in the case of international law, the larger world. The central function of courts is the enforcement of law, or more specifically, the resolution of disputes through and within law. This means that judges can shape the law through how vigorously they enforce, interpret, and, in some legal systems, create it. In many countries, courts have the ability to block or influence actions by other parts of the state by invoking the law, most notably the constitution and rights. This means that courts exercise power. There are also power and politics within the judiciary itself, as judges are typically selected, and can face discipline or even removal, by political actors who often control the budget funds allocated to courts. And there is politics between judges, as when higher courts (such as the Supreme Court of Canada) overturn lower-court decisions, or when multiple judges must work together to produce a ruling.

This chapter begins by explaining what we mean by **law** and distinguishing between various kinds of law. We next explore the role of courts and judges, paying attention to both democratic and non-democratic regimes, and the various kinds of disputes courts are asked to resolve. As we will see, different types of disputes and legal systems raise different expectations for

the role of judges. Independence and impartiality are central to the judicial function, so we then turn to those concepts with an eye to understanding how they are defined and related, and how to reconcile the need for independence with demands for judicial accountability. Following that, various methods for selecting judges are examined along with a host of related issues: political patronage, representation of diversity, and how selection methods may influence judicial decision-making. The final sections are concerned with two of the leading concerns for those who study law and courts: the impact of courts on public policy, and access to justice. The policy impact of judicial decisions has direct implications for the nature of the relationship between courts and the other branches of the state, while limits on access to the courts have profound social consequences for those who are unable to realize their legal rights and protections.

> **Law:** Rules governing behaviour by societal and state actors, adopted and enforced by the state.

WHAT IS "LAW"?

Although people routinely use the term "law," there is a surprising amount of disagreement about what that term means, beyond the common understanding that laws are rules of some sort that govern behaviour. There are a few factors that cause confusion. First, who makes law? Second, how are laws enforced? And third, what is the content of law, that is, what does law make rules about?

On the first question, laws are made by a recognized authority. That could still include a lot of rules that we do not usually think of as "laws," such as your university's rules about academic misconduct, or the official rules of sporting associations like the National Hockey League or the International Olympic Committee. Of particular note are the rules of religious faiths or organizations, such as the doctrines of the Catholic Church, or the Halakhah and sharia (the bodies of Jewish and Islamic law, respectively). Many people refer to religious rules as law (in particular, "sharia law"), and in some theocratic states, as discussed below, these rules definitely *are* laws. However, we usually reserve the term "law" for rules that are created and applied by state actors, that is, governments. In theocratic regimes, such as the Islamic Republic of Iran, religious laws are adopted and enforced by the state, but one could argue that it is this latter fact that gives the rules their distinctly "legal" nature. Similarly, **international law**, which includes treaties and conventions, is the product of agreements between states, or is created by international organizations of member-states (such as the United Nations, the European Union, or the Organization of the Petroleum Exporting Countries).

> **International law:** The body of treaties and conventions created by agreements between states or by international organizations of member-states.

There are many who argue that the distinguishing characteristic of law is its *enforcement by state authorities*, most notably courts but also the police and prosecutors with respect to criminal law. This separates law from the sorts of rules found in sports and purely religious institutions. The issue of enforcement also helps us to see the difference between law and norms. Norms (or values, customs, and conventions) are broadly-held beliefs in a society about what is right or proper behaviour, but they are enforced at the social rather than state level. For example, a norm against public nudity is reinforced by people shunning or criticizing nudists, or some other form of peer pressure. A *law* against public nudity, in contrast, is enforced when the police arrest you for public indecency, a prosecutor brings charges against you in court, and you face a penalty such as a fine or imprisonment. While the focus on state enforcement

is a useful perspective in the context of domestic law, it is more problematic with respect to international law, where enforcement mechanisms are often lacking. A good example is the failure, without any official consequences, of many countries to meet their obligations under the Kyoto Accord to reduce carbon emissions. In recognition of this fact, some states "import" international law such as treaties into their domestic laws, so that they can be enforced in their own courts. This is notably the case in the European Union, which has produced a staggeringly large body of international law. Another alternative is for states to create supranational courts to enforce international law, such as the International Criminal Court within the UN or the EU's European Court of Justice.

The greatest disagreement among legal philosophers, however, is over the content of law. The dominant view today, known as positivism, is that law is any rule created and enforced by a recognized state authority. According to positivists, laws do not need to be beneficial, wise, just, fair, moral, consistent with a society's norms, or even effective. Those things are desirable but laws lacking these characteristics are laws nonetheless. In contrast, those who hold the natural law perspective, which has its roots in ancient Greece and Rome, believe that laws must reflect certain "universal" principles (such as fairness) to be truly considered law. Contemporary variations on this tradition, recognizing that agreement on universal principles is elusive in diverse societies, often argue that laws must reflect a society's norms or advance human prosperity. The problem with these non-positivist approaches is that there is considerable disagreement possible about norms and what produces prosperity. More importantly, philosophical debates about whether something is "really law" are irrelevant to those who are subject to that law. Sadly, history is littered with discriminatory, ineffective, and just plain silly laws, but there is no question that for those subject to legal persecution—such as Jews in Nazi Germany; Aboriginals in Canada, America, or Australia; or gays and lesbians in Uganda today—these laws were or are very real. So too are laws that do not enjoy widespread public support (such as those creating some taxes, or in Canada as of this writing, the former ban regarding physician-assisted suicide[1]).

Nevertheless, a society's laws generally do reflect the dominant norms and values of that society at the time the law was adopted, as well as the interests of the leading political and economic elites. Norms and elites typically change over time, however, sometimes faster than the law does. When this happens, it can provoke social protest or legal challenges against outdated laws, or public authorities may cease trying to enforce them. A good example of the former is public acceptance of same-sex relationships, which has led to successful social and legal campaigns in many countries to legalize same-sex marriage (see Figure 9.1). It should be noted, however, that in some cases the judiciary appeared to drive public opinion on gay rights and not the other way around. In Canada, for example, after judges ruled that the equality rights in the constitution's Charter of Rights and Freedoms protect sexual orientation, there was a significant increase in public opposition to discrimination on the basis of sexual orientation. Ultimately, this led provincial legislatures and Parliament to prohibit such discrimination, and for Parliament to legalize same-sex marriage. In other words, sometimes one part of the law (such as a judicial interpretation of the constitution) can shape public opinion in ways that produce changes

in other parts of the law. This underlines a key point that we will return to throughout this chapter, that the relationship between law, courts, and politics is often complex and fluid.

Types of Law

Laws govern a wide variety of actions, relationships, and disputes, and societies have developed specialized types of law and legal systems accordingly. To begin, we can distinguish between domestic and international law. Domestic law consists, primarily, of all the laws created by a state's governing institutions and applied to those within its borders (in some cases, however, it may be applied to those acting on behalf of the state while abroad), while international law is the body of rules produced by agreements (treaties and conventions) among states, or by international organizations that govern inter-state relations or relations between individuals and organizations residing in more than one state. The North American Free Trade Agreement

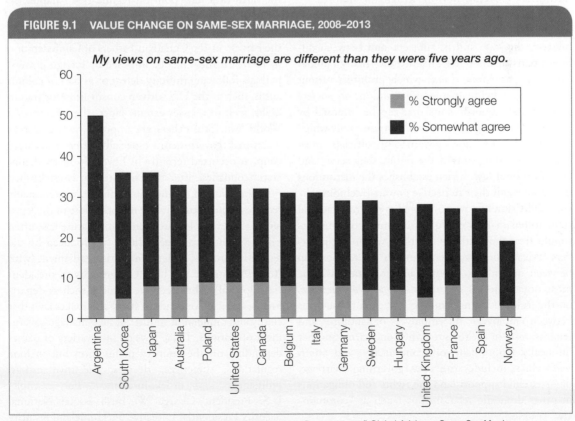

FIGURE 9.1   VALUE CHANGE ON SAME-SEX MARRIAGE, 2008–2013

My views on same-sex marriage are different than they were five years ago.

Legend:
- % Strongly agree
- % Somewhat agree

Countries (left to right): Argentina, South Korea, Japan, Australia, Poland, United States, Canada, Belgium, Italy, Germany, Sweden, Hungary, United Kingdom, France, Spain, Norway

Source: "My views on same-sex marriage are different than they were five years ago," *Global Advisory: Same-Sex Marriage* (Toronto: Ipsos, 2013), 7.

(NAFTA) is an example of international law created by an agreement between a small number of states (Canada, Mexico, and the United States), while the International Covenant on Civil and Political Rights (ICCPR), a human rights accord within the United Nations, involves 168 states. The neat distinction between domestic and international law is considerably blurrier in practice, however. In addition to the fact that some international laws apply as if they were domestic law (as in the EU), some states—particularly the U.S.—have passed domestic laws intended to apply to people beyond its borders, even non-U.S. citizens. A good example is the Helms-Burton Act (1996), which the U.S. government passed to limit trade with communist Cuba—*all* trade, even by individuals from other countries! Under the Act, the leaders of any non-U.S. company that trades with or invests in Cuba can be barred from entering the U.S. (several individuals have, in fact, been barred), and those companies can be sued in U.S. courts. Although other countries have objected to this law and even passed legal counter-measures, the Helms-Burton Act remains in force.

Another key distinction is between **public law** and **private law**. Public law governs the relationship between the state and its subjects, and between different parts of the state. This includes many familiar forms of law: *criminal law*, which prohibits various actions by individuals and organizations in society and identifies punishments that can be imposed by the state for transgressions; *administrative law*, which creates rules for how government officials must behave, including toward the public they serve; and **constitutional law**, which establishes the institutions of the state and their respective powers (including the federal division of powers), as well as the foundational rules (often in bills of rights) for how governments should treat their citizens or others within their borders. Private (or "civil") law governs the relationship between individuals, groups, and corporations. The most notable forms of private law are *contract law*, or the rules defining binding agreements, such as between employers and employees or landlords and tenants; *torts*, or the rules for when one harms another physically, emotionally, or economically; and *family law*, which includes the rules governing marriage, divorce, child support, and the rights and obligations in other domestic relationships (such as "common-law" couples).

Public law: The body of law that governs relations within the state and the relationship between the state and individuals or organizations, including criminal law, administrative law, and constitutional law.

Private law: The body of law that governs the relationship between private individuals and organizations, such as contract law.

Constitutional law: Law that establishes the institutions of the state and their respective powers, and often fundamental limits on state behaviour as well. It is usually entrenched by demanding amending formulas.

Laws can also be classified according to which part of the state makes them. Constitutional laws, which are typically the highest form of law in a state, are initially created by political elites, often during the birth of a new political regime (see Chapter 6). They may be the product of negotiation, as with the American framers following their revolution against the British, or the Canadian Fathers of Confederation in 1867. Or they may be imposed by foreign powers, perhaps following military defeat or as part of colonialism, such as the U.S.-driven constitution for Iraq in 2004, and, to a lesser extent, Japan after the Second World War. Still others are imposed by a country's dictatorial government, especially after a military coup, as occurred recently in Egypt. In many democratic countries, after the constitution is established it can be changed through amendment, which usually requires more than a simple majority vote of the legislature (for example, a referendum). Statute law, often called "statutes" or "legislation," is produced by the legislative process, such as the British Parliament (with Royal Assent) or the U.S. Congress (with presidential approval). The executive branch (such as departments, agencies, or heads of state) also makes laws that clarify and implement statutes or help manage government operations. These laws go by a variety of names depending on the country in question but include regulations, directives, decrees, executive orders, ordinances, and orders-in-council. For example, U.S. President George W. Bush issued National Security Presidential Directive 54/Homeland Security

Presidential Directive 23 (NSPD-54/HSPD-23) in 2008, which ordered the creation of stronger defenses against cyberattacks. This included the construction of the $1.5 billion Utah Data Center to process the massive amount of information collected by the National Security Agency (NSA) through its controversial program of spying on Internet and phone traffic, as revealed by whistleblower Edward Snowden in 2013. Finally, in some legal systems, common law or case law is the body of law created through judicial rulings and interpretations.

There are four main types of *legal systems* in the world: common law, civil code, religious law, and customary law. The common law system originated in medieval England and later spread with the British Empire to such countries as Australia, Canada, Jamaica, India, New Zealand, Singapore, South Africa, and the United States. The defining feature of common law is that judges decide cases by reasoning from well-established principles or ethics, rather than applying a pre-existing rule designed by political leaders for the specific set of facts before the court. To ensure consistent rulings amongst similar cases—that is, a "common" law across the country—judges look to previous court decisions involving similar legal issues and facts, or precedents. This approach is known as **stare decisis** (Latin for "to stand by things decided"). In common law systems, when the law is unclear, or there are gaps in precedent or statute law, judges are expected to reason from analogous precedents or basic principles, such as fairness. In other words, the common law system entails some judicial creativity and flexibility.

> **Stare decisis:** A Latin phrase which means that similar cases should be decided similarly; it is the central principle in common-law systems, in which judges are expected to follow prior judicial decisions involving similar facts and law, or precedents.

At least in theory, this contrasts with civil code systems, which promote legal consistency though the adoption of comprehensive statutory codes. Here, judges are expected to apply the code as established by legislators, who are also tasked with updating the code to address any perceived gaps. Codified bodies of law date to ancient antiquity, as exemplified by the Code of Hammurabi from Babylon (1772 BCE),

carved on a stone obelisk that can be viewed in the Louvre. Modern civil code systems have their roots in the Justinian Code of the late Roman Empire, which collected and standardized what had become a sprawling and contradictory set of laws. This tradition was revived during the European Renaissance in an effort to design more rational legal systems, and civil codes were adopted in most continental European countries, most notably in France by Napoleon Bonaparte in 1804. The civil code system spread to the rest of the globe with European colonialism, the legacy of which can still be found in the former French colonies Quebec and Louisiana, but also Latin America and much of Asia and Africa. Civil code systems are in fact the most prevalent in the world, although several jurisdictions (such as Nigeria, the Philippines, Quebec, and Scotland) use a mix of common law and civil code systems, using one, for example, for criminal law and the other for private law disputes. Indeed, this merging in practice can be more generally seen with judges in civil code systems increasingly looking to past judicial rulings for guidance, and governments in common law systems codifying parts of their laws, as exemplified by Canada's Criminal Code.

There are also states that base their legal systems on religious texts and doctrines, most notably **sharia law** in Islamic countries like Iran and Saudi Arabia, but other examples include the separate "personal" or family laws for Hindus, Muslims, and Sikhs in India. In the Middle Ages, European countries had ecclesiastical courts to enforce Catholic Canon law (church rules over a wide variety of topics, many of which had little to do with religion), though these were slowly replaced by secular courts and civil codes. This is not to say that there are no religious influences remaining in common or civil law systems—principles from pre-Christian Scandinavian and Germanic as well as Christian belief systems are evident in both, as well as Confucian and Buddhist values in some Asian civil codes—but truly religious legal systems explicitly base their laws on holy texts and their interpretation by leading religious authorities. It is noteworthy that despite a common basis in the Qur'an, religious legal systems using sharia are in fact quite diverse, with countries emphasizing different parts of the text, or competing interpretations, such as those that give rise to disagreements between Sunni and Shia Muslims.

Sharia law: Sharia is the Islamic system of law, both civil and criminal, that is based on the Qur'an (the holy book of Islam); the life example and hadiths (sayings) of the Prophet Muhammad; and on subsequent scholarly interpretations and writings. This system of law prescribes the correct behavior for Muslims across different areas of life and the punishments for transgressions. Importantly, Sharia law is not uniform throughout the Muslim world as it is influenced by different schools of jurisprudence, among other factors.

Finally, there are the oft-overlooked customary legal systems found among indigenous communities, such as Aboriginals in Australia and the Americas, and tribal groups in Africa. Customary laws are essentially well-established community standards, often applied and shaped by elders, which evolved where there was little government beyond the immediate community. As such, customary laws are usually indistinguishable from the group's religious or "political" laws. In some countries, such as Nigeria, these laws are officially recognized along with common law and/or civil codes, and have been upheld in the "regular" judiciary. Customary laws are particularly important in weak or failed states, where communities may be effectively self-governing (a good example is the Xeer system in Somalia).

Regardless of the type of law or legal system, what is important to remember is that laws are about *control*—they are how a government regulates its citizens and manages disputes, and even how it orders its own component parts. It is not a coincidence that some of the best-known conquerors in history—such as Napoleon and the Roman Empire—relied heavily on legal reform to consolidate their military victories. They introduced institutions to ensure that their laws, and thus their values and commands, were applied down to even the smallest villages, often displacing local customs and laws. The most important institutional innovation in that process was what we have come to know as *courts*, staffed by judges, and known collectively as the **judiciary**.

Judiciary: The body of all judges and courts in a country, or the judicial branch of government.

COURTS AND THE JUDICIAL FUNCTION

Laws are enforced by a host of state institutions and actors, including courts and judges but also police, prosecutors, and some bureaucrats (such as tax collectors or regulatory agencies). But courts are distinguished by their *dispute resolution* function, and more specifically by the way they resolve disputes. Courts and judges perform **adjudication**, which is a form of "third-party" dispute resolution. In third-party dispute resolution, two parties with a dispute—a divorced husband and wife fighting over child custody, the state prosecuting an accused criminal, one state accusing another of violating a treaty—turn to a third party to help them resolve it peacefully when negotiation has failed, rather than resorting to force. The third party must be neutral or impartial; that is, they must have no direct stake in the outcome. They should also be someone whose authority or expertise is respected. There are several forms of third-party dispute resolution, which vary based on how much authority the neutral party has to resolve the dispute. In mediation, for example, the mediator only assists the parties in negotiation and cannot impose a solution, whereas in arbitration the parties ask the third party to devise a solution (which they may or may not be bound to follow, depending on the arrangement). Arbitrators may look to previous disputes or existing rules to fashion their decisions but are not required to and may focus instead on an outcome that both parties will accept or perceive as fair. In adjudication, the third party imposes a binding decision based on a set of previously established rules, although sometimes the rules themselves are open to interpretation by the adjudicator. Although all three forms of third-party dispute resolution are common, adjudication has achieved preferred status in Western societies, as evidenced by the fact that mediation and arbitration are commonly referred to as "alternative" dispute resolution (ADR), that is, alternatives to adjudication. The logic of adjudication is familiar and found in many contexts, including sports refereeing, grade appeals in universities, and misconduct hearings within professional associations for doctors or lawyers. Adjudication is also, of course, performed by judges in courts, where the "previously established rules" are laws.

> **Adjudication:** A system of dispute resolution in which an impartial third party applies the law to decide the outcome, or what is more commonly known as "judging."

The judiciary does not exercise a monopoly over adjudication based on the law, however. Both the legislative and executive branches have developed court-like institutions, often known as tribunals, to enforce and resolve disputes arising from particular laws or government programs. Human rights tribunals in Canada, for example, are technically part of the legislative branch and hear claims under the respective provincial or federal statutory human rights codes (these are in addition to the rights found in the constitution) concerning discrimination. Executive-based administrative tribunals are more common, and may deal with very high volumes of important cases. In the U.S., for instance, disputes about immigration applications are processed almost entirely via administrative tribunals. Applications to immigrate are decided initially by United States Citizenship and Immigration Services, which is part of the Department of Homeland Security, but those decisions can be reviewed by "immigration courts" and the Board of Immigration Appeals (both part of the Executive Office for Immigration Review), which are actually tribunals within the Department of Justice. Administrative tribunals in Canada also hear some disputes about immigration, as well as landlord-tenant relations, broadcasting, parole, workplace health and safety, and much more. While tribunals have the advantage that their members may be more specialized experts in the field in question—and are not restricted to being trained in law—they often do not possess the same level of institutional independence as the judiciary, thus raising concerns about their fairness. In response to this concern, some countries (including Canada and the U.K.) have adopted protections for tribunals that largely mirror those for courts. We will return to the issue of judicial independence later in this chapter.

The Role of Courts: Law Enforcement and Interpretation

The main function of courts is thus dispute resolution via adjudication, which has the effect of enforcing the law. It is worth emphasizing the remarkable variety of disputes addressed by courts: those between states, between component parts of states (as in federations; see Chapter 6), between private individuals and groups in private law, and between the state and individuals and groups in public law. It is not surprising then that most political systems have developed complex judiciaries with specialized courts—criminal and family courts for instance—staffed by those trained in particular areas of law.

Judicial participation in law enforcement is almost always passive; that is, courts rule on cases brought to them by others.[2] In typical private law disputes, one person, group, or organization takes another to court by suing them, which highlights that, for at least one party, adjudication is not undertaken voluntarily. Examples include divorce proceedings, a landlord suing a tenant for failing to pay rent, or someone injured in a fight suing the person responsible for the cost of their medical expenses. The judge's job in such cases is to decide whether the person or organization is liable according to the law, and to issue a remedy—usually this means one side giving the other money, or performing some sort of service. In criminal law, police must first find evidence of wrongdoing and make an arrest, and prosecutors must decide to lay charges, before judges are asked to determine whether the person or organization is guilty under law and what sentence (punishment) they should receive if so. In some courts, most notably in the U.S., decisions about liability, remedy, guilt, and sentencing may be made by a jury (a collection of laypersons), with judges limited to ensuring that the court's procedural rules are followed (such as about how evidence may be used, or witnesses treated). As well, in some countries, including Canada and the U.S., many criminal cases are resolved without reaching the courts, when the accused person agrees to plead guilty in exchange for a lighter sentence. Such plea bargains are extremely efficient and help to reduce backlogs in prosecutions and courts, but there are concerns about what is lost when the more rigorous court system is by-passed. In particular, some worry that police errors and rights violations may be overlooked, leading to innocent people being convicted, or guilty people receiving lighter sentences than if they had gone before a judge.

For cases that make it to court, the role of the judge depends on the system used. In the adversarial approach employed in common-law systems, the judge is truly a "neutral" party: two opposing sides present the facts of the case, make legal arguments, and question witnesses. The judge is expected to ensure that the court's procedural rules are followed, and—unless there is a jury—to decide the case on the basis of what the opposing sides present and how well they critique each other's arguments. The adversarial system is based on the belief that the truth of what happened is more likely to emerge from a competitive approach in which the judge and jury, like referees, do not take sides. In contrast, many civil law systems use an inquisitorial approach in which the judge and jury actively participate in the case, including the questioning of witnesses, and there may be several parties to the case. In France, for example, criminal cases can involve lawyers representing the state, the accused, and the victim's family. Yet another approach, known as restorative justice, uses more informal procedures to bring together everyone affected by a dispute, to determine its root causes and to fashion a remedy to help repair the harm done to everyone involved. Judges may play a relatively small role in this approach, being just one voice in the conversation, or helping to pull together the group's decision and to ensure that commitments and legal standards are honoured. Restorative justice has its roots in how small, tightly-knit communities, such as indigenous North Americans, traditionally resolved internal conflicts but the approach has gained popularity and is now used in some mainstream justice systems or as part of ADR.

One key way in which courts enforce the law is against the state itself, and in doing so they uphold the **rule of law**. This principle's precise meaning is debated but the central idea is that the government must act through laws which are made known to the public before they are enforced (no "retroactive" laws), apply these laws equally to all, and ensure that disputes under law are heard by fair and impartial judges. This means that governments are bound by their own rules, and that no one—not even political leaders—is above the law. It is a powerful idea, and one that is central to democratic government, though as discussed below, there

are good reasons for even non-democratic governments to respect the rule of law. The law can limit state actors in a variety of ways, but two main categories stand out. First, it can create what we call procedural limits, which regulate who or which part of the state can do what, and how it must be done. For instance, a court might block a government body from regulating something when the legislation that creates the body does not give it that authority, or *jurisdiction*. An example is provided by former Toronto mayor Rob Ford who, before his highly-publicized drug problems came to light, was ordered in 2010 by Toronto City Council to repay $3,150 in donations he solicited from lobbyists for his football charity. He subsequently voted on a motion to rescind that order even though it concerned himself, an action for which he was temporarily removed as mayor by the courts. Ford was later reinstated to office after another court ruled that the City of Toronto Act did not permit Council to order the repayment in the first place.[3] As discussed in Chapter 6, jurisdictional limits on governments characterize federal systems, which divide authority for various policy issues between central and regional governments. As well, especially in new democracies, there are frequently disputes about the precise boundaries of executive versus legislative power. It often falls to courts to resolve such jurisdictional disputes. The law may also place substantive limits on government, or *what* governments may do. The most familiar examples are constitutional rights such as freedom of expression or equality rights, which respectively prohibit censorship and discrimination by the state (both are found in the Canadian Charter of Rights and Freedoms and the U.S. Bill of Rights, for example). But courts may also punish governments for corruption or for violating the democratic process. As examples of the latter, Thailand's constitutional court ordered the entire government to resign in May 2014 for alleged corruption (a military coup followed shortly after), while the Ukraine Supreme Court voided presidential elections in 2004 marred by corruption and electoral fraud and ordered a new round of voting, which resulted in a change of government.

THINK AND DISCUSS

Why do political elites create and empower courts in the first place? Why do elites tolerate judicial checks on their power? Is the answer the same for democratic and non-democratic regimes?

Rule of law: The principle that government must act through laws that are made known to the public before they are enforced and that are applied equally to all, and where disputes under law are heard by fair and impartial judges. In short, no one is above the law, even leaders.

All of this raises a puzzling question: Why do political elites tolerate the restrictions of the rule of law and of judicial checks on legislative and executive power? A few possible explanations have been offered. One is that courts are a form of "insurance" against the day when a social group or political party loses office, providing a way for those outside government to continue to influence public policy.[4] Similarly, some argue that elites may empower courts and staff them with like-minded individuals to defend their values against popular political movements that threaten those values. For example, Turkey's courts have tried to protect that country's official secularism against "political Islam," and Israeli courts have sought to prevent ultra-Orthodox Jews from undermining the country's liberal democracy.[5] Another explanation stresses that the rule of law and empowered courts provide benefits to political elites, even as they produce checks on their power. These benefits can be significant and diverse.[6] First, courts are efficient at dispute resolution, from the perspective of political elites, because they relieve political leaders of this complicated and time-consuming task. Judicial expertise and specialization allow courts to process cases relatively quickly; in effect, they enjoy economies of scale. Second, as noted earlier, law (especially criminal law) is a form of state control over society, and extensive networks of court systems ensure that laws are applied throughout the country, even in the smallest communities. Third, the existence of impartial and qualified courts increases the legitimacy of the law and the political regime, more than would be the case if legal disputes were resolved by political (or military) leaders. A clear (if cynical) indication that leaders appreciate this fact is the phenomenon of "show trials" against political rivals, such as the recent mass convictions of Muslim Brotherhood members after Egypt's military overthrew the elected government. The decision to embrace courts and the rule of law may also

be directed toward the international community, to assure foreign investors and companies that there are predictable rules and dispute resolution mechanisms regarding the country's economy—in particular, that the government will not seize foreign assets. Fourth, courts provide a way for political leaders to enforce standards and policies across the various departments and agencies of the state itself, and to monitor the bureaucracy. This is especially important in authoritarian regimes where there is no free press to expose administrative misdeeds, especially corruption. The Chinese Communist Party, for example, has encouraged the growth of administrative law courts for this reason. Finally, political leaders often find it politically advantageous to delegate controversial issues to courts. This type of delegation (what some criticize as "buck-passing") has occurred in several countries on heated topics such as same-sex marriage, abortion, and euthanasia. Some legal systems facilitate this more than others. In Canada, several U.S. states, and many civil law systems, politicians can send legal questions directly to the judiciary, in what is known as abstract review or reference cases. The U.S. Constitution, in contrast, forbids the U.S. Supreme Court from hearing hypothetical legal questions.

In enforcing the law, courts often interpret it as well—sometimes to such a degree that judges effectively create law. Some judicial interpretation is inevitable as laws have gaps, ambiguous wording and contradictions, become outdated, or use language that society interprets differently over time. Vague wording is especially common in constitutional law. Even the 1st Amendment of the U.S. Constitution, which famously states that "Congress shall make no law…abridging the freedom of speech, or of the press," suffers from imprecision. What are "speech" and "the press"? Someone hearing those words today might assume this meant only verbal communication and the news media. Someone with more historical background might point out that this was written in 1791, long before electronic media, when public communications consisted largely of spoken words and written works produced via printing press. As such, they might argue, it was intended to protect most communication in existence. But even when the 1st Amendment was adopted, there was music and visual arts—drawing, painting, sculpture, dance: were these excluded? More importantly, are there really no limits on this freedom? What about speech that is inappropriate for children, or words that are likely to cause harm to others? The 1st Amendment is silent on these questions. In such cases, judges cannot simply apply or enforce the law—they must first figure out what it means. But legal interpretation by judges is not restricted to constitutional law. As noted above, common-law judges are expected to fill in legal gaps by reasoning from related precedents; for example, if it is already established in criminal law that killing in self-defense is allowed, then is it also permissible to *plan* to kill your abusive spouse who you sincerely believe is going to murder you or your children someday?[7] Judges in civil code systems are discouraged from interpretation, as the codes are meant to be exhaustively detailed. According to this view, if the code is so unclear as to require judicial interpretation, then it should be amended. But absolute precision is impossible and judges in these systems frequently turn to interpretations published by legal academics and, increasingly, previous court decisions. The question is thus not whether judges should interpret the law but when and in what manner.

The degree to which a court engages in enforcement versus interpretation depends largely on where that court is located in the judicial system. Earlier it was noted that there is usually specialization within the judiciary, and this includes a hierarchical dimension: there are trial courts that first hear the facts of the case and apply the relevant law, and appeal courts that review the decisions of trial (and lower appeal) courts. Appeal courts exist primarily for two reasons: error correction and legal interpretation. Countries may have multiple layers of appeal courts, with a single final court of appeal for all legal questions, like the Supreme Courts of Canada and India. Or, they may have specialization even at the highest levels, as is typical in countries with civil law systems. Many countries have a Constitutional Court whose sole function is to interpret the constitution; in such systems, other courts (such as the criminal courts) are barred from interpreting or sometimes even applying constitution law, and simply refer such issues to the Constitutional Court. Figure 9.2 illustrates an example of both an integrated appeal system (Canada) and one that retains specialization (Germany).

Judicial Review

When judges enforce legal limits on government, it is known as **judicial review**. As noted above, judicial review can involve the enforcement of a variety of procedural and substantive limits in statutory, case, and constitutional law. In much of the democratic world, judicial review is associated with upholding the rule of law and thus protecting the public from the abuse of government power. Court decisions that prohibit state-sponsored discrimination, such as the U.S. Supreme Court's ruling in *Brown v. Board of Education* [1954] that banned racial segregation in public schools, are famous. Equality rights have emerged as a major limitation on state power in many countries, joining older liberal rights to free speech, religion, assembly, and association, and the legal rights to counsel, to be presumed innocent, and to receive a fair trial, for example. Some countries have also adopted rights that protect certain cultural groups—Aboriginal treaty rights or language rights, for example—as well as "positive" or social rights, such as healthcare, shelter, and clean drinking water. Judicial review that focuses on jurisdiction is also implicitly about preventing the concentration of power that can lead to abuse. Some federations, such as Canada and the U.S., divided powers between a national and several regional governments precisely for this reason, and in the case of Canada, to better protect the distinctive language, culture, and religion of Quebec. Similarly, the "separation of powers" between the legislative, executive, and judicial branches was advocated by political thinkers such as Montesquieu and the framers of the American Constitution as necessary to prevent tyranny.

> **Judicial review:** When judges determine whether state actions are legally permissible, for example, in light of rights protections or the federal division of powers.

It must be re-emphasized, however, that judicial review has sometimes been a tool used by the central government to controls its parts, or to keep

FIGURE 9.2   UNIFIED AND SPECIALIZED FEDERAL JUDICIAL SYSTEMS: CANADA AND GERMANY

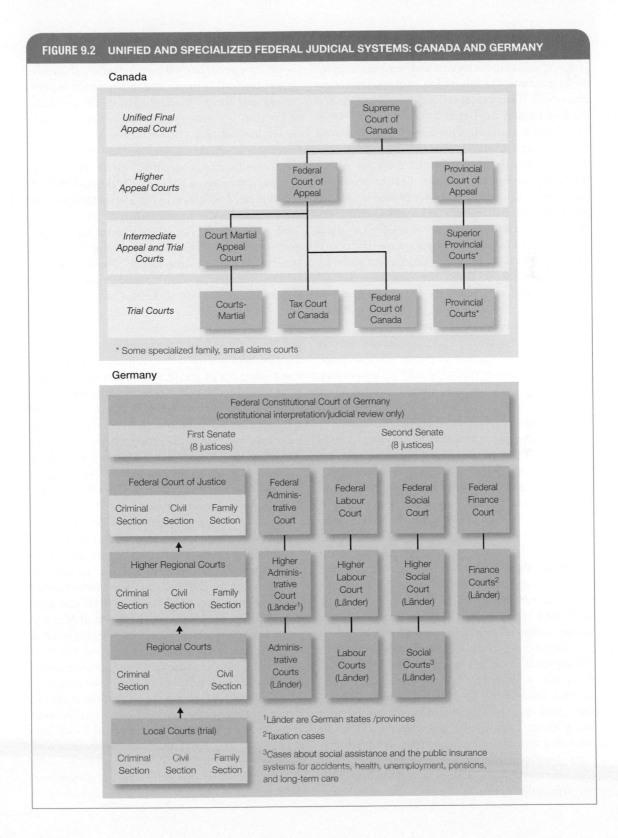

Canada

Unified Final Appeal Court	Supreme Court of Canada	
Higher Appeal Courts	Federal Court of Appeal	Provincial Court of Appeal
Intermediate Appeal and Trial Courts	Court Martial Appeal Court	Superior Provincial Courts*
Trial Courts	Courts-Martial / Tax Court of Canada / Federal Court of Canada	Provincial Courts*

* Some specialized family, small claims courts

Germany

Federal Constitutional Court of Germany
(constitutional interpretation/judicial review only)

First Senate (8 justices)   Second Senate (8 justices)

Federal Court of Justice — Criminal Section, Civil Section, Family Section

Higher Regional Courts — Criminal Section, Civil Section, Family Section

Regional Courts — Criminal Section, Civil Section

Local Courts (trial) — Criminal Section, Civil Section, Family Section

Federal Administrative Court — Higher Administrative Court (Länder[1]) — Administrative Courts (Länder)

Federal Labour Court — Higher Labour Court (Länder) — Labour Courts (Länder)

Federal Social Court — Higher Social Court (Länder) — Social Courts[3] (Länder)

Federal Finance Court — Finance Courts[2] (Länder)

[1] Länder are German states / provinces

[2] Taxation cases

[3] Cases about social assistance and the public insurance systems for accidents, health, unemployment, pensions, and long-term care

sub-national governments in line—what some have termed "rule by law."[8] While this may conjure up images of authoritarian regimes and "kangaroo courts," we have examples of rule by law in democratic countries as well. When President Charles de Gaulle oversaw the formation of the French Fifth Republic in 1958, he included the creation of the Conseil Constitutionnel (Constitutional Council) with the intention that it would protect the powers of the president against encroachment by the legislative branch.[9] Similarly, the Supreme Court of Canada was created—and then appointed—by the federal government in 1875 primarily to help resolve federal–provincial disputes about jurisdiction, when other measures used by the central government to block provincial assertions of authority proved ineffective.[10] (In neither case, however, did the courts ultimately follow the expectations of their designers, instead embracing rights and a more balanced approach to power relations.)

Even when aimed at rights protection or preventing the concentration of power, judicial review is frequently controversial, especially in democracies, and some countries such as Australia, the Netherlands, and Sweden have vigorously opposed the expansion of judicial power. There are three main criticisms of judicial review. The first is that, as just noted, courts are often called upon to enforce ambiguously-worded legal limits on government, which means that they have to interpret those limits first. There is a heated debate in many countries about which approach to interpretation judges should take. In broad terms, there are two main camps: "originalists" and "living constitutionalists" (or "purposivists"). Originalists hold that judges should adhere as strictly as possible to the plain meaning of the law's text, and, where the text is unclear, should look to what the law's authors most likely meant in light of their historical context or any additional writings they left behind (such as memoirs and speeches). One well-known version of this approach in the U.S. is labelled "framers' intent." From this perspective, the law—especially constitutional law—is the product of negotiated agreement, and thus courts are illegitimately *creating* new law without using proper procedures (such as an amending formula) if they develop novel interpretations. Possibly the most aggressive example of this argument can be found in the state of Missouri, which has repeatedly drafted amendments to that state's constitution that would compel state judges to use the original intent approach, most recently in 2014 (voters have yet to ratify the amendment). Those who oppose originalism argue that this approach burdens current and future generations with the prejudices of the past, and that the historical record is usually incomplete and contradictory because laws have many framers. Instead, they argue, it is better to interpret the constitution in a way that reflects the values of contemporary society. For example, although the U.S. "equal protection" clause in the 14th amendment did not envision gender equality when it was adopted in 1868, courts should not follow this original interpretation in the post-feminist era. According to this view, laws are "living" documents that should be allowed to develop organically with society, thus protecting the underlying purpose of the law (in the case of the 14th Amendment, the promotion and protection of equality). This approach has become the dominant one in Canada (where it is known as the "living tree" doctrine, and was used to recognize same-sex marriage) and parts of the U.S., but also further afield, as in Israel's and France's constitutional courts. The main criticism of this organic approach is that laws and especially constitutions then become what the judges say they are, with little to constrain judicial interpretations. Examples of controversial judicial "creativity" are numerous: the Judicial Committee of the Privy Council (JCPC), the British body that was Canada's highest court of appeal until 1949, reshaped Canadian federalism by greatly expanding provincial jurisdiction, contrary to the intent of the Fathers of Confederation; the U.S. Supreme Court found a right to privacy and later to abortion in the "penumbras" or shadows of the Bill of Rights; the French Conseil Constitutionnel asserted its authority to enforce rights from the 1789 Declaration of the Rights of Man and of the Citizen; the High Court of Australia reversed years of precedent to recognize Aboriginal title, or a right of Aboriginals to access, use, and partially control territory; the Supreme Court of India found a right to clean drinking water within the constitutional right to life; and the European Court of Justice ruled, without any explicit textual basis, that European Union laws can be claimed by residents of member-states in their domestic courts.

A second reason that judicial review is controversial is that when judges enforce substantive limits it can have profound effects on public policy. When a court enforces procedural or jurisdictional limits, it does not prevent government action but merely insists that government follow its own rules; in the context of federalism or the separation of powers, an unfavourable judicial ruling against one unit of government necessarily means that another unit of government can act. For example, if provincial governments in Canada cannot print money, then the federal government can. But in substantive review, the court can block action by *any* government body. Although the term **judicial activism** has many competing definitions, the least controversial is that it occurs when a judge restricts the actions of government, or through their interpretation of the law expands the legal limits on government. Judicial restraint occurs when a judge defers to government or narrows the legal limits upon it. In light of the wide discretion that they enjoy over interpretation, courts can have a very broad and powerful influence on public policy, even to the point where they are effectively making policy. The U.S. courts provide many examples of detailed judicial policymaking in such varied areas as abortion, affirmative action, and election campaign regulation. Judicial activism is considered problematic because it concentrates power in the judiciary, and judges may not have the expertise or information to devise good public policy.

> **Judicial activism:** When judges restrict the actions of the executive or legislative branches, or expand the limits on government through legal interpretation. Judicial restraint is when judges do the opposite.

A third and related criticism of judicial review in democratic countries, or where the leadership is popular, arises when courts are seen as blocking the "will of the people." As almost no countries have elected judges—the U.S. and Bolivia are two notable exceptions—courts are not directly authorized to act by the people, and as detailed in the next section, judicial independence means that they are not directly accountable either. Although this criticism can be applied to any type of legal limit that courts enforce, the greatest concern is reserved for judicial review based on constitutional law because it is usually the hardest to undo. If the court interprets case law or a statute in a manner that the government does not support, then the government can simply amend the law. This is not the case for constitutional law, which is protected by complex amending formulas (or cannot be amended at all, like many parts of the German Basic Law). This is a powerful criticism, but there is undeniably a conflict of interest if legislatures and executives are responsible for enforcing legal limits on themselves. The basic logic of third-party dispute resolution still applies when government bodies disagree over jurisdiction or when individuals claim that government actions violate their rights, and so it is no surprise that courts around the world practice judicial review.

Precisely because judicial review empowers courts, it can also be dangerous for them. Unpopular decisions can swing public opinion against the judiciary, or antagonize political leaders. Probably for this reason, it has been noted that courts are rarely too far out of step with the mainstream values of the society that they serve.[11] This is especially evident during times of war or crisis. Even in the U.S., which has a very strong tradition of judicial activism, the judiciary was unwilling to limit sweeping executive powers assumed in the name of security during wartime or shortly after 9/11, allowing such human rights abuses as the mass internment of Japanese-Americans and the removal of due process for "enemy combatants" imprisoned in Guantanamo Bay. In the context of resolving jurisdictional disputes, courts can get drawn into power struggles between the legislative and executive branches which is a particularly treacherous terrain, as siding with either risks

THINK AND DISCUSS

Your court has been asked to decide on a rights claim that, if successful, would protect someone who is deeply offensive and unpopular—for example, a free speech claim by a child pornographer. Supporting the rights claim will open the court to intense criticism from the public and the government. What do you do?

alienating the other. Worse yet, judges may choose the wrong side, to their peril. Judges on the Russian Constitutional Court learned this hard lesson when they supported the parliament against President Yeltsin in the constitutional crisis of 1993, when Yeltsin tried to dissolve the legislature, including with military force. Although the Court was legally correct—Yeltsin did not have the authority to close down parliament—Yeltsin emerged victorious. He retaliated by suspending and then replacing the Court with one packed with more like-minded judges. Since that crisis, the Court has been significantly more sympathetic to the president, including Yeltsin's successor, Vladimir Putin.

JUDICIAL INDEPENDENCE AND IMPARTIALITY

To adjudicate effectively, the single most important characteristic required of a judge is, as it has been famously said, to not only be impartial but to be seen as impartial. **Judicial impartiality** means that the judge is free of bias (such as racism or sexism) and indifferent to the outcome of the case; impartiality is thus a subjective state of mind (This is reflected in the public confidence in the courts, shown in Figure 9.3.). Humans are not machines, however, and it is widely acknowledged that judges are shaped by their upbringing and environment, a perspective known as **legal realism** (in contrast to legal

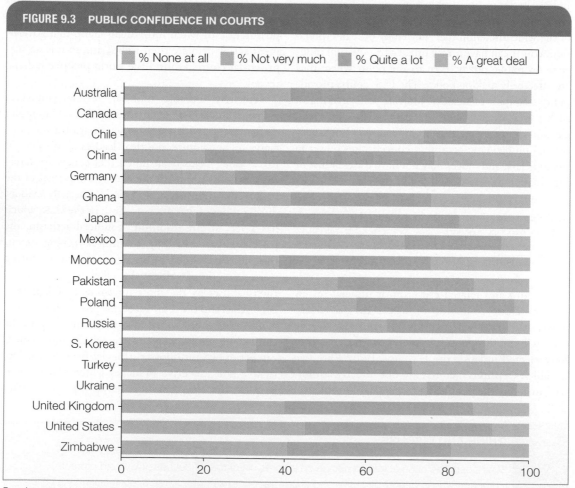

FIGURE 9.3   PUBLIC CONFIDENCE IN COURTS

People were asked, "How much confidence do you have in the courts?"

Source: Data from World Values Survey 2010-2014, except Canada and the U.K. (2005–2009), online at http://www.worldvaluessurvey.org/WVSOnline.jsp.

positivism or formalism, which holds that judges can and should simply apply the law). This produces judges who differ in their attitudes about values and the proper role of the judiciary—how else to explain the frequent disagreements amongst Supreme Court Justices in Canada (or the U.S.) in the face of the same facts and applicable laws? As such, when we speak of judicial impartiality we do not mean strict neutrality but rather the narrower expectation that judges will decide cases with an open mind and apply the law as fairly as possible, and that they have nothing personally to gain or lose through their rulings. The logic of third-party dispute resolution breaks down if a judge is not impartial, as participants will not respect the decision or see it as fair (this also helps to explain why judicial interpretation generates so much controversy, because it appears to be an expression of the judges' personal attitudes rather than the application of law, particularly when the judges disagree).

> **Judicial impartiality:** A subjective state of mind in which a judge is free of bias and indifferent to the outcome of the case, in that he or she has nothing personally to gain or lose by the decision.

> **Legal realism:** A school of legal philosophy which contends that judges' backgrounds and values shape their decisions, and that these values are able to manifest when judges have flexibility, as when they interpret the law.

Judicial independence refers to the institutional structures, or relationships between the judiciary and executive and legislative branches, that encourage judicial impartiality. Although there is considerable disagreement over the precise requirements for judicial independence, it is commonly accepted that judges must enjoy a high degree of job security (tenure) and financial security in order to be insulated against pressures to decide cases based on material self-interest rather than the law. This means that judges need to be free from either punishments or rewards from other political actors. Tenure and financial security are also intended to encourage the recruitment of highly-qualified judges, and to discourage corruption in the form of bribes from both public officials and private actors. In addition, judicial independence requires some judicial control over the operations of the court,

such as the hiring of administrative staff, budgeting, the docket (which cases will be heard and when), and the allocation of judges to cases.

> **Judicial independence:** The institutional structures, or relationships between the judiciary and executive and legislative branches, intended to encourage judicial impartiality, such as tenure, financial security, and some degree of administrative autonomy.

Tenure does not necessarily mean a "job for life," however, or that a judge cannot ever be removed. The length of a judicial term needs to be long enough to encourage strong candidates to take the job, to give them time to learn the position, and to gain the confidence to assert the rule of law where necessary. While there are judges who serve for life (e.g., the U.S. Supreme Court, the regular French judiciary), it is more common that they serve until an advanced age of mandatory retirement (75 years old for the Supreme Court of Canada, for instance). Long terms are preferable from the perspective of legal stability and therefore predictability, but this can come into conflict with the desire for judges to reflect society, and, in democratic systems, to have judges selected by those with a recent electoral mandate. It is for this reason that judges on constitutional courts in many civil law systems serve relatively short terms of 8–12 years. It is also necessary to be able to remove judges for just cause, such as criminal or unethical behaviour including corruption, mistreatment of staff, or the failure to perform duties in a professional and timely manner. More controversially, some argue that judges should be removed for failing to "follow the law," which sounds reasonable when the law is very clear and should have been applied, but is troubling when it involves grayer areas such as when to follow a precedent or whether to adhere to original intent.

Even if we could agree on *why* judges should be removed, there is still the question of *who* should decide whether removal is warranted. One option is to leave it entirely to the executive or legislative branch, but this could lead to abuse and risks undermining the main reason for judicial independence. More importantly, it is not at all clear that officials in those branches are qualified to determine whether judges deserve to be removed, at least where there is no flagrant criminality or bias on the part of the judge. At the other end of the spectrum, decisions about judicial discipline and removal can be made entirely by the judiciary, as in some civil law systems, including France. The solution that many countries have developed is a middle ground that combines peer review—that is, judges judging judges—with legislative and/or executive authority over removal. In peer review, a panel of judges reviews the judge's conduct and recommends—usually to the executive or legislative branch—whether it qualifies as misconduct worthy of discipline or removal. In Canada, for example, the Canadian Judicial Council (CJC) is a body of senior judges, chaired by the chief justice of the Supreme Court of Canada, which hears complaints about federally-appointed judges and makes disciplinary recommendations to Parliament. Parliament will not attempt to remove a judge without a CJC recommendation that it do so, and in fact, no federally-appointed judge has ever been removed (a few have resigned before they could be fired, however). The "middle-ground" approach ensures the involvement of impartial judges to assess the merits of the complaint but leaves the final authority over discipline with the elected branches. This protects against rivalries within the judiciary itself, but it still leaves the system vulnerable to the problem that judges may be reluctant to "police" each other (the CJC and other judicial councils have permitted some questionable conduct by judges, such as criticizing the government from off the bench on high-profile political issues).

The major concern regarding financial security surrounds who sets judicial salaries. If the political executive or legislature crafts the overall state budget, then it typically falls to these branches to allocate funds for judicial salaries. This can clearly lead to conflicts of interest, or the appearance of government interference with the courts, if salaries are frozen or even reduced. This touches on the distinction between individual and collective financial security for judges. Individual security means that individual judges cannot be targeted with financial penalties or rewards for their decisions; collective security refers to penalties or rewards that target the judiciary as a whole. An example of the latter might be a five percent reduction in pay for all judges by a government that has criticized the judiciary for being too lenient when sentencing criminals. Not all across-the-board pay freezes or reductions are necessarily problematic, however. For example, there

may be nothing wrong with freezing or reducing judicial salaries if the salaries of all public officials in every branch are being frozen or reduced to the same degree. The key is that there should be no suggestion that judges are being targeted. As with judicial discipline and removal, some countries have placed judicial salaries at arm's length from political leaders to avoid both abuse and the appearance that judges are haggling with government over their salaries. In Canada, judicial salaries are now effectively set by a third-party body composed of members representing both judges and the government (Judicial Compensation Commissions); governments can attempt to reject JCC salary recommendations as unaffordable or excessive, but they have to win the approval of an independent court of law (some have been able to do so).

With respect to administrative independence, judiciaries in some civil law systems are essentially self-governing branches, while those in common-law systems tend to be more dependent on the executive branch, particularly regarding budgets. In Canada, administrative independence has emerged as the next big issue related to judicial independence, as judges have intensified their lobbying for more control over how their courts are run.[12] While there is little agreement over how much administrative control courts require to protect judicial independence, recent events in Hungary illustrate well the potential problems of weak administrative independence. In 2012, the Hungarian government created a judicial "czar" (President of the National Judicial Office of Hungary) who, in addition to having the power to appoint all judges, can transfer cases between courts. Some high-profile cases against the country's main opposition party have since been shifted to judges known to be favourable to the government. Such tampering can only erode the legitimacy of the judiciary.

There are a variety of additional threats to judicial independence, such as government officials contacting judges privately about cases before the courts, or governments threatening to change the structure of the judiciary (for example, to increase the number of judges on the court, which would allow the current government to "stack" it with appointees). A government might also threaten to change how judges are selected in ways that undermine the quality and independence of the bench. Regardless of the type of threat, history shows us that judicial independence is protected best by public opposition to such government interference. Where public support for courts is low or absent, as in some Latin American countries, it is easier for political leaders to ignore or weaken formal rules protecting judicial independence. Conversely, some countries with relatively weak formal protections but strong public support for courts have quite robust judicial independence, such as Britain and Pakistan. This fact underlines that it is crucial for courts to retain strong public support (for a sense of how public support can vary across countries, see Figure 9.3, above).

It must also be stressed that there is often a gap between independence "on paper" and "in fact" or practice, in at least three senses. First, as noted above, judges may have formal protections that are not well observed in practice by government officials—threats and incentives may be used even where clearly forbidden. Second, judges may decide not to exercise their independence, even though they have it (in Japan, for example[13]). Third, and conversely, judges may act independently even when they *do not* have strong protections, as seen in Pakistan during the rule of President (formerly General) Pervez Musharraf in the early 2000s. These phenomena underline the important point that the relationship between judicial independence and impartiality is not automatic, and that we do not, in fact, know how much of the former is needed to ensure the latter.

Pakistani lawyers in 2007 protest the suspension of the Supreme Court's chief justice by President Musharraf; the president's actions severely undermined his legitimacy, and he resigned from office the next year.
© *REUTERS/Ibrar Tanoli*

JUDICIAL SELECTION

Throughout the world there are a wide variety of systems for selecting judges, and there is no agreement about which is best. What we do know is that who sits on the bench matters, because the background and personal values of judges shape their decisions. If the judiciary is drawn from only a narrow slice of society—as is often the case—it may undermine the legitimacy of the institution, and also frustrate the judiciary's ability to reflect society's values. Thus, judicial selection relates directly to not only the quality of the institution but also broader issues about the place of the judiciary within the society it serves.

Qualifications

There are two big issues to consider when analyzing selection systems: What qualifications are needed to be a judge? (in other words, on what basis are judges chosen?); and who selects the judges? These issues are often closely related. Where the political executive selects judges, for example, the most important qualification is often that the candidate supports the government's political party or faction, or what is known as **political patronage**. This was the case in Canada for much of its history, and patronage is still a factor in some cases (such as the appointment in 2014 by Prime Minister Stephen Harper of former Conservative Minister of Justice Vic Toews to the Manitoba bench). Patronage may be motivated by a desire to ensure that judges share the values of the appointers, or it may be a reward for supporting those in power, or both. Such appointments are frequently criticized on the assumption that partisan affiliation outweighed considerations of merit, such as training, experience, and character. Patronage and merit are not necessarily mutually exclusive, however, as the government's choice may be just one of many highly meritorious candidates. Nonetheless, patronage appointments are problematic because they undermine the appearance of judicial impartiality in court cases involving the government or individuals who appointed the presiding judge.

Political patronage/patronage appointment: When those in power favour political supporters or party members in making appointments to state offices.

Judicial selection is also often influenced by concerns about representing social diversity, such as sex, ethnicity, religion, or regional affiliation. On one hand, this is a natural extension of legal realism: if judicial backgrounds shape decisions, then it stands to reason that people with different backgrounds will have different values and perspectives that should be reflected on the bench. For example, there is mounting statistical and anecdotal evidence that, on average, male and female judges decide cases somewhat differently, particularly with respect to human rights, criminal, and family law cases.[14] But even if the judges' backgrounds do not influence their rulings, there is still an argument that the judiciary should reflect social diversity to enhance the perception of fairness and to foster stronger public identification with the institution (parallelling the arguments for improving diversity in the legislative and executive branches). No matter how open-minded or fair they might be, rulings by all-male judges about abortion, or by non-Aboriginal judges about Aboriginal law, are open to criticism that the court does not represent the people affected by the ruling. Of course, as with patronage, many argue that selecting judges based on representation undermines the commitment to "merit." Again, however, diversity and merit are not mutually exclusive, and unlike in the case of patronage, there are strong arguments that diversity actually improves the quality, fairness, and legitimacy of the bench. This said, arguments in favour of diversity for the judiciary *as a whole*, or where there are multiple judges hearing the case, are problematic when applied to the level of a single judge in a trial court. If judicial backgrounds matter, then it suggests that the justice one receives at trial varies with the judge hearing the case—not a thought that encourages respect for a "fair and impartial" ruling. Ignoring diversity issues when selecting judges does not make this problem go away, either. One solution might be to have panels of judges even at the trial level, as is the practice already in some countries, such as France.

A final issue related to qualifications is the training or educational background of judicial candidates, which is crucial because, as noted earlier, the legitimacy of adjudication is based on both the judge's impartiality and his or her perceived expertise at resolving legal disputes. In common law systems, judges are typically drawn from the legal profession; that is, they are lawyers. While this approach has the

obvious benefit of ensuring that judges have a legal education, it immediately restricts the judiciary to those who can afford the often exorbitant cost of law school. As well, law schools train people to be lawyers (that is, advocates or legal advisors), not judges, and the roles of each in the justice system are distinct (notably, many countries have supplemental judicial colleges to train those who become judges). In contrast, many civil law systems train people specifically to be judges. A good example is France, which has centralized judicial training in the École Nationale de la Magistrature (ENM). There is also a growing trend in common-law systems toward "lay benchers," or non-lawyers performing more routine judicial tasks such as hearing applications for warrants by police or resolving disputes where only relatively small amounts of money are at stake (in Canada, Justices of the Peace are an example). While lay benchers are considerably cheaper, they raise concerns about the quality of justice and in some cases they enjoy less independence than "full" judges.

Who Selects?

The power to staff one of the branches of the state is incredibly important, and countries around the world have devised an astonishing variety of approaches. One key distinction is between systems that give this power to political leaders (whether democratically-elected or not) and those that give it to the legal profession or the judiciary itself. France is a classic example of the latter, where the judiciary is considered part of the civil service and run like a bureaucracy: French judges thus not only train their own profession (in the ENM) but recruit, appoint, and promote judges to their positions. In another version of a professionalized approach, judges on the recently-created Supreme Court of the United Kingdom are chosen by independent selection commissions composed of lawyers and laypersons. In federations, there is the additional question of the role that regional governments should play when selecting judges to courts that interpret and enforce the federal division of powers. Regional input is often achieved by giving a formal role to a legislative upper house which is a body of regional representation (for example, the U.S. Senate, the German Bundesrat, or the Russian Federation Council).[15] In democratic regimes, we can make a further distinction based on how much power the voters have over judicial selection, either directly or through elected representatives. Direct popular election of judges is exceptionally rare, being restricted to state-level courts in the U.S. and, since 2009, Bolivia. Appointment by elected politicians is more common, but here again there are many variations based on who can *nominate* judicial candidates, who can *screen* or *vet* candidates, and who can *confirm* the selection, that is, make the final decision. Some countries follow the U.S. Supreme Court model, where justices are first nominated by the president (the executive branch) but then screened by a committee of the Senate (part of the legislative branch) in public interviews with the candidate, with the full Senate voting on whether to confirm the appointment. In sharp contrast, appointments to the Supreme Court of Canada are made solely by the prime minister (officially the governor general, but in practice the prime minister provides the name) with no formal role for Members of Parliament or provincial governments (although in recent years some appointees were interviewed by a parliamentary committee, but for informational purposes only, and inconsistently, as not every appointee was asked to appear before a committee). This astonishing concentration of power over the selection of the highest court in the land is virtually unparalleled among democracies, and is more commonly associated with dictatorial regimes.[16] Although Canada has enjoyed highly-qualified Supreme Court justices for many years, the appointment system is vulnerable to abuse and has been widely criticized. Curiously, the lower federally-appointed courts in Canada have (slightly) thicker procedures: judges are also chosen by the prime minister but candidates can nominate themselves, and a screening committee composed of representatives from the federal and provincial governments, the judiciary, and the legal profession screen applicants to ensure that they have the minimum qualifications. Some other countries permit the legislature to elect judges, as in Switzerland, Nicaragua, and Germany's Federal Constitutional Court. Many U.S. state courts in which the judges are initially appointed by politicians add an element of direct democracy by having retention elections after the judge has served a fixed number of years. Judges who have made unpopular rulings on such heated issues as capital punishment and abortion

Marshall Rothstein, nominee for appointment to the Supreme Court of Canada, awaits his appearance before a parliamentary committee in 2006, the first of its kind in Canadian history. This approach has not been used consistently since.
© *REUTERS/Dave Chan*

have sometimes, as a result, found themselves out of a job after such elections.

Popular election of judges is based on a strict democratic philosophy that all parts of the state which wield power in the name of the people should be chosen by the people. The problem is that this view is in tension with the equally-important principle of the rule of law, that judges should follow the law *even when it is unpopular.* Otherwise, legal protections for unpopular groups, such as criminals, or human rights for minorities, become meaningless. The tension is especially acute if judges must face re-election or retention elections (or re-appointment by politicians), when they may be punished for respecting the rule of law, and there is evidence that U.S. judges facing imminent election alter their behaviour to appeal to voters, for example by issuing harsher sentences to convicted criminals. Furthermore, judicial election campaigns cost money—quite a lot of money in the U.S.—which means that candidates must either be independently wealthy or solicit donations from the public, usually businesses. Recent evidence confirms the worrying suspicion that judges who receive more money from business donors are more likely to rule in favour of business.[17] For all these reasons, it is difficult to reconcile judicial elections with judicial impartiality and independence.

Leaving appointment entirely to unaccountable judicial bureaucrats is also not without its flaws. For one, it can breed an insular judiciary that is out of touch with society, particularly if judges are drawn from an unrepresentative elite. Notably, most civil law countries with highly bureaucratized selection systems for their regular judiciary use more democratic systems for their constitutional courts, to ensure that those interpreting and applying the country's most important law, the constitution, are more representative of the citizenry. For another, judges may either consciously or unconsciously appoint judges who share their views, creating a judiciary with little diversity of thought or experience. While few would desire the kind of sharp ideological battles currently seen on the U.S. Supreme Court (where the judges regularly split evenly along partisan lines), new ideas and perspectives are valuable to ensure that judges and legal interpretation remain current. Importantly, no selection system is free of politics, so the question is *whose* politics is more in play—that of politicians in the executive and/or legislative branches, or those in the bureaucracy, judiciary, or professional organizations?

PHOTO ESSAY

© The Canadian Press/Adrian Wyld

Terri-Jean Bedford flashes a victory sign after learning that the Supreme Court of Canada had struck down the country's prostitution laws in Ottawa on December 20, 2013.

THE BEDFORD CASE

Terri-Jean Bedford had good cause to celebrate in the Supreme Court of Canada on December 20, 2013. For several years the dominatrix, with several other sex workers, had waged a legal battle against the federal government for the right to operate a brothel in her Toronto-area home. All of the Court's justices—even the five Justices appointed by Prime Minister Stephen Harper—had agreed with her argument that laws which prohibited "bawdy-houses" and hiring security staff violated the rights of sex workers to "life, liberty and the security of the person" under the Charter of Rights of Freedoms in Canada's constitution, since prostitution itself was legal in Canada. The Court struck those laws down and told Parliament to craft a new approach to regulating the sex trade that would protect the safety of sex workers.

The *Bedford* case reflects many important themes related to courts and politics. In line with some leading theories about why people go to court, the case was brought by those marginalized by the traditional legislative process, namely sex workers, most of them women. The court exercised judicial review using a constitutional bill of rights to find that the government's law was illegal, illustrating the potential power of the courts. The ruling was probably influenced by recent "real-world" events, namely the deaths of dozens of street prostitutes in British Columbia at the hands of serial killer Robert Pickton. Bedford's celebration, like those of many other litigants, reflects the view that court decisions can produce clear "wins."

But there are other important lessons here as well, which Bedford probably didn't anticipate on that wintry day in Ottawa. Six months after the Court's decision, the federal government introduced new legislation which criminalized prostitution by making it a crime to pay for sex, or for sex workers to advertise their services "near" where children live (which is almost everywhere). In other words, the government's response, far from loosening the rules around the sex trade as Bedford and her colleagues had hoped, introduced greater restrictions, many of which will make life *less* safe for prostitutes. This underlines the important point that court decisions are never the end of the story, and that compliance with the court is not guaranteed.

THE POLICY IMPACT OF COURTS AND NON-COMPLIANCE

There is an unfortunate tendency amongst media and other commentators on law and courts to report judicial rulings as though they were the end of the story. The reality is more complicated: judicial decisions require lower courts, political actors in the executive and legislative branches (including police), and the public to comply, and this is far from automatic. With respect to lower courts, an old Chinese proverb sometimes applies: "the mountains are high and the emperor is far away," meaning that there may be little risk that non-compliance by a local trial court will be detected and overturned. As in most countries, only a tiny proportion of trial court rulings are appealed in Canada, and the Supreme Court of Canada hears appeals from only about two per cent of the cases in the senior appellate courts across the country. This is not to suggest that lower courts regularly ignore appeal court rulings, but this form of non-compliance occurs everywhere, and the problem is a serious one in some countries.

There are many examples of politicians refusing to comply with courts, particularly when the ruling was widely unpopular. One famous study revealed that even the landmark ruling in *Brown v. Board of Education* [1954], which ordered the racial desegregation of public schools in the United States, had little practical effect until the national government threatened non-complying school boards with funding cuts.[18] In that case, the school boards had simply refused to change their policy after *Brown*. Governments may also respond to a court decision with a new policy that does not respect the ruling. The photo essay on Terri-Jean Bedford provides a recent example, as the Canadian government sought to eliminate prostitution entirely after the Supreme Court struck down sex trade restrictions which endangered the life and health of sex workers. The ability of governments to respond with non-compliance has led some to describe the relationship between the judicial and other branches as a "dialogue," a back-and-forth about the meaning of law and what is allowed. While somewhat accurate, the dialogue metaphor downplays the power and material consequences involved in these exchanges: at some point one interpretation must prevail (at least for a time) to guide law enforcement officers and the public. Moreover, some court decisions are quite difficult to challenge, such as interpretations of the constitution which would require a formal amendment or drastic regime change to undo.

The main reason that courts experience compliance issues with other parts of the state is that the judiciary has a fundamental institutional weakness. This

Several key policy initiatives by Prime Minister Stephen Harper's government have been struck down by the Supreme Court of Canada. In 2014, his government began openly criticizing Chief Justice Beverley McLachlin, and adopting new policies that do not appear to comply with the Supreme Court's earlier rulings.

© Theo Moudakis. Reprinted by permission of Artizans.com.

weakness is most memorably summarized by American framer Alexander Hamilton in *Federalist No. 78*, where he describes the judiciary as "the least dangerous branch" because it "has no influence over either the sword or the purse.... It may truly be said to have neither FORCE nor WILL, but merely judgment." In other words, courts do not control the police, the military, or the bureaucracy, nor do they collect taxes and make budgets. Given this, it is a wonder that anyone complies with the courts! That so many people do, around the world, tells us some important things about our societies. First, it speaks to a deep desire for order and the rule of law. Second, the broad acceptance of adjudication suggests that the basic logic of third-party dispute resolution is indeed valid. Third, it emphasizes how strong the reasons are for governments to comply, which were noted earlier in this chapter. It must be stressed, however, that the institutional weakness of courts means that they rely heavily on public support, which is directly related to the perceived legitimacy of the judiciary (Canadian trust in various political institutions, including the Supreme Court, is shown in Table 9.1.). In countries where trust in and support for courts is low relative to elected politicians, it is easier for the latter to ignore judges or to violate judicial independence. There is thus a fundamental dilemma for courts, which must maintain public confidence yet also enforce laws that may not be popular.

This tension, along with the structural weaknesses of the judiciary, have led some to conclude that it is a "hollow hope" that court decisions can produce meaningful social change.[19] It is true that courts tend to reinforce dominant social values and structures, but others point out that court decisions—both wins and losses—can provoke social groups to organize and take political action. The gay and lesbian rights movement experienced this in many countries as repeated early losses in court helped to galvanize supporters, and American pro-life groups mobilized after the U.S. Supreme Court legalized abortion in *Roe v. Wade* [1973], eventually electing like-minded politicians and judges in many states (including President Ronald Reagan in 1980, who in turn appointed anti-abortion judges to the Supreme Court). Court decisions may also shape the way we talk about political issues, for example, transforming "gay rights" into the more sympathetic framework of "equality rights," or "prostitution" into a matter of "workplace safety" or "public health." All of which re-emphasizes the point that court decisions are rarely the last word.

ACCESS TO JUSTICE

Most of us live in a "law-thick world,"[20] with our relationships, jobs, political activity, and leisure governed by a staggering number of legal restrictions and obligations. It is not surprising that most people, at some point in their lives, will therefore need to interact with the legal system, and many will have a dispute requiring adjudication. However, the degree to which courts are used, and perform the many functions identified in this chapter, depends on the ability of potential litigants to access them, although many are pulled into the legal system involuntarily (such as accused criminals or people who are sued). The complexity of the law and the judicial process means that those who interact with them—voluntarily or otherwise—should have professional legal advice and representation, but this is usually expensive, even more so when cases may take years to resolve, as is common (see Table 9.2). Although justice is supposed to be blind, inequalities of income and education in society make the legal system inaccessible to many poor and middle-income individuals, which in turn contributes to biased or incorrect judicial decisions, including

TABLE 9.1	CANADIANS' TRUST OF POLITICAL INSTITUTIONS (PERCENT)				
	Great Deal of Trust	Some Trust	Not Very Much Trust	No Trust At All	Don't Know
Canadian Military	44	35	13	4	4
Supreme Court of Canada	39	35	16	6	4
Auditor General of Canada	35	35	15	5	10
RCMP	26	46	19	6	3
Provincial Government	12	32	33	19	3
Prime Minister's Office	10	27	35	25	4
Parliamentary Budget Officer	10	35	25	11	18
Senate of Canada	9	25	38	25	6
Parliament	7	44	35	9	4

Source: *News Release: Canadian Military Most Trusted Institution* (Toronto: Forum Research, 2014), 3, available at http://www. forumresearch.com/forms/News%20Archives/News%20Releases/64082_Fed_Trust_News_Release_%282014_05_26%29_ Forum_Research.pdf (accessed June 22, 2015).

wrongful convictions. This undermines the legitimacy and function of the legal system, and deepens the power imbalance between rich and poor, and between the state and the public. A good example is the phenomenon known as "SLAPPs" (systematic litigation against public participation) in which wealthy litigants, usually corporations or land developers, launch a meritless suit against an opposing community group with few resources in order to scare the group off or to ruin them financially.

The greatest expense, and thus barrier to access, is the cost of hiring a lawyer, which is why some countries (including Canada) have large numbers of unrepresented litigants. The cost of becoming a lawyer is high and the legal profession has a monopoly on legal services. Not surprisingly, this results in high fees for clients. The poorest people in many economically-developed countries can qualify for legal aid to help pay for at least some types of cases (criminal and family law, for example), and some specific disadvantaged groups may have access to free or inexpensive legal assistance—legal aid clinics for students with housing or landlord issues are an example. On the whole, however, legal aid programs are poorly funded and short-staffed, undermining the quality of legal representation that they provide. Middle-income earners are typically left to fend for themselves, and few can afford more than the simplest legal services without going heavily into debt. Some countries, again including Canada, compound the problem with

rules that require the losing party to pay the legal fees of the winning side ("fee reversal"), which greatly discourages starting a lawsuit.

Several reforms have been attempted to remedy access problems, including the expansion of simplified court systems (like "small claims courts"), which do not use lawyers or sometimes even full-time judges; class-action suits, which allow people with the same issue to combine their cases and resources under one legal team; eliminating fee reversal; adopting "contingency fees," in which the client only pays their lawyer if they win, usually a percentage of any award; free legal clinics or advice, such as through law schools, via telephone, or online; and legal expenses insurance, where people pay premiums to an insurance company, which then pays for a lawyer when needed. None of these strategies are without downsides, the biggest being that by improving access to justice they make the problem of court backlogs and delays even worse. A different approach is to divert legal disputes to alternative dispute resolution (**ADR**) like mediation, arbitration, and tribunals. However, while ADR can be effective, there is no guarantee that the outcomes will deliver what people rightly deserve under law, and it is not always cheaper; moreover, it cannot replace all need for adjudication.

ADR: Alternative dispute resolution, as in an alternative to adjudication; examples include mediation, arbitration, and tribunals.

TABLE 9.2	GLOBAL ACCESS TO JUSTICE			
	Civil Justice: Accessibility and Affordability	Civil Justice: No Unreasonable Delay	Civil Justice: Impartial and Effective ADR	Criminal Justice: Timely and Effective Adjudication
Brazil	0.53	0.30	0.52	0.32
Canada	0.54	0.55	0.80	0.69
China	0.49	0.67	0.39	0.45
France	0.60	0.60	0.69	0.65
Germany	0.63	0.77	0.80	0.62
India	0.29	0.25	0.40	0.36
Iran	0.50	0.63	0.70	0.45
Nigeria	0.47	0.37	0.59	0.34
Russia	0.49	0.54	0.53	0.44
Turkey	0.54	0.41	0.67	0.27
United Kingdom	0.54	0.69	0.77	0.76
United States	0.46	0.56	0.71	0.70

Figures represent scores on a 0-to-1 index, with higher scores constituting a more positive assessment of the judicial system.

Source: *WJP Rule of Law Index*© 2014 (Washington, DC: World Justice Project, 2014), online at http://data.worldjusticeproject.org.

Despite reforms and diversion, the unfortunate reality is that in many countries the legal and judicial systems fail to provide justice in an equitable manner, and for some people, fail to provide it all.

CONCLUSION

Laws are the formal rules that govern how people co-exist. They may be the result of cultural and religious beliefs, social needs, rational analysis, experience, political manoeuvering, or some combination thereof. They may also reflect our hopes for the society we wish to have, and contain measures that we believe are needed to get there. Laws are more than aspirations, however; they are a form of state control backed by force. While many actors enforce the law, courts and judges are arguably the most important because they possess the power to decide when laws have been broken and to assign a penalty or remedy—even when it is the state itself that is the offender. They also have the authority to interpret law. Judicial review is thus central to the rule of law, and courts are inextricably part of the policy process. To perform these tasks, courts require independence from political interference, but they must also exhibit enough impartiality in their behaviour to win and keep the public's trust. How judges are selected has an impact on public confidence in the courts and influences what

types of judges we have, although it can be difficult to reconcile highly democratic selection systems and the lessons of legal realism with the need for judicial impartiality. Finally, although courts are important political institutions that serve many crucial functions, they are vulnerable to non-compliance and are often inaccessible to people, which can lead to injustice. Lack of access to the judiciary can undermine public confidence in the courts, which in turn makes it easier for political leaders to interfere with judges or ignore court decisions. Unfortunately, there is little that courts can do by themselves to improve access problems that are rooted in socio-economic inequalities and government underfunding of the justice system. Similarly, judges are sometimes put in the position of enforcing laws, such as some minority rights, that are not popular. Thus, courts are often caught between doing what is right according to the law and what is good politically for the institution, which only goes to highlight how difficult it is to separate "law" and "politics" in practice.

DISCUSSION QUESTIONS

1. Should judges be permitted to interpret as well as enforce the law? What would the legal and judicial system have to look like if they could not?

2. Do you trust judges more than politicians? Why?

3. In what sense should judges be "accountable" for their behaviour? To whom, and for what?

4. How should we select judges? Should it be left to the public, politicians, legal professionals, other judges, or some combination? Who should have the final say?

5. What would you be willing to do to afford a good lawyer if you were charged with a crime that you did not commit?

WEBSITES

The Canadian Legal Information Institute
www.canlii.org
Provides a free, user-friendly, searchable database of laws and rulings by courts and tribunals in Canada.

Centre for Constitutional Studies
ualawccsprod.srv.ualberta.ca/ccs/
Website of the Centre for Constitutional Studies based at the University of Alberta, providing interdisciplinary, accessible commentary on major legal developments and courts cases in Canada, both in written and webcast form.

JURIST
jurist.org
An open-access site for international legal news and legal research, conducted mostly by volunteers affiliated with the University of Pittsburgh School of Law.

The World Justice Project
worldjusticeproject.org
An independent, multidisciplinary organization working to advance the rule of law around the world; its site links to research on the rule of law and access to justice, including the widely-cited *WJP Rule of Law Index.*

CONSTITUTE
https://www.constituteproject.org
A web-based search engine developed by the Comparative Constitutions Project, which allows users to search and compare the constitutions of nearly every independent country in the world.

FURTHER READINGS

Lawrence Baum, *Judges and Their Audiences.* Princeton: Princeton University Press, 2006.

Stephen B. Burbank and Barry Friedman, eds., *Judicial Independence at the Crossroads: An Interdisciplinary Approach.* Thousand Oaks, California: Sage Publications Inc., 2002.

Charles R. Epp, *The Rights Revolution: Lawyers, Activists, and Supreme Courts in Comparative Perspective.* Chicago: University of Chicago Press, 1998.

Tom Ginsburg, *Judicial Review in New Democracies: Constitutional Courts in Asian Cases.* Cambridge: Cambridge University Press, 2003.

Tom Ginsburg and Tamir Moustafa, eds., *Rule by Law: The Politics of Courts in Authoritarian Regimes.* Cambridge: Cambridge University Press, 2008.

Lori Hausegger, Matthew Hennigar, and Troy Riddell, *Canadian Courts: Law, Politics, and Process,* 2nd ed. Don Mills: Oxford University Press, 2014.

ENDNOTES

1. CBC News, "Doctor-assisted Suicide Supported by Majority of Canadians in New Poll," October 8, 2014, online at http://www.cbc.ca/news/health/doctor-assisted-suicide-supported-by-majority-of-canadians-in-new-poll-1.2792762.

2. An interesting exception involved the Supreme Court of India, where some of its leading judges developed programs to educate the public about their legal rights and even to help fund litigation, thus creating cases that the judges would then hear. See Charles R. Epp, *The Rights Revolution: Lawyers, Activists, and Supreme Courts in Comparative Perspective* (Chicago: University of Chicago Press, 1998), p. 85.

3. *Madger v. Ford*, [2013] 113 OR (3d) 241 (Ont. Div. Ct.).

4. See, for example, Tom Ginsburg, *Judicial Review in New Democracies: Constitutional Courts in Asian Cases* (Cambridge: Cambridge University Press, 2003), and Jodi S. Finkel, *Judicial Reform as Political Insurance: Argentina, Peru, and Mexico in the 1990s* (Notre Dame: University of Notre Dame Press, 2008).

5. Ran Hirschl, *Towards Juristocracy: The Origins and Consequences of the New Constitutionalism* (Cambridge, Mass.: Harvard University Press, 2004).

6. This section draws heavily from Tamir Moustafa and Tom Ginsburg, "Introduction: The Functions of Courts in Authoritarian Politics," in Tom Ginsburg and Tamir Moustafa, eds., *Rule by Law: The Politics of Courts in Authoritarian Regimes* (Cambridge: Cambridge University Press, 2008).

7. This issue is raised by the "battered wife syndrome" defense. This psychological syndrome arises when a severely abused spouse believes that they cannot escape their abuser, and that they or their children will be murdered in the near future (the abuser has typically threatened to do so repeatedly). Canadian courts have accepted this defense in some cases.

8. Ginsburg and Moustafa, eds., *Rule by Law*.

9. See Francois Luchaire, *Le Conseil constitutionnel* (Paris and Aix-en-Provence: Economica, 1980) and Alec Stone, *The Birth of Judicial Politics in France: The Constitutional Council in Comparative Perspective* (Oxford: Oxford University Press, 1992).

10. Jennifer Smith, "The Origins of Judicial Review in Canada," *Canadian Journal of Political Science* 16 (1) (March 1983), pp. 115–34.

11. Robert A. Dahl, "Decision-Making in a Democracy: The Supreme Court as a National Policy-Maker," *Journal of Public Law* 6 (1957), pp. 279–95.

12. Lori Hausegger, Matthew Hennigar, and Troy Riddell, *Canadian Courts: Law, Politics and Process*, 2nd ed. (Don Mills: Oxford University Press, 2014), ch. 6.

13. J. Mark Ramseyer and Eric B. Rasmusen, *Measuring Judicial Independence: The Political Economy of Judging in Japan* (Chicago: University of Chicago Press, 2003).

14. See Lori Hausegger, Troy Riddell and Matthew Hennigar, "Does Patronage Matter? Connecting Influences on Judicial Appointments with Judicial Decision Making," *Canadian Journal of Political Science* 46 (3) (September 2013), pp. 665–69.

15. Bundesrat representatives are selected by their respective *Länder* (state) government, and the Bundesrat selects, by a two-thirds majority vote, half of the 16 judges on the Federal Constitutional Court of Germany. Each U.S. state elects two senators, regardless of the state's population, and the Senate screens candidates for the U.S. Supreme Court and must approve their appointment. Similarly, each of Russia's 83 sub-national governmental units sends two representatives to the Federation Council, which must confirm the president's nominees to the Constitutional Court of Russia.

16. Appointments to the High Court of Australia are also effectively by the prime minister or national attorney-general, although by law he or she must at least consult with the attorneys-general of the state governments. New Zealand's Supreme Court, created in 2003, is appointed by the governor general on the advice of the attorney-general.

17. Joanna Shepherd, *Justice At Risk: An Empirical Analysis of Campaign Contributions and Judicial Decisions* (American Constitution Society for Law and Policy, 2013), online at www.acslaw.org/state-courts/justice-at-risk.

18. Gerald Rosenberg, *The Hollow Hope: Can Courts Bring About Social Change?*, 2nd ed. (Chicago: University of Chicago Press, 2008).

19. Ibid.

20. Gillian Hadfield, "Higher Demand, Lower Supply? A Comparative Assessment of the Legal Landscape for Ordinary Americans," *Fordham Urban Law Journal* 37 (2010), p. 133.

PART

4

POLITICAL PARTICIPATION

© Moodboard/AP Images

10

DEMOCRACIES IN ACTION: ELECTIONS, POLITICAL PARTICIPATION, AND CITIZENS' POWER

Amanda Bittner

© AP Photo/Anja Niedringhaus

Although they are conducted in more and less democratic political systems, elections are considered an essential feature of democratic government in the world today. They are, however, very difficult to conduct in a manner that is both free and fair, a fact understood not only in new democracies such as Afghanistan but in well-established ones such as Canada and the United States.

INTRODUCTION

Elections play a central role in politics and are often one of the first things that come to mind when the topic of politics arises. During elections, party leaders, campaign promises, debates, advertising, and public opinion polls dominate the airwaves for a few weeks, a few months, or even a couple of years, depending on the country and election in question. Elections play a crucial role in linking citizens to politics and for many may even constitute their only avenue of formal political engagement.

While elections are of central importance, there are many factors that affect whether or not they function properly. In many countries, elections are well-established and run fairly smoothly, but citizens living in some countries around the world do not have the same experience. Elections are only in their infancy in Afghanistan, for example, where they have taken place in the contemporary republic since 2004 (before this, democracy was spotty at best, and although there were some elections in the 20th century, a long history of kingships, one-party rule, and religious domination prevailed). It would be difficult to argue that elections are running "smoothly" today, given that they have exhibited numerous election violations, including fraud, intimidation, and violence (including murder). In the 2010 Parliamentary election, voter turnout was almost 50 percent but varied substantially from region to region. In Andar, an eastern district in the Ghazni province, for example, only three people are said to have voted in a population of a little over 100,000

because of threats, violence, and the resulting citizen disengagement from the political process.[1] In such an unstable environment, much will need to be done if elections are to become a functioning and central part of politics in Afghanistan.

Even in well-established democracies, however, it is important to consider such questions as: (a) how elections work; (b) why we have them in the first place; (c) how they affect which parties compete for votes; and (d) how voters decide who to vote for (or even whether to vote at all). As we work through these issues in this chapter, you will see that elections are an integral part of democratic political systems, and shape our everyday experiences as citizens. Furthermore, there is substantial variation within the democratic world, which has important implications for power and representation. In this vein, it is worth thinking about how the "rules of the game" affect how we interact with the political system.

TURNING UP VERSUS STAYING HOME: ACTIONS ON ELECTION DAY

Elections are a key component of representative democracy. Wars have been waged and struggles have taken place to ensure that countries have elections, and yet, even though they are integral to the functioning of democratic politics, many citizens opt not to participate when they have the chance. Consider the 2011 federal election in Canada, for example. Did you vote? It is possible that you were not eligible—maybe you were too young, or maybe you were not a Canadian citizen. But there are plenty of people in Canada who were eligible but did not vote (see Figure 10.1 for a breakdown by region). According to Elections Canada, of the 24,257,592 individuals on the voter's list, only 14,823,408 cast ballots: voter turnout was only about 61 percent, meaning that less than two-thirds of registered voters actually cast a ballot (almost nine-and-a-half million people opted out)! As can be seen in Figure 10.1, turnout was even lower for voters from Newfoundland and Labrador, where less than 53 percent marked their preference in the election. Not very high, is it? Newfoundland and Labrador had the lowest turnout rate of all the provinces, followed by Alberta (56 percent). If that seems low, consider the turnout for people between the ages of 18 and 24: 39 percent.

So, why is voter turnout so low, and does it matter? Some say yes, others say no. Part of the answer may depend on what you think about the next related question: *Do elections matter?* So let's talk about elections and then revisit the question about turnout later in the chapter.

Functions of Elections

Elections provide a primary "access point" through which citizens can participate in a representative democracy, giving them a say over how they are governed. There are many other ways that citizens can try to influence decision-making and the distribution of collective goods, of course: working with community groups, organizing protests and marches, writing letters to representatives and the media, and so on (see Chapter 12). However, while political participation is not limited to elections, elections are fundamental and necessary components of modern **democracy**.

> **Election:** An official process through which citizens communicate their preferences about who will form government. Individual choices are combined to determine the makeup of government.

> **Democracy:** A regime where every eligible adult citizen has the right to select the leader in free and fair elections.

At the root of democracy is the idea that citizens ought to participate in governing and decision-making, and that elections should function in a number of ways to facilitate this. First, elections should provide voters with an opportunity to express a *choice and a voice* over who should represent them and the types of laws and policies that should govern society. Democracies should allow different views to be expressed in the political system, and when citizens vote, they express their views.

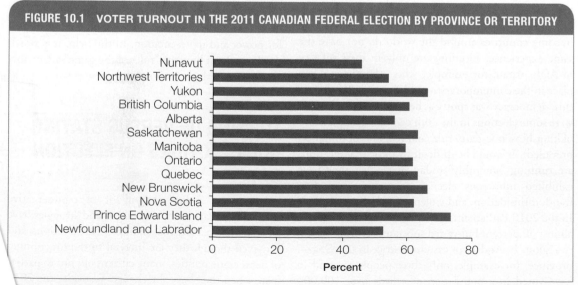

FIGURE 10.1 VOTER TURNOUT IN THE 2011 CANADIAN FEDERAL ELECTION BY PROVINCE OR TERRITORY

Source: Elections Canada, 2011. Official Voting Results, Forty-First General Election 2011, online at http://www.elections.ca/scripts/ovr2011/default.html.

Furthermore, because parties and candidates compete in an election, and because they have different political positions, electoral outcomes help to establish which views we hear more or less of in the daily business of government. The idea is that citizens get a voice on election day, and that the most popular views should receive a greater voice in the legislature. Elections, therefore, should influence how ideas and interests are put together and represented in a given political system. Because we all have different ideas and values, how we express our values on election day should influence what ends up happening in government.

Elections also allow for governments and policies to evolve, to reflect changing values and interests in society. Because voters get a clear opportunity to signal their support for parties and representatives every few years, there is less risk that laws and policies will become stagnant. New ideas, candidates, and parties have an opportunity to compete for the approval of voters, and may—with enough voter support—be transferred into the government itself. Many laws passed today would not have been initiated by previous governments, and new parties and representatives bring new societal values into the legislature, even if these new parties do not actually form government. For example, many have cited the Canadian New Democratic Party in federal politics as a major contributor to the country's publicly funded healthcare system. In France, the rise in popularity of the right-wing National Front Party has been a consistent force in raising anti-immigrant and isolationist perspectives, and is partly responsible for steering discussions and policies in those directions. For better or for worse, then, elections provide a mechanism to translate the voice of the people into the government.

Second, elections allow us to *determine the makeup of the legislature* and help to *determine who governs.* When an election takes place, citizen preferences are translated into legislative seats, giving each party a different level of presence in the legislature, which influences who forms government and the types of laws and policies that emerge. As is made clear in Chapter 7, the strength of government and its ability to pass legislation depends on the structure of institutions but it also is a reflection of the voice of the people. For example, an elected majority government in a parliamentary system has substantially more power to initiate and pass laws, while a minority or coalition government faces different challenges and must

accommodate a wider array of voices in order to make laws. Similarly, in presidential systems, the strength of a party's presence in the legislature, and whether or not the majority party is also the party of the president, has an important influence on the nature of political debate in the legislature and profoundly affects the president's ability to realize his or her political agenda.

Relatedly, elections also influence the number of parties and the types of parties that actually compete in the political system. As will be seen in the following section on electoral rules, elections themselves make it easier for some parties to succeed over others, and this is often dependent on the type of electoral system in place. There is a reason, for example, why the U.S. really only has two major parties competing in elections, while Holland has 11 different parties holding seats in the Dutch House of Representatives, as of the 2012 general election. Political institutions matter, and they influence who competes for your votes.

Third, elections have the essential function of *conferring legitimacy on governments.* By registering their preferences on election day, citizens indicate support for a given candidate, leader, and/or party. This means that until the next election, citizens essentially agree to abide by the policies and laws that are passed by the legislature. The legislature that emerges from a given election is deemed to have the authority to initiate and pass laws. This does not mean, of course, that citizens necessarily approve of all the decisions that a legislature makes. In a well-functioning democracy, however, citizens have an opportunity to register their dissent, call for new laws, and make their voices heard at a subsequent election.

This brings us to the fourth main function of elections: they provide a way of *ensuring the accountability of those who are in government.* Elections provide a stable and frequent mechanism by which voters can judge the activities and performance of those elected to office in the past. If voters are satisfied with the **incumbents**, then they can re-elect them, but if they are not content then they have the opportunity to "throw the rascals out." This process of regular and periodic elections gives legislators a limited level of job security (they need time, after all, to accomplish some of their goals), while providing citizens an opportunity to change their leadership. Elections make legislators accountable to voters: they know that they have to face the people again in a few years, and they know that if they want to keep their jobs, then they need to consider (at least generally) the electorate's wishes. This does not mean that governments only ever make popular decisions, but it does mean that they need to keep voters in mind as they govern.

> **Incumbent:** An individual or party currently holding office.

The Rules of the Game

A recurring theme in this book is the idea that political institutions have an influence on how politics plays out. This effect is most clear in relation to constitutions, which establish the fundamental structures of the political system. When we think about the political executive, legislatures, and the judiciary, the effect of institutions on politics is quite evident. Similarly, as institutions, elections have an important impact on how politics works.

The "rules of the game" are either determined by statute (laws created in legislatures) or enshrined in the country's constitution. Regardless of the origins of the rules themselves, they have a direct and substantial impact on electoral outcomes. Some examples of "rules" that influence elections include restrictions on fundraising and spending, the process for becoming a candidate, and whether there is any mandated debate coverage by the media.

The design of the ballot and the order in which names appear on it are other aspects of electoral rules that have an important impact on election outcomes. Many voters do not possess a high degree of political knowledge about the campaign, the candidates, the parties, or the issues. Studies have shown that the candidate whose name appears first on the ballot has a substantial edge over the other listed candidates. This is not really surprising given what we know about human behaviour. Think, for example, of the yellow pages section of your telephone directory. You may not know much about local companies, but you know you need a plumber to fix your toilet. You look at the list of plumbers, and "A1 Plumbing" appears first on the list. If you have not had any experience with plumbers in the past, or recall any advertisements from other plumbing companies, you are likely to pick up the phone and call the first name that you see. It is for this reason that many countries around the world have legislated requirements surrounding

how names are listed on ballots: often, they require randomization of candidate names so that not all ballots have candidates in the same order.

The prevalence of advertising during electoral contests calls attention to another major influence on election outcomes: campaign finance. Simply put, money talks, primarily because it leads to increased advertising exposure. As a result, many countries place limits on how much spending can take place in an election, who can donate to campaigns (e.g., individuals? corporations?), and the maximum amount of each individual donation. Candidates and parties have an incentive to raise as much money to finance their campaigns as possible so that they can get their messages out to as many people as possible, spending as much as they can on things like advertising and travelling across the country to meet and speak to citizens, and to attend public events. In the two-year lead up to the 2012 American presidential election, for example, Mitt Romney (Republican) raised and spent over $483 million dollars, while Barack Obama (Democrat, incumbent) raised and spent over $738 million.[2] The idea behind more stringent regulations surrounding finance and spending is the desire to ensure that money cannot be used to buy an election. In contrast to American campaign finance rules, France limits both how much can be contributed to campaigns and how much can be spent. The result is that substantially less is spent in an election: in the 2007 presidential election, for example, the two main contenders spent approximately $54 million in total, less than the permitted amount of $49 million each.

In addition to finance regulation, and perhaps most notably, one of the major political institutions that affects electoral outcomes is the **electoral system** in place. Electoral systems establish how individual votes are translated into legislative seats. There is a bit of math involved in electoral systems, as millions of votes in a single country may need to be translated into only a few hundred seats (or fewer).

> **Electoral system:** Electoral rules, often included in the constitution of a country, that outline the manner in which votes in an election are translated into legislative seats.

The British House of Commons, for example, currently has 650 seats to represent a national population of about 65 million. The Netherlands has 150 seats in its House of Representatives, with a national population of about 16 million. In both cases, millions of votes are translated into substantially fewer seats, but each country performs this calculation differently. How votes are tallied and then distributed across parties into legislative seats obviously has an impact on who gets elected but it also has an impact on how parties behave and compete, as well as on how voters understand parties and candidates. What this means is that elections in Britain are really different from elections in the Netherlands, even though both countries are democratic and hold free and fair elections.

Put simply, elections look and work differently in every country around the world. As a result, citizens think about elections in varied ways, and react accordingly to the menu of options put before them come election time. All institutions shape how people interact with the political system and there is no one perfect way of structuring institutional design. As we will see, there are tradeoffs to all institutional choices, including the choice to implement one electoral system over another.

TYPES OF ELECTORAL SYSTEMS

Electoral systems were likened earlier to the rules of the game. Instead of Monopoly or Risk, or baseball or basketball, the game is the election, and the goal for parties and candidates is usually winning legislative seats. In this game, success is generally measured by the number of seats that a party wins. One of the interesting features of the electoral game is that different sets of rules can be used, and these different rules change the nature of the game substantially, much like playing poker when it is the "dealer's choice." In poker, each time new wildcards, betting minimums, betting limits, trade limits, and so on are introduced, the game changes considerably, and the types of decisions and calculations made by the players alter along with these shifts. Similarly, different rule configurations affect how elections play out, and influence the considerations made by parties, candidates, and voters.

Although electoral systems have been categorized in plenty of different ways (for example, David Farrell[3]

has perhaps most comprehensively divided them into five families of systems; a sense of the diversity of systems used can be seen in Figure 10.2), for our purposes we can classify them into three main categories. The first is **proportional systems**, where legislative seats are distributed according to the popular vote share of each of the parties competing in the election. Under this set of rules, a party that receives 30 percent of the ballots cast will get roughly 30 percent of the seats in the legislature. This is in contrast with the second main category, consisting of **non-proportional systems**. With this set of rules, the seats in the legislature are not directly linked to a party's total share of the national vote. Thus, while a party may win 30 percent of the population's votes across the country, depending on how the votes are distributed across constituencies or districts, the end result in the legislature may not be even remotely close to 30 percent—the party might get 30 percent of the seats, but it could also receive 15 percent or 55 percent, for example. This is why these systems are labelled non-proportional: the seats are not necessarily distributed proportionately to the vote share won in the election. The third category (and an increasingly popular one around the world) is **mixed systems**, which combine proportional and non-proportional elements.

Proportional systems: Electoral systems designed to ensure a close match between a party's share of the popular vote and its share of legislative seats. Roughly speaking, if a party gets 30 percent of the vote, then it will receive around 30 percent of the legislative seats.

Non-proportional systems: Electoral systems that do not ensure a close match between a party's share of the popular vote and its share of the legislative seats. The most prominent non-proportional systems are majoritarian and plurality systems (e.g., Single Member Plurality systems).

Mixed systems: Electoral systems that combine elements of different types of electoral systems. This is often done to increase proportionality in non-proportional systems.

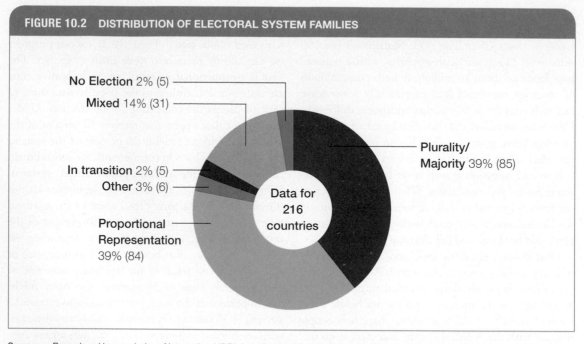

FIGURE 10.2 DISTRIBUTION OF ELECTORAL SYSTEM FAMILIES

No Election 2% (5)

Mixed 14% (31)

In transition 2% (5)

Other 3% (6)

Proportional
Representation
39% (84)

Data for
216
countries

Plurality/
Majority 39% (85)

Source: Reproduced by permission of International IDEA from Electoral System Design © International Institute for Democracy and Electoral Assistance 2015. Online at www.idea.int

Plurality Systems

Non-proportional systems can be divided into two main categories. The first contains Single Member Plurality (SMP) systems, as used in Canada and Britain, where voters mark an "X" on the ballot for their preferred candidate, and the candidate who wins more votes than anybody else in a given **constituency** (also sometimes called a district or riding) wins the seat. Say, for example, that in a riding of London, England there are candidates from three parties: the Labour Party, the Liberal Democratic Party, and the Conservative Party. They each receive 35 percent, 25 percent, and 40 percent of the votes in the riding, respectively – thus, no candidate won a majority (50 percent +1) of the votes. Who wins the seat? The Conservative candidate, who received 40 percent of the votes. Because this candidate won more votes than either of the other two, under the rules of the game, she wins the seat. Horse race metaphors are frequently used to describe this type of electoral system, often called a "first-past-the-post" system because the first person past the "post" or finish line is the winner, even if they win by only one vote and receive fewer votes than the other candidates combined.

Constituency: An electoral district or riding. For the purposes of elections and government, countries are divided into constituencies, or geographic regions, and the population of each constituency elects a representative (or representatives) to the legislature.

The contest just described took place in a single electoral constituency. In the SMP system, individual races take place in all constituencies across the country at the same time, and the winner in each takes a seat in the legislature. Generally speaking, the party with the most seats (again, not necessarily the party with a majority of the seats) will be the party that forms government.

So in plurality systems, the rules of the game are such that candidates aim to win the most votes but need not win a majority of votes. Moreover, the main political parties tend to focus more on winning enough seats to form a government rather than worrying about the total number of votes that they win in the election. This is because it is possible to form the government by winning more seats than all the other parties combined, even if the other parties collectively received more of the national vote share; this is called a false majority. Moreover, cases can arise in which a party can form government even though another party won a majority of the popular vote share, producing a "wrong winner." In a true majority situation, in contrast, the party receives both the most seats and a majority of the national vote share. A number of provincial elections in Canada over the past few decades have produced false majority results, including New Brunswick in 2006, Quebec in 1998, BC in 1996, and Saskatchewan in 1986. Such outcomes demonstrate the important influence that the rules of the game have on the nature of electoral competition—parties and candidates understand that to gain a seat they need to win the most votes within an individual district rather than summing up votes across the country, and may therefore focus their attention on "winnable ridings," sacrificing constituencies where a win would be more difficult. If the total number of votes across the country was more important, then the campaign would play out quite differently.

Majoritarian Systems

The second main type of non-proportional system is called a majoritarian system, which is used in a few countries around the world, including France and Australia. Under this set of rules, a candidate who obtains a majority—that is, at least 50 percent plus 1—of the votes in a constituency wins the seat. If nobody gets a majority in the first round of voting, then a majority can be achieved in one of two ways. The first way involves an additional round of voting, as happens in France: a run-off election is held between the two candidates with the most votes to see which can win a majority.

The second way that majorities are obtained involves a different type of ballot, as happens in Australia. Instead of marking an "X" for your preferred candidate, as you do in an SMP system, you rank-order your preferences. So, if we extend the earlier example of an election in a British district, while you may really want the Labour Candidate to win, you might nonetheless prefer the Conservative candidate over the Lib-Dem candidate. So on your ballot, you would rank the Labour candidate first, the Conservative candidate second, and the Lib-Dem candidate third. When all the votes get tallied, the

last place candidate is knocked out of the running. Next, the second preferences marked on all the ballots for that knocked out candidate are tallied. Some of the voters who had the Lib-Dem candidate (who came in third in the first count) as their first choice may have chosen the Labour candidate second, while others may have listed the Conservative candidate second. These second place preferences are added to the first preference totals for the candidates still in the running. If a candidate wins a majority of the votes with this second round of counting, then the counting is over and the candidate wins the seat. If no candidate has a majority yet in this round, then we eliminate the lowest remaining candidate and continue the process. Under our two majoritarian sets of rules, the process can take some time, so the election results may not be known for a few days. Proponents, however, like such systems because they result in governments formed as a result of seats won by majorities. Some argue that this is fairer than winning by a plurality, as occurs under "first-past-the-post" rules, because more than 50 percent of the voters in a district support the winning candidate.

All the same, a candidate winning a seat with a majority of the votes within a riding is not the same as a party winning a total number of seats in proportion to the national vote share that it receives. Because the "real" contest still takes place at the district level and individuals win their seats based on their success in a given district, it is still possible for the overall results to be disproportionate to the distribution of the popular vote share across the country. Parties may still do much better in some districts over others, and as a result they may not "win" the national vote even as they win the most seats in the legislature. In short, needing a majority to win a seat at the district level does not mean that a party must win the majority of seats in the legislature or a majority share of the national vote in order to form government. Generally speaking, the party with the most seats forms government, as in SMP systems. Because of the potentially disproportionate electoral results in such cases, some countries have opted for even greater levels of "fairness" by adopting proportional electoral systems.

Proportional Systems

In proportional electoral systems, the share of legislative seats won by a party reflects the share of votes it receives in the election. Thus, if a party wins 30 percent of the popular vote, then it obtains about 30 percent of the seats. The end result of the translation of votes to seats is very different under proportional rules in comparison to majoritarian, or in particular plurality, systems. For example, if we compare the outcome of the 2011 Canadian federal election under different types of systems, the impact of the electoral system on the distribution of seats becomes fairly evident. In this case, the Conservative Party only won 40 percent of the national vote, and did substantially better in some ridings than others, but was able to form a majority government as a result of the electoral rules of the SMP system. The Conservative Party had a plurality—that is, it got *the most* votes—in 54 percent of the constituencies across the country. Because of the way votes are translated into seats, this meant that the party won 166 of 308 seats, or 54 percent of the seats in the legislature, even though it only received 40 percent of the national vote. Similarly, the NDP benefited from the rules of the game, winning 33 percent of the seats with 30 percent of the national vote share. The other parties did not fare so well: the Liberals won 11 percent of the seats with almost 19 percent of the popular vote, the Bloc Québécois won six percent of the popular vote share and only four seats (1.2 percent), while the Green Party won almost four percent of the vote share but received just one seat (0.3 percent of the legislative seats). While the results for none of the opposition parties was as skewed as those for the Conservative Party, the results indicate that it is not only the governing party that can benefit or lose from the way that votes are translated into seats.

In contrast, under a proportional system, the 40 percent of the national vote received by the Conservatives would have translated into around 40 percent—or 123—of the seats in the House, leading to either a minority or coalition government as they would not command a majority of seats. This would have significantly altered the political picture in Canada as, you will recall from the discussion in Chapter 7, a majority government is very different from either a minority or coalition government. If you do the math based on the vote share for the other parties provided in the previous paragraph, you will see that their seat share in the legislature would have changed as well. For our purposes here, this helps to underscore that the way politics works in a country is very much dependent on what type of electoral system that is in place.

It is important to note, however, that while it is fun to imagine what the distribution of seats might look like under a variety of electoral systems, in actuality this is not a foolproof method of understanding the impact of changing systems. Because political actors behave according to the rules of the game, parties and candidates are likely to wage distinct types of campaigns in plurality versus proportional systems: in a proportional system, parties aim to achieve a higher national vote share, and therefore rather than focusing on small district contests, they pitch issues and policies at a national level. This is in contrast to plurality systems, where the local contest is a bigger focus such that more money and resources are invested in local campaigns. The outcome of an election is therefore likely to be quite dissimilar in the two systems, and not simply because we are doing the math differently. Nonetheless, the benefit of doing the calculation outlined above in the case of the Conservative Party in 2011 is that it helps to contrast the two types of systems more clearly.

It also important to note that there are various types of proportional systems found around the world. One type is a "pure" Proportional Representation (PR) List system in which legislative seats are distributed based on the party's popular vote share in the election. In this system, districts are large, with many representatives elected from each (we call these multi-member districts). Some places use the entire country as a single district, like Israel and Holland, while others divide the country into regions, with numerous legislative seats assigned to each. This type of electoral system puts parties at the forefront of politics—citizens vote for parties on their ballots rather than marking an "X" next to a candidate's name.

During an election in a PR List system, parties publish a list of their candidates for each district. Generally, voters mark an "X" on their ballot for their preferred party, and individual candidates are elected based on where they are ordered on the party's list. For example, in a 100-seat legislature, where there is only one constituency to cover the whole country, if a party wins 31 percent of the national vote, the first 31 people on the party's candidate list are awarded a seat in the legislature. A party's list is published prior to the election and usually the most important members of the party are at the top of the list (for example, the individual who would become prime minister is ranked first). Conversely, those listed last are unlikely to receive a seat in the legislature. The party would have to win nearly all of the votes in the country for that to happen!

A second type of proportional system is called Single Transferable Vote (STV), which is used in Ireland and in elections for the Australian Senate. There are three key components of the STV system: **district magnitude,** ballot structure, and electoral formula. First, electoral districts are multi-member, meaning that multiple candidates are elected within each district. District magnitude is a term that reflects the number of candidates elected from each district: for example, if three representatives can win in a given district, then its district magnitude is three. In SMP systems, in contrast, all district magnitudes are one since only one member is elected from each. The multi-member districts lead this type of system to be proportional, and the greater the number of representatives elected from each riding, the more proportional it is. So the electoral results from a riding with a district magnitude of three are not as proportional as one with a district magnitude of 11, and it is generally believed that a district magnitude of at least five is necessary for the results of an election to be proportional.

> **District magnitude:** Reflects the number of legislative seats available in an electoral district. In a Single Member Plurality system, the district magnitude is one; in Single Transferable Vote systems, the district magnitude is always greater than one. Generally speaking, the higher the district magnitude, the more proportional the electoral result.

The second main component of the STV system is ballot structure: voters rank-order their preferences on the ballot rather than simply marking an "X". Much like some majoritarian systems, then, STV makes use of more than voters' first preferences when determining which candidates win a seat. Determining how many votes each candidate needs to win is based on the electoral formula, the third component, and it is probably easiest to understand how this (somewhat complicated) system works by walking through a mock election in a single Irish district.

Let's imagine that an election is taking place in a district with a magnitude of three. In this mock election, six candidates are competing for those three legislative seats, and those six candidates are competing for a portion of the 100 voters who turn out on election day. The portion of votes that a candidate needs to win is based on an electoral formula called the "Droop Quota," which is calculated as follows:

$$\text{votes needed to win} = \left(\frac{\text{valid votes cast}}{\text{seats to fill} + 1} \right) + 1$$

In this mock riding of three seats and 100 votes, the quota breaks down as follows:

$$\text{Droop Quota} = \frac{100}{(3) + 1} + 1$$

Thus, to win a seat, a candidate needs to win 26 out of 100 votes (or 26 percent).

In this mock election, six candidates are competing for votes: Siobhan O'Leary (Fianna Fail), Seamus O'Connor (Fianna Fail), Michael Browne (Labour), Aisling Whelan (Labour), Mary Callaghan (Fine Gael), and Sean Flanagan (Fine Gael). Once the polls have closed, the ballots are counted. First preferences (recall, it is a rank-ordered ballot) are counted first. For the six candidates, first preferences were as follows:

Siobhan O'Leary (Fianna Fail) – 39 votes
Seamus O'Connor (Fianna Fail) – 26 votes
Michael Browne (Labour) – 13 votes
Aisling Whelan (Labour) – 9 votes
Mary Callaghan (Fine Gael) – 7 votes
Sean Flanagan (Fine Gael) – 6 votes

Two Fianna Fail candidates (Siobhan O'Leary and Seamus O'Connor) meet the quota of 26, obtaining 39 and 26 votes, respectively. This means that they automatically get a seat in the legislature. But there is still one seat to be filled, and since none of the other candidates has enough votes to get there, second preferences are tallied and transferred. In order to do this, the 13 "surplus" votes for Siobhan O'Leary are transferred; that is, the second preferences on these ballots are tallied and transferred to the other candidates during the second round of counting.

When second preferences are tallied, four of O'Leary's second preference votes go to Michael Browne (Labour), and nine votes go to Mary Callaghan (Fine Gael).

The tally for the remaining candidates is thus as follows:

Michael Browne (Labour) – 17 votes
Mary Callaghan (Fine Gael) – 16 votes
Aisling Whelan (Labour) – 9 votes
Sean Flanagan (Fine Gael) – 6 votes

After the second round of counting, none of the remaining candidates has reached the quota of 26 and therefore a third round of counting is necessary. Since there are no "surplus" votes at this time, the candidate with the fewest votes is eliminated and second preferences from his/her ballot are counted and transferred to the remaining candidates. In this case, Aisling Whelan (Labour) has received nine votes and Sean Flanagan (Fine Gael) has received six. Normally we would drop the candidate with the lowest number of votes (Flanagan), but since six second preference votes will not be sufficient to bring either Browne or Callaghan up to the required quota of 26, Whelan is also dropped, with second preferences on their ballots being tallied in a third round of counting.

In this third round, two of Flanagan's second preferences go to Callaghan and four go to Browne, bringing those two candidates to 18 and 21 votes, respectively. The second preferences on Whelan's nine ballots go to both remaining candidates: one to Browne, bringing him to 22, and eight to Callaghan, bringing her to 26, thereby bringing her to the quota. Mary Callaghan (Fine Gael) is thereby elected. All three seats in this district have now been filled, and the counting ends. Had a seat not been filled after the third round, the next candidate with the lowest number of votes would have been eliminated, and the second, third, and fourth (and so on) preferences from those ballots would have been tallied until another winner was declared.

The STV system is seen by many to be a bit confusing, which might explain why so few countries use it. Indeed, in a recent effort at electoral reform in British Columbia, voters in a referendum decided not to adopt the STV system and chose instead to keep the existing SMP electoral system.

Mixed Systems

Some countries, like New Zealand and Germany, have opted for mixed systems that combine parts of proportional and non-proportional approaches. Germany, for example, uses a Mixed Member Proportional (MMP) system. Voters are given two votes on the ballot: a local constituency vote, with winners determined by a first-past-the-post or plurality system, and a party vote, calculated in a proportional manner. Seats in the legislature are divided into two categories: local riding seats and "top-up" seats. Voters are therefore able to elect a local representative in their district, while the party vote is used to determine the total number of seats that a party will win in the legislature, including both local seats and top-up seats.

On election day, all local district votes are tallied and whoever wins the most votes (plurality) in the riding wins a seat in the legislature. Next, the party votes are counted. If there is a gap between a party's national vote share and how many seats it won locally, then the gap is filled from the party's list of candidates (as in the PR List system described earlier: top-up seats are allocated based on candidates' positions on the party list). As an example, let's look at a hypothetical 100-seat legislature. In the election, one party won 30 percent of the party votes but only won a plurality in 20 ridings, receiving 20 seats in the first count. This party would get a "top-up" of 10 more seats in the legislature (that is, the first 10 candidates on the party's list would win seats), so that the overall number of seats won by the party is proportional to its share of the national vote.

While MMP combines elements of SMP and "pure" PR, a "mixed" system is really just that: a mix. Just about any combination of systems is possible: for example, both Germany and Hungary have used a Mixed Member Majoritarian system in the past (note, not Mixed Member *Plurality*), which combined elements of majoritarian single member districts with a proportional list system. Often countries mix elements according to their particular needs. New Zealand, for example, adopted the MMP system in time for its 1996 General Election after years of using SMP, because it was felt that "false majorities" were a significant problem in the legislature, and a more "fair" system was desired. MMP allowed for more proportional outcomes while still maintaining close ties to a local representative.

PHOTO ESSAY

Diversity in the Legislature.

© AP Photo/Susan Walsh

DESCRIPTIVE VERSUS SUBSTANTIVE REPRESENTATION

Scholars often differentiate between "descriptive" and "substantive" representation. The idea behind descriptive representation is that those who represent us should "look like" us (whether physically or in terms of religion, sexual orientation, class, gender, and so on), and a number of reasons have been put forward to justify this expectation. First, scholars suggest that group members are more likely to pursue the interests of that group than are other representatives.[4] Second, descriptive representation is seen to create the belief among various groups in society that they have an "ability to rule," since they see people with whom they share important characteristics in the legislature. Third, and relatedly, descriptive representation is said to increase a group's political legitimacy, especially in the context of past discrimination.[5] When a group is included in the legislature, there is

a sense that the group has the right to be there and ought to have a voice. Having members of marginalized groups in the legislature is important, therefore, on many levels. Taken to its extreme, the theory of descriptive representation suggests that if the population of a country is 51 percent women (as in the United States), for example, then the legislature should have the same proportion of women. The U.S. census indicates that the current population of the United States is 13 percent Black or African American, 16 percent Latino, and 4.9 percent Asian.[6] As of July 2014, 82 women sat in the House of Representatives, alongside 42 African Americans, 33 Hispanic or Latinos, and 10 Asian American or Pacific Islanders.[7] This means that the House consists of 19 percent women, 10 percent African American, 7 percent Latino, and two percent Asian members. These figures suggest that the U.S. House is not meeting the expectations of "descriptive representation" as all of the above groups are underrepresented in that chamber.

Some people see such underrepresentation of groups as a problem, while others suggest that, in fact, descriptive representation does not guarantee that groups will be represented in policy-making. Margaret Thatcher is often pointed to as an example of a female leader who did not really stand up for women or advance feminist policies. Rather than focusing on descriptive representation, some argue, we need to focus on substantive representation, which takes place when representatives actively "stand for" various groups. There is no reason to expect a woman to always support policies that are "pro-woman" (indeed, there is likely to be debate over what exactly it means to be "pro-woman") and it is conceivable that a white man may support policies aimed to benefit African American men and women. This has led some political theorists to articulate criteria for evaluating descriptive representatives, suggesting that descriptive representation on its own is not a sufficient condition for the effective substantive representation of groups. Whether or not descriptive representatives have "mutual relations" with the groups they represent is one possible criterion for evaluating the effectiveness of representation.[8] From this point of view, whether or not a representative recognizes and is recognized by a group and whether they have shared goals are essential to determining how well group interests will be represented through a particular representative.

Representation is a contested concept (indeed, some do not believe in group representation at all and instead propose that individual interests should be the core of representation), and while both proponents of descriptive and substantive representation believe that representation of group interests is important, they have different visions of how this can and should take place.

SYSTEM TRADE-OFFS

There are advantages and disadvantages to all political institutions, including electoral systems. When it comes to proportional systems, a significant benefit cited by proponents is the idea of proportionality itself: the fact that the distribution of legislative seats more closely reflects the popular vote is held to reflect the "will of the people" better. As well, proportional systems tend to lead to increased inclusion of smaller parties and minority voices in the legislature, because even a party that receives five percent of the popular vote will receive around five percent of legislative seats. In contrast, in less proportional systems, receiving five percent of the popular vote usually does not translate into any seats. Thus, there are fewer of what are called "wasted votes" in proportional systems—votes that do not help to elect a candidate. The issue of wasted votes is seen to be particularly important for voters who support smaller, less popular parties, because if they vote for their preferred candidate in a non-proportional system, then their vote has little chance of leading to representation in the legislature. In PR systems, proponents argue, all votes have a more direct impact on the makeup of the legislature. PR systems also tend to promote coalition and minority governments because the electoral formula results in fewer false majorities and more parties are likely to be present in the legislature. You will recall that minority and coalition governments require more cooperation between parties in order to govern, which many argue is beneficial as such discussion and the policies that are thereby produced are likely to encompass more voices and perspectives.

Proportional systems also generally lead to more representation of women and other traditionally marginalized groups (see Figure 10.3). If we compare the presence of women in majoritarian systems with women in PR systems around the word, it is clear that PR systems are more conducive to the election of women legislators. Furthermore, if we look at the experiences of New Zealand both before and after MMP was adopted, we can see that the increased proportionality has benefited women's presence, and that under the new system women tend to be elected in greater numbers from the party list than they are in the SMP districts. (See the Photo Essay for more about the advantages of diverse representation.)

The main reason why women (and minority groups) tend to benefit from PR is linked to societal pressure on political parties. Think about the party lists we talked about earlier. If the top candidates of a party's list are the ones who may ultimately win a seat, then parties really have to think about the order in which they place their candidates. If, for example, the first 30 people are all 60-year-old, rich, white men, and the last 15 are black women, then the party is going to look pretty bad, and voters may choose to support a party with a more carefully balanced list. This means that parties that integrate candidates into their lists in a more egalitarian manner may be rewarded at the polls, and thus have an electoral interest in being seen to respond to that incentive. Some parties "zipper" candidates into the list, alternating between women and men, even at the top of the list, as well as integrating people of different ethnic, racial, and religious backgrounds. Consequently, members of those groups are more likely to be elected in proportional systems.

Of course, no system is perfect, and there are problems that can arise with proportional systems as well (see Table 10.1). For example, if you

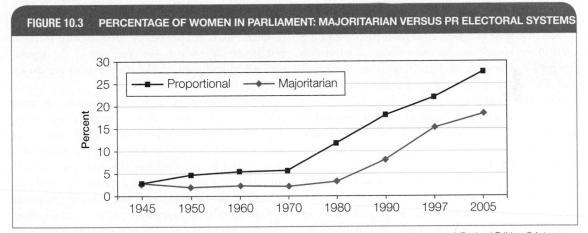

FIGURE 10.3   PERCENTAGE OF WOMEN IN PARLIAMENT: MAJORITARIAN VERSUS PR ELECTORAL SYSTEMS

Source: Reproduced by permission of International IDEA from Women in Parliament: Beyond Numbers. A Revised Edition © International Institute for Democracy and Electoral Assistance 2005. Online at www.idea.int

TABLE 10.1   PROS AND CONS OF PROPORTIONAL SYSTEMS

Pros
Fairer, no "false majorities" or "wrong winners"
Increased voice for smaller and minority parties
Tendency toward coalition and minority governments
Increased representation for women and other traditionally marginalized groups
Fewer "wasted votes"

Cons
More difficult to understand
Less connection to local representatives
Tendency toward coalition and minority governments; harder to "get things done"
Gives too much power to small parties that represent narrow, particular interests
More difficult to hold government to account when a coalition

have fewer ridings, or even a single riding for the entire country, then it diminishes the close ties that can be formed with an individual representative based in your local community. Some suggest that the larger the geographical area that an individual has to represent, the less likely people are to feel a connection to that individual, especially if the representative is from a place far from where you live. Critics also point to the tendency of PR systems to produce minority and coalition governments, which—because the constitutive parties must negotiate with one another more—have a harder time "getting things done" than majority governments, which can all but ignore other parties. Italy is frequently identified as an example of a PR system gone bad: with 10 or more parties winning seats in the lower house in most elections, governing has proven to be difficult. Finally, some are concerned that PR systems give small parties too much power, as they may hold the handful of seats that a major party needs to secure the political support required to govern. Indeed, in giving a voice to fringe and radical parties, the system might prompt greater societal and political fragmentation within the country.

Of course, so much of what is seen to be positive or negative depends on your personal beliefs about what you expect representatives to do and how you would like the legislature to work, and so when we compare proportional and plurality systems, often the positives of one are seen as the negatives of the other, and vice versa. Thus, proponents of plurality systems argue that these are familiar and simple to understand, that you can easily identify your local representative, who comes from the same part of the country as you do, and that the systems tends to produce majority governments, meaning that it is easier to "get things done."

Critics of plurality systems note that SMP distorts the vote too much and may result in a false majority (when a party gains a majority of the seats in the legislature without a majority of the popular vote). Furthermore, the system can produce "wrong winners" when a party forms government even though another party had more of the national popular vote share (as occurred in New Zealand in 1978 and 1981). Wasted votes are also seen to be a problem, as is the tendency for minority interests and smaller parties to get shut out of the legislature. (Pros and cons of plurality systems are shown in Table 10.2.)

Which system you prefer depends on your priorities and values: if you value cooperation, negotiation, and having more voices heard in the legislature, then you might prefer a proportional system. If a local candidate is really important to you, or if you prefer decisive governments with the power to "get things done," then you might prefer a plurality system. Neither is perfect, and deciding which system a country should employ is not easy. Given that so much is at stake in deciding on the rules of the game, it comes as no surprise that it is generally quite difficult to change from one system to another.

TABLE 10.2	PROS AND CONS OF PLURALITY SYSTEMS
Pros	
Familiar and simple to understand	
Easy to identify local representatives	
More majority governments, and thus more political stability	
Governments are able to "get things done"	
Easier to hold government to account at the next election	
Cons	
Less fair, more "false majorities" and "wrong winners"	
More limited voice for smaller and minority parties	
Less representation of women and other traditionally marginalized groups	
More "wasted votes"	

THINK AND DISCUSS

Over the years, many efforts have been made in Canada to reform the electoral system.
Should Canada change from SMP to something else? What would that "something else" look like?
What trade-offs would have to be made in any choice that you would recommend?

BOX 10.1

RECENT EFFORTS TO MOVE TOWARD PROPORTIONAL REPRESENTATION IN CANADA

In Canada, a number of efforts to move away from the country's first-past-the-post system have taken place in recent years, none of which has succeeded:

- British Columbia 2004-2005 (Citizens' Assembly recommended STV, did not pass in referendum in 2005, another referendum in May of 2009, did not pass)
- Prince Edward Island 2005 (Commission recommended MMP, did not pass in referendum in 2005)
- New Brunswick 2005 (Commission recommended MMP, but the new government elected in 2007 opted not to conduct the referendum originally scheduled for 2008)
- Quebec 2006 (Commission recommended MMP, no action taken)
- Ontario 2007 (Citizens' Assembly recommended MMP, did not pass in referendum in 2007)

For example, there have been a few attempts in Canada to change the electoral system, largely at the provincial level, but plurality systems are still used at provincial and federal levels. In every case of reform in Canada over the last 20 years (see Box 10.1), efforts were made to move to a more proportional system, often because of the problems with SMP outlined above. These reform efforts failed for a number of reasons, depending on the province. While proponents of change were enthusiastic about the benefits of greater proportionality, some people were confused by the proposed changes and felt that the existing system was easier to understand, while others were concerned about the potential loss of a local representative or did not like the idea of more coalition and minority governments.

There are tradeoffs with every type of electoral system, and the characteristics of each can be seen as positive or negative, depending on your preferences and priorities. Nonetheless, the rules of the game are important because they have an impact on how politics actually operates. They affect how parties compete, how governments organize and operate, and how citizens perceive the legitimacy of the elections themselves.

Citizens in the System

The democratic system that developed around the 5th century in Athens was one of the world's first known democracies, and is seen in some respects to be the gold standard of democracy: citizens were engaged directly in the activities of governing, and participated directly in making collective decisions, rather than electing officials to make those decisions on their behalf. At the time, the population of "citizens" in Athens was not very large—fewer than 50,000 because women, slaves, and foreigners were not eligible to vote—and therefore this system was more feasible than it is today, certainly at the national or regional level. Contemporary democracies have much larger populations and territories, and citizens are generally quite busy doing other things, and therefore being involved in the day-to-day operations of government is not very practical. This is why we have **representative democracy**, wherein citizens delegate power and authority to selected representatives to make public decisions on their behalf: we choose them, and they conduct the business of government for us.

> **Representative democracy:** A system of government in which voters elect candidates to represent them and make collective decisions on their behalf.

Elections therefore allow us to choose representatives and governments. Indeed, this is the first real function of elections mentioned earlier in this chapter. Recall, we established that elections (a) offer citizens a choice and a voice, (b) help to determine the makeup of the legislature, (c) confer legitimacy upon governments, and (d) provide voters with an accountability mechanism. All of these functions combined suggest that elections are quite important, especially if you believe that the role of legislators as something mandated by the people is desirable and important.

In addition to these vital functions, it is during elections that we often learn the most about politics, issues and policies, candidates, parties, and party leaders. Generally, citizens pay very little attention to what is going on around them when it comes to politics. This is not really surprising: we all have other things to think about. Our jobs, families, schoolwork, hobbies, and so on all take up a lot of our time, leaving little opportunity (or brain power!) to think about complex issues such as how to regulate the financial industry or how much money should be spent on healthcare or the military.

During elections, however, politics seems to come alive. Parties and candidates are knocking on doors, talking about what governments have been doing, what they would do if elected into office, trying to get regular citizens interested in politics. They want volunteers and donations, and they want you to come to their rallies and events. It is during elections that we tend to talk with others around us about politics—friends, family, co-workers, acquaintances—and that we find out what others think, engage in discussions about policies and issues, and maybe even do a little research and thinking on our own by reading blogs, newspaper articles, and having discussions with others about our findings on Facebook or Twitter. This flurry of activity tends to die down between elections, but some citizens will hold onto some of the enthusiasm that was generated during the campaign.

So if Aristotle was right and we are political animals (recall the discussion in Chapter 2), and participating in politics allows us to reach our better selves, then elections can really help this process along as we become more informed, engaged, and involved. This is not to say that elections have the same effect on all of us, or that everybody will be focused on the campaign, but elections do tend to increase our interest in and awareness of politics, overall.

Understanding Voters

In politics, how voters think is a topic that seems to intrigue many of us more than anything else. Consider all the newspaper coverage of polling during elections, for example. Tracking the "horse race" between party leaders, monitoring the "undecided" vote over the course of a campaign, and trying to predict what will happen on election day are all major features of news stories during elections around the world, and give some idea about the importance of the election and, in particular, voter decision-making.

In fact, voting is not even just about the choice between, for example, Barack Obama and Mitt Romney. There is a lot more involved. Part of the decision-making process involves whether or not to even show up on election day and cast a ballot. So what influences our decisions? What convinces us to turn up to vote (or stay home)? And why do we choose one candidate or party over another?

There are many factors that we can point to that play a role in how we make such decisions. Think about a past election. What influenced your vote (if you were eligible to vote), or the votes of your family and friends? Maybe a particular conversation convinced you to vote a certain way. Or maybe you grew up in a household that always votes for a particular party and you took that on as well. Or maybe you just had a gut feeling about a particular candidate or party. There are many possible explanations for why we vote the way we do, and researchers have spent years trying to identify and unpack them.

Probably the best way to understand voters' decisions comes from some famous research conducted in the United States. *The American Voter*[9] analyzed voters' thinking during three presidential elections (1948, 1952, and 1956), drawing on face-to-face interviews with American voters. This work has had a lasting legacy, since much of our understanding of voter attitudes and behaviour today is based on its findings. Indeed, many studies have confirmed that the bulk of its conclusions remain accurate, especially its **funnel of causality** model of voter behaviour (see Figure 10.4).

> **Funnel of causality:** A model to explain the factors influencing vote choice and public opinion, in which long- and short-term factors are situated in relation to their influence on one another as well as the vote.

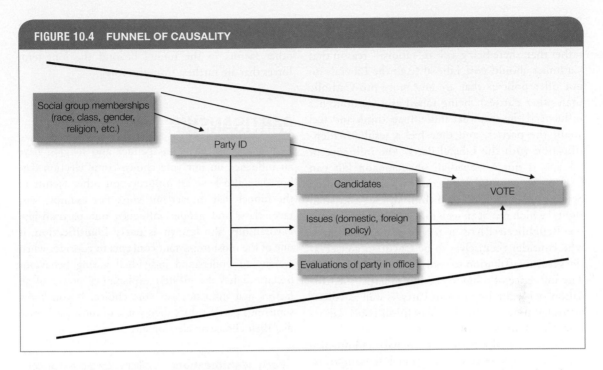

FIGURE 10.4   FUNNEL OF CAUSALITY

As we move from the mouth to the stem of the funnel we are moving through time, closer and closer to the actual vote itself. Factors that influence the vote are grouped into categories based on how far or close they are to a person's decision on voting day. Long-term forces (like religion) are found furthest away from the vote at the mouth of the funnel, while short-term forces (like our impressions of candidates) are found closer to the stem. The main principle behind placement in the funnel is that longer-term forces influence our perceptions of both shorter-term forces and the vote itself, helping us to arrive at a decision. Much of the impact of these various forces is subconscious as we do not even realize that they are influencing our choices. Recent (controversial) studies have even pointed to the role of genetics in affecting our electoral decisions, suggesting a likelihood that participation through voting may in part be something that we inherit.[10] If these studies are right, then this would be the ultimate in long-term (and subconscious) forces!

Long-Term Forces

When considering long-term forces, we can think of a category loosely called the "unchangeables." Generally speaking, most individuals' demographic characteristics do not change throughout their lives, and these types of characteristics, such as race, religion, ethnicity, class, and gender, are found at the mouth of the funnel. The impact of these variables can be traced back to what we call **political socialization** (as explored in Chapter 1). We grow up surrounded by friends and family and are raised certain ways, going to certain churches or mosques, for example, and as a result we are socialized into different communities or groups with their attendant values and attitudes.

Political socialization: A process of inheriting and disseminating norms and customs in society. This begins in childhood and continues throughout our lives as we are influenced by family, friends, the organizations we belong to, and so on.

The socialization process helps to shape who we are, including how we feel about various political issues, parties, candidates, and so on. We can point to the impact of religion, for example, in the Canadian context. It has long been understood that Catholics and Protestants (Canada's two largest religious denominations) vote differently: Catholics tend to support the Liberal Party, while the Protestant vote is more spread out across parties.

What is not really understood is why.[11] We suspect that what is happening here reflects "group think" rather than there being a clear "rational" reason that Catholics should vote Liberal (e.g., the Liberals do not offer policies that are any more pro-Catholic than other parties). Being raised as a Catholic has influenced the way that individuals think and feel about the parties, and they feel a resultant identification with the Liberal Party. The influence of religion is not a Canadian phenomenon but can be found in a number of countries. In the United States, for example, we can think of the "Christian right," which has been seen to control and influence the Republican Party in recent years: individuals who consider themselves to be Christian conservatives feel an affiliation toward the Republican Party. The influence of religion extends to both "identification" with the Republican Party as well as voters' attitudes about a number of political issues (abortion, for example).

Gender has also been shown to have an influence on the way people vote, with women tending to be more left-leaning on issue attitudes and party preferences. A number of scholars have made endeavours to understand the impact of this "gender gap" and a variety of explanations have surfaced, including gendered patterns of employment in the workforce, women's reliance on the welfare state, the role of feminism as a mobilizer of women, differences in men's and women's values, and the existence of a women's political culture.[12] All of these explanations provide insight into the gender gap, although none taken individually can explain everything. In the past it was found that women tended to be more conservative than men[13] but this seems to have reversed in the 1980s, when women were seen to be more likely to lean to the left of the political spectrum in their opinions and vote choice. This pattern has continued and has also led to increased support for female candidates: for example, 1992 is often labelled the "year of the woman" in the United States[14] because a record number of women were elected to Congress that year.

Because individuals belong to more than one social demographic group (called "cross-cutting memberships"), predicting how a person will vote based solely on these long-term forces is tricky and certainly not foolproof. Different memberships (e.g., religion, gender, age, etc.) can pull individuals in more than one direction. This is why it is important to consider other factors in the funnel beyond the long-term forces that are furthest from the vote.

PARTISANSHIP

Long-term forces such as gender and religion have an influence on our vote choice come election day, but they also have an influence on other factors in the funnel that impact our vote. For example, our race, class, and gender influence our partisanship. Partisanship, also known as **party identification**, is one of the most important concepts to consider when seeking to understand individual voting behaviour because it has the greatest explanatory power of all factors that influence our vote choice. If you know someone's partisanship, then you can most easily predict their choice on election day.

> **Party identification:** An affinity toward a political party. Such partisanship is not simply about who an individual votes for but which party the individual identifies with. Voters can identify with one party and still vote for another.

Party identification boils down to a feeling of affiliation with a political party. First introduced in electoral studies in the 1960s in the United States, the idea behind party identification is that it has a major (and often subconscious) influence on our vote choice.[15] We often vote on the basis of partisanship, *even if we are not familiar with the party's candidates or policies.* That is, the impact of partisanship on our vote choice happens automatically. We talked earlier about the fact that most voters have jobs, hobbies, families, friends, and things to do, and that, as a result, most citizens do not spend much time discussing, studying, or thinking about politics. Thus, people generally do not have a lot of awareness of issues, candidates, and parties, and this has been the case for quite some time: lack of knowledge is not a new phenomenon.[16] Party identification, then, is one way that voters can overcome their lack of information and make a decision on election day. While the concept of partisanship originated in the United States, it has been found to have a profound influence on voters' decision-making processes around the world. For example, recent comparative research on voting in Africa (see Table 10.3, below) suggests that partisanship is an important predictor of vote choice, and that large portions of the population in many countries identify closely with political parties. The African experience with contemporary electoral democracy is a relatively recent phenomenon, and one might expect partisan ties to be less strong and less influential.

Thus, partisanship is an important force in elections, and this process of deciding with the help of party identification is often subconscious: we do not even know that we are making decisions this way, and if somebody were to ask us, "what made you vote for party x?" we might have a "real" answer for them based on something else (we might point to issues, the candidate's competence, or some other factor that we think was important to us). Studies have shown that more often than not these so called "other" factors lead back to partisanship (take another look at the funnel of causality to see the influence partisanship itself has on these other factors). Furthermore, research in psychology indicates that we may not really be aware of the origins of our choices or attitudes,[17] and that, when prompted, we attribute factors to our decisions that

may not have been at play in reality. Put simply, as individuals we are not very good at knowing why we act or think the way that we do.

Partisanship is like a filter through which we perceive new information. Being a partisan is akin to being a sports fan. You have your team and you love them, even if they have a really terrible season. You perceive every penalty, goal, and referee's call through the lens of being a fan. The same goes for partisanship. You tend to prefer the candidates of your party and you side with them on the issues of the day. While you may sometimes vote for someone else, you still generally "feel" like a partisan of your party, and you absorb new campaign information through the lens of your party identification.

Campaign Effects

That partisanship and other long-term forces have an important effect on election results is not to say that campaigns do not matter. They do. There is a reason why parties and candidates spend so much money on election campaigns.

While long-term forces (including both social group membership and party identification) have a large and discernible impact on voters' decisions,

TABLE 10.3 PARTY IDENTIFICATION IN AFRICA		
	Percent reporting feeling close to a political party	Percent reporting feeling close to the ruling party
10 African countries	55.9	70.7
Botswana	75.3	60.5
Lesotho	57.4	66.3
Malawi	82.2	56.8
Mali	57.7	72.4
Namibia	71.1	80.1
Nigeria	36.8	64.3
South Africa	44.7	75.5
Tanzania	79.2	78.7
Zambia	36.8	70.6
Zimbabwe	45.3	70.7

Source: Michelle Kuenzi and Gina M.S. Lambright, *Party Politics* (17, 6), pp. 767–799, copyright © 2011 by SAGE. Reprinted by Permission of SAGE.

these factors do not do a very good job of accounting for short-term changes in elections. Think about it this way: if partisanship is fairly stable and does not change much, and if our social group identity does not really shift either (for example, people generally do not convert from one religion to another), then our vote choice should remain fairly stable over time. This would make election results quite predictable and similar over time. In reality, however, we sometimes see dramatic changes from one election to the next, and parties and candidates that have been in office (the incumbents) are often defeated and replaced by new ones. So, long-term forces cannot possibly represent all factors affecting our vote decisions. Something else has to be at play. This "something else" boils down to "short-term" forces, which include the types of topics that get talked about the most during election campaigns: candidates, party leaders, issues, the economy, and so on.

These short-term forces are the closest to the stem of the funnel, meaning that they are the most proximate to our decisions on election day. These factors are much more changeable, and how we think about them tends to fluctuate with the times (and the menu of options put before us in a given campaign). Party leaders, for example, play an important role in determining which party we will vote for, and new elections will often have new leaders for us to consider. Our perceptions of party leaders, then, can be considered a short-term force. As the funnel model suggests, these perceptions both (a) have an impact on vote choice and (b) are influenced by partisanship and social group identity. For example, a recent study examined voters' perceptions of party leaders across seven countries and 35 elections, and found that voters tend to think about leaders' personality traits in two main categories: "character" (which includes traits like "caring" and "trustworthy") and "competence" (which includes traits like "intelligence" and "strength of leadership").[18] Voters around the world thought about these characteristics when they went into the voting booth, which helped them to decide who to vote for. At the same time, voters partially formed their opinions about leaders' traits based on the long-term forces in the funnel of causality: an individual's party identification influenced his or her perceptions, as did their social group identity. Partisans tended to

view the characteristics of leaders of their own party more favourably, and gender and social class characteristics (e.g., employment status, education) also had an influence on how voters perceived different party leaders.

Leaders are one of the biggest examples of short-term forces that influence voters, but there are certainly others. The media increasingly helps to facilitate the importance of short-term factors, as we are able to see and hear so much more during an election campaign today than we could even just a few years ago. One of the most famous examples of the impact of technological innovation is the Kennedy–Nixon debate during the American presidential election of 1960. This was the first televised presidential debate (prior to this, debates were only broadcast over the radio for citizens to listen to at home). The story might be familiar to you: those who listened to the debate on radio thought that Richard Nixon had won. But on television, Nixon looked pale, sweaty, and sickly (he had recently been hospitalized), while John F. Kennedy looked confident and calm, and even sported a bit of a tan. Those who watched the debates on TV thought that Kennedy had carried the debate, and Kennedy himself credited the televised debates with helping him to secure his narrow win (Kennedy won this election with a little over 100,000 votes—a margin of only 0.1 percent of the popular vote!). This marked a turning point in the type of attention that parties and party operatives paid to the appearance of their candidates.

Indeed, the Kennedy–Nixon example points to the importance of the election campaign more generally, not only in terms of debates but in terms of party and candidate visibility overall, be it in relation to advertising or mobilization on the ground, including lawn signs, ribbon cutting, and handshakes. Campaigns cost money, and money talks. Evidence suggests that campaign spending has a major influence on electoral outcomes, and that those who spend more money are more likely to win. Recent research by Gary Jacobson[19] on candidate spending in elections to the House of Representatives in the United States, for example, breaks down spending across incumbents and challengers, and finds that voters recognize and recall the names of candidates who spend more (see Figure 10.5).

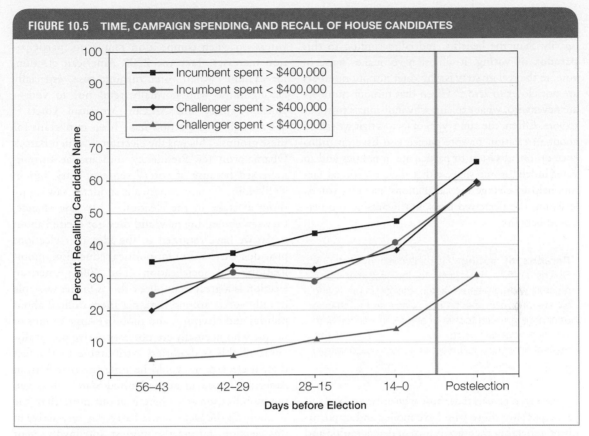

FIGURE 10.5   TIME, CAMPAIGN SPENDING, AND RECALL OF HOUSE CANDIDATES

Source: Gary C. Jacobson, "Measuring Campaign Spending Effects," in H.E. Brady and R. Johnston, eds, *Capturing Campaign Effects* (Ann Arbor, MI: University of Michigan Press, 2006), 210. © University of Michigan Press

Closest to the stem of the funnel, then, are short-term forces (like candidates and campaign events) that influence the choices that we make at the ballot box. Parties seek to influence voters as much as possible during the campaign, mobilizing their partisan "base" (long-term, reliable supporters) as well as others (who may not identify with the party but might respond to short-term factors in a given election).

So in a given election, all kinds of forces come together to influence how we vote, and while some are long-term and fixed, others are variable and change with the times. Locating the position of a particular force in the funnel helps us to figure out what kinds of influence it may have had on vote choice. What is interesting about the funnel is that it not only helps to explain voter behaviour but public opinion in general. Thus, the same factors that influence our vote affect how we think about different political issues that arise between elections. How we react to issues such as abortion, same-sex marriage, and capital punishment, as well as less exciting issues such as tax policy, can all be explained using the same principles.

PARTICIPATION AND TURNOUT

We now have a general sense of the types of things that help to explain how we decide who to vote for, but what influences whether or not we vote in the first place?

A major starting point in the voter turnout literature suggests that people decide to vote based on their rational calculations about whether or not it is worth their while.[20] This "rational" model of participation suggests that turnout should usually be low because one ballot is rarely decisive and the cost-benefit analysis of voting always leaves the costs weighing more heavily than the benefits. Indeed, according to this **paradox of voting**, it almost never makes sense to vote, so the real mystery is why voter turnout numbers are not closer to zero.[21] Given that turnout numbers are never zero, what explains why individuals turn out to vote? Often, the same types of factors that we talked about in relation to vote choice also have an influence on our decision to participate in politics and to vote. Indeed, some suggest that these additional factors help to change the calculations made by voters, lessening the perceived costs and increasing the perceived benefits.

> **Paradox of voting:** First identified by Anthony Downs (1957), this refers to the fact that for a rational, self-interested actor, the costs of voting always outweigh the benefits, because the chance of changing the outcome of any given election with just one vote is next to none. Yet, even with this rational-actor calculus, people do turn out to vote in significant numbers.

Research reveals that those who are most likely to participate are those who have money and opportunities, reflecting the importance of demographic and socioeconomic characteristics. In a nutshell, at least in the Western world, white working men who are older and have higher incomes tend to be the most politically involved. Their higher socioeconomic status provides them with the resources to be more active in politics—the costs are smaller for them than for other citizens. In addition to resources, however, scholars point to a number of other factors that can influence turnout. Some argue that the people who have the strongest sense of duty are likeliest to vote: these individuals feel bad if they do not vote, and they feel like it is their responsibility as citizens to turn out on election day.[22] In the language of costs and benefits, for these citizens, the benefits that come from being a good citizen outweigh the perceived costs.

In addition to resources and a sense of duty, it is also possible that people participate in elections more when they think that there is something at stake: voters believe that the benefits of having "their" party win (or the costs of having another

party win) are substantial enough to encourage them to head to the ballot box. Competition drives voters, so when competition ramps up, participation increases. Take the 2008 American election, for example, when voter turnout rose, especially among those who normally tend not to vote—youth, Latino, and African American voters.[23] Why would this election have been important for these groups? This was the election in which Barack Obama won the Presidency, and maybe turnout increased because of voters' sense of duty, but in all likelihood, many Americans suddenly saw something at stake in the election. They saw change, they saw something new, and they got excited about it. So we have returned to the idea that elections provide a mechanism for political education, mobilization, and socialization. The 2008 American election is a great example of this. Obama was able to rally voters around him, get them excited about politics and elections, and mobilize large groups of people who normally are not very active politically. Some of this is doubtless attributable to the fact that, if elected, he would become the first African American President of the United States. However, the mobilization story here is about more than the symbolism: the Democratic Party was very active in this election, raising the interest and involvement of "regular" citizens. The Obama campaign broke fundraising records, collecting the bulk of its funds from individual donations of $200 or less through a very active social media campaign.[24] In 2008, elections—and more generally politics—became important to people, and thus more people became involved and, in the end, turned out to vote.

Unfortunately, the effect was not long-lasting. In 2012, voter turnout dropped again, falling to a greater extent among youth than it did for the rest of the population. The 2012 American election saw only 38 percent of youth voters cast a ballot. (see Figure 10.6) This is very similar to the 39 percent of Canadian youth voters who turned up to vote in the 2011 federal election, noted at the beginning of the chapter.

As Figure 10.6 below makes clear, with the exception of a few temporary increases, turnout rates have seen a steady decline in the United States over time, for all age groups except senior citizens. Some argue that this decline is because elections have become less competitive, while others maintain that

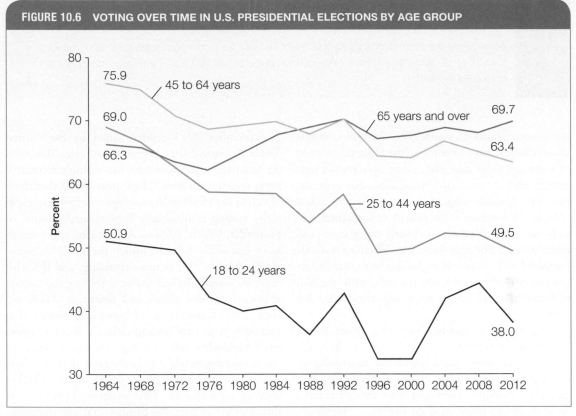

FIGURE 10.6   VOTING OVER TIME IN U.S. PRESIDENTIAL ELECTIONS BY AGE GROUP

Source: Thom File, *Young-Adult Voting: An Analysis of Presidential Elections, 1964–2012* (Washington, DC: U.S. Census Bureau, 2014), online at http://www.census.gov/prod/2014pubs/p20-573.pdf.

it is the result of a cultural change, where younger people feel less duty-bound to vote. Some suggest that voters (especially youth) have become disenchanted with politics and disengaged from the political system, while others propose that it might be a sign of complacency. The complacency theory maintains that voters are relatively satisfied with the state of their democracy and therefore do not worry or feel that they need to get involved. Some argue that more individuals are shying away from identifying as feminists for much the same reason—the major battles have been won, there is no need to worry about equality anymore. Others see these explanations as problematic insofar as they sideline numerous reasons why people might feel marginalized from contemporary politics.

Low levels of political knowledge and interest are also often cited as sources of declining turnout, especially among youth. Scholars have suggested that unless youth participation is taken seriously,

turnout decline is likely to be a long-term problem, as it is the earliest elections in a citizen's life that are formative: once eligible to vote, if youth 18 and older vote in their first three elections, the activity is likely to turn into a habit, and these citizens will vote throughout their lives. If they do not participate early, then not voting is more likely to become a lifelong habit.[25] Capturing and engaging youth in those formative years, then, is probably particularly important for long-term voter turnout rates, and thus the health of our democracies overall. Generally speaking, it is likely that some combination of factors (both institutional as well as perceptual) is to blame for declining turnout rates—no one theory has "universal" support among scholars. This is one reason that voter turnout continues to captivate scholars around the world.

In response to such trends, substantial efforts have been made to increase voter turnout around the world, including grassroots/non-profit "rock the vote"

THINK AND DISCUSS

Some argue that Canadian voter turnout might increase if the minimum voting age were reduced from 18 to 16. What do you think? Would this make a difference? Is this a change that ought to be considered seriously?

movements aimed at youth. The electoral commissions (charged with organizing the electoral process) of some countries have even taken on a role of promoting and encouraging participation. For example, Elections Canada created a new initiative called "Inspire Democracy"[26] to provide information and in-house research related to youth engagement and participation. For this initiative, Elections Canada partnered with grassroots organizations to share information, including academic research, with the aim of fostering youth engagement and increasing voter turnout.

Legislation is another way that governments can influence voter turnout, and this can have the effect of increasing participation or decreasing it, depending on the nature of the measures put into place. For example, some countries require citizens to vote, fining those who do not (e.g., Australia). This has the effect of increasing voter turnout, and indeed, turnout in Australia averages about 95 percent, substantially higher than the global average. There are other institutional "fixes," however, that are not as drastic as mandatory voting. Some suggest opening up elections to e-voting as one possibility, which would allow individuals to vote easily from the comfort of their homes. This would help to facilitate voting for those who face mobility challenges, but it may also help to attract younger voters who either live away from home (in university residences, for example) or who may find it easier to vote online since they already spend a substantial amount of time "plugged in" to the Internet.

On the opposite end of the spectrum, legislation can have a negative impact on voter turnout. One issue that is becoming more prominent in the North American context concerns voter registration laws, particularly those requiring voters to present government-issued photo identification when registering to vote and when voting, ostensibly introduced because of concerns over voter fraud.

A September 2014 report issued by the United States Accountability Office[27] indicates that over 33 American states now have increasingly restrictive voter registration laws. The report found that these laws had the effect of *depressing* voter turnout, especially among traditionally less-engaged groups. In particular, youth, African Americans, and Latinos were less likely to vote under the more stringent electoral laws. This is not surprising, and fits with what we already talked about regarding the impact of socioeconomic status and resources. Many see such restrictions as a substantial problem that increases inequality among citizens, and the report itself highlights this as a negative consequence of the laws. In general, it is fairly clear that the more restrictions we have in place, the less likely it is that individuals will vote. This dynamic is even more pronounced among the groups that are traditionally less likely to vote (e.g., younger voters, less wealthy voters, and less educated voters).

If we go back to thinking about the functions of elections, and in particular the idea that elections provide citizens with a *choice and a voice*, allowing them to have a say over the makeup of the legislature and how the country is led, then it becomes clear that declining turnout is a significant problem. Moreover, non-participation is not random: one can predict based on demographic and socioeconomic characteristics which groups in society are most and least likely to vote. If the bulk of citizens who opt to exercise their choice and voice are wealthier, of the dominant race/ethnic group, and have more formal education, while those who are traditionally marginalized (poorer, with less formal education, from non-dominant ethnic groups, immigrants) stay at home, then the voices of the latter may become even further marginalized in the legislature and in the resulting policies initiated by governments. This is a major cause for concern, and can have a lasting legacy.

CONCLUSION

Elections perform a number of important functions, including providing citizens with the opportunity to have a say in how they are governed. Elections can take many forms, however, and electoral rules are quite varied from jurisdiction to jurisdiction. These "rules of the game" are important because they shape how politics "works" in a country, including how parties compete and how voters interact with the political system. Voters tend not to have a lot of information about politics, and making electoral decisions is complicated: in an election they need to decide both whether to vote and who to vote for. Some systems make this clearer and easier than others, and some scholars argue that certain types of electoral systems may actually boost voter turnout.[28] The important point to keep in mind is that democratic systems are exactly that: democratic. This means that they can be evaluated, reevaluated, and changed, if need be, in consultation with citizens. We can adapt our systems to evolving societal needs, and indeed it is important that we regularly examine the foundations that structure politics, and identify what works and what needs to be improved. Big changes are not always necessary: small tweaks can have a marked impact on how politics "works."

DISCUSSION QUESTIONS

1. Electoral institutions have an important impact on the way that politics works. Describe some of the differences we might expect in the legislature if we have a proportional electoral system versus a single member plurality system.

2. Why do proponents of descriptive representation believe that it matters, even if they understand the principles behind substantive representation?

3. If voters lack so much information about politics, should we feel comfortable with the state of democracy? Should uninformed citizens play a role in determining who forms government?

4. Some scholars have recently attempted to explain voting behaviour using a model that points to the importance of genetics. How might this fit with understandings of voter decisions based on the funnel of causality, especially the role of socialization?

5. Do you think that low levels of voter turnout are a problem? Why? What steps could be taken to increase voter turnout?

WEBSITES

IDEA (International Institute for Democracy and Electoral Assistance)
http://www.idea.int
Contains data and reports about the state of electoral democracy around the world.

Interparliamentary Union (Women in Parliaments Initiative)
http://www.ipu.org/iss-e/women.htm
Provides a database of information about women's role in elections and parliaments around the world.

Canadian Election Study
http://ces-eec.org
Data from surveys conducted during national elections in Canada. A great place to look at public opinion and voting behaviour trends over time.

Ontario Citizens Assembly
http://www.citizensassembly.gov.on.ca
This website chronicles efforts to reform the electoral system in the province of Ontario, and includes background information on electoral systems and the 2007 proposal made by the assembly.

United States Census
www.census.gov
For population data and information about the United States.

FURTHER READINGS

Larry M. Bartels, *Unequal Democracy: The Political Economy of the New Gilded Age*. Princeton: Princeton University Press, 2008.

Angus Campbell, Philip Converse, Warren Miller, and Donald Stokes, *The American Voter*. New York: John Wiley and Sons, 1960.

David Farrell, *Electoral Systems: A Comparative Introduction.* Houndsmills, Basingstoke: Palgrave MacMillan, 2001.

Richard Johnston, André Blais, Henry Brady, and Jean Crête, *Letting the People Decide: Dynamics of a Canadian Election.* Montreal and Kingston: McGill-Queen's University Press, 1992.

Mebs Kanji, Antoine Bilodeau, and Thomas Scotto, *The Canadian Election Studies: Assessing Four Decades of Influence.* Vancouver: University of British Columbia Press, 2013.

Hanna Pitkin, *The Concept of Representation.* Oakland: University of California Press, 1967.

Larry J. Sabato, *The Year of Obama: How Barack Obama Won the White House.* Toronto: Pearson, 2009.

Manon Tremblay and Linda Trimble, eds., *Women and Electoral Politics in Canada.* Toronto: Oxford University Press, 2003.

ENDNOTES

1. Ray Rivera, "Taliban Challenge U.S. in Eastern Afghanistan," *The New York Times,* December 26, 2010, online at http://www.nytimes.com/2010/12/26/world/asia/26ghazni.html?pagewanted=all.

2. Federal Election Commission, *2011–2012 Election Cycle Data Summaries through 12/31/12,* 2013, online at http://www.fec.gov/press/summaries/2012/ElectionCycle/24m_PresCand.shtml.

3. David Farrell, *Comparing Electoral Systems* (London: Prentice Hall, 2001).

4. Jane Mansbridge, "Should Blacks Represent Blacks and Women Represent Women? A Contingent 'Yes'," in Mona Lena Krook and Sarah Childs, eds., *Women, Gender, and Politics: A Reader* (Toronto: Oxford University Press, 2010).

5. Ibid., p. 201.

6. United States Census Bureau, *Profile of General Population and Housing Characteristics,* 2010, online at http://factfinder.census.gov/faces/tableservices/jsf/pages/productview.xhtml?src=CF.

7. Jennifer Manning, "Membership of the 113th Congress: A Profile," *Congressional Research Service,* 2010, online at http://fas.org/sgp/crs/misc/R42964.pdf.

8. Suzanne Dovi, "Preferable Descriptive Representatives: Will Just any Woman, Black, or Latino Do?," in Krook and Childs, *Women, Gender, and Politics,* pp 215–24.

9. Angus Campbell, Philip E. Converse, Warren E. Miller, and Donald E. Stokes, *The American Voter* (Chicago: John Wiley and Sons, 1960).

10. Christopher T. Dawes and James H. Fowler, "Social Preferences and Political Participation," *SSRN,* February 14, 2007, online at http://dx.doi.org/10.2139/ssrn.1008205.

11. André Blais, "Accounting for the Electoral Success of the Liberal Party in Canada: Presidential Address to the Canadian Political Science Association London, Ontario, June 3, 2005," *Canadian Journal of Political Science* 38 (4) (2005), pp. 821–40.

12. Elisabeth Gidengil, André Blais, Richard Nadeau, and Neil Nevitte "Women to the Left? Gender Differences in Political Beliefs and Preferences," in M. Tremblay and L. Trimble, eds., *Women and Electoral Politics in Canada* (Toronto: Oxford University Press, 2003), pp. 140–60.

13. Ronald Inglehart and Pippa Norris, *Rising Tide: Gender Equality and Cultural Change around the World* (Cambridge: Cambridge University Press, 2003).

14. Kathleen Dolan, "Voting for Women in 'The Year of the Woman'," *American Journal of Political Science,* 42 (1) (January 1998), pp. 272–93.

15. Campbell, Converse, Miller, and Stokes, *The American Voter.*

16. Philip E. Converse, "The Nature of Belief Systems in Mass Publics," in E.E. Apter, ed., *Ideology and Discontent* (New York: Free Press, 1964), pp. 206–61.

17. Timothy D. Wilson and Elizabeth W. Dunn, "Self-Knowledge: Its Limits, Value, and

Potential for Improvement," *Annual Review of Psychology*, 55 (1)(2004), pp. 493–518.

18. Amanda Bittner, *Platform or Personality? The Role of Party Leaders in Elections* (Oxford: Oxford University Press, 2011).

19. Gary C. Jacobson, "Campaign spending effects in U.S. Senate elections: Evidence from the National Annenberg Election Survey," *Electoral Studies*, 25 (2) (2006), pp. 195–226.

20. Anthony, Downs, *An Economic Theory of Democracy* (New York: Harper, 1957).

21. Ibid.

22. André Blais, *To Vote or Not to Vote: The Merits and Limits of Rational Choice Theory* (Pittsburgh: University of Pittsburgh Press, 2000).

23. United States Census Bureau, "Voter Turnout Increases by 5 Million in 2008 Presidential Election, U.S. Census Bureau Reports Data Show Significant Increases Among Hispanic, Black and Young Voters," 2009, online at https://www.census.gov/newsroom/releases/archives/voting/cb09-110.html.

24. Geoff Norquay, "Organizing Without an Organization: The Obama Networking Revolution," *Policy Options* (October 2008), online at http://archive.irpp.org/po/archive/oct08/norquay.pdf.

25. Mark Franklin, *Voter Turnout and the Dynamics of Electoral Competition in Established Democracies since 1945* (Cambridge: Cambridge University Press, 2004); Richard Johnston, J. Scott Matthews, and Amanda Bittner, "Alienation, Indifference, Competitiveness, and Turnout: Evidence from Canada, 1988–2004," *Electoral Studies*, 26 (4) (2007), pp. 735–45.

26. http://inspirerlademocratie-inspiredemocracy.ca/

27. United States Government Accountability Office, Report to Congressional Requesters, "Elections: Issues Related to State Voter Identification Laws," September 2014, online at http://www.gao.gov/assets/670/665966.pdf.

28. André Blais, Louis Massicotte, and Agnieszka Dobrzynska, "Why Is Turnout Higher In Some Countries Than Others," *Elections Canada*, March 2003, online at http://elections.ca/res/rec/part/tuh/TurnoutHigher.pdf.

11

POLITICAL PARTIES: IMPERFECT BUT ESSENTIAL

Anna Esselment

© ROMEO GACAD/AFP/Getty Images

Political parties are central mechanisms through which "the will of the people" can be translated into executive and legislative bodies. Although the competition of political parties structures democratic political life to a significant degree in many countries around the world, in some—such as Canada—many citizens feel that such institutions are unable or even unwilling to represent their interests effectively.

INTRODUCTION

Would it surprise you to learn that most readers of this chapter do not belong to a **political party**? Probably not. Across most western democracies, the number of citizens who actively seek out membership in a political party has declined dramatically.[1] Interest in parties may spike when a new leader is being selected, or when nominees are vying to be chosen as a candidate to stand for public office. Overall, however, fewer and fewer people are members of political parties between elections. This stands in stark contrast to earlier generations, such as your grandparents' or great-grandparents' in the mid part of the 20th century, when it was unusual if you did *not* belong to a party. Political parties were a key source of political information, a social network; voters felt more strongly about their attachments to parties.

> **Political party:** An organization of like-minded individuals interested in winning power, organizing government, and implementing their preferred policies.

The decline of active participation in political parties, and reasons why this has occurred, raise intriguing questions that we will explore throughout this chapter. We will begin with a discussion about whether parties even matter anymore, and then analyze their roles, functions, and organization. We will also examine different types of parties and the systems in which they compete for power. New trends in election campaigning by parties will also be studied as an introduction to the concept of political marketing. This should provoke some discussion about whether treating citizens as consumers is contributing to negative perceptions of parties. The chapter will conclude with some thoughts about the future of political parties in existing and emerging democracies.

DO PARTIES MATTER?

If we accept that parties are less prominent in the daily lives of citizens than before, then the next logical query is whether parties are still important. Do they really *matter*? If we did not have parties, then how would you imagine government to work? How would our leaders be selected and dismissed? How would it affect the way that we vote? In the absence of parties and the platforms that they put forward, how would local, provincial, and national problems such as transit gridlock, youth unemployment, and a changing climate be addressed?

The fact is that parties *do* matter; they are a key part of the political process. Scholars have long argued that political parties, and the functions that they perform, are essential to sustaining democratic states. In 1888, the American scholar James Bryce proposed that "no free country has been without [parties]. No one has shown how representative government can work without them."[2] E.E. Schattschneider later wrote that "modern democracy is unthinkable save in terms of parties,"[3] and Clinton Rossiter has likewise asserted: "No America without democracy, no democracy without politics, and no politics without parties."[4]

Party scholars in the 21st century still support this **party consensus**, maintaining that "vital, resilient democracies are not possible without strong, prosperous parties."[5] We can see how this consensus holds by examining countries that have fledgling, or transitioning, democratic systems. In Russia, for example, political parties are not firmly entrenched and even major parties are frequently prone to changing their name, organization, and membership. For this reason, Russia's party system has been called "floating," a situation often cited as a reason why the country's democracy has been slower to take shape.[6]

> **Party consensus:** The agreement among scholars that modern democracy requires entrenched and stable political parties to articulate political interests and organize government.

We see similar struggles to consolidate democratic systems in other countries that have weak parties and weak party systems, such as Indonesia, the Philippines, and Thailand.[7] Similarly, the institutionalization of parties is complicated in countries where parties may exist but are ineffective because of restrictions on genuine political participation and competition by an authoritarian (non-democratic) state, such as Egypt under Hosni Mubarak or Zimbabwe under Robert Mugabe. For countries that have been able to foster political party organizations as legitimate expressions of political interests, such as Chile and Morocco, the transition to democracy is having more success.

The important point to remember is that almost all countries have political parties. However, while parties are everywhere, the degree to which they have long-term stability, ideological consistency, dependable supporters, and the ability to compete for power in a free and fair election is determined by the adherence to democratic principles in the country in which they operate. What we will find is that stable parties and vibrant democratic systems are mutually reinforcing; to have one is usually a condition to having the other. In this way, parties matter very much.

WHAT IS A POLITICAL PARTY?

If a political party is so important to democracy, then what exactly is it? And what roles does it play? A common understanding of a political party is that it is an organization of like-minded individuals who are interested in winning power, organizing government, and implementing their preferred policies. There is often an emphasis on electoral competition and success.[8] The desire to win office and pass laws separates political parties from interest groups or social movements (see Chapter 12). The central goal of interest groups is to *influence* policy makers. Political parties want to *be* those policy makers.

Not all political parties are in the position to win enough votes or legislative seats to form government, of course. Think of the Green Party or Bloc Québécois in Canada. Why do they continue to contest elections when they know that controlling the House of Commons is highly unlikely? These parties have ideas and positions that they want to promote, often resulting in the major parties (such as the Conservatives, Liberals, and NDP) responding in some way. The environment is a good example here. Since the Green Party has become more popular in Canada (but only electing one member of parliament—leader Elizabeth May—so far[9]), all the major parties have made efforts to include environmental policy in their platforms. Similarly, the Bloc was formed to voice the concerns of Quebec, particularly francophones, at the national level. Historically, Quebec has always had an impact on the development of national policies, but since the BQ formed in 1990, the major parties have been particularly sensitive to the needs of the province. This was aptly illustrated in the 2006 federal election, when Conservative Party leader Stephen Harper, in a bid to win more support from voters in Quebec, campaigned in that province on the concept of "open federalism." Open federalism meant that a Conservative federal government would not interfere with the constitutional responsibilities of the provinces. The BQ has continually pressed this position in the House of Commons and the Conservative Party's position in 2006 was a welcome response.

In short, political parties generally exist in order to compete for power by electing candidates to office. Some parties are in a stronger position to do so, but even those that are not can have an impact on policy-making by promoting issues or positions that prompt consideration by the other major parties.

POLITICAL PARTY DECLINE?

The challenge for political parties in a number of western democracies is that for many citizens, parties are no longer the centre of political life. Representative assemblies are still composed of parties (whether the governing party or opposition parties, or the "majority" or "minority" parties as found in the U.S. Congress). But whereas parties used to play a strong mediating and integrating role between citizens and their governing institutions, there are now countless other ways to find out what is going on in Canberra, London, Ottawa, or Washington, or to advocate for policy change. If, for example, you want to find out the Conservative government's position on legalizing marijuana, contacting your Member of Parliament may not be your first move. It is more likely that you would turn on your computer, Google "legalizing marijuana" and "Conservative Party of Canada" or "Conservative government of Canada," and then investigate the trail of hits that appears on your screen. Or you might watch a newscast on the issue, stumble upon a blog on what the various parties think about decriminalizing marijuana, or find a Facebook group dedicated to that issue. Discovering the governing party's stance would probably not involve attending a policy convention held by the party, sitting in on a constituency association meeting, or participating in a telephone town hall. Because we have the technological capabilities to uncover information quickly on our own, an important role that political parties used to play has been undercut.

Challenges to parties can be seen in other ways as well. Fewer of us are members of parties even though it is easy and inexpensive to join one; every university, for example, has campus party groups that are eager to sign up new members. Another option is to simply visit a party's website and click "join" to become involved. Declining memberships means that parties no longer have a strong base of party supporters on which to rely during elections. The lack of a reliable and consistent group of partisans in the electorate makes it harder for parties to make unpopular but perhaps necessary decisions, such as advocating for increased levels of taxation or spending cuts to healthcare. Without a dependable cushion of party members to turn to, party leaders would rather avoid angering citizens whose votes may be needed in the next election.

We can also see a decline in parties in terms of policy innovation. Even if you are a party member, novel ideas for parties to consider are more likely to come from outside organizations, such as think tanks (the Fraser Institute or the Centre for Policy Alternatives, for instance), interest groups, or academic policy papers. This can diminish the incentive to join a party, since your own policy prescriptions may be cast aside in favour of such expert advice.

Perhaps most importantly, scandals that have affected parties or individual politicians within parties lessen our attachment to, and respect for, political parties. Good examples here are former Italian prime minister Silvio Berlusconi, who was convicted of tax evasion and soliciting minors for sex, and former premier of Alberta Alison Redford, who used the government jet for personal reasons. When this kind of behaviour hits the headlines, some are discouraged from even bothering to *vote*, much less join a party.

It is significant that Canadians are not alone with respect to the decline in political parties. We may not understand or think much of parties, but trends suggest that neither do most other citizens in comparable countries. Indeed, party scholars Russell J. Dalton and Martin P. Wattenberg have observed a decline in party memberships, party identification, and trust in parties across many countries around the globe.[10] The public is more skeptical of parties, primarily due to media attention that focuses on party and government scandals and instances of corruption. We are also more critical of our leaders and less willing to believe that they are working on our behalf. The fifth wave World Values Survey (2005–2008) showed that a majority of citizens surveyed across European, Nordic, and Westminster countries had "not very much" confidence in political parties. In four countries, between 23 and 36 percent of respondents declared that their confidence level was "none at all" (France [36.7 percent], Germany [33.1 percent], Italy [27.8 percent], and Great Britain [23.4 percent]). About 22 percent of Canadians had "quite a lot" or "a great deal" of confidence in their parties but an overwhelming majority (72.5 percent) had "not very much" confidence or "none at all."

The attitudes captured by the World Values Survey may reflect some of your own (see Figures 11.1 and 11.2). But is it possible that our focus is centred too much on the stories that help to sell newspapers (such as political scandals and gaffes) or increase the advertising revenues on websites? Is it possible that a greater understanding of the roles that parties play in sustaining democracy would increase your level of support for them? Perhaps even convince you to join one? Looking more closely at party functions may provide you with a greater appreciation of just what it is they do.

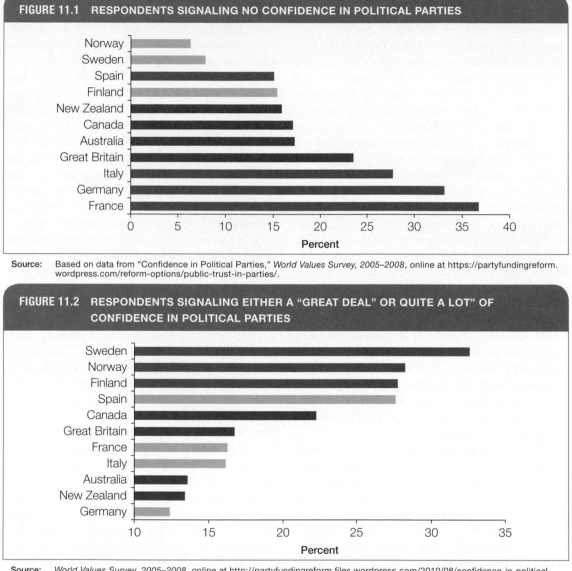

FIGURE 11.1   RESPONDENTS SIGNALING NO CONFIDENCE IN POLITICAL PARTIES

Source: Based on data from "Confidence in Political Parties," *World Values Survey, 2005–2008*, online at https://partyfundingreform. wordpress.com/reform-options/public-trust-in-parties/.

FIGURE 11.2   RESPONDENTS SIGNALING EITHER A "GREAT DEAL" OR QUITE A LOT" OF CONFIDENCE IN POLITICAL PARTIES

Source: *World Values Survey, 2005–2008,* online at http://partyfundingreform.files.wordpress.com/2010/08/confidence-in-political-parties.pdf.

THINK AND DISCUSS

What is your own confidence level in our political parties? Is it high, low, or have you never thought about it? Why or why not? Think about it now and discuss where you land on the confidence barometer.

A THREE-LEGGED STOOL: THE ROLES AND FUNCTIONS OF PARTIES

The American scholar V.O. Key conceived the political party in three ways: the party as an organization, the party in the electorate, and the party in government (PO, PIE, PIG).[11] Each facet had roles or functions to fulfill; put differently, each constituted a leg of a three-legged stool.[12] The question we now consider is how well parties are actually fulfilling these functions today.

Party as Organization

Think of a news report in which numerous Canadians are dressed in similar colours, wearing buttons, waving placards, and cheering for Liberal leader Justin Trudeau. One of the roles of the party as an organization is to *choose its leader and candidates*. Usually you have to join a party and be a member in good standing in order to cast a vote for party leader. In a bid to widen its net of potential voters and encourage Canadians to become involved in the process, the Liberal Party of Canada created a new category of "supporter" for its last leadership race in 2013; "supporters" did not have to become full-fledged members of the party but could still vote in the leadership race. In return, the Liberal Party was able to amass a large number of new names and the contact information of many Canadians who were "supportive" of the Liberals or its leadership candidates and thus who could potentially vote for the party at election time.

A similar process exists for a citizen who wants to be a party candidate. In order to get on the ballot, the person has to win a nomination contest (in Canada) or a primary race (in the U.S.) by securing the most support from members of the party in their particular riding or district. For citizens in countries using proportional electoral systems, potential candidates must get on a party's "list" (as described in Chapter 10). The popular vote will determine the number of seats won in the assembly and the party list will determine who gets to take those seats. List systems are used in the Netherlands, Israel, Serbia, and South Africa, among others. In non-proportional systems, party members usually elect the person they think will best represent the party and who they believe has the greatest chance of beating the candidates from the other parties. If you want to get around the party, you can certainly run as an Independent; in many parliamentary systems, however, independent candidates are rarely successful. This is also the case in the U.S., particularly in presidential races.

Recruiting and choosing leaders and candidates is a critical role of the party organization. We should, however, point out that the preference of party members, particularly in candidate selection, is not always respected by party elites. In Canada, leaders have the power to bypass local riding associations and simply appoint the candidates whom they favour, often to the dismay of local party members (although in doing so, and in doing so too frequently, they risk alienating party members and supporters in the public). Likewise, new research on candidate selection in Ireland, New Zealand, and Scotland suggests that scholars have underestimated the degree of struggle that takes place between a party's leadership and the wider membership on who should stand as candidates.[13] So while this particular task of parties continues to be fulfilled, there appear to be significant intra-party disagreements over how it should be done. This matters because clashes along these lines can have the effect of driving members out of the party, compounding the problem of declining participation in political parties.

Political parties also *articulate political interests*— they take positions on issues that best reflect the views of both their members and those voters whose support they would like to attract. We can detect the latter by simply listening to keywords that party leaders use, such as "middle-class families," "small business owners," or "students." Sometimes it can be difficult to discern differences in positions between the parties. This can lead to the common refrain that parties are "all the same." On some matters, various parties are often in agreement. It would be a challenge to find a major party in Canada that would advocate the dismantling of the public healthcare system. Likewise, most parties agree that a balanced budget is preferable to financing deficits. But on other issues differences are more readily apparent. The Liberal Party has long been in favour of a national firearms registry to track gun ownership which it created in 1995 when it was in power. The Conservatives opposed the firearms registry and scrapped it after they became the government. The Democratic Party in the U.S. is in favour of same-sex marriage, while the Republicans have mostly been against it. The point is that political parties articulate the political interests of their membership and also *aggregate those interests* into a larger platform that they present to citizens during an election. Aggregating interests is a process that helps parties to connect voting segments of the citizenry based on issues, regions, language, and values in order to form a coalition of support. In 2006, for example, the Conservative platform aggregated the interests of Canadians who wanted tax cuts, justice reform, and more accountability in government. There were enough voters in Canada who agreed with those platform planks for the party to win a plurality of seats in the House of Commons.

The ability of parties to aggregate interests effectively can fluctuate. A general indicator of effectiveness in the Canadian context is if a party is able to win seats from all parts of the country. When parties are unable to do this, their support tends to be more regionally isolated. This was certainly the case after the 1993 federal election. Brian Mulroney's Progressive Conservatives had won majority governments in 1984 and 1988 by carefully balancing the interests of the West with those in Quebec. Over time, however, a series of political problems and missteps detrimentally affected the delicate equilibrium that Mulroney had struck between those two regions. One problem was extending a lucrative government contract to build CF-18 aircraft to a firm in Quebec over a more competitive bid tendered by a firm in Winnipeg. This angered voters in the West, who perceived the government's decision as pandering to voters in *la belle province*. Another problem was two failed constitutional negotiations (the Meech Lake Accord and the Charlottetown Accord) that had attempted to address demands from the Quebec government in order to entice that province to sign the 1982 Constitution. In the end, the Conservatives managed to fuel discontent in the West *and* Quebec, as well as other areas of the country. The 1993 election witnessed the burgeoning success of two new parties: the Bloc Québécois and the western-based Reform Party. The Liberals won a majority government, but mostly from a strong base of support in Ontario, while the NDP lost 35 seats, tumbling from 44 to just nine, and the Progressive Conservatives went from holding

a majority to winning only two seats. Competently aggregating interests is thus a critical function of party organization, but one that is done more or less well depending on the particular issues and political context of the day.

Party in the Electorate

While fewer people are choosing to become members of parties, the role of the political party in the larger electorate is still critical. Political parties remain a key link between citizens and the democratic process in several respects. First, parties *simplify choices for voters.* How do they do this? Well, think about the Democrats and the Republicans in the United States. When you hear the word "Democrat," what phrases or words come to mind? What about "Republican"? Because the two main parties in the U.S. have taken fairly consistent policy positions year after year, decade after decade, we do not need to know a lot about them to have a general idea of what they stand for. The same is true for the Conservatives and Labour in Britain. The party names themselves provide a clue to their ideological orientation. This makes it easy for voters to make a preliminary match between their own beliefs and outlooks and those of the parties.

Parties also *provide symbols of identification and loyalty.* Partisan identification reflects a psychological attachment to a political party.[14] It is akin to loyalty to your favourite sports team—that team may consistently lose, but you cheer for it regardless. The loyalty that voters feel for a particular party helps to stabilize the system; parties are less likely to dissolve and reorganize (as they often do in destabilized or transitioning democracies), providing some continuity to the choices offered to the electorate. At the same time, in some countries (Canada is an example here) there is a shrinking pool of citizens who have stable and strong partisan identification. In other words, it is increasingly likely that you will choose to vote for different parties in different elections; you may vote for the NDP in the next federal election but for the Liberals in the election following that one. Even though you voted NDP federally, you may choose to support the Green Party in the provincial election. There are fewer people who consistently vote for the same party, election after election, and at both levels of government.

In contrast, while there is some growth in the number of those who claim to be "independent" in the U.S., most Americans are either strong Democrats or strong Republicans, or at least "lean" in those directions.[15] The Canadian experience is a little different, for several reasons. At both the federal and provincial levels, we have more than just two parties that compete for power, so there is a greater variety of political choice for voters. Furthermore, party labels—"Liberal" or "Conservative"—may not reflect ideological consistency at both the federal and provincial levels either, meaning that the provincial Liberal Party in British Columbia may be quite different from the Liberal Party of Canada. This can result in a provincial Liberal Party voter in BC also supporting the federal Conservative Party. Furthermore, Canadian voters appear to be influenced by short-term election dynamics, such as party leadership and particular issues raised during the election. In short, we seem to be more "flexible" in our partisanship when compared to Americans.[16] It is worth noting, however, that there remain enough voters with consistent partisan attachments that Canadian parties are clearly still a focus for identity, loyalty, and thus party system stabilization.

A third function of parties in the electorate is to *mobilize citizens to vote*. Because parties want to win control of the government, it is in their interest to get supporters to the polls to cast a ballot. Considering that the potential coalition of support based on aggregated interests may be different for each party, it is likely that at some point each voter will be asked by at least one party to participate politically. Parties may send volunteers to knock on doors and drop off pamphlets outlining party policies; they may set up call centres where volunteers (and professionals) phone voters to remind them of the election and inquire whether they will be supporting the party's candidate; they may also send e-mail messages or texts to people who have indicated that they will be voting for the party in order to ensure that they get to the polling stations.

Voter turnout in most democracies is trending downward, which raises the question of how well parties are able to persuade citizens to vote. Only 58 percent of eligible voters cast their ballot in the 2012 U.S. presidential election; 61 percent of Canadians turned out for the 2011 federal election;[17] and 65 percent of Britons voted in the 2010 general election. This is a decrease from earlier decades, when voter turnout reached 75 percent or more in the U.K. and Canada, and closer to 65 percent in the U.S. At the provincial level in Canada, turnout can be even worse: 58 percent in British Columbia in 2013, 52 percent in Ontario in 2014, and 59 percent in Nova Scotia in 2013, although some provinces (such as Quebec and New Brunswick) have traditionally experienced higher rates of participation (Quebec reached 71 percent in the 2014 provincial election).

There are also other countries (Austria, Chile, Germany, and Sweden, for instance) where participation remains comparatively higher. These larger turnout rates are not a result of mandatory voting laws, as can be found in countries like Australia, Luxembourg, and Singapore. What makes Chile different from Canada and the U.S.? Why are the Swedes more likely to participate politically? The type of electoral system matters, as do regulations that determine how easy it is to vote (see Chapter 10). But the ability of parties to mobilize is also important; falling rates of turnout can be an indication that parties are having a more difficult time reaching voters and persuading them to come out on election day.

Finally, parties in the electorate *educate citizens*. For example, parties regularly raise issues for public discussion that they deem important, publish reports and policy papers that citizens may consider, draw attention to what the government is doing in either a positive or negative way, and try to connect with citizens by providing them with information through public meetings, mailings, e-mail, and their websites. As with their mobilization function, the role of parties as educators has diminished. This is due in large part to advanced technology in most western democratic countries. Political parties have always been a source of information for citizens interested in certain issues, but now they must compete with exponentially more points of access for news, many of which also offer commentary and analysis on topics of political relevance. Widespread access to the Internet and the reams of data uploaded to it each day from around the world means that citizens can more easily educate themselves on matters that they deem important (although the reliability of that information can often be questioned). There are also interest groups, think tanks, academics, the traditional media, and social media such as Twitter, Facebook, and YouTube, all of which contribute to debate and discussion on policy issues.

These new sources of information are beyond the control of parties and, arguably, contribute to a healthy democracy. Considering the lower levels of trust that plague parties, they are in a weaker position to compete for voters' attention. At the same time, political parties are also trying to harness these new social media and information-dispersing tools in order to continue their education function. Parties now routinely send tweets, e-mails, and push notifications on various matters to members and citizens who have indicated an interest in receiving the information. You can "follow" leaders and members of Parliament on Twitter, access their YouTube channels, and "friend" them on Facebook. In these and other ways, parties can still interact directly with citizens and continue their role as educators, but it remains clear that this function has contracted over the last several decades.

Party in Government

The final leg of the tripod is the party in government. Once the party organization has selected its leader and candidates, articulated its political positions, aggregated interests, and fought an election by relying on loyal and mobilized voters, it may have won enough seats to form a government.

After citizens have elected their representatives, the first function of the parties is to *create a government*. In the U.S. presidential system, the political executive is elected through an Electoral College. In parliamentary systems, the party with the most seats usually forms the governing caucus and the cabinet is selected from members of that party. If a majority of seats have been won by representatives of the same party, then stability over the course of the next four or five years is more or less assured. If a party has won only a plurality of seats (more seats than any other single party but not a majority of seats), then it will be a minority or coalition government.

Unlike a minority government where a single party controls the political executive, a coalition government requires that two or more parties come together and combine their seat shares to produce a government. Agreement must be reached regarding leadership roles, the composition of the cabinet, and the policy agenda to be pursued, since these items require a common, cooperative spirit. Coalition governments are in place throughout the world, including Indonesia (five parties ruling together), Israel (four

parties ruling together), and Japan (two parties ruling together). These types of governments occur most frequently in electoral systems that have incorporated a degree of proportionality, such as Italy, Germany, New Zealand, Norway, Poland, and Ukraine. They are less frequent in countries that continue to employ a Single Member Plurality (SMP) system because, in most cases, SMP decreases the number of competitive parties, although coalitions still occur. In 2010, the United Kingdom's general election resulted in a coalition government between the Conservatives and the Liberal-Democrats that governed effectively until it was replaced by a majority Conservative government in 2015. Creating governments has long been a key function of parties and they continue to fulfill this role.

Once the government has been created, the party in power must *organize the government*. The party leader (now prime minister) selects a cabinet; the cabinet consists of those members of parliament in charge of departments, such as justice, foreign affairs, and finance. Organizing the government also involves choosing which legislative proposals will be considered first in order to *implement the party's policy objectives*. Initial policy objectives will largely emanate directly from the party's campaign platform (or, in the case of a coalition, their platforms); others will arise over the course of the party's mandate. The role of the party in government also extends to *providing an alternative government* through organized opposition. Parties in "opposition" rigorously question and debate the

Conservative leader David Cameron and Liberal Democrat leader Nick Clegg forge a coalition government after the May 2010 British election.

© Nils Jorgensen/Rex Features/The Canadian Press

policy choices of the government. This provides some degree of transparency to the public but it is also a way of demonstrating that, should they become tired of the government, there is a "government in waiting" that citizens can vote for in the next election. One advantage of party government in parliamentary systems is the provision of a clear line of accountability—citizens generally know who to blame or praise for policy choices. This is less the case in systems with separated powers, such as the United States. The executive branch (the president and vice-president) can blame the legislative branch (Congress) for action or inaction, especially when the two branches are controlled by different parties. If there is gridlock between the branches, government can shut down altogether; this has happened three times since 1994, most recently in October 2013. Regardless of these occasional, albeit serious, clashes, political parties in the U.S. must still create and organize government (at least organize the House and Senate), implement an agenda, and offer themselves to the public during elections as an alternative governing choice.

Of the three-legged stool described here, the assessment of the ability of political parties to fulfill their various roles and functions is mixed. Parties do well at selecting their leaders and candidates, but are not consistently effective at aggregating and articulating interests. Parties certainly simplify choices for voters, but no longer command the same attachment from citizens. Getting people out on election day has also suffered, alongside the role of educator. At the same time, political parties are effectively creating, organizing, and providing alternative governments. While some roles are more or less prominent than others, the point to remember is that political parties remain key players in the management of politics and the political system. With this in mind, we will now take a closer look at the different types of parties and the systems in which they compete for power.

PARTY TYPES

Not all parties are the same. Some are small, tight-knit groupings, while others have hundreds of thousands of members. Some focus mainly on winning elections, while others are devoted to their ideological orientation. The type of party is important because

categorization allows for the comparison of parties over time and gives us an idea of how parties may evolve from one type to another. Party classification helps to sort parties according to certain characteristics, such as their level of inclusiveness regarding membership, their intensity of activity both during and between elections, or even their degree of professionalization. While scholars tend to quibble about the appropriateness of each category in terms of capturing the essential characteristics of different parties effectively, this section will help familiarize you with both traditional and new categories of party types.

Party scholar Maurice Duverger provided the first categorization of two specific party types: cadre and mass parties.[18] **Cadre parties** developed in the 19th century and were small organizations with membership confined mostly to representatives who held seats in parliament. The "extra-parliamentary" party (the party organization we are familiar with that includes regular citizens as members who are not elected to parliament themselves) was largely non-existent. Cadre parties were fairly exclusive and mostly interested in ensuring that they attracted notable candidates to stand for election and attend to parliamentary business. The party was not wed to any particular ideology nor did it adhere to any doctrine that shaped its thinking. Financing came from private sources, whether from the personal wealth of the representatives or from supporters in the business community. The origins of the Liberals and Conservatives in Canada and the Democrats and Republicans in the United States are based on the cadre-style party. It is noteworthy that most of these elite-type parties have now evolved through a process of internal democratization: they have both larger memberships and a broader fundraising base. For the most part, cadre parties have morphed into catch-all and/or electoral-professional parties, discussed below.

> **Cadre party:** Nineteenth-century small party organizations of local notables with membership confined mostly to representatives who held seats in the legislature.

The opposite of the cadre party was the **mass party,** which originated in Europe at the beginning of the 20th century as suffrage expanded to include a wider range of citizens. Its organization was based on attracting a very large membership. The German Social Democratic Party, for example, had over a million members in 1913. Used successfully by socialist, communist, and (to a lesser extent) fascist groups, the mass party was doctrinaire in its political approach. Alongside an electoral imperative, its purpose was to provide political education to "the masses" in order to have "increasing influence over all the spheres of the individual's daily life."[19] All party members financed the party through dues or fees, since many of its representatives were not wealthy and it could not depend on donations from businesses. For mass parties, organizational success usually came before electoral success. While less prevalent today, mass parties can still be found in various jurisdictions, including Argentina (Justicialist Party) China (Communist Party of China), India (Bharatiya Janata Party), and South Africa (African National Congress).

> **Mass party:** Political parties that emerged in the early 20th century that had a large membership base, a strong ideological orientation, and internal funding from dues and fees.

Party types continued to evolve—mass parties based on fascist or ultra-nationalist ideologies became far less appealing after the Second World War, and cadre types became more open to entice a larger number of voters and attract good candidates. Mass parties often headed in the direction of becoming **catch-all parties**, a term first used by Otto Kircheimer to describe a loosening of their ideological adherence (in order to "catch all" voters), more emphasis on the party's leadership, and a greater commitment to securing electoral success.[20] The focus on elections became more apparent in the 1970s and 1980s and a new party type was developed by Angelo Panebianco, called the **electoral-professional party**.[21] This type puts even more emphasis on the role of elections; campaigns are capital intensive and largely run by professional consultants who have a greater appreciation of how to win power. The role of ideology is further marginalized, and the party's platform is geared less toward its membership base and more toward voters who can be persuaded to support the party in the election. Richard Katz and Peter Mair have also identified what they call *cartel parties*.[22] Cartel parties are established parties that engage in a form of collusion with

the state to keep themselves well-funded and prevent new parties from becoming competitive. Cartel parties receive public subsidies (taxpayer dollars) to not only assist them with the expenses of an election, but also to help maintain their party organizations year over year. State-imposed institutional barriers (usually through electoral laws) can also limit the emergence of new parties into the party system, which helps to keep the competition for power among those few established parties.

> **Catch-all party:** Political parties in the post-war era that shed much of their ideological adherence, placed more emphasis on the party's leadership, and focused on securing electoral success.

> **Electoral-professional party:** A political party focused on winning elections; party membership tends to be small and there is little to no identifiable ideological adherence.

Key to the Canadian context is the **brokerage party**. Due to the country's history of divisions based primarily on language, region, and religion, a consistent challenge for the three main parties—Conservative, Liberal, and New Democrat—has been to preserve national unity. Political parties in Canada—particularly the Liberals and Conservatives, since they are the only two that have formed the national government—are thus far less ideological than parties in almost any other country. Their job is to broker interests among voters from the different regions, between the two official languages, and across the dominant religions (although the religious divide between Catholics and Protestants is far less prevalent today) in order to win power. As brokers, Canadian parties tend to be called "big tents" since their lack of strong ideology means that many Canadians are comfortable voting for either party and occasionally being members of one or the other at different times.

TABLE 11.1	SELECT PARTY TYPES	
Cadre	Electoral-Professional	Ideological
Mass	Brokerage	Interest
Catch-All	Cartel	Franchise

Other party types exist as well: there are more *ideological parties* in many African, European, and Latin American countries—these parties strongly adhere to an ideological perspective on either the left or right of the political spectrum and may occasionally hold the balance of power in a coalition government (the far-right Progress Party in Norway, for example). These parties are organized mostly because they believe in their doctrine, even if winning power remains an elusive goal.

Interest parties are somewhat similar in that the party wants to advance a particular issue, such as the environment (Green parties) or separatism (the Scottish National Party or the Bloc Québécois), or animal rights (the Dutch Party for the Animals), or the legalization of marijuana (the Marijuana Party). One intriguing interest party is the growth of the Pirate organization. Founded in Sweden but now registered in 43 countries across the world, the Pirate Party advocates for "the protection of human rights and fundamental freedoms in the digital age," including freedom of information, transparency, and protection of personal and confidential communication.[23] The Pirate Party routinely wins less than five percent of the popular vote in the elections that it contests, but its proliferation in countries around the globe suggests that it has some appeal. An interest party is more likely to be part of a coalition since the narrowness of the particular issue that led to its creation is unlikely to attract broad enough support for the party to win power on its own.

There are also *ethnicity-based parties* whose purpose is to bring more state attention and benefits to a group based on its common ethnicity, such as the Inkatha Freedom Party in South Africa, or to build support and connections with other ethnic groups in the electorate, such as the Congress Party in India. *Nationalist parties* are similar in this respect, but they often promote a vision for the country based on a nationalist ideology that can include a "master race" or, at the very least, a country that does *not* include certain other ethnicities, races, or religions. Hungary's Jobbik Party, for instance, which won 20 percent of the popular vote in

that country's 2014 general election, wants to rid the country of Jews and Romani.

Aside from the types enumerated above, there are also quirky parody and protest parties like the Rhinoceros Party. This Canadian party was founded to make fun of other political parties and politicians; the key promise of the Rhino Party is not to keep any of its promises. Russia has a Beer Lovers Party, Sweden has a Donald Duck Party, and the United Kingdom has an Official Monster Raving Loony Party.

By this point it should be clear that there are many kinds of political parties, and not all have been listed here. Parties are both numerous and variable, and for those citizens who live in countries where they are free to join parties, they are likely to find at least one party that reflects their values, their ideological orientation, or the interests that are important to them.

PARTY SYSTEM

No matter the type, all political parties must operate within a larger system. The United States has been called a "two-party" system, India a "multiparty" system, and the province of Alberta a "one party dominant" system. What does this mean? The combination of parties competing with one another in order to win power is called a **party system**, but how the party system is classified (one, two, or multiparty) is open to interpretation.

Some argue that classification should be based on the number of parties. But which number? Registered parties? If that is the case, then Canada (and many other countries) would have an extreme multiparty system since 18 parties contested the 2011 election (including the Pirate party)![24] Others maintain that only parties able to win legislative seats should be considered part of the larger "system." However, 11 parties had at least one legislative seat in the British House of Commons in 2014, but few would suggest that the U.K. has an 11-party system.

Party scholar Giovanni Sartori developed a useful method of classifying party systems: to be placed in the party system, a political party has to both win seats *and* affect government formation. Larger parties that consistently win numerous seats are obviously part of the system (such as the Australian Labor Party or New Zealand's National Party). But Sartori also counts parties with "coalition" or "blackmail" potential. If a party is a potential coalition partner (the Liberal-Democrats in the U.K., for example, or the Green Party in Germany), then it is considered part of the system. The same is true for those that affect how other parties in the legislature cooperate. For example, few mainstream parties in the position of seeking coalition partners want to do so with a communist or fascist party. But the mere existence of a fascist party affects the behaviour of larger parties by compelling them to seek support from other, more palatable parties that have won seats, such as a Green party or a social democratic party.

Using this method, the number of parties that qualify to be in a system is greatly reduced. The United States is thus accurately portrayed as a two-party system, particularly in the contest for the White House. Britain can be viewed as having a two-and-a-half party system, since the traditional third party—the Liberal Democrats—has never won power on its own but has been a coalition partner with the Conservatives and could play that same role for the Labour Party. Canada, along with many other countries, is a multiparty system, with most of the competitive edge belonging to the Conservatives, Liberals, and NDP since these parties have either formed government or the official opposition.

There are also instances where one party remains dominant in a system, even if on occasion other parties provide some semblance of a competitive challenge. The African National Congress in South Africa, for example, has governed since 1994. In Japan, the Liberal Democratic Party has wielded power for most of the last 60 years. A Canadian example can be found in the province of Alberta. Until 2015, the provincial Progressive Conservatives had formed the government since 1971; that's over four decades of uninterrupted power. Until very recently, few other parties have been able to pose any effective competitive challenge. The PCs' dominance was challenged during the 2012 provincial election, however, by the newly-established Wildrose Alliance. However, at the end of the day, the election results witnessed a loss of only five seats for the PCs and a gain of 13 for Wildrose; in other words, the PCs managed to win another commanding majority in the legislature. In an interesting turn of events, the bulk of Wildrose's caucus defected to the governing PCs in December 2014 (including its leader, Danielle Smith). This move suggested that the Progressive Conservative Party would continue to dominate Alberta's politics for the foreseeable future. But party systems will change—and often in unanticipated ways—when voters have had enough of the status quo and see a viable alternative. In the spring 2015 election, Albertans overwhelmingly supported the NDP and its plan for the province's fiscal future in the face of plummeting oil prices and stalled economic growth. Under leader Rachel Notley, the NDP won 53 of the 87 seats in the Alberta legislature, a historic change. If over the next several years the Wildrose Alliance and PCs decide to merge into one party, future electoral contests in this western province may shift from being one-party dominant to a very competitive two-party system.

In short, party systems provide a good way to assess the competitiveness of the political parties within them. These systems can have long-term stability, but in many cases they also evolve as institutional and societal changes occur. Two-party systems may become multiparty systems if proportionality is introduced into the electoral rules, such as when New Zealand moved from a first-past-the-post to a Mixed Member Proportional system in 1996. Likewise, some parties may collapse and exit the system because of new social cleavages or an inability to maintain traditional areas of voter support. The federal Progressive Conservative Party in Canada was a major player in the party system until its devastating loss in the 1993 general election, which reduced its legislative seats from 156 to just two. The PC party never recovered and eventually merged with another party (the Canadian Alliance) to form the new Conservative Party of Canada.

PARTY ORGANIZATION
Party Structure

How a party is structured can depend on a variety of factors, both internal and external. If it is an interest party (such as the Marijuana Party), then the structure may be quite loose, with a few executive positions, limited membership, and flexibility over the degree of involvement in a campaign. If the party conforms to the catch-all or electoral-professional model, then there may be strict control from the executive and leader, a larger and more active membership involved in leadership and candidate selection, and some role for members in policy debate (but usually to ratify decisions that have come from the leader, **parliamentary caucus**, or political and campaign professionals employed by the party).

> **Parliamentary caucus:** A group of elected representatives in the legislature who belong to the same political party.

Structure can also be affected by external factors, such as whether the party operates in a unitary or federal political system. A federal system can complicate party organization. With two levels to consider, does a party stay *integrated* and offer the same brand and policy ideas at both levels? (The NDP in Canada is an example here.) Or is it better to be *confederal*, and allow two independent organizations to exist, one concentrating federally and the other provincially? (The Conservative Party is an example here, where the Ontario Progressive Conservatives and the Alberta Progressive Conservatives are distinct from the federal party.)

Whether integrated or confederal, the internal organization of parties in most western democracies tends to be similar. Political parties have constitutions or charters that set out, among other things, the party's principles, executive council, affiliated organizations, fundraising arm, annual meeting, committees, and the process for leadership selection. The executive council is usually composed of a president or executive director (which in Canada is a separate position from the leader of the party), vice-presidential positions (people in charge of heading up policy, memberships, fundraising, youth), as well as a chief financial officer or treasurer.

Some parties also have commissions or branches dedicated to women, youth, students, Indigenous peoples, and others. This is an illustration of how parties try to recruit members and entice them to stay by offering meaningful participation. In the Liberal Party of Canada, members between 14 and 25 can join the "Young Liberals." The Young Liberals can put forward their own policy resolutions, are guaranteed spots at party conventions, and have representation on the party's national executive. Likewise, the Canadian NDP has commissions and committees for women, people with disabilities, Aboriginals, LBGT members, and visible minorities. The Canadian federal Conservative Party, in contrast, has not established such affiliated associations, maintaining that each person is an equal member of the party, regardless of age, gender, ethnicity, ability, or sexual orientation. There is a "Campus Conservatives" organization for universities in Canada, but its focus is on supporting Conservative ridings, representatives, and candidates in elections.[25]

The structure of federal political parties in Canada also includes operations at the national and local level. If you buy a membership in the Liberal Party, you will belong to a local riding association that corresponds with where you live (for example, Calgary Centre, Hamilton Mountain, or Cape Breton-Canso). Each electoral riding has its own party executive to keep track of local members, develop policy ideas, throw fundraisers, and, when required, hold nomination contests to choose a party candidate for election. In fact, the local nomination and national leadership contests tend to increase a party's membership significantly, sometimes by 200 or 300 percent as nominees race to sign up new members to help them win.[26] Unfortunately, the swelled numbers are usually temporary, and in spite of commissions and committees that reach out to specific groups of Canadians, parties find it increasingly hard to recruit and retain members.

Party Members

The foundation of most parties is their membership. Have you ever thought about joining a party? What would motivate you to seek out a membership? As noted at the beginning of this chapter, across advanced industrial nations fewer people are choosing to do so.[27] Two Canadian scholars, William Cross and Lisa Young, conducted a survey of party members to uncover descriptive information about party members as a whole, as well as details about why people join a party in the first place. They found that party members hardly reflect the socio-demographic make-up of Canada. The majority of members are older, male, well-educated, and born in Canada.[28] There are more women and youth in the Liberals and NDP, but male members are still the majority. While there is clearly some homogeneity to the "average" party member, the other significant fact is that few Canadians maintain their membership year over year. In fact, the survey found that only one to two percent of Canadians renew their membership annually, placing Canada "at the bottom of the list of Westminster democracies."[29]

What are parties doing wrong? Cross and Young argue that "the likely reason for the low membership rate is that Canadians do not see any great benefit to be gained through party membership."[30] If we examine some of the traditional roles that party members have played in parties, we may be able to pinpoint where there are diminishing returns for members. This appears to be the case in two areas in particular: party policy and elections. At the same time, party members remain significant in the areas of party finance as well as leadership and candidate selection.

Party Policy

One of the most common responses to "reasons for joining a political party" in the Cross and Young survey was belief in the party's policies (84 percent).[31] Almost 20 percent of respondents indicated a desire to influence party policy as a "very important" reason for seeking membership.[32] The influence that members have over policy, however, is usually quite minimal. As parties have moved toward the electoral-professional type and political marketing approaches have become the preferred method of product development for parties (discussed later in this chapter), the role of regular members in shaping policy has been curtailed sharply.

Reducing the policy influence of party members has much to do with the fact that partisans tend to be more ideological than voters in the larger electorate; party elites recognize that the prescriptions to policy problems emanating from a convention of dedicated Conservatives (perhaps advocating for the privatization of healthcare) or Liberals (perhaps advocating for a rise in the GST and income taxes) may not be acceptable to other Canadians, many of whom lack partisan identification and may be "persuadable voter targets" for any one of the parties. Party leaders are thus caught between their desire to raise membership

levels (which helps to stabilize support for the party and increase its legitimacy and credibility within the public) and giving members more influence over the direction of party policy (which could have the unintended consequence of alienating certain segments of the electorate).

Elections

Alienating voters is problematic for parties hoping to win power. For many parties, the point of their existence is to control the government. A long-held role of party members has been to help their party win elections. But much like policy development, here we see a traditional task constrained because of new ways of conducting campaigns. Party member volunteers are obviously required when fighting an election, particularly at the local level. A party needs people to canvass neighbourhoods, go to rallies, help raise funds, make telephone calls to potential supporters, and get out the vote on election day.

But technology has replaced some of the labour that was required just a few decades ago and this has sidelined the role of on-the-ground volunteers. Parties can hire companies that will make automated calls to contact voters and find possible party supporters for election day; campaign strategy, branding, messaging, and the leader's tour are controlled by party professionals attached to the executive; advertisements on TV and radio highlight the party's promises; and local candidates are forbidden from developing their own policy positions or prescriptions—they must follow the campaign "messages" given to them by the party headquarters to ensure consistency in what candidates are saying across a province or country. Strict control over how elections are conducted, in addition to the technology available to improve the efficiency of voter contact, can dampen the enthusiasm that some volunteers have for campaigning in their constituencies.

Party Financing

How do parties raise the money that they need for elections and for inter-election party activities? This is one area where party members retain a preeminent stature since they have a greater inclination to donate money to their party. In fact, for almost all parties in Canada, contributing funds was the most likely activity in which members participated.[33]

To comply with the principles of fairness, transparency, and accountability, there are parameters placed on how much parties can raise from individual Canadians in a year, and limits on how much a party can spend during an election campaign. The fairness principle maintains that there should be a level playing field for parties competing for power. In other words, a party's ability to raise and spend money should not be a determining factor in the outcome of a campaign. Placing limits on party and candidate spending is not uncommon. In a 2012 survey of 180 countries, the International Institute for Democracy and Electoral Assistance found that 29 percent imposed restrictions on party spending and 44 percent limited candidate spending (with European countries being the most likely to do so).[34] Transparency and accountability also matter, and the same survey found that just over 50 percent had regulations that demanded political parties report on their election expenses and identify donors.

In Canada, campaign finance legislation first took effect in 1974. These initial reforms established spending limits during elections as well as rules for disclosing contributions. The next dramatic change in political party funding occurred in 2003. For many years, the major parties had turned to corporations and unions to provide them with the money necessary to contest elections and keep their party headquarters running from year to year. In 2001, for example, the six largest Canadian banks donated $350,000 to the Liberal Party, $211,000 to the Progressive Conservative Party, $140,000 to the Canadian Alliance, and nothing to the NDP, which instead received over $1.3 million from trade unions.[35] The 2003 changes capped the amount that corporations and unions could donate to political parties, and further legislative changes in 2006 banned corporate and union donations outright. Parties now have to fundraise solely from members and reach out to other Canadians for extra donations, with limitations on the amount that an individual can donate each year. To ease the parties into this new regime, the changes made in 2003 included the introduction of public subsidies based on votes won in the election. For every vote that a party won, it would receive $1.75 from the public purse.[36] The public subsidy scheme lasted just a decade. A fourth round of party financing reforms in 2012 provided for the elimination of this subsidy

by 2015. The change seriously disadvantages the Bloc Québécois and Green Party, since they were highly dependent on the subsidy. It will advantage those parties that have become sophisticated at raising small amounts of money from a large number of donors. To this point, the Conservatives have been the most successful in this respect, attracting over $17 million from just over 87,000 donors in 2012.[37] That same year, the Liberals raised just $8.1 million from 44,466 donors while the NDP gathered $7.7 million from 43,500 donors.[38] Being in power certainly helps a party's ability to attract donors, but the fact is that the Conservatives (and their predecessors in the Canadian Alliance and Reform Party) have always been very good at raising money from individual Canadians since they could not rely on substantial contributions from either banks or unions.

To put party financing into some perspective, the impact of money on elections in the Canadian system appears quite minimal when compared with the United States. In the 2011 Canadian federal election, each party fielding candidates in all 308 ridings had their spending capped at $21 million over the five-week campaign.[39] In contrast, after a series of successful constitutional challenges to campaign finance laws in the U.S., there are few remaining legislative limits on raising or spending money during an American election. Consequently, the 2012 general election in the United States resulted in over $6 billion in expenditures by parties and candidates to win office.[40] This dwarfs the amount spent in most other countries.

Candidate and Leadership Selection

In addition to donating money, party members continue to play a prominent role in selecting both candidates for elections and party leaders. Choosing candidates has long been a jealously guarded right of local associations, especially since the ability of party members to influence policy has waned considerably. In a competitive bid for the nomination, a local riding association can welcome hundreds of new members and raise significant sums of money to fund the subsequent campaign.

Scholars have called this bargain between party elites (who control policy) and grassroots members (who oversee candidate selection) a "stratarchy," which describes an organization where each strata (or group) has areas of control independent of the other.[41] New evidence, however, reveals that it is rare to find a party in which mutual autonomy is strictly respected vis-à-vis candidate selection. In countries such as Australia, Canada, Ireland, and New Zealand, the reality is organizational interdependency.[42] This is readily apparent in the Canadian context. Party leaders can appoint candidates in ridings, regardless of what the local association desires. They may choose to do this, for example, if there is a "star" candidate and the leader wants to shield the person from a nomination race. Diversity in representation is another reason for appointing candidates—to ensure that members of traditionally underrepresented groups such as women and visible minorities have an opportunity to run in the general election.

Party leaders can also prevent someone from running for a nomination. This may be the result of a background review that reveals a criminal history, or perhaps the potential nominee has controversial views that are not in line with party policy. The central party may also interfere in ways that are less obvious, such as controlling the timing of the nomination, protecting incumbents by automatically allowing them to run again, or vetoing the choices of the local constituency association by refusing the formal endorsement of the party leader, a requirement of the Canada Elections Act. In countries where the electoral system involves a list, leaders and other party elites can play an active role in determining who is on the list or, at the very least, where on that list a name is placed. This can be crucial in a closed list system, since candidates placed at or near the top of the list are the first to be allocated legislative seats based on the party's popular vote.

It is important to note that interference in local nomination races can backfire. The precious few party members who have a vested interest in these nomination contests may resent the involvement of party elites. In some cases, it can result in the party losing both members and campaign volunteers. So while it is wrong to suggest that local ridings have *exclusive* control over candidate selection, it is still a key area of responsibility that most party members take very seriously and in which party leaders must think carefully before meddling.

Leadership selection is another domain where the membership has taken an active role. In the late 19th and early 20th centuries, party leaders in most Westminster systems were chosen (and removed) by the parliamentary caucus. This is still the case in Australia. Before the 2010 Australian general election, Labor MPs voted to remove their leader Kevin Rudd, who also happened to be the prime minister, and replace him with the more popular Labor MP Julia Gillard. Gillard won the 2010 election but three years later Rudd successfully replaced *her* to become prime minister again.

Selection and removal of the leader by the parliamentary caucus is less popular in other democracies, and there has been movement toward greater inclusivity for party members in the larger party organization to have a say in who becomes leader. In Britain, choosing a leader combines both exclusive and inclusive processes. The Labour Party, for example, creates a shortlist of candidates determined by the parliamentary caucus—to get on that shortlist you must have the support of at least one-sixth of the parliamentary caucus. An electoral college decides who ultimately wins the leadership by combining votes from MPs and members of the European Parliament, the broader party membership, and affiliated organizations. The presidential nominees (and thus leaders) of the Democratic and Republican parties in the United States are determined through a succession of state primaries that facilitate the participation of millions of Americans. In non-democratic countries, leadership selection processes tend to be less inclusive. In China, for example, the leader of the Communist Party is still selected through a delegated process at the party's congress, held every five years. However, extensive succession plans for a new leader are the norm and it is well known who the favoured candidate is in advance. The selection by delegates is less a real competition and more a vote of approval for the choice made by the out-going leader and Politburo, the most powerful committee of the Communist Party.

Leadership selection in Canada has become an increasingly open process. The traditional method of selecting leaders exclusively through the parliamentary caucus has been abandoned for decades. Neither do the federal parties use a delegate model of selection, where party members are elected by fellow members as "delegates" who attend the convention and vote for a new leader. The federal parties have expanded the inclusive nature of leadership selection to embrace the one-member/one-vote system, in which each party member (or, in the case of the 2013 Liberal Party leadership selection, any "supporter" of the party) can cast a vote for their favoured candidate, often using a preferential ballot to rank their choices. The Conservatives and Liberals allot each riding 100 points, and how many points a candidate wins from an electoral district is allocated proportionally by first preference votes of members in that riding. With 308 ridings in the 2013 Liberal election, a candidate had to win 15,401 points to be victorious. Justin Trudeau did so on the first round with 24,668 points (80 percent support of the 104,552 votes cast by party members and supporters).

As noted earlier, becoming a party member is easy and affordable. Sometimes there is a requirement of being a member for a certain length of time before you are eligible to vote in a leadership selection (usually a few months). In other cases, you can buy a membership and vote right away. Ways of casting a ballot have also been expanded. Party members can vote in person at sites dedicated to the leadership election, they can vote by phone, and most parties have also implemented online voting. These new ways of voting are aimed at increasing the number of members participating in the selection of their leader.

In summary, what we see is heavier involvement by party members in candidate and leadership selection

Justin Trudeau handily wins the 2013 Liberal Party leadership race.

© The Canadian Press/Ryan Remiorz

and raising money for elections, but a declining role in developing party policy. We also see some side-lining of party members in the development of election campaign strategies. The next section will detail new trends in contesting elections and how they are reshaping party politics into something that resembles a permanent campaign. We need to think about whether aspects of the permanent campaign could have the effect of further dampening enthusiasm for politics and parties by members and citizens alike.

NEW TRENDS FOR PARTIES IN CAMPAIGNS

One of the more interesting and rapidly changing areas of party politics is how parties contest elections. Electioneering has evolved dramatically over the past few decades, primarily due to the advent of Web 2.0 and the technology available to reach voters with very targeted messages.

When we think back to the party types outlined earlier, we see that campaign techniques have actually enhanced aspects of the electoral-professional party. For parties in Australia, Britain, Canada, New Zealand, the United States, and elsewhere, winning power remains the primary goal of the organization. Party members are important to achieving success during a campaign through their work as door-to-door canvassers, calling supporters from phone banks, and even driving people to the polls to get out the vote. But how parties develop policies, build a brand, create a strong image of their leader, and uncover which segments of voters will be most receptive to their messages (such as soccer mums, small business owners, or young professionals in urban centres) is called **political marketing**, and it is becoming the predominant way that successful parties "do" politics in the 21st century. A market-oriented party is different from other parties. Instead of simply creating policies and trying to "sell" them to the voting public, a market-oriented party uses market intelligence such as public opinion polls, focus groups, survey data, and consumer reports to gauge the needs and wants of the electorate—and how best to present them—*before* designing their "product." The product itself can be all or any combination of the policies, the leader's image, the brand, party symbols, and candidates. In this way, a political party has a good idea of what "consumers" want and can respond accordingly.[43]

> **Political marketing:** The application of business marketing concepts to the practice and study of politics and government. Strategies and tools include branding, focus groups, opposition research, get out the vote efforts, polling, public relations, voter segmentation, voter profiling, and strategic product development.

In the years leading up to the 1997 general election, Britain's Labour Party under Tony Blair used market intelligence to transform the party into "New Labour" by responding to what British voters said they wanted. As a result, New Labour was less socialist, less influenced by unions, less "tax and spend," more business-friendly, and more mainstream, and offered policy outcomes that were measurable so that the public could hold the party to account at the next election.[44] Other marketing tools—such as direct mail, TV and radio ads, e-mail, and online social networking—were used to direct political communications at the voter segments that market research indicated would respond most favourably to the party's product, mostly because those segments had informed its development in the first place (for example, working-class women with children, or self-employed middle-class men). Using such a market-oriented approach, New Labour won a landslide in 1997 and secured subsequent majority governments in 2001 and 2005.

The more information a party can access, the better it can combine data sources, discover trends and patterns between personal characteristics and political beliefs (for example, voters who subscribe to magazines like *Field and Stream* are more likely to vote Republican), design products that respond to those voters, and then target them specifically for political messages. Barack Obama's 2008 presidential campaign, for example, used market research in a way that revealed which bus routes should have ads because a handful of target voters rode those routes each day.[45] His brand of "hope" and core "Yes We Can" message were developed based largely on data about his key voter segments.[46]

The Conservative Party of Canada is considered a market-oriented party,[47] with the NDP and Liberals

still playing catch up. By using market research to help prepare the party for the 2006 election, Stephen Harper presented himself as a less rigid leader, made five promises that the data suggested would appeal to core and persuadable voters, and shaved off the harder ideological edges that had characterized the Canadian Alliance and its predecessor, Reform.

The Conservatives only achieved a minority government in 2006, but over the ensuing two elections the party was able to build support to win a majority in 2011. What differentiates the parties in Canada from those in the United States is a more limited access to consumer data. Privacy laws in Canada restrict parties from buying consumer data in the same way that American parties can. To get around this problem, the Conservatives have built their own database (the Constituency Information Management System) so that they can successfully segment and target voters. Each day information is inputted into the CIMS by party volunteers, MPs, and party staff, based on such sources as party membership lists, donors, people who have signed up to receive information through the party's website, calls from the public, and information gathered from door-to-door canvassers during elections. When the details gathered by the party are combined with public opinion polls and other datasets from Statistics Canada, party strategists can sort Canadians into useful voter profiles.

With more parties adopting a market-oriented approach, there is growing debate about whether it is appropriate to treat citizens as consumers. A consumer, for example, usually has rights but few

In 2006, Canadian voters wanted Stephen Harper to have a softer image.
© Ingrid Rice

responsibilities or obligations in the marketplace. This is not true for citizens, who possess both rights *and* responsibilities in a democracy. When voters are perceived as consumers, parties are more likely to respond to their wants, but not necessarily to their *needs*. Few people want to pay more taxes, but greater revenue may be required to provide healthcare to an aging population. Consumerism, in other words, is about the individual; citizenship is about the collective. If we only think about "what's in it for me," then we risk losing the benefit of thinking about others, which has long been a core principle of strong, democratic political systems.

There are also drawbacks of the market-oriented approach for party members. We have learned that political parties in Canada and elsewhere are losing members. We also know that for those who do join it is largely because they like the policies or want to influence policy development. The market-oriented party is fixated less on the policy desires of its membership and more on having members support policies divined from the market research. This marginalizes members from the policy role that most say attracted them to the party in the first place. How will parties recruit new members if a market orientation diminishes the policy influence of the party membership?

The Permanent Campaign

When an election is over, some parties will have won enough seats to form government while others will sit in opposition and try to hold the government accountable. The representatives settle into their respective roles and they and their parties will wait until the next election before fighting it out again. Or will they?

An interesting development in a number of western democracies is the advent of the **permanent campaign**. If you consider such factors as a shrinking pool of voters and party members, the use of market intelligence to guide the development of policy and party decisions, a saturated 24-hour media environment, and the desire for error-free government in which successful candidates-now-MPs are under the same strict messaging command to maintain a party's brand in the public mind, the arrival of constant campaigning does not seem so surprising. The permanent campaign is an approach to government whereby party elites apply strategies and techniques usually confined to election campaigns to the process of governing itself. In order to maintain public approval and improve chances for re-election, every issue, decision, legislative vote, policy announcement, and public opinion is viewed as a mini-contest with a winner and a loser. The governing party wants to be on the winning side more often than not, and can use the resources that government provides to secure partisan advantage.

> **Permanent campaign:** An approach to government whereby partisan elites who control government apply strategies and techniques that are usually confined to an election campaign to the process of governing itself.

The permanent campaign originated in the United States in the late 1970s and 1980s.[48] In the 1990s, President Bill Clinton hired the pollsters and strategists from his campaign to work in the White House.[49] For Clinton and successive presidents, presidential travel was planned strategically to target states needed to win re-election.[50] Political communications were aimed more at the public than Congress, since public approval of presidential policy could influence Congressional votes more effectively than direct negotiations with legislators themselves.[51]

The phenomenon of the permanent campaign has crept into other countries as well, with evidence demonstrating its existence in Australia, Britain, Ecuador, and Italy.[52] Canada is no exception. Since the mid-2000s, we see, among other indicators, the prime minister's office obsessed with communications spin and rapid responses to any criticism of government policies

THINK AND DISCUSS

Should parties treat citizens like consumers? Does this lead to more responsive politics? Does it leave anyone out?

and decisions; the growth in political staff in certain branches of the PMO such as communications, tour and scheduling, and issues management; the prime minister's aircraft painted with party colours; the firing of public servants who speak without prior approval of the PMO or who go wildly off-message; parliamentary debate that consists almost solely of government speaking points; refusal by the government to produce requested documents to Parliament; and the increase in government partisan advertising. Another clear indication of the permanent campaign is advertisements attacking successive Liberal leaders between elections since 2006. Because of the Conservatives' fundraising prowess, the party has had plenty of money to create and air commercials intended to plant seeds of doubt about the leadership capabilities of their parliamentary opponents. Since the ads were launched in the inter-election period, spending limit legislation did not apply (parties can spend as much as they wish when there is no election). As detailed in this chapter's photo essay, both Stéphane Dion and Michael Ignatieff, as well as their parties, suffered in the polls because of the ads. The point to take home is that the new context in which politics takes place means that the campaign never ends. The party in government has the advantage of numerous resources to provide assistance in that task; parties in opposition have taken the role of fund-raising more seriously so that they can mount attacks and counter-attacks when required.

The critical question for citizens and voters is whether the advent of the permanent campaign has diminished the quality and quantity of substantive policy debate between and among parties. If the imperative is to maintain high public approval, sustain a certain image, and tear down party opponents through inter-election advertising, do we still get good policy? Or is policy only aimed at core voters? This raises a question of good governance and how these new election trends are impacting the operation of party government. Can we be confident that the party in power is really governing on behalf of us all?

Where Do Parties Go from Here?

At this point, it should be clear that political parties are still important to sustaining democracies. Parties compete with one another to provide choices to the electorate, form the government, and keep government accountable by watching what it is doing, asking questions of those in power, and offering citizens alternative policy views. At the same time, political parties are losing the confidence of citizens and failing to attract members and a dependable base of voters. This has much to do with the increasing sources of information about government and politics that citizens can access instead of turning to parties, a more educated and critical electorate, and various political scandals that turn many people off from political parties. So what can parties do to become more relevant in the day-to-day lives of citizens? How do parties compete with the myriad of other distractions and commitments that people have? Three possibilities come to mind.

First, the move by the Liberal Party to create a new category of "supporter" is a good development and something that could be emulated by other party organizations. The supporter was not a full-fledged member and did not have to buy a membership but did have to provide contact information and register with the party to cast a ballot in the leadership race that resulted in Justin Trudeau's win. Party supporters have been characterized as "tire kickers," people who want to get a sense of the party and what it is about without making a full commitment. The data collected by the party suggests that many of those who signed up as supporters were young people. Party strategist John Duffy noted that "that's not just very young people… but the pool of people who've never voted, many of them are now in their early 40s. They represent a huge…reservoir of potential political energy."[53] While the Liberal Party's experiment with supporters is still new, this approach has potential for attracting more citizens to become more engaged in political parties.

Second, while the trend is toward more powerful, centralized, and professionalized parties, for those organizations that depend on financial contributions from members (making membership highly important), it is clear that greater policy involvement by the grassroots is a critical factor. A major incentive to joining a party is having influence over policy; if parties can make good on this commitment, then there is a higher likelihood of growing and maintaining their membership rolls, particularly between elections.

This is where the move away from public funding for political parties is also important. In many European countries, for example, parties are becoming increasingly reliant on the state to provide

PHOTO ESSAY

Inter-election attack ads feature prominently in the permanent campaign.

THE PERMANENT CAMPAIGN IN PRACTICE

Stéphane Dion was elected leader of the Liberal Party of Canada in December 2006. The Conservative Party, governing with only a minority, wanted to brand Dion as a weak leader as early as possible. If Canadians came to view Dion as rather hapless and pathetic, then this would certainly help Conservative fortunes with voters. Since spending limits only apply to the writ period (from the time when an election is called to voting day), and since the Conservatives had amassed a large financial war chest through successful fundraising efforts, the party wasted little time creating ads that assailed the newly elected Dion.

Using footage from an actual Liberal leadership debate where Dion had commented that setting priorities was not easy, the Conservatives launched a television ad that emphasized the requirement of strong leadership to "get things done" and that Dion was "not a leader." The ad aired during the 2007 Super Bowl, reaching a wide swath of voters. The attack had its desired effect: Dion's polling numbers plummeted and never recovered and the Conservatives went on to win the subsequent 2008 election. The formula was repeated when Michael Ignatieff took over as Liberal leader in 2009 (the Conservatives also won the 2011 election), and again when Justin Trudeau took the helm of the party in 2013.

The aggressive offensive against these Liberal leaders by the Conservative Party was significant because nothing of that magnitude had occurred in Canadian politics before; the ads were evidence that a permanent campaign was well underway. The degree to which these types of attacks will continue depends on party coffers—it is costly to buy air time, especially during major sporting events or awards shows. The precedent has been set, however, and Canadian voters should not be surprised to see more of this type of permanent campaigning in the future.

Want to see the ads described here? See the websites at the end of this chapter.

their organizations with funds to support their work. This can lead party elites to ignore grassroots members and their contributions, since the party is not dependent on them for finances. Where the *only* source of funds is from members and supporters, they are not as easily ignored by the party leadership. Of course, some balance may be required. The Green Party of Canada will suffer more than other parties with the elimination of government support to parties in Canada, and this is true of other small or new parties in other countries. Social media may be of some help here, since it is becoming increasingly affordable for parties to reach out to the public and solicit support through official websites and social media channels.

The third, and most difficult, possibility is to encourage a softening of the hyper-partisanship that has taken over politics in countries around the world and is fuelling the permanent campaign. The United States is perhaps the most obvious example here. Because the Democratic and Republican parties have difficulty compromising on issues, the government has, on several occasions, verged on total dysfunction. To compromise is *not* to lose but of late this is the way that politics is framed. Since the media feeds on controversy, disagreements between parties and politicians are broadcast, analyzed, and replayed, preventing productive discussions about policy options. Increasing polarization between parties threatens good governance and reinforces the negative views of parties held by citizens, which in turn can weaken the quality of democracy. How to encourage a change in hyper-partisanship is the critical question since it will have to involve more than institutional reforms, such as changing the electoral system.

CONCLUSION

Political parties are critical to the study and practice of politics. They come in many varieties and compete in different party systems. Two points about political parties are particularly important to remember. First, we should be concerned about their weaknesses, especially the ones that lead to lagging memberships and a general decline of confidence in parties by citizens. As the chapter has shown, these are problems plaguing political parties in numerous countries around the globe and they deserve on-going attention.

Second, our misgivings about parties should not overshadow the important role that they play in democratic governance. It is through parties that interests are articulated and put to the public as policy choices, leaders are selected, voters are mobilized, citizens are elected as representatives, and peaceful transitions of power are assured. Furthermore, we know that parties can evolve. If we do not like the way that political parties function, if we want to increase our levels of confidence and trust in them, then we can change them. This will require us to become more involved; the more that people become interested and engaged in our parties and party system, the greater the ability to affect change from within.

Whether we like parties or not, we need them. Strong, stable parties are a vital component of a vibrant democracy—having one is contingent on having the other. As citizens we must understand that while parties may not be perfect, they are essential to representative government. Put simply, the party will live on. It is up to us whether we will join in.

DISCUSSION QUESTIONS

1. Why do you think young people are more likely to join interest groups instead of political parties?

2. How can political parties regain the confidence of citizens?

3. Should the parliamentary caucus be able to remove the party leader or should that power remain with party members?

4. Is the amount of money in American political campaigns a problem? Should there be restrictions on the amount of money that a party can spend in an election?

5. Is the "permanent campaign" a positive or negative development for political parties? Why or why not?

WEBSITES

Manifesto Project Database
https://manifestoproject.wzb.eu
For access to data, reports, and publications on comparative party platforms and party positions.

National Democratic Institute
https://www.ndi.org/political-parties
For information about political parties around the world.

Political Marketing
http://www.political-marketing.org
Online resources for literature and audio-visual material on new campaign techniques used by political parties.

Political Party Database
http://www.politicalpartydb.org
Working Group for comparative analyses of political parties and their role in representative democracies.

Attack Ads on the Liberal Leaders
https://www.youtube.com/watch?v=yEH_hprcs6g
Dion Attack Ad

https://www.youtube.com/watch?v=COeNW8K_1e8
Ignatieff Attack Ad

https://www.youtube.com/watch?v=1qKps7uG6eM ()
Trudeau Attack Ad

FURTHER READINGS

William P. Cross and André Blais, *Politics at the Centre: The Selection and Removal of Party Leaders in the Anglo Parliamentary Democracies.* Oxford: Oxford University Press, 2012.

Russell J.Dalton and Martin P. Wattenberg, *Parties without Partisans: Political Change in Advanced Industrial Democracies.* Oxford: Oxford University Press, 2000.

Royce Koop, *Grassroots Liberals: Organizing for Local and National Politics.* Vancouver: University of British Columbia Press, 2011.

Kay Lawson, ed., *Political Parties and Democracy.* Santa Barbara: Praeger, 2010.

Jennifer Lees-Marshment, *Political Marketing: Principles and Applications.* London and New York: Routledge, 2009.

ENDNOTES

1. William Cross and Lisa Young, "Are Canadian Political Parties Empty Vessels? Membership, Engagement, and Policy Capacity," *Choices* 12 (4) (June 2006), pp. 14–28; Russell J. Dalton, *Citizen Politics: Public Opinion and Political Parties in Advanced Industrial Democracies,* 6th ed. (Washington, DC: CQ Press, 2013); Russell J. Dalton and Martin P. Wattenberg, eds., *Parties without Partisans: Political Change in Advanced Industrial Democracies* (Oxford: Oxford University Press, 2000).

2. Quoted in Leon D. Epstein, *Political Parties in the American Mold* (Madison: University of Wisconsin Press, 1986), p. 18.

3. E.E. Schattschneider, *Party Government in the United States* (New York: Rinehart, 1942), p. 1.

4. Clinton Rossiter, *Parties and Politics in America* (Ithaca: Cornell University Press, 1976), p. ix.

5. Kay Lawson and Peter H. Merkl, "Political Parties in the 21st Century," in Kay Lawson and Peter H. Merkl, eds., *When Political Parties Prosper* (Boulder: Lynne Reimer, 2007), pp. 1–2.

6. Richard Rose, Neil Munro, and Stephen White, "Voting in a Floating Party System: The 1999 Duma Election," *Europe-Asia Studies* 53 (3) (May 2001), pp. 419–43.

7. Allen Hicken, "Stuck in the Mud: Parties and Party Systems in Democratic Southeast Asia," *Taiwan Journal of Democracy* 2 (2) (December 2006), pp. 23–46; Paige Johnson Tan, "Indonesia Seven Years after Soeharto: Party System Institutionalization in a New Democracy," *Contemporary Southeast Asia* 28 (1) (April 2006), pp. 88–114.

8. Leon D. Epstein, *Political Parties in Western Democracies* (New Brunswick, New Jersey:

Transaction Books, 1980), p. 9; Joseph A. Schlesinger, *Political Parties and the Winning of Office* (Ann Arbor: University of Michigan Press, 1991).

9. At the time of writing (early 2015), there were actually two Green Party MPs: Elizabeth May, who was elected in the 2011 federal election, and Thunder Bay-Superior North MP Bruce Hyer, who left the NDP caucus in 2012 to sit as an independent but chose to join the Green Party in December 2013.

10. Dalton and Wattenberg, *Parties without Partisans*; Russell J. Dalton, *Democratic Challenges, Democratic Choices: The Erosion of Political Support in Advanced Industrial Democracies* (Oxford: Oxford University Press, 2004).

11. V.O. Key Jr., *Politics, Parties, and Pressure Groups*, 5th ed. (New York: Crowell, 1964).

12. The particular roles and functions are drawn from Dalton and Wattenberg, *Parties without Partisans*, pp. 5–10.

13. William Cross, "In Search of Stratarchy: An Examination of Intra Party Democracy in Four Westminster Systems." Paper presented at the annual meetings of the Canadian Political Science Association. St. Catharines, Ontario, May 2014.

14. Angus Campbell, Philip Converse, Warren Miller, and Donald Stokes, *The American Voter* (New York: John Wiley and Sons, Inc., 1960).

15. Bruce E. Keith et al., *The Myth of the Independent Voter* (Berkeley: University of California Press, 1992).

16. Laura B. Stephenson and Cameron Anderson, *Voting Behaviour in Canada* (Vancouver: University of British Columbia Press, 2010).

17. Elections Canada, "Voter Turnout at Federal Elections and Referendums," online at http://www.elections.ca/content.aspx?dir=turn&document=index&lang=e&section=ele.

18. Maurice Duverger, *Political Parties* (New York: John Wiley and Sons, Inc., 1963).

19. Sigmund Neumann, ed., *Modern Political Parties: Approaches in Comparative Politics* (Chicago: University of Chicago Press, 1956), p. 404.

20. Otto Kircheimer, "The Transformation of the Western European Party System," in J. LaPalombara and M. Weiner, eds., *Political Parties and Political Development* (Princeton: Princeton University Press, 1966), pp. 177–200.

21. Angelo Panebianco, *Political Parties: Organization and Power* (Cambridge: Cambridge University Press, 1988).

22. Richard S. Katz and Peter Mair, "Changing Models of Party Organization and Party Democracy: The Emergence of the Cartel Party," *Party Politics* 1 (1) (January 1995), pp. 5–28.

23. Pirate Party International, online at http://www.pp-international.net.

24. Elections Canada, "Final Election Expenses Limits for Registered Political Parties," online at http://www.elections.ca/content.aspx?section=ele&document=index&dir=pas/41ge/limpol&lang=e.

25. See Campusconservatives.ca, online at http://www.campusconservatives.ca/who-we-are/.

26. William Cross and Lisa Young, "Political Parties as Membership Organizations," in William Cross, ed., *Political Parties* (Vancouver: University of British Columbia Press, 2004), p. 15.

27. Peter Mair and Ingrid Van Biezen, "Party Membership in Twenty European Democracies, 1980–2000," *Party Politics*, 7 (1) (January 2001), pp. 5–21; Paul Webb, David Farrell, and Ian Holliday, eds. *Political Parties in Advanced Industrial Democracies* (Oxford: Oxford University Press, 2002).

28. Cross and Young, "Political Parties as Membership Organizations," pp. 14–31.

29. Cross and Young, "Are Canadian Political Parties Empty Vessels?," p. 16.

30. Cross and Young, "Political Parties as Membership Organizations," p. 19.

31. Ibid., p. 24.

32. Ibid.

33. Ibid., p. 27. Liberal Party members were more likely to display an election sign, attend a local meeting or nomination contest, and volunteer in an election campaign.

34. Magnus Ohman, "Political Finance Regulations Around the World: An Overview of the International IDEA Database," *International Institute for Democracy and Electoral Assistance*, 2012, online at http://www.idea.int/publications/political-finance-regulations/upload/Political-Finance-Regulations-Overview-of-IDEA-database.pdf.

35. Elections Canada, *Political parties' financial reports, 2001*, online at http://www.elections.ca/scripts/ecfiscals2/default.asp?L=E&Page=SummariesResult&FP=213&SS=2; Parliament of Canada, *Political contributions by the six largest Canadian banks, 1982–2003*, online at http://www.parl.gc.ca/parlinfo/pages/PartyContributionBank.aspx.

36. The subsidy would only be paid if the party won more than two percent of the popular vote nationally or five percent of the vote in ridings where the party ran candidates.

37. Elections Canada, "Registered Party Financial Transactions Return," online at http://www.elections.ca/WPAPPS/WPF/PP/PP/SelectParties?act=C2&period=1&returntype=1.

38. Ibid.

39. "Elections Canada sets $21 million campaign spending limit," *CBC News*, March 31, 2001, online at http://www.cbc.ca/news/politics/elections-canada-sets-21m-campaign-spending-limit-1.1101493.

40. Congressional races cost $3.6 billion and the presidential race $2.6 billion. See opensecrets.org at https://www.opensecrets.org/bigpicture/.

41. R. Kenneth Carty, "Parties as Franchise Systems: The Stratarchical Organizational Imperative," *Party Politics* 10 (1) (January 2004), pp. 5–24; R. Kenneth Carty and William Cross, "Can Stratarchically Organized Parties be Democratic? Evidence from the Canadian Experience," *Journal of Elections, Public Opinion and Parties* 16 (2) (2006), pp. 93–114.

42. Cross, "In Search of Stratarchy."

43. Jennifer Lees-Marshment, *Political Marketing: Principles and Applications* (London and New York: Routledge, 2009).

44. Jennifer Lees-Marshment, *Political Marketing and British Political Parties*, 2nd ed. (Manchester: Manchester University Press, 2008), pp. 181–203.

45. Sasha Issenberg, *The Victory Lab: The Secret Science of Winning Campaigns* (New York: Crown Publishers, 2012).

46. Brian M. Conley, "The Politics of Hope: The Democratic Party and the Institutionalisation of the Obama Brand in the 2010 Mid-Term Elections," in Jennifer Lees-Marshment, ed., *Routledge Handbook of Political Marketing* (London and New York: Routledge, 2012); David Plouffe, *The Audacity to Win* (New York: Penguin Books, 2010).

47. Daniel Paré and Flavia Berger, "Political Marketing Canadian Style? The Conservative Party and the 2006 Federal Election," *Canadian Journal of Communication* 31 (1) (2008), pp. 39–63.

48. Blumenthal, Sidney, *The Permanent Campaign: Inside the World of Elite Political Operatives* (Boston: Beacon Press, 1980).

49. Kathleen Shoon Murray and Peter Howard, "Variation in White House Polling Operations: Carter to Clinton," *Public Opinion Quarterly* 66 (4) (February 2002), pp. 527–58; Karlyn Bowman, "Polling to campaign and to govern," in N. Orstein and T. Mann, eds., *The Permanent Campaign and Its Future* (Washington, DC: American Enterprise Institute and the Brookings Institution, 2000), pp. 4–74.

50. Corey Cook, "The Permanence of the 'permanent campaign': George W. Bush's Public Presidency," *Presidential Studies Quarterly* 32 (4) (December 2002), pp. 753–64; Brendan Doherty, "The Politics of the Permanent

Campaign: Presidential Travel and the Electoral College, 1977–2004," *Presidential Studies Quarterly* 37 (4) (December 2007), pp. 749–73.

51. C.O. Jones, *Passages to the Presidency: From Campaigning to Governing* (Washington, DC: Brookings Institution, 1998); Samuel Kernell, *Going Public: New Strategies of Presidential Leadership*, 3rd ed. (Washington, DC: Congressional Quarterly, 1997).

52. Kathy MacDermott, "Marketing government: The public service and the permanent campaign," *Report No. 10* (Melbourne: School of Social Sciences, Australian National University, 2008), pp. 1–118; Peter Van Onselen and Wayne Errington, "The Democratic State as a Marketing Tool: The Permanent Campaign in Australia," *Commonwealth and Comparative Politics* 45 (1) (February 2007), pp. 78–94; Margaret Scammell, "Political Brands and Consumer Citizens: The Rebranding of Tony Blair," *The Annals of the American Academy of Political and Social Science* 611 (1) (May 2007), pp. 176–92; Catherine Conaghan and Carlos de la Torre, "The Permanent Campaign of Rafael Correa: Making Ecuador's Plebiscitary Presidency," *International Journal of Press/Politics* 13 (3) (July 2008), pp. 267–84; Franca Roncarolo, "Campaigning and Governing: An Analysis of Berlusconi's Rhetorical Leadership," *Modern Italy* 10 (1) (May 2005), pp. 75–93.

53. Leslie MacKinnon, "Liberals' 'supporter' experiment put to the test," *CBC News*, April 13, 2013, online at http://www.cbc.ca/news/politics/liberals-supporter-experiment-put-to-the-test-1.1366977.

12

CIVIL SOCIETY: THE STUDY OF POWER. INTRIGUE. PASSION.

Rachel Laforest

© REUTERS/Olivier Jean

Through such mechanisms as interest groups, social movements, and voluntary organizations, people can find ways—beyond elections and political parties—of representing themselves in politics. Here, thousands of students and their supporters took to the streets in Montreal to oppose—successfully—the Quebec government's 2012 plan to raise university tuition.

CHAPTER OBJECTIVES

After you have completed this chapter, you should be able to:

- define civil society and describe the main functions of civil society actors
- compare and contrast the characteristics of interest groups, social movements, and voluntary organizations
- distinguish insider strategies from outsider strategies

- identify new trends in civil society organizing and how they are impacting civil society groups
- discuss the effects of civil society organizing on the state of democracy

INTRODUCTION

We live in a democracy where "the rule of the people" through periodical elections is the key mechanism through which citizens exercise power. But what if the elections are not all that fair and competitive, allowing a relatively small group of leaders to possess real political power? What if public participation in the electoral process is limited and largely indirect? What if elections favour candidates that have exceptional resources, education, and connections, thereby limiting the ability of minority voices to be represented and heard? What would you do if your political opinions were not echoed in the policy choices put forward by political parties because they tailor their platforms to majority opinions in an effort to appeal to as many voters as possible? What if you didn't see yourself, your gender, your ethnicity, your language, or your economic interests reflected in the candidates running in your constituency? What if the issues and values that mattered the most to you, such as the environment, religious practices, or international human rights, reached beyond the jurisdiction of your national government? Would you question whether elections were enough to secure the real basis of democracy?

Every day, people fight for ideas and interests that they do not see reflected in the political systems in which they live. They do not want to govern and take over power, but they want to affect change either by influencing the state directly or public opinion more generally. If the ultimate authority in the political sphere rests with citizens, then they need to be able to access channels and mechanisms to express themselves when they have concerns and preoccupations that are not being addressed through the electoral system. Civil society research focuses on the many ways that individuals come together to do just that. For this reason, it is an essential focal point for studying politics. This chapter addresses the following questions: What is civil society? Why do individuals participate in collective action? What are some of the main forms and functions of civil society organizing? What impact does civil society research have on the study of politics? This chapter provides an introduction to the concept of civil society and the rich diversity of actors that compose it, and offers an overview of how the field has grown and evolved over time in response to broader societal changes. While pondering these dynamics, we will also discuss critically the impact that civil society organizing can have on democracy. On the one hand, civil society organizing can bring about important and meaningful change by drawing attention to inequities and fostering democratic values. On the other hand, civil society organizing can be used by dominant groups to reinforce existing power dynamics and, therefore, have potentially harmful or detrimental effects on democracy. Both aspects of civil society organizing need to be acknowledged.

CIVIL SOCIETY

Civil society is a social sphere, distinct from both the state and the market, which includes a wide range of social institutions and organizations around which people pursue common interests. These can include formally organized groups such as labour unions, professional associations, nonprofits, charitable organizations, community-based organizations, and voluntary organizations; but they can also include spontaneous, loosely organized networks and social movements. All such manifestations of collective action are critical vehicles for the transmission of interests and ideas into the policy arena, particularly the voices of disadvantaged and marginalized communities.

> **Civil society:** The social sphere, distinct from both the state and the market, which includes a wide range of social institutions and organizations around and through which people organize and pursue common interests.

Just in the past five years, a number of high-profile civil society mobilizations around the world have drawn attention to the power that political, financial, and economic elites yield. In 2010, a revolutionary wave of protests known as the Arab Spring spread through northern Africa and the Middle East, toppling a number of governments. In 2011, 4,000 people occupied Zuccotti Park in New York to protest government policies that benefited the richest percentile of earners—the one percent—at the expense of the remaining 99 percent. Since then, the "Occupy movement" has become a worldwide phenomenon with protests organized in 951 cities and across 82 countries, emphasizing the growing concentration of income and wealth among top earners. In 2011 in Quebec, half-a-million people marched to support the student movement[1] in its fight to stop a tuition increase announced by the provincial government. This was not only "the longest and largest student strike in the history of North America," but also "the biggest act of civil disobedience in Canadian history."[2] Across Canada in 2012–2013, the Idle No More movement[3] used teach-ins and flash mobs to protest

violations of Indigenous treaty rights after the federal government introduced legislative changes that removed protections for forests and waterways, some of which pass through First Nations land. Solidarity protests were held around the world in the U.S., the U.K., Sweden, Germany, and New Zealand to support Indigenous peoples in Canada. These movements have left an indelible mark on politics today.

But civil society organizing also takes place in the shadows of the political arena. YMCAs across Canada provide services and engage communities every day in order to improve peoples' living conditions and to promote personal growth, accessibility, and inclusivity. Many people have sponsored a child in a developing country through World Vision to help fight world hunger. These are also examples of **collective action** because they involve individuals acting in similar ways in the hopes of achieving a common goal.

> **Collective action:** Any action taken together by two or more individuals whose goal is to achieve a common objective.

According to Miriam Smith, "there is no agreement among political scientists specifically or social scientists in general about the best ways to study group and social movement politics."[4] Indeed, the diversity in scale, scope, level of organization, and the nature of their relationships with political parties and other organized groups make it difficult to delineate and circumscribe the characteristics of civil society organizations with precision. As a result, within this field of research, different strands of the literature focus on specific forms of organizing within civil society. This diversity in approaches has fostered important debates and often radically different ideas about the role of civil society in politics. This next section introduces you to a variety of civil society actors and discusses how research has evolved through each of the main strands of the literature.

THINK AND DISCUSS

Make a list of some of the civil society organizations that you can think of that have an effect on our political world. Consider at least three ways in which these organizations are similar, and three ways in which they differ from each other. What strikes you?

WHAT ARE INTEREST GROUPS, SOCIAL MOVEMENTS, AND VOLUNTARY ORGANIZATIONS?

Within the civil society sphere, there are different entities with distinct characteristics. This section looks specifically at three categories in turn: interest groups, social movements, and voluntary organizations.

One way people can have their voice heard is to find and work with others who share similar concerns. **Interest groups** are defined by Paul Pross as "organizations whose members act together to influence public policy in order to promote their own interests."[5] Contrary to a political party, an interest group does not want to govern but rather seeks to influence those who do. In this sense, a group's primary objective is to persuade policy-makers to support or undertake actions that will help, or to oppose or refrain from policies that will harm, members of the group and their interests. An interest group will also usually seek to influence public opinion and educate the public on the issues that concern the group and the positions that it supports. For example, trade unions like the Canadian Auto Workers Union and the Canadian Labour Congress attempt to influence labour market policies by meeting with elected officials face-to-face or by publishing research aimed at the broader public.

> **Interest group:** An organization that brings together people with common interests and concerns in order to influence public policy.

Because a key function of interest groups is to promote the interests of their members, they can also be referred to as "pressure groups" or "lobby groups." One of the most powerful interest groups in the United States is the National Rifle Association (NRA), which boasts more than 2.5 million members. It represents and defends the interests of gun owners before government. It also seeks to promote good marksmanship and to educate the public on firearms use, especially in the context of a constitutional "right to bear arms." With such an impressive membership base, the NRA carries considerable political clout in the U.S. and works hard to persuade decision-makers to take its side on important policy issues surrounding gun control. In fact, the NRA has traditionally been "one of the biggest spenders in congressional elections."[6] It ranks congressional candidates on the basis of their positions on gun rights, lobbies for judicial and Senate appointments, and funds the political campaigns of like-minded candidates who support the NRA's policy agenda.

An important trend in the field of interest group research over recent decades has been the recognition of the internationalization of interest group activity and the rise of mobilizing beyond national borders. Globalization has transformed the balance of power among interest groups in favour of economic interests. In global markets, businesses can move their operations to countries with less stringent regulations, lower taxation levels, and a less expensive workforce. Even small businesses no longer have to sell their products in domestic markets; they can easily export to overseas markets. This process of globalization has shifted the site of decision-making. With global markets, there is an increasing need for national governments to coordinate their policies. As a result, international agencies like the World Trade Organization (WTO), the United Nations (UN), and the European Union (EU) are increasingly important political spaces. Globalization has also prompted various groups to organize themselves to seek representation before these bodies in the hope of redressing these power imbalances. For example, new interest groups at the European level abound, such as the European Trade Union Confederation, the European Women's Lobby, and the European Federation of National Organisations Working with the Homeless (FEANTSA).[7]

Interests groups can be divided into four different types. *Economic associations* bring together members who share a common economic interest, such as local chambers of commerce. *Professional associations* bring together members that belong to a particular profession; for example, the Canadian Medical Association represents Canadian physicians. Other interest groups serve wider public interests. They are called *public interest groups* and they are distinct because their goals benefit people beyond their membership. They are said to pursue a broader public purpose. A great example is Friends of the Earth. It aims to protect the environment and the benefits of its activities are shared beyond the membership of the organization. A final type of interest group is a *special interest group*, which—as opposed to a public interest group—defends a narrow set of interests. The concept of "special interest group" emerged in response to concerns over the influence of interest groups in politics. Because interest groups, by definition, pursue policies that benefit their members, they may promote interests that are too narrow and particular, against those that might benefit a broader spectrum of society. Economist Mancur Olson feared that these groups could exert undue influence and distort the allocation of resources to the detriment of the general public good.[8] However, the distinction between a public interest group and a special interest group can be fraught with difficulty. For example, in advocating on behalf of "the right to bear arms," the National Rifle Association would argue that it is serving the broader public interest. Opponents would maintain, however, that its policy agenda reflects a particular view of society, one that may not be shared by the majority of the population, and that may not be in the best interest of the public.

This concern reflects a common overarching theme in the literature, which has been to understand the changing nature of the relationship between interest groups and the state. Civil society is a political space that is independent of the state, yet state and society are connected and mutually influence each other. This interaction has led to multiple theories that aim to understand how interest group representation is both affected by and influences the larger political context.

Early writing in the pluralist tradition—which recognized the importance of having a policy process that is open to different voices—attributed the emergence of interest groups to dynamics outside the political environment. Writing in 1951, political scientist David Truman, for example, described groups forming through the "spontaneous coalescence of interests" in society as issues came to the fore.[9] Under this model, the strength of groups reflected the constellation of interests across society, and the state, as a neutral arbitrator, made policy decisions that reflected this natural distribution. It was not too long, however, before the pluralist approach was criticized for not recognizing that groups did not have equal access to the political arena or to organizational resources.[10] This, in turn, suggested that public policies were more likely to reflect particular (powerful, influential) interests rather than mirror the broader "public interest."

Not surprisingly, given these concerns, an important preoccupation of scholars of interest groups has been to study what factors affect the degree of influence that interest groups exercise on the state. One way to approach this has been to focus on the relational dimensions within policy fields; that is, on the nature of the contacts that groups have with the state and with one another, and the tactics that they use. William Coleman and Grace Skogstad[11] use the concept of **policy communities** in Canada to capture how different interests and institutions seeking to influence policy in a particular field are organized and structured, and how they relate to each other. Building on Paul Pross's work, Coleman and Skogstad make a distinction between "the attentive public," which shares an interest in a given policy field but is not actively engaged in policy-making, and the "sub-government," which is directly involved in policy discussions, decisions, and implementation. This has proven to be a very powerful tool to analyze and compare how patterns of state/interest group relations vary across policy fields.

> **Policy community or policy network:** Organized interests and institutions that seek to influence public policy in a particular field.

For instance, the "policy community" in the poverty field includes anti-poverty groups in the sub-government but it also includes members of the attentive public such as women's organizations, child care facilities, and unions, among other societal actors. While they may have varied interests, all of these groups seek to improve conditions for those living in poverty and they are regularly in contact with one another, as well as with other actors in the sub-government and attentive public. This research has led scholars like Coleman and Skogstad to develop typologies to describe patterns and structures of policy communities. They have identified characteristics such as membership, resources, organizational structure, and degree of institutionalization, which are all critical to a group's ability to influence policy. In a similar vein, Evert Lindquist and Michael Howlett use the concept of **policy networks** to emphasize the particular relationships between actors with specific policy expertise within the "sub-government."[12] Such modelling of interest group behaviour can not only incorporate the rich array of actors and interests at the domestic level, but it can also identify them along an international dimension as well.

The interest group literature captures some but not all aspects of civil society organizing. While it has contributed important typologies that have generated insight on the organizational and structural features of the relationship between groups and the state that can affect policy outcomes, not all civil society mobilization is formally organized or can be explained through an emphasis on shared interests. When we turn our attention to other parts of civil society, we start to move away from structural and organizational explanations of mobilization to a focus on the emergence and persistence of collective action.

A **social movement** is an informal network of individuals and groups who embrace and bring awareness to a particular vision of social change. It is distinct from an interest group because it is not a formal entity with a governance structure. Ralph Runer and Lewis Killian have defined a social movement as "a collectivity acting with some continuity to promote or resist a change in the society or organization of which it is a part. As a collectivity, a movement is a group with indefinite and shifting membership and with leadership whose position is determined more by informal response of the members than by formal procedures for legitimating authority."[13] Although social movements can comprise organizations, one does not need to be a member of any particular organization to join a social movement. For example, Greenpeace is an organization that is part of the environmental movement but one does not need to be a part of Greenpeace to identify with the environmental cause and join a public action to support it.

> **Social movement:** An informal network of individuals and groups who embrace and bring awareness to a particular vision of social change.

Much like the interest group literature, a major strand of the social movement literature explores the relational dimensions of social movement interactions between state and society. Early research focused on the labour and anti-poverty movements, but—as will be seen shortly—the literature has broadened considerably since then. Social movements reflect the context and environment in which they mobilize. In the industrial period, when modern industry and manufacturing flourished, relations between working people and elites changed significantly. The mechanization of production brought in a larger number of wage labourers in low-skilled jobs during the production process. As profits for business owners grew, inequality deepened, and class issues and economic concerns rose on the policy agenda once people began to mobilize around economic issues. However, in the 1960s, collective action shifted from these material concerns and focused more on post-materialist values—with a greater emphasis on quality of life, belonging, and social identity.[14] The environmental movement, the peace movement, and the lesbian, gay, bisexual, and transgender (LGBT) social movement are examples of what have come to be known as "new social movements." Apart from the issues and visions for change that define them, they are also distinct from older social movements because they challenge existing social norms.

These shifts generated a new wave of scholarship focusing on the emergence and significance of contemporary social movements in post-industrial societies and specifically the question of identity. Until then, scholarship on social movements, similar to that on interests groups, treated class interests as given. That is, the literature did not question why people came together and mobilized. It was assumed that class structures would generate class identity and interests naturally. But with new social movements, as Scott Hunt and Robert Benford note, "collective identity replaced class consciousness as the factor that accounts for mobilization and individual attachments to new social movements."[15] The rise of identity-based mobilizations such as the LGBT and feminist movements brought scholars to focus on why these movements emerged and how they formed around these issues. Alberto Melucci was one of the first social movement scholars to focus on the cognitive process of identity-building and investigate how collective action emerges through the negotiation and interaction of individual beliefs and meaning systems.

Social movements distinguish themselves from interest groups because they are identity-based. An identity is different than an interest because it is broader, more encompassing, and speaks to one's sense of self. Thus, participation in a social movement is more closely tied to personal identity, and for this reason collective identity is a focal point of mobilization. David Snow notes that collective identity's "essence resides in a shared sense of 'one-ness' or 'we-ness' anchored in real or imagined shared attributes and experiences among those who comprise the collectivity and in relation or contrast to one or more actual or imagined sets of others. Embedded within the shared sense of we is a corresponding sense of collective agency."[16]

Take, for example, Canada's National Action Committee on the Status of Women (NAC), an interest group that was quite powerful in the 1970s and 1980s. NAC was regularly consulted on policy matters by government and its goal was to draw attention to how gender relations affected policy problems. On poverty matters, NAC was an influential actor in the policy field because it was able to advise governments on important gender dimensions, such as the fact that many single mothers were unable to find full-time work, leaving their households vulnerable to poverty. Thus, NAC provided expertise in order to gain political concessions for such women. The feminist movement, by contrast, struggles for equality at a broader level. It seeks recognition of women's collective identity and mobilizes for greater gender consciousness. Although it also seeks to influence policy by expressing political demands, its main objective is to change the political terrain permanently. In that sense, feminist activists challenge existing gender relations by drawing attention to how societies have constructed the role of women through identities such as "mother" or "wife." The very goal of their mobilization campaign is to generate awareness concerning gender-related barriers and to empower women to overcome them.

What these examples illustrate is that social movement research provides lessons on power and how it is distributed within our political system. Because civil society is a space where we engage as citizens in coming to terms with some of the major challenges of our time, it sheds light on the broad representation of different interests in mainstream politics, as well as their systematic exclusion. Civil society mobilization stems from existing social, economic, and political cleavages. This has enabled political scientists to understand better how various systems of power, such as gender and race, structure our daily interactions.

Social movements also question the assumptions on which societal decisions are made and challenge entrenched ideals. They render visible inequalities that are hidden in our everyday world, reflecting existing social, economic, and political cleavages. For this reason, they tend to engage in more contentious forms of collective action and adopt strategies that are more confrontational, such as demonstrations, strikes, and riots.[17] Social movements often mobilize in ways that mirror and reflect power dynamics and inequalities within our political systems. If the revolutions sweeping the Middle East and Occupy protests sprouting around the world are any indication, one of the biggest issues of our times will likely be the deepening national and worldwide growth in income inequality.

A great example of a social movement closer to home is the Quebec student movement. Table 12.1 details the steps in the progression of the movement. On the surface, one could argue, as many media commentators did, that the student conflict began with three interest groups opposing tuition hikes in order to defend the interests of their members—students. However, a social movement lens focuses on collective frames that underpin the claims being made. It brings us to ask why a public call for change in policy from the three student body organizations (FEUQ, FECQ, and La CLASSE) in the province turned into daily marches that regularly drew over 200,000 people? To answer this question, we need to look at the collective frames of the student movement, which reveals that it was actually a debate not just about tuition but about the role of the university in society. The post-secondary education system in the province was developed during the Quiet Revolution,[18] at a time when educational attainment levels in Quebec were lower than in any other province and poverty levels were high. Higher education was framed as a collective good for the purpose of advancing Quebec society as a whole. The promise of the post-secondary education system was that it would be accessible and that tuition should remain low. These became important symbols of the Québécois collectivity and became part of a sense of shared solidarity. Hence, it is not surprising that the student movement mobilized against tuition hikes, and it has done so since the 1980s. But it is important to recognize that not just students—with a direct interest and stake in the tuition hike—mobilized. So did a variety of other actors who shared the common vision of a society in which education remains accessible for all as a collective good.

While the organization of these marches was a collaborative effort between the three student organizations, environmental, labour, social justice, and women's groups also used their own networks to mobilize people. Most of the protesters who joined the marches, as a result, were not members of the student organizations; some sympathized and shared a concern for the state of the education system and wanted to express that concern in solidarity with other members of the movement. Others saw the mobilizations as an opportunity to challenge the existing government with whom they had ideological and policy differences. In that sense, the marches became a magnet for a variety of issues. These fluid boundaries illustrate the informal nature of social movement networks.

This example also helps us to see the fluidity of social movements, composed of both organizations and individuals. The participants who join a social movement and mobilize often do not do so under the direction of any specific organization. What is more, multiple organizations can have different perspectives and strategies with regard to the issues, even as they mobilize together within the movement. In the case of the student movement, the FEUQ and the FECQ are more formalized, institutionalized organizations that have a long history of engaging with the Quebec government. They are both traditional interest groups

with a president at their head who has the authority to make decisions in the name of the organization. La CLASSE, however, is a more decentralized organization with no formal hierarchy. Instead, it has two spokespersons conveying student concerns to the provincial government. As such, they have no authority to work beyond the mandate given to them by the members of La CLASSE. This situation complicated interactions with government, particularly when the Quebec government asked student organizations to condemn acts of violence. The FEUQ and FECQ presidents could do so because they had the authority, but la CLASSE spokespersons could not without going back to the governance table and asking members to provide them with such a mandate.

After months of protests, the Liberal government lost the election in the fall of 2012 and the newly elected Parti Québécois announced a tuition freeze by ministerial decree, which brought an end to the protests. While tuitions were indexed to the cost of living, the increase remains far lower than had originally been anticipated. Was the student movement successful in meeting its objectives? Yes, in the sense that it has left an imprint on the collective imaginary and reminded the public of the importance of the post-secondary education system as a collective good that needs to be protected. In this vein, the student movement continues to fight alongside other policy actors against broader austerity measures and against cuts to public services.

TABLE 12.1 TIMELINE OF QUEBEC STUDENT STRIKES	
March 17, 2011	Quebec Liberal government's provincial budget contains plans to increase university tuition fees by $325 a year for five years.
March 18, 2011	Students take to the streets to protest, arguing that the tuition increase will result in high student debt levels.
November 10, 2011	More than 20,000 students boycott classes and march to Premier Jean Charest's Montreal office.
February 17, 2012	Protesters break into and vandalize the CEGEP Vieux–Montreal and 37 students are arrested. This marks the start of weeks of daily protests.
February 20, 2012	36,000 post-secondary students desert their classes in protest. This marks the beginning of the class boycott.
February 23, 2012	Thousands of students shut down Montreal's Jacques Cartier Bridge during rush hour.

(Continued)

TABLE 12.1	TIMELINE OF QUEBEC STUDENT STRIKES (CONTINUED)
March 7, 2012	One thousand students organize a sit-in in front of Loto-Québec's head office. Police uses tear gas and flash-bang grenades against protesters.
March 20, 2012	Two hundred students block access ramp to Montreal's Champlain Bridge. One hundred students are fined for contravening the Highway Safety Act.
March 22, 2012	An estimated 200,000 people take to the streets in downtown Montreal. The crowd spans over 1.8 km and 50 city blocks.
April 16, 2012	Premier Jean Charest announces that the government will not invite the student group la CLASSE to the negotiation table with the province's education minister because the group refuses to condemn acts of vandalism.
April 19, 2012	Police arrest 151 students in Gatineau after busloads of protesters arrive from Montreal as part of province-wide demonstrations against the Quebec government's proposed tuition increase.
April 27, 2012	Premier Jean Charest announces that his government will stretch the $1,625 tuition hike over seven years instead of five. Student groups reject the offer.
May 6, 2012	Student leaders and the Quebec government reach a tentative deal to end the class boycott. In addition to stretching the tuition hike over seven years, students will have input on a committee that will be established to look for savings in university budgets. Those savings could then be passed along to students through lower fees.
May 11, 2012	After putting it to a vote, all three student groups in Quebec (FECQ, FEUQ, La CLASSE) reject the tentative agreement.
May 14, 2012	Line Beauchamp, Education minister, resigns her cabinet position and her legislative seat. Premier Charest announces that Michelle Courchene will replace her in an effort to kick start negotiations with student leaders.
May 15, 2012	Fifty students obtain a court injunction allowing them to return to class at Collège Lionel-Groulx. A group of protestors blocks the doors, which leads to a standoff after the police declare the protest illegal.
May 16, 2012	Administrators at UQÀM try to resume classes in the undergraduate law program. After hundreds of protesters storm the university's building, classes are suspended.
May 16, 2012	The Quebec government announces that it will table special legislation, Bill 78, to suspend the semester for many CEGEP and university students and allow all students to finish their academic term in August. The legislation also proposes heavy fines for students and their organizations, and strict regulations governing demonstrations.
May 18, 2012	Members of Quebec's National Assembly vote 68-48 in favour of the emergency law. In a separate move, city of Montreal councillors approve a by-law that bans the wearing of masks at public protests.
May 20, 2012	For the 27th night in a row in Montreal, students hit the streets. Police declare the demonstration illegal under the province's new emergency law. About 300 people are arrested and 20 injured as protesters clash with police.

(Continued)

TABLE 12.1 TIMELINE OF QUEBEC STUDENT STRIKES (CONTINUED)	
May 22, 2012	Tens of thousands of students and their supporters march to mark the 100th day of the student movement. Montrealers in several urban neighbourhoods take to the streets with pots and pans, banging them to support Bill 78 protests. Approximately 1,000 people are arrested. Related events take place in New York, Paris, Toronto, Calgary, and Vancouver, where protesters march in solidarity.
May 23, 2012	Nightly tuition protests ramp up after the adoption of Bill 78, with civil rights groups joining students and their supporters in the streets. Montreal authorities arrest at least 518 people—a record for a single night since the beginning of the conflict.
May 31, 2012	The Quebec government pulls out of talks with student leaders.
June 22, 2012	100,000 people march in Montreal in opposition to the tuition hikes and Bill 78.
September 5, 2012	The newly elected Parti Québécois government announces a tuition freeze by ministerial decree and that Bill 78, now known as Law 12, will be repealed.

As a field of research, social movement analysis is also a study of intrigue and strategy. For interest group scholars, as we discussed earlier, interests are given and groups emerge because people come together around existing common interests. The relative strength of an interest group reflects the distribution of interests across society. So according to this explanation, if NAC is influential and has secured a solid resource base, it is because women's concerns are widely shared. Social movement scholars, on the other hand, believe that the existence of grievances is not enough to explain why some protests are successful and others are not. Societies are diverse and citizens will always have concerns and discontent that they want to express. What needs to be explained is why people mobilize around some forms of discontent and not others.

Resource mobilization theory, a strand of social movement research that emerged in the 1970s, attempts to explain how social movements respond to their environment and strategize to acquire resources and alliances. Early researchers such as John McCarthy and Mayer Zald were the first to consider that social movements were rational actors and that their success or failure was dependent on their ability to secure resource flows to participating organizations. They identified financial resources, leadership, networks, and organizational skills as potentially decisive strategic resources at the disposal of social movements.[19]

As the field developed, researchers came to recognize that changes in the political context can also affect social movement organizing in important ways. Institutional arrangements, like the laws regulating group activities, shape the context within which groups organize. According to Sydney Tarrow,[20] the political context can enable or constrain social movement activity through its relative openness of access to participation by new actors, governing political alignments, the presence or absence of possible allies within governing elites, and the state's capacity or will to repress dissent. The concept of the *political opportunity structure* was developed to capture each of these dimensions and can be defined as the "consistent— but not necessarily formal or permanent—dimensions of the political environment that provide incentives for collective action." A great example of the political opportunity structure facilitating the emergence of a social movement can be found in Spain with the rise of the Indignados movement protesting against corruption in the political and financial sector as well as the precarious employment situation for youth. On the May 15, 2011, 1.5 million people mobilized in Spain under the slogan "Real Democracy Now."[21]

The timing of the movement was a defining factor in its success. The police announced that they would not intervene to block the mobilization efforts out of fear that this would foster negative media attention leading up to local and regional elections scheduled on May 22nd. The movement used new social media tools such as Twitter and Facebook, which reduced the costs of getting its message out and increased the success of its mobilization efforts. The movement also found an ally in the Partido Popular political party, which ultimately won the national elections.

This example also illustrates how new social media and information technologies have become important resources that can affect the opportunities for and effects of collective action. Indeed, many commentators argue that technology is driving a new wave of organized activity. The speed and impact of recent waves of contention mobilizing citizens in the Middle East, Europe, and North America, for example, have surprised many observers. In non-democratic countries where the level of repression and cost of mobilization are high, the Internet and social media provide opportunities for movements to emerge in a closed institutional context. These technologies can help movements build transnational connections and identify allies in ways that are accessible, fast, and cheap. However, it is important to recognize that their utility as an organizational tool is also limited.

The 2009 "Green Revolution" in Iran, a movement that emerged under a regime of repression and in response to fraudulent elections, is a case in point. For the first time in history, international observers and journalists had access to real-time information about protests being held in a country known for strong government control over the media. Western newspapers claimed that Twitter was revolutionizing protests in Iran. The United States State Department took the unusual step of asking Twitter to delay a scheduled maintenance on its website to ensure that the citizens of Tehran could communicate via social media and coordinate their activities easily during protests. Clearly, Twitter had come to be seen as an instrument of democracy. Whether it had a meaningful impact on the ground in Iran, however, is another matter. For one, most of the tweets were in English, not in Farsi—the local language. For this reason, many commentators argue that these social media tools were used almost exclusively to garner international solidarity, not local solidarity.[22] Critics have also noted how difficult it is to communicate on issues using only 140 characters. Indeed, Evgeny Morozov argues that "to ascribe such great importance to Twitter is to disregard the fact that it is very poorly suited to planning protests in a repressive environment like Iran's. The protests that engulfed the streets of Tehran were neither spontaneous nor were they 'flashmobs'; they were carefully planned and executed by the [the opposition]."[23] What the Iran example teaches us is that we need to probe more deeply into political dynamics on the ground, and that as a field of research, we are just beginning to understand the impacts that these new communication technologies are having on social movement organizing.

While most civil society research has focused on interest group and social movements to date, a third and more contemporary strand of research into civil society mobilization examines the role and place of voluntary organizations. A **voluntary organization** exists to serve a public benefit, is independent from government, does not distribute any profits to members, and relies (but not necessarily entirely) on volunteers—at the very least to serve on its board. Examples of voluntary organizations include a wide variety of organizations such as churches, sports organizations, YMCAs, and the Canadian Cancer Society. In some countries, the term **nonprofit** is used to emphasize the fact that such organizations are not constituted as profit-making entities, but in Canada the preferred designation within the sector is voluntary organization. In developing countries, the term "NGO"—which stands for non-governmental organization—is also commonly used to label groups that are not part of government or the private sector. It is important to note that these organizations assume important responsibilities in the provision and financing of a variety of services, such as healthcare, aid to victims of war, and famine and natural disaster relief, to name a few.

Voluntary organization: An organization that exists to serve a public benefit, is independent from government, does not distribute any profits to members, and relies on volunteers to a certain degree—at the very least to serve on its board.

Nonprofit organization: A group that comes together to achieve a social purpose, rather than to make a profit.

Charities are a distinct category of voluntary organization because they fundraise and issue tax receipts in exchange for donations. Because of their impact on tax collection, permission to issue tax receipts must be obtained from the government. In Canada, this authority lies with the Canada Revenue Agency and charities must submit to particular rules and conditions, the most important being that their political activities are monitored and restricted.

Charity: An organization that has charitable purposes and that is registered (under the Income Tax Act in Canada) so that it can issue charitable receipts to donors, who are in turn allowed to deduct amounts from their personal income tax.

In Canada, there are over 161,000 charities and voluntary organizations, which together account for 8.6 percent of the country's GDP in terms of the revenue they generate. In addition, over two million people are employed in voluntary organizations.[24] When one factors in the millions of volunteers who donate their time, voluntary organizations make up a considerable, yet distinct, element of the Canadian labour force. It is clear that voluntary organizations are a significant social, political, and economic force in Canada, as in many countries. However, voluntary organizations also exist beyond state borders. Think of all the international aid organizations, such as Free the Children, which works in more than 45 countries. When we factor that in, the impact of voluntary organizations in the world is both significant and extensive.

A key research question for scholars has been to examine what accounts for the differences in size and scope of voluntary sector activities within countries. Some of the earliest efforts in social movement analysis involved attempts to understand why people engaged in collective action and what conditions were necessary for it to emerge, and this strand of research has influenced the study of voluntary organizations. Indeed, Mancur Olsen first raised the dilemma of collective action when he argued that individuals are more likely to "free ride" than to engage in collective

action because their marginal contribution would not likely affect the final outcome and would come at a cost in terms of time, energy, and resources. For example, if an individual knows that there are people mobilizing for clean air, and that he can reap the benefits of their efforts without investing his own time and energy, then the rational decision would be not to participate. Economist Burton Weisbrod used Olson's work to explain that voluntary organizations emerged when government failed to meet the demand for these "collective goods"—goods that nobody else can be excluded from enjoying once provided to one person. Elected officials, who are also rational actors and want to be re-elected, will tend to provide collective goods only when a majority of the population demands the good in question. This theory is called the "government failure theory." This reasoning led Weisbrod to argue that the voluntary sector will be larger in countries where the population is homogenous and smaller in countries where the population is heterogeneous because in the latter there will be more minority groups that have unmet demands. Examine Figure 12.1 on the next page. Does Weisbrod's hypothesis hold?

Lester Salamon, one of the leading researchers in the field, has argued, in contrast, that the government failure argument does not follow international trends. If the voluntary sector is a substitute for government when it fails, then we would expect the size and scope of the voluntary sector to vary proportionally with the size of the state. However, data in Figure 12.1 illustrates that countries with big governments and generous social programs, like the Netherlands, also have large voluntary sectors.

According to Salamon, one notable trend has been the growing importance of voluntary organizations in the delivery of various services that we have come to expect and rely on. Since the 1990s, governments have been contracting out services to third parties in an effort to cut down the scope and size of government machinery. Salamon has aptly referred to this phenomenon as the rise of "third party government."[25] Many of these contracts are awarded to voluntary organizations that, as a result, are now increasingly reliant on this source of funding to support their activities. These contracts, however, impose great burdens on participating groups in terms of government oversight in the form of regulation, governance requirements, and accountability. In their study

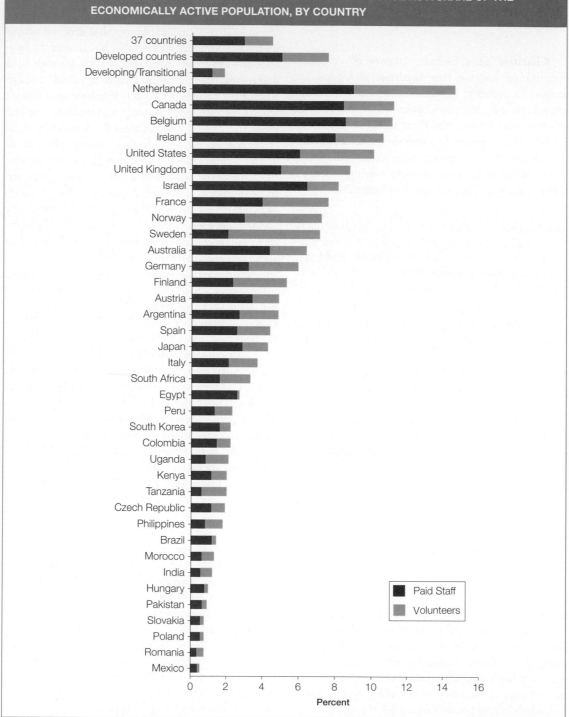

FIGURE 12.1 **NONPROFIT AND VOLUNTARY ORGANIZATION WORKFORCE AS A SHARE OF THE ECONOMICALLY ACTIVE POPULATION, BY COUNTRY**

Source: Michael H. Hall et al., "Nonprofit and Voluntary Organization Workforce as a Share of the Economically Active Population, by Country," *The Canadian Nonprofit and Voluntary Sector in Comparative Perspective* (Toronto: Imagine Canada, 2005), 10, online at http://sector-source.ca/sites/default/files/resources/files/jhu_report_en.pdf.

of voluntary organizations in the United States, Steven Rathgeb Smith and Michael Lipsky illustrate how the American government has altered the environment of service provision, which in turn has affected nonprofit behaviour.[26]

Indeed, numerous studies demonstrate that government funding of voluntary organizations can have an effect on their structures, leading to greater professionalization and bureaucratization, greater demands for accountability and performance measures, and a displacement of power away from communities and boards of directors and toward the funder—government. These trends are important because they can erode the autonomy of voluntary organizations—an important defining feature of such groups. Voluntary organizations exist because they emerged to fulfill certain needs within communities. The fear is that, as they distance themselves from their community base, they may become vulnerable to having their mission appropriated by the state.

The field of voluntary sector research has also begun to recognize that the old model of governance, whereby governments make policy and bureaucrats execute it, is important but outdated. Instead, governing is much more collaborative and dynamic. In fact, the boundaries between voluntary organizations, the state, and the market are increasingly blurring. We can now observe voluntary organizations adopt new organizational forms—like a social enterprise using a business model to generate revenue to meet its social mission. An example of how voluntary organizations and the market are mixing in new ways can be seen with the award-winning Santropol Roulant, which runs a restaurant and a meals-on-wheels program. The initiative was first created by McGill students who worked at the Café Santropol and were concerned by the lack of meaningful employment opportunities available for youth in Montreal. They also wanted to foster cross-generational interaction between youth and seniors in the city to combat the social isolation of both groups. In order

to do so, they launched a meals-on-wheels program whereby youth volunteered to deliver meals to, and spend time talking with, seniors. They created a separate social enterprise named in honour of the Café where they worked and which gave them access to a kitchen to prepare meals. Over time the social enterprise began developing more intergenerational activities and programs. It is self-sufficient financially, covering its operational costs by charging a modest fee for meals and generating supplementary funds through programming.

The blurring of the boundaries between the public, private, and voluntary sectors raises an entire new set of questions in the field, such as: How are voluntary organization practices changing? How can we distinguish between private and voluntary sector organizations? Are these categories still relevant? Because this blurring of the boundaries is new, the field is just beginning to build knowledge on what the impacts may be on the political arena.[27] Some of the major debates revolve around the organizational impact of adopting new business models to achieve social goals that lead to more professionalization within the sector. One concern is that adopting these new models will create cultural changes within organizations as they take on more entrepreneurial values, and that gradually economic motivations will come to trump social functions at the heart of their missions. That being said, voluntary organizations see huge potential in the social enterprise model as a way to generate new resources in the wake of significant government cutbacks to the sector.

The rise and growth of the voluntary sector is not just a Western phenomenon. Even in authoritarian political systems, voluntary organizations have come to play an important role in governing. In Box 12.1, you can see the increasingly powerful and variegated role that such organizations play in Chinese society and policy as the country works through an unprecedented historical juncture of economic growth and political change.

BOX 12.1

CHINA'S GROWING NONPROFIT SECTOR

Portrayed by some as a "quiet revolution," China's civil society sector has expanded rapidly since the government launched its economic and political reforms some 30 years ago. Today, there are over 460,000 officially registered nonprofit organizations (NPOs) with nearly six million employees, as well as millions of unregistered grassroots organizations.

Chinese nonprofits do not fit neatly into the definitions of nonprofit organizations commonly used among Western scholars and practitioners. According to the current classification system developed by the [Chinese] Ministry of Civil Affairs (MOCA), the more than 460,000 officially registered NPOs fall into three broad categories:

1. "Social organizations," which include economic groups (trade unions and chambers of commerce, etc.), social groups (social clubs, research organizations, hobby groups, etc.), religious groups, and membership-based public-benefit organizations;
2. "Private non-enterprise organizations," which include nonprofit schools, hospitals, and social service organizations, among others; and
3. "Foundations," which include public fundraising foundations (such as Soong Chingling Foundation, [established in memory of the Honorary President of the People's Republic

of China, Soong Soong Ching Ling, providing funding to support various social projects in China], the China Foundation for Poverty Alleviation, etc.) and non-public fundraising foundations, often referred to as private foundations.

While the majority of NPOs serve a public- or mutual-benefit purpose, these registered nonprofits vary in the extent to which they are autonomous and voluntary. In fact, many nonprofit organizations currently registered with MOCA are actually "government-organized nongovernmental organizations" (GONGOs). Nearly all of the national associations are GONGOs, as are many NPO service agencies. There are also many organizations *not* included in the 460,000 registered NPOs noted above that operate on nonprofit principles but are registered as for-profit businesses, as in the case of some private schools and social welfare NPOs. Though still young and fragile, the emerging nonprofit sector in China in the past 25 to 30 years has clearly demonstrated its potential in providing social services and leisure activities, as well as influencing public policy.

Source: Excerpted from Chao Guo, Jun Xu, David Horton Smith, and Zhibin Zhang, "Civil Society, Chinese Style: The Rise of the Nonprofit Sector in Post-Mao China," *Nonprofit Quarterly* 19, no. 3, Fall 2012.

In addition to looking at the evolving relationship between government and the voluntary sector, research in this field has also been concerned with understanding why individuals volunteer and make donations to support the public good. Alexis de Tocqueville, in *Democracy in America*, written in 1840, first referred to civil society organizations as "schools of democracy," where citizens come together to discuss, exchange, and learn from each other.[28] Through political participation and engagement, he observed, citizens gained a better understanding of issues and learned skills that were essential to politics.

Since then, research has confirmed that civil society is a vital pillar in the promotion of active

citizenship practices and social cohesion. Through political participation and volunteering, citizens come into contact with others, building bonds and bridging their differences. The trust relations that can flow from these contacts are important ties that bind society together. The resultant "social capital"—that is the value created through these norms of reciprocity—is essential to democratic governance and to fostering a compassionate and caring society.[29] Robert Putnam, who popularized the idea of social capital in his 2000 book, *Bowling Alone: The Collapse and Revival of American Community* (see further below), defines it as "the features of social organization, such as networks, norms, and trusts, that facilitate coordination and cooperation for mutual benefit."[30] Social capital involves both bridging and bonding ties. Bridging involves developing links between socially heterogeneous groups—across differences. Bonding is a more powerful form of social capital, involving building connections between socially homogeneous groups. Both are important for democracy because they foster trust, and it has been found that trusting people are more comfortable with others, as well as being more tolerant and accepting of them. Increases in social capital have been linked to many benefits, such as lower crime rates, better health indicators, lower tax evasion, greater tolerance for gender and racial equality, support for civil liberties, as well as greater economic and civic equality.[31] In fact, Putnam proposes that joining an organization will cut an individual's chance of dying in the next year by half!

However, not all social capital is positive. Imagine a situation where there are high levels of bonding between individuals who are like-minded but no bridging across differences. A typical example is the Ku Klux Klan (KKK), which reflects considerable bonding but very little bridging. The forms of social capital that the KKK generates are not, therefore, beneficial for society as a whole. For this reason, it is important to ensure that society has many organizations that promote bridging ties and not just those that engage in bonding.

Most of the research on social capital has focused on the United States. Putnam relies on measures of confidence in government, the number of associations that people belong too, and various forms of engagement in civil life such as voting, reading the newspaper, and participating in marches. Other scholars also look at levels of volunteering and charitable donations within countries as indicators of civic participation. In Canada, in addition to data on voting patterns, we have had a number of surveys on giving, volunteering, and participating.

As you will have already seen in Chapter 10, we know that there has been a steady decline in the rate of voter turnout in federal elections over the past 20 years or so. In contrast, Canadians seem to be doing better in terms of civic participation. Indeed, as Table 12.2 indicates, 84 percent of the population aged 15 and over made a charitable donation and 47 percent volunteered in 2010, and these numbers have remained stable over time. What is more, Canadian tax filers claimed $8.3 billion in donations in 2010, an increase of approximately $500 million from 2009.[32] So both in terms of giving and volunteering, civic engagement in Canada is relatively stable.

However, the data obscures another reality. While the total amount of donations made has increased, the number of donors has actually declined, from 30 percent of tax filers in 1990 to 23.4 percent in 2010.

TABLE 12.2	DONORS, DONATIONS, VOLUNTEERS, AND VOLUNTEER HOURS, POPULATION AGED 15 AND OLDER, CANADA, 2007 AND 2010	
	2010	**2007**
Total population (thousands)	28,285	27,069*
Donors and donations		
Donors (thousands)	23,789	22,841*
Donor rate (percent)	84	84
Total amount of donations** (thousands of dollars)	10,609,533	10,429,330
Volunteers and hours volunteered		
Volunteers (thousands)	13,282	12,478
Volunteer rate (percent)	47	46
Total hours volunteered (millions)	2,067	2,067

* Represents a statistically significant difference (α=0.05) between 2007 and 2010.

** 2007 dollar amount is adjusted to 2010 dollars.

Source: Statistics Canada, 2013. Donors, donations, volunteers and volunteer hours, population aged 15 and older, Canada 2007 and 2010. Canada Survey of Giving, Volunteering and Participating, 2007 and 2010, online at http://www.statcan.gc.ca/ pub/89-640-x/2011001/tbl/tbl01-eng.htm (accessed June 22, 2015).

In effect, the base of donors in Canada has been steadily shrinking over the past decade. This trend is further aggravated by the fact that a high proportion of the total amount of charitable contributions is borne by a few individuals. The *2004 Canada Survey of Giving, Volunteering and Participating* shows that nine percent of donors are responsible for 62 percent of charitable donations. Moreover, seven percent of the Canadian population undertakes 73 percent of all the volunteer work.[33] Together, this small group of individuals accounts for more than two-thirds of all volunteering, giving, and community activities in Canada. These contributory behaviours, which support the public good, are linked, as you can see in Figure 12.2 below. What this data indicates is that the social capital created through civic engagement in Canada depends to a large extent on a small proportion of Canadian adults, known as the "civic core."[34]

Another challenge affecting the voluntary sector is a generational shift in the world of volunteering, and it is compounding the difficulties engendered by declining financial resources. Members of the civic

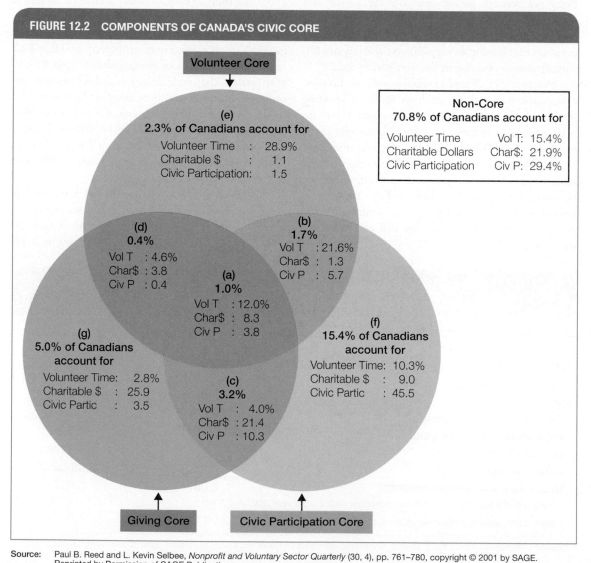

FIGURE 12.2   COMPONENTS OF CANADA'S CIVIC CORE

Volunteer Core

(e)
2.3% of Canadians account for

Volunteer Time	:	28.9%
Charitable $	:	1.1
Civic Participation:		1.5

Non-Core
70.8% of Canadians account for

Volunteer Time	Vol T:	15.4%
Charitable Dollars	Char$:	21.9%
Civic Participation	Civ P:	29.4%

(d)
0.4%

Vol T   : 4.6%
Char$: 3.8
Civ P   : 0.4

(b)
1.7%

Vol T   : 21.6%
Char$: 1.3
Civ P   : 5.7

(a)
1.0%

Vol T   : 12.0%
Char$: 8.3
Civ P   : 3.8

(g)
5.0% of Canadians account for

Volunteer Time	:	2.8%
Charitable $	:	25.9
Civic Partic	:	3.5

(c)
3.2%

Vol T   : 4.0%
Char$: 21.4
Civ P   : 10.3

(f)
15.4% of Canadians account for

Volunteer Time:	10.3%
Charitable $	:	9.0
Civic Partic	:	45.5

Giving Core   Civic Participation Core

Source: Paul B. Reed and L. Kevin Selbee, *Nonprofit and Voluntary Sector Quarterly* (30, 4), pp. 761–780, copyright © 2001 by SAGE. Reprinted by Permission of SAGE Publications.

core tend to be older, religious, well-educated, in higher status and income occupations, with children between the ages of six and 17 in the home, and living in communities outside major metropolitan centres. We also know that the generation of individuals born before 1945 tends to be particularly generous because it lived through the Great Depression. Two of these characteristics are significant if we are to make projections about the future of our donor base in Canada. First, our population is aging. While individuals tend to volunteer more as they retire, what is problematic is that the generation of donors born before 1945, who are amongst the most generous, is rapidly shrinking. The generation that succeeds it will not, as it ages in turn, match these high levels and thus there will likely be a decline in volunteer activity as the pre-1945 generation dies. Second, we are facing a decline in religious belief, which may have implications for overall levels of charitable giving in the future as we lose more of our generous givers. According to the 2011 National Household Survey and the Canada census, the percentage of Canadians who identify as Catholic has dropped from 47 percent to 39 percent since the 1970s, the percentage who identify as Protestant has fallen from 41 percent to 27 percent. Perhaps most importantly, the percentage of Canadians who declare themselves religiously unaffiliated has grown from four percent to 24 percent over this period.

These trends point to a decline in social capital in Canada that could potentially have an impact on the health of our democracy. Putnam identified a similar erosion of social capital in the United States in *Bowling Alone*, the title of which reflects the fact that Americans are less likely today to bowl in leagues, but increasingly bowl on their own. More generally, he presents evidence from 500,000 interviews conducted over the last quarter century that indicates that Americans are more isolated from one another in many ways; for instance, they belong to fewer organizations that meet, do not know their neighbours as well, and socialize with their families less often.

The nature and causes of such changes remain a hot topic of scholarly debate because of the central importance of the bonds and social norms that are formed when engaging in these types of activities (recall the discussion of political socialization in Chapter 1). Putnam argues that people are spending more time watching television as opposed to interacting

face-to-face with each other. If he is right, then the social media revolution could further erode social capital as individuals communicate online rather than through meeting face-to-face. Theda Skocpol, on the other hand, attributes this shift to the changing institutional infrastructure within civil society, arguing that organizations have become increasingly dominated by a professional class and have lost their connections to their grassroots.[35] Both theories point to important transformations in civil society that could significantly impact the vitality of our democratic systems and that therefore deserve more attention.

FUNCTIONS OF CIVIL SOCIETY ACTORS

Civil society actors fulfill several important functions in the political system. The first and most basic function is that of political representation. This involves both the articulation of interests—the act of giving meaning and shape to one's interests—and the aggregation of interests—the act of bringing together individual interests into one broad vision. Whereas political parties aggregate interests within geographical spaces, civil society organizations aggregate interests along interest (e.g., healthcare, the environment, taxation) and identity (e.g., race, gender, class) lines. By engaging in political representation, civil society actors provide alternative channels for citizens to express their views in the political arena. In this way, they are critical to building a strong and vibrant democracy in which disadvantaged and marginalized communities can be heard alongside more politically powerful players.

The second important function of civil society actors is education. Interest groups, social movements, and voluntary organizations educate citizens about public issues and their rights. Not all civil society actors even target the state; some are more interested in changing public opinion and generating awareness with regards to the issues that concern them. Civil society actors also provide spaces and forums in which people can come together to discuss, exchange, and learn from each other. Through these interactions, citizens can develop civic skills such as tolerance, cooperation, and compassion.

Civil society actors also bring the expertise and knowledge of different communities to the public-policy process. As such, they provide additional and often unappreciated or ignored perspectives on a wide range of policy issues. For example, interest groups, like the Canadian Chamber of Commerce, and think tanks, like the Canadian Centre for Policy Alternatives, publish data and reports on policy issues that are widely used by government, the public, and the media. In doing so, they become essential vectors in democratization and in maintaining the health of democracies.

While some forms of contentious politics remain controversial, civil society actors increasingly play a critical role in democratic government. Indeed, they are active in all phases of the policy process: from agenda-setting and policy-making through to policy implementation, monitoring, and evaluation. For example, in the field of immigration, voluntary organizations are responsible for the delivery of services on behalf of federal and provincial governments to help newcomers settle and adjust to life in Canada. Not only are these groups at the frontline of service delivery, but because they have important ties with the immigrant community, they have a significant role to play in advising government and informing policy-making. In addition, they assess and evaluate the success of settlement services in Canada.

Civil society actors also provide legitimacy to the policy process. They can serve as watchdogs, monitoring the actions of governments, business organizations, and even international agencies. In doing so, they can both support the claims of the state to be acting on behalf of the public good and can also challenge them. In fact, civil society actors play an important role in channeling citizens' voices and fostering participatory democracy on a global scale. Although the European Parliament is elected, those who lead powerful international organizations such as the UN, International Monetary Fund (IMF), G20, and World Bank are not legitimated through national elections, and therefore they are not accountable directly to citizen constituents. Civil society organizations can help such organizations build those bridges. For example, the Directorate General for Employment, Social Affairs and Inclusion, one of the committees under the responsibility of the European Commission, was among the first to recognize the need to strengthen links with civil society groups to make progress on social policy issues—such as those revolving around gender, youth, social exclusion, disability, and racism—because these groups can provide information and insight into the experiences and needs of various segments of society, and in doing so help in the design of more appropriate and effective public policies.[36]

Each of these functions has been under enormous pressure in recent years as civil society has had to come to terms with the challenges of new and growing demands, fewer resources, a more competitive funding environment, and evolving relationships with the state and the private sector. However, such pressures have also created new opportunities to do things differently, especially in terms of using new tools—such as social media—in order to engage with citizens more effectively.

TOOLS OF CIVIL SOCIETY

Civil society actors use many different instruments in their efforts to influence government. These can be organized into two broad categories: insider and outsider strategies. An *insider strategy* refers to techniques employed when one has access to policymakers. An *outsider strategy*, by contrast, refers to mobilizing forces outside the state and exercising pressure indirectly on policy-makers. Wyn Grant first came up with the distinction between insider and outsider strategies in order to qualify the types of contacts that groups have with government and the tactics that they use.[37] He argued that insider groups have privileged access to government and are regularly consulted on policy, thereby exercising more direct influence over government. Outsider groups, in contrast, are either unable or unwilling to use insider strategies and enter into dialogue with government.

Traditional interest group politics are usually associated with insider strategies. For example, lobbying is an insider strategy that involves organizing a face-to-face meeting with decision-makers in order to share the group's interests and concerns. At these meetings, groups provide information to decision-makers in the hopes that a decision will be taken that benefits the group's members. Lobbying may also involve testifying at legislative hearings, helping draft legislation, alerting decision-makers to the effects of a proposed or enacted law, mounting grassroots campaigns, and writing letters to elected officials. Groups may also generate research and evidence in order to challenge existing conventions.

Wealthy interest groups, like tobacco companies, generally hire professional lobbyists to defend their interests. In Canada, lobbying activities are regulated by the state. Lobbyists must register if they meet with government officials to influence them to take a particular stance, unless they are invited to share their views. In 2006, as a result of concerns with regards to the rising influence of political advocacy groups in electoral campaigns, the Conservative government made changes to the regulations under the Lobbying Act and adopted the Federal Accountability Act. One important consequence was the creation of a Commissioner of Lobbying as an independent Officer of Parliament responsible for maintaining a register of lobbyists and conducting reviews to ensure compliance with the Lobbyists' Code of Conduct. As an effort to preserve the democratic process, this legislation has provided greater clarity and transparency with regards to who communicates with government agencies and on what issues.[38] Canada is not alone in regulating lobbyist activities more heavily. For example, the U.K. has recently introduced similar legislation to restrict and monitor lobbying. Although greater transparency is generally welcomed, some critics fear that the new register could stifle the voice of voluntary organizations that may fear losing their funding in a broad sense because they are perceived to be engaging in advocacy activities if they are registered.

Another insider strategy is to donate money to a candidate's electoral campaign, endorse a candidate, or issue a public rating of candidates. In all three cases, interest groups hope that the candidates, if successful in achieving office, will be more sympathetic to the views of the group, if they are not already. Not everyone agrees on whether allowing financial donations to electoral campaigns is beneficial for democracy. For some, making a donation is a valid way of supporting a cause or an issue. For others the concern is that it may give groups too much influence over elected officials, which could distort the political system in favour of wealthier and more powerful groups. In Canada, new campaign finance laws have restricted the ability of interest groups to make contributions to national electoral campaigns and to engage in political advertising, and therefore very few Canadian interest groups donate to political campaigns at the federal level today. As for the provinces, most limit the amount that a person or organization can donate, but these limits range from $30,000 in Alberta to $100 in Quebec. British Columbia, Saskatchewan, Prince Edward Island, and Newfoundland and Labrador are the only provinces with few rules governing political donations. Quebec, Manitoba, and Nova Scotia have also gone further than most by banning corporate and union donations.

In the United States, similar laws have been passed but interest groups have created broad coalitions—**political action committees** (**PACs**)—to pool campaign contributions from members and donate to electoral candidates (see Table 12.3), a practice that has found support in a 2010 Supreme Court ruling on laws restricting campaign spending. Overall, American campaign finance laws have been less effective at bringing in greater transparency and interest groups remain much more influential in the country's electoral politics. While the U.S. and some countries in Europe allow political donations by groups, corporations, unions, and other organizations, only recently have they been strictly banned from making donations in Canada.

Political Action Committees (PACs): American organizations that pool campaign contributions from members and donate those funds to particular electoral candidates.

A third insider strategy is to attempt to use the courts to influence change. Since the entrenchment of the Charter of Rights and Freedoms in the Canadian constitution in 1982, groups representing Aboriginal people, women, and same-sex couples have increasingly used the courts as a channel for political change. In his book *Friends of the Court: The Privileging of Interest Group Litigants in Canada*, Ian Brodie identifies four categories of groups that generally seek access to the courts (governments, economic interests, citizen

TABLE 12.3	TOP 10 PAC CONTRIBUTIONS, 2013–2014	
Rank	**Committee**	**Amount**
1	Honeywell International PAC	$3,707,375
2	International Brotherhood of Electrical Workers PAC	$3,445,540
3	American Federation of Teachers, AFL-CIO Committee on Political Education	$3,412,000
4	National Association of Realtors PAC	$3,244,326
5	Engineers Political Education Committee (EPEC)/International Union of Operat II	$3,071,791
6	Employees of Northrop Grumman Corporation PAC	$3,060,750
7	Senate Conservatives Fund	$2,989,079
8	Lockheed Martin Corporation Employees' PAC	$2,953,500
9	AT&T Inc. Federal PAC	$2,910,500
10	National Beer Wholesalers Association PAC	$2,891,000

Source: Federal Election Commission, PAC Table 4c, Top 50 PACs by Contributions to Candidates and Other Committees January 1, 2013-June 30, 2014, online at http://www.fec.gov/press/summaries/2014/tables/pac/PAC4c_2014_18m.pdf (accessed June 22, 2015).

groups, and individuals). Particularly notable is the increase in economic interests such as business groups, professional groups, unions, and corporations seeking representation before the Supreme Court of Canada. Access to the courts requires resources and time, of course, which may disadvantage some groups. Up until 2006, Canada had a Court Challenges Program that facilitated access to the judicial system by providing financial assistance for important court cases that advanced language and equality rights under the constitution. However, the program was abolished out of concern that it supported and gave unfair weight to claims made in the name of particularistic interests. Prime Minister Stephen Harper even characterized the program as "subsidizing lawyers to bring forth court challenges by left-wing fringe groups."[39]

Globalization has created further opportunities for civil society actors to influence policy. Interest groups can appeal to a wide range of international organizations in order to gain support for their causes, from the WTO, the UN, the World Bank the IMF, to the EU; there are more institutional access points for groups than ever before. These institutions can also be used by interest groups to influence domestic politics. For example, the United

States government had to reverse its decision to ban shrimp caught by countries using fishing nets that are harmful to endangered sea turtles because the WTO ruled it illegal in light of existing trade agreements. As countries become increasingly bound by international agreements and collaboration through international agencies, it is likely that civil society organizations will increasingly direct their activities toward both national and international levels.

In a political system that is relatively open, an organization might choose to adopt a more conventional strategy to advocate for its concerns. However, if a system is relatively closed, then organizations may have little choice but to use less conventional approaches to draw attention to their causes (see Table 12.4). Outsider strategies range from conservative to more confrontational and radical activities. On the conservative end, civil society actors can attempt to use the media to influence public opinion and thereby exert pressure on decision-makers. The media provides an outlet to reach a potentially large number of people, while new technologies have increased the speed at which messages can be picked up and distributed. One individual's action can quickly translate into global support for a cause (see the Photo Essay box). For

PHOTO ESSAY

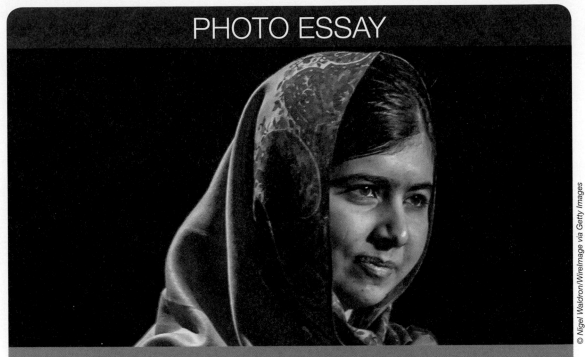

Nobel Peace Prize winner Malala Yousafzai of Pakistan.

I AM MALALA

Malala Yousafzai is a Pakistani activist from Swat Valley in the province of Khyber Pakhtunkhwa (PKP) in Northern Pakistan. This is a remote mountain area with many tribes that are not subject to the authority of the Pakistani government at the moment. It is a very difficult area to police. Because it was governed by the old tribal order, the Taliban was able to come into the area and impose their rule. One rule was to ban girls from attending school. At the age of 12, Malala started writing a blog under a pseudonym about her experiences under Taliban rule. She raised concerns about the lack of access to education for young girls in her community. As she gained prominent attention for her views, she was targeted and shot in 2012. This assassination attempt sparked an outpouring of support for Malala and for worldwide access to education. Since then, the "I am Malala" slogan has been used by the United Nations Special Envoy for Global Education to advocate that all children worldwide, between the ages of six and 11, be in school by the end of 2015. She has effectively become the face of the movement. In 2014, Malala's activist efforts were recognized when she was awarded the Nobel Peace Prize. She is currently the youngest ever Nobel Peace Prize winner and she continues to speak eloquently about education and injustice:

> Though I appear as one girl, though I appear as one girl, one person, who is 5 foot 2 inches tall, if you include my high heels. (It means I am 5 foot only) I am not a lone voice, I am not a lone voice, I am many. I am Malala. But I am also Shazia. I am Kainat. I am Kainat Soomro. I am Mezon. I am Amina. I am those 66 million girls who are deprived of education. And today I am not raising my voice, it is the voice of those 66 million girls.*

___

* © The Nobel Foundation 2014

example, Pat Quinn from Boston had a friend who was diagnosed with the disease amyotrophic lateral sclerosis (ALS). He took it upon himself to generate awareness of the disease and wanted to raise funds for research to find a cure. He created the Ice Bucket Challenge—the challenge of pouring ice cold water over your head and then nominating others to do the same in an effort to raise awareness and funds—the challenge quickly went viral and global via social media. Pat's idea has generated over $100 million dollars—so far—for the fight against ALS. Moving toward a more radical strategy, organizations may resort to direct action to reach out to citizens, encouraging them to participate through petitions and mobilizations. A particularly effective strategy to foster a shared understanding of an issue is to use symbols to draw attention to the significance of the problem. For example, the Quebec student movement used the symbol of a red square that people could wear on their lapel. The red square was first introduced in the anti-poverty movement as a symbol of "being financially in the red" (i.e., in debt). By adopting the "red square" as a brand, it strategically enabled the student movement to connect and build allies within the anti-poverty movement by emphasizing that they had a shared vision.

Outsider strategies, however, can also be quite confrontational, and may even involve breaking the law. They can include such tactics as strikes, demonstrations, picketing, occupying public spaces, sit-ins, road blockades, civil disobedience, occupations, and even armed insurgency. Because social movements are informal networks, actions can take on a life of their own. While some may be critical of these confrontational strategies because they are disruptive, Stephen D'Arcy, in his book *Language of the Unheard,* makes a compelling case that outbursts of rebellion and revolts often have their roots in a democratic impulse, and that they are frequently the symptoms of real tensions and inequities.[40] For example, the Arab Spring began in 2010 with a street vendor in Tunisia, Mohamed Bouazizi, who set himself on fire in protest against his autocratic government. This set in motion a number of protests that spread through North Africa and the Middle East, which ultimately contributed to the toppling of governments in Tunisia, Egypt, Yemen, and Libya.

A social movement can develop spontaneously and illegally without approval from leadership within the movement, like a wildcat strike. For example, in 2012 in Toronto, 15 employees spontaneously blocked the main exit in the carousel section of Pearson airport without the sanction of their union. What had prompted the incident was the fact that some workers had noticed Labour Minister Lisa Raitt, who had just passed back-to-work legislation and sent a contract dispute with the airline to arbitration, coming off a flight from North Bay. The wildcat strike action at the airport created travel chaos for 24,000 customers across North America. Such strikes, by their nature, are unpredictable and rarely occur. They can be risky because they are generally reactive and unplanned. As a result, they can turn public opinion against the protesters rather than drawing sympathy for the cause.

There is no clear evidence as to whether insider or outsider strategies are more effective. In fact, the distinction may not be entirely useful since most civil society organizations adopt, at various times, both strategies depending on the issue and the context they face. There are, of course, some advantages to being on the inside. Over time, organizations can develop long-term relations with decision-makers and gain trust, legitimacy, and recognition. They can also develop a better understanding of the issues and the perspective of government. However, not all actors have the ability to work the system from the inside. Access to decision-makers depends in large part on the availability of resources, reputation, and connections necessary to obtain access. What is more, not all actors want to work on the inside. Some fear that insider strategies can lead to co-optation if organization leaders come to associate more closely with policy-makers than with their members or their base. As they become accustomed to working on the inside, they may adopt the values of decision-makers rather than preserve those that led to the creation of the organization in the first place. Ultimately, the choice of tactics will involve some trade-offs.

NEW TRENDS IN CIVIL SOCIETY ORGANIZING

While there has been a strong record in the field of civil society research, there are still many dynamics

TABLE 12.4 INSIDER AND OUTSIDER TACTICS	
Insider	**Outsider**
• Lobbying	• Petitioning
• Meeting with elected officials and bureaucrats	• Mounting media and education campaigns
• Producing research	• Striking (including wildcat strikes)
• Testifying at legislative hearings	• Demonstrating
• Letter-writing to elected officials	• Picketing
• Funding electoral candidates	• Occupying public spaces
• Ranking electoral candidates	• Conducting sit-ins
• Supporting judicial and senate nominations	• Setting up road blockades
• Appearing before the courts	• Engaging in civil disobedience
	• Undertaking armed insurgency

that puzzle us, particularly as concern new trends in civil society organizing. In fact, the scope of changes to representational practices since the turn of the century are so striking that they necessitate a reappraisal of current approaches to understanding state–society relations. They constitute a profound shift in both the substance and practice of state–society relations.

Resource mobilization theory has shown us that resources—time, money, skills, human resources—and alliances are vital to the success of a mobilizing effort. However, the pace of change is happening exponentially. New technologies and social media have increased the potential for connection. Citizens now have more tools to organize quickly, to share their ideas, and to have their voices heard in the political arena. We have seen positive experiments in state–civil society interaction in recent years. In the United States, for example, the Obama administration launched a website called "We the People" in 2011 to allow citizens to submit petitions online. If 100,000 people sign a petition in 30 days, then it gets reviewed.[41] In 2012, the government of Finland similarly opened up the legislative process using collaborative online tools to allow ordinary citizens to comment on draft legislation and offer their own proposals.[42] There will likely be more such initiatives and experiments to increase access for citizens to the policy process in the future.

However, even if people have increased opportunities to participate, will they actually take advantage of these and become involved? Although the tendency for citizens to "free ride" remains, new technologies can significantly lower the costs of participation. But in order for that to happen, we need to address the digital divide. A huge proportion of the world's population still does not have access to these new tools. In Table 12.5, Statistics Canada data reveals that while 83 percent of all Canadians use Internet wireless services, only a quarter of lower-income Canadians do. Access to Internet wireless services is also particularly difficult for Aboriginal communities in remote areas. Political literacy and digital literacy need to be priorities if we are to leverage these new opportunities. As the complexity of both the world and our engagement with it increases, so too must our approaches.

ARE INTEREST GROUPS TOO POWERFUL?

Interest groups are important to democracy because they can help governments to be more representative of and responsive to different voices and interests in society. This is particularly true when there is healthy competition among interest groups so that no single

TABLE 12.5	CANADIAN INTERNET USAGE BY HOUSEHOLD INCOME, 2010, 2012	
	2010	**2012**
Lowest quartile household income	59.2	62.5
Second quartile household income	73.4	77.8
Third quartile household income	85.5	90.2
Highest quartile household income	94.3	94.5

Source: Statistics Canada. *Table 358-0152 - Canadian Internet use survey, Internet use, by age group and household income for Canada, provinces and census metropolitan areas (CMAs), occasional (percent)*, CANSIM (database).

viewpoint or interest dominates the debate. Interest groups support democracy insofar as they offer channels outside elections through which citizens can participate in the political process and have their views heard.

At the same time, some observers fear that civil society actors can distort politics by giving disproportionate meaning to an issue that concerns only a minority of citizens. These observers often believe in the primacy of the electoral process in pursuing the public good, whereby elected officials are selected by the citizenry to be legitimate representatives of the public interest. A second concern is that these groups may seek to achieve their objectives at the expense of society as a whole. The term "special interest groups" has widely been used to refer to organizations that are perceived to represent very limited and narrow interests. In fact, when the government of Canada terminated the Court Challenges Program, it raised the concern that this program enabled such special interest groups to take elected governments to court on taxpayers' dollars. Finally, some are concerned that interest groups may not genuinely speak for those who they claim to represent.

However, as we saw early on in this chapter, it is not always easy to determine whether an interest group represents a "special interest" or a "public interest" because there is generally some overlap between public and self-interest. It is also worth noting that there can be an ideological dimension to the debate, as "special interest group" is often used as a derogatory term by political commentators who wish to undermine the cause of a group with which they disagree.

Beyond rhetoric, the same tools that can be used to encourage political participation can also

be used in efforts to limit it. While we know that civil society makes an important contribution to advancing political debate, there are signs of growing restrictions being placed on the capacity of civil society actors to advocate and mobilize. For example, in Quebec, the provincial government introduced a law during the student protests requiring that every event of more than 50 people be reported to the police and that the route and mode of transportation be revealed at least eight hours before it starts. The law also gave police the authority to order protesters to change their route and to impose fines on the leaders of the mobilization in the event that a mishap happens during the event. The proposed fines of $100,000 are so steep that if imposed they would threaten the very existence of almost any civil society organization. Although this law was eventually repealed, it was a significant constraint on the vitality of key democratic freedoms, such as freedom of assembly, freedom of the press, and freedom of expression, at a very time when citizens where availing themselves of those freedoms.

Unfortunately, all around the world, a growing number of governments are trying to regulate democratic freedoms to limit the power of organizations and movements that challenge the status quo. Tactics used by governments include increased media oversight, tighter accountability rules, and declining funding for specific advocacy activities. For example, in January 2014, the Ukraine government passed legislation that banned public assembly and regulated the flow of foreign investment to civil society groups. We have also observed a tightening of regulations that significantly limit the ability of voluntary organizations

Protesters clash with riot police during an opposition rally in the centre of the Ukrainian capital Kiev in 2014 in a show of defiance against strict new curbs on protests.

© SERGEI SUPINSKY/AFP/Getty Images

to engage in advocacy activities. In Canada, for example, a number of high-profile national organizations in the areas of international development and the environment lost public funding after speaking out against government policies. This "advocacy chill" even prompted the famous Canadian environmentalist David Suzuki to step down from the board of directors of his own organization, the David Suzuki Foundation, out of fear that it would be punished for his political activism.[43] In response, many organizations have moved away from political representation activities toward a more service-oriented focus in order to secure potential government contracts and develop social enterprise models.

That being said, there has been over the past decade some evidence of a reversal of trends in youth disengagement. While young people are far less likely to vote than older Canadians, they are more likely to volunteer than any other age group and this is on the rise now that mandatory volunteering has been introduced in a number of school curriculums (see Table 12.6). Initiatives such as the "Me to We" movement have been leading the charge through projects such as the "We Day" movement to inspire and motivate youth. We Day is an annual event held across cities in Canada and the U.S. that brings together international speakers and celebrities to launch the beginning of a year of educational programs and activities to empower youth and develop their ability to change the world. Me to We is now one of the biggest youth culture movements, mobilizing tens of thousands of individuals toward achieving social change in areas such as eliminating child labour. What is also interesting in this movement is that it is teaching youth that small contributions can bring about significant social change, as the average donation received by the organization is eight dollars. While we are used to thinking of Bill Gates and Warren Buffet as the great philanthropists, movements like Me to We, Avaaz.org, and MoveOn.org are impressive because they focus on the potential of ordinary people to change the world and, moreover, are having a meaningful impact by training a new generation of leaders.

TABLE 12.6	VOLUNTEERING (PERCENT PARTICIPATION) IN CANADA BY AGE GROUP		
Age Group	2004	2007	2010
15 to 24 years	55	58	58
25 to 34 years	42	40	46
35 to 44 years	51	52	54
45 to 54 years	47	48	45
55 to 64 years	42	40	41
65 years and over	32	36	36

Source: Vezina, Mireille and Susan Crompton. 2012. *Volunteering in Canada*. Statistics Canada Catalogue no. 11-008-X. Ottawa, Ontario. 21 p. http://www.statcan.gc.ca/pub/11-008-x/2012001/article/11638-eng.pdf (accessed June 22, 2015).

CONCLUSION

Whether through funding cuts or more stringent regulations on the ability of groups to advocate, it is clear that the voice of some civil society groups in policy-making has been weakened in recent years. When we place these dynamics in the context of broader shifts in political participation, such as the decline in voter turnout and the growing constraints on lobbying and advocacy activities in Canada, there is cause to worry about the overall state of our democratic polity. Political representation is central to democratic processes, and civil society is an important locus for shaping and changing discourses, ideas, and interests. Yet there has been a great democratization of political participation facilitated by globalization and new communications technologies. This has created new patterns of interest mobilization and new waves of contentious politics. Each of these trends deserves further investigation. Perhaps you can be a part of the next generation of research in this field.

DISCUSSION QUESTIONS

1. Choose one interest group, one social movement, and one voluntary organization and compare the instruments that they could use to influence decision-makers.

2. Describe how the relationship between government and civil society organizations has evolved. What are some of the challenges facing the ability of civil society to mobilize to effect change today?

3. Should we be worried about declining levels of volunteering, giving, and participating in the political sphere, and what could be done to reverse this trend?

4. Have the new tools of social media reinvented civil society organizing? Can Internet communications have the same effect as face-to-face contact?

5. Name three ways that civil society organizations support democratic politics, and three ways that they can undermine it.

WEBSITES

The Digital Activism Research Project (DARP)
http://digital-activism.org/resources/open-access-activism-data-sets/
Gathers data on global digital activism, civic engagement, non-violent conflict, and citizen journalism. It provides open access data sets on activism.

Sector Source
http://sectorsource.ca/
An online portal that provides resources, information, and up-to-date data on the voluntary sector in Canada. It is managed by Imagine Canada, a national charity that aims to support and strengthen the voluntary sector in Canada.

Charity Village
http://charityvillage.com/
An online portal that brings together news and how-to resources to help voluntary organizations. If you are interested in pursuing a career in the voluntary sector, it is also the number one source to view job postings from across Canada.

The Johns Hopkins Center for Civil Society Studies
http://ccss.jhu.edu/
Houses international data that compares the size and scope of the voluntary sectors around the world. It is a great source of information to observe and analyze emerging trends in civil society.

FURTHER READING

James Cairns and Alan Sears, *The Democratic Imagination: Envisioning Popular Power in the Twenty-First Century.* Toronto: University of Toronto Press, 2012.

Donatella della Porta and Alice Mattoni, eds., *Spreading Protest: Social Movements in Times of Crisis.* Colchester: ECPR Press, 2014.

Darren Halpin, *The Organization of Political Interest Groups: Designing Advocacy.* London and New York: Routledge, 2014.

Rachel Laforest, *Voluntary Sector Organizations and the State.* Vancouver: University of British Columbia Press, 2011.

Miriam Smith, ed., *Group Politics and Social Movements in Canada,* 2nd ed. Toronto: University of Toronto Press, 2014.

Miriam Smith, *A Civil Society? Collective Actors in Canadian Political Life.* Peterborough: Broadview Press, 2005.

Suzanne Staggenborg, *Social Movements.* Toronto: Oxford University Press, 2012.

ENDNOTES

1. See *Theory & Event: Special Issue on the Quebec Student Movement* 15 (3) (2012).

2. Peter Hallward, "The Threat of Quebec's Good Example," *Socialist Project,* e-Bulletin No. 647 (June 6, 2012), online at http://www.socialist-project.ca/bullet/647.php.

3. Ken Coates, *#Idle No More and the Remaking of Canada* (Regina: University of Regina Press, 2014).

4. Miriam Smith, *A Civil Society? Collective Actors in Canadian Political Life* (Peterborough: Broadview Press, 2005), p. 19.

5. A. Paul Pross, *Group Politics and Public Policy* (Toronto: Oxford University Press, 1986), p. 13.

6. John Bruce and Clyde Wilcox, *The Changing Politics of Gun Control* (Maryland: Rowman and Littefield, 1998), p. 158.

7. Caroline De La Porte and Philippe Pochet, "Participation in the Open Method of Coordination," in Jonathan Zeitlin and Philippe Pochet, eds., *The Open Method of Coordination in Action: The European Employment and Social Inclusion Strategies* (Brussels: PIE Peter Lang, 2005), pp. 353–89.

8. Mancur Olson, *The Logic of Collective Action: Public Goods and the Theory of Groups* (Cambridge, Mass.: Harvard University Press, 1965).

9. David Truman, *The Governmental Process* (New York: Knopf, 1951).

10. Peter Bacharach and Morton Baratz, *Power and Poverty* (New York: Oxford University Press, 1970).

11. William D. Coleman and Grace Skogstad, eds., *Policy Communities and Public Policy in Canada* (Toronto: Copp Clark Pitman, 1990).

12. Evert Lindquist, "New Agendas for Research on Policy Communities: Policy Analysis, Administration, and Governance," in Laurent Dobuzinskis, Michael Howlett, and David Laycock, eds., *Policy Studies in Canada: The State of the Art* (Toronto: University of Toronto Press, 1996), pp. 219–41; Michael Howlett, "Do Networks Matter? Linking Policy Network Structure to Policy Outcome: Evidence from Four Canadian Policy Sectors 1990–2000," *Canadian Journal of Political Science* 35 (2) (June 2002), pp. 235–67.

13. Ralph H. Turner and Lewis M. Killian, *Collective Behavior* (Englewood Cliffs, New Jersey: Prentice Hall, 1972), p. 223.

14. Post-materialist values mainly concern lifestyle choices. As economic development and prosperity increase, individuals become less concerned with their daily survival and material conditions, but rather start to focus on quality of life values instead. See Neil Nevitte, *The Decline of Deference: Canadian Value Change in Cross-National Perspective* (Peterborough: Broadview Press, 1996); Ronald Inglehart, *Culture Shift in Advanced Industrial Society* (Princeton: Princeton University Press, 1990).

15. Scott Hunt and Robert Benford, "Collective Identity, Solidarity, and Commitment," in David Snow, Sarah Soule, and Hanspeter Kriesi, eds., *The Blackwell Companion to Social Movements* (Oxford: Blackwell, 2004), p. 437.

16. David Snow, "Collective Identity and Expressive Forms," University of California, Irvine escholarship repository, 2001, online at https://escholarship.org/uc/item/2zn1t7bj#page-4.

17. Sydney Tarrow, *Power in Movement: Social Movements, Collective Action and Politics* (Cambridge: Cambridge University Press, 1994).

18. The Quiet Revolution refers to a period in Quebec's history, in the 1960s, when the province underwent profound social, economic, cultural, and political change. The Quiet Revolution was tied to the rise of nationalism in Quebec as the state took on the sole responsibility for the provision of welfare programs and the Catholic Church began to lose its hold on society.

19. John McCarthy and Mayer Zald, *The Trend of Social Movements in America: Professionalization and Resource Mobilization* (Morristown, New Jersey: General Learning Press, 1973).

20. Tarrow, *Power in Movement*, p. 77.

21. For more information, see http://www. democraciarealya.es/.

22. See, for example, Malcolm Gladwell, "Small Change: Why the revolution will not be tweeted," *The New Yorker*, October 4, 2010, online at http://www.newyorker.com/ magazine/2010/10/04/small-change-3.

23. Evgeny Morozov, "Iran: Downside to the "Twitter Revolution," *Dissent* (Fall 2009), p. 12, online at http://www.evgenymorozov.com/ morozov_twitter_dissent.pdf.

24. Michael Hall et al., *Cornerstones of Community: Highlights of the National Survey of Nonprofit and Voluntary Organizations* (Ottawa: Ministry of Industry, 2004); see also Statistics Canada, *Satellite Account of Non-profit Institutions and Volunteering, 2007* (Ottawa: Ministry of Industry, 2009).

25. Lester Salamon, *Partners in Public Service: Government-Nonprofit Relations in the Modern Welfare State* (Baltimore: Johns Hopkins University Press, 1995).

26. Steven R. Smith and Michael Lipsky, *Nonprofits for Hire: The Welfare State in the Age of Contracting* (Cambridge, Mass.: Harvard University Press, 1993).

27. David Billis, *Hybrid Organizations and the Third Sector: Challenges for Practice, Theory and Policy* (London: Palgrave MacMillan, 2010).

28. Alexis de Tocqueville, *Democracy in America*, edited and introduced by Isaac Kramnick, trans. by Gerald Bevan (London: Penguin Books, 2003). Originally published in two volumes in 1835 and 1840, respectively.

29. Robert D. Putnam, *Making Democracy Work: Civic Traditions in Modern Italy* (Princeton: Princeton University Press, 1993).

30. Robert D. Putnam, "Bowling Alone: America's Declining Social Capital," *Journal of Democracy* 6 (1) (1995), pp. 65–78.

31. To view the data on social capital benefits, see Robert D. Putnam, "Social Capital: Measurement and Consequences," online at http://www.oecd.org/innovation/ research/1825848.pdf.

32. Imagine Canada, *Research Bulletin*, 15 (1) (December 2011), p. 1, online at http://www. imaginecanada.ca/sites/default/files/www/en/ researchbulletins/rb1501en.pdf.

33. See Statistic Canada, *Caring Canadians, Involved Canadians: Highlights from the 2004 Canada Survey of Giving, Volunteering and Participating* (Ottawa: Ministry of Industry, 2006).

34. Paul Reed and Kevin Selbee, "The Civic Core in Canada: Disproportionality in Charitable Giving, Volunteering, and Civic Participation," *Nonprofit and Voluntary Sector Quarterly* 30 (4) (December 2001), pp. 761–80.

35. Theda Skocpol, *Diminished Democracy: From Membership to Management in American Civic Life* (Norman: University of Oklahoma Press, 2003).

36. Stijn Smismans, "European Civil Society: Shaped by Discourses and Institutional Interests," *European Law Journal* 9 (4) (September 2003), pp. 473–95.

37. Wyn Grant, "Insider Groups, Outsider Groups and Interest Group Strategies in Britain," University of Warwick, Department of Politics *Working Paper no. 19*, 1978.

38. Margaret Malone, "Regulation of Lobbyists in Developed Countries, Current Rules and Practices," online at http://www.environ.ie/en/Publications/ LocalGovernment/Administration/ FileDownLoad,2048,en.pdf.

39. Stephen Harper, speech in Sault Sainte-Marie, Youtube video at 3:38, online at https://www.youtube.com/watch?v=COsA_m-c0XY&feature=player_embedded.

40. Stephen D'Arcy, *Languages of the Unheard: Why Militant Protest is Good for Democracy* (Toronto: Between the Lines, 2013).

41. Note that the original threshold was 5,000 signatures. It was increased to 25,000 in 2011 and to 100,000 in 2013.

42. For more information, visit http://oikeusministerio.fi/en/index/currentissues/tiedotteet/2012/01/kansalaisaloitekayttoonmaaliskuunalusta.html.

43. To see David Suzuki's open letter, visit http://www.davidsuzuki.org/blogs/panther-lounge/2012/04/an-open-letter-from-david-suzuki/.

PART

5 INTERNATIONAL POLITICS

© Courtney Keating/Getty Images

13

THE POLITICS OF DEVELOPMENT

Michelle Bonner

© BSIP/UIG via Getty Images

Development can be seen in many different lights around the world and can be promoted through many different techniques. Some of the greatest strides may be through such means as the promotion of education and the provision of health services, which in turn can empower people to determine the forms of development most appropriate to their needs.

INTRODUCTION

From Bono to Bill Gates, many celebrities draw media and public attention to the problem of global poverty. We see images on television and online of starving and sick children, refugees fleeing wars, and citizens standing up to their governments. The solutions to these problems appear simple. For example, we can donate money, provide technology, build a school, or adopt a child. But are these the right answers? Are we even asking the right questions?

The study of the politics of development suggests that we should back up and ask bigger questions, such as: Why is there so much inequality and poverty in the world? Why are some countries rich and others poor? Does international development make a positive difference? Which approaches are best? Will technology solve these problems? Can I make a difference?

The answers to these questions do not fit neatly into media sound bites, but they are much better at helping us to understand the political context of the images that we see in the news. This chapter will introduce you to some answers to these questions. It begins by asking you to think about what "development" means, dissecting the words used to describe the areas of the world in need of "development," and looking at different types of development. The chapter next lays out ways in which colonialism and independence have shaped politics and economics in these countries. We then move on to examine the major theories of how countries develop and the roles played by women, aid from countries in the Global North (such as Canada), international banks, and media and technology.

LABELLING THE REGIONS OF STUDY

The politics of development tackles important issues that affect the well-being of people living in particular regions of the world: Africa, the Middle East, Latin America, the Caribbean, and most of Asia. These regions are comprised of the majority of countries in the world and the majority of the world's population. They are also incredibly diverse.

These regions represent many different languages, religions, and cultures. There is also a lot of variation within countries between social classes, cities, rural areas, and climatic regions. Some countries are financially richer than others. For example, Brazil is considerably wealthier than Bangladesh. Some countries, like India, have long histories of democracy while others, such as China and Uganda, have mostly experienced authoritarian rule. Some countries are relatively peaceful, such as Uruguay and Costa Rica, while others, like Syria and Afghanistan, are not.

However, despite such diversity, we need a term that refers to all these countries together so that we can discuss how to solve their common challenges. Finding an appropriate label for such a vast proportion of the world is very challenging and immediately forces us to ask what we mean by "development."

You can see the difficulty of labels in the way that professors over the years have changed the title of second-year courses on the politics of development. From the 1970s to the early 1990s, such courses were commonly called "Third World Politics" and then "Comparative Politics of Developing Areas" (still sometimes used); more recently, you find titles such as "Politics of the Global South" or "Politics of Development." This last title nicely sidesteps the need to label the area of the world being discussed. But why do these differences matter? According to some scholars, labels are more than just names because they signal the problems that need to be addressed, and the possible solutions that might be pursued. Let's look more closely at the history of labels to understand better what this means.[1]

The first term used to identify the regions of the world in need of international development was **underdeveloped**, and can be traced back to a speech given by United States President Harry Truman in 1949. However, this term soon fell out of favour as many scholars and practitioners felt that it was pejorative because it suggested that these countries lacked something or were somehow "backward." In an attempt to be more positive, the term **developing** countries emerged, which suggested a trajectory toward progress and is still sometimes used. It has been criticized, however, for being too optimistic; not all countries are necessarily improving the well-being of their citizens. Some international organizations, such as the United Nations, use **less developed countries (LDCs)**, which escapes the problem of over-optimism but leaves us wondering which countries are the benchmark of achieved development. Similarly, today we often hear terms such as **emerging economies** and **newly industrialized countries (NICs)** that suggest movement toward a global market-based economy.

> **Underdeveloped/developing/less developed countries (LDCs)/emerging economies/newly industrialized countries (NICs):** Terms used to refer to the regions of study in development that emphasize economic development.

To avoid any evaluation of whether a country or region is lacking in or progressing to a particular definition of development, some scholars have taken a different approach in labelling the areas of the world studied in the politics of development. The first such term, the **Third World**, was rooted in the Cold War. At that time the First World was defined as the countries of Western Europe along with the U.S., Canada, Australia, and New Zealand. The Second World referred to the Soviet bloc countries in Eastern Europe. Originally coined by a French scholar in 1952 to describe the rest of the world, the Third World gained meaning as a political bloc when many of these countries joined together to form the Non-Aligned Movement to distance themselves from the Cold War rivalries between First and Second World countries. However, with the end of the Cold War, the meaning of the Third World largely lost its relevancy (after all, there is no more Second World) and concerns arose that the term suggested a sort of third class status for these countries.

> **Third World:** A term from the Cold War that refers to countries that were not part of the First World (Western Europe, the United States, Canada, Australia, and New Zealand) or Second World (USSR and Soviet bloc countries in Eastern Europe).

More recently, the **Global South** has emerged as one of the most common ways to refer to the countries of study in the politics of development, as these countries are largely located in the southern hemisphere. This is the term that will be used in this chapter. In response to the criticisms raised with previous labelling efforts, it allows us to study this area of the world without passing judgment on its level or type of development and instead simply refer to the geographic location of these countries. It remains, of course, imprecise. Thus, there are countries in the Global South that are not usually studied in terms of development, such as Australia and New Zealand. And there are countries in the North that share similar challenges with the Global South, as can be seen in Eastern Europe. Yet, of the terms we have today, it appears to be the least problematic. Of course, when possible it is preferable to name and compare specific regions or countries to highlight the diversity in these parts of the world better.

> **Global South:** A recent term used to refer to those regions of the world that are the focus of study in the politics of development (Africa, Latin America, the Caribbean, the Middle East, and most of Asia).

THINK AND DISCUSS

Is development only an issue for the Global South? The Global South is the focus of most of the literature on development. However, some scholars and practitioners argue that we need to talk about poor parts of the world that exist in all countries. For example, Indigenous communities in Canada share many experiences with the Global South, such as colonialism and poverty.

WHAT IS DEVELOPMENT?

The idea of development has gone through many changes over the years. Prior to the mid-20th century, the term generally used was "civilizing" rather than "developing" the Global South. At the time, most of the Global South was colonized and many European colonizing powers debated how to "civilize" the "barbarous" or "primitive" populations under their rule. Others debated if it was even possible to civilize them. Civilization was associated with such things as living in cities, European culture and religion, reason, whiteness of skin, and masculinity.[2] If you read old comic books such as *The Adventures of Tintin*, for example, or colonial literature such as Joseph Conrad's *Heart of Darkness*, this civilizing message is apparent. In each case, the hero is from Europe, travels to the colonies, and encounters the "primitive" people who live there. Such ideas often defined the work of missionaries, who were among the first "development workers" as they saw it as their job to contribute to this civilizing project by converting colonial subjects to European religions, particularly Christianity. With the onset of decolonization in many parts of the Global South (on this process, the timing of which varied greatly depending on the country in question, see further below), the vocabulary changed from "civilizing" to "developing the Third World." Decolonization meant that European powers had less political and social control over their former colonies. However, they were able to offer economic assistance and proposals for "development" as a way, in part, to maintain ties with their former colonies.

As you may have identified in this brief historical overview, "development" can refer to economic, social, or political development. Thus, if we want to contribute to "development" then we need to be clear about what type of development we would like to see. In what follows, we examine what is meant by economic, social, and political development.

Economic Development

The dominant definition of development was and remains **economic development**. With decolonization, development efforts focused on how to raise a country's per capita Gross Domestic Product (GDP). **GDP per capita** is a measure of a nation's total production (goods and services), or how rich the country is in economic terms, divided by its population. Gross National Income (**GNI**) is GDP plus income received from overseas (e.g. when a national company makes money from property they own in another country). GDP, GDP per capita, and GNI are common measures of economic growth (to what degree a country's overall economy has grown or shrunk).

Economic development: Development defined in terms of economic indicators such as GDP and GNI.

GDP per capita: A measure of a nation's total production (goods and services), or how rich the country is in economic terms, divided by a country's population.

GNI: A measure of a country's GDP plus income received from overseas.

This approach to development contends that if a country's GDP per capita rises then it will be able to address issues such as employment, poverty, education, and health. However, GDP per capita does not tell us how well the economic wealth of a country is distributed. It does not tell us how much poverty there is in a country. In this case, poverty is defined as the number of people in a country who do not earn enough money to pay for basic needs such as food, sanitation, and shelter. It is possible, in other words, for a country to have a high GDP per capita alongside extensive poverty. Indeed, this is the case in many countries, such as Nigeria, Brazil, and Chile. It is also possible for a country to have a modest GDP but relatively low levels of poverty, as in China, Indonesia, and Jordan. For this reason, it is a limited indicator of development if our concern is reducing poverty.

The **Gini Coefficient** is a measure of inequality of wealth in a country. It is a measure from 0 to 1 in which those countries scoring closer to 0 are more equal (Norway is one of the lowest at approximately .25) than those scoring closer to 1 (South Africa is one of the highest at .63). Combined with a country's GDP per capita, the Gini Coefficient can tell us not only how wealthy a country is but also how evenly that wealth is distributed. For example, relative to other regions in the Global South, most Latin American countries have strong per capita GDPs alongside some of the highest inequalities of wealth in the world (most with Gini Coefficients between .55 and .60). Thus, the issue for Latin America is less the generation of wealth and more its distribution. In this way, the Gini Coefficient helps us to identify and understand levels of poverty in a given country better.[3]

> **Gini coefficient:** A measure of inequality of wealth in a country.

Social Development

Discussions of wealth distribution lead us to ask what we mean by poverty and if poverty is just an economic condition. In the late 1960s, many scholars and practitioners began to investigate other dimensions of poverty related to issues of inclusion, well-being, and the ability of people to participate more fully in the political and social life of their societies. Social services, such as education and healthcare, help people to do this.

In an attempt to capture this broader idea of development, the United Nations Development Programme (UNDP) introduced an alternative measure of development in 1990, the **Human Development Index (HDI)**. The HDI is used in the annual UNDP Human Development Report, which evaluates changes in development in all countries around the world. The HDI measures development in terms of not only a country's national income (GDP per capita) but also dimensions of **social development** such as life expectancy, education attainment, and gender equality (see Table 13.1).

> **Human Development Index (HDI):** Measures development in terms of not only a country's national income but other factors such as life expectancy, educational attainment, and gender equality.

> **Social development:** Includes not only economic indicators of development but also issues such as education, sanitation, health, and infant mortality.

The HDI reflects a definition of poverty that is multidimensional, including but not limited to economics. From this perspective, eliminating poverty requires more than simply increasing a country's per capita GDP. It also involves addressing issues such as eliminating discriminatory laws (for example, laws that prohibit women from owning or inheriting property), improving access to education, and expanding state-provided health services, all of which are related to the distribution of wealth. For example, when a woman can inherit property she is less likely fall into poverty if her husband dies. The idea of social development is consistent with the idea of the welfare state in the Global North, which views the state as responsible for taking care of those who are most vulnerable in our current economic system.

Social development is also the focus of the Millennium Development Goals (MDG). In 2000, 189 countries made a commitment to free people from extreme poverty. This commitment turned into eight development goals referred to as MDG. The eight goals are:[*]

1. Eradicate extreme poverty and hunger
2. Achieve universal primary education
3. Promote gender equality and empower women
4. Reduce child mortality
5. Improve maternal health
6. Combat HIV/AIDS, malaria, and other diseases
7. Ensure environmental sustainability
8. Develop a global partnership for development

Many development organizations (NGOs, state and international organizations) currently focus their

---

* Millennium Development Goals, *United Nations*, online at http://www.un.org/millenniumgoals/ (accessed June 23, 2015).

TABLE 13.1 HDI AND COMPONENTS, BY REGION AND HDI GROUP, 2012				
Region and HDI group	HDI	Years life expectancy at birth	Mean years of schooling	Expected years of schooling	Gross national income per capita (2005 PPP $)
Region					
Arab States	0.652	71.0	6.0	10.6	8,317
East Asia and the Pacific	0.683	72.7	7.2	11.8	6,874
Europe and Central Asia	0.771	71.5	10.4	13.7	12,243
Latin America and the Caribbean	0.741	74.7	7.8	13.7	10,300
South Asia	0.558	66.2	4.7	10.2	3,343
Sub-Saharan Africa	0.475	54.9	4.7	9.3	2,010
HDI group					
Very high human development	0.905	80.1	11.5	16.3	33,391
High human development	0.758	73.4	8.8	13.9	11,501
Medium human development	0.640	69.9	6.3	11.4	5,428
Low human development	0.466	59.1	4.2	8.5	1,633
World	0.694	70.1	7.5	11.6	10,184

Note: Data are weighted by population and calculated based on HDI values for 187 countries. PPP is purchasing power parity. HDI scores range from 0 to 1, with 1 being the better score.

Source: Khalid Malik et al., *Human Development Report 2013* (New York: UNDP, 2013), 25, online at http://hdr.undp.org/sites/default/files/reports/14/ hdr2013_en_complete.pdf (accessed June 23, 2015).

work on these goals. However, success and commitment has been uneven. For example, the 2008 global financial crisis and subsequent austerity measures led many countries in the Global North to reduce their financial contributions to official development assistance (ODA).

Political Development

While poverty is often thought to be the central concern of development and is easily conceived of as an economic and social issue, it is also political. That is, without effective political institutions that can mediate conflict, develop policy, and provide needed services, it is very difficult for a state to tackle poverty. This is the concern of **political development**. Samuel Huntington was one of the first to highlight the importance of strong institutions for successful development, and even argued that these institutions did not need to be housed immediately within a democracy.[4] This produced a lively debate on whether authoritarian or democratic regimes were better able to produce economic and social development.

Political development: The establishment of functional and effective political institutions that can mediate conflict, implement policy, and provide the services needed to tackle poverty. It can include the establishment of democracy.

Some authors, such as Huntington, argued that if democracy, while desirable, was pursued before economic development, then newly elected governments would lack the resources to meet citizen demands, or violent conflict between ethnic groups might erupt as groups competed for scarce resources. Others, during the Cold War, saw authoritarian Communism as a better path to development as it was thought that such a state could ensure the distribution of economic wealth as well as the provision of services needed for social development. Since the end of the Cold War and the fall of many authoritarian regimes in the Global South, scholars and practitioners have increasingly accepted democracy as both an ends and means for development.

Amartya Sen is one of the leading scholars to have linked development with democracy, arguing that we should conceive of **development as freedom**. Sen sees democracy and human rights as central to this concept of development. "Development as freedom" includes basic needs such as freedom to satisfy hunger, to have access to basic healthcare, and to clothe and house oneself. It also reflects more ambitious freedoms such as educating oneself, finding employment, and being safe from violence. Sen argues that democracy is more likely to provide these freedoms and, where it has not, the issue is the need for more democracy, not less.[5] Responding to this shift in understanding democracy as key to development, many scholars, states, NGOs, and international organizations dedicate their work to promoting the building of effective democratic political institutions such as elections, judiciaries, and legislative bodies.

> **Development as freedom:** A concept developed by economist Amartya Sen that sees democracy and human rights as central to development. It includes basic needs such as people's freedom to satisfy hunger, to have access to basic healthcare, and to clothe and house themselves. It also reflects more ambitious freedoms such as educating oneself, finding employment, and being safe from violence.

The concepts of economic, social, and political development offer us different ways of approaching the question: What does development mean? Yet they do not help us to answer some of the more basic questions we asked at the beginning of this chapter: Why

are some parts of the world rich and others poor? Or why is there so much inequality in the world? To answer these questions we will start with colonialism.

COLONIALISM, DECOLONIZATION, AND NEOCOLONIALISM

Most countries in the Global South were at one time colonies of countries in the Global North. This is why scholars sometimes refer to the Global South as **post-colonial**. The term draws our attention to the fact that what all these regions have in common is their experiences of long periods of European colonization. **Colonialism** is the territorial conquest, ownership, occupation, and direct administration of one country by another. The term post-colonial emphasizes that colonialism has had and continues to have an important impact on these regions. It has affected borders, state structures, military practices, cultures, and economies, and fostered what some call a "colonial mindset" both in the Global North and South.[6]

> **Post-colonial:** A term used to refer to countries in the Global South that have previously experienced long periods of colonization by countries in the Global North.

> **Colonialism:** The territorial conquest, ownership, occupation, and direct administration of one country by another.

Indeed, all theories of development, which we will discuss further below, agree that colonialism has had an important impact on the political and socioeconomic realities that these countries face today. That is, there is a relationship between colonialism and development. Given this consensus, it is important to devote some time to understanding colonialism: Why did it happen? What were the similarities and differences between colonizers? What are some of the legacies of colonialism?

Many European countries, including Spain, Portugal, France, Britain, Belgium, the Netherlands, Italy, and Germany—and, later, the United States and Japan—colonized countries in the Global South. Together their colonies spanned all regions of the

Global South and some countries were colonized by more than one colonizer. For example, the Philippines was colonized first by Spain and then the United States. Colonialism had many similar features but also varied depending on the region colonized, the resources found, when colonization occurred, and how local people reacted to colonial rule.

Similarities across Colonial Regimes

1. The goal of colonialism was to make European powers rich

Colonial powers competed to control resources available in the Global South, such as gold, silver, and other minerals, as well as foodstuffs like sugar, coffee, and tea. Goods such as cotton that supported 19th-century European industrialization were also popular. The goal was to move these products from the Global South to the European power as easily as possible.

2. Rule on the cheap

Since the goal of colonialism was to make the colonizing country rich, it was important that the costs of colonialism not outweigh the economic gains. European investment in colonial infrastructure, political institutions, and economic systems was therefore limited to the minimum needed to extract the desired goods. For example, railways were often built to facilitate the transportation of goods to ports where they could be shipped to Europe. Sometimes colonizers pursued interests in the colonies beyond the extraction of wealth, such as educating locals in European languages, customs, and religion, but usually with some ambivalence.

3. Colonialism established territories and territorial boundaries

Colonialism created countries, and borders for these countries, based on the interests of the colonizers. They did not represent the territories used by the people indigenous to the area. They were established to address power imbalances between European countries (e.g., provide a European country territory in Africa so as to discourage it from invading another European country in order to expand its territory) and divide peoples in the Global South. The latter tactic facilitated colonial power.

For example, the Treaty of Tordesillas (1494) was an agreement between the Spanish and Portuguese to share South America by dividing the continent

in half, along what is now the border of Brazil. This fragmented the territory of Indigenous peoples such as the Guaraní, whose territory is now divided between Paraguay, Argentina, Uruguay, and Brazil. Similarly, the Berlin Conference (1884–1885) legitimized ground rules for a competitive European land grab of territory in Africa. No African was at the Berlin Conference and Africans were not part of the negotiations that established territorial borders. While the Organization of African Unity has pledged to respect the borders established by European colonizers, many conflicts in the region stem from problems created by imposed borders, such as the separation of similar ethic groups into different countries and the forced clustering of too many diverse ethnic groups in a single territory that did not exist as a single political entity prior to colonization. For example, Nigeria holds one-sixth of Africa's population and 389 ethnic groups.

4. Colonialism established states and political orders that were hierarchical and authoritarian

To maintain control of colonies and ensure that desired goods were moved as easily as possible from the colonies to the colonizer's country, systems of governance were established. The institutions put in place varied from country to country but were always authoritarian and hierarchical (even if the colonizer practiced democracy at home) to ensure the control of resources and the local population.

Conference of Berlin, 1884–1885
© akg-images

5. European colonialism believed in the superiority of European peoples

European powers justified the economic exploitation of their colonies and the people indigenous to those colonies through arguments that asserted European moral, racial, cultural, and religious superiority.

6. Colonialism established, formally and informally, new social attitudes, institutions, and communication

Through colonialism, European languages became a common means of communication. Yet other practices aimed to create social divisions that had not previously existed. Colonial administrators often favoured some groups within a country over others, a practice that often still shapes relations between these groups today. In Sri Lanka (formally British Ceylon), the British gave preferential treatment to the Tamil minority for positions in colonial governance. The Tamils then lost these privileges to the Sinhalese majority with independence. This is an important part of the ongoing conflict between the Tamils and Sinhalese in Sri Lanka.

Differences in Colonial Regimes

Of course, there were also many differences between colonial regimes. These differences help us to understand the variety of challenges that former colonies face today. The following offers a brief overview of some of the unique characteristics of the regimes of three of the largest colonizers, the Spanish, French, and British.

Spanish Most Spanish colonies (primarily in Latin America) were established in the 16th century and achieved independence around 1820, much earlier than colonies in Africa and Asia, where independence came in the late-1800s to the early 1960s.

Spanish colonialism had two main objectives. The most important was to bring gold and silver from the colonies back to Spain in order to increase the wealth of the Spanish monarchy and, in turn, enhance the country's power vis-à-vis other European countries. Most of the original Spanish colonists were men who went to Latin America to become wealthy and, in turn, make Spain wealthy. In doing so, most intended to return to Europe. While the original idea was not to settle the Americas, many Spaniards ultimately stayed for reasons

of intermarriage and social mobility. Second, and of lesser importance, many clergy went to Latin America to "civilize" Indigenous populations by converting them to Catholicism. In many respects this goal was simply an extension of Spanish politics in Europe. Spain began its infamous Inquisition to rid the country of non-Catholics around the same time that it entered the Americas.

The Spanish colonial hierarchal system placed God at the top, followed by the Spanish Monarch, colonial governors (vice-roys) who were born in Spain but living in the colonies, and local governors who were either born in Spain or of Spanish descent. At the bottom of the hierarchy were Indigenous people and the African slaves brought by the Spanish to the Americas. In practice, the divisions within this structure could become blurred but its purpose was to ensure that the wealth found in the Americas made its way to Spain to, in part, fund wars in Europe. In this way, like colonialism generally, Spanish colonialism was rooted in a belief of European superiority, and was both hierarchical and authoritarian.

French The French established colonies in South-East Asia, Africa, the Middle East, and the Caribbean. Inspired by the French revolution of 1789, French colonialism aimed not only to exploit the colonies for their economic wealth but, at least in rhetoric, to assimilate the local people culturally and politically as well. While the Spanish and British saw their colonial subjects as racially inferior, the French instead viewed them as culturally inferior. In principle, if the colonized abandoned their culture and language, and adopted French culture, language, and nationality, then they could become "civilized" or "modern."

Hence, whereas the Spanish were very clear that only people born in Spain (not even people of pure Spanish decent) could rule over their colonies, it was possible, although not common, for a well-assimilated African to become the governor of a French colony. Moreover, unlike both Spanish and British colonies, some French colonies were eventually able to elect their own representatives to the French National Assembly.

Theoretically, French colonialism required a great deal of economic and administrative resources in order to ensure assimilation (for example, public and accessible education in French language and customs); yet, in practice, few resources were invested in the education of the colonized, rendering the ideal of assimilation nearly impossible to achieve. Thus, in a similar but different manner to other colonial regimes, French colonialism justified its actions in European superiority, was hierarchical and authoritarian, but was also assimilationist.

British By the late 19th century, Britain was the largest colonizer, with territories across the globe. In contrast to the French, British colonial rule was not assimilationist and instead believed in the racial superiority of the British. Culturally, this meant that each British colony could, for the most part, maintain its culture(s) and religion(s), and each colony was understood as distinct, albeit inferior. Economic exploitation was facilitated politically by minimizing the number of British administrators and working with indigenous authorities, when possible. This form of governance was called **indirect rule**. Generally, the British maintained control over national politics and left local politics to the people of the country. When local authorities were unwilling to work with the British, they were overthrown, as occurred in Burma in 1942, when Premier U Saw was suspected of meeting with Japanese officials in Lisbon in 1942 (during the Second World War) and the British had him arrested and replaced by the pro-British Premier Paw Tun.

> **Indirect rule:** A form of colonial governance used by the British that legitimized local political leaders and legal systems as long as they remained subordinate and useful to the colonial power.

Thus, while the British, like the French, were developing liberal democracy and the rule of law at home, their colonial administrations remained accountable to Britain, not to the local populations. Unlike the French, who envisioned that their colonies would eventually become a part of France, or the Spanish, who did not plan for colonialism to end at all, the British saw their colonies becoming independent when the British viewed them to be "ready." Again, like other colonial powers, British colonialism legitimized its rule through the idea of European superiority, and was hierarchical and authoritarian in its own distinct ways.

INDEPENDENCE

The end of colonialism came as a result of both push and pull factors at home and in the colonies.

For colonizing states, maintaining colonies was an expensive, administratively challenging, and morally taxing endeavour. Thus, most colonial regimes ended in part due to challenges faced by European colonizers at home; challenges that undermined their economic, administrative, and moral authority. For Spain, this occurred when the French Emperor Napoleon Bonaparte invaded the Iberian Peninsula in 1807, deposed the King of Spain, and placed his brother, Joseph-Napoleon Bonaparte, on the throne. For Britain and France, decolonization began after the Great Depression and the two World Wars. These events were expensive for the colonizing powers, disrupted the administration of their colonies, and revealed the European powers to be fallible.

However, even before these developments, people within colonized countries had begun to organize for independence by asserting their own political identities through nationalist movements.

Independence and Nationalist Movements

Independence and nationalist movements were attempts by people within colonized countries to gain freedom in order to realize their own identities through their language, religion, territory, history, or culture. They also often aimed to address related issues pertaining to the unequal distribution of land, wealth, and control over resources.

Many independence and nationalist movements promised dignity, human rights, self-determination, and a more equitable distribution of wealth. Movies like *Gandhi* (1982) capture the romance and excitement of a people fighting an authoritarian colonial power and reclaiming control of their own futures.

Yet, as the film also depicts, very often during or after independence, cleavages emerged between groups that had very different visions of what the new nation should look like, or who had benefited differently from colonialism. For example, Pakistan separated from India in order to form a Muslim state and there has been violent conflict between Hutus and Tutsis in Rwanda, and between white settlers and non-white settlers in Kenya, South Africa, and Algeria.

Many newly independent countries have also struggled in their transition to a more autonomous national economic system. This has allowed former colonizers and other countries, such as the United States, to assert economic control in ways that limit the autonomy of these new governments. This is sometimes referred to as **neocolonialism**. In such cases, the country is officially independent but is constrained in its choices by a foreign power that may use economic or military might to ensure that the country follows economic policies consistent with the interests of the neocolonial power. For example, the U.S. supported coups in Guatemala (1954) and Chile (1973) when its interests in bananas and mining, respectively, were threatened by the election of socialist governments.

> **Neocolonialism:** When a country is officially independent but remains constrained in its choices by a foreign power that may use economic or military might to ensure that the country follows economic policies consistent with the interests of the neocolonial power.

In sum, colonialism, independence, and neocolonialism tell us a lot about global inequality and why some countries are rich and some are poor. This history does not, however, adequately answer the question: How can countries in the Global South develop? To answer this, we need to turn to the major theories of development.

THEORIES OF DEVELOPMENT

A large number of countries became independent after the Second World War and during the Cold War. Many former colonizers hoped to maintain trade relations with their former colonies and worried that these new countries might succumb to Communism. This was an important motivating factor for countries in the Global North to shift their concern from "civilizing" to helping former colonies "develop." For this reason, new theories emerged aimed at understanding how countries in the Global South could "develop." There are four main theories of development, each of which views the problem of development and its solution differently: modernization theory, dependency theory, post-development theory, and neoliberalism (see Table 13.2).

Modernization Theory

Modernization theory was developed in the 1950s based on an analysis of how Britain's economy had developed. It was thought that this model, as exemplified in W.W. Rostow's *The Stages of Economic Growth* (1960), could be used by countries in the Global South.[7] Rostow proposed that there are five stages of economic growth. Countries begin as "traditional societies" defined primarily by their reliance on subsistence agriculture. Modernization starts when the local population begins to question these traditional practices. This can happen when people become exposed, perhaps through colonialism, to "modern" technology (such as the plough). With this exposure, they enter the second stage: "Pre-conditions for Take Off." At this point, countries in the Global North can assist the Global South through financial and infrastructure investments. These, combined with investments made by local business owners who have financially benefitted from new technology, facilitate the third stage: "Take-off." Further re-investment, such as a factory owner using profits from one factory to open others, leads the country to the "Drive to Maturity" stage and, with continued investment, the final "Age of Mass Consumption" stage. Countries in the Global North are thought to be in this last stage.

From the perspective of modernization theory, the problem of development is low economic productivity and the solution is capitalist development. According to this theory, a government (or state) can lead the country to development and the Global North can assist through financial, technological, and infrastructure investments. That is, the state can assist the market to achieve development. The idea that "there are stages of capitalist economic growth that lead to modernity" remains influential in international development and financial organizations, such as the World Bank, today. However, there is less support for state involvement, as former advocates of modernization theory now predominately favour neoliberalism.

Dependency Theory

Dependency theory emerged in the 1960s in Latin America as a neo-Marxist critique of modernization theory, led by scholars such as Andre Gunder Frank, Theotonio Dos Santos, and Walter Rodney.[8] Many

TABLE 13.2 MAJOR THEORIES OF DEVELOPMENT					
Theory	Date	Key authors	Definition of development	Problem	State versus Market-Led Solutions
Modernization	1950s	Rostow, Lewis, Huntington	Economic, GDP	Traditional societies	Modernization through stages of economic growth (state-assisted, market-led)
Dependency	1960s	Frank, Cardoso, Rodney, Wallerstein	Economic, distribution of wealth	World economic system	De-link or socialist revolution (state-led)
Post-Development	1970s	Escobar, Ferguson	Economic, social, political	The Global North	Up to local communities, social movements (community-led)
Neoliberalism	1970s	Friedman	Economic, GDP	State intervention	Free markets (market-led)

authors, such as Argentine sociologist Atilio Borón, continue to write from the perspective of dependency theory today.[9] Dependency theory argues that the Global South has been underdeveloped by the Global North. Through colonialism and capitalism, the Global North, referred to as the "core" of the global economy, has extracted raw materials and foodstuffs from the "periphery" (Global South). The world economic system itself, then, ensures that countries on the periphery are dependent on the core. For example, while the Global South provides raw materials and foodstuffs for low prices, it pays high prices for finished products and technology from the Global North. Thus, while modernization theory sees development as within the control of national governments, with assistance from the Global North, dependency theory disagrees.

From the perspective of dependency theory, the problem of development is dependency and the solution for countries on the periphery is to disconnect from the world economic system. Some theorists argue that this can be done through socialist revolution while others argue for countries in the Global South to establish protectionist measures to facilitate the growth of local industry and shelter their economies from global competition. In either scenario, the state has a central role to play in development. Like modernization theory, the definition of development

employed is economic but there is greater concern for the distribution of wealth both within and between countries. From the perspective of dependency theory, if you want to help with development then you need first and foremost to address these inequalities, and the state will play a key role in this process.

Post-Development Theory

Post-development theory emerged in the 1970s when scholars influenced by post-modernism and the work of the French philosopher Michel Foucault began to question the very idea of development. Key scholars of post-development theory include Arturo Escobar and James Ferguson, who still write on these issues today.[10] While there are many strands of post-development theory, they share a basic concern that the term "development" is usually defined by people in the Global North who then, based on their definition, advocate or pursue corresponding solutions (the "development workers"). Yet these definitions of and solutions to the problems of development may not correspond with the needs and priorities of people in the Global South. Or worse, these definitions and solutions might prioritize the needs of people in the Global North (e.g., facilitate Canadian mining interests in the Global South). Instead, post-development theory argues that local communities in the Global South should define development and the corresponding paths to achieving it. If people from the Global North want to be involved, then they should provide assistance when requested by communities in the Global South.

For post-development theory, the problems of and solutions for development are many and range well beyond economics, including issues pertaining to the environment, health, education, democracy, and security. Leadership needs to be given to local communities or social movements in the Global South to define which issues are most pressing and what solutions will work best. Many development NGOs today, such as Oxfam, put this theory into practice by partnering with and following the lead of organizations in the Global South. National states can play a role in development as well by supporting local community and social movement initiatives. Of course this approach raises questions concerning the continued power of organizations in the Global North (and national states) to choose which organizations in the Global South they will support and whether the chosen organizations indeed represent the communities that they claim to represent.

Neoliberalism

Neoliberalism is really an anti-development theory that has become increasingly dominant since the 1970s. Its ideas are based in the writings of economist Milton Friedman but remain prominent in the work of many recent scholar such as that of Zambian economist Dambisa Moyo.[11] Essentially, neoliberalism views development aid as unnecessary. It holds that each country should open its economy to free trade, reduce the size of the state (that is, reduce the provision of social services, regulations, and taxation), and compete on the global market. It holds that if a country's economy is weak then it is because its market is not free enough. Fewer regulations on businesses and trade will result in more trade and the generation of more wealth.

For neoliberalism, development pertains to economics, defined by GDP, and the solution is a free market economy. There will be some countries that do better than others in this system but inequality is not itself a problem as it is thought to spur innovation. Those countries that do less well will be motivated to find new products and services to provide, or further reduce state regulations and spending in order to become more competitive. From this perspective, a national government alone has the ability to direct a country's development prospects by reducing its own size and freeing the market. Unlike modernization theory, neoliberalism does not see a role for the state or the Global North in providing financial, technological, or infrastructure investments. These investments should emerge naturally through the market.

As you can see, each theory views the problems of development and their solutions quite differently. Once you are familiar with the theories you can hear them being used by actors engaged in development practice today. For example, in a conflict over mining in a country in the Global South you might hear business owners and government talking about how the mine is good for development because it will increase the country's GDP and provide local jobs. Community members and some international NGOs such as Mining Watch, in contrast, might contest the mining project using a definition of development that instead focuses on the impact on the environment, health, human rights, and indigenous relationships to the land. Sometimes the development theories will be slurred together, as when companies or World Bank projects provide venues for community participation in development projects that are neoliberal in orientation. Some scholars argue that such participation is used to legitimate neoliberal policies, not to meet the needs or demands of affected communities. Research and debate on the impact of combining community participation and neoliberalism is ongoing (see photo essay).

GENDER AND DEVELOPMENT

All these theories, except perhaps post-development theory, assume a gender-neutral position on development. Yet, when we look closer at available statistics, we see that development is not gender-neutral. Women, girls, as well as men and boys who do not conform to dominant gender roles, disproportionately live in extreme poverty, attain lower levels of education, and have poorer health. Why is this the case?

The dominant development theories do not have much to say here. So, the next logical question is: Does

PHOTO ESSAY

Community members affected by Goldcorp's Marlin Mine operations in their territories protest through the streets of Guatemala City.

James Rodríguez/MiMundo.org

THE MARLIN MINE

Goldcorp, a Canadian mining company, has projects around the world but one of its most controversial is the Marlin mine in Guatemala. The Marlin mine is an underground and open pit mine in a rural part of the country that once relied on subsistence agriculture. The dispute highlights how different definitions of development can clash in important ways. The company and the World Bank Group (which has provided loans to support the project) claim that the mine is contributing to development both in the community within which the mine is located and the country as a whole. Goldcorp claims to have provided the community with 800 jobs and invested in social projects that go beyond the needs of the mine itself, such as building roads, bridges, churches, and hiring school teachers. The company is the largest taxpayer in Guatemala.

In short, the company, the World Bank, and the Guatemalan government all view the mine as positive to development because it contributes to economic development primarily defined in terms of the country's GDP, with some attention to building community resources. However, many local community organizers, international NGOs, academic studies, and international organizations oppose the mine, using a definition of development that emphasizes social development. They argue that the mine has had a significant negative impact on the environment, the health of community members, and respect for human rights. For example, independent studies have found unacceptable levels of arsenic in groundwater that the community uses for drinking. On the basis of environmental, health, and human rights concerns, in 2011, the Organization of American States' (OAS) Inter-American Commission on Human Rights called for the mine to be shut down.[12]

considering gender change our approach to development? If so, how? This has been the focus of a substantial amount of research and debate between scholars, development practitioners, state actors, and development activists. Today it is hard to find an international development organization or development NGO that does not devote attention to gender. There remains, however, significant debate on how best to address gender and development.

Unlike one's sex, **gender** is not biologically determined. It is constructed and varies in practice from country to country. Gender is about what is expected from a woman or man in terms of how to behave and dress, their legal status, etc. Women and men can choose not to conform but there are often consequences of not conforming (social and/or legal). In *all* societies gender incorporates some degree of female subordination, and this exists at *all* levels of society (household, regional, national, international). For example, in Canada women have been permitted to join the RCMP since 1974. However, recently many female officers have been coming forward with cases of gendered workplace abuse (such as sexual abuse) that suggest that the idea that "policing is a male profession within which women are not welcome" may still persist within the force.

> **Gender:** What is expected from a woman or man in terms of how s/he is to behave and dress, their legal rights, social norms, etc.

That said, not all women experience subordination in the same way, even within the same territorial boundaries. A woman's experience may vary based on such factors as ethnicity, race, religion, class, ability, age, and sexual orientation.

The challenge for development is that while gender has the most significant impact on women's life expectations, it is highly political as it is often closely intertwined with dominant understandings of national identity, culture, and/or religion. Challenging gender requires challenging social, religious, and/or legal hierarchies. It is politically much easier for state, international, and NGO development actors to address poverty—and women's poverty in particular—as separate from gender relations (see Box 13.1).

So how have scholars, state actors, practitioners, and activists attempted to address this challenge? There have been six major approaches:

BOX 13.1

WOMEN AND DEVELOPMENT

Development and poverty affect women differently:

- Six out of 10 of the world's poorest people are women
- Global GNI per capita (2013) for women is 8,956; for men it is 18,277
- Global HDI (2013) for women is 0.655; for men it is 0.712
- Percent of women holding seats in parliament: 21.1

Source: Khalid Malik et al., *Human Development Report 2013* (New York: UNDP, 2013), 152-155, 160-161, online at http://hdr.undp.org/sites/default/files/reports/14/hdr2013_en_complete.pdf (accessed June 23, 2015).

---

1. Welfare Approach

In the 1950s–1970s, influenced by modernization theory, a dominant idea of development was that countries in the Global South needed to move away from their "traditional societies." This approach saw women in traditional societies as being primarily mothers who had too many children. The problem for development was overpopulation and thus women's fertility needed to be controlled. This led to the adoption of policies such as female sterilization (sometimes forced).

This approach viewed women as objects of development policy. That is, no consideration was given to why women were having so many babies, how they felt about it, or if these women had other ideas about the reasons for their poverty. Some state governments continue to be concerned with women's fertility as an issue of development, such as China, which maintains a now slightly loosened one-child policy. However, in the 1970s, thinking on women and their relationship to development began to change.

2. Women in Development (WID)

The global feminist movement of the 1960–1970s contributed to the UN taking on the issue of women's equality. It also led to Ester Boserup's seminal *Women's Role in Economic Development* (1970), in which women were made—for the first time—visible in development. For example, Boserup observed that in some regions women had traditionally done most of the agricultural work until colonial regimes introduced cash crops (large-scale farming of a single crop for export) and taught *men* how to use the plough. As a result, the plough was either not used (as it was considered women's work) or women's participation in agricultural work decreased.

Boserup's work, combined with the feminist movement and the 1975 UN World Conference on Women, contributed to development agencies across the Global North adopting policies to include women in development (WID). Influenced by modernization theory, most WID programs aimed to move women out of "traditional society," but this time, instead of controlling fertility, doing so by providing them with better education, skills, and access to credit and agricultural technology. In this way, women could be taken out of the home and subsistence agriculture, and incorporated into the capitalist economy.

3. Women and Development (WAD)

Given the heated debates on development in the 1970s between modernization theory and dependency theory, it is not surprising that another approach emerged around the same time inspired by the latter theory. Arguing against WID, the Women *and* Development (WAD) approach holds that women are already integrated into development, albeit in a subordinate role.

Drawing on Marxism, WAD argues that capitalism is intrinsically tied to patriarchy; it relies on the subordination of women. Thus, the only way to address women's poverty in development is to abolish capitalism. Indeed, many women in the Global South have joined communist revolutionary movements in the hopes that such revolutions would bring about gender equality.

Some revolutionary governments have taken steps to entrench gender equality in government policy. In China, Vietnam, and Cuba, governments used education and propaganda in an effort to transform traditional cultural values concerning gender. For example, in China, the revolutionary government ended the practice of binding women's feet. In Cuba, a Family Code was passed that required men and women to share equally in household chores and childrearing.

However, in such regimes, it is common for women's demands for equality to be subordinated to the primary goal of revolution and class equality. In some cases, women's demands have been labelled anti-revolutionary, middle class, or Western. Moreover, many Communist countries have focused on including

Photo of a woman used in Nicaraguan revolutionary posters celebrating women's contribution to the revolution as soldiers and mothers.
© *Larry Towell/Magnum Photos*

women in the paid workforce outside the home without considering women's **double burden** (work outside the home in addition to continued responsibilities for childrearing, eldercare, and domestic labour).

> **Double burden:** When women work outside the home in addition to continued responsibility for childrearing, eldercare, and domestic chores.

4. Gender and Development (GAD)

Gender and Development emerged in the 1980s as an attempt to provide a more holistic approach, stressing the social relations that contribute to inequality. Inspired by the initiatives of women living in the Global South, the goal of GAD is to change social relations in order to improve the lives of both women and men of all backgrounds. That is, it calls into question that which is labelled "feminine" and "masculine" as well as the structures of power that result from those classifications.

GAD is particularly interested in empowering women as a way to change dominant social relations and in gaining the support of men for gender equality. This involves giving women the tools that they need (such as education, changes in child-rearing responsibilities, etc.) that allow them to pull themselves out of their situation. For example, an Asian Development Bank 2013 GAD project seeks to bring lower secondary school education to girls in disadvantaged areas of rural Vietnam. The project includes building separate washrooms for girls that are located close to the teacher's office in order to address the safety concerns of the community.

5. Effectiveness Approach

In the 1980s, the International Financial Institutions, such as the World Bank and International Monetary Fund (IMF), developed an approach to gender that was consistent with neoliberalism, called the Effectiveness Approach, which promoted the consideration of women in neoliberal development projects in order to increase productivity.

One of the most well-known projects that reflects this approach is micro-credit aimed at women, such as the Grameen Bank in Bangladesh. Micro-credit involves providing small loans (usually a few hundred dollars or less) to the poor so that they can start small businesses. Women have been targeted as borrowers because they have been shown to be much better at paying back such loans than men. The repayment success rate of women (97 percent) has contributed to international actors viewing micro-credit as an important tool in fighting poverty. The Grameen Bank, and its founder, economist Muhammad Yunus, were awarded the Nobel Peace Prize in 2006.

However, most micro-credit projects do not take into account gender relations. Many women struggle with the double burden of domestic responsibilities and starting a business. Some women face abuse from husbands for neglecting their domestic responsibilities. In the majority of cases, men take the money that women receive and women are left with the responsibility of paying it back. In less than 37 percent of cases do women maintain control over the loan.[13]

Like WID, the Effectiveness Approach can provide women with training, education, and access to financial resources. However, the neoliberal basis of the approach creates some internal tensions. For example, it does not address how the reduction of social services that result from neoliberal policies disproportionately affect women, how gender relations affect the ability of women to participate in the economy, or the realities of women's unpaid labour at home.

6. Mainstreaming Gender Equality (MGE)

This approach emerged around the time of the 4th UN World Conference on Women in Beijing in 1995, where the women in attendance, representing 189 countries, agreed that gender equality is essential for development.

Instead of having WID programs operate as but one of many programs pursued by development organizations, mechanisms were proposed to ensure that all development programs consider gender in their projects. Gendered assessments of programs include an evaluation of how women are included, the potential impact on women, and the potential impact on gender relations (including an assessment of how to gain men's support for gender equality). For example, the World Health Organization uses gender mainstreaming in its HIV projects by assessing how HIV affects men and women differently and how men's and women's gender roles affect HIV policy outcomes.

In many ways, gender mainstreaming builds on GAD by offering practical ways in which gender relations can be challenged in a regular and institutionalized manner. However, critics argue that it bureaucratizes gender and in so doing may make it easier for organizations to avoid challenging politically sensitive gender norms.

All scholars and practitioners agree that women matter in development, and that no development theory is gender-neutral. All development projects need to consider gender relations and women's empowerment, and to include men in the goal of gender equality. Moreover, gender needs to be considered along with other power systems, such as ethnicity, race, ability, religion, class, and global capitalism. However, the development field remains very divided on how best to do this. All of the approaches reviewed here, usually in various combinations, continue to be used by different state, NGO and international organizations. Moreover, considerable practical challenges remain, as the 2012 shooting of Malala Yousafzai's, the young girl fighting for girls' education in Pakistan whose example was reviewed in the previous chapter, so vividly highlights.

CANADIAN FOREIGN AID

Of course, the politics of development is not just theoretical. There are many actors involved in development in very concrete ways. The Canadian government is one such actor.

How Has Canada Been Involved in International Development?

Prior to 1959, Canada's involvement was primarily limited to contributions to international organizations such as the United Nations. However, Canada slowly began to provide its own assistance in the form of **bilateral aid**. Bilateral aid is assistance given by a donor country to a specific recipient country. In 1968, Canadian foreign aid was expanded and the Canadian International Development Agency (CIDA) was created to manage and coordinate Canadian overseas development goals. Canadian aid to the Global South grew (albeit unevenly) until the 1990s, when it was cut dramatically from 0.45 percent of the country's Gross National Income (GNI) to 0.25 percent.[14] In contrast, the United Nations target for official development assistance (ODA) is 0.7 percent of GNI and the most generous countries are spending more. In 2008, Sweden spent 0.98 percent, Norway 0.88 percent, and Denmark 0.80 percent. In 2013, the Canadian government amalgamated CIDA into the Department of Foreign Affairs and International Trade (DFAIT), creating the new Department of Foreign Affairs, Trade and Development. While combining CIDA and DFAIT could be helpful to the provision of aid, many scholars and NGOs are concerned that it will result in changes in foreign aid that render it less effective.

Bilateral aid: Development assistance given by one country (the donor) to another.

Indeed, Canada's reduction in foreign aid over the last 20–30 years and the recent change in administration may reflect a government shift toward a neoliberal approach to development that emphasizes less aid and a more free market. For example, a 2013 federal government press release states: "The private sector, including firms from Canada, is the driving force behind sustainable economic growth and as such can play an important role in reducing poverty around the world."[15]

What Type of Aid Has Canada Provided?

It is often assumed that foreign aid involves countries, religious organizations, and NGOs in the Global North generously providing money and goods to the Global South in order to help the less fortunate in other countries. While sometimes this is the case, bilateral aid is also provided out of self-interest by donor countries, including Canada. Aid can be directed to specific countries in the Global South for such reasons as diplomacy, commerce, and security.

For example, until 2002 it was common for Canada to provide **tied aid**. Tied aid is the practice of making ODA conditional on the receiving country buying goods and services from the donor country. Accordingly, Canadian agricultural aid has been provided to countries in the Global South on the condition that they buy Canadian tractors and parts for those tractors. Tied aid benefits the donor country and in 2002 comprised the majority of aid provided by Canada. By 2007, international pressure against tied aid had led many donor countries to untie their aid. Following their lead, Canada announced in 2008 that it would untie all aid by 2012–2013. By March 2013, 99.9 percent of Canadian aid was untied.[16]

Tied aid: The practice of making development assistance conditional on the receiving country buying goods and services from the donor country.

While tied aid has declined, other forms of aid can also support Northern businesses in the South. For example, Canada announced in 2012 that it will provide development aid to communities in the Global South where Canadian mining companies are active. Canada is an important actor in global mining. These mines are argued by some scholars, states, corporations, and NGOs to bring jobs and money to poor communities in the Global South. In addition, some mines engage in Corporate Social Responsibility (CSR), which involves mining companies investing in development projects in the communities affected by the mines, as a way to give back further. Other scholars, states, corporations, and NGOs, however, raise significant concerns regarding the environmental and human rights impact of many mines (see photo essay). Canadian aid to mining-affected countries and communities comes in the form of schools and roads but also money to encourage local governments to reduce legislation governing mining.[17] As was seen earlier, such actions are consistent with a neoliberal approach to development.

The motivations of donors, such as Canada, can affect where aid money goes. A country may receive aid because it is strategically important and not because it is the most in need. For example, after Canada shifted its priorities toward supporting mining, aid money moved from poorer countries in Africa to relatively well-off countries in Latin America, such as Colombia and Peru. Canada's post-9/11 security interests also contributed to the provision of significant levels of development aid to Afghanistan, where the Canadian military had been sent to fight the Taliban.

The major theories of development, particularly neoliberalism, help us to make sense of the choices made by governments regarding the allocation of funds for ODA. Yet history also sheds light on how and why some theories of development have become dominant over others. The debt crisis, in the 1980s, is one such important event.

THE DEBT CRISIS AND INTERNATIONAL FINANCIAL INSTITUTIONS (IFIs)

Individual governments are not the only actors that provide foreign aid. Since 1982, International Financial Institutions, notably the International Monetary Fund (IMF) and World Bank, have been important development actors in the Global South. The debt crisis initiated their heavy involvement.

What Is the Debt Crisis?

In the early 1970s, the global price of oil went up. Oil-producing countries made significant profits and wished to invest these profits in international banks. International banks, in turn, saw countries in the Global South as good places to invest because their economies were growing and the banks thought that the returns on their investments would be strong. Latin America was seen to be a particularly attractive place to invest. Private international banks encouraged governments in the Global South to take out large loans at very low interest rates (almost zero percent). Many governments, including authoritarian ones, took advantage of the loans to invest in large infrastructure development projects. External debt in Latin America rose from approximately $30 billion

in 1970 to more than $230 billion in 1980 (in U.S. dollars). The idea was that these projects would fuel the economy, making the repayment of the loans easy (especially at the low interest rates).

However, in 1979 there was a second oil boom, only this time countries in the Global North responded by dramatically increasing interest rates. Suddenly, countries in the Global South were unable to make their debt payments. Mexico was the first country to announce that it could not repay its loans, beginning the debt crisis. To this day, many countries struggle with large amounts of foreign debt (see Table 13.3). Some international civil society organizations, like Jubilee 2000, maintain that the single most important action that the Global North can take for development in the Global South is to forgive these loans. In 1996, the IMF and World Bank responded to this pressure by providing some debt relief for what it calls Highly Indebted Poor Countries, which are a small number of the most indebted poor countries (primarily in Africa).

The IMF and World Bank are banks of last resort. When a country has a balance-of-payments problem (they owe more than they can pay) and is unable to secure a loan through private banks or a bilateral loan from another country, it can approach the IMF and World Bank. This was the case for a large number of countries in the Global South as the debt crisis grew in the 1980s.

TABLE 13.3	TOTAL EXTERNAL DEBT OF DEVE-LOPING COUNTRIES, 2005–2012
Year	$billions
2005	2,338.0
2006	2,534.4
2007	2,993.5
2008	3,262.1
2009	3,542.1
2010	3,987.5
2011	4,437.8
2012	4,829.6

Source: The World Bank. 2014. *International Debt Statistics 2014.* © International Bank for Reconstruction and Development/The World Bank. https://openknowledge.worldbank.org/bitstream/handle/10986/17048/9781464800511.pdf License: Creative Commons Attribution license (CC BY 3.0 IGO). This is an adaptation of an original work by The World Bank. Responsibility for the views and opinions expressed in the adaptation rests solely with the author or authors of the adaptation and are not endorsed by The World Bank.

However, loans provided by the IMF and World Bank come with conditions and in the 1980s and 1990s this involved **structural adjustment loans (SALs)**. Consistent with neoliberalism, the IMF and World Bank believed that in order for countries to develop and become financially strong enough to pay back the loans, their governments needed to reduce the size of the state and its involvement in the market. Typical conditions of SALs included reducing export and import duties, eliminating state subsidies, reducing taxes, flexibilizing labour (this means making it easier to hire and fire employees, and hire them on a contract-to-contract basis), reducing state spending (including on social services), and privatizing state-owned businesses. Countries receiving SALs also were encouraged to join free trade agreements in order to further facilitate the unencumbered flow of goods between countries.

> **Structural adjustment loans (SALs):** Loans provided by the IMF and World Bank to countries in the Global South beginning in the 1980s that were conditioned upon the implementation of various neoliberal reforms.

While SALs have been successful in some cases at stabilizing inflation and increasing GDP, they have also contributed to greater inequalities in wealth and deteriorating health and education outcomes. In this way structural adjustment illustrates some of the tensions between definitions of development discussed earlier in the chapter.

SALs also reveal the power that the Global North has over the Global South, as noted in dependency and post-development theory. The IMF and World Bank are led by its members, and a member's influence is proportionate to the amount of money it provides the organizations. As significant contributors, therefore, the United States and to a lesser extent European countries determine the policies of these institutions.

Many in the Global South have pushed back against the control that the Global North has exerted on their economies through SALs and the impact that these have had on their lives. Resistance has come in the form of street protests, the election of anti-neoliberal presidents, and attracting loans and investment from other countries in the Global South (most notably China and Venezuela). For example, in 2009, former Venezuelan president Hugo Chávez led the establishment of BancoSur (Bank of the South) as an alternative to the World Bank for countries in Latin America not wanting to pursue neoliberalism.

In response, the IMF and World Bank have moved away from SALs and instead offer Poverty Reduction Strategy Papers (PRSP), which emphasize the participation of actors from the Global South in deciding the best paths toward reducing poverty. While couched in the vocabulary of post-development theory, critics argue that the results of PRSPs are similar to structural adjustment owing to the disproportionate power of the IMF and World Bank in this North-South dialogue. Thus, from this perspective, PRSPs have changed little in practice from SALs.

The debt crisis made the IMF and World Bank important actors in the politics of development. Governments needing loans had little room to resist the requirements set by these International Financial Institutions. This has contributed to the dominance of the theories of development supported by the IMF and World Bank (notably neoliberalism) in discussions of development. This situation persists.

MEDIA, TECHNOLOGY, AND DEVELOPMENT

There is a great deal of hype in the news media about the exciting new world of information technology and its liberating potential. From the Zapatistas who used the Internet to communicate to the world in 1994 to the Arab Spring in 2011, the media has celebrated the way people around the world have used new

THINK AND DISCUSS

Should International Financial Institutions simply forgive Global South debt? This could free money up for states to meet their citizens' basic needs. Yet there are concerns regarding the impact that this would have on the world economy and on the credit rating of countries whose debt is forgiven.

communications technology to try to free themselves from oppression.

Our media also celebrate the spread of "modernization" as farmers in rural Africa use cell phones to check prices for their crops in the city, or as increasing numbers of people are hired in call centres in India and the Philippines. These reports can lead us to believe that the answer to world economic and political inequalities lies in the spread of new technology and media.

But to what extent is this true? What are the benefits of media and information technology and what are the drawbacks? What do the dominant development theories have to say about it?

As has been the case throughout history, the effects of new communications technologies are both positive and negative today. Indeed, the iconic Canadian communications theorist, Harold Innis, argued that the most successful societies in history have been those that achieve a balance between old and new means of communication.

Communications media refers to a wide variety of forms, including pamphlets, books, films, newspapers, magazines, telegraphs, radio, television, e-mail, texting, websites, blogs, social media, telephones, cell phones, and tablets. Historically, whenever new communications media have been introduced, they have changed the ways in which people interact with each other even as people have adapted the technology in ways that suit their needs.

> **Communications media:** A wide variety of different media, including pamphlets, books, films, newspapers, magazines, telegraphs, radio, television, e-mail, texting, websites, blogs, social media, telephones, cell phones, and tablets.

For example, literacy, a persistent problem of development today, only became a concern with the technological invention and availability of paper (12th and 13th centuries) and the printing press (15th century). While these technologies expanded the number of people who could receive written communication, to have an impact two shifts needed to occur: more people had to learn how to read and write, and writing had to be done in a commonly spoken language, the vernacular, instead of Latin. These shifts both occurred but slowly and unevenly, and inequalities in literacy persist even today. For example, less than half of the adult population is literate in Haiti (49 percent), Niger (29 percent), Sierra Leone (42 percent), and Benin (42 percent).[18]

All new technologies—from paper to Twitter—can have both positive and negative consequences for development. Moreover, the same communications technology will not necessarily have the same impact on all societies or even on all people within the same country. The usefulness of particular media for development varies based on geography (e.g, rural versus urban areas), the costs of particular technologies in different countries, and the characteristics of the potential user (his or her education, employment, age, and social environment), for example. The media technology that is going to have the most significant positive impact on development is the technology that makes the most sense or is the most appropriate for the specific issues of development or people for whom it is targeted. The appropriate communications technology could be social media but it also could be radio or pamphlets. There is no need to get caught up in the latest technologies unless they make sense in the given context.

That said, new media technologies have not been ignored by development scholars, NGOs, states, and international organizations. The manner in which new media technologies are integrated into development scholarship and practice varies not only between the local contexts within which they work, but also in accordance with the theory of development that influences the scholar or practitioner's work.

Modernization Theory, Neoliberalism, and New Media Technology

From the perspective of modernization theory and neoliberalism, new media is symbolic of modernization. It is a technology that could assist a country to move through or even skip stages of economic growth. For example, Internet technology could bring jobs as people can work remotely (their employer might be in a different country) and can sell products more easily to customers all over the world. Since 1998, India has seen its Internet technology business sector make an increasing and important contribution to the country's GDP.

Internet technology can also foster democratization by allowing people to hold authoritarian leaders accountable. Social media, for example, is thought by some scholars and international organizations to have played an role in the end of the authoritarian regime in Tunisia in 2011. Larry Diamond and Marc Plattner, in their book *Liberation Technology* (2012), provide many more cases that highlight the potential role of the Internet in democratic political development. However, other scholarly work disagrees and instead finds that social media alone does not lead to revolutions or the overthrow of authoritarian regimes. Such political change requires a well-organized network of people who work off-line in a more long-term and face-to-face manner. Authoritarian regimes, such as the Chinese government, also have proven to be quite skilled at controlling and monitoring Internet activity.

From the perspective of neoliberalism, the most significant barrier to the potentially liberating impact of Internet media technology is the state. When the state interferes, by censoring or repressing people using new technologies, this inhibits democracy and modernization. In contrast, dependency theory suggests that the market itself limits the contribution of the Internet to development.

Dependency Theory and New Media Technology

For dependency theory, new media technologies are often seen to reinforce existing inequalities inherent in capitalism, producing a **digital divide**. The digital divide refers to the greater access to information technology that some have over others. This can exist both between and within countries.

> **Digital divide:** The greater access to information technology that some people have over others. This can exist between countries but also within countries.

For example, even in primarily agriculturally based societies there is usually a socio-economic class (the wealthy) that has regular access to the Internet. In Afghanistan, from 2009–2013, 5.9 percent of the population had access to the Internet (the wealthiest Afghans). In contrast, in Canada, approximately 86 percent of the population had access (98 percent of the wealthiest Canadians had home Internet as compared to only 58 percent of the poorest Canadians).[15]

The digital divide within countries is particularly concerning if a government chooses to save money by, for example, replacing employment assistant centres with websites or closing libraries that offer free Internet access. Moreover, new media technologies may mean that people now need not only literacy (a persistent problem in many countries) but also computer literacy, and possibly even need to read and write English since this is the dominant language of the Internet.

Dependency theory also cautions us to be wary of the impact of business on political development. The Internet, like all media technologies, is not neutral. Big businesses such as Microsoft, Google, and Facebook make decisions about who has access, what information they can access, when they have access, etc. They make these decisions not in pursuit of the greater good or democracy but for their businesses. Thus, from this perspective, business, as much as the state, may play an important role in controlling citizens' access to information, which can impact democracy.

Finally, dependency theory asks to what degree new media technology should be a priority for communities struggling to meet basic housing, health, security, and educational needs. That is, does bridging the digital divide promote development, or does it take resources away from more important priorities? For example, in 2010, the state in Argentina provided all school children with a laptop to help with their digital literacy. Yet many children still go to school with empty stomachs and in buildings that are not heated properly and are falling apart.

Post-Development Theory and New Media Technology

From a post-development perspective, the best approaches ask local people or civil society organizations what their most important development concerns are and what they see as the solutions. Within this framework, an array of possible relationships exists between development and media technologies.

One approach is to allow local community organizations to choose for themselves the appropriate technologies that meet their needs, which may or may not include the Internet. All new technologies change the ways in which people interact with each other and, in turn, potentially change local social, cultural, and political practices. Each community should choose for itself which media technologies make sense for them and how they want to use them.

For example, for some communities a local radio station may be the best communication technology as it requires no literacy, radios are fairly inexpensive, content can easily be shared, and people can engage in other activities while listening. The programming can highlight issues of particular concern to that community in their own language. In Mexico, community radio has been an important vehicle for Indigenous peoples to preserve their language and culture, as well as to connect isolated communities through sharing information, news, and ideas.

Second, if Internet technology is chosen locally, then it may allow communities to network with others in the Global South in order to share ideas and strategies for development (avoiding the dominance of the Global North). It may also be used by local organizations in the Global South to attract the attention of media, governments, and NGOs in the Global North.

If local grassroots organizations want to use new Internet-based media technologies, however, there remain significant challenges. It costs money and there may be difficulties obtaining computers. Organizations also need someone with the knowledge and time to set up and maintain a website, listserv, blog, Facebook page, Twitter account, etc. Ideally this will be someone who will do this work well and do it for free. Even if all of this is accomplished, the reality is that the organization is just one of many on the Internet and may struggle to get the attention of the state, NGOs, or international development organizations.

Thus, from the perspective of post-development theory, media technologies are a tool that could be helpful in building local alternatives but the decision as to their usefulness and how they are useful should be left to local organizations.

There is no perfect or best media technology for development and none is likely to solve all the pressing issues associated with development. However, with careful consideration for context, audience, and development theories, media technologies may bring some important benefits for some people.

CONCLUSION

This chapter has provided an introduction to the study of the politics of development. We began by dissecting what we mean by development and some of the major theories of how to achieve it. Using these building blocks we looked at some challenges to development as they relate to the issues of Canadian foreign aid, the debt crisis, and media technology. Hopefully, these discussions enable you to question some of the stereotypes about development and the Global South that are often found in the mainstream media, and perhaps encourage you to pursue upper-level classes on development and politics in the regions of the Global South.

DISCUSSION QUESTIONS

1. Find a news story on development. What development theory or theories inform the story? How do you know?

2. If you were to do something to help with development in the Global South, what would it be and why? What ideas from this chapter informed your choice?

3. Why is it important to discuss gender when addressing the issue of development?

4. Some governments in the Global South and international organizations have provided all school children in the country with a free laptop computer in order to help bridge the digital divide. What are the benefits and drawbacks of such programs?

5. What are some of the legacies of colonialism today?

WEBSITES

United Nations Development Programme (UNDP)
undp.org
The UNDP publishes yearly Human Development Reports, available as PDFs on its website.

World Bank
worldbank.org
The World Bank publishes yearly World Development Reports, available as PDFs on its website.

Foreign Affairs, Trade and Development Canada
www.international.gc.ca
Under the tab "development" you can learn about Canadian government priorities for international development.

Jubilee Debt
http://jubileedebt.org.uk/
This is an international NGO working on the issue debt in the Global South.

FURTHER READING

Stephen Brown, ed., *Struggling for Effectiveness: CIDA and Canadian Foreign Aid.* Montreal and Kingston: McGill-Queens University Press, 2012.

Arturo Escobar, *Encountering Development: The Making and Unmaking of the Third World.* Princeton: Princeton University Press, 1996.

Paul A. Haslam, Jessica Schafer, and Pierre Beaudet, eds., *Introduction to International Development: Approaches, Actors and Issues*, 2nd ed. Toronto: Oxford University Press, 2012.

Janet Henshall Momsen, *Gender and Development.* New York: Routledge, 2010.

Amartya Sen, *Development as Freedom.* New York: Alfred Knopf, 1999.

ENDNOTES

1. For more on labelling the regions of study in the politics of development, see Martin Lewis, "Is There a Third World?," *Current History* 98 (631) (November 1999), pp. 355–58.

2. For more on this, see Catherine V. Scott, *Gender and Development: Rethinking Modernization and Dependency Theory* (Boulder: Lynne Rienner, 1995), pp. 1–21.

3. The numbers and ranking in this paragraph and the one before are from the UNDP's *2013 Human Development Report*, pp. 152–55, 160–61, online at http://hdr.undp.org/en/2013-report.

4. Samuel Huntington, *Political Order in Changing Societies* (New Haven: Yale University Press, 1968).

5. Amartya Sen, *Development as Freedom* (New York: Anchor Books, 1999).

6. For more on the colonial mindset, see Edward W. Said, *Orientalism* (New York: Vintage Books, 1978).

7. W.W. Rostow, *The Stages of Economic Growth: A Non-Communist Manifesto* (New York: Cambridge University Press, 1960).

8. See Andre Gunder Frank, "The Development of Underdevelopment," in Charles Wilber and Kenneth Jameson, eds., *The Political Economy of Development and Under-Development* (New York: McGraw-Hill, 1991), pp. 107–18; Theotonio Dos Santos, "The Structure of Dependence," *American Economic Review* 60 (2) (May 1970), pp. 231–36; Walter Rodney, *How Europe Underdeveloped Africa* (London: Bogle-L'Ouverture Publications, 1972).

9. Atilio Borón, *Twenty-First-Century Socialism: Is There Life After Neo-Liberalism* (Winnipeg: Fernwood Publishing, 2014).

10. See Michel Foucault, *Power/Knowledge: Selected Interviews and Other Writings, 1972–1977* (Brighton: Harvester Press, 1980); Arturo Escobar, *Encountering Development: The Making and Unmaking of the Third World* (Princeton: Princeton University Press, 1995); James Ferguson, *The Anti-Politics Machine: 'Development,' Depoliticization, and Bureaucratic Power in Lesotho* (New York: Cambridge University Press, 1990).

11. See Milton Friedman, *Capitalism and Freedom* (Chicago: University of Chicago Press, 1962); also, see Dambisa Moyo, *Dead Aid: Why Aid is Not Working and How There is a Better Way for Africa* (New York: Farrar, Straus and Giroux, 2009).

12. Lyuba Zarsky and Leonardo Stanley, *Searching for Gold in the Highlands of Guatemala: Economic Benefits and Environmental Risks of the Marlin Mine.* Report published by the Global Development and Environment Institute, Tufts University, 2011; World Bank, "Glamis Gold Ltd.'s Montana Exploradora Marlin Project in Guatemala," online at http://web.worldbank.

org/WBSITE/EXTERNAL/TOPICS/EXTOG
MC/0,,contentMDK:20421886~pagePK:21005
8~piPK:210062~theSitePK:336930,00.html.

13. See L. Mayoux, "Vers un nouveau paradigm
dans les programmes de micro-crédit," in Jeanne
Bisilliat and C. Verschuur, eds, *Genre et économie:
Un premier éclairage. Cahiers genre et développe-
ment no.2* (Paris/Genève: Harmattan, 2001),
pp. 25–31; Lamia Karim, *Microfinance and
Its Discontents: Women in Debt in Bangladesh*
(Minneapolis: University of Minnesota Press,
2011).

14. From Stephen Brown, "Aid Effectiveness and the
Framing of New Canadian Aid Initiatives," in
Stephen Brown, ed., *Struggling for Effectiveness:
CIDA and Canadian Foreign Aid* (Montreal and
Kingston: McGill-Queen's University Press,
2012), p. 80.

15. Foreign Affairs, Trade and Development Canada,
"Harper government consults experts on private
sector-led international development," Press
release, February 11, 2013, online at http://
www.acdi-cida.gc.ca/acdi-cida/acdi-cida.nsf/eng/
NAT-211114228-MLL.

16. CIDA's *2012–2013 Departmental Performance
Report*, online at http://www.international.gc.ca/
department-ministere/assets/pdfs/dev/DPR-
2012-13-eng.pdf.

17. See Elizabeth Blackwood and Veronika Stewart,
"CIDA and the Mining Sector: Extractive
Industries as an Overseas Development
Strategy," in Brown, *Struggling for Effectiveness*,
pp. 217–45.

18. The numbers and ranking in this paragraph
and the one before are from the UNDP's *2013
Human Development Report*, pp. 170–73.

19. World Bank, "Internet users (per 100 people),"
online at http://data.worldbank.org/indicator/
IT.NET.USER.P2; Statistics Canada, "Canadian
Internet Use Survey, 2012," online at http://
www.statcan.gc.ca/daily-quotidien/131126/
dq131126d-eng.htm.

14 REGIME CHANGE AND PERSISTENCE
Arjun Chowdhury

© REUTERS/KCNA

While the emergence of more democratic forms of government around the world during the past few decades has been remarkable, the persistence of authoritarian political regimes—as in North Korea, pictured here—cannot be ignored. Moreover, a number of transitions toward more democratic practices have stalled or shown signs of reversal, making the study of regime change especially important.

CHAPTER OBJECTIVES

After you have completed this chapter, you should be able to:

- understand the difference between democratic and non-democratic regimes

- realize how non-democratic leaders stay in power

- know how rebellions happen in non-democracies

- recognize the difficulties involved in transitions from non-democratic rule

INTRODUCTION

As you saw in Chapter 3, a **regime** is the constitutional principles and arrangements according to which government decisions are made. A regime can be democratic or non-democratic in the sense that either every eligible adult has the right to select the leader (a **democracy**) or not (a **non-democracy**). In the last 30 years, the world has seen a large number of regime changes: after 1989, almost 50 nation-states went from non-democracy to democracy. By the early 1990s, with the transition of many communist regimes to democracy, many people thought that every nation-state would eventually become democratic. But since 2000, not only has the number of electoral democracies worldwide stayed at the same level, but some have turned back toward non-democracy.

Regime: The constitutional principles and arrangements according to which government decisions are made; the political system.

Democracy: A regime in which every eligible adult citizen has the right to select the leader in free and fair elections.

Non-democracy: A regime in which a very limited section of the population is able to select the leader

We now know that transitions to democracy are more complicated than we had thought. We also know that the type of regime in place is very important for the economic and political prospects of a nation-state. Democracies rarely fight wars against other democracies, for example, but they do fight non-democracies, while non-democracies fight wars against both other non-democracies and democracies. In the 20th century, Canada fought in 10 wars, but never against a democratic state. This is one reason why Canadian and other democratic leaders would like democracy to spread: they believe that the world will be a more peaceful place if there are more democratic regimes. However, when states move from non-democracy to democracy, the risks of unrest and civil war actually increase because those in power often seek to hold on through force. So understanding different types of regimes and how they change is extremely important: regimes affect the prospects for war and peace between states, and the prospects for freedom and prosperity within states.

In this chapter, we will explore the simplest way of understanding the differences between democracies and non-democracies. Rather than look at individual characteristics of leaders, we will look at the rules of the game, also called **institutions**. The key institutional difference lies in the ability of citizens to select their leaders. In democracies, the rules of the game—elections, the right to protest, and free media, for example—allow citizens to voice opposition to their leaders and provide regular opportunities to vote them out. In non-democracies, the rules of the game—such as falsified elections, crackdowns on protest, and state-controlled media—prevent citizens from voicing opposition, and deny them the opportunity to remove those in power. Instead, non-democratic leaders are often removed by force, through coups or revolutions, and so we will explore the tools that they use to stay in power.

> **Institutions:** The rules of the game—which can be formal or informal—by which a society functions.

DEFINING DEMOCRACY AND NON-DEMOCRACY

Democracy means "rule of the people" (from the Greek *demos* [people] and *krátos* [power or rule]). But it is quite hard to establish what "rule of the people" means in practice. Does it mean that all citizens have a direct input into each government policy that affects them, from tax rates to emissions standards to what should be taught in the schools? This would be impossible in a modern state as there are so many policies and because people leading busy lives find it hard to follow the daily news, much less keep track of complicated legislative changes and policy proposals. So how do citizens in a democracy have input into the policies that affect their everyday life?

Today, when we say "democracy," we mean that all eligible adults, regardless of gender or race or whether they own property, have the right to choose their leaders in "free and fair elections."[1] A "free" election means that individuals can vote or run for office without onerous restrictions. A "fair" election means that citizens' votes are secret, the voting is not falsified, and the process is ideally regulated by an independent body like an election commission. In addition, "free and fair elections" require a certain level of freedom of speech and of the press, so that those running for office can campaign freely and citizens can be informed of the campaigns by the media (such freedoms are often called "civil and political liberties"). The ability to select leaders allows citizens to have some input into the policies that affect their everyday lives, because they can support leaders who will implement policies that are agreeable to them. **Democratization**, or transition to democracy, in practice means an increase in the number of citizens who have the right to select their leaders. Democratization can be gradual—like the slow extension of the vote in the United States, first to white men without property, starting in 1812, followed by the enfranchisement of non-white men in 1870, then the granting of the vote to women in 1920 and Native Americans in 1924—or sudden, like the establishment of universal suffrage after the 1974 fall of the Portuguese dictatorship, before which there was no meaningful voting in Portugal. This definition of democracy is a "procedural" or "institutional" definition because it looks at the rules of the game by which leaders are chosen.

> **Democratization:** A group of transitions from non-democratic to democratic regimes, involving the relaxation of authoritarian political control by political leaders, the expansion of political and civil liberties, and the creation of institutional mechanisms that open up the political system to greater public representation and participation.

This is not the only possible definition of democracy. A different, "substantive" definition looks at the amount of influence that citizens have on policy-making. Namely, do all voters have the opportunity and ability to get elected officials to implement the policies that they want? The institutional and substantive definitions of democracy, because they look at different things, can produce differing assessments of the level of democracy in a given country. For example, scholars have recently argued that while all American citizens can vote, elected officials seem to respond primarily to the demands of wealthier citizens because it is the wealthy who donate to election campaigns. As these officials are concerned with the needs of wealthier citizens, for tax cuts, for example, they pay less attention to policies like the minimum wage that affect poor citizens, effectively ignoring their needs.[2] The U.S. can thus be a democracy according to the "institutional" definition—citizens can select their leaders—but many of those citizens may have no influence on important policies, which means that the U.S. may fall short of "substantive" democracy.

As the example of the United States indicates, the criterion for democracy as free and fair elections open to all citizens regardless of gender, race, or wealth has developed relatively recently. With the exception of New Zealand, it has only been since the early 20th century that women have been able to vote in the world's long-standing democracies, and there have been many restrictions on the voting rights of racial and ethnic minorities as well as people who do not own property. Switzerland, for example, is seen as an early democracy (from 1848 onwards), but women in Switzerland only gained the right to vote in federal elections in 1971. In Canada, members of First Nations were barred from voting till 1960 because they were seen as "wards" of the state, meaning that they were like children to be cared for by the government, not adult citizens capable of participating in it. It is important to keep in mind that when we talk of "democratization" in the 19th century, we generally mean that more and more males gradually became eligible to vote, starting with property-owners from outside the nobility and then extending to other males, and eventually to women.

A non-democratic regime, or a non-democracy, is one in which large numbers of citizens cannot choose their leader. This could be because the leader is decided by hereditary succession, as in a monarchy. It could be because a small group of citizens, like the members of a political party or the high command of the military, select the leader. In addition, civil and political liberties such as freedom of speech, freedom of the press, and freedom of association are restricted in non-democracies, and there is often censorship of citizen opinions, regime control of the media, and restrictions on citizens running for office (for example, the banning of political parties). There are several names for non-democratic regimes in common usage. Each has a specific meaning but they are often used interchangeably.

We will use most of these terms (with the exception of "totalitarian," which has become less common after the fall of the USSR) more or less as synonyms. This is mostly for convenience; it is easier to write "**dictator**" instead of "authoritarian ruler" and "**autocracy**" rather than "authoritarian regime."

> **Dictator/dictatorship:** An individual who wields absolute power. A dictatorship is a regime headed by a dictator.

> **Autocrat/autocracy:** The opposite of "rule by the people" because it means "rule by oneself." An autocrat is an individual who wields absolute power. An autocracy is a regime headed by an autocrat.

Many regimes claim to be democratic: the Democratic People's Republic of Korea (North Korea) is an example. In North Korea, elections are held but the leader runs unopposed and often wins with 100 percent of the vote! Such an election is certainly not what anyone would call "free and fair" because there is no way for citizens to vote out the leader if they are dissatisfied. While it is quite clear by this standard that North Korea is not a democracy (and, conversely, it is evident that Canada is a democracy), it is not so obvious in the case of other regimes. Iran, for example, held competitive elections for the presidency between 1997 and 2004, but a group of Islamic scholars, the Council of Experts, could block candidates from running for office (i.e., not everyone was free to run for office in Iranian elections). So defining democracy is not always straightforward.

In Iran there are some features of democracy, such as meaningful if restricted elections, but these have fluctuated over time. If we simply classify Iran as a non-democracy, this would obscure from our view the democratic practices that do occur in Iran, and the changes that have happened over time. Iran is less democratic than Canada but more democratic than North Korea. Is there a way to represent this? One way of classifying regimes is to position them along on a continuous scale. This means that rather than see regimes on a binary scale: democracy (1) or non-democracy (0), we assess them on a scale of more or less democracy.

One such classification system that uses a continuous rather than binary scale is called the Polity Index.[3] In the Polity Index, each state is assessed by experts on three criteria—how the leader is selected; the level of checks and balances, or constraints, on the power of the leader; and whether there are free and fair elections. Each criterion is given a score, and all three are added together to yield a total between −10 and 10. A score between −10 and −6 reveals a "full autocracy," in which leaders are not selected through free and fair elections, there are few checks and balances on the leader like an independent judiciary, and ordinary citizens are not allowed to compete freely for office in elections. North Korea is an example of a full autocracy. A score between 6 and 10 represents a "full democracy," in which every eligible adult can vote to select the leader, there are checks and balances on the leader, and eligible adults can run for office if they so choose. Canada is an example of a full democracy. Between autocracy and democracy is a third, interesting category: "anocracy" (scores of –5 to 5). **Anocracy**, sometimes called "partial democracy," refers to a mixed regime in which there are aspects of both democracy and autocracy.[4] To understand how an anocracy combines aspects of democracy and autocracy, we can look at the example of Iran in the chart below.

Anocracy: A mixed regime that combines democratic and non-democratic institutions.

In Figure 14.1, there are two **X**s (for regression from democracy), in 1953 and in 2004–2005, and one **R** (for revolution), in 1979. The first **X** represents the coup that overthrew Prime Minister

Mohammed Mossadegh and put Shah Reza Pahlavi on the throne, hence the Polity Index Score was reduced from –1 to –10. In 1953, Iran went from being an anocracy, a regime in which there were some democratic practices like elections, to being a full autocracy in which a hereditary monarch, the Shah, was the ruler. This situation persisted until 1979, when the Islamic Revolution led by the Ayatollah Khomeini occurred and a group of Islamic clerics took power (the **R** in the chart). After the Revolution, Iran was still an autocracy but the monarchy was abolished, hence the Polity Score increased from –10 to –6. In the mid-1990s, when elections were held and reformist politicians took power, Iran was no longer an autocracy—its score increased to 3—but it was not fully a democracy either. Rather, Iran was once again an anocracy, in which citizens could elect the president but the Council of Experts, a group of religious leaders, could change the leaders chosen by citizens if they decided to, or block citizens from running for office. Remember, a "free and fair" election

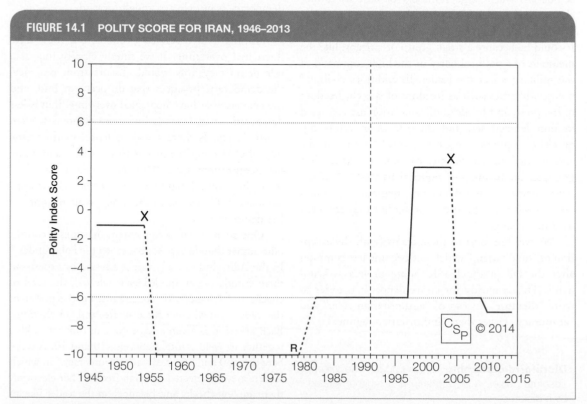

FIGURE 14.1   POLITY SCORE FOR IRAN, 1946–2013

Dashed line signify periods of transition.

Source: Center for Systemic Peace, "Authority Trends, 1946-2013: Iran," *Polity IV Individual Country Regime Trends, 1946–2013*, online at http://www.systemicpeace.org/polity/irn2.htm (accessed June 23, 2015).

means that any citizen can be a candidate for office. If the Council bars individuals from running, then the election is not free and fair. This is sometimes called "partisan democracy" because only partisans, those belonging to a particular group or political party, are allowed to compete for office. In 2004, the second **X** represents the decision by the Council of Experts to restrict elections to partisan candidates. Indeed, the Council of Experts blocked 2,500 candidates from running for office, including 80 who were already sitting in the Parliament. That is, the Council disqualified 25 percent of sitting parliamentarians from running for re-election! Since then, Iran has become increasingly less democratic. In 2009, after presidential election results were seen to be rigged to ensure the victory of Mahmoud Ahmadinejad, it was reclassified as a full autocracy. Iran's recent history shows us that regimes can change over time, and that the change is not always toward democracy.

Regime change can occur in either direction: toward democracy or non-democracy.

> **Regime change:** A shift from one type of regime to another.

Using the Polity classification system, we can see how the level of democracy worldwide has changed over time. You can see in Figure 14.2 that that there were almost no democracies until the mid-19th century. Most regimes for which we have information were autocracies, like the Tsarist monarchy in Russia, and the large number of anocracies consists of regimes, particularly in sub-Saharan Africa, for which there is very little information until the 20th century. We can also see from this figure that there have been three big upward shifts in the number of democracies: the first began in the early- and mid-19th century, the second began after the Second World War, and the biggest

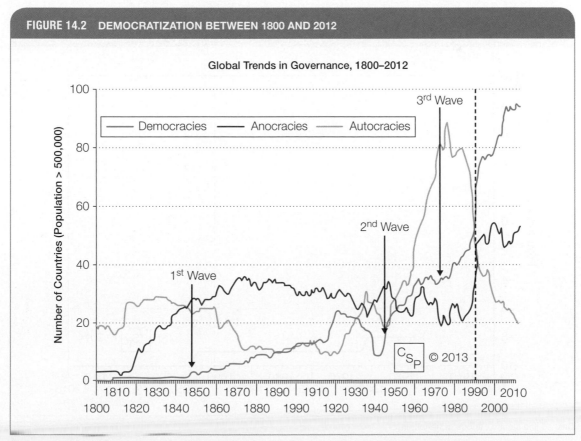

FIGURE 14.2 DEMOCRATIZATION BETWEEN 1800 AND 2012

Global Trends in Governance, 1800–2012

Source: Center for Systemic Peace, "Global Trends in Governance, 1800–2012," online at http://www.systemicpeace.org/polity/polity1.htm (accessed June 23, 2015).

started in the mid-1970s. These are often called the "three waves of democracy."[5] The first wave saw the expansion of the franchise in Europe and North America to males outside the nobility. The second wave was a short-lived period after the Second World War, when some of the states conquered by the Fascist powers became democratic (although the number of autocracies also increased). The third wave, which is the most significant, began in 1974 with the downfall of the Portuguese dictatorship, after which a number of other southern European and Latin American states became democratic. The third wave really picked up steam after the Soviet Union fell in 1991. Currently, a little more than 50 percent of states with a population of 500,000 or more are classified as full democracies, 33 percent are anocracies, and about 15 percent are full autocracies. This is a very different world from even 50 years ago, when many decolonized states, especially in Africa, were autocratic. That is one reason

that you see a big increase in autocracies after the second wave around 1950, peaking at almost 50 percent of all states in the late 1970s. There were many new states created after the fall of the European empires, like Ghana and Nigeria, which gained independence under autocratic or authoritarian regimes. Over time, many of these, including Ghana and Nigeria, have become either anocracies or democracies. We will discuss anocracies in greater detail in the last section of this chapter.

Even as they show us how much regime change has occurred over time, these Polity Score charts also reveal that autocratic regimes can last for a long time. The North Korean regime, for example, has persisted since 1948, through three generations of Kims! Indeed, as Figure 14.3 shows, North Korea has become increasingly autocratic over time.

There are no **X**s or **R**s in this chart because there have been no coups or revolutions in North Korea since 1946. Over time, while many other states have

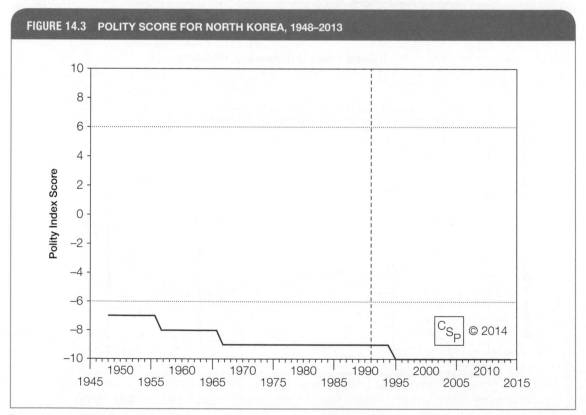

FIGURE 14.3 POLITY SCORE FOR NORTH KOREA, 1948–2013

Dashed line signify periods of transition.

Source: Center for Systemic Peace, "Authority Trends, 1948–2013: North Korea," *Polity IV Individual Country Regime Trends, 1946–2013*, online at http://www.systemicpeace.org/polity/prk2.htm (accessed June 23, 2015).

become more democratic, North Korea has remained an autocracy. How has this happened?

DICTATORSHIP 101

When watching news coverage of dictators (which is what we will call authoritarian leaders for convenience), you often hear some bizarre stories. For example, former North Korean dictator Kim Jong-il was a movie buff who admired a certain South Korean director. So he had the director kidnapped and brought to North Korea, where he made him direct movies that Kim wrote! Muammar Gaddafi of Libya was known for living in a tent when he went on diplomatic trips because he saw himself as a nomadic warrior. Gaddafi also had an interesting sense of style, which you can see here in a photo taken in one of his tents.

Both dictators are easy to laugh at. But don't underestimate them! Each was able to hold onto power for a long time: Gaddafi ruled for over 40 years, and Kim Jong-il succeeded his father, Kim il-Sung, and ruled for over a decade until he died, at which point his son, Kim Jong-Un, succeeded him. How do dictators maintain power?

Let's simplify by putting ourselves in the shoes of a dictator. What does the dictator want above all else? A dictator wants to stay in power. Why? Obviously any leader, whether democratic or non-democratic, wants to stay in power because being in power enables him or her to implement policies that they believe in or that reward supporters. But for a dictator, staying in power is even more important because that is how he—dictators are almost always male[6]—can stay alive or out of jail. The risks are very real. In the 2011 Arab Spring, dictators lost power in Egypt, Libya, and Tunisia. Egypt's Hosni Mubarak was jailed for corruption, Libya's Gaddafi was killed during the civil war, and Tunisia's Zine Abedine Ben-Ali fled to Saudi Arabia and lost most of his wealth (he has been sentenced to life in prison in absentia). Even dictators who avoid jail, like Chile's Augusto Pinochet, can still be charged after they leave office for crimes conducted while they were in power (Pinochet died before the court case against him concluded). By contrast, when a democratically elected leader loses power, he or she can remain in politics or retire without risking imprisonment (unless they break the law) or execution. For example, after losing the 2006 Canadian federal election, former prime minister Paul Martin has continued to be active in business and has started his own non-profit, the Martin Aboriginal Initiative, to improve education for Canadian First Nations. Dictators cannot leave office and start non-profits; the stakes are much higher for them!

So now we know that a dictator wants to stay in power. But he is only one person. Surely others, from within his government or as citizens outside government, can join forces and depose him. In a dictatorship, there are two ways in which the dictator can lose power against his will: a coup d'etat (**coup**, for short) or a **rebellion**. We will deal with coups first, and discuss rebellions in the next section.

> **Coup (or coup d'état):** An attempt by those inside the government to remove a national leader and install a new leader.

> **Rebellion:** An attempt to remove a leader conducted by those outside the government.

A coup d'etat sees the replacement or overthrow of the autocrat or dictator by people within his government. A coup can be violent or non-violent. A very famous example of a coup is the story of Julius Caesar. After Caesar had declared himself the "dictator in perpetuity" of ancient Rome, a group of senators, including Caesar's close friend Brutus, conspired to kill him and take power. William Shakespeare wrote a

Gaddafi in his tent.
© Konstantin Chernichkin/Reuters/Corbis

play about this conspiracy. In the climax, when Brutus stabs Caesar, the fallen dictator says, "Et tu [you, too] Brute? Then fall, Caesar!" Caesar's surprise at this betrayal indicates an important feature of how dictators lose power: they are often deposed by those close to them, whose support they need to stay in power. Between 1946 and 2008, more than half of the dictators who lost power (68 percent) did so as a result of a coup.[7] Sometimes, as with Caesar, they lost power at the hands of their most trusted supporters, even members of their own family: President Park Chun-Hee of South Korea, for example, who himself came to power through a coup in 1961, was assassinated by his head of the Korean intelligence services in 1979, and Sheikh Khalifa, the monarch of Qatar, was ousted by his own son while vacationing in Switzerland in 1995.

So a dictator must be able to command sufficient support. This is extremely important to remember. No dictator rules alone. He is always maintained in power by some section of the population even as he is opposed by others. When his supporters turn instead to favour a rival, the dictator loses power. Therefore, in every dictatorship there is a section of the population—sometimes broad and sometimes narrow—that *selects* the dictator or his replacement. We will call this group the **selectorate** (it is also referred to as the "ruling circle").[8]

> **Selectorate:** The group of people that can select the leader in any regime.

Every type of regime has a selectorate: in a democracy, every eligible voter is a member of the selectorate because each has a vote. Every voter, in other words, is able to participate in the selection of the leader. If you are eligible to vote, then you are a member of the Canadian selectorate! In dictatorships, only certain people are members of the selectorate, and the criterion for membership varies across dictatorships, depending on the institutional makeup of the dictatorship. Sometimes, the selectorate is composed of elite members of a political party. In China, for example, the Politburo of the Communist Party selects the leader. Members of a political party that selects a dictator can also be from an ethnic group. Let's take the case of Daniel Arap Moi, Kenya's dictator between 1979 and 2002. Moi's supporters came from the KADU political party, a coalition of the Kalenjin, Maasai, Turkana, and Samburu ethnic groups, which excluded the more numerous Kikuyu and Luo groups. To be a member of the Kenyan selectorate, you had to be a KADU party member and thus a member of one of the first four ethnic groups; if you were Kikuyu and Luo, you could not be in the selectorate. In military dictatorships, the selectorate is the military high command, sometimes called a junta. Military dictatorships used to be very common, especially in Latin America and Africa, where they ruled in Brazil, Argentina, Nigeria, and Uganda, among other countries. More recently, the Pakistani military has taken power on three occasions, and each time the leader of the military became president of Pakistan. In these states, you have to be a member of a certain group—the party or the military high command—to be a member of the selectorate.

The selectorate is another way to understand dictatorship and democracy on a continuum—like the Polity Scale—rather than as opposites. In a complete dictatorship, the selectorate is just one person: the dictator himself. In a complete democracy, the selectorate is every eligible adult (the electorate). Even in states classified as democracies from the 19th century, like Canada, the selectorate has increased over time. In the first federal election in Canada, only 12 percent of the population was eligible to vote. As the franchise was expanded over time, the proportion of eligible voters increased, to 23 percent of the population in 1900, 50 percent in 1921 (women were allowed to vote in 1918), and over 75 percent in the 2011 federal election.[9] If in the future Canada allows 16-year-olds to vote, for example, it would expand the selectorate even further. Thus, the selectorate in democracies has changed over time (and may change further). This sort of change is another reason why it helps to see regimes on a continuum, where change is measured in terms of "more or less" rather than on a binary "yes or no" scale.

As the example of voters in a democracy suggests, any leader has to keep his or her selectorate happy by implementing policies that benefit its members. These benefits might include making healthcare or education accessible, tax breaks, subsidies on fuel, or direct cash handouts. Or these benefits may be about the supporter's personal beliefs, for example, as they pertain to the teaching of certain topics in schools. The point is that the leader must direct government policy—spending and legislation—to conferring benefits on those who have the power to keep him or her in power—the selectorate. For example, in a military dictatorship, if the leader does not increase the military budget, then members of the selectorate may try to remove the leader. The primary way in which a dictator keeps his selectorate happy is to write laws that favour their interests and direct government spending toward them. In practice, the power to write laws and spend money is tightly connected, as we will see.

Now, the dictator has a lot more control over government spending than a democratic leader. In a democracy, leaders have to get spending bills passed by the legislature and members of her party. This limits their ability to reward only those who immediately voted for them. Let's say that the ruling party in Canada, led by a prime minister and finance minister from Toronto, unveiled a federal budget in which the bulk of the spending was directed to Toronto and its suburbs. This budget would anger MPs from outside Toronto and the 905 area code, even members of the prime minister's own party from southern Ontario, never mind other provinces! If a majority of MPs vote against the budget, then this would constitute a vote of "no confidence" in the government, and would likely result in an early election, or prompt the governor general to ask another party to form a new government. Therefore, leaders in Canada, to get their spending bills passed, must spread the wealth across a broader swathe of society. This is another example of the checks and balances on the leader, or executive, in a democracy that you read about in Chapters 6, 7, and 8. By contrast, the dictator does not have to get the approval of a legislature (although he may seek to obtain it). He thus has a lot of control over how the government spends money, and the economy more generally.

To understand just how a dictator uses his control over the economy to benefit a narrow selectorate, let's look at the case of Tunisia's former dictator Ben-Ali, who lost power after popular protests in 2011.[10] Like any government, the Tunisian regime wrote laws affecting trade and investment. One way in which it did so was to set a quota for the import of foreign cars. Quotas are not unusual; democracies like Australia and India have previously restricted automobile imports. Quotas on cars are designed to benefit the local car industry and those who work for it, by reducing competition from foreign carmakers, but they raise the cost for consumers looking to buy cars. However, the Tunisian regime manipulated these rules to benefit its supporters, not the Tunisian car industry. After Ben-Ali's son-in-law decided to buy a car dealership in 2004 for $16 million, the quota on car imports was quadrupled! Ben-Ali's son-in-law's dealership was now able to sell more cars, and when the son-in-law wanted to sell a part of the company, its value had increased to $33 million. When it came to foreign investment the story was similar: McDonald's was looking to open fast food restaurants in Tunisia, but the regime demanded that one of Ben-Ali's family members be granted the sole franchise. When McDonald's refused, the regime denied it permission to invest in Tunisia. The Tunisian regime used its power to make laws concerning the economy—like quotas or licenses to operate—to benefit the selectorate. Those outside the selectorate were harmed when the regime manipulated the laws to stifle competition in those sectors where regime supporters were doing business, driving up costs for consumers and reducing the quality of the goods. For example, the Ministry of Education shut down a private school in Tunis, the Bouebdelli School, because it had not complied with "regulations." Where would the unfortunate students go? The Ministry invited them to seek admission at the International School of Carthage, founded by none other than Leila Ben-Ali, the dictator's wife! Tunisia actually had a high economic growth rate under Ben-Ali but most of these gains from economic activity in Tunisia were captured by the selectorate.

If those in the selectorate continue to reap rewards while the rest of the population suffers, then a dictator's supporters will have less reason to mount a coup and depose him. So the dictator's primary focus when it comes to the economy is to increase the rewards for his supporters, not to increase the general welfare. Indeed, when a dictator rewards supporters, there is less left over for citizens outside the selectorate. This is why in some dictatorships the members of the selectorate enjoy a lavish lifestyle while the citizens are very poor. In the late 1990s, for example, North Korea suffered a famine in which 600,000 people died, and many became dependent on food supplied by international aid agencies. Yet then-dictator Kim Jong-il and his selectorate continued to import expensive Hennessey cognac—in fact, Kim Jong-il was the single biggest customer of Hennessey, spending $700,000 a year on it! Because the government controlled imports and North Korea does not have a car industry, in 2007 there were estimated to be only 20,000–25,000 passenger cars in North Korea, most owned by government officials, for a population of 24 million (by comparison, in Vancouver there were over 300,000 registered vehicles in 2007 for a population of 600,000). When Kim Jong-il gifted someone a car, its license plate began with 216 to signify his birthday (February 16),[11] making the rewards for loyalty obvious for all to see.

Another dictator who spent government money to reward himself and his cronies was Joseph Mobutu, who ruled Zaire (now the Democratic Republic of Congo) between 1965 and 1997. Mobutu's selectorate was known as Les Grosses Legumes (the Big Vegetables) because they got fat on government money. Mobutu's excesses are legendary: he used to rent a supersonic Concorde jet to fly himself and his close supporters to Europe. He even used to bathe in Chanel perfume! But while he and his selectorate lived the good life, the income of the average Congolese declined from $742 a year in 1965, when he took power in a coup, to $256 a year in 1997, when he lost power. Mobutu's rule did not just impoverish his citizens; after he fell, Congo descended into a nightmarish civil war.

Similarly, citizens outside the selectorate in North Korea have become much poorer under the three generations of Kims (il-Sung, Jong-il, and now Jong-Un) who have ruled in succession since 1948. This is partly because these regimes have spent government funds to reward their respective selectorates and reduced spending to meet the needs of the general population. But there is another important problem. Look at the type of goods that these regimes spent money on: Hennessey cognac, Mercedes Benz vehicles, and Chanel perfume are consumer goods, not investment goods. Consumer goods provide returns in the present; investment goods are aimed at providing returns in the future. (Think about your decision to invest in your university education rather than start working immediately after high school.)

When a dictator spends money on consumer goods for his selectorate, he is diverting resources that could be spent on his citizens in two ways. First, he is not providing them consumer goods such as food in the present. In the case of North Korea, this has led to widespread malnutrition and starvation. Second, by spending money on consumer goods for his selectorate, he is not providing investment goods such as education and healthcare, which would improve the welfare of his citizens in the future. Because dictators focus on rewarding their selectorate, they often neglect investments that will benefit citizens over the longer term.

The logic of this is quite straightforward: more money for the selectorate means less money for everyone else. The dictator is always facing a choice to reward his selectorate with consumer goods like cognac and cars, or investing in goods like healthcare, sewage systems, and schools. We can see a stark example of how dictators choose to spend money in the case of Argentina, when it fluctuated between military dictatorship and democracy between the 1960s and 1980s (see Figure 14.4). From 1962 to 1973, Argentina was a full autocracy (military leaders led a coup in 1962, then held restricted elections won by a civilian in 1963 but overthrew the civilian president in another coup in 1966). After protests against military rule, elections were held in 1973 and Argentina became a full democracy, but then became an autocracy again in 1976 when the military overthrew the government led by Isabel Perón.

Now let's look at an example of an investment good provided by the government that would benefit a large number of people in Argentina: safe drinking water. In 1970, when Argentina was under military rule, only 12 percent of rural Argentinians had access to safe drinking water.[12] In 1975, two years after a democratic government took power, this figure doubled: 26 percent of rural Argentinians had access to safe drinking water. In 1984, eight years after the military had retaken power, the number of rural Argentinians who had access to safe drinking water had fallen to 17 percent. Why did these changes happen? It was most likely because, once in power, each regime rewarded its selectorate. The democratic regime wanted to reward the rural people who had voted for it—and had to do so to maintain their support—so it spent money on providing safe drinking water. But rural citizens do not select the leaders of the military. So the military regime spent less money on the needs of rural citizens, including improving their access to safe drinking water. This pattern can be seen elsewhere. In 1983, a military dictator, Muhammadu Buhari, took power in Nigeria. Between 1982 and 1985, the rate of immunization for infants

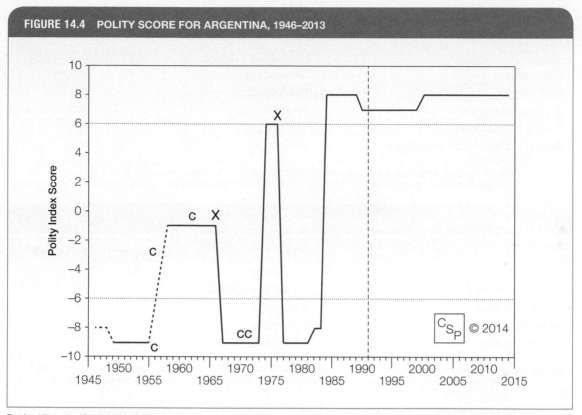

FIGURE 14.4   POLITY SCORE FOR ARGENTINA, 1946–2013

Dashed line signify periods of transition.

Source: Center for Systemic Peace, "Authority Trends, 1946–2013: Argentina," *Polity IV Individual Country Regime Trends, 1946–2013*, online at http://www.systemicpeace.org/polity/arg2.htm (accessed June 23, 2015).

against diphtheria, pertussis, and tetanus fell from 20 percent to nine percent. Again, a military ruler's primary interest is the children of his own supporters not of the rest of the population! As spending on immunization for the whole population was reduced, the rate of immunization in Nigeria as a whole fell. This was one indicator of a bad period for ordinary citizens in Nigeria. The GDP per capita in Nigeria dropped from $634 in 1983, when military rule began, to $537 in 1999, when military rule ended.[13] In general, dictators invest less in goods that benefit everyone than democratic leaders: this is because their selectorate is much smaller, and often demands consumer goods for personal enrichment.[14]

Let's compare two sets of leaders on two dimensions: economic growth and length of time in office. Table 14.1 shows us the leaders between 1955 and 1999 whose economies saw the highest growth while they were in power. Table 14.2, in turn,

reveals the leaders who stayed in power the longest (minimum 36 years).

Like the Kims in North Korea, dictators like Enver Hoxha of Albania and Reza Shah of Iran stayed in power a long time without making their citizens' lives better off. By contrast, higher rates of growth were generally delivered by leaders of democracies and anocracies.

As the example of Spain's Franco in Table 14.2 suggests, not all dictators neglect the needs of citizens outside the selectorate. Some make significant investments which benefit their citizens in the long term. In Cuba, the Castro regime has built one of the best systems of primary healthcare in the Caribbean. Under the South Korean military dictatorship, the regime provided significant support to local export industries, which have now become world-class conglomerates like Samsung and Hyundai. There may in fact be institutional features of dictatorship that allow

TABLE 14.1 LEADERS THAT DELIVERED HIGH RATES OF ECONOMIC GROWTH, 1955–1999		
	Regime	Growth rate in power
Sato (Japan)	Democracy	9.8
Meir (Israel)	Democracy	9.3
Bin Onn (Malaysia)	Anocracy	8.3
Castro (Honduras)	Autocracy	8.3
Balaguer (Dominican Republic)	Anocracy	8.1

Source: Bueno de Mesquita, Bruce, Alastair Smith, Randolph M. Siverson, and James D. Morrow, *The Logic of Political Survival*, pp. excerpt from growth rate tables, pages 274–275, © 2003 Massachusetts Institute of Technology, by permission of The MIT Press.

TABLE 14.2 LEADERS WHO STAYED IN POWER LONGEST, 1955–1999		
	Regime	Growth rate in power
Mwambutsa (Burundi)	Autocracy	2.4
Ibn Talal (Jordan)	Autocracy/Anocracy	6.2
Hoxha (Albania)	Autocracy	2.1
Reza (Iran)	Autocracy	0.5
Franco (Spain)	Autocracy	6.7

Source: Bueno de Mesquita, Bruce, Alastair Smith, Randolph M. Siverson, and James D. Morrow, *The Logic of Political Survival*, pp. excerpt from growth rate tables, pages 274–275, © 2003 Massachusetts Institute of Technology, by permission of The MIT Press.

a dictator to make policy decisions that are unpopular in the short term, but pay off years later. Indeed, intellectuals in China have argued that democratic leaders often engage in unwise short-term spending prior to elections to convince voters to vote for them. A famous example of this can be seen in the 1972 American presidential election. In October of that year, 25 million Americans received Social Security checks that had grown by 20 percent, courtesy of a new statute passed by Congress and signed into law by President Richard Nixon, who was also asking these same citizens to re-elect him a month later! Unburdened by the pressure of winning elections—an "institutional feature" of dictatorships—Chinese leaders do not have to engage in such short-sighted spending, and instead are able to focus on the long term and make investments in roads, schools, and

universities. Because of these investments, China has been able to reduce the number of its citizens living below the poverty line—$1.25 a day or less—from over 80 percent of its population in 1981 to below 20 percent today. In the same time that Congolese and Nigerians became poorer on average, Chinese GDP per capita tripled. Chinese leaders and intellectuals are justly proud of the fact that China has lifted so many people out of poverty.

Yet looking back at Chinese history reminds us that dictators do not always make such wise decisions. Under Mao Zedong, China saw not one, but two catastrophic events—the Great Leap Forward of 1958–1962, and the Cultural Revolution of 1966–1976—in which millions of people died because of decisions made by the regime. The Great Leap Forward was a campaign to ban private farming and collectivize

THINK AND DISCUSS

Should Canada and its allies provide aid to dictators? What are the pros and cons of aiding dictators over democratic leaders?

farms to produce food for urban areas. In addition, the regime forced rural workers to set up "backyard furnaces" to melt everyday tools, like pots, into iron and steel for industrial production.[15] These decisions led to widespread starvation in rural areas as agricultural output fell and what was produced was sent to the cities. Because the regime punished any form of criticism—in 1959, a high-ranking military leader was fired for criticizing the policy at a Party Congress—very few officials dared to report that villagers were starving (all media outlets were also controlled by the Party). When Mao toured Xushai province in 1958, as people had already begun to starve, he had the following discussion with the provincial Party leader, who had falsely reported huge grain surpluses:[*]

MAO: How are you going to eat so much grain? What are you going to do with the surplus?

ZHANG GUOZHING (leader of Xushai province): We can exchange it for machinery.

MAO: But you are not the only one to have a surplus, others too have too much grain! Nobody will want your grain![16]

The provincial official was so frightened of Mao that he lied to Mao himself! Now think of thousands of other such officials submitting reports of big grain surpluses rather than admitting that their villagers were starving, and you get a famine of epic proportions. Let's trace the steps that led to this catastrophe:

1. The leader chose a bad policy.
2. Because the regime punished criticism, no official reported that the policy was bad.
3. Because the citizens could not vote out the leader, he continued the bad policy.

You can immediately see that any leader, regardless of regime, can choose a bad policy; the first step in the process can happen in a democracy or a non-democracy. But the second and third steps are particular to non-democratic regimes.

Therefore, the initial bad decision by the Chinese regime to collectivize agriculture was made far worse by the nature of the regime, namely that it punished criticism and that the starving villagers could not vote Mao out of

office. These last two are institutional features of non-democratic regimes. In contrast, in democratic regimes there is a free press and political opponents can compete for power, for example. Indeed, the economist Amartya Sen has argued that no democracy has ever experienced a famine because the news that people are starving gets publicized by the media, and citizens would vote out a leader that puts them at risk of starvation.[17] But in non-democratic regimes, these institutional features do not exist, and hence decisions that can ultimately cause the starvation of millions (Mao), or lift millions of citizens out of poverty (Mao's successors), are entirely up to those within the regime. Citizens cannot influence these decisions, unless they rebel.

So, it is undoubtedly the case that non-democratic regimes can invest for the long-term welfare of their citizens. However, the decision to invest is entirely up to the regime (the dictator and his selectorate); if they want to spend money on wasteful consumer goods, then there is nothing to stop them in their lifetime short of a revolution or a coup. By contrast, in a democracy, citizens can vote out a government that rewards its own supporters to the exclusion of others. This puts a limit on the length of time that any democratic leader can loot the public treasury. But in a dictatorship, the lack of elections means that a dictator can loot the public treasury to reward himself and his selectorate for decades if he is able to maintain power!

HOW DO CITIZENS OVERTHROW REGIMES?

Thus far, we have not talked about the citizens outside the selectorate. In a dictatorship, these citizens are usually a majority and they are unable to exercise a variety of rights that citizens in democracies take for granted. Now, even in a democracy, a majority of the population may not actually vote. In the 2011 Canadian federal election, only 47 percent of the total population voted, meaning that a majority did not participate in the selection of the leader (30 percent of the population who were eligible to vote did not, while another 23 percent, mostly those under 18, were ineligible to vote). But the majority—some 75 percent of the population in Canada—had the opportunity to vote, and thus select their leaders. By contrast, the majority of

---

[*] Quoted in Frank Dikotter, *Mao's Great Famine* (New York: Walker and Co., 2011), p. 41.

the population in a dictatorship has no opportunity to select their leaders. In addition, they are often denied the freedom to protest; the media is either censored or controlled by the regime; and checks and balances on the dictator, like an independent judiciary, are rare. On the economic front, democratic citizens are not always richer than those in dictatorships. Indeed, the state with the highest per capita income is an autocracy (Qatar), and the average citizen in other oil-producing dictatorships like Saudi Arabia is much wealthier than citizens in democracies like India. It is on the political side—the ability to select a leader; freedom of speech; access to media—that citizens in dictatorships are generally worse off than citizens in democracies. But the economic and political are related. If citizens in a democracy are unhappy with the economic performance of their government—if unemployment has increased a lot, for example—they can vote out that government and select another. But when economic conditions worsen in a dictatorship, the citizens must suffer in silence: think of the North Koreans, for example. Or they can choose to rebel. A rebellion or **revolution** is therefore an attempt to remove the dictator conducted by those outside the selectorate, in contrast to a coup, which is an attempt to remove the leader conducted by members of the selectorate.

> **Revolution:** A sudden, drastic, and usually violent change in the government of a state; the overthrow and replacement of existing political institutions and principles, not merely the forcible removal of the current ruler or government.

Therefore, we would expect citizens in dictatorships to want to rebel against the dictator, especially when economic conditions worsen. Yet rebellions do not happen very often, and when dictators are overthrown, it is much more likely to happen through a coup than a rebellion. Of dictators who were overthrown between 1946 and 2008, over 60 percent were removed in a coup and only 10 percent by a popular rebellion.[18] This seems odd: citizens excluded from the spoils of power should be the most likely to overthrow the leader. Much of the time, they have become poorer while the members of the selectorate have become richer, and almost all of the time, they are denied civil liberties like freedom of speech and association. Why are rebellions not more common?

The basic problems for protestors or rebels are twofold: protest and rebellion are individually costly and dangerous; and it is hard to join forces (often called **collective action**) with other protestors or rebels in a dictatorship. Put yourself in the position of a citizen living in a dictatorship. You are upset that your child has to learn roller skating in school rather than play soccer, because the dictator likes roller skating (this actually happened in North Korea!). Would you go to the public square and protest? Well, it depends. You might protest if, first, you thought the police would not beat you up, and if, second, you thought that other citizens would join you, so that the police could not beat up all of you. Hence, you would protest if protesting was not too costly to you as an individual, and if you were confident that enough other citizens would join you to make the protest collectively less costly.

> **Collective action:** Any action taken together by two or more individuals whose goal is to achieve a common objective.

Putting yourself in the shoes of a citizen living in a dictatorship requires thinking about two types of costs: the costs that you and other citizens are willing to pay, and the costs that the dictator can impose on you. Citizens vary in terms of the costs that they are willing to pay. Some will protest on principle, no matter the cost, because they care so much about their cause. Think of a Tibetan monk who immolates himself to protest Chinese rule. Another way of putting this is that the monk does not allow the personal costs of his action to prevent him from acting (suicide bombers are similar). But most people are very concerned about the prospects of death, injury, or imprisonment; they are sensitive to the costs, or "cost-sensitive." So while some monks sacrifice their lives, not only do the vast majority of Tibetans not self-immolate, but many do not even protest. This means that while there will always be some citizens who accept the costs, the vast majority decide not to protest after taking the costs into account.

Dictators know this, and so they make an effort to impose heavy costs on protestors. The Soviets under Joseph Stalin would arrest any individual even suspected of criticizing the regime, declare them a "traitor," and ship them off to the gulag, a network of prison camps in remote areas where prisoners were forced to do grueling hard labour. The regime found these "traitors" by encouraging everyone to report any criticism they heard in the workplace or home to the authorities. Children were encouraged to inform on their parents if they heard the latter say anything negative about Stalin, and were rewarded when they did so in school by becoming members of the Pioneers, an elite youth group. The fear of being reported to the authorities for a throwaway comment about Stalin or his regime was so prevalent that the writer Isaak Babel wrote that "today a man talks freely only with his wife—at night, with the blankets pulled over his head."[19] In keeping with a long Russian tradition of dark humour, Soviet citizens would make jokes about this:[*]

QUESTION: "Was it possible to criticize Hitler?"

ANSWER: "Sure. The same way as you criticized Stalin. You had to lock yourself in your bedroom, hide under two, or better three covers, place a pillow, or better two pillows on top of the blankets over your head, and then whisper whatever your soul wishes about the dictator, strictly adhering to a five-minute limit."[20]

Gulags are not ancient history. The North Korean regime maintains a network of prison camps (known as the *kwan-li-so*) to which individuals can be dispatched for any suspicion of opposition. While information about these camps is hard to come by, estimates about the total number of prisoners run as high as 150,000 to 200,000.[21] Worse, the families of these individuals are imprisoned as well, including children who are forced to do hard labour.

The USSR under Stalin and the North Korean regime are among the worst offenders, but dictatorships in general rely on **coercion** or force—torture, imprisonment, extra-judicial killing—and the threat of force to stifle protests. In Argentina during the Dirty War (1976–1983), the military dictatorship's forces would abduct and murder opponents before disposing of their bodies in unmarked graves. No one knew where these individuals had gone; hence they were called "The Disappeared." While democracies have certainly used force against their citizens—the Indian armed forces have been accused of

"disappearing" suspected rebels in Kashmir and burying them in unmarked graves much like what happened in Argentina, for example[22]—they also allow some level of protest and have non-violent modes of dispute resolution such as the courts. Further, because democratic leaders have to face their citizens at the polls, they are less likely to anger them by using force. Dictatorships, by contrast, do not allow protest and rely on force to resolve disputes with their citizens. Therefore, a protestor in a dictatorship is more likely to be imprisoned, tortured, or even killed than a protestor in a democracy. Put another way, in a dictatorship the cost of protest for the average citizens is much, much higher than it is for the average citizen in a democracy.

> **Coercion:** The use of force to achieve desired objectives and outcomes.

Now you know that the average citizen is sensitive to costs, and dictators often impose very high costs on regime opponents. Let's raise the stakes of the protest. You, the average citizen, are plotting to overthrow the dictator by force. Would you attack a police station? Again, the answer is: *it depends*. If you attack on your own, you are likely to be killed or imprisoned. Therefore, you will only do so if you think that you could survive, and for that you would need to be confident that others would join you. We call this a **coordination** problem. Coordination requires a sufficient number of rebels to make the same choice, if all are to benefit.

> **Coordination:** An interaction in which all participants have to cooperate or choose the same course of action for each to benefit.

The coordination problem was initially analyzed by the French philosopher Jean-Jacques Rousseau in his *Discourse on Inequality* (1755) through the example of the stag hunt. Three individuals are hunting for food. If they all agree to hunt a stag, and cooperate in the hunt, they can all eat for a week. If they break the agreement, one of them can catch a hare and can eat for a day as the others go hungry. While everyone is better off if everyone cooperates, if any one person does not, the others will suffer. Obviously, the individuals will cooperate if they are confident that the

---

[*] Jokes copyright Mark Perakh. Reprinted by permission of Valentina Perakh.

others will also do so; if any thinks another will not cooperate (i.e., will instead chase the hare), then she will too.

The rebel is facing a similar problem as the participants in the stag hunt. If others join the rebel, then they can together overthrow the dictator. But if others do not join, then the rebel will be left fighting the regime on her own. (Think about attacking a police station on your own to get a sense of how risky these individual decisions to rebel can be.) This is a hopeless cause, and so if the rebel thinks that no one will join her, then she is better off not rebelling in the first place. So much depends on what the rebel thinks other citizens will do.

Up till now, we have just been talking about individual citizens and what they think other individuals will do. What happens when we add up these individual perceptions to get collective action? Interestingly, we get two entirely different outcomes when we add up individual perceptions in a stag hunt. If all three hunters think that the others will cooperate, then they all cooperate and capture the stag: they coordinate. But if each thinks that the other will not cooperate, then none will cooperate: there is no coordination. Therefore, in the stag hunt, you either get everyone cooperating, or everyone not cooperating.

Let's think of some situations where cooperation is more likely. Obviously, if you know the other hunters personally and trust them, then cooperation is most likely. Conversely, if you know the other hunters and know that they are untrustworthy, then cooperation is least likely. Here we have identified two crucial features—knowledge of the other people and trust in them—that determine whether cooperation is likely or not. Because rebellions require hundreds or even thousands of participants, individuals do not have personal knowledge of each individual rebel. Therefore, they must depend on other characteristics to figure out whether they can trust their fellow participants or not. One such characteristic is the group identity, for example ethnic or religious identity, of the other

participants. We know that in dictatorships, members of certain groups are excluded from power—they are outside the selectorate—and repressed in case they protest. Therefore, individuals in this group know that, if a rebellion occurs, then the regime will punish them purely because they are members of that group, whether or not they actually rebel. During the Iran–Iraq War, some Kurds in northern Iraq rebelled against Saddam Hussein's Iraqi regime with the support of Iran. To destroy the rebellion, the Iraqi regime targeted all Kurds, even those who were not fighting, in genocidal acts like the use of chemical weapons against the city of Halabja in 1988. In such a situation, members of a group like the Kurds must cooperate with other group members against the regime: they must participate in the rebellion even if they do not know who the other rebels are personally because the costs will be imposed upon them by the regime regardless of whether they participate or not. Group identity thus is one way to solve the coordination problem.

Therefore, the most important factor for a rebellion to occur is not whether citizens are angry with the regime or whether the regime has impoverished or repressed citizens—both of these occur in dictatorships. It is whether citizens expect others to join them in rebellion. That is why rebellions are often unexpected: people may have been angry at the regime for a long time but feel that they are isolated and that no one will join them in venting their anger (remember, if they are the only one protesting, they may be beaten up, imprisoned, or even killed). Then one person protests, or a few protest, and many realize that others are willing to risk the costs, at which point very large numbers of citizens who were passive suddenly become active in protest.

Let's take two examples of unexpected rebellions. In 1989, the Berlin Wall fell and within days the East German leaders had resigned. The fall of the East German regime surprised most observers: Radio Free Europe commented, "our jaws cannot drop any lower."[23] In 1990, German researchers conducted

THINK AND DISCUSS

Should Canada and its allies provide aid to rebels? What are the pros and cons of supporting rebels against a dictator?

a survey in Berlin to figure out how the Wall fell. Were the protests the product of a secret conspiracy unknown to the world? Or were they spontaneous, coming as a surprise to the protestors themselves? The results were very interesting: a majority of those polled (78 percent) said that they were themselves surprised by the protests, and had barely even imagined that the regime would fall so quickly. Yet many of those polled had probably participated in the protests, and were happy to see the regime collapse.

The fact that East Germans were surprised at their own protests teaches us that while the regime's behaviour may lay the seeds for rebellion by angering citizens, those seeds do not inevitably flower into rebellion (if they did, then the North Koreans would have rebelled a long time ago!). East German citizens had been unhappy at the regime for a long time. Not only had their standard of living declined, but the East German secret police, or Stasi, tapped phones and kept records of citizens' everyday lives (there is a great movie made about this: *The Lives of Others*).[24] Many East Germans had tried to flee to West Germany (indeed, the Berlin Wall was built to stop East Berliners from crossing over to West Berlin, and dozens were shot trying to cross the wall). But they did not engage in collective protest until they were confident that others would join them.

Our second example is more recent. In the picture below, you see Tahrir Square in Cairo. On January 25, 2011, there was a protest in Tahrir Square against police brutality, which thousands of protestors attended. When the images of the protestors were broadcast on TV and over the Internet, other citizens unhappy with the regime realized that there was strength in numbers and joined. That is why you see tents in the middle of the square in the photo: some protestors had been there for days, and others joined once they realized that the square was full. As more people joined, participants set up stalls to feed the protestors and even a "kindergarten" for the children who had been brought! The kindergarten indicates that, first, people were confident that their children would not be hurt in the protest, and second, that once they brought children, police and soldiers would be even less willing to use force against the protestors (very few people willingly hurt children). That is why once protests or rebellions start, they can move like a snowball rolling down a hill, picking up more protestors (or rebels) along the way. The dictator then faces three difficult choices: he can step down by handing power to a caretaker regime (this is what Mubarak did in 2011), he can allow fair elections in which he runs for office but faces the risk of losing (this is unusual because dictators generally rig elections in which they are running), or he can crack down on the protests, which can lead to violence or even a civil war (this occurred in Syria in 2011, and as of writing, the civil war has claimed over 200,000 lives, according to the United Nations).

If you are a dictator, then letting protesters camp out in Tahrir Square is a bad idea. That is why dictators ban public demonstrations, censor the news media, and crack down on protests with force. They do not do this because they are sensitive souls whose feelings are hurt when people criticize them! Rather, dictators worry that if citizens are able to communicate to each other that they are willing to protest, then they may be able to solve the coordination problem. Once they do so, there are suddenly hundreds of thousands of protestors in the square, which is the dictator's worst nightmare.

Three scholars conducted an ingenious analysis of censorship in China to test if non-democratic leaders censor because their feelings are hurt by criticism of the government, or if they censor because they are trying to stop citizens coordinating protests, or even a rebellion.[25] In China, there are many Twitter-like microblogs, the biggest being Sina Weibo with over 500 million users. The Chinese regime engages in a lot of Internet

The protests in Tahrir Square, Cairo, in spring of 2011.
© REUTERS/Dylan Martinez

censorship, including deleting microblog posts. The scholars, however, were able to download millions of posts in real time, *before they could be censored*. The scholars then monitored the microblogs to observe which posts the Chinese regime censored or deleted. They reasoned that if the regime was sensitive to criticism because the leader's feelings would be hurt, then it would censor all posts critical of the regime. Alternatively, if the regime was concerned about coordination, then it would censor only those posts that could lead citizens to protest together. To understand the difference, here is a hypothetical example. A Chinese citizen goes to her district's Department of Motor Vehicles and is treated rudely by the official. She then gets on her cellphone and posts either "DMV officials are so rude! May all DMV officials rot in hell!" (**POST 1**) or "DMV officials are so rude! Let's protest at the DMV at 6pm!" (**POST 2**). If the Chinese regime is concerned about the feelings of the DMV official, then it will censor both posts. If the Chinese regime is concerned only about coordination, and not so much about the feelings of the DMV official, then it will censor only **POST 2**. When the scholars analyzed millions of posts, which posts did they find were censored and which were allowed?

They found that the Chinese regime censored posts like **POST 2** and allowed posts like **POST 1**. The regime allowed criticism, as long as that criticism did not encourage citizens to coordinate collective protest. When the regime was worried that citizens might coordinate with one another, such as during protests in Inner Mongolia, they censored all posts, even those supportive of the regime! Consider two actual posts from citizens. The first, **A**, is a post about corruption in a city government. The second, **B**, is a post reacting to a bombing carried out to protest unpopular building demolitions by the government:[26]*

> **A.** This is a city government [Yulin City in Shaanxi province in northwest China] that treats life with contempt, this is government officials run amok, a city government without justice, a city government that delights in that which is vulgar, a place where officials all have mistresses, a city

government that is shameless with greed [it goes on in this vein for a while].

> **B.** The bombing led not only to the tragedy of his death but the death of many government workers. Even if we can verify what Qian Mingqi [the bomber] said on Weibo that the building demolition caused a great deal of personal damage, we should still condemn his extreme act of retribution.

Which one was censored? **A**, despite criticizing the city government in scandalous terms (accusing officials of having mistresses!), was not censored. **B**, which is actually supportive of the regime, was censored. The reason is that **A**, while critical of the regime, did not threaten any type of collective protest. **B**, although supportive, occurred at a time when the regime was very concerned about collective protest against the building demolitions that they had conducted. So they allowed **A**, and censored **B**.

Sometimes, such censorship seems absurd: during the Jasmine Revolution (another name for the Arab Spring in 2011), the sale of jasmine flowers was banned in Chinese cities because the regime was worried that people were wearing jasmine flowers to signal to others that they were willing to protest! But there is a serious lesson here: what Chinese censorship reveals is the importance that such regimes place on preventing coordination from starting in the first place. Let's go back to the example of Tahrir Square. Because the regime did not remove the early protestors (who stayed so long that they needed to set up tents, food stalls, and a kindergarten), other citizens realized that they were not alone. Once they realized that others were protesting, they participated. For major collective protest or rebellion to occur, it is not enough that the citizens are poor and angry. If this was the case, then we would have seen far more protest and rebellion in North Korea (and conversely, the Chinese government, which has overseen huge improvements in living standards, would not be so worried about protests). Protests and rebellions, including armed rebellions, occur when citizens solve the coordination problem (see Photo Essay). Once people believe that others are joining the protest, they protest too, and the regime might fall very quickly. This is what happened in Berlin in 1989, and also in the Arab Spring in 2011.

---

* King et al., pp. 13–14. Reprinted by permission of Gary King.

PHOTO ESSAY

The "Tank Man" in Tiananmen Square, 1989.

THE TANK MAN

In 1989, one man—whose identity is still unknown, but who is often called "Tank Man"—tried to obstruct a column of tanks advancing in Tiananmen Square in Beijing during student protests. The tanks tried to maneuver around him, and he continued to obstruct them. This picture, and how it is represented in China today, encapsulates the importance of coordination and coercion in non-democracies.

In April 1989, student groups demanding more political freedoms, especially of speech and the right to select their leaders, began to assemble in Tiananmen Square, a public space adjacent to the tomb of Mao Zedong. In the following weeks, thousands of people joined them—they had solved the coordination problem—and the authorities initially promised a dialogue. On May 17, hundreds of thousands of people, possibly even a million, assembled in the Square. Immediately after, the Chinese government announced martial law, and on June 4 and 5, cracked down with force. We do not know how many people were killed, but the estimates range from hundreds to several thousand. The tanks in the picture remind us that non-democratic regimes, when faced with protests, often resort to coercion, and coercion is often successful in ending protests, and avoiding regime change. The individual facing the tank reminds us of the costs and sacrifices that those opposing such regimes pay, and why widespread rebellion is so hard and rare under dictatorship.

You have most likely seen this photo. *Life Magazine* named it one of the "100 Photos that Changed the World" in 2003. But many Chinese, particularly young Chinese, have not: the photo and references to Tiananmen Square have been censored in China for the last two decades. On the 25th anniversary of the protests, the Chinese government censored 64 terms from microblogs, including "Tiananmen," "June 4th," and "Tank Man."[27] The protestors in 1989 had mobilized many thousands for their cause, and the violent crackdown claimed many lives. But some of the events are shrouded in mystery—we are still not sure who "Tank Man" is, or what happened to him—and officially off-limits in China. The Chinese government has censored these photos and cut the protestors out of official history to prevent future protestors mobilizing around the memory or symbol of Tiananmen Square. If the protestors in 1989 solved the coordination problem for a brief period of time, then the Chinese government, through censoring the memory of this event, is trying to create a coordination problem for contemporary protestors. This shows us that a non-democracy's effort to prevent coordination is an ongoing one, and that it involves surveillance and censorship of everyday activities.

For more information about "Tank Man," visit the websites listed at the end of this chapter.

WHAT HAPPENS AFTER THE DICTATOR IS OVERTHROWN?

Since 1989, we have seen an almost 50 percent reduction in the number of autocracies and, consequently, a large number of transitions to democracy. In recent years, we have noticed two interesting features in these transitions. First, as you saw in Figure 14.2, these transitions have often not led to a full democracy, like you see in Canada; there is a large number of anocracies (about a third of all regimes), which combine features of autocracy and democracy. Second, as you saw in the case of Iran, anocracies can change in either direction. Sometimes, a transition to democracy is followed by a return to autocracy.

Earlier, we described anocracy as a mixed regime. There could be elections, for example, but the candidate list remains restricted. There is a more systematic way of understanding the difference between an anocracy and a full democracy. Consider two parties competing in a Canadian election. When one loses, they accept the results. Why? A loser in a Canadian election knows that even though she lost the election, there will be another in the future and she will be able to compete again. Future elections will happen regardless of what the prime minister wants. This is because Section 4 of the Canadian Charter of Rights and Freedoms guarantees that there will be an election at least every five years, and the election will be administered by a non-partisan body (Elections Canada). No Canadian prime minister can ignore these rules of the game. So our electoral loser accepts her defeat, licks her wounds, and gets ready to campaign again in a few years. We call this "institutionalized democracy" (or full democracy in the Polity Scale) because the rules of the game—also called institutions—guarantee that electoral losers are not permanently excluded from taking power. In fact, the rules are set up to give electoral losers the opportunity to compete for power in the future.

As the existence of the Charter of Rights and Freedoms and Elections Canada imply, in democracies there are tools that are independent of the central government that electoral losers can use to pursue their interests. They can appeal to the courts for redress, broadcast their grievances in the media, and ask government employees like the bureaucrats of Elections Canada to investigate suspected breaches of electoral rules. The independence of the courts, media and, to a lesser extent, the bureaucracy (for bureaucrats are expected to implement the policies of the government unless it clashes with their mandate) is, again, part of the rules of the game in democracies.

These rules do not exist in an anocracy. In the absence of such rules, electoral winners are able to restrict political competition if they so wish. Therefore, a loser in an election is often worried that the winner will not hold another in the future, rig any future election, or bar the loser from competing. There are many tactics used to restrict political competition in anocracies, as you can see in Table 14.3.

These are a lot of tactics—including using government bodies that should be independent of political interference—that can be employed to restrict political competition! Faced with the prospect of not being able to compete fairly in the future, electoral losers in anocracies often do not accept their defeat. Instead, they do one or both of two things. First, they take to the streets and create unrest. Second, they support an autocratic takeover. The basic problem is institutional: electoral losers do not have institutional guarantees that free and fair elections will be held in the future.

TABLE 14.3	SOME TACTICS USED TO RESTRICT ELECTIONS IN ANOCRACIES
Category	**Examples of tactics**
Manipulating voting as it happens	1. Intimidating or harassing voters 2. Falsifying voter lists, so opposition supporters cannot vote 3. Falsifying the vote count 4. Appointing supporters to election commission
Restricting political completion	5. Banning or jailing opposition candidates 6. Threatening to punish donors to opponents
Using government resources to campaign	7. Using government workers as campaign workers 8. Using government funds to bribe voters
Control of the media during elections	9. Using state-owned media for political advertisements 10. Preventing independent media from operating

Source: Adapted from Paul d'Anieri, "Electoral Tactics and Autocratization," *American Political Science Association Comparative Democratization Newsletter* 11(2): 2013, pp. 5–6.

Let's take an example of what can happen when electoral losers are worried about future restrictions on elections. In the lead-up to the 1991 elections in Algeria, leaders of the Islamic party (FIS) declared as part of their campaign that if they won power they would cancel future elections as democracy was un-Islamic. The FIS won the first round of parliamentary elections in 1991, and it looked like they would take power in 1992. In response, the army, with the support of the ruling party, the FLN, dissolved the government and took power, jailing the FIS leaders. The FIS fought back and Algeria descended into a civil war that claimed around 100,000 lives. Later, the leaders of the FIS claimed that they had no intention of restricting elections, but what is important is that their opponents thought they would. That is, there were no institutional guarantees in Algeria—no rules of the game like the Canadian Charter—that would prevent the FIS from restricting or banning elections if it wanted. Fearing this, the rivals of the FIS in the military and the FLN blocked the elections from going forward.

So for a state to move from anocracy to full democracy, it is necessary for rules to be established that guarantee free and fair elections *in the future*. These rules can be formal, as in the United States, where a president can only serve two consecutive terms and there will always be a presidential election on the Tuesday after the first Monday in November every four years. Or the rules can be enforced by a neutral government body, like an election commission (Elections Canada is an example). In many full democracies, beyond formal rules, there are various informal norms in play as well, such as the expectation that the government will not meddle with the election commission. If the government interferes with the independence of the election commission, then it will likely be subject to criticism by opponents, the media, as well as ordinary citizens, and may suffer, as a result, at the polls. In full democracies, formal rules are augmented by informal norms shared broadly among citizens. We sometimes call this a "democratic culture" or a "culture of democracy," when citizens, regardless of wealth or race, expect their leaders to follow certain rules of the democratic game. When citizens have confidence in the rules of the game, they believe that—in some sufficiently meaningful way—their voices matter and their votes count. In India, despite great poverty and inequality, the 2014 elections saw 553 million voters cast their votes, out of 834 million eligible to vote, for a turnout rate of 66 percent (voter turnout in Canada in the last 50 years has ranged from 58–75 percent). In anocracies, by contrast, voter turnout is generally low and/or sections of the population do not vote.

In Egypt, after the military deposed President Mohammed Morsi of the Muslim Brotherhood party, they called an election for 2014 in which the former army chief, Abdel-Fateh el-Sissi, ran for office. Voter turnout, at 38–44 percent, was much lower than the 52 percent who had voted in the 2012 election, and el-Sissi won easily. Many supporters of the Muslim Brotherhood boycotted the election as they felt that they had no real chance to compete, so the only voters left were el-Sissi's supporters. Election boycotts, street protests, and, in the rare instance, civil war result when citizens do not feel that the rules of the game give them a meaningful opportunity to select their leader.

The examples of Algeria and Egypt show that rules guaranteeing free and fair elections are often not established in anocracies. When we look at why they are not established, we have to look at the incentives of those competing for power after the fall of a dictator. Remember from our discussion of how the dictator rewards his selectorate that the regime has significant control over the economy, and with this control can reward supporters. All leaders, democratic or non-democratic, have supporters: in a democracy, these are members of your party and your voters. When a dictator falls, his successor, even if they came to power as a result of an election, has a difficult choice. The first, democratic choice is to establish institutions and rules of the game that guarantee that she will hold a free and fair election in the future, and that she will step down from power if she loses that election. Obviously, if she loses power, she loses the ability to spend government money to reward her supporters, who will be unhappy. But her opponents will be happy, because they will get a fair opportunity to compete for power. The second, non-democratic choice is to not establish these institutions or to subvert them in some way, through such means as those listed in Table 14.3. The non-democratic choice is for a democratically elected leader to restrict the selectorate to favour the influence of her own supporters. If she chooses this path, then many of her supporters will be happy, because they will control power and continue to be rewarded in the future. Her opponents, however, will certainly be unhappy, and may take to the streets or worse.

One example of how democratically elected leaders can make the non-democratic choice comes from recent events in Ukraine, which went from being a democracy in 2010 to an anocracy in 2014 on the Polity Scale. How did this happen? Victor Yanukovich won a free and fair election in 2010, but a year later he jailed his opponent, Yulia Tymoshenko, and several officials from her party on corruption charges. The European Union and non-governmental organizations criticized the Yanukovich government for these actions on the grounds that they served to restrict political competition. The government lost much of its credibility because of that decision, and after it made an unpopular agreement with Russia in 2013, protestors took to the streets in Kiev. After months of protests, the government stepped down and Yanukovich fled to Russia, after which it was discovered that he had enriched himself and his supporters in eastern Ukraine significantly. With Yanukovich gone, Russia began to support separatists in eastern Ukraine, resulting in a civil war which, by the middle of 2014, had resulted in several thousand dead and tens of thousands of refugees. This pattern, when electoral winners restrict the ability of electoral losers to compete in the future so that those in power can continue to reward their supporters, is characteristic of an anocracy, and can lead to broader instability.

The choice to establish democratic rules of the game (to "institutionalize democracy") thus boils down to deciding whether you want to make your supporters happy or make your opponents happy. Naturally, many leaders make the choice to keep their supporters happy, and do not set up democratic rules of the game! That is why we see so many anocracies, and why we often see disruptive street protests and civil unrest in these anocracies. In rare instances, like Algeria, this can escalate to civil war.

For more democratic rules to develop, leaders must make credible commitments to giving up power. To encourage African leaders to step down, a Sudanese entrepreneur, Mo Ibrahim, has established a $5 million dollar prize for African leaders who govern well and then leave office at the end of their term, whether because they lose an election or because they have reached the term limit.[28] The first recipient of the Ibrahim Prize was President Joaquim Albert Chissano of Mozambique, who received the prize because he presided over Mozambique's successful transition to multi-party democracy after a 16-year civil war that ended in 1992. After being elected twice to the presidency, Chissano declined to seek a third term. When long-serving leaders stand down voluntarily, it indicates to the opposition and ordinary citizens alike that political power is open to competition, and not to be monopolized by a few. While Mozambique is still not a full democracy (it is currently "4" on the Polity Scale), it has made huge strides in two decades, from a society torn apart by a civil war that killed approximately 800,000 people to one that holds regular elections. Without leaders committing to stepping down from power, these types of transitions prove to be very difficult.

If a leader does not establish democratic rules of the game (or institutionalize democracy), then the regime either remains an anocracy or it can move back into autocracy. Both have occurred since 2000, and hence scholars and policymakers worry that we are seeing a period of "democratic backsliding" or "democratic regression."

Figure 14.5 is compiled by Freedom House, an American organization that examines the extent to which democratic and civil liberties like freedom of speech change over time. It is different from the Polity scores that we have been using, which do not include civil liberties. By the Freedom House measure, every year for the last eight years, more states have seen declines in democratic and civil liberties than have seen increases. What does this mean?

In many states, even though elections are still held, civil and political liberties that are necessary for democracy have been curtailed in recent years.

For example, in 2013 the operations of non-governmental organizations in Indonesia were restricted. This curtailed the freedom of association necessary for the exercise of democracy. In other places, like Russia, opponents of the government, whether politicians or journalists, have faced threats and censorship, which is a restriction on freedom of speech and the press. Neither Indonesia nor Russia is an autocracy, but in both states there has been a restriction on the liberties associated with democracy. When we add up all the states in the system, the trend of democratization is either flat or marginally negative: that is, since 2000, democratic and civil liberties have not increased at a worldwide level, and may have regressed slightly. We have seen that this is mostly because of the changes within anocracies, where democratically elected leaders have too often chosen to restrict political competition so that they can hold on to power and reward their supporters. This shows us that there is nothing inevitable about the advance of democratic and civil liberties. While the record of the last two decades is, overall, very positive, there is still much to be done to institute democracy in many parts of the world, and it is important to remain vigilant to prevent regression from democracy where it already exists.

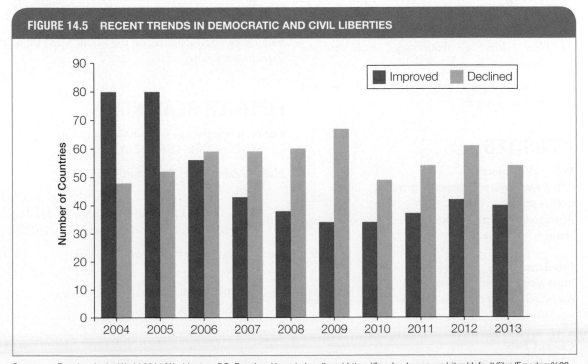

FIGURE 14.5 RECENT TRENDS IN DEMOCRATIC AND CIVIL LIBERTIES

Source: *Freedom in the World 2014* (Washington, DC: Freedom House), 4, online at https://freedomhouse.org/sites/default/files/Freedom%20 in%20the%20World%202014%20Booklet.pdf (accessed June 23, 2015).

CONCLUSION

While there have been significant increases in the number of democracies around the world, non-democracies still exist and have proven enduring in some cases. Non-democracies can last for a long time if leaders are able to use government funds to reward their supporters, and to use force to prevent citizens from coordinating protest and rebellion. There is also a large number of regimes—anocracies—that combine features of democracy and autocracy. Within such regimes, democratic practices have not been sufficiently institutionalized, and are diminished when leaders restrict political competition and manipulate elections. Thus, the expansion of democracy is not inevitable, and, just like leaders in non-democracies, democratically elected leaders in anocracies face pressures to reward their supporters. As a result, they often choose to restrict political competition to stay in power, just like non-democratic leaders do. The difference between democracy and non-democracy therefore lies not so much in the nature of leaders—leaders in any regime want to stay in power, whether to implement policies they believe in or reward their supporters. The difference between democracy and non-democracy lies in the rules of the game that guarantee that citizens can choose their leaders through free and fair elections, or not. These rules of the game—also called institutions—are still being built in many places.

DISCUSSION QUESTIONS

1. What do we mean when we say "democracy" in the contemporary world, and how has this understanding changed over time?

2. If you were a dictator, how would you rule so that you could stay in power for a long time?

3. If you were a rebel in a non-democratic regime, how would you get the average citizen to join you to overthrow the government?

4. How does a democracy come to be "institutionalized"?

5. What happens when democracy is not institutionalized?

WEBSITES

Polity IV Project
http://www.systemicpeace.org/polity/
polity4.htm
A research project that tracks levels of democracy and changes of regime.

Freedom House
https://www.freedomhouse.org/
An NGO that documents civil and political liberties worldwide.

China Chats
https://china-chats.net/
A website that tracks censorship in China.

Orlando Figes
http://www.orlandofiges.com/whisperers.php
This website has testimonies of ordinary life under Stalin, and how people coped, as described in his book *The Whisperers*.

"Tank Man" Documentary
http://www.pbs.org/wgbh/pages/frontline/tankman/
PBS Frontline released a documentary in 2006, with background material, on the "Tank Man" from Tiananmen Square.

FURTHER READINGS

Daron Acemoglu and James Robinson, *Why Nations Fail*. New York: Crown, 2011.

Hannah Arendt, *On Revolution*. New York: Viking, 1963.

Bruce Bueno de Mesquita and Alastair Smith, *The Dictator's Handbook*. New York: Public Affairs, 2012.

Orlando Figes, *The Whisperers*. New York: Picador, 2008.

Alexis De Tocqueville, *Democracy in America*. New York: Harper, 1969.

ENDNOTES

1. However, even in democracies this right can be restricted. In the United States, convicted felons are restricted from voting in many ways: in 48 states, they cannot vote while imprisoned, in 35 states, they cannot vote while on parole, and in four states they are forbidden from voting even after serving their sentence.

2. Larry Bartels, *Unequal Democracy: The Political Economy of the New Gilded Age* (Princeton: Princeton University Press, 2008).

3. The Polity Index is available at http://www.system-icpeace.org/polity/polity4.htm. On the website, you will find a chart and a report for each country, which provides a history of major events, like coups or revolutions, which change the type of regime in the state. The index is the product of research funded by the U.S. Central Intelligence Agency.

4. David Epstein et al., "Democratic Transitions," *American Journal of Political Science* 50 (3) (July 2005), pp. 551–69.

5. Samuel Huntington, *The Third Wave* (Norman: University of Oklahoma Press, 1990).

6. With the exception of four interim leaders— Queens Dzeliwe and Ntombi in Swaziland in the early 1980s, Ertha Pascal-Trouillot in Haiti in 1990, and Ruth Perry in Sierra Leone in 1996—authoritarian leaders have been men; Jennifer Gandhi and Adam Przeworski, "Authoritarian Institutions and the Survival of Autocrats," *Comparative Political Studies* 40 (1) (November 2007), pp. 1279–1301.

7. Milan Svolik, *The Politics of Authoritarian Rule* (New York: Cambridge University Press, 2012), p. 5.

8. Bruce Bueno de Mesquita, Randolph Siverson, Alastair Smith, and James Morrow, *The Logic of Political Survival* (Cambridge, Mass.: MIT Press, 2003).

9. Elections Canada, "Voter Turnout at Federal Elections and Referendums," online at http://www.elections.ca/content.aspx?dir=turn&document=index&lang=e&section=ele.

10. All the information in this paragraph is drawn from Bob Rijkers, Caroline Freund, and Antonio Nucifora, "All in the Family: State Capture in Tunisia," *World Bank Policy Research Working Paper 6810*, 2014, online at elibrary.worldbank.org/doi/pdf/10.1596/1813-9450-6810.

11. Bradley Martin, "In Kim's North Korea, Cars Are Scarce Symbols of Power, Wealth," *Bloomberg*, July 9, 2007, online at http://www.bloomberg.com/apps/news?pid=newsarchive&sid=a31VJVRxcJ1Y.

12. David Lake and Matthew Baum, "The Invisible Hand of Democracy: Political Control and the Provision of Political Goods and Services," *Comparative Political Studies* 34 (6) (August 2001), pp. 587–621.

13. All GDP numbers are 2005$ from the World Bank World Development indicators, available at http://data.worldbank.org/data-catalog/world-development-indicators.

14. Bueno de Mesquita et al., *The Logic of Political Survival*, pp. 129–213.

15. For a look at this period, see the 1994 movie *To Live* (dir. Zhang Yimou). *To Live* won awards in Europe but was banned in China, and its director was subsequently not allowed by the Chinese government to make films for two years.

16. Quoted in Frank Dikotter, *Mao's Great Famine* (New York: Walker and Co., 2011), p. 41.

17. Amartya Sen, "Democracy as a Universal Value," *Journal of Democracy* 10 (3) (July 1999), pp. 3–17.

18. Svolik, *The Politics of Authoritarian Rule,* p. 5.

19. Quoted in Orlando Figes, *The Whisperers: Private Life in Stalin's Russia* (New York: Picador, 2008), p. 251.

20. You can find many more similar jokes at http://www.johndclare.net/Russ12_Jokes.htm.

21. David Hawk, *The Hidden Gulag* (Washington, DC: Committee for Human Rights in North Korea, 2012), p. 27. You can explore this

report and see satellite images of these camps at http://www.hrnk.org/uploads/pdfs/HRNK_HiddenGulag2_Web_5-18.pdf.

22. Amnesty International, "If They are Dead, Tell Us," March 2, 1999, online at http://www.amnesty.org/en/library/asset/ASA20/002/1999/en/153ef5a8-e34c-11dd-a06d-790733721318/asa200021999en.html.

23. Timur Kuran, "Now Out of Never: The Element of Surprise in the East European Revolution of 1989," *World Politics* 44 (1) (October 1991), pp. 7–48.

24. It was released in 2006, and is directed by Florian Henckel von Donnersmarck.

25. Gary King, Jennifer Pan, and Margaret Roberts, "How Censorship in China Allows Government Criticism But Silences Collective Expression," *American Political Science Review* 107 (2) (May 2013), pp. 1–18. Scholars at the Medialab at the University of Toronto have developed a searchable database of microblog censorship in China, available at https://china-chats.net/.

26. King et al., "How Censorship in China Allows Government Criticism," pp. 13–14.

27. Megan Garber, "There are 64 Tiananmen terms censored on China's Internet Today," *The Atlantic*, June 4, 2014, online at http://www.theatlantic.com/technology/archive/2014/06/china-has-found-64-tiananman-related-terms-to-block-on-its-internet-today/372137/.

28. Information on the Ibrahim Prize is available at http://www.moibrahimfoundation.org/ibrahim-prize/.

15

INTERNATIONAL RELATIONS: GLOBAL ANARCHY, CONFLICT, AND COOPERATION

Claire Turenne Sjolander

© John Nordell/The Christian Science Monitor via Getty Images

There is not just one way of looking at politics between states but many, and each calls our attention to certain dynamics and proposes certain explanations for how government and non-government forces and factors act and interact at the global level. The theories that are thereby developed and debated address some of the most important issues that we face as human beings, such as war and peace.

INTRODUCTION

International Relations courses often attract the largest enrolments in university Political Science departments. Students signing up for these courses imagine that they will learn everything there is to know about wars, revolutions, terrorism, and any other manner of threat to world peace and stability. Who can blame students for being drawn to a subject matter that is glorified in countless Hollywood blockbusters? It often comes as a surprise to students, therefore, to discover that the study of International Relations seems to have less to do with identifying Hollywood's global "good guys" and "bad guys"—that is, those with the potential to take the world to the brink—than it does with learning about different theoretical models and approaches that provide contrasting and sometimes contradictory interpretations of the reasons for, and the possible solutions to, global problems.

What is the field of International Relations? Despite the fact that it is usually taught as part of Political Science programs, most scholars of International Relations argue that it is a distinct academic discipline—related to Political Science, of course, but also connected to Economics, History, Sociology, Anthropology, and Geography. Well before it was ever considered as a self-contained area of study, however, the major themes that have continued to preoccupy the discipline since its inception had long been identified. Questions of global order and anarchy had consumed generations of philosophers, historians, and economists. Concerns over injustice and inequality had motivated social revolutions and brought about regime change throughout the world. In other words, the major issues of International Relations—and the basic range of options or choices confronting the international system (as Leo Tolstoy wrote in 1869: *War and Peace*)—are, and have always been, widely understood. We know *what* the choices are. What has been less clear is the question of how we, as analysts and scholars, should interpret the meaning of the circumstances that condition these choices. What are the best ways to achieve peace, justice, equality, and order? Is it even possible to achieve all of these ends? Is it desirable to try to do so? How do we interpret the reasons that the world is able, or unable, to achieve that for which humanity strives?

Theories, Approaches, and Facts

What should be clear immediately is that if the problems posed by International Relations seem obvious, then the answers are far less so. These are big questions that are global in scope. The world is a very complicated place and it is hard to judge which information is relevant in affecting both the choices that need to be made and the reasons that particular outcomes have been reached. It is simply hard to know where to start in the search for explanation and understanding. Facts can be confusing, partial, and contradictory. They do not "speak for themselves"—too often, when facts "speak," we cannot figure out what they are saying because there are too many facts claiming our attention at once. That is why theoretical models and approaches are so important in Political Science in general and in International Relations more specifically; it is theory that helps us to make sense of the complexity of the world. Theory is what helps us to know what is relevant and what does not need to be taken into account, at least not as a primary explanatory factor. This chapter will present some of the different theories in International Relations and explain some of the reasons for their emergence in the field. Before we do this, however, two cautionary notes are needed.

First, if we know what the choices in international relations are, but we have many different theories guiding us in our interpretation of the conditions that give rise to them or the factors that we need to take into consideration, it should seem obvious that theory is not necessarily a perfect reflection of reality. Theories are *interpretations* of reality. Because there are many possible interpretations, there are many theoretical approaches and perspectives. This can make the study of International Relations seem terribly confusing—the answer to the question of "what is the truth?" inevitably has to be "well, it depends." Theories are prisms that allow us to make sense of the world, but as with any prism they invariably distort the world, at least to some extent. Theories tell us what to look for and what is important. Different theories point to different things as being the most important in understanding a particular aspect of international reality. Theories are more than our opinions, of course. They have an important relationship to reality in the sense that we need to find evidence to support our theories. But theories are not, in themselves, unvarnished reality. They are not facts speaking for themselves, but instead they are simplifications of the world. The problem for us as scholars is that the world is too complex for us to understand without theory. We have to accept that different perspectives tell us different (sometimes contradictory) things about the world, and that no one theory is able to tell us everything about the world.

The second cautionary note follows from the first. Theories are distinct from facts; they are systems of interpretation that allow us to make sense of facts. Because of this, one of the most important Canadian scholars of International Relations, Robert W. Cox, argued that: "theory is always *for* someone and *for* some purpose."[1] In saying this, Cox was reminding us that theories are anchored in normative

positions. Many theories in International Relations claim to advance arguments about the way the world *is*—scholars refer to theory that does this as "positive theory." The arguments might be correct or they might be wrong (because they do not correspond to the evidence we uncover), but in telling us how the world *is*, a theorist does not appear to be advancing a judgment about the world (either approval or disapproval). A theorist can say: "states are prone to conflict, and the only way to reduce the chance of conflict is to make sure that one state is more powerful than all the others." This appears to be a positive statement, or a statement of fact; even the theorist authoring the statement could say that he or she does not agree with what has been observed, but that it is nonetheless the way the world is.

Cox argues, however, that even positive theories are normative; that is, that they are theories that advance a judgment or a position: they are for someone or for something. A theory that tells us that the only way to reduce the possibility of international conflict is to ensure that there is a global superpower, for example, is implicitly arguing a number of normative positions: that conflict is always bad and that reducing the possibility of conflict is always good, and therefore having a global superpower is beneficial because it is the only way to reduce the chance of conflict. Even though they do not appear as such, Cox would say that these are also statements about the way the world *should* be—it *should* be defined by an unequal distribution of power and resources (this, after all, is what defines a superpower), and this unequal distribution is the best way to ensure that the world remains as stable and conflict-avoiding as possible. While stability seems to be a good thing, stability also means that the distribution of power and resources in the world will not change, and that the superpower will always be the superpower, even if other states have to remain poor and marginal as a result. In this positive theoretical statement about the necessity of a global superpower (or a global hegemon), there are clear normative choices that define stability as more important than equality or justice. Thus, debates in International Relations theory are less about the truth of specific facts (although these debates do take place) than they are about the merits of particular normative positions and whether or not these positions are actually made explicit by the theorist.

THINK AND DISCUSS

What is theory? What is the difference between theory and fact? Why is theory important to the study of International Relations? Is it possible to study International Relations without using theory?

Expansion of the Field

What does this mean for the student of International Relations? To begin, the field must be thought of as very fragmented; there are many different approaches and many different theories. There is no one "truth" about the way the world works. This is not only because scholars hold different normative positions; it is also, as we will see, because the object of study that is International Relations has become much more complicated over the past seven or so decades. International Relations might be about contending theoretical approaches, but theoretical approaches evolve and change as a result of the changing world, however partially we can observe these changes. As a result of globalization, the end of the Cold War, the growth of new information technologies, the rapidity with which information is shared across borders, and the realization that many of the most pressing issues in the world today (such as the environment or health; think of climate change or the Ebola epidemic) have causes and consequences beyond the capacity of any one state to manage, our object of study has grown exponentially. It is increasingly difficult to know where the boundaries between national and international politics, economics, and society are drawn. Because the object of the study is so vast, International Relations, bluntly put, can be confusing and the analyses can seem ambiguous. There are no readily apparent "right" or "wrong" answers—at least, if what we are trying to identify are answers that are *always* right or *always* wrong, no matter where or when they are applied. In the midst of the confusion and ambiguity, however, International Relations is a field of study characterized by vigorous debate, touching on some of the questions that are most important to the survival of our planet and the quality of life of its people. In that respect, there might be no more important field of study, despite—and perhaps because of—its messiness.

© Jerry King. Reprinted by permission of Artizans.com.

WAR AND PEACE

What we have discussed above elaborates some of the reasons for the importance of theory and the seemingly never-ending debates that characterize the development of International Relations. Beyond this, however, what is the field of International Relations about? Unlike some disciplines related to Political Science (and unlike Political Science itself), International Relations is largely a post-Second World War phenomenon. This does not mean, of course, that no scholars were interested in International Relations before 1945, but rather that those who were interested defined themselves as scholars of something else—history, international law, economics, or philosophy, for example. Yet, if something was very clear in the period between the start of the First World War and the end of the Second, it was that international developments were critically important and profoundly reshaped societies throughout and beyond Europe. Understanding the causes of the international conflicts which had so significantly engulfed substantial parts of the world twice in 25 years quickly seemed to be one of the most pressing scholarly concerns.

This is not to say that there had not been attempts after the First World War to avoid the conflagration brought about by the Second World War. The League of Nations had been proposed by U.S. President Woodrow Wilson as a solution to the instability that had brought about the first war. According to Wilson, "a general association of nations… [needed to] be formed under specific covenants for the purpose of affording mutual guarantees of political independence and territorial integrity to great and small states alike."[2] The League was hampered from the start—not least by the refusal of the United States Senate to permit the U.S. to join. In the absence of the United States, the authority of the League was weakened and major powers (Germany, Japan, and Italy) began to withdraw from the League rather than to respect its decisions. The collapse of the promise of the League of Nations as a dispute-resolution mechanism was epitomized by the start of the Second World War—the League had been unable to forestall the very event that it was created to prevent.

The Realist Approach

The failure of the League of Nations to prevent the Second World War raised two issues upon which the discipline of International Relations was founded: first, the problem of **security** (can interstate conflict be avoided?), and second, the problem of **global governance** (can an international organization enable states to resolve their differences, thereby preventing interstate conflict?). The approach to the study of International Relations that initially gained ascendancy was the approach identified as "realist"—that is, the approach that argued that it was naïve to think that international organizations could assist states in finding a peaceful resolution to their differences. The perspective of realists made a great deal of sense at the time, given the cumulative experiences of the failure of the League of Nations and the disasters of the two world wars. These experiences are critical in understanding the focus of **realist theory**—if the failures of great power politics had led to two devastating world wars, then surely a sustained focus on great power politics and the instability of the international system was needed. It is within the context of these experiences that realists began to define the basis of their positive

theory of International Relations. For realists, the problem with the League of Nations and other similar efforts to find collaborative solutions to international differences was simple: the League could not work because it was designed on the basis of ideals—on the promise that the world could change and become a better place—rather than on a hard-nosed "realistic" assessment of the way the world *really* is.

Security: The peace of mind that comes with a sense of safety from harm to what one values; a sense of well-being that can have economic, environmental, social, linguistic, or cultural dimensions. It can be seen in terms of both individual and community safety.

Global governance: Collective policy-making aimed at addressing global problems in the absence of a formal governing structure for the whole world.

Realist theory: A foundational theory in International Relations, usually identified with Hans J. Morgenthau, that emphasizes the anarchy of the international system and the interaction of states based on their respective power.

As realists, these theorists argued, we needed to understand that states were conflict-prone by nature, just as individual human beings can be seen to be conflict-prone. For realists, human nature has its real limits: human beings are fundamentally selfish and will—in the end—always act to protect themselves above all. States are just like human beings, and will always seek to protect their own self-interest in the final instance, particularly if that self-interest is wrapped up in national survival (however that might be defined). Further, even if states tried to avoid conflict, defending oneself (and preparing for that defence by having available the needed military capability) can sometimes be the only choice—particularly if the state's very survival is at stake. The absence of a world **government** to resolve disputes between states made it more likely that states would have to resort to behaving in their nature if they felt threatened. The "true" nature of states, early realist theory told us, made international conflict inevitable. International organizations could not stop states from pursuing their own national interests and taking steps to ensure their national survival. As a result, it was simply wrong-headed to think that such organizations could be guarantors of world peace. Rather, a "realistic" assessment of the world dictated that we try to determine the best ways to bring about international stability, even if that stability could not be a permanent feature of the international system given the true nature of states.

> **Government:** The set of institutions and practices that make and enforce collective public decisions for a society.

Anarchy and Power

While not the first "realist," Hans Morgenthau quickly became the best-known realist scholar, and his principles became the bedrock of the new discipline of International Relations. His book, *Politics Among Nations*, first published in 1948 (but reissued many times in revised editions),[3] became the most widely used textbook in International Relations courses in the United States as well as in many other countries. Born in Germany to a Jewish family and educated in Germany and Switzerland, Morgenthau had immigrated to the United States in 1937 and accepted a teaching position at the University of Chicago. Morgenthau's contribution to realist theory, and thus to the entire discipline of International Relations, was powerful in its simplicity. Reflecting on the experience of European states in the 19th century (the balance of power system known at the Concert of Europe) and the world wars of the 20th century, Morgenthau argued that **states** were the central and most important international actors, and that the concern of states (and indeed, of the entire field as a scholarly enterprise) was **power**. Morgenthau emphasized the importance of national interest as the determinant of state behaviour (with the ultimate national interest being national survival), and defined that interest in terms of power. For Morgenthau, the field of International Relations was really about international politics. The field at its inception, therefore, was narrowly defined; it was concerned with the ultimate political actors—**nation-states**—and their interactions in a sphere characterized by the absence of any central authority. In other words, International Relations as a field of study would look at states and their interactions in the international arena under conditions of **anarchy**. States, power, and anarchy became the realist trinity of the study of International Relations.

> **State:** A modern form of organizing political life that is characterized by a population, territory, governing institutions, and a government that claims a monopoly of legitimate force; recognition by the international community of states (most often by the United Nations) may also be key.

> **Power:** The ability of one actor to impose its will on another, to get its own way, to do or get what it wants.

> **Nation-state:** A term sometimes used synonymously with state but which implies that citizens share a common ethnic or cultural background. In the modern world, few such homogeneous states remain, most either being multicultural, multiethnic, or multination states.

> **Anarchy:** A system of social, political, and economic relations without formal institutions of governance to define enforceable rules or exact obedience from the governed. Realist scholars use this term to characterize the international system, where there is no authority above the state that can solve interstate conflict. Anarchy does not mean chaos.

For these early realists, domestic politics did not play a role in the analysis of a state's international interactions because domestic politics are not played out under the same circumstances as international politics. Domestic politics do not take place under conditions of anarchy; in the domestic arena, the state holds the legitimate monopoly over the use of force in a defined national territory. There is no analogous situation in the international realm—whatever the different domestic circumstances of individual states, their behaviour internationally would adhere to the same logic: that dictated by anarchy. Without a **supranational** authority, states could only rely on themselves and their allies to ensure their ultimate national interest (survival) in what became known as a system of self-help. Self-help requires states to acquire and maintain the power resources that might conceivably be necessary to protect their national interests from potential threats emanating from other states. For a number of realists, writing three decades after Morgenthau, the anarchic structure of the international system was seen to be a more important determinant of state behaviour than their "true" nature as conflict-prone. For these realists, led by Kenneth Waltz,[4] the structure of anarchy compelled states to behave under the self-help logic, no matter how "nice" a state might be or how altruistic its foreign policy intentions. Anarchy determined state behaviour.

> **Supranational:** A sphere of politics and political institutions that exists "above" the nation-state but usually "below" the global level. The only supranational polity in the world is the European Union.

Given that under conditions of anarchy a threat can come from any direction (as each state pursues its own national interest), the prospects for peace are fragile at best. International stability, however, could emerge from coalitions of states with similar interests balancing coalitions of states with opposing interests. This effort to achieve a "balance of power" would contribute to stability, in realist thought, because it would diminish risk—a state in one coalition would know who its enemies might be (those in opposing coalitions), and so it would not need to protect itself from all states. Threats would no longer come from anywhere or from everywhere; instead, they would come from a specific set of opposing states.

The Cold War

Despite the fact that realist theory was first elaborated using European politics of the 19th and 20th centuries as examples, the period of the **Cold War** seemed to confirm what realists were saying about the nature of states and their power-balancing behaviour under conditions of anarchy. The decades-long "cold" confrontation between the United States and the Soviet Union appeared to illustrate the importance of states and power in the international system, as well as the precariousness of the international stability that could emerge as a result. For realist theory, it did not really matter that the United States was a **capitalist** democracy or that the Soviet Union was a **socialist** dictatorship. What was important was that both countries, as leaders of their respective coalitions—the North Atlantic Treaty Organization, or NATO, in the case of the United States, and the Warsaw Pact, in the case of the Soviet Union—behaved following the logic of self-help under conditions of anarchy. Waltz went so far as to argue that because the international rivalry was bipolar

(between two superpowers), this distribution of power and resources made the international system more stable than could be achieved under any other distribution of power and resources: both the United States and the Soviet Union were clear on who the enemy was, so both could focus their attention on protecting themselves from the threat presented by the other (see Box 15.1).

> **Cold War:** The period in international relations between 1945 and 1990 that was dominated by global political conflict and economic competition between the United States and the Soviet Union, each with its ideology and allies, in which major wars were precluded by a military balance between the two superpowers, but which was marked by many regional proxy conflicts.

> **Capitalism:** An economic system in which the means of production (land, factories, technology, etc.) are privately owned and operated according to a profit motive. Decisions about production, investment, and distribution of resources are determined according to market forces (i.e., whether a profit can be made producing and marketing a product), rather than collective or community priorities. In capitalism, workers exchange their labour for wages or salary. Although it is often called the "free enterprise system," capitalism can exist even where there is little freedom, politically or socially, and where the state controls the system (i.e., in "state capitalism").

> **Socialism:** The doctrine advocating economic equality of the classes and the use of government to serve the collective good of the whole society. Socialists value the collective good over the private interests of individuals, and thus emphasize cooperation over competition. Socialists advocate public ownership of key industries, regulation of the market, redistribution of resources, and protection of fundamental social rights and freedoms. There is a wide variety of socialist practice. Social democrats insist on working within the parliamentary system and achieving socialism through democratic and evolutionary change, while communists and other radical socialists believe in the need for total, revolutionary change, often through the violent overthrow of the existing regime. Since 1989, however, officially communist regimes have either collapsed or reframed their ideological positions to provide for a greater role for the market in the economy.

BOX 15.1

FROM THE COLD WAR TO THE WAR ON TERROR

For many realists, the period of the Cold War (1945–1991) between the United States and the Soviet Union represented the classic example of the workings of the balance of power system fundamental, at least from their perspective, to international stability. The Cold War rivals differed in their systems of government (liberal democracy versus one-party rule), in their opposite understandings of the hierarchy of rights (individual rights, especially rights to property, versus collective rights), and in their dissimilar economic systems (a capitalist free market versus a centrally-planned economy, otherwise known as communism). These fundamental differences in worldview or ideology set the stage for a global rivalry which largely defined international politics in the second half of the 20th century.

During the period of the Cold War, both the United States and the Soviet Union developed formal military alliances—NATO in the case of the United States, comprising most of the western half of Europe and North America, and the Warsaw Pact in the case of the Soviet Union, comprising the eastern half of Europe. Each alliance represented a formidable military bloc targeting the other. Both the United States and the Soviet Union amassed huge stockpiles of nuclear weapons that targeted the military installations and major population centres of the opposite alliance. Estimates suggested that each side had enough nuclear firepower to destroy not only each other but the world, many times over, if the Cold War ever became a "hot" confrontation.

Despite the fact that the United States and the Soviet Union conducted "proxy" wars through their client states in various areas of the world (especially Southeast Asia and Africa), the two superpowers and their alliances never engaged in a direct confrontation—although they did come close during the Cuban missile crisis of 1962. For a number of realist scholars, the military power at the hands of each alliance and the threat that this power posed to the other contributed directly to stability between the two superpowers during the Cold War. The threat of "mutually assured destruction" (MAD) should one side launch a nuclear strike against the other was one of the most significant reasons for this bipolar stability, as the realist balance of power was equally a balance of terror. For such scholars, the fact that the Cold War was a bipolar rivalry also

simplified international politics, because each superpower always knew who the enemy was. When the Cold War ended with the collapse of the Soviet Union, John Mearsheimer lamented that "we will soon miss the Cold War"[5] as the world moved toward what would be, in realist eyes, a less stable multipolar system.

Indeed, for realist scholars, international politics since 1990 have been more confusing and threats have emerged from different parts of the world. Not only are there more players on the international stage (we can think of the rise of China, India, Brazil, and South Africa as very important state actors, emerging as regional powers and, in the case of China, potentially rivaling the United States), but states are not the only actors able to affect international security seriously. One of the most important changes in the post-Cold War era is found in the ability of non-state actors to pose serious threats to global peace and security. The rise of Al-Qaeda in the Middle East and Southeast Asia, or of ISIL (Islamic State of Iraq and the Levant; also known as ISIS, or Islamic State of Iraq and Syria), in Iraq and Syria, has mobilized an international coalition of states to combat non-state forces, something that traditional realist scholars would have found difficult to predict or explain. When the terrorist attacks of September 11, 2001 occurred, and Al-Qaeda claimed responsibility for them, state policy-makers were confronted with a major challenge: how to respond militarily against a non-state actor? The United States, the United Kingdom, and many other countries, including Canada, took military action against a state (Afghanistan) known to have strong links with Al-Qaeda, and suspected to have been harbouring its leader, Osama Bin-Laden (at least for a time). In that sense, Afghanistan was a proxy for Al-Qaeda, even if Al-Qaeda was launching attacks in many different countries, including Sudan, Somalia, Yemen, and Indonesia. While realism conceives of conflict in the international system as a state-against-state phenomenon, the war on terror confronts the very difficult and different problem of targeting states as proxies for non-state actors. The same is true of the emergence of the war against ISIL in which an international coalition of military forces, including Canada, is engaging in military operations in and over Iraq and Syria through airstrikes, air support, and ground forces performing training.

The focus on the centrality of the state and the importance of anarchy became defining characteristics of the study of International Relations. Because realism seemed to be able to account for the persistence of the Cold War, it was lent theoretical credibility in the field. This does not mean, however, that there were no critiques of realism, or that serious problems with this theoretical approach were not identified. One of the most powerful critiques argued that realism best corresponded to an analysis of how a superpower might conduct its foreign policy. At one level, this is hardly surprising. Morgenthau's work was quite explicit in that respect; he saw his book as a manual for U.S. foreign policy-makers. *Power Among Nations* was radical for its day: Morgenthau was telling the United States that it needed to understand that all nation-states behave in the same way in the international system, and have the same basic national interest—survival. The political rhetoric that often accompanies international conflict (the demonization of the enemy, whether Adolph Hitler's Germany or Saddam Hussein's Iraq) was not helpful from Morgenthau's perspective. Such rhetoric tended to cloud the fact that all states want to protect themselves and to ensure their survival, and that they will all take the steps that they deem necessary to do so. Morgenthau wanted to teach American foreign policy-makers to be prudent and to engage in wars only if national survival was truly at stake. (As such, Morgenthau was a passionate opponent of the U.S. intervention in Vietnam, which he did not believe could be justified on the grounds of national interest).

Over the decades, however, realism had insisted upon its nature as positive theory, particularly when it evolved toward a structural understanding of state behaviour (whereby anarchy defined the parameters of state action). Positive theory tries to be general theory; realism identified the "reality" of the international system (anarchy) and the necessary impact of anarchy on state behaviour. Realist theory claimed applicability to all states or, at the very least, to all great powers. This, of course, was a source of frustration for scholars who were *not* primarily interested in the foreign policy of the United States (or other larger powers). The stability of the bipolar period really depended on where you lived; it might have seemed to be a relatively stable period if you lived in the United States or Canada or even Western Europe, but it looked a lot less stable to those living in any number of other countries where wars killed hundreds of thousands, if not millions, of people (Korea, Vietnam, Cambodia, Laos, Rwanda, Burundi, Nigeria, Bangladesh, Ethiopia, Afghanistan, Sudan … the list goes on). Realism, however, was interested in telling us that the *world* was stable in the bipolar era.[6]

Actors Other Than States

Other scholars reproached realists for their excessive focus on states as the primary actors in the international system. They pointed to a number of problems with this premise, such as its inability to recognize the importance of **social movements** because of its unwillingness to treat domestic politics seriously. As a result, these critics argued, realism was unable to predict the end of the Cold War—which seemed ironic given the importance of the Cold War in realist thought. The lack of attention paid to social movements blinded many realists to the social **revolutions** taking place in many Eastern European countries as well as in the Soviet Union at the end of the 1980s, just as some realists have been surprised by the social revolutions taking place in a number of Middle Eastern and North African countries since 2011. These social movements within the Soviet Union and in Eastern Europe, however, were critical to the evolution of the world's political and economic structures because their ability to push for fundamental political change effectively ended the Cold War. In addition, traditional realists underplayed the ability of non-state actors to have a significant impact on international relations; the shock in response to the terrorist attacks of September 2001 was felt in the theoretical world of realism as well as in the "real" world.

Social movement: An informal network of individuals and groups who embrace and bring awareness to a particular vision of social change.

Revolution: A sudden, drastic, and usually violent change in the government of a state; the overthrow and replacement of existing political institutions and principles, not merely the forcible removal of the current ruler or government.

The lack of attention paid to social movements and non-state actors was not the only criticism levelled against the state-centricity of realism. Its early unwillingness to take the global economy seriously limited its capacity to understand the power and influence of **transnational corporations** (many with annual budgets and revenues greater than those of a significant number of states). Further, the lack of attention paid to the global economy, critics argued, led realists to overstate the importance of the anarchic features of the international system; because trade and investment relations created powerful webs of interdependence between countries, the potential to constrain state behaviour (limiting the prospects of armed conflict between countries with largely interdependent economies, for example) existed. Focusing on the state, they argued, created an artificial "billiard-ball" model of International Relations and made it appear that states were hermetically sealed units, bumping into each other along their own independent trajectories. This model seemed to be increasingly and fundamentally incompatible with the growing interdependence of a **globalizing** world economy.

> **Transnational corporation:** Business firms that are headquartered in one country but have plants or places of operation around the world, permitting them to integrate their business activities on a global scale.

> **Globalization:** The movement of goods, capital, ideas, and people across geopolitical boundaries today and in the past. Contemporary patterns of globalization involve a deepening constellation of economic, technological, and cultural changes that are worldwide in scope and that challenge the sovereignty of the state. These processes are leading to ever closer economic relations among the countries of the world, based on increased trade, foreign direct investment, activity by multinational corporations, and financial flows.

Terrorism in New York City, September 11, 2001.
© AP-Todd Hollis/The Canadian Press

Social movements and patterns of economic exchange were not the only factors marginalized by realist theory, according to its critics. As we have seen earlier, the events of September 11, 2001 underscored the extent to which states were not the only international actors capable of deploying deadly force.

The international webs of the **terrorist** network Al-Qaeda could not be understood easily in statist terms, although the international community reacted militarily against one state (Afghanistan) in seeking to avenge the attacks on the United States. Both realist theory and the foreign policy actions of states seemed to have difficulty moving beyond the state centricity of their understanding of the relationship between states and the global distribution of power. For many scholars, realism's difficulty in responding to an evolving global reality was due to the fact that, in its essence, it was a theory of great power politics that responded to the interests of those powers when it argued that great powers were necessary to the stability of the international system. In response to Cox's observation that theory is always for someone and something, realism appeared to be a theory for the status quo defined in terms of the unequal distribution of resources and power between states. While realism has been able to integrate some of these criticisms in order to broaden its focus, other issues still remain.

> **Terrorism:** The threat or use of violence, usually directed at civilian populations, in order to create some form of political change.

The Role of Ideas

Realist scholars were also challenged by those who pointed out that realism did not take seriously the role of ideas in shaping the world. Where realists pointed out that we needed to know which states (or, eventually, non-state actors) possessed weapons of mass destruction so that we could identify the next potential threat, constructivist scholars pointed out that not all weapons of mass destruction were created equal. For the United States, or the Western alliance more generally, nuclear weapons in the hands of France or Britain were not a concern—while the same bombs in the hands of the Soviet Union, North Korea, or China were a greater worry. While realists would point to alliance structures, constructivists suggested that the issue was more fundamental than shifting alliances. The way in which we understand something as a threat or as benign depends on how we "construct" that threat socially. In other words, our understanding of the way the world works, of who is an enemy and who is a friend, and of what enemies and friends represent, defines how we act.

In his celebrated work *Social Theory of International Politics*, Alexander Wendt makes the argument that "anarchy is what states make of it." Different from Waltz, who argued that the structure of the international system (bipolarity, multipolarity, or unipolarity) causes states to behave in certain ways and to perceive certain threats, or Morgenthau, who argued that the very nature of states is to be mistrustful, Wendt proposed that states can understand anarchy in different ways, and thus behave differently. Wendt argues that there are different cultures of international relations and that depending on how states understand security, they do not need to follow the egotistical roadmap of self-help painted by classical or structural realists. Rather, if states believe that security is cooperative

(so that my security does not negatively impact on your security) or that it is collective (so that I have an interest in your security as being valuable to me), then anarchy does not mean that you will threaten me. Anarchy cannot tell us whether two states will be friends (the U.S. and Britain) or foes (the U.S. and the Soviet Union during the Cold War), and it cannot tell us how states will necessarily behave. Ideas, and the ways in which they structure our understanding of the world, are critical in explaining why states behave in one way rather than another.

ORDER AND ANARCHY

As we noted, the original realist premise was based on the idea that the true nature of states existing in an anarchic international system precluded their ability to cooperate over any significant period of time. States, realists argued, would cooperate but only so long as this cooperation was seen to be in their national interests. As soon as cooperation no longer responded to the national interest, states would defect and either leave the international organizations to which they belonged, or ignore their engagements to these organizations in the pursuit of their own interests. The prospects for **international organizations**, therefore, seemed quite slim—at least, from a realist perspective. Despite this, however, international organizations multiplied in the period after the Second World War. The **United Nations** (UN) was created (although through the attribution of a veto in the Security Council to the post-war great powers, the UN exempted certain states from the obligation of respecting the will of the broader international community) and a host of specialized agencies were brought under the UN's umbrella, each endeavouring in a specific sphere of international activity (global health, children's welfare, the rights of women, aviation, the global environment, the AIDS pandemic, among many others; see Figure 15.1). While the Security Council of the United Nations has not always been able to act (or to prevent the action of one of its members), the UN's specialized agencies have demonstrated the extent to which states are able to cooperate along a vast range of issues in pursuit of transnational solutions. Further, the network of international financial organizations created in the post-war period, known collectively as

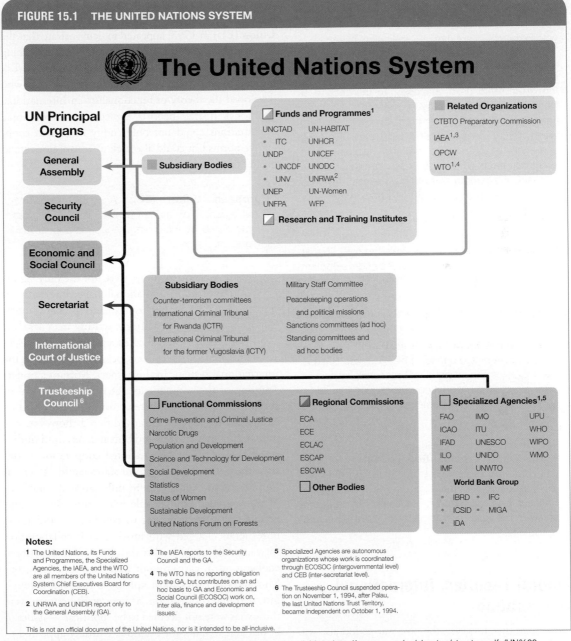

FIGURE 15.1   THE UNITED NATIONS SYSTEM

The United Nations System

UN Principal Organs

- General Assembly
- Security Council
- Economic and Social Council
- Secretariat
- International Court of Justice
- Trusteeship Council [6]

Subsidiary Bodies (→ General Assembly)

Funds and Programmes[1]

UNCTAD	UN-HABITAT
• ITC	UNHCR
UNDP	UNICEF
• UNCDF	UNODC
• UNV	UNRWA[2]
UNEP	UN-Women
UNFPA	WFP

Research and Training Institutes

Related Organizations

CTBTO Preparatory Commission
IAEA[1,3]
OPCW
WTO[1,4]

Subsidiary Bodies

Counter-terrorism committees
International Criminal Tribunal
  for Rwanda (ICTR)
International Criminal Tribunal
  for the former Yugoslavia (ICTY)

Military Staff Committee
Peacekeeping operations
  and political missions
Sanctions committees (ad hoc)
Standing committees and
  ad hoc bodies

Functional Commissions

Crime Prevention and Criminal Justice
Narcotic Drugs
Population and Development
Science and Technology for Development
Social Development
Statistics
Status of Women
Sustainable Development
United Nations Forum on Forests

Regional Commissions

ECA
ECE
ECLAC
ESCAP
ESCWA

Other Bodies

Specialized Agencies[1,5]

FAO	IMO	UPU
ICAO	ITU	WHO
IFAD	UNESCO	WIPO
ILO	UNIDO	WMO
IMF	UNWTO	

World Bank Group

- IBRD • IFC
- ICSID • MIGA
- IDA

Notes:

1 The United Nations, its Funds and Programmes, the Specialized Agencies, the IAEA, and the WTO are all members of the United Nations System Chief Executives Board for Coordination (CEB).

2 UNRWA and UNIDIR report only to the General Assembly (GA).

3 The IAEA reports to the Security Council and the GA.

4 The WTO has no reporting obligation to the GA, but contributes on an ad hoc basis to GA and Economic and Social Council (ECOSOC) work on, inter alia, finance and development issues.

5 Specialized Agencies are autonomous organizations whose work is coordinated through ECOSOC (intergovernmental level) and CEB (inter-secretariat level).

6 The Trusteeship Council suspended operation on November 1, 1994, after Palau, the last United Nations Trust Territory, became independent on October 1, 1994.

This is not an official document of the United Nations, nor is it intended to be all-inclusive.

Source: Adapted from United Nations, "The United Nations System," available at http://www.un.org/en/aboutun/structurepdfs/UN%20 system%20chart__letterbw_2013.pdf (accessed June 23, 2015).

the Bretton Woods organizations (the **World Bank** and the network of regional development banks; the **International Monetary Fund [IMF]**; the General Agreement on Tariffs and Trade, later supplanted by the **World Trade Organization [WTO]**), were *not* predicated on a vision of the international system defined by anarchy but rather on an understanding of international relations as a system of rules, patterns of behaviour, expectations, and norms that could and should be enshrined in international organizations.

International organization: An organization, such as the United Nations, the WTO, or NATO, whose members are typically sovereign states.

United Nations: An international organization formed in 1945 as a successor to the League of Nations; it has become the largest and most ambitious international governmental organization in world history, consisting of a vast array of organs and agencies. Its membership now includes almost every country in the world. Less than a world government, it attempts to promote peaceful relations among states and economic and human rights for all people.

World Bank: A bank closely linked to the IMF that is one of the world's largest sources of development assistance. Through loans, policy advice, and technical assistance, it aims to improve the living standards in the developing world.

International Monetary Fund (IMF): A sister of the World Bank and a branch of the United Nations that regulates the international monetary system in order to stabilize national currencies, and that, subject to certain conditions, makes loans to developing countries.

World Trade Organization (WTO): An organization created during the Uruguay Round of GATT negotiations whose goal is to provide liberal trading practices and to reduce protectionism through the development and enforcement of global laws and regulations.

Liberal Theories: International Cooperation

More than this, however, the post-war period also witnessed the growth of regional economic organizations which not only sought to define and codify the rules of exchange in a specific geographical region, but which attempted to facilitate greater exchange and integration within that region as well. The progression of integration in Europe, beginning with the establishment of the European Coal and Steel Community in 1951, through to the creation of the European Economic Community in 1957 and then the ongoing expansion and deepening of integration with the establishment of the **European Union (EU)** in 1993, appeared to demonstrate that the international system might be structured by something more than anarchy. Inspired by the pioneering work of theorists David Mitrany[7] and Ernst Haas[8] (who developed the theory of functionalism in International Relations), liberal theorists argued that international organizations could not only codify or embed cooperative norms but could also seek to advance or extend greater cooperation between states.

European Union (EU): A unique supranational organization made up of 28 member states, characterized by increasing economic and political integration.

For these theorists, states were not the only significant actors on the international stage; international organizations could be just as, and perhaps more, important than states. Mitrany, writing in *A Working Peace System* (first published as a pamphlet in 1943), saw states as an obstacle to cooperation or peace in the international system. In this respect, Mitrany's understanding of the consequences of the "true nature" of states was not widely different from that proposed by Morgenthau. Where Mitrany differed, however, was in his belief that citizens and bureaucrats could understand the merits of transnational cooperation better than the political leadership of states could. A certain number of problems require international solutions, Mitrany argued, and people know this. As a result, people will pressure states to collaborate, and those bureaucrats charged with moving such collaboration forward will begin to realize the virtues of international cooperation in carrying out necessary functions. For Mitrany, the issues most apt to be resolved through international cooperation, at least at the outset, were those that were not deemed to be "political"—issues of health and welfare, for example. Mitrany appeared to be arguing that while there was little to be done with the state's obsession over the "high politics" of conflict, much cooperation could and did take place under the surface in those areas of everyday life of most interest to ordinary citizens. Over time, the habits and benefits of cooperation would become ever more apparent and state power would become marginal by comparison to the extensive webs of international cooperation.

For Ernst Haas, writing more specifically about the prospects of European integration, politics could not so easily be separated from economics or other spheres of human activity—*all* spheres were inherently political. For Haas, though, this was not an obstacle to cooperation or integration because states could genuinely choose to collaborate. The European project was not one in which states had stood aside as bystanders, but rather one in which states had been active participants, choosing to "share" power with and within a regional organization and to cede authority when it made sense to do so according to both national and regional interests. Cooperation rather than conflict was the key to prosperity and growth, and cooperation was a source of predictability and order in the international system, even if, for some, anarchy remained an underlying feature of the system.

As with the realists, liberal theorists were and are interested in providing solutions to the problem of how to make the existing international system function more effectively. This is hardly a bad thing, and is in fact what most positive theory in International Relations

attempts to do. Robert Cox named this positive theory "problem-solving theory." Problem-solving theory "takes the world as it finds it, with the prevailing social and power relationships and the institutions into which they are organized, as the given framework for action. The general aim of problem-solving is to make these relationships and institutions work smoothly by dealing effectively with particular sources of trouble."[9] Liberals try to theorize the ways in which states can cooperate more effectively, but they do not question the relationships and institutions in which such cooperation takes place. The fact that cooperation may work to deepen patterns of inequality, exploitation, and injustice, as scholars in some developing countries would argue has been the result of international financial and economic cooperation, goes beyond the scope of problem-solving theory—which in this case is to enhance the prospects for cooperation (see Box 15.2).

The focus on international organization met with new interest once the Cold War came to an end. At that point, it was felt that the United Nations system

---

BOX 15.2

THE TECHNICAL SIDE OF THE UNITED NATIONS SYSTEM

As liberal theorists such as David Mitrany suggest, international cooperation has been possible and successful in a number of areas that might be considered to be more "technical" in nature. The United Nations system currently includes 15 of these agencies, known as specialized agencies, which reflect the compartmentalization of international relations into a large number of specialized areas. These agencies are generally less well known than the United Nations General Assembly or the Security Council and yet they arguably have been more significant to the day-to-day functioning of international affairs than either of these two much more explicitly political bodies. Two of these organizations, the International Civil Aviation Organization (ICAO) and the World Health Organization (WHO), are profiled here but a list of all 15 agencies can be found at http://www.un.org/en/aboutun/structure.

For example, the ICAO is headquartered in Montreal. Formally established in 1947 (although an interim agency existed between 1945 and 1947), the ICAO is responsible for the development of procedures

and regulations governing international civil aviation, including "generally applicable rules and regulations concerning training and licensing of aeronautical personnel both in the air and on the ground, communication systems and procedures, rules for the air and air traffic control systems and practices, airworthiness requirements for aircraft engaged in international air navigation as well as their registration and identification, aeronautical meteorology and maps and charts."[10]

The rules and regulations that the ICAO developed enabled air navigation to become truly international—not to mention that these rules ensure that commercial aircraft from everywhere in the world do not run into each other in flight! The ICAO establishes procedures permitting the orderly growth of an international air transport system to which all countries with a commercial aviation industry belong.

The WHO is another example of a specialized agency that has proven to be very significant to the functioning of the international system. Created in 1948, it is the public health arm of the United Nations system. At the first World Health Assembly, held in June 1948, leaders agreed that the WHO's priorities would be malaria, women's and children's health, tuberculosis, venereal disease, nutrition, and environmental sanitation. Many of these issues are still relevant today, although the WHO's work has also grown to cover health problems that were not known in 1948, including relatively new diseases such as HIV/AIDS. In addition, the WHO sends response teams to contain the outbreak of disease (as during the SARS epidemic that affected Toronto in 2002, and the more recent and ongoing Ebola crisis), provides emergency assistance to people affected by disasters, and organizes mass immunization campaigns to protect children from disease. The WHO also does work which is less visible, including monitoring health trends throughout the world in order to inform the development of public policy, and establishing a single international name for drugs so that individuals can be assured that prescriptions filled away from home will be what the doctor ordered (http://www.who.int/about/brochure_en.pdf).

would be able to realize its full potential as it would not be mired in Cold War politics. Because both the United States and the Soviet Union (now Russia) have veto power in the UN Security Council, the United Nations remained peripheral to many serious conflicts during the Cold War, since the U.S. or the U.S.S.R. would threaten to use its veto to stop UN action (and did, at times). The potential of international cooperation seemed limited by the bipolar confrontation. Once the Cold War ended, though, international organizations came under closer scrutiny because they might now be able to function as intended. Many countries began by questioning whether it was appropriate that the Security Council's veto powers continued to reside in the hands of fading European powers (notably France and the United Kingdom), rather than be given to economic powers (Germany or Japan, for example) or to major regional powers (such as Nigeria, South Africa, India, or Brazil).

Other critics suggested that international organizations were too limited if they did not integrate non-state actors in major decisions and their implementation. The United Nations Development Program, for example, partners with a wide range of civil society organizations (including social movements, volunteer organizations, indigenous peoples' organizations, mass-based membership organizations, non-governmental organizations, and community-based organizations, as well as communities and citizens acting individually and collectively) in order to provide services, to implement programs, and to engage in policy advocacy. The integration of these non-state actors into issue-specific policy sectors (international development, the global environment, or the fight against HIV/AIDS, for example) allows the formal structure of international organizations to better respond to emerging global challenges, and extends the resources of the international community in developing new modes of global governance (see the Photo Essay in this chapter).

Marxist Theory

It should come as no surprise, given that both theoretical approaches are preoccupied with making the "problem" of conflict and disorder a less threatening one, that certain realist and liberal theorists have been able to forge common ground in a debate over the extent to which national interest permits cooperation even under conditions of anarchy. Other theorists concerned with patterns of economic exchange have rejected entirely the notion that the international system can ever be seen as defined by anarchy. These scholars, inspired by more radical Marxist and neo-Marxist writings, have argued that the world is not anarchic—it is capitalist. Further, these authors contend that the capitalist system of exchange has rules and patterns, supported by states but not defined by them. Rather, capitalist interests (the interests of large firms and banks, for example) have worked together with states to structure an international system that is most profitable to their economic and political interests.

In this vein, Immanuel Wallerstein produced a very important three-volume work (*The Modern World-System*)[11] in which he argued that global capitalism defined the nature of the modern international system. The exchange relationships embedded within the capitalist world-system were unequal, however, and contributed not only to the creation of richer and poorer regions in the world but equally to their maintenance. Wallerstein proposed that countries of the wealthy centre (the developed countries) remained wealthy because they benefited from a pattern of

PHOTO ESSAY

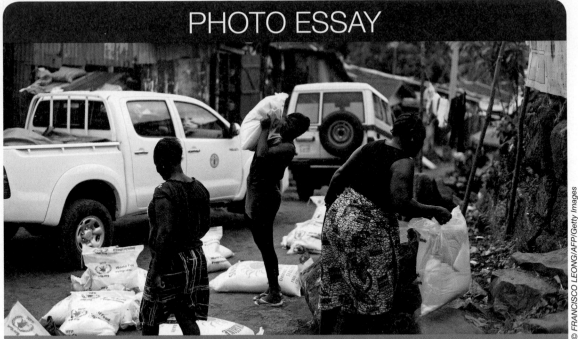

Quarantined citizens in the Dwarzac neighbourhood of Freetown, Sierra Leone, carry supplies delivered by the UN's World Food Program.

© FRANCISCO LEONG/AFP/Getty Images

THE GLOBAL EBOLA RESPONSE

The United Nations General Assembly and the Security Council of the United Nations created the United Nations Mission for Emergency Ebola Response on September 19, 2014. The first-ever UN emergency health mission, it was set up to help meet needs related to the unprecedented global fight against Ebola. The United Nations Secretary General appointed a Special Envoy on Ebola and established the Global Ebola Response Coalition to provide strategic coordination of the global Ebola response.

The Coalition includes a number of different types of global actors, including representatives of key international organizations (such as UNICEF, the UNDP, the World Food Programme, the WHO, and the World Bank), ministers from the affected countries, donor countries (especially the United States),

the private (business) sector, and representatives from key non-governmental organizations (including the Red Cross, Doctors without Borders, and InterAction, a large alliance of U.S.-based NGOs). Membership in the Coalition can change over time, though, as the nature of the Ebola crisis changes. This form of international cooperation allows many different stakeholders at different levels (from the international to the local, and from the governmental, business and non-governmental sectors) to coordinate their actions and devise strategy in response to the Ebola epidemic. Focusing on stopping the outbreak, treating the infected, ensuring essential services, preserving stability, and preventing further outbreaks, the strategy is premised on the idea that international action must be responsive to the needs of the local communities, and that these communities must be involved fully in working to end the Ebola epidemic.

unequal exchange with poorer countries (countries of the periphery, or less developed countries). Countries of the semi-periphery situated themselves somewhere between these two extremes and shared some of the characteristics of wealthier economies (some industrial production, for example) as well as some of the characteristics of the periphery (such as a heavy dependence on resource extraction). For Wallerstein, the primary role of the semi-periphery was political: to mitigate the potential for conflict between the centre and the periphery, since the semi-periphery made it appear that it might be possible to progress from the one category (the periphery) to the other (the centre).

Wallerstein's Marxist theory of the international system was heavily criticized as being static and largely incapable of explaining the emergence of dynamic economies in what has been labelled the "developing world" (economies such as Singapore, South Korea, and Thailand, for example). His contribution was influential in International Relations, however, in so far as it reminded scholars that realists had not developed the first theory of conflict in the international system—Marxists had. Well before Morgenthau, Marxist scholars—from Rosa Luxembourg to Lenin— were arguing that war was the natural consequence of rivalry between capitalist countries seeking to expand in order to find new markets and new wealth in the interests of their national capitalist classes. Here, conflict was not the product of anarchy but was the inevitable result of capitalist expansion.

Marxist-Inspired Theory

Marxist-inspired theory has moved far beyond Wallerstein's contributions. Work of scholars such as Robert Cox (his most influential book is *Production, Power and World Order*)[12] nuanced the static portrait painted by Wallerstein to explore the relationships between forms of capitalist production, forms of state power, and forms of world order. Cox brings international organizations squarely into focus in his analysis, and he identifies them as the crystallization of moments of hegemony. Where realists speak of the hegemony of states, however, Cox speaks of the hegemony of dominant classes working with and through dominant states. The international financial institutions created after the Second World War, therefore, represent particular patterns of hegemonic

consensus (the principles of non-discrimination and reciprocity in international trade, for example). This hegemonic consensus permitted not only the systemic hegemon (the United States) to reap the rewards of trade liberalization but permitted other states (such as Canada) and their dominant social classes, wholly integrated into the American economic system, to benefit as well. The threat of conflict, always present in Wallerstein's scholarship as well as that of earlier Marxists, is considerably muted here, as Cox reminds us of the power and influence of these institutionalized international norms. As long as they represent a hegemonic consensus, they do not need to be backed up by the threat of force because they are seen as normal and inevitable. While this radical scholarship differs substantially from that of both the realists and the liberals in that it is explicitly normative, asking whose interests are being supported by a particular configuration of world order (rather than the implicitly normative assumption that the order of the international system is simply a given), Cox's work reminds us that even when an order is working to the advantage of particular interests, those who are disadvantaged might well simply accept the situation as normal or as one for which there is no alternative. Cox's work, as well as the work of other critical scholars, was reflective of a trend to normative or "critical theory," rather than problem-solving theory. Critical theory "is critical in the sense that it stands apart from the prevailing order of the world and asks how that order came about. Critical theory, unlike problem-solving theory, does not take institutions and social and power relations for granted but calls them into question by concerning itself with their origins and how and whether they might be in the process of changing."[13] The explicitly normative focus of this critical scholarship underscore the extent to which its objectives were not defined in terms of the maintenance of the status quo.

While Marxist scholarship in International Relations has, in some respects, been transcended by a new generation of scholarship (some of which we will discuss in the next section of this chapter, looking particularly at the contributions of feminist scholarship in International Relations), the insights of Marxist scholarship continue to resonate in some aspects of international practice. Just as realism continues to capture some elements of great power foreign policy and liberalism contributes to our understanding of some processes relating to integration and regional cooperation, Marxist-inspired theories provide a lens through which we can assess the evolution of aspects of the relationship between developed and developing economies. The Doha Round of trade negotiations launched in 2001 under the auspices of the World Trade Organization, for example, became known as the "Doha Development Round," or the "Doha Development Agenda," under pressure from developing countries seeking trade rules that would be fairer to their economies. Underlying this pressure was the analysis by a significant bloc of developing countries that the trading system has worked to entrench the interests of the industrialized world and to ensure that developed economies prosper disproportionately from international trade when compared to developing countries, notably, but not exclusively, in agricultural trade. For these countries, the problem of the international system is hardly the instability that is the consequence of anarchy; rather, it is the *stability* of international trade rules and practices that have consistently discriminated against developing economies and ensured that the benefits of capitalism return disproportionately to the rich. The difficulty in concluding the Doha Round of negotiations (which at the time of this writing are still ongoing—into its 14th year!) suggests the extent to which the international trade rules and practices seem almost intractable. The Occupy movement, protesting against global social and economic inequality, argues that current trade rules and practices, as well as the global financial order, have concentrated wealth and power in the hands of transnational corporations and a few wealthy individuals (the one percent) rather that in the hands of the vast majority of people and their governments, with serious consequences for the viability of democracy.

INJUSTICE AND EQUALITY

Marxist-inspired theories of International Relations are explicitly normative and critical; in identifying the interests that are served by the workings of the international capitalist system they also identify those segments of the global economy that suffer in the bargain. Their insights lead them to point to injustice and inequality as being a fundamental feature of the international system and a consequence of the workings

A Syrian refugee looks outside her tent at the Al Zaatri Syrian refugee camp in the Jordanian city of Mafraq, near the border with Syria. As of the end of January 2013, donor countries had pledged more than $1.5 billion to aid Syrians affected by the civil war.

© REUTERS/Majed Jaber

of global capitalism. International policy efforts, for these authors, must be targeted toward reducing the inequalities (in the short, "problem-solving" term) and planning for system transformation in the longer term. The normative component of Marxist-inspired theories is much easier to identify than in realist or liberal theories, since Marxist theories are explicit about their normative concerns.

Over the past two decades, International Relations theory has seen an important normative turn with the advent of many different critical approaches to the study of International Relations. Inspired in part by the Marxist concern for inequality and injustice, various schools of thought new to International Relations have begun to make their mark. What unites these theories is a concern with injustice, as well as the way in which the practice of international politics is represented in speeches, media reports, television images, and popular culture. For these critical scholars, the study of International Relations must be concerned with far more than state-to-state relations, the role of international organizations, or the formal workings of the global economy. The practice of international relations is made possible and is sustained by the ways in which the world and those within it are represented. Where international practices produce injustice or inequality, these are caused, permitted, and sustained by the representations of what is "normal" practice in International Relations. This common orientation of critical scholarship brings us back to the beginning of the chapter; if facts cannot speak for themselves, then how do we understand them through theory? In other words, how do we make them speak and what do we make them say? Further, since we are making the facts speak, should we not listen to what the theories are saying when we do so? After all, our theories help to construct the prevalent interpretations of the world. In order to examine some of the ways in which this is done, we will turn our attention to some of the feminist interventions in the field of International Relations, all the while recognizing that this represents but one of the critical turns in International Relations.

Feminist Approaches

Feminist scholars of International Relations began by asking a series of questions about where women are to be found in international politics and economics (why are so few leaders, foreign ministers, generals, and diplomats women?). Realist International Relations included very few spaces to speak about people but there was never any doubt that the individuals who "counted" in international practice (the above mentioned leaders, foreign ministers, generals, and diplomats) were largely men. More specifically, pioneering scholars such as Cynthia Enloe[14] asked if the places in which women are more often found (from the household to the brothel) sustain international relations, and if so, how it is that women are also made invisible by the same theories of International Relations. For example, many feminist scholars have argued that the war-making capacity of states could not be sustained if mothers were not prepared to allow their children (mostly their sons) to enlist in the military to be sent off to war. The willingness of mothers to do so makes women an integral part of the foreign policy machinery of states; however, when we speak about the military we tend not to mention the women who bear, nurture, and raise the manpower staffing those very military forces. The wives of diplomats have played and continue to play a substantial role—at little cost to the public purse—in the intricacies of the state's foreign representational activities.[15] Spouses (read: wives) are seen as part of the "package deal" when a man—the husband—is posted abroad to represent his country. (Despite the increasing number of women in the foreign service, spouses are still understood to

Mary Robinson, former President of Ireland; Margot Wallstrom, Vice President of the European Commission; Kim Campbell, former Prime Minister of Canada; and Jenny Shipley, former Prime Minister of New Zealand at the International Women Leaders Global Security Summit in New York, November 2007, evaluate meaningful strategies for global security.

© AP-David Karp/The Canadian Press

be women who are largely occupied with the task of raising children at home—to the profound frustration of the men who are following their diplomatic wives abroad).[16] The (unpaid) labour of the spouse is assumed and is neither compensated nor remarked upon in an analysis of International Relations, despite the fact that international diplomatic practice could not function (at least not at the highest levels) without the spouse.

Feminism: A belief in the full equality of men and women, and the insistence that all barriers to such equality be removed.

Gender and Race

In a similar way, international financial negotiations to restructure developing economies in order to enable them to service their debt are not only about arrangements made between national leaders and international financial institutions. The very success of these austerity and restructuring measures depends on the capacity of women—with disproportionate responsibilities for household management—to absorb the additional burdens that will result from cutbacks in social spending.[17] Authors such as Marianne Marchand have pointed to the ways in which globalization is itself premised on a gendered and **racialized** division of labour. The image of the (mainly white, male) risk-taking captains and warriors of the global financial industry (even if their risks are sometimes too great, as the 2008–2010 financial crisis revealed) conceals the extent to which this industry depends on an "internationalized service economy in both the public and private spheres."[18] These services are characterized by large numbers of migrant (non-white) women employed in the world's financial centres as domestic help and nannies, and by (non-white) migrant men who clean the offices of financial institutions, mostly overnight or who work in low-paying jobs as data-entry clerks for these institutions' offshore offices. International Relations, however, both as an academic discipline and as political and economic practice in the "real world," makes these racialized women and men invisible, even in discussions of global financial restructuring and globalization. It does not ask how the financial warriors with all their riches and the financial institutions that they lead depend on an invisible racialized and gendered class of people earning very little indeed. While Marxist-inspired International Relations theorists pose questions about which **classes** are exploited in global capitalist exchange, they have had less to say about the extent to which such exploitation and inequality is also a function of gender and race, rather than exclusively or predominantly one of class.

> **Racialization:** The historically and culturally specific processes associated with representations or assertions of superiority by one group over another on the basis of purported biological and/or cultural characteristics.

> **Class:** A concept that describes hierarchical groupings within societies based on social and economic factors such as income, occupation, education, and status.

Beyond asking where the women are in the practice of international politics, however, feminist critical scholars have also pointed to the ways in which representations of International Relations are themselves profoundly gendered. Addressing realist theory, for example, Ann Tickner has raised the issue of the extent to which Hans Morgenthau's principles of realism reflect a masculinist understanding of the world. While Tickner takes on all aspects of Morgenthau's theorizing, we will limit ourselves to the discussion of only part of his theoretical framework, that which looks at power. Morgenthau's conception of power as the control of man over man, Tickner argues, represents a very narrow understanding of power typically associated with masculinity. Yet this is not the only understanding of power possible. She identifies other ways in which power has been understood: as the human ability to act in concert, or as persuasion and coalition-building.[19] These are collaborative behaviours that can lead to positive outcomes and those who are able to encourage such collaborative behaviours demonstrate a form of power often associated (because of its non-combative nature) with women. Yet this understanding of power is completely absent from Morgenthau's discussion of International Relations; power is control and domination, not collaboration and persuasion. For an account of the importance of gender on the international agenda, see Box 15.3.

Other feminist scholars have looked at the ways in which international politics and economics are represented in the public sphere in very gendered ways. For example, Sandra Whitworth has brought an important feminist contribution to those scholars interested in critical security studies. Emerging after the end of the Cold War, critical security studies began to ask if the state was the only, or even the most important, object of security (as was the clear consensus in realist analyses of International Relations). Who should be secured? The state? Privileged groups? All people? And from what should they be secured? Finally, who gets to decide what constitutes a security threat, what does not, and who is the object of security?[20] This subject is explored in greater detail in Chapter 16. Whitworth's study of **peacekeeping** picks up on these questions in order to raise fundamentally political concerns about the nature of peacekeeping and the contradictions upon which it rests. She contrasts the way in which peacekeeping is represented, not only in Canada but also internationally, as "benign and altruistic," with the reality that peacekeeping is performed by soldiers who have been taught to kill.[21] This contradiction, Whitworth describes, is the result of the incoherence between "the messages a soldier receives about appropriately masculine soldierly behaviour" and peace operations (often

BOX 15.3

THE STATUS OF WOMEN AS AN INTERNATIONAL ISSUE[22]

The United Nations system, pressured by many women's organizations working both with the UN and as critics of it, has worked to address issues surrounding the status of women internationally. In 1975, the United Nations observed the first International Women's Year and held the first of four UN conferences on women, in Mexico City. The Mexico City conference was held to remind the world that discrimination against women continued to be a problem in most areas of the world. In addition to leading to the declaration of the United Nations Decade for Women (1976–1985), the Mexico City conference launched a new global dialogue on gender equality. In particular, the United Nations General Assembly identified three key objectives that would become the basis for the work of the United Nations on behalf of women: (1) full gender equality and the elimination of gender discrimination, (2) the integration and full participation of women in development, and (3) an increased contribution by women in the strengthening of world peace.*

In 1980, the Second World Conference on Women was held in Copenhagen. Halfway through the UN Decade for Women, this conference was spurred by the adoption by the General Assembly in late 1979 of the United Nations Convention on Elimination of All Forms of Discrimination Against Women (CEDAW), a very powerful international instrument for women's equality. Despite this important milestone, however, the Copenhagen conference noted a significant gap between the legal breakthroughs in favour of women's equality internationally and the practical ability of women to exercise these rights. As such, the conference built upon the general areas identified as the basis for work stemming from the previous Mexico City meeting by adding three specific areas where action needed to be taken if the goal of women's equality was to be reached—equal access to (1) education, (2) employment opportunities, and (3) healthcare services.*

The 1985 Third World Conference on Women, held in Nairobi, Kenya, unleashed a powerful push for women's rights. Observing that NGOs championing women's rights and women's equality were increasing in numbers and scope, the conference hosted 1,400 official delegates and 15,000 NGO delegates. The issue of violence against women was given focused attention as an essential component of the promotion and maintenance of peace internationally. The Nairobi Conference established a set of Forward Looking Strategies to address outstanding obstacles in the path of women's equality—and it was notable for the fact that the 157 governments participating put their many differences aside and unanimously adopted these strategies.

The impetus provided by the Nairobi Conference laid the groundwork for the Fourth World Conference on Women, in 1995, better known as the Beijing Conference. This was the most important and most influential of the world conferences on women, and it was attended by nearly 180 government delegations and 2,500 NGO delegations. The Beijing Platform for Action laid out 12 critical areas for concern:**

1. The persistent and increasing burden of poverty on women
2. Unequal access to and inadequate educational opportunities
3. Inequalities in health status, and unequal access to and inadequate health-care services
4. Violence against women
5. Effects of armed or other kinds of conflict on women
6. Inequality in women's access to and participation in the definition of economic structures and policies and the production process itself
7. Inequality between men and women in the sharing of power and decision-making at all levels
8. Insufficient mechanisms at all levels to promote the advancement of women
9. Lack of awareness of and commitment to internationally and nationally recognized women's human rights

---

* *The Four Global Womens' Conferences 1975–1995: Historical Perspective* (United Nations Department of Public Information, 2000), online at http://www.un.org/womenwatch/daw/followup/session/presskit/hist.htm (accessed June 23, 2015).

** "Twelve Critical Areas of Concern," *The United Nations Fourth World Conference on Women: Platform for Action* (United Nations Entity for Gender Equality and the Empowerment of Women, 1995), online at http://www.un.org/womenwatch/daw/beijing/platform/plat1.htm (accessed June 23, 2015).

10. Insufficient mobilization of mass media to promote women's positive contribution to society
11. Lack of adequate recognition and support for women's contribution to managing natural resources and safeguarding the environment
12. The girl-child

The Beijing Declaration set out clear objectives and commitments on behalf of international organizations and national governments to address the critical areas for concern. In so doing, the Beijing Declaration provided a global benchmark against which policies for women's equality are measured. Five-year annual reviews of the international community's progress in meeting the Beijing commitments have been held (known as Beijing +5, +10, +15). In October 2000, the United Nations Security Council adopted a special resolution on Women, Peace and Security (Security Council Resolution 1325), which reaffirms the important role of women in the prevention and resolution of conflicts, peace negotiations, peace-building, peacekeeping, humanitarian response, and post-conflict reconstruction, and stresses the importance of their equal participation and full involvement in all efforts for the maintenance and promotion of peace and security. It also calls on all parties in situations of armed conflict to take special measures to protect women and girls from gender-based violence, particularly rape and other forms of sexual abuse. The International Criminal Tribunal for the former Yugoslavia and the International Criminal Tribunal for Rwanda were the first to prosecute rape as a war crime. Since 2006, pressure has been increasing from the global women's NGO community to convene a 5th World Conference on Women, and this pressure continues in the lead-up to the Beijing +20 conference.

with restrictions imposed as to the use of force) which are neither fully nor properly militaristic.[23]

Peacekeeping: An undertaking by any group of governments, usually under the sponsorship of the United Nations, to put the forces of a third party between warring parties who have come to a cease-fire, in order to encourage them to keep the peace.

Whitworth's inquiry, therefore, goes beyond the traditional questions of International Relations in that it asks how our understandings of what it is to be masculine (and feminine) inform the military and military operations, and what happens when the representations of gender and the expectations of appropriate militarized gender roles do not coincide with the mission on the ground. Gender here is not so much about women and men as biological subjects but about the ways in which representations of what it is to be "masculine" in the military have practical consequences. These are illustrated in Whitworth's study, whether in the outburst of sexualized or racialized violence by military troops, or in the increase in cases of post-traumatic stress disorder (PTSD) in soldiers who have not been able to respond to violence in the defensive ways in which they have been trained as soldiers because the peace mission cannot and does not permit it. These practical consequences raise real questions about who is being made secure in International Relations. Using gender or race as a prism through which to view International Relations both as a field of study and as an international "reality" leads us to pose questions about the way in which we construct what is legitimate and what is not on the international stage, as well as the consequences of so doing. What are the injustices and inequalities that are perpetuated by maintaining specific gendered or racialized ideas of what is appropriate and legitimate or not?

THINK AND DISCUSS

What or who are the most important actors and/or forces in International Relations today and why?

CONCLUSION

As we have seen, International Relations as a field of study is characterized by a series of different theoretical interventions in the study of the international arena. These theories put their emphasis on states, anarchy, and power, or on collaboration and order, or on justice and inequality (through examinations of class, gender, or race, for example). In a field of study as complex as International Relations, it is no surprise that the number of theories far surpasses the few we have been able to examine here. The point of this chapter has not been to provide a comprehensive survey of the various approaches to International Relations, however, but to highlight the ways in which the discipline evolves through theoretical debate. These theories structure the ways in which we understand the world and therefore colour our understanding of what is possible in that world.

As Cox reminds us, theory is always for someone and for some purpose, and his observation heightens the distinction between positive (problem-solving) and normative (critical) theory. As the field of International Relations has evolved and broadened its scope, normative or critical theory has begun to play a greater role. This form of theorizing turns the discipline on its head because instead of trying to develop theories that explain the world the way it *is*, critical theory asks us to think of the consequences of the way we theorize or represent the world to ourselves. If our theories blind us to the ways in which the international system produces and sustains patterns of class, racial, and gender inequalities (among others), or habits of environmental exploitation and degradation, then our theories are complicit in perpetuating the very injustices that we as scholars should strive to overcome. As Steve Smith argues, "International Relations theory has concentrated almost exclusively on a particular world of international relations, and that has not been a world that most of the world's population could relate to. Their concerns, the violences that affected them, the inequalities they suffered, were all invisible to the gaze of the discipline, and in that very specific way the discipline, my discipline, my work, was culpable in serving specific social interests and explaining their agenda."[24] While the critical or normative turn in International Relations does not make the discipline more coherent or less messy, it can be hoped that it contributes to a greater ethic of responsibility and theoretical humility. The world as it *is*, is also the world as we make it.

DISCUSSION QUESTIONS

1. Did the Cold War contribute to global stability? What promotes international stability in the world today?

2. Do you agree with the realist theory of International Relations? Why or why not?

3. How realistic is the liberal theory that emphasizes international cooperation? Do the functional accomplishments of the United Nations justify its existence?

4. To what extent do Marxist and Marxist-inspired theories explain international relations?

5. What has the feminist approach added to the study of International Relations?

WEBSITES

United Nations
http://www.un.org/en

A comprehensive overview of the current issues facing the global community, as well as the roles and responsibilities of the United Nations, its principal organs, funds, bodies, and agencies.

United Nations Development Program Human Development Reports
http://hdr.undp.org/en
The leading reports on global and national quality of life indicators, as well as global and national inequality.

Committee on the Elimination of Discrimination Against Women
http://www.ohchr.org/en/hrbodies/cedaw/pages/cedawindex.aspx
This website details the progress (both internationally and nationally) toward the elimination of discrimination against women worldwide, as per the UN Convention on the Elimination of Discrimination Against Women.

Europa.eu
http://europa.eu/index_en.htm
The official website of the European Union, including sections on how the EU works and on EU law.

The World Trade Organization
http://www.wto.org
The official website of the WTO, including membership, ongoing trade negotiations, trade dispute resolution, implementation and monitoring of agreements, and building trade capacity.

FURTHER READING

Barry Buzan and Lene Hansen. *The Evolution of International Security Studies.* Cambridge: Cambridge University Press, 2009.

Greg Donaghy and Kim Richard Nossal, eds., *Architects and Innovators: Building the Department of Foreign Affairs and International Trade, 1909–2009.* Montreal and Kingston: McGill-Queen's University Press, 2009.

Cynthia H. Enloe, *Bananas, Beaches and Bases: Making Feminist Sense of International Politics.* Berkeley: University of California Press, 1990.

Mitrany, David. *A Working Peace System.* Chicago: Quadrangle Books, 1966.

Claire Turenne Sjolander, "Adding Women but Forgetting to Stir: Gender and Foreign Policy in the Mulroney Era," in Kim Richard Nossal and Nelson Michaud, eds., *Diplomatic Departures: The Conservative Era in Canadian Foreign Policy.* Vancouver: University of British Columbia Press, 2001.

Kenneth N. Waltz, *Theory of International Politics.* New York: Random House, 1979.

ENDNOTES

1. Robert W. Cox, "Social Forces, States and World Orders: Beyond International Relations Theory," *Millennium: Journal of International Studies* 10 (2) (June 1981), p. 128.

2. Woodrow Wilson, "Fourteen Points: President Woodrow Wilson's Address before a Joint Session of the United States Congress, January 8, 1918," *Virginia Center for Digital History,* online at http://www.vcdh.virginia.edu/solguide/VUS09/vus09b05.html.

3. Hans J. Morgenthau, *Politics among Nations: The Struggle for Power and Peace,* 5th ed. (New York: Knopf, 1978; first published in 1948).

4. Kenneth N. Waltz, *Theory of International Politics* (New York: Random House, 1979).

5. John J. Mearsheimer, "Why we will soon miss the Cold War," *The Atlantic Monthly* 266 (2) (August 1990), pp. 35–50.

6. See, for example, ibid.

7. David Mitrany, *A Working Peace System* (Chicago: Quadrangle Books, 1966).

8. Ernst B. Haas, *Beyond the Nation-State: Functionalism and International Organization* (Palo Alto, California: Stanford University Press, 1968).

9. Cox, "Social Forces, States and World Orders," pp. 128–29.

10. See http://www.icao.int/cgi/goto_m.pl?icao/en/hist/history02.htm

11. Immanuel Wallerstein, *The Modern World-System, Vol. I: Capitalist Agriculture and the Origins of the European World-Economy in the Sixteenth Century* (New York and London: Academic Press, 1974); *The Modern World-System, Vol. II: Mercantilism and the Consolidation of the European World-Economy, 1600–1750* (New York: Academic Press, 1980); *The Modern World-System, Vol. III: The Second Great Expansion of the Capitalist World-Economy, 1730–1840s* (San Diego: Academic Press, 1989).

12. Robert W. Cox, *Production, Power and World Order: Social Forces in the Making of History* (New York: Columbia University Press, 1987).

13. Cox, "Social Forces, States and World Orders," p. 129.

14. See, in particular, Cynthia H. Enloe, *Bananas, Beaches and Bases: Making Feminist Sense of*

International Politics (Berkeley: University of California Press, 1990).

15. See, for example, Cynthia H. Enloe, "Diplomatic Wives," in *Bananas, Beaches and Bases*; for a Canadian take on the question, see Claire Turenne Sjolander, "Adding Women but Forgetting to Stir: Gender and Foreign Policy in the Mulroney Era," in Kim Richard Nossal and Nelson Michaud, eds., *Diplomatic Departures: The Conservative Era in Canadian Foreign Policy* (Vancouver: University of British Columbia Press, 2001), pp. 220–40.

16. See Claire Turenne Sjolander, "Margaret Meagher and the Role of Women in the Foreign Service: Groundbreaking or Housekeeping?," in Greg Donaghy and Kim Richard Nossal, eds., *Architects and Innovators: Building the Department of Foreign Affairs and International Trade, 1909–2009* (Montreal and Kingston: McGill-Queen's University Press, 2009), pp. 223–36.

17. Cynthia H. Enloe, "Just Like of the Family: Domestic Workers in World Politics," in *Bananas, Beaches and Bases*, pp. 184–85.

18. Marianne Marchand, "Gendered Representations of the 'Global': Reading/

Writing Globalization," in Richard Stubbs and Geoffrey Underhill, eds., *Political Economy and the Changing Global Order* (Toronto: Oxford University Press, 2000), p. 223.

19. J. Ann Tickner, "Hans Morgenthau's Principles of Political Realism: A Feminist Reformulation," *Millennium: Journal of International Studies* 17 (3) (December 1988), p. 434.

20. For a summary of the changes in the field of security studies, see, for example, Barry Buzan and Lene Hansen, *The Evolution of International Security Studies* (Cambridge: Cambridge University Press, 2009).

21. Sandra Whitworth, *Men, Militarism and UN Peacekeeping: A Gendered Analysis* (Boulder: Lynne Rienner Publishers, 2004), pp. 183–87.

22. Descriptions and documentation on the various conferences reviewed here can be found online at http://www.5wwc.org/index.html.

23. Ibid., p. 16.

24. Steve Smith, "Singing Our World into Existence: International Relations Theory and September 11," *International Studies Quarterly* 48 (3) (September 2004), p. 514.

16

SECURITY IN PIECES: APPROACHES TO THE STUDY OF SECURITY IN INTERNATIONAL POLITICS

Sandy Irvine

© DMITRY SEREBRYAKOV/AFP/Getty Images

At the outset of 2015, there were an estimated 59.5 million people worldwide who had been forcibly displaced from their homes, including those internally displaced within their own country and refugees who had crossed an international border. Here, refugee children play in a camp established for those fleeing the conflict in Ukraine.

INTRODUCTION

On June 28, 1914, a teenager in Sarajevo fired a shot that sparked the First World War (1914–1918), one of the most significant events in modern history. Since that time we have seen tremendous change in our understanding of security. At the end of the war, over 20 million had been killed and 21 million wounded, including as many as 10 million civilian deaths.[1] Post-war efforts to create a lasting international peace—the most prominent being the establishment of the League of Nations—failed to prevent the outbreak of the Second World War (1939–1945), which saw 61 million killed and the genocide of six million Jews. The end of the Second World War ushered in a 45-year Cold War during which two global superpowers, the United States and the Soviet Union, were poised to engage in a third world war, but this time with enough force to wipe each other—and most other countries—off the face of the planet. While coming very close to a "hot" war, in periods like the Cuban Missile Crisis, the Cold War did not result in these two states, or their close allies, directly engaging each other in combat. However, the pursuit of their interests and their efforts to contain the advancement of the other side's power saw both superpowers contribute to a wide range of conflict across the globe. For those in the Global South, the superpower rivalry exacerbated a long history of conflict fuelled by colonization, decolonization, and nation-building. The abrupt end of the Cold War in 1989 gave way, for a short period of time, to optimism that states could

build a more peaceful and cooperative global system. This hope dissipated very quickly during the 1990s, however, as new threats emerged, and it was shattered after 9/11 when states became pre-occupied by the threat of international terrorism.

International politics over the last century has provoked considerable debate amongst political leaders and academics about what security is and how it can be achieved. The desire for security is not limited to our political leaders. Increasingly, we as individuals are inundated with reasons to fear for our personal security in the face of international threats. This is evidenced by recent worries about the spread of Ebola, renewed tensions with Russia, the rise of the Islamic State of Iraq and the Levant (ISIL), and the potential for internationally inspired "homegrown terrorism." The study of security offers important insights into how we understand this insecurity and how we collectively choose to respond. This chapter lays out the main contending perspectives on security organized around three interrelated questions. These have been answered in different ways by those who consider security at the international and, in the end, the domestic level.

The first question asks: Who or what needs to be secured? "The state" has been the answer of traditional approaches to the study of international politics. In this view, state leaders and citizens first and foremost need to ensure the security of the state because the state in return protects its members and their way of life. Insecure states, and states at war, prevent citizens from living peacefully and pursuing their interests. Pursuing state security is often thought of as protecting the most fundamental aspect of the "national interest." In contrast, those who employ a human security approach focus on the security of people. This is a much broader definition of security, one that holds that individuals feel insecurity in very personal and immediate ways. In many situations, before experiencing threats to national security, individuals feel insecure from a lack of food, clean drinking water, or employment, for example.

"Who or what needs to be secured?" raises two additional questions: What causes insecurity? And, how is security achieved? For those who focus on the security of the state, war has been a leading cause of insecurity. In response, traditional approaches to the study of international politics have developed numerous theories of international conflict that attempt to explain the causes of war and prescribe policies to prevent them from occurring. Alternatively, a focus on human security points to different sources of insecurity, such as poverty and economic under-development, that require international cooperation in fields such as trade, the environment, and human rights, and focus less directly on the prevention of conflict. Critical security approaches, also discussed in this chapter, challenge traditional explanations of insecurity. They maintain that it is the way that powerful actors talk about security and the systems of power in society—such as patriarchy, class, and racism—that shapes our understanding of who needs to be secured and how that can be accomplished. In response, these scholars argue that security is achieved by challenging the dominant understandings of security and the practices that they support.

In the first section, the chapter opens up these questions by considering traditional approaches that address state-based understandings of **national security**. This section looks at the causes and evolution of conflict as well as the implications of techno-logical change for national security, and explores new and developing security threats that states face today, including the rise of transnational criminal networks, terrorism, and cyber-security. In the next section, the chapter outlines the human security approach, con-sidering what human security looks like, important sources of human insecurity, and how human security might be achieved. The chapter then explores whether the international community should be required to intervene in the internal affairs of sovereign states to ensure human security. Finally, the chapter turns to the rise of critical security approaches to global insecurity, which challenge traditional understandings of security, how security is talked about, and the role of the state in providing security.

> **National security:** Reflects a focus on the state and its interests. Among other aspects, national security includes protecting state territory, institu-tions, economic interests, as well as citizens and their core values. Traditional approaches to the study of security in international politics focus on national security.

NATIONAL SECURITY

Ever since the end of the First World War, much of the study of international politics has been motivated by the desire to understand why conflict between states occurs, how it can be prevented, and, if not, how the state can protect itself and its interests. Academics are not alone in seeking answers to these questions. State leaders have also been driven by concerns of secu-rity. One of the most fundamental responsibilities of these leaders is to ensure the protection of their respec-tive states. The U.S. presidential oath of office requires the president to swear to "preserve, protect and defend the Constitution of the United States." The Russian presidential oath is even more assertive: "I swear in exercising the powers of the President of the Russian Federation to respect and protect the rights and free-doms of man and citizen, to respect and defend the Constitution of the Russian Federation, to protect the sovereignty and independence, security and integrity of the state." Publics also commit to protecting the state. When they sing their national anthem, Canadians promise to "stand on guard for thee." National mili-tary service requirements in some countries, such as Finland and Israel, are a clear demonstration of citi-zens' obligations to serve and protect the state. Indeed, in every state there is an expectation that in a time of dire need citizens should be prepared to die to defend their country. For many of us in the Global North, such sacrifice seems almost unimaginable. Our per-sonal experiences of war, for the most part, are very distant compared to those who lived through the two world wars, or the reality of those who today live in conflict zones. Nonetheless, the fear that our states are not secure remains one of the public's greatest concerns in society and tops our politicians' agendas.

While citizens have obligations to the state, the state's central responsibility is to protect its citizens. At the domestic level, this may involve providing conditions under which people can exercise their rights, ensuring public safety and stability, and creating the structures through which citizens can pursue their interests peacefully. In the face of international uncertainty or war, states are expected to be able to protect their people and territory. While states understand their responsibility to protect citizens differently, a central role has been to protect the physical territory of the state from invasion or conquest and to ensure that national cultures, languages, and values—the things that define who citizens are as a nation—are preserved.

Threats to national security often arise in disputes over claims to territory. For example, control over the Rhineland was at the centre of disputes between France and Prussia/Germany for more than a century before the Second World War. Iraq's 1993 invasion of Kuwait was in part precipitated by Iraqi claims to Kuwaiti territory. Similarly, in 2014, Ukraine and Russia fought over control of the Crimea. While territory is a central factor it is rarely the only issue. States often fight over territory because of its economic or geopolitical significance—a seaport that will allow states access to maritime trade, natural resources such as oil, for example, or a strategic military location. At other times, political leaders may believe that people living in a foreign territory are actually members of the state's national community and that they are responsible for their well-being. In such territorial disputes the motivations for conflict are often intertwined and clouded. For example, the 2014 conflict between Ukraine and Russia was partially the result of an ethno-Russian movement within Crimea. At the beginning of the conflict a referendum—the authenticity of which was disputed by Ukraine and its allies—in the Crimean city of Sevastopol showed overwhelming support for the city's separation from Ukraine and absorption into the Russian Federation. Russia used this vote to bolster its claim that a majority of the people of Crimea saw themselves as Russian and that their wishes to be repatriated to Russia should be respected. However,

Russia also had territorial interests in Crimea, since Sevastopol is a key naval base for the Russian Black Sea Fleet. It has been further argued that the Crimea conflict was a small piece of a broader effort by Russia to assert its strategic influence in the region against moves by Ukraine to increase its economic ties with Europe.

While focus is often placed on conflicts between states, conflict over the last half century has frequently been between factions within states. Over the last 20 years, the majority of deaths due to conflict globally have occurred through internal wars or internal wars that have then been regionalized (that have begun within a single state but spilled over the state's borders to include warring factions from neighbouring states), and often in post-colonial states. In such cases, it is domestic conflict that has been the cause of insecurity. A primary source has been over control of the state itself, often referred to as **regime security**. Weak or fragile states that cannot provide citizens with the basic conditions to sustain a productive life or to secure the regime are especially susceptible to this type of insecurity. The 2014 surge in conflict in Iraq—which caused concerns about wider regional conflict and international involvement—arose over competing groups' attempts to gain control of the state. Secession movements, in which a group seeks to separate from the existing state and create an independent political structure on behalf of a given community, are a common source of such internal conflict. These movements create numerous forms of insecurity, from full-scale civil war (as was seen in the break-up of the former Yugoslavia) to the use of terrorist tactics (as in Northern Ireland or the Basque region of Spain). At its extreme, this type of ethno-nationalist conflict within a state can result in genocide, where one faction attempts to eradicate another group, often on the grounds of their ethnicity. The genocide of 800,000 Tutsis in Rwanda in 1994 is a clear and troubling example of this type of conflict.

> **Regime security:** Focuses on the stability of the government of a state. Challenges to regime security come from internal or external sources seeking to overthrow the existing government. Weak and failed states are particularly susceptible to regime insecurity.

Underlying many of these conflicts is the idea of nationalism. **Nationalism** is an ideology that is used by leaders to motivate members to support efforts to advance the nation and its interests. The nation reflects a shared set of ideas about who belongs to a particular community, and who is excluded. Such membership is built around the perception of common core characteristics, such as language, ethnicity, religion, and culture as well as shared territory and historical experiences. Members of the nation, with encouragement from their leaders, are often prepared to fight for its preservation. This may include defending the territory that they possess or fighting to acquire territory that they believe is rightfully theirs. It may also include efforts to protect members of the nation who reside in other states. Nationalism is therefore a very powerful tool that can be used by leaders to initiate and sustain conflict. Religion, sometimes used in conjunction with nationalism, is also a potent source of conflict, as can be seen in the partition of India and Pakistan, the Israel–Palestine conflict, and recent efforts to establish an Islamic State of Iraq and the Levant.

> **Nationalism:** An ideology used by state leaders to promote the interest of the nation, including defence of the state in times of war. Alternatively, it can be used by secession movements against the state. In the extreme, nationalism can be used to motivate ethnic cleansing and genocide. Nationalism has been a leading cause of conflict.

Regime insecurity and internal conflict have been central to the experiences of many former colonial states. As seen in Chapter 13, colonization often arbitrarily imposed an unsuitable model of the European state onto diverse communities. Colonial administrations were designed to facilitate the extraction of natural resources and often ensured that powerful local elites, who were unresponsive to the needs of those living in these territories, could quell dissent and ensure that access to natural resources remained unimpeded. Many of these colonies acquired independence as the decolonization movement took hold after the Second World War. However, rather than being a positive experience, independence often unlocked old conflicts and produced new forms of insecurity. Postcolonial states have been susceptible to authoritarian regimes that control internal dissent through force, often at the expense of human rights. These states have also regularly experienced revolution/counter-revolution as competing groups have sought to control the state. The Democratic Republic of Congo, which since independence in 1960 has suffered fierce ethnic conflict, multiple military coups, and the spillover of conflict with the neighbouring states of Uganda and Rwanda, is a prime example of the history and potential for conflict in post-colonial states. It has been estimated that the recent conflict has caused as many as six million deaths—nearly 10 percent of the population—as well as widespread human rights violations and war crimes.[2] External influences often further exacerbate these internal conflicts. For example, during the Cold War, the two superpowers frequently supported opposing sides in a number of conflicts in or between countries of the Global South. Driven by economic interests and access to resources like oil, powerful actors from the Global North continue to influence the internal affairs of post-colonial states, at times contributing to conflict and insecurity around the world today. In many cases, the trade in local commodities such as Colten or diamonds has fuelled conflict by providing funds for local combatants.

While traditional approaches to the study of security have focused on national territorial security, states have also understood security threats in other ways. For example, national economic security ensures that citizens have the resources and conditions to prosper, which in turn strengthens the state. Economic security could be threatened by unstable access to resources or markets in other countries, or as a result of an unpredictable trading regime. Against such uncertainties, states have been prepared to use military power to secure their economic interests. For example, the 1956 Suez Crises saw Britain and France invade Egypt after it nationalized the Suez Canal, a major shipping route between Europe and the Indian Ocean that had been controlled by Britain. Issues of economic security continue to exist in the region today. Piracy in the Gulf of Aden off the coast of Somalia has resulted in a large international military response by states seeking to protect the economic interests of businesses that use the waterway for commerce. The Gulf of Aden is a major international shipping lane through which a significant proportion of the world's trade flows. The cost of piracy, which includes the payment of ransoms, increased insurance premiums, and vessels' increased security or re-routing, have been considerable. The World Bank estimates that between 2005 and 2012, as much as $385 million

(U.S.) has been spent on ransoms for hijacked ships.[3] In response, major counter-piracy operations by the United States, Canada, and NATO as well as by China have been undertaken. In 2011, these operations have cost $1.27 billion (U.S.) collectively.[4] In total, the World Bank estimates that Somalia piracy costs the world economy $18 billion (U.S.) annually.[5]

The nature of insecurity has also changed in response to technological innovations. As a human race we have made remarkable advances in how we can do each other harm. The last century in particular has witnessed significant changes in our use of new technology in the pursuit of national security. In the First World War, new technologies sparked significant shifts in how warfare was conducted. The construction of a European rail system quickened the movement of soldiers and military supplies, increasing the speed of mobilization and the difficulty in stopping

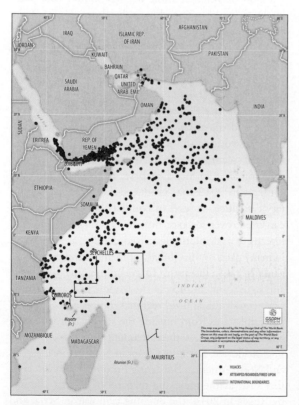

Somalia Piracy Hijackings and Attempted Hijackings (2000–2012).

The World Bank Regional Vice-Presidency for Africa. 2013. The Pirates of Somalia: Ending the Threat, Rebuilding a Nation. © International Bank for Reconstruction and Development/World Bank. http://siteresources.world-bank.org/INTAFRICA/Resources/pirates-of-somalia-main-report-web.pdf. License: Creative Commons Attribution license (CC BY 3.0 IGO)

the march to war. As well, mounted cavalry units gave way to armoured tanks, while the development of the airplane saw its application to warfare first in surveillance and then in aerial bombing. Even the widespread use of barbed-wire for the first time changed the face of conflict by contributing to trench warfare—a new and defining feature of 20th-century conflict. Similar innovations continued through to the end of the Second World War, culminating in the development of the atomic bomb.

The advent of nuclear weapons significantly altered the level of destruction that states could achieve in conflict. The first use of a nuclear bomb on the Japanese city of Hiroshima on August 6, 1945 was believed to be 2,000 times the strength of any previous detonation and was estimated to have killed between 60,000 and 80,000 people instantly. The eventual death toll from the blast is thought to have been as high as 135,000 people.[6] During the Cold War, the ability to use intercontinental ballistic missiles armed with nuclear devices to attack enemies on the other side of the globe contrasted sharply with the more contained battlefield tactics of previous wars. Although only five states possessed nuclear weapons by the mid-1960s, the existence of such weapons globalized conflict as the use of nuclear weapons would be catastrophic not just for the states involved but would have effects across the planet. As a result, nuclear technology changed relations between states, especially the United States and the Soviet Union, which became locked in an arms race driven by the perceived need to ensure that the enemy did not gain a nuclear advantage. States invested trillions of dollars to develop more powerful nuclear detonations, better delivery systems, and defensive systems to shield the state from nuclear attack. While fuelling inter-state rivalry, the fear of the awesome destructive power of this technology also prompted states to cooperate with one another, and resulted in several international treaties to limit testing, decrease nuclear warhead stockpiles, prevent the weaponization of space, and stop the spread of nuclear capabilities to non-nuclear states. Furthermore, the fear of mutually assured destruction through nuclear war may have restrained major conflict between the superpowers, helping to keep the Cold War from igniting into a hot war. Although the end of the Cold War lessened fears over nuclear war between states, these weapons continue to generate concerns amongst policymakers, especially with regards to nuclear proliferation.

In particular, there have been fears that states such as North Korea and Iran have acquired, or are in the process of acquiring, nuclear weapons, thus enhancing their military and political influence in unstable regions such as the Middle East. As well, there have been concerns about countries such as India and Pakistan, which are members of the nuclear club. Relations between these two states have been unstable for many years, raising fears of a nuclear arms race and perhaps even a nuclear conflict.

Technological innovations in warfare continue to be made. The increased use of drones over the last decade has been one of the most important developments and has raised vital questions about the methods used by states to ensure their security. Drones are unmanned, remotely controlled aircraft that have widespread applications, from environmental surveying to policing and border control. As a military tool, drones have evolved from surveillance and reconnaissance vehicles to surgical attack aircraft that can carry laser-guided "hellfire" missiles. The technical ability of drones is impressive. For example, nano-drones, such as the "black hornet" used by the British Army, are the size of a pop can and provide tactical reconnaissance to ground troops. Larger "reaper" drones can be controlled from anywhere in the world, removing the risk associated with deploying comparable military personnel in the field of combat. From high altitudes, undetected from the ground, these drones can be used to identify accurately and hit targets with less risk to surrounding populations than traditional attacks by piloted fighter jets. Despite these benefits, there is great unease concerning the use of drones. For some, there is an unfairness in the use of this technology, which can be used to kill without warning and from which there is little defence. However, it is not clear why drones are any less fair than the overwhelming force of other technologies of war. Critics also worry that the next step in the development of drones might be unmanned aerial "robot killers" that select their own targets. An October 2014 report of the Institute for Conflict, Cooperation and Security at the University of Birmingham argues that these robot killers would raise serious ethical question about how targets are selected and the oversight of these decisions.[7] Criticisms of the current use of drones often focus on the targeted killings of suspected terrorists. The United States in particular has rapidly increased its uses of drone strikes for such purposes in places like Yemen, where it is believed that as many as 902 militants have been killed, and Pakistan, where between 1,675–2,855 militants have been killed.[8] While drone technology arguably enables more efficient killings, the question of whether these killings should take place in the first place, outside a judicial process, is at the root of many concerns about these practices. It is clear that, like technological developments in the past, the rapid development of drone technology has presented decision-makers and societies more broadly with many new legal, ethical, and governance questions.

Despite the rise of a more integrated, globalized world, and the absence of a major global conflict like the two world wars or the Cold War, the focus on national security remains warranted. According to the Uppsala Conflict Database, there were 32 active conflicts in 2012 that produced around 38,000 military casualties—a level of conflict that has been fairly consistent over the past decade.[9] As suggested, regime insecurity and internationalized conflict are the norm in many parts of the Global South and are likely to continue to cause insecurity for years to come. There are also significant conflicts in the Middle East and Eurasia that could destabilize regional peace and entangle powerful states from outside the region. A rogue state like North Korea, with its frequent threat to develop a nuclear device, has raised fears in South Korea, Japan, and North America. Bordering Europe, significant conflict such as the annexing of parts of eastern Ukraine by Russia in 2014, the ongoing civil war in Syria, and the rise of ISIL have caused concerns among European leaders. While our experience of traditional warfare in North America has been limited, threats to international security and the potential for conflict remain prevalent and continue to demand serious attention.

U.S. Reaper Drone in Afghanistan 2007.
Staff Sgt. Brian Ferguso acquired from United States Air Force.

EXPLAINING NATIONAL SECURITY

The continued possibility of interstate conflict makes efforts to explain and prescribe ways to avoid conflict important. This is complicated, however, by the variety of factors that can lead to conflict and theories that point to different sources of conflict and insecurity. A common method of ordering these explanations is to look at three sources of conflict: at the international, the state, and the individual levels. Explanations that focus on the international level claim that it is the make-up and nature of the international system of states that causes conflict. One such explanation is found in the realist approach to International Relations. As explained in Chapter 15, realists maintain that states attempt to become as powerful as they can to ensure their security. States do this because they exist in an international system defined by **anarchy**, in which there is no higher authority that sovereign states can turn to when they need to resolve disputes or require protection from other states. This is unlike the domestic sphere of politics, where conflicts between citizens are managed by the state—through laws and institutions such as the police and the judiciary. In contrast, on the world stage, states operate in a context of continual uncertainty as to whether other states will harm their national interests or even outright conquer them. Under such conditions, the realist prescription for ensuring state security is captured in the advice of the 4th century Roman military strategist Vegetius, who stated "Si vis pacem, para bellum"— "if you want peace, prepare for war." Since no other state can be trusted to protect a given state's national interests, each state needs powerful militaries to protect itself. The pursuit of such power, however, produces a further problem—often called the **security dilemma**. This dilemma arises when state A's efforts to develop the resources to protect itself are perceived by state B as an aggressive act. In response, state B will try to increase its military might to become more secure. This, in turn, re-enforces state A's fear of state B and motivates state A to obtain even greater power. The perpetuation of this cycle fosters an arms race, as was seen during the Cold War. The dilemma, then, is that efforts to increase security can result in greater insecurity for each party.

Anarchy: A system of social, political, and economic relations without formal institutions of governance to define enforceable rules or exact obedience from the governed. Realist scholars use this term to characterize the international system, where there is no authority above the state that can solve interstate conflict. Anarchy does not mean chaos.

Security dilemma: A situation that arises from the belief that the global system is anarchic. In such a system, states feel compelled to ensure their own security by increasing their military power. This, in turn, is likely to encourage other states, as a defensive response, to increase their own military capacities. This can generate an arms race, in which each state tries to gain enough strength to defend against the other, which is trying to accomplish the same goal. Thus, the dilemma is that a state's attempt to secure itself leads to its own greater insecurity.

Realists are not the only theorists who focus on the international level to explain the sources of insecurity. Within liberal approaches to International Relations, there are arguments that the condition of anarchy can be overcome by creating international laws and institutions that constrain conflict between states, akin to what occurs at the domestic level. In another approach, Alexander Wendt, a constructivist scholar, suggests that the condition of anarchy does not have to produce fear and conflict between states. Instead, he proposes that the international system can be altered by interaction between states, which can lead to states learning to trust each other, cooperate, and thereby manage to resolve conflicts peacefully.

A second set of explanations suggests that conflict is caused by the characteristics of states and the politics within them. Factors such as secession movements, ethnic conflict, and regime change all fit within this state-level explanation of the causes of war. Another prominent state-level explanation has been offered by advocates of the **Democratic Peace Theory**, who argue that it is the particular system of government of the state that makes it more or less likely that it will go to war. This theory points to the fact that since the early 1900s no longstanding liberal democracy has fought a war with another liberal democracy. Different domestic factors are used to explain this fact. For example, it is argued that leaders in liberal democracies need to consider the interests of their citizens in order to get voted into office, and that those citizens generally prefer that leaders avoid wars which lead to citizen casualties and the disruption daily life. Democratic leaders also usually have to consult with other actors—especially legislative bodies—before going to war, which slows down decision-making and the rush to war. In contrast, leaders of authoritarian states need not be as concerned about the impact of war on their citizens and are less constrained by other political institutions. There are criticisms of the Democratic Peace Theory. For instance, critics argue that the evidence used by the approach is overstated. Canada and Australia have not gone to war with one another, but this might just as likely be explained by the vast geographic distance between them rather than their systems of government. Furthermore, over the last century there have been so few liberal democracies that it is difficult to draw the conclusion that democracies produce peace. Finally, the theory does not suggest that liberal democracies are less war-prone. For instance, there is evidence that publics in liberal democracies at times push for war and reward leaders who enter into conflict with non-democracies. A "rally around the flag" effect was seen in the case of British Prime Minister Margret Thatcher, whose leadership in the 1982 Falklands war with Argentina resulted in an increase of popular support that helped her to win the 1983 general election. Thus, it is clear that peace is not necessarily produced by publics who want peace, as the theory suggests. Nonetheless, the Democratic Peace Theory has been used in support of policies that push for the spread of democracy and it provides a good example of a state-level explanation of war.

> **Democratic peace theory:** A theory that explains why democratic states do not go to war with one another. This theory fits within a liberal approach to international politics in emphasizing domestic characteristics of the state—democratic institutions.

Other explanations point neither to the international system nor the characteristics of states but rather to individual leaders. Scholars studying individuals as a source of conflict point to the importance of individual-level decision-making that may be influenced by misperception, miscommunication, and poor information

as potential factors that lead to international conflict. Such factors affect both authoritarian and democratic leaders, who in periods of crisis have extraordinary powers to direct a country into conflict. Other scholars point to the personal characteristics of leaders, such as their beliefs or ambitions, that might contribute to their propensity to engage in war. For example, Adolf Hitler's leadership is often cited as a leading cause of the Second World War. Although there were other precipitating causes, such as the settlement of the First World War, which put very difficult conditions on the German state, it was Hitler's ambition and willingness to pursue conflict that led to the war. Explanations of the 2003 Iraqi War also point to the actions of individual leaders, especially Presidents Saddam Hussein and George W. Bush, which created the conditions that led to war. In contrast, the leadership of President John F. Kennedy and Soviet Premier Nikita Khrushchev have been credited with averting nuclear conflict during the 1962 Cuban Missile Crisis. In each of these examples, the decisions of powerful leaders are understood as being important in explaining the causes of conflict, as well as its avoidance.

9/11, GLOBALIZATION, AND NEW THREATS TO NATIONAL SECURITY: TERRORISM, INTERNATIONAL CRIMINAL NETWORKS, AND CYBER THREATS

New and evolving threats, especially global terrorism, ensure that national security remains a continuing preoccupation for states. Although there has been difficulty finding agreement on how to define terrorism, it is often identified by the tactic, frequently used by non-state actors, of targeting civilians or symbolic targets with the goal of provoking fears in a wider audience of a future attack. Terrorists hope that this tactic will achieve certain political goals. For example, the 2004 attacks on four Spanish commuter trains, which killed 191 people and injured 1,800 more, were conducted by terrorists who wanted Spanish troops to leave Iraq. Shortly after, and following intense popular pressure, a newly elected Spanish government quickly removed Spanish troops from Iraq. While terrorism is generally seen as a tactic used by weaker actors, there are arguments that states also use terror-like tactics to instil fear in their own populations as a means of control, or in foreign states to pressure them to alter their behaviour.

As a tactic of conflict, terrorism is not new and continues to be used routinely in many conflicts globally. However, the use of terrorism at the international level has become a significant feature of states' security concerns over the course of the last 30 years. The 9/11 attacks, like the two world wars and the Cold War, were a defining moment in global politics, one that has had effects far beyond their initial impact. Several factors contribute to their importance. First, in comparison to most single terrorist events, these attacks killed a large number of people. More importantly, they did this while being broadcast live around the world; as individuals fell from the World Trade Towers, a global audience witnessed these events in real time. However, most significant was the fact that the attacks took place on American soil. Previously, the United States— despite its active involvement in conflict globally—had not suffered, with the exception of Pearl Harbor, from large-scale foreign attacks on its own territory. The realization that it was vulnerable to the effects of global conflict, despite its immense power, sparked fear and refocused Americans' attention on terrorism and the country's insecurity in the 21st century. In response, the most powerful state in the global system sought to secure its citizens through an aggressive foreign policy that sparked wars in Afghanistan and Iraq, as well as the pursuit of terrorists in an ill-defined global war on terrorism. As we will see later in the chapter, fear of terrorism has also produced significant changes in how the American government pursues security domestically. For many, the responses to 9/11 have been seen as a failure rather than a success and have produced a more insecure global system. Indeed, it has been suggested that the rise of ISIL in 2014 is partially the result of the invasion of Iraq in 2003. Thus, the attacks of 9/11 can be seen to have created, for many, greater insecurity and a less stable international system.

Apart from terrorism, there are many other transnational sources of insecurity for states, such as internationalized criminal networks. Crimes such as money laundering, drug or human trafficking, and counterfeiting are undertaken by criminals who do not respect borders and who operate beyond them as it suits their needs. These actors have significant financial motivations. Although difficult to calculate (given the hidden nature of such transactions), recent estimates of the global markets of trafficking (drugs and human) and counterfeiting, the two largest illegal activities, put the value at around $602 billion (U.S.).[10] The networked nature of international crime is clearly evident in the case of human trafficking, in which numerous criminal organizations often perform different tasks across the globe in moving an individual from one part of the world to another. At the point of origin, criminals lure, buy, or kidnap victims to be trafficked while others provide false travel documents. Operating across borders, different criminal organizations may be used to transport victims or bribe border officials. Once in the destination state, a new set of criminals might conceal, control, and exploit the victims. Central to the expansion of international criminal activity is the ability of these networks to use global spaces to expand their markets and circumvent state control. In response, states have been less effective in combating these activities, inhibited by jurisdictional boundaries and a hesitation to cooperate at the international level.

Threats to state interests have also arisen out of an increased reliance on electronic data and communications. This dependence was first widely demonstrated with Y2K at the end of the 20th century, when many believed that a computer programming glitch would result in global disruptions. This fear provoked both widespread concerns and considerable private and state investment in efforts to solve the problem. Either through this preparation or because of an overstatement of the problem, Y2K did not have significant effects. However, concerns over cyber-security have only increased since then. Vital government operations pertaining to everyday activities as well as areas such as defence and security, alongside the systems employed by private sector actors, are all vulnerable to cyber-attacks from both state and non-state actors. Such threats are difficult for states to assess because the degree of vulnerability is generally not clear, especially given the rapid evolution of technology. It is also often hard to determine who is perpetrating a given attack. The complexity of cyber threats can be seen in the different types of attacks that have occurred. For instance, in April 2014, the Royal Canadian Mounted Police arrested a teenager in an alleged cyber-attack that forced Canada's online tax collection system to shut down for five days. In 2011, a cyber-attack raised worries that sensitive information from the Department of Finance, the Treasury Board, and the Defence Research and Development Canada Agency had been stolen by international hackers. In 2009–2010, "Stuxnet," a computer virus allegedly developed by the Israeli and U.S. governments, was used in a cyber-attack on Iran, causing extensive damage to its nuclear program.[11] In the fall of 2014, the protest movement Anonymous used cyber-attacks to access the KluKluxKlan's twitter account and to "unhood" (make public) the identities and online activities of alleged Klan members.

Cyber-activities like these have raised more questions about the control of the Internet. For some, groups such as Anonymous should be seen as an online protest movement—or "hacktivist"—that uses cyber-attacks to draw attention to issues and to effect wider change. However, Anonymous often acts outside of established legal systems and has targeted states and corporations around the globe, leading national and international security organizations to argue that members of Anonymous represent a global security threat. Beyond cyber-attacks, the Internet has also been used by organizations like Wikileaks—driven by a belief that publics have a right to know about the secret activities of their states—to collect and disseminate large amounts of information damaging to state interests. Wikileaks allows individuals to upload documents anonymously to its website, which are then made available to the public. Tens of thousands of secret military,

intelligence, and diplomatic documents have been published by the organization to date. Cyber-attacks and the importance of the Internet as a platform of domestic and global politics have made states increasingly aware of the need to address cyber-security as part of their national security focus.

International terrorism, criminal networks, and cyber-attacks are significant not only because of the harm that they do but also because they directly challenge the state's ability to control its borders and provide security for its citizens, two of the central functions of sovereign states. Moisés Naím, a renowned international columnist, former Venezuelan Minister of Trade and Industry, and executive director of the World Bank, has argued that international criminal networks and terrorists, spurred on by globalization, provide a particular challenge to the state because they are flexible and unconstrained by the same rules that dictate how states must act in international relations.[12] Furthermore, while traditional national security threats could often be attributed to other states or fairly well-defined groups, new threats often come from within, across, and beyond borders and are perpetrated by both state and non-state actors. The globalized nature of these threats renders them post-territorial (going beyond the traditional system of states), which makes it very difficult for states to locate sources of insecurity and develop responses to them. As a result, states have in part altered their security focus from the protection of territorial borders to internal security threats that originate from beyond the state. This focus on **public safety** encompasses not only threats to national security but also broader threats to public health, water and food, as well as the impacts of natural disasters.

THINK AND DISCUSS

For many, the freedom of the Internet has clashed with state efforts to control it in what they perceive to be the interest of protecting the state and its citizens. Should states be allowed to limit individuals' freedom and the activities of organizations like Wikileaks or Anonymous on the Internet in the name of protecting state security?

Public safety: An environment that is obtained when citizens can go about their lives secure from major disruptions to society and unthreatened by crime and violence. Public safety often focuses on the internal security of the state. Threats to public safety come from a variety of sources, including natural disasters, systemic failure of national economic infrastructure, civil unrest, terrorism, and widespread threats to public health.

INSECURITY AND DOMESTIC POLITICS

The pursuit of national security raises important political questions. One relates to the balance between the uses of resources to ensure national security and the potential that these resources could be put toward other national interests such as healthcare, education, and infrastructure. In the post-9/11 period, the United States has committed vast resources to its international efforts to pursue its security. According to the Cost of War Project conducted by the Watson Institute for International Studies at Brown University, the United States had spent $3.7 trillion on wars in Iraq and Afghanistan/Pakistan by 2011, while the cost of medical and disability claims of American veterans from the Afghanistan and Iraq campaigns had reached $134.7 billion by 2013.[13] In 2011, 20 percent, or $718 billion, of the total budget of the United States went to defence and security operations.[14] While this number is set to decline, with a $575 billion expenditure for security projected in 2015,[15] the country's financial commitment to security remains very high. Some have questioned the need for these expenditures and have suggested that the United States' budgetary crisis and ailing economy has been exacerbated if not caused by the cost of it security commitments. Others, however, maintain that in an increasingly insecure and unpredictable world, the United States needs to spend even more to ensure its security both at home and abroad. While Canada spends considerably less than the United States, its security spending in the decade after the attacks of 9/11 also increased significantly. One estimate suggests that defence spending doubled while public security spending tripled over pre-9/11 levels, resulting in an additional $92 billion than what would have been spent if pre-9/11 levels had been maintained.[16]

The costs of security go beyond the financial commitments of states. The defence of the state often involves, and can be weighed against, the costs borne by its citizens. Most starkly this trade-off is demonstrated in wartime, when it is believed that the pursuit of national interests justifies the loss of citizens' lives. However, as we will see later in this chapter, the pursuit of security also compromises individual liberties as people are often asked to give up rights—such as the right not to have their communications monitored by the state—in the name of increased security.

Central to the politics of security are efforts to convince publics that the costs of providing security is necessary and worth it. This raises a difficult question of risk, which underlies many of these debates. Insecurity is often based on speculation about the risk of certain threats to national security. Agreeing what constitutes a risk is difficult, especially with respect to new and emerging sources of insecurity. Donald Rumsfeld, United States Secretary of Defence from 2001 to 2006, famously captured this problem when explaining the Bush administration's concerns over connections between Iraq and the potential use of WMDs by terrorists. In speaking of this threat, he claimed that there were "known unknowns; that is to say we know there are some things we do not know. But there are also unknown unknowns—the ones we don't know we don't know."[17] For Rumsfeld this uncertainty and its associated risks helped to justify American intervention in Iraq, although we now know that Iraq did not possess WMD and had no connections to the 9/11 attacks. The unclear definition of the risk that states face makes security difficult to achieve. Open-ended understandings of risk may provoke political leaders to overreact in ways that increase insecurity. Indeed, from another perspective, explored later in the chapter, leaders may manipulate and unnecessarily raise fears in order to justify receiving additional powers or to use extra-ordinary security measures that themselves produce insecurities. The spectre of insecurity can also be used to shut down debate about how to respond to the perception of insecurity. Politicians opposed to increased security measures find it difficult to argue against these as the public might see them as weak or irresponsible on national security issues, especially in periods of perceived heightened insecurity. Furthermore, no politician wants to risk being held responsible for serious breaches of security if they were to take place. Increasingly, the rise in the perceived risk of new threats to public safety and national security require state leaders to walk a fine line between doing too much to protect their population and the possibility that they have done too little. One final problem of the unclear nature of the risk of insecurity is that it makes it very difficult to know when we are indeed secure. Even when threats may be very low, the potential of an attack can make us feel insecure and may require that we are always on our guard.

Human Security

Changes have taken place in the study of security in global politics that move the focus away from the state and national security. An important example of this change began in 1994, when the United Nations Development Program (UNDP) asked states to consider the issue of **human security**. Human security answers the question of "who is security for" differently than a traditional emphasis on national security. Rather than centring on the state, concerns about human security focus primarily on the individual, who—particularly outside times of war—feels insecurity differently than states. The 1994 *Human Development Report* of the UNDP captured this shift, declaring that:

> For too long, the concept of security has been shaped by the potential for conflict between states. For too long, security has been equated with the threats to a country's borders. For too long, nations have sought arms to protect their borders.
>
> For most people today, a feeling of insecurity arises more from worries about daily life than from the dread of a cataclysmic world event. Job security, income security, health security, environmental security, security from crime— these are the emerging concerns of human security all over the world.[18]*

Human security is premised on the idea that individuals should experience daily life free from the threat of personal violence and with the resources to pursue a healthy and fulfilled existence. The UNDP lists seven dimensions of security that individuals should experience: economic, food, health, environmental, community, personal, and political. The threats to these aspects of security can be very specific and acute, such as fears of persecution due to one's political beliefs, race, religion, or sexual orientation, or the fear of becoming a victim of crime. However, human security is also undermined by broader underlying conditions. Factors such as poverty, environmental degradation, economic collapse, and the lack of access to education all can undermine an individual's security.

> **Human security:** Reflects a focus on the security of the individual. Security concerns are defined broadly and fall primarily into one of two categories: freedom from threats of violence to the individual, and freedom from poverty and hunger that limit an individual's ability to reach their potential. Although linked, human security is often contrasted with national security.

The focus on human security reflects the empirical realities of insecurity globally. As has been seen, global conflict continues to threaten not just states but the security of many people around the world. However, while the deaths and potential for death from conflict are great, causes of death and suffering that stem from sources identified by the human security approach are a more regular and continual source of insecurity for individuals. Take, for instance, the issue of hunger. Statistics provided by the United Nations World Food Program show that 795 million people, predominantly in the Global South, survive on less food than they require. Indeed, one out of six children globally is underweight and 3.1 million children die annually because of malnutrition.[19]

A different conception of security also requires different responses than are found in traditional security studies. Proposed solutions to human insecurity are multiple and complex, and raise many problems of development in the Global South that have been surveyed in Chapter 13. As with underdevelopment, there are competing explanations of insecurity. Many proposed solutions from the international community include, amongst other ideas, supporting vulnerable populations by providing states with the capacity

---

* United Nations Development Programme, *Human Development Report 1994* (New York: Oxford University Press, 1994), p. 3.

to meet the needs of their constitutive populations, addressing climate change and other environmental problems, finding agreement on and protecting human rights, and increasing access to clean drinking water and medicines to cure and prevent disease. Such solutions require reforming the way we govern ourselves at the global level. Reform is needed in the structures of global governance to ensure that the interests of states in the Global South are expressed and reflected in the actions of powerful global institutions such as the World Bank and the World Trade Organization. For many, this includes supporting the participation of states from the Global South in the global economy by ensuring that market access for the goods that they produce is fair. For instance, one important step would be to end agricultural subsidies that protect actors in the Global North from competition and which prevents states in the Global South from profiting in areas of agricultural production in which they have a clear advantage.

Such international cooperation, however, has been difficult to achieve. Powerful actors rarely agree on the sources of human insecurity and, even if they did, there is often little incentive (at least in terms of their immediate perceived self-interest) for them to find solutions to these problems. Furthermore, states in the Global North have been inclined to overlook their own role in creating these insecurities. Indeed, a common counterargument is that human insecurity is primarily caused by unstable and corrupt authoritarian regimes in the Global South. The case of Nigeria, which possesses the natural resources to be a very strong economic power, is indicative of this problem. In 2012, the country ranked fifth in the world in export of crude oil.[20] At the same time, it ranked 153rd on the **Human Development Index**, a commonly used marker of human security that includes indicators such as life expectancy, literacy, and access to healthcare to measure and rank citizens' quality of life.[21] This discrepancy between resources and human security has occurred in part because of domestic corruption in the oil industry and government. The 2013 Transparency International report on corruption ranked Nigeria 144th,[22] placing it among the most corrupt countries globally. However, Nigeria's problems are not simply of its own making. A long history of colonization, superpower interference during the Cold War, poor lending practices by international banks, and destructive

engagement by international companies competing for natural resources in the country have all contributed to the deeper problems faced by the Nigerian people. This underscores the complex causes of human insecurity, and the difficulty in designing and implementing effective solutions to them.

> **Human Development Index (HDI):** Measures development in terms of not only a country's national income but other factors such as life expectancy, educational attainment, and gender equality.

While the substantial reforms necessary to address human insecurity seem unlikely to emerge in the near future, some efforts have been made in this area. International organizations such as the UN and many of its sub-organizations such as the UNDP and the United Nations International Children's Emergency Fund (UNICEF) have made significant attempts to deal with different aspects of human security. The UNDP in particular monitors the sources of insecurity, develops policies to address these, and supports the work of other agencies to increase human security. One of the most ambitious UN undertakings has been the establishment of the Millennium Project in 2002, which created eight Millennium Development Goals (MDGs) with quantifiable measures that were to be met by 2015. The eight goals are the eradication of extreme poverty and hunger; universal primary education; the promotion of gender equality; the reduction of child mortality; improvement of maternal health; combating of HIV/AIDS, malaria and other diseases; promoting environmental sustainability; and developing global partnerships to promote development.[23]

The Millennium Project's eight Millennium Development Goals (MDGs)
UNDP Brazil

While these goals are unlikely to be met by the original 2015 target, and although results have varied across different countries and regions, there has been important success in reducing the insecurity of many. For example, in the case of improving maternal health, a MDG which the Canadian government has prioritized since 2010, there have been marked improvements, including a 47 percent reduction in maternal mortality from 1990 levels.[24] Supporters of the MDGs would also point to the fact that by working to meet these specific goals the international community has established a focused international process through which broader goals of human security can continue to be pursued. Efforts to address human security have also been aided by non-governmental organizations (NGOs) such as Oxfam and Human Rights Watch. Among other activities, such NGOs have raised public awareness about the causes of human insecurity and the need for action, motivating publics and providing them with channels to address these issues either by lobbying governments or by making donations to programs that directly alleviate the sources of human insecurity.

While it is useful to highlight human insecurity as a distinct concern, national security and human security are often linked. States that are unable or unwilling to provide for their people often produce the conditions that result in instability and violent conflict. Similarly, conflict itself leads to conditions of human insecurity. In contrast, individuals who feel secure may be more likely to contribute to secure and prosperous states that in turn have the capacity to foster the conditions for human security. The strength of the human security approach is that it expands our focus and highlights important sources of insecurity that are overlooked by a traditional focus on national security. A difficulty arises, however, from the fact that while we might be more aware of the causes of human insecurity, possible solutions go to the core of some of the most substantial problems of global politics.

HUMANITARIAN INTERVENTION

The need to address human security has at times presented the international community with the difficult question of whether it should intervene in the internal affairs of states. As the name suggests, the motive of **humanitarian intervention** should be aimed at

relieving the suffering of a population rather than fulfilling the self-interest of an intervening state. The most intrusive form of intervention is humanitarian military intervention, whereby the international community attempts to use military force to stop conflict, protect populations from being displaced, provide military protection for efforts to distribute aid, and stop crimes against humanity, human rights abuses, and/or genocide. The mandate of humanitarian intervention is broader, more complicated, and more active than the traditional peacekeeping approach used in the Cold War period, when the international community was invited to monitor peace settlements after a given conflict had ended.

> **Humanitarian intervention:** Intervention in the affairs of another state for the purposes of resolving a humanitarian concern. While humanitarian intervention may take a number of forms, the most controversial is intervention that contravenes state sovereignty and that applies the use of force to accomplish its goals.

Starting in the early 1990s, emboldened by the end of the Cold War and the growing sense of interconnectedness that came with globalization, the international community became increasingly willing to undertake such interventions. Most prominent amongst these were the military interventions to protect the delivery of humanitarian aid to the people of war-torn Somalia in 1992 and to prevent ethnic cleansing in the former Yugoslavia from 1992 to 1995. While these interventions were criticised extensively in the end, and even though the early enthusiasm for intervention has more recently waned, intervention continues to be an important question that the international community struggles with in countries such as Libya and Syria. In the latter case, violations of human rights, such as the reported use of chemical weapons on Syrians by the al-Assad regime, could have been used to justify military intervention by the international community.

Interventions are viewed as more legitimate when they are undertaken by the international community—which, it can be argued, has certain obligations and/or powers with respect to threatened populations under the United Nations Charter and other international treaties and laws. A difficult issue of humanitarian intervention lies in determining when the international community has an obligation to intervene, especially when it is against the will of the target state. The international state system is premised on the principle of state sovereignty; that the internal affairs of states should not be meddled in by external actors. Sovereignty, codified in Article 2.7 of the UN Charter, has never been absolute in practice, with states regularly experiencing interference from beyond their borders. However, the increased interest in humanitarian intervention has given rise to calls for more explicit guidelines outlining when and how the international community can override sovereignty to ensure the safety of people within a state. At the end of the 1990s, the international community, through the International Committee on Intervention and State Sovereignty, began to rethink these conditions, leading to the creation of the **Responsibility to Protect (R2P)** doctrine adopted by the UN in 2005. This doctrine challenges traditional understandings of state sovereignty and has been used to argue that sovereignty entails not only a state's right to non-interference but also its responsibilities, especially with respect to the protection of its citizens. Glyn Berry, former Minister-Counsellor to the United Nations and the first civilian Canadian official to be killed in the recent Afghanistan campaign, captured this commitment clearly in arguing that "No state, government, or institution has a legitimate rationale for its existence apart from the interests of the individual human beings for whose benefit they are supposed to act."[25] Under R2P, in cases where mass crimes against humanity, ethnic cleansing, or genocide are being committed by a state, or the state does not have the capacity to stop these from occurring, the state's claim to non-interference is overridden and the international community is obligated to intervene to protect the population.

Responsibility to Protect (R2P): A doctrine adopted by the United Nations in 2005 that places an obligation on the international community to intervene in the affairs of states to stop serious human rights violations and crimes against humanity. Thus, R2P refocuses sovereignty, placing an increased onus on the state to ensure the security of its members, not just to protect its own interests.

Despite the development of R2P, wide international backing for interventions has been difficult to obtain. For instance, in February 2012, Russian and Chinese vetoes prevented the United Nations Security Council from passing a resolution condemning the violence in Syria, never mind finding agreement on whether intervention was necessary. As a result, intervention is often carried out by particular states or alliances of states that agree upon the circumstances that require intervention. For example, the North Atlantic Treaty Organization (NATO), an alliance originating in the Cold War that consists of predominantly western European and North American states, has undertaken intervention on its own, as in the case of Kosovo in 1999. At other times, interventions that do not have the backing of the United Nations, such as the 2003 invasion of Iraq, have been led by powerful states such as the United States and the United Kingdom. For the United States, the 2003 Iraq war was primarily motivated by the claim that regional and international security required that Iraq be prevented from acquiring WMDs or passing such technology on to terrorist organizations. For Tony Blair, then prime minister of the United Kingdom, it was also an invasion that would address humanitarian concerns raised by Saddam Hussein's mistreatment of the Iraqi people. Many, however, did not accept these justifications and argued that the war was not a humanitarian intervention but rather an attempt by the United States, and to an extent the United Kingdom, to pursue their own national security and resource interests in the region.

The case of Iraq highlights a frequently used criticism of humanitarian intervention: that it is actually not very humanitarian at all but instead a façade for self-interested acts, such as stabilizing a region to suit a strategic military, economic, or resource objective. The role of self-interest has also been used to criticize non-intervention, as with the Rwandan genocide in 1994 and the heightened crisis in Darfur beginning in 2003, where action was necessary but not forthcoming. This point has been made by Lieutenant-General Roméo Dallaire, the Canadian leader of UN forces in Rwanda and later a Canadian senator, whose calls for action to the international community at the beginning of the Rwanda genocide were not answered. Dallaire has argued that at its heart, the Rwandan story is the story of the failure of humanity to heed a call for help from an endangered people. The international community, of which the UN is only a symbol, failed to move beyond self-interest for the sake of Rwanda. While most nations agreed that something should be done, they all had an excuse why they should not be the ones to do it. As a result, the UN was denied the political will and material means to prevent tragedy.[26]*

In such cases the failure to intervene and protect vulnerable populations in real need has been attributed to the belief that a region possesses no strategic interest and therefore the international community will not act. This has led some to argue that humanitarian intervention, especially by the Global North, in the affairs of states in the Global South reflects a form of neo-imperialism, whereby powerful states establish a system of engagement with weaker states to serve their own interests and in a manner that exploits those weaker states.

As in the case of war, states make strategic decisions about intervening based on the potential costs and domestic impact. Interventions are very expensive and require considerable resources that states could use to address the needs of their own citizens. Military intervention also often results in casualties that politicians must justify to their citizens. This leads to difficult political and ethical questions, such as how many of a state's own citizens should be sacrificed to save the lives of others? Furthermore, undertaking humanitarian intervention is never straightforward. The mandates often change during the mission as leaders respond to challenges on the ground. At times it is unclear under what conditions a humanitarian intervention can be deemed successful, and when an exit from the campaign is feasible. As a result, interventions are often extended in ways that increase the costs and diminish public support. Leaders contemplating intervention need to be prepared to address these issues and respond to increasingly attentive publics who might not be willing to support such costs. This was the case for the British public, who at the height of the Syrian crisis in August 2013 pressured politicians to vote against a government motion to

send British troops to support an intervention. Thus, even if the international community accepts a responsibility to protect, states may not be willing or able to back such action.

In addition, there is the important question of whether humanitarian intervention is effective or whether it exacerbates existing problems. Tragedies, like the massacre of Srebrenica during the Yugoslavian conflict, damaged the international community's reputation to intervene effectively. In July 1995, Bosnian Serb forces captured the city of Srebrenica and killed over 8,000 unarmed Bosniak men and boys.[27] Prior to the massacre, the United Nations had declared Srebrenica a "safe area" where Muslim Bosniaks, who took shelter by the thousands, would be protected by UN forces. Despite this promise, the ill-equipped UN peacekeepers were unable to prevent Bosnian Serb forces from taking the city. In fact, several thousand Bosniaks who had fled Srebrenica to a nearby Dutch UN peacekeeping compound were turned over to Serbian forces as the massacre took place.

The 1992–1995 UN intervention in Somalia is another prominent example of a more generalized failure of intervention. Initially undertaken to provide humanitarian aid, the rise in internal fighting between local militias led to increased international military engagement in an effort to create conditions under which aid could be delivered. This military engagement reached a critical point in the summer of 1993, when 24 Pakistani peacekeepers were killed by members of a leading militia. In response, the international community, led by the United States, sought to capture those responsible for the attacks. This resulted in a further crisis for the international force when, in October 1993, 18 American soldiers were killed after two American Black Hawk helicopters were shot down in Mogadishu, the capital of Somalia. These events led to the withdrawal of American troops and then the United Nations from Somalia, with no improvement in security for Somalis as a result of the intervention. Although undertaken with good intentions, the intervention in Somalia starkly revealed the new challenges of making peace in the face of difficult and evolving conditions on the ground.

Not all interventions, however, are necessarily military. Indeed, more often than not, other forms of

---

* Roméo Dallaire, "Rwandan Genocide: The Failure of Humanity," online at http://www.romeodallaire.com.

intervention such as monitoring, diplomacy, or sanctions are used. In the case of the ongoing Syrian crisis, the international community has undertaken diplomatic intervention to pressure the state to change its behaviour toward its own citizens and find a negotiated solution. This has included numerous diplomatic efforts such as high-level diplomatic meetings with former UN Secretary General Kofi Annan and pressure from the Arab League—an important international organization representing many Arab states from North Africa and the Middle East. In addition, sanctions, a more intrusive method of intervention, have been used to pressure the Syrian leadership.

Non-military intervention can also be undertaken by non-state actors such as prominent individuals, journalists, and NGOs whose goals are to address a variety of humanitarian needs. For instance, human rights groups can raise awareness of human rights violations by monitoring and reporting on abuses perpetrated within a state, in the hope that the international community will put pressure on the government. In the case of the Syrian crises, in addition to UN monitoring of the situation, organizations such as the Red Cross and Doctors without Borders as well as members of the media have reported on events and called for action against the al-Assad regime.

Intervention today seems to have arrived at a problematic intersection. On the one hand, the international community has developed the principle of R2P, which highlights its obligations and provides tools to circumvent the traditional role of sovereignty in impeding intervention. On the other hand, recent history demonstrates how difficult interventions can be in practice, which undermines the willingness of states to participate. Publics in particular have become increasingly prepared to scrutinize the decisions of their leaders in terms of the costs, effectiveness, and justifications for military humanitarian intervention. Moving forward, in the face of serious threats to human security around the world, intervention remains an important option that the international community should be prepared to use. However, ways need to be found to increase the rates of success. Ultimately, the most effective solutions—also highlighted in the R2P doctrine—might be to prevent the conditions that lead to the need for intervention from arising in the first place.

CRITICAL APPROACHES TO SECURITY

The expansion of our understanding of security, represented by the case of human security, has been helped by the rise of critical academic approaches to the study of International Relations that challenge core assumptions about security. While these critical approaches vary in their treatment of security, there are some underlying similarities. First, like those who adopt a human security approach, they expand the analysis to consider the insecurity of individuals and groups—based on characteristics such as economic class, gender, ethnicity, and religion—who are marginalized in the state and international system. Second, they recognize that the state, rather than providing security, can itself be a source of insecurity for its own citizens. Third, they share an interest in security discourse—the way actors talk about security. For critical security scholars, it is the labelling of a problem as a threat to security that often makes it a threat. In turn, the fear raised by this discourse provokes security responses that exceed the original problem and can be used more widely to shape and control society. Finally, critical approaches suggest that discourse and practices around the issue of security predominately reflect the interests of powerful actors at the expense of less powerful and more vulnerable actors. In these ways, critical scholars draw attention to and challenge dominant understandings of security studies in the hope of changing them.

The possibility that the state can be a source of insecurity for individuals is a central feature of these critical approaches. For instance, critical scholars fear that a state's pursuit of security may compromise individual rights. Recent criticisms of anti-terrorism and border security policies are indicative of these concerns. For instance, the use of torture at Guantanamo Bay in the post-9/11 period raised the question: is it justifiable to torture a suspected terrorist if the information obtained could prevent another terrorist attack? While the information might provide security, torture violates individual rights and personal security. Extraordinary measures that extended beyond Guantanamo—such as increased government surveillance, arbitrary arrest, and rendition—justified by the need to protect the state, produced considerable insecurity in a much wider community.

Advances in modern security technologies have given states and other powerful actors immense and unprecedented resources to identify, profile, track, and control individuals. A 2008 report of *The Sunday Telegraph* estimated that the average citizen of the United Kingdom had their personal information recorded 3,254 times each week. In a day, that same citizen was likely to be captured on closed-circuit television over 300 times.[28] Not all such surveillance is undertaken by the state but states have been very active in pursuing new technologies for security purposes. One important example involves the use of biometrics, "a measurable, physical characteristic or personal behavioural trait used to recognize the identity or verify the claimed identity [of a person]."[29] Biometric indicators include facial and voice recognition, fingerprints, and the gait of an individual's walk. States also employ advanced techniques to track wireless and electronic communications. The potential intrusiveness of these technologies was seen in the Ontario Government's 2007 proposal to embed wireless technology in provincial driver's licences, which would emit the card holder's personal information to external readers. In another case, the Canadian state, in a trial run and citing the protection of Canadians, has used free Internet services at major Canadian airports to tag mobile electronic devices and trace them as they move across the country.[30] The advantage of these technologies is that they have the capacity to collect and read information related to an individual without direct interaction, and that they can do this for large groups of people simultaneously. The information generated by these technologies allows states to identify and track suspected threats and concentrate security resources in areas where they are considered to have the most impact.

Although very efficient, this kind of technology runs the risk that state actors might misuse the information, discriminating against certain individuals or groups. Those identified as threats may have done nothing wrong and may not be aware that they are being monitored. Furthermore, the suspicions upon which such surveillance is initiated may reflect a state or society's prevailing fears and prejudices. In the aftermath of the 9/11 attacks, for example, Muslim communities in the United States were targeted by the state and monitored using these types of technologies. Like other states, Canada has also compromised individual rights in the pursuit of national security. One of the most public cases was that of Maher Arar, a Syrian-born Canadian who was intercepted in New York on his way home to Canada in September 2002. American officials, believing that he was associated with Al-Qaeda, sent him to Syria, where he was tortured and detained despite his Canadian citizenship. A subsequent public inquiry found that Canadian security officials had passed along misleading information that might have prompted American officials to deport Arar to Syria. In 2007, Canadian Prime Minister Stephen Harper publically apologized for Canada's mistreatment of Arar. While the potential for misuse is greatest for vulnerable communities, all citizens run the risk that their rights might be affected by these technologies.

The misuse of these technologies is all the more likely in a context in which fear justifies their use. As a result, critical security approaches point to the importance of the effects of discourse on security. They argue that saying an issue—like illegal immigration—is a security problem, or labelling a particular community as a security threat, can actually make them a threat and affects policy choices by raising fears that might not exist or do not exist to the degree to which they are presented. This in turn provides justification for policies that might not have been considered appropriate if this fear did not exist. For instance, the post-9/11 discourse around the threat of international terrorism created an environment in which violations of detainee rights in Guantanamo were seen as acceptable and necessary.[31] Thus, critical scholars challenge the very understandings of insecurity that the state and other significant actors in society such as the media claim exist. Although security discourse often evolves in very subtle ways, at times the rhetoric of fear is quite stark. At the height of Britain's post-9/11 response to terrorism, one newspaper ran a headline calling on all Britons to search their hedges for terrorists who could be hiding there. The idea that the threat of terrorism was so close—in one's own backyard—is indicative of how discourse contributed to an overall fear of terrorism within the population that could be used to justify increased state security measures.

The expansion of the security discourse has been captured by the term **securitization**. Securitization is a process through which normal issues of policy are given heightened importance by being labelled issues of security. As such, security officials demand extraordinary powers that in the past may have been reserved for periods of national crisis, such as wartime. Key to the securitization process is that the broader society accepts both the label of a given policy issue as a security concern and that extraordinary responses are necessary and appropriate. At their extreme, policy areas that have been securitized are not even subject to normal political debate about what might be an appropriate response to a security concern. In short, when an issue becomes securitized, publics trust that their governments will ensure their security whilst behaving in a proper and ethical manner. For critical scholars, as will be shown below, this public trust has been misplaced and has created the conditions under which states have undermined the rights and the security of their populations. Today, issues such as health, popular protest, and immigration have been increasingly securitized. For instance, the presentation of citizen protest as a security threat has resulted in laws and enforcement measures that have limited citizen expression and access to government.

> **Securitization:** Occurs when an issue area becomes understood as a security issue rather than a more routine matter of policy. This process develops through the use of a security language by leaders which is accepted by publics. Once an issue is securitized, more powerful security measures that enhance the power of the state (many of which may constrain individual rights) are taken for granted as being necessary.

Another example can be seen in how states in the Global North manage migration. While the vast majority of migrants entering states in the Global North are not violent criminals, public discourse has been predominantly framed in terms of the threat that migrants present to the receiving state and society. Addressing the arrival of one well-publicized group of migrants in Canada, several of whom were later recognized as refugees needing protection, one Canadian parliamentarian asked "is it not fair to assume then that having these people walk away and not being adequately tracked poses a threat to national security and a danger to the Canadian public?"[32] This type of discourse, the norm in many states, has led to severe laws and practices around border control, including interdiction, arbitrary detention, decreased assistance for refugee claimants, and limitations on the legal rights of migrants. In turn, these policies have threatened the lives and well-being of migrants, and even—some argue—contributed to migrant deaths. François Crépeau, a Canadian academic and UN Special Rapporteur on the Human Rights of Migrants, highlights in his 2013 report to the UN General Assembly the dangers for irregular migrants:

> …growing numbers of migrants are embarking on dangerous journeys in order to enter the European Union irregularly … They are doing so by taking unseaworthy vessels not only across the Mediterranean and Atlantic oceans, but also by risking their lives through precarious overland routes, in order to seek out such opportunities. Indeed, it is estimated that in 2011, over 1,500 persons lost their lives in attempting irregular border crossings in the Mediterranean Sea. Between 1998 and 2012, more than 16,000 persons have been documented to have died in attempting to migrate to the European Union. It should be noted that this statistic includes not only deaths caused at sea, but also in various other ways, including suffocation in trucks, car accidents, frostbite, police violence, hunger strikes, landmines, or suicide in detention, highlighting many of the dangers involved in irregular migration pathways.[33]*

Similar concerns have been raised about expanded American control policies along the Mexican-U.S. border, which have forced migrants to cross at increasingly more dangerous points such as the Sonora Dessert, where from 2000 to 2013 the bodies of over 2,000 migrants have been recovered.[34]

In these and other ways, critical scholars trace how the perception of insecurity can produce real insecurities for individuals. Another concern arises from the fact that today in both the experience and discourse of insecurity it is increasingly difficult to define clearly when we have achieved security. Security threats seem to be present continually in one aspect of our lives or another, making it difficult to feel that we are—or even can be—secure. Traditionally, wars have been won with

---

* François Crépeau, "Report of the Special Rapporteur on the Human Rights of Migrants," Human Rights Council of UN General Assembly, April 24, 2013.

clearly demarked events such as ceasefires and surrenders. The war on terrorism or the fight to control illegal migration, in contrast, stem from problems that suggest no such definitive ends. Thus, it is very unclear what it will take for decision-makers to say: "The war on terrorism is over! We are secure!" This creates the conditions under which states continue to justify extraordinary security policies that over time are treated as being normal and which, for critical scholars, ignore the way these insecurities are perpetuated by this discourse.

Other critical scholars point to the role that broad societal values and beliefs, such as racism or gender stereotypes, contribute to insecurity. The use of rape in war reflects both of these ideas. Understandings of women as the mothers of the nation who give birth to new members of an ethnonationalist community have produced a belief that rape as a weapon of war can be used to "breed-out" a nation's ethnic purity. Consider the experience of one victim of systematic rape in the war in the former Yugoslavia, who recalls soldiers shouting "Look at how many children you can have. Now you are going to have our children. You are going to have our little Chetniks."[35] Gender-based violence and violence against sexual minority groups take many other forms, such as domestic abuse and the deprivation of rights, which produce conditions that harm the security of individuals and groups. Critical scholars propose that we can understand the sources of insecurity and violence better by identifying the underlying values held by publics, the media, and among our political leaders that render such acts possible. By seeking to change those values, they propose, we can increase security.

PHOTO ESSAY

© REUTERS/Sergei Karpukhin

Russian Security Personnel at the 2014 Sochi Winter Olympics.

SECURITY AND WORLD SPORTING EVENTS

Major international entertainment events, especially international sporting competitions, have gained prominence as venues where concerns about security have been heightened. International sporting events are seen to pose substantial risks, especially to the threat of terrorism and anti-globalization protest, and as a result very large amounts of resources are committed to ensure the safety of participants and spectators. These events are significant targets because they are highly visible. Take, for example, two major international sporting events in 2014: the Winter Olympics held in Sochi, Russia, and the Fédération Internationale de Football Association (FIFA) World Cup held in Brazil. In the case of the Olympics, the heads of 66 states and international organizations alongside 2,900 athletes and an estimated viewership of 500 million people worldwide meant that the impact of an attack would be significant.[36] Estimates for the Winter Olympics, a three-week event, placed the security cost at $3 billion (U.S.),[37] although many think that the actual cost was much higher. These expenditures covered a variety of security measures, from the use of the Russian Navy to the deployment of as many as 100,000 security personnel.[38]

Critical scholars might ask whether publics have adequately questioned the need for such a high level of security. Publics seem to accept the existence of threats that are used to justify significant security efforts but this might be part of an unfounded yet widely accepted fear generated by powerful actors. Critical security scholars might also question the widespread use of intelligence and surveillance to monitor and search for threats leading up to and during these events, arguing that these infringe on the rights of visitors and citizens of the host country. These powers are also open to abuse and have been misused to stifle free speech and protest, as seen in the treatment of LGBT and environmental activists at the Sochi Olympics.

Critical security approaches might also raise alternative understandings of insecurity at these events. Efforts to secure these events have disproportionately focused on ensuring the security of affluent and powerful actors such as wealthy spectators, global media companies, large corporations who use these events to market their brands, and global organizations like FIFA and the IOC which can consolidate their image and capacity to provide a safe and secure platform for these profit-making activities.

In contrast, the events involve significant costs for publics and create insecurity for vulnerable members of society. States with significant levels of poverty, such as Russia and Brazil, might be served better by using the resources put toward security at major sporting events to other, more immediate areas of public interest, like education and healthcare. Furthermore, many individuals' lives are directly made more insecure as a result of these events. For example, Brazil's preparation for the World Cup involved "cleaning up" large urban slums—the homes of many of the country's poorest citizens. There is also evidence that major international sporting events create insecurity for women, who are rendered more vulnerable to human trafficking, sexual exploitation, and violence. In recognition of such insecurities at the World Cup in Brazil, a NGO campaign—"It's a penalty"—raised awareness about the sexual exploitation of children by spectators attending the event.[39]

For critical scholars, the sources of insecurity may extend beyond the state. Some critical approaches, especially those that focus on class conflict, suggest that insecurity is caused by the rise of a global economy in which the spread of an aggressive capitalist system places profits over the interests of people. This contributes to a number of types of insecurity at both national and individual levels. (This idea is expanded in the Photo Essay for this chapter.) States themselves are less able to control their economies, which are more susceptible to the demands of international economic actors. The need to have a competitive economy also pushes state leaders to cut spending and has left citizens across the globe with less-secure employment, lower wages, and less state protection at difficult points in their lives. The reduction of social support—as seen in decreased access to healthcare,

education, and child care—has a particularly negative impact on women. States that have opened their economies to global markets have also experienced resource depletion, diminishing access to clean water, pollution, and the fear that commercial farming and genetically modified crops will negatively impact local agricultural production and the ability of farmers to provide for their families. The problem of Somali piracy, raised earlier from the perspective of national security, is illustrative. A critical perspective on piracy argues that piracy arises out of the local and long-running insecurities of the Somali people caused in part by global politics. This includes the experiences of colonialism, the failure of intervention in the early 1990s, and the short-comings of the international community's support of Somalis in their efforts to create a stable country in which people can live safely and provide for their families. Furthermore, in specific instances the international community has failed to prevent companies based in the Global North from exploiting the absence, for much of the 1990s and 2000s, of a central government in Somalia, or to punish them for having done so. These companies have been accused of damaging fishing grounds, where Somalis traditionally made a living, through overfishing and the dumping of waste.[40] For critical scholars, the national security discourse purposefully misses the underlying problems of insecurity and serves the most immediate interests of powerful actors in these situations.

Critical security approaches are effective at challenging the **normative position** of traditional security approaches and identifying other sources of insecurity, especially in relation to the actions of the state and powerful economic actors in the global system. In doing so, these approaches call on members of the public to question what they are being told about insecurity and to recognize the implications of the discourse of security on how policies are chosen and how these policies in turn can create further insecurity. They hope that by doing this, deeper and more problematic sources of insecurity might be addressed. Of course, critical security

perspectives have themselves been challenged. One criticism is that they do not deal with real issues of global security. For instance, traditional scholars have argued that these approaches do not help to explain important aspects of interstate politics that lead to war or that influence whether international cooperation between states can be accomplished. In short, critical approaches often do not provide policy options that decision-makers find useful. Security practitioners want solutions, often immediately, to problems like nuclear proliferation and internationalized ethnic conflict, and advice on defence budgets in response to potential threats. While critical perspectives help to understand the sources of conflict and offer potential long-term solutions, the ideas are often not seen as being useful to the specific and immediate issues of national defence and security that traditional scholars are interested in addressing.

> **Normative position:** The ideas and values upon which approaches to politics are grounded. These ideas and values reflect beliefs about good and bad as well as understanding of what is desirable or what ought to be done in a given situation.

CONCLUSION

Read the website of any news agency and it quickly becomes clear that security is at the top of the agendas of our political leaders. As members of the public, we are regularly told that we live in an insecure world. These concerns about security have had significant impacts on the decisions that we have made as a society. Not surprisingly, the focus on security has shaped our foreign and defence policies and has resulted in tough decisions that have sent troops overseas—many of whom have been killed or wounded—into conflict which has itself produced death and significant insecurity for local populations. Our need for security has

also affected our approach to many other issues. We have altered, for example, our approaches to immigration and citizenship policy, policing and intelligence gathering, human rights, the environment, and health policy. While security can be important in each of these areas, we do not often agree on the sources of our insecurity or how we should respond to them—these themselves are deeply political questions. As a result, the study of security is an important part of understanding both domestic and international politics, and the choices about the type of society and state that we will live in.

DISCUSSION QUESTIONS

1. What makes you feel most insecure? What aspects of domestic and international politics contribute to your sense of insecurity? In what ways would an individual, living in a state in the Global South, feel differently about insecurity?

2. Do you live in a more secure world today than students did 50 years ago? What has changed, for better or for worse?

3. Consider a political issue that has recently been in the news, such as healthcare, the environment, or immigration. Has this issue been presented as

a security issue? Do you think that the framing of this issue as a security concern changes how people respond to the issue or how public figures attempt to address it?

4. In what ways is the state a source of security? How does it cause insecurity?

5. How far should individual rights be limited to provide state security?

WEBSITES

The United Nations Trust Fund for Human Security
http://unocha.org/humansecurity/
A United Nations website that highlights the organization's activities to promote human security globally.

The United Nations Millennium Development Goals
http://www.un.org/millenniumgoals/
A United Nations website that describes the history of and the current efforts to meet the Millennium Development Goals.

Uppsala Conflict Data Program, Department of Peace and Conflict Research, Uppsala Universitet
http://www.pcr.uu.se/research/ucdp
The Conflict Data Program at Uppsala University in Sweden provides access to extensive data and research on current and historical trends in global conflict.

Global Peace Index, Institute for Economics and Peace
http://www.visionofhumanity.org
The website of the Institute for Economics and Peace, a think tank that provides an annual ranking of the relative peacefulness of states using 22 different indicators.

Lieutenant-General, The Honorable Roméo A. Dallaire
http://www.romeodallaire.com
The homepage of the Honourable Roméo A. Dallaire, which details his experience and current work to address global security issues.

FURTHER READING

Peter Andreas, "Illicit Globalization: Myths, Misconceptions, and Historical Lessons," *Political Science Quarterly* 126 (3) (Fall 2011), pp. 403–25.

Tara Brian and Frank Laczko, eds., *Fatal Journeys: Tracking the Lives Lost during Migration.* Geneva: International Organization for Migration, 2014.

Ronald Deibert, *Black Code, Surveillance, Privacy, and the Dark Side of the Internet.* New York: Signal, 2013.

Christian Enemark, "Drones over Pakistan: Secrecy, Ethics, and Counterinsurgency," *Asian Security* 7 (3) (2011), pp. 218–37.

Veronica Kitchen and Kim Rygiel, "Privatizing Security, Securitizing Policing: The Case of the G20 in Toronto, Canada," *International Political Sociology* 8 (May 2014), pp. 201–17.

Joseph S. Nye and David A. Welch, *Understanding Global Conflict and Cooperation*, 9th ed. Toronto: Pearson, 2013.

ENDNOTES

1. Nadège Mougel, "World War I casualties," trans. by Julie Gratz, *Reperes – Explanatory Notes*, Robert Schumann Centre, 2011, online at http://www.centre-robert-schuman.org/reperes-explanatory-notes.

2. International Coalition for the Responsibility to Protect, *Crisis in the Democratic Republic of Congo*, online at http://www.responsibilitytoprotect.org/index.php/crises/crisis-in-drc.

3. Quy-Toan Do, "The pirates of Somalia: Ending the threat, rebuilding a nation" *The World Bank*, 2013, p. xxi, online at http://documents.worldbank.org/curated/en/2013/01/17672066/pirates-somalia-ending-threat-rebuilding-nation.

4. Ibid., p. 158

5. Ibid., p. xxiii.

6. "1945: U.S. drops bomb on Hiroshima," *BBC News*, online at http://news.bbc.co.uk/onthisday/hi/dates/stories/august/6/newsid_3602000/3602189.stm; "WW2 People's War," *BBC News*, online at http://www.bbc.co.uk/history/ww2peopleswar/timeline/factfiles/nonflash/a6652262.shtml.

7. The Birmingham Policy Commission, "The Security Impact of Drones: Challenges and Opportunities for the U.K.," The Institute for Conflict, Cooperation and Security at the University of Birmingham, October 2014, pp. 64–65, online at http://www.birmingham.ac.uk/Documents/research/policycommission/remote-warfare/final-report-october-2014.pdf.

8. Ibid., pp. 26–27.

9. Lotta Themnér and Peter Wallensteen, "Armed Conflicts, 1946-2013," *Journal of Peace Research* 51 (4) (July 2014), p. 543.

10. Daily Charts, "Illegal markets," *The Economist* (April 29, 2013), online at http://www.economist.com/blogs/graphicdetail/2013/04/daily-chart-19.

11. David E. Sanger, "Obama order sped up wave of cyber attacks against Iran," *The New York Times*, June 1, 2012, online at http://www.nytimes.com/2012/06/01/world/middleeast/obama-ordered-wave-of-cyberattacks-against-iran.html?pagewanted=all&_r=0.

12. Moisés Naím, "The Five Wars of Globalization," *Foreign Policy*, January 1, 2003, 28–37.

13. Daniel Trotta, "Iraq War could cost U.S. more than $2 trillion: study," *Reuters*, March 14, 2013, online at http://www.reuters.com/article/2013/03/14/us-iraq-war-anniversary-idUSBRE92D0PG20130314.

14. Brad Plummer, "America's staggering defence budget, in charts," *The Washington Post*, January 7, 2013, online at http://www.reuters.com/article/2013/03/14/us-iraq-war-anniversary-idUSBRE92D0PG20130314.

15. Peter Apps, "U.S. military to face growing crises, falling budgets," *Reuters*, July 2, 2014, online at http://www.reuters.com/article/2014/07/02/us-usa-iraq-analysis-idUSKBN0F71VM20140702.

16. Media Release, "The Cost of 9/11 and the Creation of the National Security Establishment," *Rideau Institute*, September 7, 2011, online at http://www.rideauinstitute.ca/2011/09/07/the-cost-of-911-and-the-creation-of-a-national-security-establishment/.

17. David A. Graham, "Rumsfeld's Knowns and Unknowns: The Intellectual History of a Quip," *The Atlantic*, March 27, 2014, online at http://www.theatlantic.com/politics/archive/2014/03/rumsfelds-knowns-and-unknowns-the-intellectual-history-of-a-quip/359719/.

18. United Nations Development Programme, *Human Development Report 1994* (New York, Oxford University Press: 1994), p. 3.

19. http://www.wfp.org/hunger/stats, June 25, 2015.

20. Central Intelligence Agency, *World Factbook*, online at https://www.cia.gov/library/publications/the-world-factbook/rankorder/2242rank.html.

21. See https://data.undp.org/dataset/Table-1-Human-Development-Index-and-its-components/wxub-qc5k.

22. See http://cpi.transparency.org/cpi2013/results/.

23. See http://www.un.org/millenniumgoals/.

24. United Nations Fact sheet, "We Can End Poverty: Millennium Development Goals and Beyond 2015," United Nations, online at http://www.un.org/millenniumgoals/pdf/Goal_5_fs.pdf.

25. Glyn Berry, "Sovereignty as a Responsibility to Prevent, Protect and Rebuild," *The Ploughshares Monitor* 25 (1) (Spring, 2004), online at http://ploughshares.ca/pl_publications/sovereignty-as-the-responsibility-to-prevent-protect-and-rebuild/.

26. Roméo Dallaire, "Rwandan Genocide: The Failure of Humanity," online at http://www.romeodallaire.com.

27. James Meikle, "Serbians say sorry for 1995 Srebrenica massacre," *The Guardian*, March 31, 2010, online at http://www.theguardian.com/world/2010/mar/31/serbians-sorry-1995-srebrenica-massacre.

28. Richard Gray, "How Big Brother watches your every move," *The Sunday Telegraph*, August 16, 2008, online at http://www.telegraph.co.uk/news/uknews/2571041/How-Big-Brother-watches-your-every-move.html.

29. United State Department of Homeland Security, "Biometrics: The future of security," *CBC News Online*, December 14, 2004, online at http://www.cbc.ca/news2/background/airportsecurity/biometrics.html.

30. Greg Weston, Glenn Greenwald, and Ryan Gallagher, "CSEC used airport Wi-Fi to track Canadian travellers: Edward Snowden documents," *CBC News*, January 31, 2014, online at http://www.cbc.ca/news/politics/csec-used-airport-wi-fi-to-track-canadian-travellers-edward-snowden-documents-1.2517881.

31. Richard Jackson, "Language, policy and the construction of a torture culture in the war on terrorism," *Review of International Studies* 33 (3) (July 2007), pp. 353–71.

32. Rob Anders, *Standing Committee on Citizenship and Immigration Evidence*, 36th Parliament, 2nd Session Meeting 2, November 3, 1999, p. 1600.

33. François Crépeau, "Report of the Special Rapporteur on the Human Rights of Migrants," Human Rights Council of UN General Assembly, April 24, 2013, p. 6, online at http://www.ohchr.org/Documents/HRBodies/HRCouncil/RegularSession/Session23/A.HRC.23.46_en.pdf.

34. Edward Helmore, "'Death map' of deserts aims to save lives of desperate Mexican migrants," *The Observer*, June 1, 2013, online at http://www.theguardian.com/world/2013/jun/01/map-us-mexico-migrant-deaths-border.

35. Robert Fisk, "Bosnia War Crimes: 'The rapes went on day and night'," *The Independent*, February 8, 1993, online at http://www.independent.co.uk/news/world/europe/bosnia-war-crimes-the-rapes-went-on-day-and-night-robert-fisk-in-mostar-gathers-detailed-evidence-of-the-systematic-sexual-assaults-on-muslim-women-by-serbian-white-eagle-gunmen-1471656.html.

36. David Bond, "Sochi 2014: World watches Winter Olympics that are 'Putin's Games'," *BBC News*, February 7, 2014, online at http://www.bbc.com/sport/0/winter-olympics/26083154; Karolos Grohmann, "Sochi Games global broadcast output dwarfs Vancouver," *Reuters*, February 19, 2014, online at http://www.reuters.com/article/2014/02/19/us-olympics-sochi-broadcasting-idUSBREA1I0L020140219_linger_with_olympics_near_dimanno.html.

37. Rosie DiManno, "Sochi 2014: Security fears linger with Olympics near," *The Toronto Star*, January 28, 2014, online at http://www.thestar.com/sports/sochi2014/2014/01/28/sochi_2014_security_fears_linger_with_olympics_near_dimanno.html.

38. Matt Lundy, "Why the Sochi Olympics are the most expensive Games ever," *Yahoo! Sports Canada*, February 7, 2014, online at https://ca.sports.yahoo.com/blogs/eh-game/why-sochi-hosting-most-expensive-olympics-ever-133051945.html.

39. See http://www.itsapenalty.com.

40. Emmanuel Kisiangani, "Somali pirates: villains or victims?," *South African Journal of International Affairs* 17 (3) (December 2010), pp. 361–74.

GLOSSARY

Aboriginal self-government Diverse arrangements whereby the authority of Aboriginal or Indigenous groups to govern themselves is recognized; such authority (over various aspects of community life) would have to be consistent with the laws operating within existing states. (p. 89)

Absolute monarchy A system of government ruled, at least in name, by one individual whose authority is unchecked, final, and permanent. (p. 72)

Adjudication A system of dispute resolution in which an impartial third party applies the law to decide the outcome, or what is more commonly known as "judging." (p. 254)

Administrative tribunals Boards or commissions established by the government to adjudicate certain disputes by applying laws to the facts; also called quasi-judicial tribunals or regulatory agencies. Not being proper courts, these tribunals are not headed by judges. (p. 209)

ADR Alternative dispute resolution, as in an alternative to adjudication; examples include mediation, arbitration, and tribunals. (p. 271)

Affirmative action An American policy and term designed to increase the representation of targeted groups in such areas as employment and education. Critics may view it as "preferential treatment" or "reverse discrimination" but proponents say it redresses the effects of past discrimination. Affirmative action began in the U.S. in the 1960s, focusing mainly on increasing opportunities for African-Americans. In the 1970s, it started to be used to increase the number of women in professional and managerial positions. In Canada, a policy of "employment equity" has been used to encourage the representation of women, visible minorities, Aboriginal people, and persons with disabilities in government or companies doing business with the government. (p. 46, 105)

Agents of political socialization Those groups of people or institutions that convey political attitudes and values to others in society. (p. 15)

Amending formula The procedure by which a constitution can be amended; it is usually more onerous than procedures in place to amend ordinary legislation. (p. 171)

Anarchy A system of social, political, and economic relations without formal institutions of governance to define enforceable rules or exact obedience from the governed. Realist scholars use this term to characterize the international system, where there is no authority above the state that can solve inter-state conflict. Anarchy does not mean chaos. (pp. 71, 451)

Anocracy A mixed regime that combines democratic and non-democratic institutions. (p. 394)

Aristocracy Government by an elite or privileged class or by a minority regarded as those best fit to rule. For the Ancients, the term was reserved for the rule by the few "best" (*aristos* in Greek)—the most educated, wise, brave, and selfless people, who would rule in the interests of the whole society rather than their own. During the Middle Ages in Europe, the term became associated with hereditary rule by a particular social class, otherwise known as "the nobility." The term aristocracy has generally lost its original positive connotation and it now commonly carries a pejorative meaning in liberal-democratic societies. (p. 44)

Authoritarian government A non-democratic form of government that is not based on free and fair elections, severely curtails public participation in political life, and holds the actions of the state to be above the law; such regimes often commit gross human rights violations in order to maintain their power. (p. 86)

Autocrat/autocracy The opposite of "rule by the people" because it means "rule by oneself." An autocrat is an individual who wields absolute power. An autocracy is a regime headed by an autocrat. (p. 393)

Bilateral aid Development assistance given by one country (the donor) to another. (p. 381)

Bill A proposed law introduced into a legislature. Bills must go through a long review process, usually involving several votes and numerous amendments (additions to the bill), before being passed into law. (p. 219)

Brokerage party Political parties in the Canadian national context that expend much effort to broker regional, linguistic, and cultural cleavages in order to create winning coalitions of support. (p. 315)

Brokerage party system A description of Canada's national party system, which holds that ideological polarization is less pronounced in Canadian politics than in many other countries; instead, the main political parties are said to attempt to aggregate enough diverse interests to win elections. (p. 139)

Bureaucracy The expert, permanent, non-partisan, professional officials employed by the state to advise the political executive and to implement government policies. (pp. 82, 205)

Cabinet The group of people chosen by the prime minister or president to provide political direction to government departments; in Canada, cabinet members act collectively to make the key government decisions. (pp. 196, 222)

Cabinet government A system of government in which the major political decisions are made by the cabinet as a whole, as opposed to one in which the prime minister or president acts with considerable autonomy. (p. 196)

Cabinet solidarity The constitutional duty of ministers to publicly support the policy of the government. Ministers who openly dissent from government policy must resign from the government. (p. 197)

Cadre party Nineteenth-century small party organizations of local notables with membership confined mostly to representatives who held seats in the legislature. (p. 313)

Capitalism An economic system in which the means of production (land, factories, technology, etc.) are privately owned and operated according to a profit motive. Decisions about production, investment, and distribution of resources are determined according to market forces (i.e., whether a profit can be made producing and marketing a product), rather than collective or community priorities. In capitalism, workers exchange their labour for wages or salary. Although it is often called the "free enterprise system," capitalism can exist even where there is little freedom, politically or socially, and where the state controls the system (i.e., in "state capitalism"). (pp. 47. 125, 424)

Catch-all party Political parties in the post-war era that shed much of their ideological adherence, placed more emphasis on the party's leadership, and focused on securing electoral success. (p. 314)

Central agencies Those agencies of the state that assist the political executive to coordinate and control overall government operations. They provide both policy advice and administrative support. (p. 203)

Charity An organization that has charitable purposes and that is registered (under the Income Tax Act in Canada) so that it can issue charitable receipts to donors, who are in turn allowed to deduct amounts from their personal income tax. (p. 343)

Checks and balances A constitutional system of power-sharing under which powers are assigned to the three branches of government (the executive, legislative, and judicial) so as to enable each branch to curb the unilateral exercise of power by the others. (p. 194)

Civil rights and liberties Those legal and constitutional guarantees, such as freedom of speech, the right of *habeas corpus*, and non-discrimination rights, that govern the conduct of the state, and some private sector actors, in their relations with individuals and certain minority groups. (p. 155)

Civil society The social sphere, distinct from both the state and the market, which includes a wide range of social institutions and organizations around and through which people organize and pursue common interests. (p. 334)

Class A concept that describes hierarchical groupings within societies based on social and economic factors such as income, occupation, education, and status. (pp. 126, 437)

Coercion The use of force to achieve desired objectives and outcomes. (p. 405)

Cold War The period in international relations between 1945 and 1990 that was dominated by global political conflict and economic competition between the United States and the Soviet Union, each with its ideology and allies, in which major wars were precluded by a military balance between the two superpowers, but which was marked by many regional proxy conflicts. (p. 424)

Collective action Any action taken together by two or more individuals whose goal is to achieve a common objective. (p. 334, 404)

Collective responsibility In Westminster parliamentary systems, members of the political executive are collectively responsible to parliament for government policy and for the overall administrative performance of the government. (p. 197)

Colonialism The territorial conquest, ownership, occupation, and direct administration of one country by another. (p. 370)

Communications media A wide variety of different media, including pamphlets, books, films, newspapers, magazines, telegraphs, radio, television, e-mail, texting, websites, blogs, social media, telephones, cell phones, and tablets. (p. 384)

Communism A political ideology based on eliminating exploitation through near complete public ownership, full state control, and central planning of the economy. (p. 55)

Concurrent powers Those fields of shared jurisdiction under a federal constitution in which both the national and subnational governments can act and pass laws. (p. 162)

Confederation An association of sovereign states that have agreed by treaty to delegate certain powers to a central governing authority. In principle a looser political union than a federation, a confederation's member-states retain the right of secession. (p. 159)

Confidence (or non-confidence) vote An explicitly worded motion indicating that the legislature either has or does not have confidence in the government, a vote on a matter that the government has previously declared to be a matter of confidence; or a vote on important measures central to the government's plans, such as the budget. (pp. 193, 224)

Congressional system A style of democracy, characterized by having a bicameral national legislature and the separation of the executive from the legislature. This system is found, notably, in the United States. (p. 220)

Conservatism An ideology defending the status quo against major social, economic, and political change. Conservatism became a clearly articulated philosophy in reaction to the upheavals caused by the French Revolution. The classic statement of this attitude can be found in the speeches and writing of the English statesman Edmund Burke (1729–1797). He argued that political order and stability will be maintained only if change is gradual and evolutionary rather than rapid and revolutionary. Today, conservatism is often used to label those who wish to protect established economic interests and social norms. (p. 59)

Constituency An electoral district or riding. For the purposes of elections and government, countries are divided into constituencies, or geographic regions, and the population of each constituency elects a representative (or representatives) to the legislature. (p. 282)

Constitution The body of fundamental laws, rules, and practices that defines the basic structures of government, allocates power among governmental institutions, and regulates the relationship between citizens and the state. (p. 154)

Constitutional convention An unwritten rule of constitutional behaviour that fills in gaps in the written constitution and conditions the exercise of legal powers under the constitution. While considered obligatory, such rules are not legally enforceable. (pp. 158, 221)

Constitutional law Law that establishes the institutions of the state and their respective powers, and often fundamental limits on state behaviour as well. It is usually entrenched by demanding amending formulas. (p. 252)

Constitutionalism The idea that the constitution should limit the state by separating powers among different branches and levels of government, and by protecting the rights of individuals and minorities, as through a bill of rights. (p. 155)

Coordination An interaction in which all participants have to cooperate or choose the same course of action for each to benefit. (p. 405)

Corporatism A political economy in which formal bargaining and compromises among leading societal interests, above all business and labour, are very important for social and economic outcomes. (p. 130)

Coup (or coup d'état) An attempt by those inside the government to remove a national leader and install a new leader. (p. 397)

Crown An often-overlooked but critical part of Westminster parliaments. Officially the head of state, the Queen (or in her absence her representative) provides non-partisan continuity in governance, including such vital aspects as proroguing and dissolving parliament and, following an election, identifying who can command the confidence of the assembly to form the government. (p. 222)

Crown corporation A corporation owned by the government that assumes a structure similar to that of a private company and that operates semi-independently of cabinet. (p. 209)

Cultural pluralism The coexistence of many ethnic and cultural groups within a country. Such diversity is the starting point in arguing that all groups in a society can maintain their linguistic, cultural, and religious distinctiveness without being relegated to the economic or cultural margins, and is achieved through the creation of a common set of values and institutions. (p. 115)

Democracy A regime in which every eligible adult citizen has the right to select the leader in free and fair elections. (p. 391)

Democratic deficit The perceived gap between the theoretical principles of democracy and the actual practice of ostensibly democratic institutions, including national governments and international organizations. (p. 72)

Democratic Peace Theory A theory that explains why democratic states do not go to war with one another. This theory fits within a liberal approach to international politics in emphasizing domestic characteristics of the state—democratic institutions. (p. 451)

Democratization A group of transitions from non-democratic to democratic regimes, involving the relaxation of authoritarian political control by political leaders, the expansion of political and civil liberties, and the creation of institutional mechanisms that open up the political system to greater public representation and participation. (pp. 85, 392)

Department of Finance Chief economic advisor of the government of Canada, this department is responsible for managing the national economy, raising revenue, preparing economic forecasts, and determining public expenditure levels. Its British counterpart is the Treasury. (p. 203)

Deputy minister A senior civil servant who acts as chief policy advisor to the minister and as general manager of the department. Known in Britain as the permanent secretaries, deputy ministers play a key role in the collective management of government operations. (p. 206)

Development as freedom A concept developed by economist Amartya Sen that sees democracy and human rights as central to development. It includes basic needs such as people's freedom to satisfy hunger, to have access to basic healthcare, and to clothe and house themselves. It also reflects more ambitious freedoms such as educating oneself, finding employment, and being safe from violence. (p. 370)

Devolution The delegation of administrative or legislative powers by a central government to regional or local governments. (p. 166)

Diaspora An ethnic group that has experienced or currently experiences dislocation across multiple states, yet typically nurtures narratives and political projects about a specific "homeland" as a place of eventual return. (p. 104)

Dictator/dictatorship An individual who wields absolute power. A dictatorship is a regime headed by a dictator. (p. 393)

Digital divide The greater access to information technology that some people have over others. This can exist between countries but also within countries. (p. 385)

District magnitude Reflects the number of legislative seats available in an electoral district. In a Single Member Plurality system, the district magnitude is one; in Single Transferable Vote systems, the district magnitude is always greater than one. Generally speaking, the higher the district magnitude, the more proportional the electoral result. (p. 285)

Dominant conformity A model of ethnic group integration holding that all groups in a society should conform to the language and values of the dominant group. In the case of Canada, this is the idea behind historical policies emphasizing Anglo conformity, which aims to have all groups assimilate by speaking English and holding the values of the dominant British-origin group. (p. 114)

Double burden When women work outside the home in addition to continued responsibility for child-drearing, eldercare, and domestic chores. (p. 379)

Dual executive A form of executive in which the posts of head of state and head of government are divided, each being held by a separate officeholder. In parliamentary systems, the head of state is a constitutional monarch or an elected president, and the head of government is the prime minister. (p. 186)

Economic development Development defined in terms of economic indicators such as GDP and GNI. (p. 367)

Egalitarianism The doctrine that advocates that people should be treated as equals regardless of differences of wealth, income, class, sex, religion, ethnicity, physical ability, and so on. At minimum, egalitarianism promotes the equality of social and political rights for all citizens; at maximum, it calls for a much greater equality of wealth and income for all persons across all divisions in society. In this regard, liberals emphasize equality of opportunity, while socialists emphasize equality of condition. (p. 43)

Election An official process through which citizens communicate their preferences about who will form government. Individual choices are combined to determine the makeup of government. (p. 278)

Electoral system Electoral rules, often included in the constitution of a country, that outline the manner in which votes in an election are translated into legislative seats. (p. 280)

Electoral-professional party A political party focused on winning elections; party membership tends to be small and there is little to no identifiable ideological adherence. (p. 314)

Enumerated powers Those areas of legislative authority in a federal state that are specifically listed in the constitution and assigned to one level of government or another, or to both. (p. 162)

Ethnic cleansing The removal of one or more ethnic groups from a society by means of expulsion, imprisonment, or killing. The term entered the political lexicon in reference to the former Yugoslavia; it was first used to describe the violent measures and policies designed to eliminate or dramatically reduce the Muslim and Croat populations in Serb-held territory. (p. 100)

European Union (EU) A unique supranational organization made up of 28 member states, characterized by increasing economic and political integration. (pp. 91, 111)

Executive The branch of government concerned with the implementation and enforcement of laws and other authoritative decisions of the state. The executive also formulates public policy and provides political leadership. (p. 184)

Executive Office of the President Offices and agencies attached directly to the president of the United States that provide advice on decisions and help develop and implement policies and programs. (p. 205)

Fascism A political system of the extreme right, based on the principles of the strong leader (dictator), a one-party state, nationalism, total control of social and economic activity, and arbitrary power, rather than constitutionalism. In 1922 in Italy, Benito Mussolini created the first fascist regime, soon emulated by Adolf Hitler in Germany. Fascist regimes also held power in Spain and Argentina. Today there are numerous neofascist movements advocating ultranationalist, racist, and anti-immigrant political positions. (pp. 61, 87)

Federalism A form of government in which the sovereign powers of the state are formally divided under a constitution between two levels of government, neither of which is subordinate to the other. (p. 161)

Feminism A belief in the full equality of men and women, and the insistence that all barriers to such equality be removed. (p. 436)

Fiscal imbalance In federal states the constitutional responsibility of subnational governments to deliver a wide range of public services often exceeds their financial capacity, thus requiring cash and other transfers from the national government. (p. 163)

Funnel of causality A model to explain the factors influencing vote choice and public opinion, in which long- and short-term factors are situated in relation to their influence on one another as well as the vote. (p. 292)

Fusion of powers In parliamentary systems, the joint exercise of legislative and executive powers by the prime minister and members of the cabinet, who simultaneously hold office in the legislative and executive branches of government. (p. 192)

GDP per capita A measure of a nation's total production (goods and services), or how rich the country is in economic terms, divided by a country's population. (p. 367)

Gender What is expected from a woman or man in terms of how s/he is to behave and dress, their legal rights, social norms, etc. (p. 378)

Genocide The deliberate and systematic extermination of a national, ethnic, or religious group. The term was developed in response to the horrors of the Holocaust. (p. 99)

Gini coefficient A measure of inequality of wealth in a country. (p. 368)

Global governance Collective policy-making aimed at addressing global problems in the absence of a formal governing structure for the whole world. (p. 72)

Global South A recent term used to refer to those regions of the world that are the focus of study in the politics of development (Africa, Latin America, the Caribbean, the Middle East, and most of Asia). (p. 366)

Globalization The movement of goods, capital, ideas, and people across geopolitical boundaries today and in the past. Contemporary patterns of globalization involve a deepening constellation of economic, technological, and cultural changes that are worldwide in scope and that challenge the sovereignty of the state. These processes are leading to ever closer economic relations among the countries of the world, based on increased trade, foreign direct investment, activity by multinational corporations, and financial flows. (pp. 91, 110)

GNI A measure of a country's GDP plus income received from overseas. (p. 367)

Government The set of institutions and practices that make and enforce collective public decisions for a society. (p. 72)

Group of 8 (G8) Canada, France, Germany, Italy, Japan, Russia (prior to 2014), the United Kingdom, and the United States, whose leaders meet once a year to discuss how they might coordinate their economic activities to ensure that the global economy functions well. (p. 141)

Head of government Officeholder, such as the prime minister in a parliamentary system, who is in effective charge of the executive branch of government. (p. 186)

Head of state Officeholder, such as a constitutional monarch, who symbolizes and represents the state but does not exercise effective political power. (p. 186)

Human Development Index (HDI) Measures development in terms of not only a country's national income but other factors such as life expectancy, educational attainment, and gender equality. (pp. 368, 457)

Human rights Rights enjoyed by individuals simply because they are human beings, primarily including the prevention of discrimination or coercion on grounds of ethnicity, religion, gender, or opinion. (p. 86)

Human security Reflects a focus on the security of the individual. Security concerns are defined broadly and fall primarily into one of two categories: freedom from threats of violence to the individual, and freedom from poverty and hunger that limit an individual's ability to reach their potential. Although linked, human security is often contrasted with national security. (p. 456)

Humanitarian intervention Intervention in the affairs of another state for the purposes of resolving a humanitarian concern. While humanitarian intervention may take a number of forms, the most controversial is intervention that contravenes state sovereignty and that applies the use of force to accomplish its goals. (p. 459)

Ideology A fairly coherent set of beliefs that not only explains what may be wrong with society, but also provides a vision of what society should look like. (p. 54)

Imperialism A broader term than colonialism that literally means "empire building," imperialism occurs when one country dominates another with the aim of controlling and/or exploiting the latter. This domination can be economic, political, social, and/or cultural. (p. 106)

Incumbent An individual or party currently holding office. (p. 280)

Indirect rule A form of colonial governance used by the British that legitimized local political leaders and legal systems as long as they remained subordinate and useful to the colonial power. (p. 373)

Institutions The rules of the game—which can be formal or informal—by which a society functions. (p. 391)

Interest group An organization that brings together people with common interests and concerns in order to influence public policy. (p. 335)

International law The body of treaties and conventions created by agreements between states or by international organizations of member-states. (p. 250)

International Monetary Fund (IMF) A sister of the World Bank and a branch of the United Nations that regulates the international monetary system in order to stabilize national currencies, and that, subject to certain conditions, makes loans to developing countries. (pp. 141, 430)

International organization An organization, such as the United Nations, the WTO, or NATO, whose members are typically sovereign states. (p. 430)

Judicial activism When judges restrict the actions of the executive or legislative branches, or expand the limits on government through legal interpretation. Judicial restraint is when judges do the opposite. (p. 261)

Judicial impartiality A subjective state of mind in which a judge is free of bias and indifferent to the outcome of a case, in that he or she has nothing personally to gain or lose by the decision. (p. 263)

Judicial independence The institutional structures, or relationships between the judiciary and executive and legislative branches, intended to encourage judicial impartiality, such as tenure, financial security, and some degree of administrative autonomy. (p. 263)

Judicial review When judges determine whether state actions are legally permissible, for example, in light of rights protections or the federal division of powers. (p. 258)

Judiciary The body of all judges and courts in a country, or the judicial branch of government. (p. 254)

Laissez-faire A French phrase meaning literally "let do"; this economic theory provides the intellectual foundation for the system of free-market capitalism. Following the principles of Adam Smith, proponents of laissez-faire believe that the economy works best when there is no government intervention. Thus, the theory rejects state ownership or control, advocates a free market, values individualism, and promotes free trade. (p. 51)

Law Rules governing behaviour by societal and state actors, adopted and enforced by the state. (p. 249)

Legal realism A school of legal philosophy that contends that judges' backgrounds and values shape their decisions, and that these values are able to manifest when judges have flexibility, as when they interpret the law. (p. 263)

Legislature The major lawmaking institution in a democracy. Legislatures can either be unicameral or bicameral. (p. 219)

Legitimacy A measure of the degree to which citizens accept and tolerate the actions and decisions of social and political actors such as governments, states, international organizations, and civil society groups themselves, usually based on the notion that the decision-makers have a right to such power. (p. 83)

Liberal democracy A form of government common to Western political systems in which there is a combination of the "liberal" right to individual freedom and the "democratic" right to representative government. Decision-making power is subject to the rule of law as established by a constitutional system that recognizes fundamental rights and freedoms (e.g., free speech, freedom of the press and religion, and freedom of association) along with certain legal rights to property, privacy, equality under the law, etc. Liberal democracies are distinguished by free and fair elections within multi-party systems, civilian rule, separation of powers between the executive and legislative branches, an independent judiciary, and a political culture of tolerance and pluralism—including protection for minorities against potentially tyrannical majorities. (p. 42)

Liberalism The ideology based on the paramount value of individual liberty. Liberalism assumes that all humans are free and equal by nature, and that society is a vehicle for the protection and enhancement of our natural rights. In its earlier form, often called classical liberalism, this ideology assumed a limited role for the state. In later years, liberals tended to advocate a larger role for the state to guarantee equality and to help foster the full development of the individual. In one form or another, liberalism is the most widely held political position across the West and has become increasing hegemonic worldwide, especially since the fall of the Berlin Wall in 1989. (p. 39)

Logrolling A method of strategic voting in which a representative agrees to vote in favour of another representative's bill or amendment in return for a vote in favour of their own bill or amendment. (p. 241)

Majority government   A government in which a single party holds a majority of seats in parliament and has exclusive control of the cabinet. (p. 192)

Marxian political economy   An approach to political economy that stresses the importance of social classes and class conflict, and that identifies the interests of the dominant class, the capitalist one under capitalism, as the main influence on social institutions, including the state. (p. 126)

Mass party   Political parties that emerged in the early 20th century that had a large membership base, a strong ideological orientation, and internal funding from dues and fees. (p. 314)

Merit principle   A system of hiring and promoting public servants on the basis of their merit (education, training, experience, and so on), rather than on the basis of party affiliation or other considerations. (p. 207)

Ministerial responsibility   The responsibility of individual ministers to answer to parliament for the administration of their departments, including the actions of public officials employed in such departments. (p. 198)

Mixed systems   Electoral systems that combine elements of different types of electoral systems. This is often done to increase proportionality in non-proportional systems. (p. 281)

Multiculturalism   A policy sometimes adopted in a state characterized by cultural pluralism that supports ethnic and cultural groups in maintaining their customs and traditions, often with public financial assistance. (p. 105)

Multination state   A state that contains more than one nation. (p. 102)

Nation   A community of people, normally defined by a combination of ethnicity, language, and culture, with a subjective sense of belonging together. (pp. 81, 101)

National security   Reflects a focus on the state and its interests. Among other aspects, national security includes protecting state territory, institutions, economic interests, as well as citizens and their core values. Traditional approaches to the study of security in international politics focus on national security. (p. 446)

Nationalism   An ideology used by state leaders to promote the interest of the nation, including defence of the state in times of war. Alternatively, it can be used by secession movements against the state. In the extreme, nationalism can be used to motivate ethnic cleansing and genocide. Nationalism has been a leading cause of conflict. (pp. 101, 448)

Nation-state   A term sometimes used synonymously with state but which implies that citizens share a common ethnic or cultural background. In the modern world, few such homogeneous states remain, most either being multicultural, multiethnic, or multination states. (pp. 79, 98)

Neocolonialism   When a country is officially independent but remains constrained in its choices by a foreign power that may use economic or military might to ensure that the country follows economic policies consistent with the interests of the neocolonial power. (p. 374)

Neoconservatism   A term applied to those on the political right who combine neoliberal economic policies (low taxes, smaller government, limited social spending) with conservative social policies (opposition to abortion, gay rights, feminism) and a "hawkish" foreign policy (increased military spending, pro-nuclear weapons, vigilant "war on terror"). The term is used primarily in the U.S., and had its greatest currency during the presidency of Ronald Reagan years in the 1980s. (p. 60)

Neoliberalism   An economic philosophy that holds that a system of free markets, free trade, and the free flow of capital is the best way to ensure the greatest social, political, and economic good. It argues for reduced taxation, reduced government regulation, and minimal state involvement in the economy. (p. 60)

New Public Management   A bureaucratic transformation occurring in many states over the past 15 years involving downsizing government, technological change, providing public services in new (alternate) ways, and forming partnerships with private sector agencies. (p. 211)

Non-democracy   A regime in which a very limited section of the population is able to select the leader. (p. 391)

Nonprofit organization A group that comes together to achieve a social purpose, rather than to make a profit. (p. 343)

Non-proportional systems Electoral systems that do not ensure a close match between a party's share of the popular vote and its share of legislative seats. The most prominent non-proportional systems are majoritarian and plurality systems (e.g., Single Member Plurality systems). (p. 281)

Normative position The ideas and values upon which approaches to politics are grounded. These ideas and values reflect beliefs about good and bad as well as understanding of what is desirable or what ought to be done in a given situation. (p. 466)

North American Free Trade Agreement (NAFTA) An agreement ratified by the United States, Canada, and Mexico that contains rules to promote the freer movement of goods, capital, and services between these countries. (p. 176)

Oligarchy A system of government ruled by a few and, according to Aristotle, in their own interests. (p. 76)

Opposition days Also known as allotted days. In a Westminster system, opposition days are when a member of an opposition party is allowed to decide the topic for debate on that particular day. This gives the opposition a tool to "set the agenda" in the legislature, and to direct attention to specific areas of government policy for scrutiny. (p. 230)

Paradox of voting First identified by Anthony Downs (1957), this refers to the idea that for a rational, self-interested actor, the costs of voting always outweigh the benefits, because the chance of changing the outcome of any given election with just one vote is next to none. Yet, even with this rational-actor calculus, people turn out to vote in significant numbers. (p. 298)

Parliament In a Westminster system, this is a common, informal name for the national lower house, though it formally encompasses both the lower and upper houses (as in Canada, where it includes both the House of Commons and the Senate). (p. 220)

Parliamentary caucus A group of elected representatives in the legislature who belong to the same political party. (p. 317)

Party consensus The agreement among scholars that modern democracy requires entrenched and stable political parties to articulate political interests and organize government. (p. 306)

Party discipline Reflected when all members in a political party vote along the same lines inside a legislature. The level of party discipline varies between countries and parties. Some parties require their members to always vote along the same lines, while others only enforce party discipline for important votes (such as during a confidence vote). (p. 225)

Party identification An affinity toward a political party. Such partisanship is not simply about who an individual votes for but which party the individual identifies with. Voters can identify with one party and still vote for another. (p. 294)

Party system The combination of parties effectively competing with one another in order to control government. Party systems can have two parties, multiple parties, or be one-party dominant. (p. 315)

Peacekeeping An undertaking by any group of governments, usually under the sponsorship of the United Nations, to put the forces of a third party between warring parties who have come to a ceasefire, in order to encourage them to keep the peace. (p. 439)

Permanent campaign An approach to government whereby partisan elites who control government apply strategies and techniques that are usually confined to an election campaign to the process of governing itself. (p. 323)

Plurality Where a party or candidate has more seats or votes than its rivals, though not a majority (50 percent or more). In a Westminster system, a government with a plurality of seats is known as a minority government, since it must rely on the support of opposition parties and MPs in order to pass legislation. (p. 226)

Policy community or policy network Organized interests and institutions that seek to influence public policy in a particular field. (p. 336)

Political Action Committees (PACs) American organizations that pool campaign contributions from members and donate those funds to particular electoral candidates. (p. 351)

Political authority The imposition of one's will on another by reason of legitimacy—because the subject regards the decision-maker as having a right to make such a binding decision. (p. 23)

Political culture The collection of understandings, values, attitudes, and principles of a community or society that relate to its political organization, processes, disputes, and public policies. Out of a society's political culture come important beliefs and values that structure the citizens' attitudes and expectations toward such political concepts as legitimacy, power, authority, and obedience. (p. 15)

Political development The establishment of functional and effective political institutions that can mediate conflict, implement policy, and provide the services needed to tackle poverty. It can include the establishment of democracy. (p. 369)

Political economy The study of the relationship between the state, as the leading authoritative actor in affluent societies, and the economy, the site in these societies where wealth is produced and exchanged. (p. 124)

Political marketing The application of business marketing concepts to the practice and study of politics and government. Strategies and tools include branding, focus groups, opposition research, get out the vote efforts, polling, public relations, voter segmentation, voter profiling, and strategic product development. (p. 322)

Political party An organization of like-minded individuals interested in winning power, organizing government, and implementing their preferred policies. (p. 305)

Political patronage/patronage appointment When those in power favour political supporters or party members in making appointments to state offices. (pp. 207, 265)

Political representation In which the interests, values, goals, etc. of citizens (and in some cases noncitizens) are represented within the political system, especially the executive and legislature. (p. 24)

Political science The study of the institutions and processes through which, and the ideas on the basis of which, individuals and groups make decisions that have consequences for the recognition, production, and allocation of public and private goods and goals. (p. 3)

Political socialization The processes through which attitudes toward and knowledge about political matters are passed on within a society. (pp. 15, 293)

Polity A system of government ruled by the many but not—as in a democracy—by all; according to Aristotle, this was the most stable system of government when it was able to balance the interests of the wealthy with those of the poor. (p. 76)

Post-colonial A term used to refer to countries in the Global South that have previously experienced long periods of colonization by countries in the Global North. (p. 370)

Power The ability of one actor to impose its will on another, to get its own way, to do or get what it wants. (p. 423)

Prime minister The head of government in a parliamentary system, who provides political leadership and makes the major political decisions, usually in concert with a cabinet. (p. 196)

Prime Minister's Office (PMO) In Canada, the office that provides political advice to the prime minister. Staffed by partisan appointees, its chief concern is to protect and promote the PM's political interests. (p. 203)

Prime ministerial government The notion that the prime minister is now so pre-eminent that the term "cabinet government" no longer accurately describes how decisions are made in the political executive, especially those based on the Westminster model. This idea is also known as the presidentialization of the parliamentary executive. (p. 198)

Private law The body of law that governs the relationship between private individuals and organizations, such as contract law. (p. 252)

Privatization Transferring a government program, agency, or Crown corporation to the private sector, for example, by selling shares in the corporation to the public at large or to a private firm. (p. 211)

Proportional systems Electoral systems designed to ensure a close match between a party's share of the popular vote and its share of legislative seats. Roughly speaking, if a party gets 30 percent of the vote, then it will receive around 30 percent of legislative seats. (p. 281)

Prorogation A prerogative power of the Crown in Westminster systems to end the current session of parliament for a certain period. Nowadays, it is generally exercised only on the advice of the prime minister. (pp. 191, 223)

Public law The body of law that governs relations within the state and the relationship between the state and individuals or organizations, including criminal law, administrative law, and constitutional law. (p. 252)

Public policy A course of action or inaction selected by public officials, usually in response to a specific problem or set of problems. (p. 184)

Public safety An environment that is obtained when citizens can go about their lives secure from major disruptions to society and unthreatened by crime and violence. Public safety often focuses on the internal security of the state. Threats to public safety come from a variety of sources, including natural disasters, systemic failure of national economic infrastructure, civil unrest, terrorism, and widespread threats to public health. (p. 454)

Question Period A period of time in a Westminster-style lower house when the opposition can ask questions of the government. This is the most common way that the opposition attempts to hold the government accountable, as Question Period is public and thus under the scrutiny of the media and ordinary citizens. (p. 223)

Race Historically, the term "race" was used to speak about differences between people that were supposedly biologically based. Today social scientists completely reject the idea that there are any significant biological differences between people that warrant the use of the term. While some suggest that in light of this the term should not be used at all, many contemporary social scientists put the term in quotation marks to refer to differences that are socially constructed and historically specific, but have important consequences in the form of racism. Contemporary discussions of racism assume that it involves a biological and/or cultural assertion of superiority by one group over another. (p. 104)

Racialization The historically and culturally specific processes associated with representations or assertions of superiority by one group over another on the basis of purported biological and/or cultural characteristics. (p. 104)

Rational choice An approach to political economy, and the study of politics more generally, that derives from economics, and in which social processes, including politics, are said to reflect the outcome of interaction among individuals and organizations that each seek to maximize their own self-interest or utility, which may include power and status as well as wealth and income. (p. 126)

Reading The general stages that a bill goes through in a legislature in the process of becoming a law. This includes the introduction of the bill to the legislature, as well as the formal debate in the legislature on the bill's components and any amendments to it. (p. 228)

Realist theory A foundational theory in International Relations, usually identified with Hans J. Morgenthau, that emphasizes the anarchy of the international system and the interaction of states based on their respective power. (p. 422)

Rebellion An attempt to remove a leader conducted by those outside the government. (p. 397)

Regime The constitutional principles and arrangements according to which government decisions are made; the political system. (p. 391)

Regime change A shift from one type of regime to another. (p. 395)

Regime security Focuses on the stability of the government of a state. Challenges to regime security come from internal or external sources seeking to overthrow the existing government. Weak and failed states are particularly susceptible to regime insecurity. (p. 447)

Representative A person who has been selected, usually through an election, to serve in a legislature. Representatives perform numerous tasks in a legislature, such as debating and proposing bills, attacking/defending the government, and meeting with constituents and lobbyists. (p. 219)

Representative democracy A system of government in which voters elect candidates to represent them and make collective decisions on their behalf. (p. 80)

Republic A system of government ruled by a head of state who is not a monarch (generally, in modern times, a president), in which citizens are entitled to participate in decision-making. (pp. 74, 172, 187)

Residual power   The power in a federal state to pass laws in relation to any matters that the constitution does not expressly assign to either level of government. This power is assigned either to the federal or provincial governments. (p. 162)

Responsibility to Protect (R2P)   A doctrine adopted by the United Nations in 2005 that places an obligation on the international community to intervene in the affairs of states to stop serious human rights violations and crimes against humanity. Thus, R2P refocuses sovereignty, placing an increased onus on the state to ensure the security of its members, not just to protect its own interests. (p. 459)

Responsible government   A defining principle of the Westminster model of parliamentary government, according to which the cabinet may only hold office as long as it has majority support in the legislature on votes of confidence. In a bicameral parliament, the government is responsible to the lower house, not the upper house. (p. 192)

Revolution   A sudden, drastic, and usually violent change in the government of a state; the overthrow and replacement of existing political institutions and principles, not merely the forcible removal of the current ruler or government. (p. 404)

Rule of law   The principle that government must act through laws that are made known to the public before they are enforced and that are applied equally to all, and where disputes under law are heard by fair and impartial judges. In short, no one is above the law, even leaders. (p. 77, 256)

Seats   Refers to the territorially defined area that an elected representative serves. In most "first-past-the-post" electoral systems, there is only one elected official per seat or district, although at the provincial level, Prince Edward Island had 16 ridings that each elected two members until 1996. The distribution of seats among the different parties will determine whether any one party can form a majority government. (p. 222)

Securitization   Occurs when an issue area becomes understood as a security issue rather than a more routine matter of policy. This process develops through the use of a security language by leaders which is accepted by publics. Once an issue is securitized, more powerful security measures that enhance the power of the state

(many of which may constrain individual rights) are taken for granted as being necessary. (p. 463)

Security   The peace of mind that comes with a sense of safety from harm to what one values; a sense of well-being that can have economic, environmental, social, linguistic, or cultural dimensions. It can be seen in terms of both individual and community safety. (p. 422)

Security dilemma   A situation that arises from the belief that the global system is anarchic. In such a system, states feel compelled to ensure their own security by increasing their military power. This, in turn, is likely to encourage other states, as a defensive response, to increase their own military capacities. This can generate an arms race, in which each state tries to gain enough strength to defend against the other, which is trying to accomplish the same goal. Thus, the dilemma is that a state's attempt to secure itself leads to its own greater insecurity. (p. 451)

Selectorate   The group of people that can select the leader in any regime. (p. 398)

Senator   A member of the Senate (the "upper house") of a country. In Canada, senators are unelected, being appointed on the advice of the prime minister. In Australia and the United States, senators are elected. (p. 228)

Separation of powers   A principle of constitutional government that is usually taken to mean that the legislative, executive, and judicial functions of the state are carried out by separate branches of government. No one may hold office in more than one branch at the same time. (pp. 193, 222)

Sharia law   Sharia is the Islamic system of law, both civil and criminal, that is based on the Qur'an (the holy book of Islam); the life example and hadiths (sayings) of the Prophet Muhammad; and on subsequent scholarly interpretations and writings. This system of law prescribes the correct behavior for Muslims across different areas of life and the punishments for transgressions. Importantly, Sharia law is not uniform throughout the Muslim world as it is influenced by different schools of jurisprudence, among other factors. (pp. 42, 78, 114, 253)

Single executive   A form of executive in which the posts of head of state and head of government are combined and held by a single officeholder. This arrangement is characteristic of presidential systems, such as those of Argentina, Mexico, and the United States. (p. 186)

Social development   Includes not only economic indicators of development but also issues such as education, sanitation, health, and infant mortality. (p. 368)

Social movement   An informal network of individuals and groups who embrace and bring awareness to a particular vision of social change. (pp. 337, 426)

Socialism   The doctrine advocating economic equality of the classes and the use of government to serve the collective good of the whole society. Socialists value the collective good over the private interests of individuals, and thus emphasize cooperation over competition. Socialists advocate public ownership of key industries, regulation of the market, redistribution of resources, and protection of fundamental social rights and freedoms. There is a wide variety of socialist practice. Social democrats insist on working within the parliamentary system and achieving socialism through democratic and evolutionary change, while communists and other radical socialists believe in the need for total, revolutionary change, often through the violent overthrow of the existing regime. Since 1989, however, officially communist regimes have either collapsed or reframed their ideological positions to provide for a greater role for the market in the economy. (p. 47)

Sovereignty   A legal authority over a population and territory commonly claimed by the government of a state but ultimately sanctioned by the international system of states. In other contexts, sovereignty can be said to reside in the people or in parliament. (p. 143)

Speaker   The Speaker is a member of a legislature (usually elected by their fellow representatives) who is responsible for the general day-to-day procedures of the legislature, such as debates and voting on bills. They are also usually responsible for maintaining decorum in the legislature. (p. 232)

Speech from the Throne   The document prepared by the prime minister and the cabinet and read by the head of state at the opening of each session of parliament; it outlines the government's legislative proposals for the session at hand. (p. 192)

Staples thesis   An interpretation of Canadian economic development that holds that, unlike most other now-affluent countries, the production of raw materials for export markets has remained central for the Canadian economy. It has not been replaced by a focus on manufactured goods and then services. (p. 138)

Stare decisis   A Latin phrase which means that similar cases should be decided similarly; it is the central principle in common-law systems, in which judges are expected to follow prior judicial decisions involving similar facts and law, or precedents. (p. 253)

State   A modern form of organizing political life that is characterized by a population, territory, governing institutions, and a government that claims a monopoly of legitimate force; recognition by the international community of states (most often by the United Nations) may also be key. (pp. 81, 101)

Structural adjustment loans (SALs)   Loans provided by the IMF and World Bank to countries in the Global South beginning in the 1980s that were conditioned upon the implementation of various neoliberal reforms. (p. 383)

Supraconstitution   In imposing on national governments a set of rules, norms, and principles from which domestic laws may not derogate, international trade and investment agreements are said by some scholars to be a form of transnational constitution. (p. 176)

Supranational   A sphere of politics and political institutions that exists "above" the nation-state but usually "below" the global level. The only supranational polity in the world is the European Union. (p. 424)

Terrorism   The threat or use of violence, usually directed at civilian populations, in order to create some form of political change. (p. 90)

Third World   A term from the Cold War that refers to countries that were not part of the First World (Western Europe, the United States, Canada, Australia, and New Zealand) or Second World (USSR and Soviet bloc countries in Eastern Europe). (p. 366)

Tied aid   The practice of making development assistance conditional on the receiving country buying goods and services from the donor country. (p. 381)

Totalitarian government A non-democratic form of government that seeks to control and transform the people though an all-encompassing ideology that speaks to their cultural, economic, political, and social roots and destiny. Totalitarian regimes were responsible for two of the worst genocides of the 20th century, in Europe during the Second World War and in Cambodia in the 1970s. (p. 86)

Transnational corporation Business firms that are headquartered in one country but have plants or places of operation around the world, permitting them to integrate their business activities on a global scale. (pp. 141, 427)

Underdeveloped/developing/less developed countries (LDCs)/emerging economies/newly industrialized countries (NICs) Terms used to refer to the regions of study in development that emphasize economic development. (p. 366)

Unicameral/bicameral A unicameral legislature has only a single legislative house that handles all lawmaking in a state, province, or country. A bicameral legislature has two houses, such as the Canadian House of Commons (the "lower house") and Senate (the "upper house"), that handle lawmaking in a state, province, or country. (p. 221)

United Nations An international organization formed in 1945 as a successor to the League of Nations; it has become the largest and most ambitious international governmental organization in world history, consisting of a vast array of organs and agencies. Its membership now includes almost every country in the world. Less than a world government, it attempts to promote peaceful relations among states and economic and human rights for all people. (pp. 83, 430)

Unwritten constitution A constitution whose subject matter is dispersed across a variety of statutes, court rulings, and unwritten political practices known as constitutional conventions. (p. 158)

Varieties of Capitalism (VoC) The foremost contemporary political economy approach to developed countries. These are divided between Coordinated Market Economies (CMEs), where firms rely on coordination with other actors, and Liberal Market Economies (LMEs), where they do not. (p. 131)

Veto The authority to block a decision or piece of legislation, especially that of a president to reject a law

passed by congress or that of a province to reject a proposed constitutional amendment. (p. 194)

Voluntary organization An organization that exists to serve a public benefit, is independent from government, does not distribute any profits to members, and relies on volunteers to a certain degree—at the very least to serve on its board. (p. 342)

Weak state The form of state that exists in countries where it did not play an important role in fostering the transition to a market and industrial economy, and in which it continues to play a modest role in guiding overall economic development. This does not mean that the institutions of government work badly or have "failed" in such states; but they do not intervene extensively and systematically. (p. 129)

Welfare state A concept that stresses the role of government as a provider and protector of individual security and well-being through the implementation of interventionist economic policies and social programs. This positive role for government stands in contrast to the minimalist government (or "nightwatchman state") that has as its only function the protection of personal property and individual security. The welfare state is regarded as having a positive role in promoting human welfare and in shielding the individual against the economic and social consequences of unemployment, poverty, sickness, old age, disability, and so on. (p. 59)

Welfare state regimes The welfare states of affluent, capitalist countries are said to come in three variants—social democratic, Christian democratic, and liberal (Anglo-Saxon)—which originated through different political party and social coalitions. These regimes are associated with different levels of poverty and inequality. (p. 133)

Westminster system A style of democracy, characterized by having a bicameral national legislature and the inclusion of the executive within the legislature. This system is found in countries like Canada and the United Kingdom. (p. 220)

World Bank A bank closely linked to the IMF that is one of the world's largest sources of development assistance. Through loans, policy advice, and technical assistance, it aims to improve the living standards in the developing world. (p. 430)

World Trade Organization (WTO) An organization created during the Uruguay Round of GATT negotiations whose goal is to provide liberal trading practices and to reduce protectionism through the development and enforcement of global laws and regulations. (pp. 92, 176, 430)

Written constitution A constitution whose fundamental provisions have been reduced to a single document or set of documents. (p. 158)

INDEX